SEXUAL INTERACTIONS

BASIC UNDERSTANDINGS

Sexual Interactions

Basic Understandings

Elizabeth Rice Allgeier

BOWLING GREEN STATE UNIVERSITY

Albert Richard Allgeier

ALLGEIER AND ASSOCIATES, BOWLING GREEN, OHIO

HOUGHTON MIFFLIN COMPANY   BOSTON   NEW YORK

Sponsoring Editor: David Lee
Senior Associate Editor: Jane Knetzger
Senior Project Editor: Janet Young
Editorial Assistant: Carrie Wagner
Senior Designer: Henry Rachlin
Senior Production/Design Coordinator: Carol Merrigan
Senior Manufacturing Coordinator: Sally Culler
Marketing Manager: Pamela Laskey

Cover design by Harold Burch, Harold Burch Design, NYC.

Credits appear following index.

Printed in the U.S.A.

Library of Congress Catalog Card Number: 97-72430

ISBN: 0-395-84600-5

2 3 4 5 6 7 8 9 - DW – 08 07 06 05 04

BRIEF CONTENTS

PREFACE xix
ABOUT THE AUTHORS xxiv

1 LEARNING ABOUT SEXUALITY 2

2 SEXUAL DIFFERENTIATION AND DEVELOPMENT 28

3 SEXUAL ANATOMY AND PHYSIOLOGY 54

4 AROUSAL AND COMMUNICATION 78

5 SEXUAL BEHAVIOR 104

6 SEXUAL DYSFUNCTION AND THERAPY 134

7 PREGNANCY AND BIRTH 158

8 PREVENTING AND RESOLVING UNWANTED PREGNANCY 186

9 GENDER AND SEXUALITY IN CHILDHOOD AND ADOLESCENCE 220

10 GENDER AND SEXUALITY IN ADULTHOOD 246

11 SEXUAL ORIENTATION 270

12 SEX FOR PROFIT 296

13 SEXUALLY TRANSMITTED DISEASES 322

14 SEXUAL COERCION 348

15 ATYPICAL SEXUAL ACTIVITY 376

16 LOVING SEXUAL INTERACTIONS 402

APPENDIX: SOURCES OF INFORMATION ABOUT SEXUALITY A1
GLOSSARY A5
REFERENCES A12
NAME INDEX A33
SUBJECT INDEX A39
CREDITS A50

CONTENTS

Preface   xix
About the Authors   xxiv

1 LEARNING ABOUT SEXUALITY   2

REALITY OR MYTH?   3

RESEARCH ON SEXUALITY   3
The Impact of Societal Beliefs, Political Attitudes, and Ethical Issues on
    Research   4
▪ ACROSS CULTURES: Beliefs About Conception and Development   5
Understanding the Process of Sex Research   8
Evaluating Results of Studies of Sexuality   13

CONTEMPORARY EXPLANATIONS OF HUMAN
SEXUALITY   14
Evolutionary Approaches   14
Psychoanalytic Approaches   17
Learning Approaches   19
Sociological Approaches   21
▪ ACROSS CULTURES: A Polygynous African Tribe   22
Theories, Politics, and Morality   24

SUMMARY OF MAJOR POINTS   25
CHECK YOUR KNOWLEDGE   27

2 SEXUAL DIFFERENTIATION AND DEVELOPMENT   28

REALITY OR MYTH?   29

FERTILIZATION   29
Meeting of Sperm and Egg   29
Cell Division   31
Chromosomes and Genetic Inheritance   31
Sex Chromosomes and Genetic Sex   31

PRENATAL DEVELOPMENT   33

TYPICAL SEXUAL DIFFERENTIATION 34
Gonadal Sex   35
Hormonal Sex   36
▪ ACROSS CULTURES: Aborting Female Fetuses as Population Control   37
Genital Sex   38
▪ HIGHLIGHT: The Major Sex Hormones   39

ATYPICAL SEXUAL DIFFERENTIATION   40
Sex Chromosome Abnormalities   40
Inconsistencies in Sexual Differentiation   40

DEVELOPMENT THROUGH THE REMAINDER OF PREGNANCY   45

SECONDARY SEXUAL CHARACTERISTICS   47
Female Maturation   47
▪ HIGHLIGHT: Meanings of Menarche   48
Male Maturation   49

SEXUAL DIFFERENTIATION AND GENDER IDENTITY   49
A Genital Accident   49
Ambiguous Genitals   50

SUMMARY OF MAJOR POINTS   52
CHECK YOUR KNOWLEDGE   53

3 SEXUAL ANATOMY AND PHYSIOLOGY
54

REALITY OR MYTH?   55

SEXUAL ANATOMY   55
The Male Sexual System   55
▪ HEALTH: Testes Self-Examination   57
The Female Sexual System   59
▪ ACROSS CULTURES: Female Circumcision   64
▪ HEALTH: Kegel Exercises   65
▪ HEALTH: Breast Self-Examination   66

HORMONES AND THE ENDOCRINE SYSTEM   67
The Endocrine Glands   67
The Effects of Hormones   68
The Menstrual Cycle   69

THE NERVOUS SYSTEM   71
The Sympathetic and Parasympathetic Nervous Systems   71
The Central Nervous System   72

SUMMARY OF MAJOR POINTS   76
CHECK YOUR KNOWLEDGE   77

4 AROUSAL AND COMMUNICATION   78

REALITY OR MYTH?   79

LEARNING TO BE AROUSED   80
Models of Arousal   81
The Two-Stage Model of Sexual Arousal   81
The Purposes of Sexual Arousal   82

SOURCES OF AROUSAL   83
Touch   83
Smell   83
Sight   84
Hearing   85
Fantasy and Sexual Arousal   85
Attitudes Toward Sexuality   87
HIGHLIGHT: **Do You Feel Guilty About Your Sexual Feelings?**   90
Gender Differences and Similarities in Arousal   90

COMMUNICATION ABOUT SEXUALITY   92
Socialization for Communicating About Sex   92
Gender Differences in the Communication of Feelings   94
Interpersonal Communication and Sexual Intimacy   94
Enhancing Interpersonal Communication   96
Informed Consent and Sexual Intimacy   97
The Management of Sexual Feelings and Behavior   99
HIGHLIGHT: **Negotiating a Sexual Relationship**   100
Honoring Agreements   100

SUMMARY OF MAJOR POINTS   102
CHECK YOUR KNOWLEDGE   103

 5 SEXUAL BEHAVIOR   104

REALITY OR MYTH?   105

SOURCES OF SEXUAL PLEASURE   106
Nocturnal Orgasm   106
Masturbation   107
HIGHLIGHT: **Mark Twain on Masturbation**   110
Mutual Masturbation   112
Oral Sex   113
"Foreplay" and Coitus   115
Coitus and Coital Positions   116
Anal Sex   121
Frequency of Coitus and Number of Sexual Partners   122
Sexual Satisfaction and Enjoyment   122
Simultaneous Orgasm: A Note   123

SEXUAL RESPONSES   124
Sexual Desire   124
Excitement/Plateau   125
Orgasm   125
Resolution   126
■ HIGHLIGHT: Physical Reactions During Sexual Response   127
Patterns of Sexual Response   127
■ HIGHLIGHT: Whose Is It?   128
Normal Variations   128

VARIETIES OF ORGASM   129
Female Orgasm: Different Types?   129
Research on Female Ejaculation   130
The Consistency of Female Orgasm   130
The Consistency of Male Orgasm   131
Multiple Orgasms in Females   131
Multiple Orgasms in Males   131

SUMMARY OF MAJOR POINTS   132
CHECK YOUR KNOWLEDGE   133

6 SEXUAL DYSFUNCTION AND THERAPY

134

REALITY OR MYTH?   135

SEXUAL DYSFUNCTION: CONTRIBUTING FACTORS   135
Biological Factors   136
Psychosocial Factors   136
■ HEALTH: Disorders, Diseases, and Other Factors That Can Affect Sexual Functioning   137
■ HEALTH: Excessive Sexual Desire   139

TYPES OF SEXUAL DYSFUNCTION   141
Sexual Desire Disorders   141
Sexual Arousal Disorders   143
Orgasm Disorders   144
Sexual Pain Disorders   146

SEX THERAPY   147
Masters and Johnson's Approach   148
Kaplan's Approach   149
Treatment of Sexual Dysfunctions   149
■ HEALTH: A Treatment Program for Orgasmically Inhibited Women   152
Qualifications and Ethics of Therapists   155

SUMMARY OF MAJOR POINTS   156
CHECK YOUR KNOWLEDGE   157

7   PREGNANCY AND BIRTH   158

REALITY OR MYTH?   159

PREGNANCY   159
Early Symptoms of Pregnancy   159
■ HEALTH: The Inability to Conceive   161
Threats to Fetal Development   161
Stages of Pregnancy   162
■ HEALTH: Tests for Identifying Fetal Abnormalities   165
Sex During Pregnancy   168

LABOR AND BIRTH   169
Preparation for Childbirth   170
■ HIGHLIGHT: A Personal Account of Childbirth   171
Labor for Childbirth   171

POSTPARTUM EVENTS AND DECISIONS   177
Feeding   177
■ HEALTH: Possible Birth Complications   178
Circumcision   180
Postpartum Adjustment   181
Postpartum Sexual Expression   181

SUMMARY OF MAJOR POINTS   183
CHECK YOUR KNOWLEDGE   185

8   PREVENTING AND RESOLVING UNWANTED PREGNANCY   186

REALITY OR MYTH?   187

THE DEVELOPMENT AND USE OF MODERN CONTRACEPTIVES   187
Selecting a Contraceptive   188
Correlates of Contraceptive Use   189
■ HIGHLIGHT: Spontaneous Sex—The Big Lie   190

METHODS OF CONTRACEPTION   192
Rhythm   192
Diaphragm and Spermicide   194
Cervical Cap   196
Condom   196
Female Condoms   198
Foams and Suppositories   198
Oral Contraceptives   199
Hormone Implants and Injections   201
Intrauterine Devices   201
Relatively Ineffective Methods   202

STERILIZATION 203
Vasectomy 203
Tubal Ligation 204

CONTRACEPTIVE TECHNIQUES OF THE FUTURE 205
Research on Future Methods of Birth Control for Men 206
Research on Future Methods of Birth Control for Women 206

UNWANTED PREGNANCY 206

ABORTION: A HUMAN DILEMMA 207
The Moral and Legal Debate over Abortion 207
■ HIGHLIGHT: **The Legal Status of Abortion in the United States** 208
Reasons for Abortion 209

ABORTION: THE PROCESS 211
Abortion Methods Early in Pregnancy 211
First-Trimester Abortion Methods 212
Second-Trimester Abortion Methods 213
Psychological Responses to Abortion 214
The Male Role in Abortion 214

UNINTENDED PARENTHOOD 215
Adolescent Parents 216
Keeping an Unwanted Child 217

SUMMARY OF MAJOR POINTS 218
CHECK YOUR KNOWLEDGE 219

9 GENDER AND SEXUALITY IN CHILDHOOD AND ADOLESCENCE

220

REALITY OR MYTH? 221

UNDERSTANDING CHILDHOOD SEXUALITY 222
■ RESEARCH CONTROVERSY: **Children's Sexual Knowledge—An Immoral Research Topic?** 223

INFANCY: TRUST VERSUS MISTRUST 223
Biosexual Development 225
Sensual Development 226
Parental Reactions to Early Sensuality 226

EARLY CHILDHOOD: AUTONOMY VERSUS SHAME AND DOUBT 227
Language, Gender, and Sexuality 227
Toilet Training and Gender: Differences in Sexual Associations 227
Awareness of Gender Differences 228

PRESCHOOL YEARS: INITIATIVE VERSUS GUILT 229
Gender-Role Socialization 229
Gender Similarities and Differences Versus Gender Stereotypes 230

Sexual Learning   230
Physical Attractiveness   233

LATE CHILDHOOD: INDUSTRY VERSUS INFERIORITY   233

Sexual Rehearsal   234
Homosociality   234
Sex Education   235
■ ACROSS CULTURES: The Relationship Between the Provision of Sex and Contraceptive Education and Unwanted Pregnancies in Western Nations   238

ADOLESCENCE: IDENTITY VERSUS ROLE CONFUSION   239

Gender-Role Identification in Adolescence   240
Sexual Exploration in Adolescence   241
The Sexual Double Standard   242

SUMMARY OF MAJOR POINTS   243
CHECK YOUR KNOWLEDGE   245

10 GENDER AND SEXUALITY IN ADULTHOOD   246

REALITY OR MYTH?   247

YOUNG ADULTHOOD   247

■ HIGHLIGHT: Back-Burner Relationships   249
The Relationship Between Sexual Intimacy and Emotional Intimacy   249
Lifestyle Choices and Shifting Norms   250

MARRIAGE AND LONG-TERM COMMITMENTS   252

Sex, Time, and Parenthood   252
Family Formation and Division of Labor   253

LONG-TERM RELATIONSHIPS   254

Sexual Pleasure and Marital Longevity   254
Attraction Versus Attachment in Long-Term Relationships   255
Extramarital Sexual Relations   256
■ ACROSS CULTURES: The Relationship of Equity to Likelihood of Having Extramarital Sex   258
Separation and Divorce   258
Adjustment to Separation: Who Suffers Most?   259

AGING AND SEXUALITY   259

Midlife Changes and Assessments   260
Menopause   261
The Double Standard of Aging   261
Midlife Challenges and Gender Roles   262

OLD AGE   263

Physiological Changes   263
■ HEALTH: Aging of the Male Sexual System   264

Social Stereotypes and Self-Image   264
■ HEALTH: Aging of the Female Sexual System   265
Decreasing Sexual Activity: Aging or Other Factors?   265

SUMMARY OF MAJOR POINTS   268
CHECK YOUR KNOWLEDGE   269

11 SEXUAL ORIENTATION
270

REALITY OR MYTH?   271

WHAT IS SEXUAL ORIENTATION?   271
Cross-Species Perspectives   272
■ HIGHLIGHT: Variations in Sexual Orientation and Gender Identity   273
Cross-Cultural Perspectives   273
■ ACROSS CULTURES: Rigid Versus Fluid Definitions of Orientation   274

HOMOSEXUAL BEHAVIOR AND GAY IDENTITY   275
Self-Definition   276
Sexual Expression   278

EXPLANATIONS OF SEXUAL ORIENTATION   281
Biological Correlates   281
Family Experiences   284
Gender-Role Nonconformity During Childhood   284

SEXUAL ORIENTATION AND ADJUSTMENT   286
Antigay Prejudice   286
Changing Views of Mental Health   288
Therapy   288

DISCRIMINATION AND LIBERATION   289
Discrimination   289
The Gay Liberation Movement   290

BISEXUALITY   291
Incidence   291
Characteristics   292
Identity Versus Experience   293
Bisexual Identity: Stable or Transitional?   293

SUMMARY OF MAJOR POINTS   294
CHECK YOUR KNOWLEDGE   295

12 SEX FOR PROFIT
296

REALITY OR MYTH?   297

VARIETIES OF SEXUAL PRODUCTS AND SERVICES   297
Magazines and Newspapers   298
Advertisements   298
Television Programs   299
Erotic Movies and Videos   299
■ HIGHLIGHT: Romance Novels—Erotica for Women?   300

Adult Bookstores   301
Telephone Sex   302
Cyberspace   302
Erotic Dancing   303
Other Forms of Erotica   304

EROTICA AND THE LAW   305

THE EFFECTS OF EROTICA   306
Nonviolent Erotica   306
■ HIGHLIGHT: Public Policy and Erotica   307
Violent Erotica   307
Prolonged Exposure   309
Cultural Variations   310
Children and Erotica   310

PROSTITUTION (COMMERCIAL SEX WORK)   311
The Oldest Profession   311
Commercial Sex Work in Contemporary Society   312
■ ACROSS CULTURES: Japanese Telephone Clubs That Offer Sex
  with Girls   317
■ ACROSS CULTURES: Sex Tourism   319

SUMMARY OF MAJOR POINTS   320
CHECK YOUR KNOWLEDGE   321

13 SEXUALLY TRANSMITTED DISEASES   322

REALITY OR MYTH?   323

ATTITUDES TOWARD SEXUALLY
TRANSMITTED DISEASES   323
Attitudes Toward People with STDs   324
■ HEALTH: How Accurate Is Your Knowledge of HIV/AIDS?   325
The Relationship of AIDS Knowledge and Attitudes   325
Attempts to Reduce STD Transmission   326

BACTERIAL INFECTIONS   326
Gonorrhea   328
Syphilis   328
Chlamydia and Nongonococcal Urethritis (NGU)   329
■ RESEARCH CONTROVERSY: Ethical Principles and the Tuskegee Study   330
Cystitis   331
Prostatitis   331
Other Bacterial Infections   332
Pelvic Inflammatory Disease (PID)   332

ACQUIRED IMMUNODEFICIENCY
SYNDROME (AIDS)   333
■ HIGHLIGHT: An Epidemic of Stigma   334
Prevalence   335

Causes   335
Risk Factors   336
Symptoms   337
Diagnosis   337
Opportunistic Infections   337
Treatment   338
■ HEALTH: Being Tested for HIV Antibodies   339
Protection Against AIDS   339

OTHER VIRAL STDs   340
Herpes Simplex Type II   340
Genital Warts/Human Papilloma Virus   341
Hepatitis B   342

PARASITIC INFECTIONS   342
Candidiasis   342
Trichomoniasis   343
Pediculosis Pubis   343

SAFER-SEX PRACTICES: REDUCING THE RISK
OF CONTRACTING STDs   343
Relationship Negotiation   344
Other Practices That Reduce Risk   345

SUMMARY OF MAJOR POINTS   346
CHECK YOUR KNOWLEDGE   347

14 SEXUAL COERCION

348

REALITY OR MYTH?   349

SEXUAL ASSAULT   349
The Magnitude of the Problem   349
Rape Stereotypes   350
The Sexual Assault Offender   350
Victims of Sexual Coercion   352
■ HIGHLIGHT: Male Rape   354
What Provokes Sexual Assault?   355
The Aftermath of Sexual Assault   357
What Should Assault Victims Do?   357
■ HIGHLIGHT: Was He Asking for It?   358
Sexual Assault and the Criminal Justice System   359
Factors Associated with Being Sexually Assaulted   360

SEXUAL HARASSMENT   363
Sexual Harassment in Occupational Settings   363
■ HIGHLIGHT: Research Findings on Sexual Harassment   364
Sexual Harassment in Educational Settings   365
Sexual Harassment in Therapeutic Settings   365

SEXUAL ABUSE OF CHILDREN   366
Prevalence of Sexual Abuse of Children   367
Risk Factors for Sexual Abuse During Childhood   367

■ HEALTH: Memories of Sexual Abuse During Childhood 368
Characteristics of Child-Adult Sexual Contacts 368
Long-Term Correlates of Child-Adult Sexual Contacts 368

GENDER DIFFERENCES IN SEXUALLY
COERCIVE BEHAVIOR 373

SUMMARY OF MAJOR POINTS 374
CHECK YOUR KNOWLEDGE 375

15 ATYPICAL SEXUAL ACTIVITY 376

REALITY OR MYTH? 377

THE PARAPHILIAS 377

THE NONINVASIVE CONSENSUAL PARAPHILIAS 378
Fetishes 378
Transvestism 379
Transsexuality 381
Sexual Sadism and Sexual Masochism 386
■ HIGHLIGHT: Pain and Sexual Arousal 387

THE INVASIVE PARAPHILIAS 388
Voyeurism 389
Exhibitionism 391
Frotteurism 393
Pedophilia 394
Zoophilia 395
Necrophilia and Miscellaneous "Philias" 396
Compulsive Sexual Behavior 396
■ HIGHLIGHT: Uncommon Paraphilias 397

TREATMENT OF THE INVASIVE PARAPHILIAS 398
Psychotherapy 398
Surgical Castration 398
Chemical Treatment 399
Cognitive-Behavior Therapies 399
Other Approaches 400

SUMMARY OF MAJOR POINTS 400
CHECK YOUR KNOWLEDGE 401

16 LOVING SEXUAL INTERACTIONS 402

REALITY OR MYTH? 403

BEING LOVED 403
Early Experience 403
■ HIGHLIGHT: Attachment Styles and Adult Relationships 407

SELF-LOVE 408
Self-Love Versus Selfishness 408

LOVING OTHERS 409
Constructions of Love 409
Forms of Love 410
Love Versus Lust 414
▪ ACROSS CULTURES: What Do You Look for in a Partner? 416

LOVE AS DEPENDENCY, JEALOUSY, AND OTHER UNLOVELY FEELINGS 416
Dependency and Control 416
Jealousy 418
▪ HIGHLIGHT: Dating Infidelity 419

LOVING SEXUAL INTERACTIONS 420
Vitality in Long-Term Relationships 421
▪ HIGHLIGHT: Make Love, Not War 422

SUMMARY OF MAJOR POINTS 423
CHECK YOUR KNOWLEDGE 424

APPENDIX: SOURCES OF INFORMATION ABOUT SEXUALITY A1
GLOSSARY A5
REFERENCES A12
NAME INDEX A33
SUBJECT INDEX A39
CREDITS A50

PREFACE

We named our text *Sexual Interactions* because of our belief that the complexity of human sexual behavior cannot be understood by reference to just one theory or to biological, psychological, sociological, historical, medical, or religious factors alone. Instead, in most instances, an individual's sexual feelings and behaviors result from the complex interactions of these factors.

Perhaps more than any other area, the field of human sexuality is filled with myths and misconceptions. We seek to provide readers with a strong research base to counter the many myths. Without the ability to communicate about many of the issues confronting individuals and couples, however, knowledge may contribute little to the quality of people's personal and sexual experience. Thus, we seek to increase readers' communication skills and comfort in sharing their feelings and desires regarding such diverse areas as birth control, sexual arousal, sexual orientation, sexually transmitted diseases, and their desire to have or to avoid sexual intimacy with a potential sexual partner. We do this by presenting vignettes, dialogues, and practical advice on negotiating sexual interactions, in each of the relevant chapters.

Since we began writing *Sexual Interactions* almost two decades ago, we have had a number of colleagues ask us about writing a concise edition. Although instructors had used our full editions in their courses, they suggested that it would be helpful to have a brief edition for their summer courses or for courses they offer in community colleges or on the quarter system. Some of our colleagues had been solving the length problem themselves by assigning only a subset of the chapters, consequently dropping some important topics entirely. We were also told that our writing level, although appropriate for advanced undergraduate and graduate students, should be made more accessible for a larger range of students. As a result, we decided to write a shorter, more accessible book. *Sexual Interactions: Basic Understandings* is the result.

We faced a number of decisions and challenges with the change in our goal, from writing a comprehensive book to providing basic and accessible coverage. One guiding principle was to avoid attempting to cover at a more superficial level everything we have in the full editions. Instead, we opted to retain the in-depth coverage of central topics but to restrict the number of topics we covered. Accordingly, there are fewer and shorter chapters in this book. Also, we have retained the strong empirical base present in the four editions of *Sexual Interactions*, but we have attempted to increase the clarity, crispness, and accessibility of the language.

Special Features

To help make the knowledge generated by research in human sexuality more accessible to students, we have developed a number of pedagogical features that run throughout the text.

Reality or Myth?   Each chapter begins with five or six statements, each of which represents either a research-based finding or an unsubstantiated myth or stereotype. In reading the chapter, students learn whether each statement is indeed reality or myth.

A symbol occurs in the margin beside the relevant discussion. With this feature, we hope to stimulate students to think critically about their own beliefs and to revise them in light of scientifically gathered data.

Issues to Consider   Each chapter contains four to six questions in the margins, in which students are asked to indicate how they would handle particular situations as individuals, citizens, and parents in the light of data presented in that section. By provoking critical thinking and values clarification, these Issues to Consider can provide the basis for engaging students in class discussion or small-group interactions.

Research Controversies   Where appropriate, we have described many of the contemporary controversies over sexual issues in boxed features that show alternative sides to these controversies. For example, in the chapter on sexually transmitted diseases we describe the bases for initial decisions in the Tuskegee experiment to prevent the treatment of Black men with syphilis. In the sexual coercion chapter, we review the recovered memory–versus–induced memory controversy.

Across Cultures   With this feature, we have attempted to broaden students' perspectives on beliefs about various aspects of sexuality, given the great diversity that can be found in looking from one culture or subculture to another. For example, we cover polygyny, aborting female fetuses, female circumcision, and sex education, among other topics.

Health   Throughout the text, we have placed a number of health-related issues in boxed Health features. Because of the link between physical and psychological health and various sexual practices and experiences, we thought it important to provide easy access to this information by highlighting it in this way. For example, we provide explicit directions and illustrations for self-exams of breasts and testes, and we give directions for doing Kegel exercises. We also describe the methods available for prenatal testing and variations in response to menarche, among other topics.

Highlight   An additional running feature involves the presentation of research findings likely to intrigue students of human sexuality. The common phenomenon of dating infidelity and the behaviors that young people perceive to be "unfaithful" are presented in Chapter 16. Another example concerns the relationship of pain to sexual arousal, described in a highlight in Chapter 15.

Boldfaced Key Terms and Running Marginal Glossary   To help students master the terminology of the field, we place key terms in boldface in the text, and we provide a running glossary of these terms in the page margins. We also provide an end-of-text glossary for students' reference.

Summary of Major Points   At the end of each chapter, we provide a narrative review of major findings and issues described in the chapter. These summaries are intended to give students a final overview of salient information.

Check Your Knowledge   The final pedagogical feature for each chapter is a brief multiple-choice quiz. These questions give students practice answering the kinds of multiple-choice questions they are likely to encounter in examinations of that kind. Instructors can readily turn these into short-answer essay questions as well.

Overview of Contents of Sexual Interactions: Basic Understandings

In *Chapter 1, Learning About Sexuality,* we begin with an overview of the interaction between social beliefs and sex research. We look at the ways in which information is obtained. Theories about sexuality are then presented, including evolutionary, psycho-analytic, social learning, and sociological theories. In the section on sociological theory, we have included a summary of feminist approaches to explaining sexuality.

Chapter 2, Sexual Differentiation and Development, contains material on typical and atypical sexual and gender differentiation. We have included information on the debate over the clinical treatment of intersexual infants (those with ambiguous genitals).

In *Chapter 3, Sexual Anatomy and Physiology,* we cover anatomy, hormones, and the nervous system. We have placed material on breast, cervical, prostate, and testicle cancers in this chapter and included instructions for self-examinations of the breasts and testes.

In *Chapter 4, Arousal and Communication,* we review sources of sexual arousal and focus heavily on communication skills. Communication issues are also discussed in other relevant chapters because of our belief that reinforcement and repetition of this crucial topic is essential for students' well-being.

In *Chapter 5, Sexual Behavior,* we describe updated information on sexual behavior, particularly the Laumann et al. (1994) national probability survey. We place special emphasis on safer-sex practices, given the prevalence of STDs in North America.

In *Chapter 6, Sexual Dysfunction and Therapy,* we present the most recent research on sexual dysfunctions and therapy. We have moved away from an emphasis on DSM-IV because of its strong medical bias.

In *Chapter 7, Pregnancy and Birth,* recent research on the process of pregnancy and birth is presented. We cover postpartum events, including the controversies surrounding breast-feeding and circumcision.

In *Chapter 8, Preventing and Resolving Unwanted Pregnancy,* we cover current information on methods of contraception and abortion. We describe early abortion methods using extra doses of oral contraceptives, DES, and RU-486. We also present interesting cross-national data on the consequences of unwanted parenthood for the parent(s) and offspring.

In Chapters 9 and 10, we review sexual development across the life span. In *Chapter 9, Gender and Sexuality in Childhood and Adolescence,* we review what is known about gender differences and similarities in sexual socialization from infancy through adolescence, ending with relationship formation that occurs during adolescence. In *Chapter 10, Gender and Sexuality in Adulthood,* we have included recent studies suggesting that monogamy may be more prevalent among married couples and cohabiting gay or heterosexual couples than was indicated by previous research. We briefly cover studies focusing on sexual expression among aging and elderly people.

Although variations in sexual orientation are covered throughout the text, in *Chapter 11, Sexual Orientation,* we review what is known about similarities and differences in the lives and experiences of heterosexual, homosexual, and bisexual individuals. A particular emphasis is placed on cross-cultural differences in the definition of what constitutes sexual orientation. We also examine the contradictions between sexual behavior and sexual-orientation identity.

In *Chapter 12, Sex for Profit,* we describe the various ways in which sex is used in advertising, the media, and sex work (prostitution). We evaluate the research on the effects of exposure to sexually explicit material. Cross-cultural aspects of sex and money are presented, including sexual tourism and telephone clubs that connect young women to men who pay for sexual services.

In *Chapter 13, Sexually Transmitted Diseases,* we present the major STDs and discuss societal attitudes that may hinder treatment of STDs and efforts to impede the transmission of these diseases. The latest research on AIDS and its treatment is presented, including the new protease-inhibitor "cocktails." We end with practical advice on the role of communication in safer-sex practices.

Chapter 14, Sexual Coercion, covers sexual assault, harassment, and child-adult sexual contact (sexual abuse). The most recent research on these violations of human dignity and consent are presented, along with advice on reducing the likelihood of these events. We describe the controversy regarding recovered versus elicited memories of childhood sexual abuse.

In *Chapter 15, Atypical Sexual Activity,* we distinguish between noninvasive paraphilias (e.g., fetishes and transsexualism) and invasive paraphilias (e.g., exhibitionism and pedophilia). We also discuss the effectiveness of various treatments of the paraphilias.

Chapter 16, Loving Sexual Interactions, ends the book with an optimistic summary of what is related to loving sexual interactions. We review the burgeoning literature on love relationships and also describe those interactions that can be harmful even though they are initiated under the guise of love. We describe the remarkable bonobo (also called pygmy chimpanzees), who appear to resolve interpersonal conflict by engaging in sexual stimulation. We also include discussion of the differences between love, jealousy, control, and dependence. Finally, we express the hope that our students will enjoy loving sexual interactions.

The *Appendix, Sources of Information About Sexuality,* contains the names of professional organizations concerned with various aspects of sexuality and a list of sexuality journals publishing research reports. In addition, we provide the names and addresses of self-help organizations for people with questions about sexual functions and products.

Ancillaries

A particularly effective set of supplemental materials is available with this text to enhance the teaching and learning processes.

Instructor's Resource Manual and Test Bank   The *Instructor's Resource Manual* features numerous lecture and discussion topics and classroom activities, provided by Elizabeth Rice Allgeier, and a test bank, written by Paul Yarab and Michelle Fuiman of Bowling Green State University. Each chapter of the test bank includes 100 multiple-choice questions and several essay questions. The multiple-choice questions are keyed to learning objectives and identified as factual, conceptual, or applied in nature. Factual questions have been kept to a minimum.

Computerized Test Bank   The test bank is also available on disk with software that allows instructors to add and edit questions and prepare exams.

Study Guide   Each chapter of the accompanying student *Study Guide*, written by Paul Yarab and Michelle Fuiman, includes a chapter overview, learning objectives, a key-terms review exercise, and a multiple-choice quiz with explanations for both correct and incorrect answers.

Transparencies   A selection of 40 full-color overhead transparencies, including images from inside and outside the text, is available.

Psychology Web Site   Houghton Mifflin's Psychology Web Site can be reached by pointing to the Houghton Mifflin home page at http://www.hmco.com and going to the

College Division Psychology page. This location provides access to additional useful and innovative teaching and learning resources that support this book.

Multimedia Policy   The Houghton Mifflin multimedia policy offers adopters a variety of videos, available through your Houghton Mifflin representative.

Acknowledgments

We remain indebted to reviewers of the first four full editions of our text, as well as those who commented on draft manuscript for this book, who include:

Judith A. Baker, Texas Woman's University
Kenneth C. Becker, University of Wisconsin at La Crosse
Roy O. Darby, University of South Carolina at Beaufort
Joseph S. Darden, Jr., Kean College of New Jersey
Beverly Drinnin, Des Moines Area Community College
Randy D. Fisher, University of Central Florida
Anthony T. Gordon, Contra Costa College
Alan Grieco, Rollins College
Bill D. Keever, Western Illinois University
Norma L. McCoy, San Francisco State University
Lynn Miller, Texas Woman's University
Patricia Owen, St. Mary's University
Calvin D. Payne, University of Arizona
Peggy J. Skinner, South Plains College
Susan Sprecher, Illinois State University
Jeffrey Stern, University of Michigan at Dearborn
Cindy Struckman-Johnson, University of South Dakota
Michael W. Wiederman, Ball State University

To fulfill the mission of this book, we relied heavily on the advice and skill of our editors. David Lee, our sponsoring editor, has been enthusiastic and unusually involved in a number of aspects of this project, and we appreciate his strong interest. Sheralee Connors, our developmental editor, was particularly gifted in helping us to increase the accessibility of our book. With Sheralee's careful work and awareness of the audience we are addressing, we were able to enhance the communicability of the ideas in the book without introducing the distortion that can occur with such a complex topic. For many months, we have been in almost daily contact (via e-mail) with our project editor, Janet Young. Her sense of humor, professional touches, and quick responsiveness to our questions have been very helpful. Jane Knetzger, our senior associate editor, has worked on the development of the ancillary materials and has been very much involved in advising us about the content of the book. We also thank Carol Merrigan for her thorough and energetic work on production, and Sandra Sevigny for her rendering of the full-color illustrations.

E. R. A.
A. R. A.

ABOUT THE AUTHORS

Elizabeth Rice Allgeier earned her B.A. from the University of Oregon in 1969, her M.S. from the State University of New York at Oswego in 1973, and her Ph.D. from Purdue University in 1976. Currently Professor of Psychology at Bowling Green State University, she has won numerous teaching awards, including the BGSU Alumni Association's Master Teacher Award in 1988, and the BGSU Outstanding Contributor to Graduate Education in 1992. In 1986, she was named the American Psychological Association's G. Stanley Hall Lecturer on Sexuality. She has taught human sexuality at Eastern Michigan University and at the State University of New York at Fredonia. Dr. Allgeier's interest in studying human sexual behavior began while she was living with the So, a preliterate, polygynous tribe in Uganda. Her study of this tribe resulted in a two-volume ethnography that she coauthored. Her current research interests include the societal regulation of sexual behavior, sexual coercion, and the relationship between gender-role norms and sexual interaction. Actively involved in The Society for the Scientific Study of Sex, she has served as national secretary and as president for that organization, and in 1991 was awarded its Distinguished Service Award. In 1994, she was also awarded the Alfred C. Kinsey Award for Outstanding Contributions to Sexual Science by the Midcontinent Region of The Society for the Scientific Study of Sex. She sits on the editorial board of four scholarly journals that publish sex research and is ending her term as editor of *The Journal of Sex Research.*

   Albert Richard Allgeier earned his B.A. from Gannon University in 1967, his M.A. from the American University of Beirut in Lebanon in 1969, and his Ph.D. from Purdue University in 1974. He has been Clinical Director at both the Northwest Center for Human Resources in Lima, Ohio, and Wood County Mental Health Center in Bowling Green, Ohio. He has served on the faculty of Alma College, the State University of New York at Fredonia, and Bowling Green State University. Currently, he is in private practice in Bowling Green. He has conducted research on interpersonal attraction and sexual knowledge, and has participated with Elizabeth Rice Allgeier, his wife, in a series of studies on attitudes about abortion. He is also interested in the implications of evolutionary theory for the study of human sexuality. He and Elizabeth Rice Allgeier have just completed the editing (with Gary Brannigan) of *The Sex Scientists.* That book features the research process experienced by 15 sexual scientists, and is part of a series of books on that topic that they are developing.

   The Allgeiers have four children and five grandchildren. They enjoy traveling, reading novels, and watching college athletics.

DEDICATION

We dedicate this book with much love to our parents, our four children, and our five grandchildren, Forrest, Laurel, Larkin, Maya, and Max. We also dedicate this book to The Society for the Scientific Study of Sexuality (SSSS). SSSS has been a major supporter of the scientific efforts of sex researchers, and we consider a number of SSSS members to be part of our own extended family.

Sexual Interactions

Basic Understandings

1

RESEARCH ON
SEXUALITY
*The Impact of Societal Beliefs,
Political Attitudes, and Ethical
Issues on Research*
**Across Cultures: Beliefs About
Conception and
Development**
*Understanding the Process of
Sex Research*
*Evaluating Results of Studies
of Sexuality*

CONTEMPORARY
EXPLANATIONS OF
HUMAN SEXUALITY
Evolutionary Approaches
Psychoanalytic Approaches
Learning Approaches
Sociological Approaches
**Across Cultures: A Polygynous
African Tribe**
Theories, Politics, and Morality

SUMMARY OF MAJOR
POINTS

CHECK YOUR
KNOWLEDGE

LEARNING
ABOUT
SEXUALITY

 REALITY or MYTH ?

1. Since the pioneering work of the Kinsey group and Masters and Johnson, opposition to sex research has almost disappeared.

2. Participants in sex research almost always report accurately about their sexual behavior.

3. Research indicates that vitamin E has no effect on sexual activity.

4. Evolutionary theorists have little to say about modern sexual behavior.

5. In Freud's theory, the superego is part of what most people refer to as the conscience.

6. Human sexual behavior is quite similar across cultures.

THE classroom atmosphere on the first day in a human sexuality course is usually charged with tension, and laughter is frequent—perhaps indicating anxiety. Many students enroll in the course with personal concerns and worries not associated with enrollment in other classes. Some have even been asked by parents or roommates to justify taking the class. The queries have ranged from "Why would you want to take a class like that?" to "How can it take a whole semester just to study sex?" One woman dropped our class after her fiancé saw it listed on her schedule. She told us apologetically: "He won't let me take it. He said he'll teach me anything I need to know about sex after we get married."

The scientific study of sexuality is very new. With the loosening of sexual taboos in the past few decades, a great deal of research has been devoted to human sexuality. This research activity produces both frustration and a great deal of excitement among scholars in the area. No sooner is a book about sexuality published than new research emerges that questions the "facts" published in the book.

RESEARCH ON SEXUALITY

When we make decisions that affect our lives, it is helpful to have information about the potential consequences of the choices available to us. Sexual decisions can have major consequences in terms of costs and benefits, but in this area many of us make decisions in the dark, so to speak. With relatively little knowledge, we make judgments as voters for or against sex education, as parents giving advice about nonmarital sex, or as consumers of contraceptives or products to promote fertility. One goal of sex researchers is to increase knowledge about the causes, correlates, and consequences of sexual attitudes and behaviors. The outcome of their work can have a direct effect on our lives, so it is important for us to have some idea about how they go about their work and the extent to which we can have confidence in their conclusions.

The Impact of Societal Beliefs, Political Attitudes, and Ethical Issues on Research

The questions researchers ask about sexuality and the methods they use to search for answers are intimately related to societal values/beliefs and ethical considerations, as well as to their own beliefs. Sometimes it is hard to see the difference between these influences. For example, sex research with children is contrary to the ethical values held by the scientific community because it violates the principle of informed consent; that is, a young child is not considered mature enough to consent to participate in sex research. Such research also violates the societal belief that sex research with children is immoral. In this instance, then, ethical values and societal beliefs are in agreement regarding the moral inappropriateness of such research. Here we separate the discussion of these influences on research, however, because sometimes societal beliefs conflict with ethical views of appropriate topics for sex research.

POLITICAL AND SOCIETAL BARRIERS TO RESEARCH.

When a few nineteenth-century physicians attempted to institute training or research procedures related to sexuality, they suffered dire consequences. In the mid-nineteenth century, for example, Dr. James Platt White allowed 20 medical students to do vaginal exams on a consenting pregnant woman prior to and during childbirth as part of training for obstetrics. Responding to objections from other physicians, who believed that it was wrong for a doctor to see women's genitals even when delivering babies, the American Medical Association expelled White in 1851 and passed a resolution against such training (Bullough, 1983). Across cultures, beliefs have varied considerably about what causes conception in the first place (see "Across Cultures: Beliefs About Conception and Development").

You might assume that such extreme reactions and beliefs are relics of the nineteenth century, but even scientists who studied sexual behavior in the mid-twentieth century paid a price for doing so, both professionally and personally. To illustrate the risks taken by sex-research pioneers, we focus on a select group of sex investigators who experienced many obstacles in their endeavors.

The Kinsey Group. In the mid-1930s Alfred Kinsey and some other Indiana University faculty members were asked to teach a course on marriage and the family. In preparing for the course, Kinsey discovered that there was little scientific information about the sexual aspects of marriage, so he decided to do his own research. Initially, he administered questionnaires to his students about their sexual experiences. By 1938 he had established a research group at Indiana, and members of the group began the first of their interviews with thousands of Americans about their sexual experiences and behaviors. Kinsey and his colleagues, Wardell Pomeroy, Clyde Martin, and Paul Gebhard (see Figure 1.1), undertook the task of describing the sexual behavior of typical Americans throughout the life span by using a combination of intensive interviews and questionnaires.

For the first several years of this project, Kinsey and his colleagues were repeatedly warned about the dangers involved in collecting sex histories, and they experienced some organized opposition. The harassment was not limited to the scientists on the project, however; a high school teacher who

Figure 1.1
Kinsey and His Colleagues
In a meeting at the Institute for Sex Research in Bloomington, Indiana, Kinsey and his colleagues discuss some of their statistical analyses. From left to right are Alfred C. Kinsey, Clyde E. Martin, Paul H. Gebhard, and Wardell B. Pomeroy.

Across Cultures

Beliefs About Conception and Development

Many ancient cultures, apparently unaware of the male's role in conception, believed that pregnancy resulted from the entrance of ancestral spirits into a woman's body. Nonetheless, men and women still engaged in sex—the activity necessary for the continuation of their group into successive generations—and created other justifications for it.

Most twentieth-century North Americans know that coitus is necessary for conception. In fact, some believe that conception is the only justification for sexual relations, an idea in line with the long-standing official position of the Roman Catholic Church. This notion that procreation is the sole justification for having sexual relations, known as *reproductive bias,* has a lengthy history in Western cultures. Beliefs about the purposes of sex are intimately tied to the religious and ideological perspectives of cultures throughout human history.

Cross-cultural research provides information about differences and similarities among groups and can help us to gain perspective on our own culture's sexual beliefs and practices. Some cultures believe that sexual intercourse is important for promoting the growth of children. For example, among the Tiwi people of Melville Island, off the northern coast of Australia, girls go at age seven to live with their future husbands, who are already adults. Within a year the girls begin to have sexual intercourse because the Tiwi believe that intercourse stimulates the onset of puberty (Goodall, 1971). The Tiwi believe that young girls are incapable of developing breasts, pubic hair, and broadened hips and of beginning to menstruate unless they experience intercourse. The Sambia of New Guinea hold a somewhat similar view, except that they think that boys, rather than girls, need sexual stimulation. Specifically, they believe that young boys need to swallow semen to achieve manhood (Herdt, 1984).

In contrast to the Tiwi and the Sambia, the Mehinaku of central Brazil believe that the sexual stimulation of children is dangerous. Although tolerant of sexual games between young boys and girls, the Mehinaku believe that as boys approach puberty, they need to practice sexual abstinence (Gregor, 1985). When a boy is 11 or 12, his father builds a palmwood seclusion barrier behind which the youth remains for most of the next three years, taking growth-producing medicines and following strict dietary rules. Although the Mehinaku idea that contact between boys and sexually mature women is dangerous resembles contemporary Western attitudes, it has a different rationale. The Mehinaku believe that women's menstrual blood and vaginal secretions can poison the growth medicines that boys are given and can even cause a fatal paralysis in boys. Girls are also secluded for a period of time following their first menstrual period, so that they will not "contaminate" the village boys.

The Mehinaku think of fathering children through sexual intercourse as a collective project by the males. The Mehinaku believe that one sexual act is insufficient to conceive a child, for the semen of a woman's husband forms only a portion of the infant. Yet at the same time, moderation is important: A woman who produces a larger-than-normal child or who bears twins has had too many lovers. Such offspring are immediately buried alive.

helped the Kinsey group find volunteers outside the school but in the same city was dismissed by his school board. In addition, there were attempts to persuade Indiana University to stop the study, censor or prevent publication of the results, and fire Kinsey. But the university's administration defended the Kinsey group's right to do scientific research. However, by the time the group published *Sexual Behavior in the Human Male* (1948) and its sequel, *Sexual Behavior in the Human Female* (1953) the United States was in the grip of the McCarthy era, years of intense political repression. Under pressure from a congressional committee, the Rockefeller Foundation withdrew its financial support of the project, and Kinsey died three years later.

The Kinsey group's findings benefited the general public by providing a basis for social comparison that previously had not existed. For instance, we now know that the

ISSUES TO CONSIDER

What are the advantages and disadvantages of knowing about the results of sex research on the variety of sexual behaviors in which people engage in your culture?

majority of people report masturbating at various times, a fact unknown before the publication of the Kinsey group's two major books. Presumably, people who realize that masturbation or other sexual behavior is typical of most people in our culture do not suffer the pangs of remorse and guilt that previous generations endured—or that still afflict those people who are unaware that most people masturbate.

William Masters and Virginia Johnson. In 1966 William Masters and Virginia Johnson (see Figure 1.2) published their first major book on sexuality, *Human Sexual Response,* which described the results of their observations of human sexual response in laboratory settings. Instead of interviewing people about what they did sexually, as the Kinsey group had done, Masters and Johnson directly observed sexual stimulation in a laboratory. They studied volunteers through one-way glass as they masturbated, had oral sex, or engaged in coitus. The two researchers measured sexual responsiveness with the use of devices that fit around the penis or were inserted into the vagina. Their work is responsible for the popularization of the finding that—contrary to Sigmund Freud's theories (see Chapter 5)—the clitoris is involved in most women's sexual responsiveness.

Despite the Kinsey group's precedent-setting work, when Masters asked Washington University authorities for permission to do sex research, "they were terrified. . . . But had they known what we were going to do, they'd have been even more so" (Allgeier, 1984). In the late 1950s Masters and Johnson experienced sabotage. Parts of their equipment disappeared, and personal attacks followed. "What we didn't expect was how they were done: They were fundamentally carried out against our children, [who] were socially ostracized [and] bitterly attacked as being sex-mongers. I had to move my daughter from St. Louis and send her to prep school" (Allgeier, 1984). Despite this early harassment, Masters and Johnson persevered, and we know of no books dealing with human sexual response that do not refer to Masters and Johnson's work—a testament to their important contributions to the field.

In this section we have considered some of the barriers and risks faced by pioneering sex researchers, but as the Kinsey group wrote in 1953 (p. 19), sex researchers are not alone in experiencing such barriers:

> There was a day when the organization of the universe, and the place of the earth, the sun, the moon, and the stars in it, were considered of such theologic import that the scientific investigation of these matters was bitterly opposed by the ruling forces of the day. The scientists who first attempted to explore the nature of matter, and the physical laws affecting the relationships of matter were similarly condemned. . . . We do not believe that the happiness of individual men, and the good of the total social organization, is ever furthered by the perpetuation of ignorance.

Having read this review of the harassment experienced by several sex-research pioneers, you may be left with the mistaken impression that hostility to sex research is behind us. In fact, contemporary efforts to gather data still face uphill battles. For example, a study that became known as the National Health and Social Life Survey was initially designed in 1988 by contract with the National Institute for Child Health and Human Development (Laumann, Gagnon, Michael, & Michaels, 1994). The study was to be the first to question a nationally representative sample of American adults about their sexual attitudes and behaviors. Funding for pilot research was awarded in July 1988, and interviews were planned for about twenty thousand people.

However, conservative politicians such as Senator Jesse Helms of North Carolina got wind of the proposed study and were able to create a political atmosphere that led

Figure 1.2
William Masters and Virginia Johnson Masters and Johnson were pioneering researchers on physiological aspects of human sexual response.

to the withdrawal of funding for the project. The flavor of the Helms opposition is revealed in the following remarks he made before the U.S. Senate:

REALITY or MYTH ? 1

> *The real purpose . . . is not to stop the spread of AIDS. . . . These sex surveys have not—have not—been concerned with legitimate scientific inquiry as much as they have been concerned with a blatant attempt to sway public attitudes in order to liberalize opinions and laws regarding homosexuality, pedophilia, anal and oral sex, sex education, teenage pregnancy and all down the line.* (Congressional Record, *September 12, 1991, pp. S12861–S12862)*

Fortunately, the investigators were able to obtain private funding, although they had to scale back the number of respondents to 3,432. Ironically, their findings—many of which are reported in our text—revealed a more conservative sexual atmosphere in the United States than had most previous studies!

ETHICAL ISSUES.   In addition to the limitations that societal attitudes and beliefs impose on the kinds of questions that can be investigated, scientists must also be concerned with the rights, safety, and well-being of those who participate in their research. Over the years several principles have been developed to safeguard the rights of volunteers for research.

The principle of *informed consent* stipulates that participants be informed of any aspects of a study that might be embarrassing or damaging to them, including all the procedures they will undergo, before they consent to participate. Prisoners, psychiatric patients, developmentally disabled adults, and children are not considered capable of giving informed consent. When children are the population of interest for a particular study, researchers must obtain the informed consent of their parents.

The principle of *freedom from coercion* requires that potential volunteers be free of undue pressure to participate in research. In the past, prison inmates have been induced by offers of shortened sentences to participate in drug research, and college students have been required to "volunteer" for research or accept an incomplete grade in particular courses. Such practices are now viewed as coercive.

The principle of *protection from physical or psychological harm* deals with a particularly thorny ethical problem. If we knew all the potential effects of a sex-therapy treatment, medical procedure, or contraceptive drug, there would be no reason to conduct research to determine these effects. But not knowing what the effects may be, researchers run a real risk of negatively affecting the physical or psychological health of research participants. This ethical principle requires that researchers be aware of this danger and design their study to minimize it. Specifically, volunteers should encounter no more risk to their physical or psychological health during the course of a research project than they would in their normal daily lives. In addition, protecting the anonymity of volunteers and the confidentiality of their responses is an important part of the research principle of protecting participants from harm.

Research on some topics poses dilemmas that cannot be adequately resolved by reference to the principle of protection from physical or psychological harm. We evaluate testing in these and similar areas on the basis of the *risk-benefit principle*. For example, after the birth control pill had been developed and tested with animals, it could not be marketed until its effects on humans had been measured (Reed, 1984). Because the researchers were trying to determine whether the pill produced serious side effects, they obviously could not give unconditional guarantees of protection from harm to volunteers for the testing program. Pregnancy itself poses a health risk, however, and the mortality rates for women and babies were known to be higher when pregnancies occurred less than two years apart than when they occurred at longer intervals. Thus development of a highly reliable contraceptive appeared to offer great potential benefits when testing began in the 1950s. In support of the application of the risk-benefit principle to this case, the maternal mortality rate from pregnancy and childbirth, as we now know, is higher than that from any form of contraception. Therefore, when the potential benefits of research outweigh the potential risks, research is considered permissible, provided the principle of informed consent is maintained.

To make sure that scientists adhere to the four ethical principles just described, ethics boards review research proposals. If an ethics review board approves a research proposal, scientists can begin their study. The results of their research may be presented at professional meetings and published in scholarly journals (see Appendix) and subsequently reported in the popular press. At that point you may become aware of the research and wonder to what extent you should make personal decisions on the basis of it. The remainder of this chapter is aimed at providing you with skills to make an educated judgment regarding the applicability of research findings to you as an individual, (potential) parent, or voter.

Understanding the Process of Sex Research

Attempting to understand the research process for the first time is a bit like making bread or making love for the first time. It is one thing to read about evaluating research in a textbook, kneading dough in a cookbook, or caressing genitals in a sex manual, but quite another to engage in these processes. Initially, you are likely to feel unsure of yourself. Exactly how do you knead dough, anyway? Are you supposed to push it or squeeze it? How hard are you supposed to knead it, and for how long? Similarly, how do you caress genitals? In regard to understanding research, what are the relevant questions, and how do you get the answers?

hypothesis (hy-PAW-theh-sis) Statement of a specific relationship between or among two or more variables.

variable Any situation or behavior capable of change or variation.

operational definition Description of a variable in such a way that it can be measured.

DEFINITION OF RESEARCH TERMS.   When researchers seek scientific evidence relevant to issues in any discipline or field, they generally begin by stating their question as a **hypothesis,** which is a statement of a specific relationship between two or more variables. Put another way, a hypothesis is an educated guess stated in such a way that it can be accepted or rejected on the basis of research results. A **variable** is anything that can vary or change. For instance, our levels of hunger, happiness, sexual arousal, and time spent studying can all change, so these can all be defined as variables.

To formulate a testable hypothesis, a scientist must operationally define the variables. An **operational definition** involves describing each variable, so that it can be measured or counted and people can agree on the definition. Given these criteria, some variables cannot be operationally defined. For example, consider the classic question "How many angels can dance on the head of a pin?" Although we could probably agree on what we mean by "head of a pin" and "dance," we might hit a snag with the term *angel.* Counting or measuring the angels is even more difficult. If we cannot operationally define a variable, we cannot study it.

independent variables Variables that are manipulated or varied by an experimenter.

dependent variables Variables that are measured or observed.

KINDS OF VARIABLES.   There are three kinds of variables: independent, dependent, and control. **Independent variables** are those that can be manipulated or varied by an experimenter. For instance, to investigate the effect of nudity on sexual arousal, we might vary the degree of nudity (the independent variable) in a series of photos, such as those in Figure 1.3.

Dependent variables are variables that are measured. Changes in dependent variables are assumed to depend on variations in the independent variable. For instance, after exposure to one of the photos in Figure 1.3, volunteers could be asked to indicate their level of arousal. Their response—their reported level of arousal—would then be

Figure 1.3
Degree of Nudity as an Independent Variable Although the degree of nudity varies in these photos, other factors vary as well. Thus responses to the photos may differ not only because of the degree of nudity but also because of the extent of body contact.

the dependent variable. Independent variables are sometimes called stimulus variables, and dependent variables can also be called response variables.

Control variables are factors that could vary but that are controlled or held constant. Because in our example we are interested in the effect of nudity on arousal, we want to hold all other variables constant if we can. A number of variables were controlled through use of the same couple in all three photos in Figure 1.3. Otherwise, differences in reported arousal might be confounded—that is, unintentionally influenced—by responses to variations in the age, attractiveness, and so forth of each couple rather than to the degree of nudity per se.

control variables Variables that are held constant or controlled to reduce their influence on the dependent variable.

OBTAINING RESEARCH PARTICIPANTS: PROBLEMS IN SAMPLING. The last time a lab technician pricked your finger to draw some blood, you were participating in a **sampling** process. When physicians order a blood sample, of course, they are not particularly interested in the properties of the small amount of blood that is drawn. Rather, they assume that the properties of that sample are the same as those of the person's entire blood supply.

Scientists conducting sex research would be delighted if they could place as much confidence in their sampling procedures as the lab technician can in blood-sampling procedures. Obtaining accurate results in the sampling of most aspects of human sexuality, however, is considerably more difficult. Most characteristics of sexual behavior are not evenly distributed throughout whatever population we might wish to sample. Further, because all potential sources of **bias** have not been identified, it is difficult to obtain a representative sample. Among the most persistent sources of sampling bias that have been identified are volunteer bias and self-report bias.

sampling The process of selecting a representative part of a population.

bias An attitude for or against a particular theory or hypothesis that influences one's judgment.

volunteer bias Bias introduced into the results of a study stemming from systematic differences between those who volunteer for research and those who avoid participation.

REALITY or MYTH ? 2

generalizability The extent to which findings from a particular sample study can be described as representing wider populations and situations.

self-report bias Bias introduced into the results of a study stemming either from participants' desire to appear "normal" or from memory lapses.

ISSUES TO CONSIDER

According to a college newspaper, 20 percent of students at that college have a sexually transmitted disease. The reporter based these results on data from students who were treated at the local health center. Is there a problem with the reporter's conclusions?

correlational method A research method involving the measurement of two or more variables to determine the extent of their relationship.

experimental method A research method involving the manipulation of one or more independent variables to determine their influence on dependent variables.

Volunteer bias refers to the differences between those who volunteer and those who refuse to participate in research. Studies of volunteer bias have indicated that, although volunteers for sex research do not differ from nonvolunteers in most personality characteristics or in level of adjustment, systematic differences do appear in their attitudes toward sexuality and in their experience with various sexual activities (Bogaert, 1996; Strassberg & Lowe, 1995). Specifically, compared to nonvolunteers, volunteers are more sexually liberal, more positive toward sexuality, more sexually curious, and more supportive of sex research. Generally, volunteers are more sexually experienced and report having had a greater number of sexual partners than do nonvolunteers. Men are more likely than women to volunteer for research on sexuality and other "unusual" topics. Among women, volunteers date more frequently and masturbate more frequently than do nonvolunteers.

After volunteers have been obtained for sex research, another kind of bias, self-report bias, can restrict **generalizability. Self-report bias** can result from participants' reluctance to provide honest answers or inability to give accurate answers. Fearing that they will appear deviant in their sexual feelings and behavior, volunteers may either fail to report or underreport (or in some cases overreport) their behavior. They may respond with what they believe is the socially desirable behavior rather than with their actual behavior (Wiederman, 1993; Wiederman, Weis, & Allgeier, 1994).

Even when volunteers want to report accurately, they may have difficulty recalling some past events. For example, you can probably remember quite accurately the first time you kissed someone erotically. But can you give as accurate an account if you are asked how many times you have kissed someone or how many different people you have kissed?

These sources of bias do not eliminate the usefulness of sex research, nor are they unique to sex research. They simply limit the extent to which we can assume that all people feel or behave precisely the way that research volunteers do. With these potential limitations in mind, let us turn to the two major methods used to gather information about sexual attitudes and behavior.

RESEARCH METHODS.   In gathering evidence relevant to the testing of a hypothesis, researchers generally rely on one of two methods: the **correlational method** and the **experimental method.** With both methods, researchers pay close attention to the bases for selection of samples of the organisms under study, whether they are people, monkeys, or egg cells.

An idea that students have brought to class for the past several decades is that vitamin E increases sexual desire and performance. How would you test this belief? Using a correlational approach, you could give a questionnaire to a large group of people regarding the frequency and quality of their sexual experiences. You could also ask them about the kinds and amounts of vitamins they take. Assume that those people who take large doses of vitamin E also report engaging in more sexual activity than those who take little or no vitamin E. This correlation between taking vitamin E and engaging in more sexual activity indicates that the two are related, but it does not tell us that vitamin E *causes* greater levels of sexual activity or higher levels of performance.

The hypothesis that vitamin E enhances sexual performance was tested with an experimental approach by Edward Herold and his colleagues several decades ago (Herold, Mottin, & Sabry, 1979). Specifically, volunteer couples were randomly assigned to one of two groups. One group received capsules containing vitamin E. The other group received capsules that were identical in appearance but, unknown to them, did not contain vitamin E. Thus the presence or absence of vitamin E—the independent variable—was manipulated. The volunteers also completed questionnaires reporting both their sexual and nonsexual feelings—the dependent variables.

The random assignment of the couples to the vitamin or nonvitamin groups provided a means to control the influence of other, irrelevant variables. We can assume that through random assignment the average level of reported sexual activity prior to participation in the study would have been about the same in both groups.

Before we reveal the results of Herold et al.'s (1979) study, note that if they found, using an experimental method, that the vitamin E group had greater levels of sexual desire and performance than the nonvitamin E group, we could conclude that vitamin E *enhances* (a causal inference) sexual performance. In fact, Herold et al. found that the vitamin E group reported increased energy and more other positive effects than did the non–vitamin E group. However, the two groups did not differ in reported levels of sexual activity.

MEASUREMENT IN SEX RESEARCH. Methods of measuring sexual responses include self-administered measures, interviews, direct observation, physiological and biochemical measures, and case studies (Beere, 1990; Davis, Yarber, Bauserman, Schreer, & Davis, 1997). When someone is designing or choosing research measures, he or she must determine their **reliability** and **validity.** If a measure is reliable, then individuals will respond the same way over a period of weeks or months. A measure is valid to the extent that scores on it accurately reflect the variable in question. If, for example, you created a self-report measure of sexual arousal in response to erotic stimuli, you might test its validity by using it in conjunction with physiological measures of arousal (for example, erection and vaginal lubrication). If physiological measures reflect greater levels of arousal as self-reported ratings of arousal increase, then confidence in the validity of the self-report measure increases.

reliability The extent to which a measure elicits the same response at different times.
validity The extent to which an instrument measures what it is designed to measure.

SELF-ADMINISTERED QUESTIONNAIRES, SURVEYS, AND SCALES. Hundreds of measures have been developed to record attitudinal and behavioral responses to various aspects of sexuality. By comparing responses to these measures across samples from different populations, researchers can get an idea of how different groups of people (for example, men versus women, adolescents versus adults, sexually experienced versus sexually inexperienced people) differ in their attitudes, knowledge, and behavior regarding such matters as contraception, abortion, homosexuality, and rape. By comparing the survey responses from samples of the same population across different time periods, researchers can get an idea of what changes occur over time.

ISSUES TO CONSIDER

Would you volunteer to participate in a research project to (a) respond to a questionnaire about your sexual attitudes and behavior, (b) observe erotic films, (c) be observed engaging in sexual behavior? Why or why not?

INTERVIEWS. Researchers also obtain information about sexual attitudes and behavior by interviewing people. This method is usually more expensive and time-consuming than pencil-and-paper measures, but it allows for greater flexibility in acquiring in-depth information.

DIRECT OBSERVATION. Direct observation involves exactly what its name implies: The behavior of interest is directly observed. For example, researchers have directly observed such sexual behaviors as flirtation in bars (Moore, 1985; Perper, 1985) and sexual activity of heterosexual and homosexual couples (Masters & Johnson, 1966, 1979). This approach is also useful with nonhuman species because they cannot respond to questionnaires or interviews.

A problem with direct observation is that the presence of an observer may alter the behavior of the organisms being observed. Many of us have experienced this phenomenon while under observation when we were learning to drive or type. Volunteer bias may also be a greater problem when researchers use direct observation than when they rely on self-reported behavior for information about sexuality (Strassberg & Lowe, 1995).

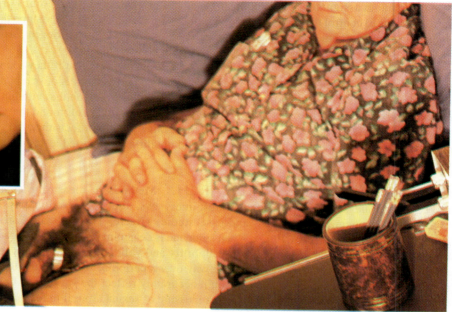

Figure 1.4
Device for Measuring Male Sexual Response In the photo to the left, a metal strain gauge has been placed on a model of a penis. It contains a measure to assess the extent of erection of the penis. In the photo to the right, a research volunteer has the device around the base of his penis prior to sexual arousal.

PHYSIOLOGICAL RESPONSE MEASURES.

Some other approaches that are used to record changes resulting from sexual arousal range from measures of general responses, such as heart rate and dilation of the pupils, to measures of genital responses. The general measures do provide information about arousal; however, they do not indicate whether sexual or nonsexual stimulation is the source of the observed arousal. Sex hormones, such as testosterone, can be measured through analysis of blood or saliva samples.

Among the devices for measuring male genital response are the penile plethysmograph, the mercury-in-rubber strain gauge, and the metal-band gauge (see Figure 1.4). All three of these devices fit partially or totally around the penis and are designed to measure changes in its circumference. The devices that are currently being used to measure female genital response are the vaginal myograph and the rectal myograph (see Figure 1.5). Both of these devices monitor the muscular activity of the pelvic floor. Although these genital measures have advantages over more general measures, their use reflects an unintended bias: that sexual response is primarily a genital, rather than a total body-and-mind, process.

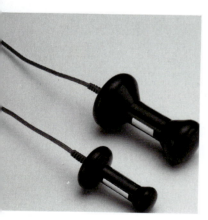

Figure 1.5
Devices for Measuring Female Sexual Response This photograph shows the current models of the vaginal and rectal myographs that monitor the muscular activity of the pelvic floor.

CASE STUDIES AND FOCUS-GROUP RESEARCH.

When a researcher studies a single person, family, or small group without the intention of comparing that person, family, or group with others in the same study, the approach is known as the case study or focus-group research. With the case study, a single individual is studied extensively via one or more of the methods described above (e.g., scales, interviews, biochemical measures). This approach does not permit cause-effect inferences, nor can the responses from a single person be generalized beyond that person. Nevertheless, the case study of one individual can disprove an always or never assertion, for example, that women never ejaculate or men always ejaculate.

Researchers using focus groups select people who share some common characteristics and interview the participants in groups. One purpose of focus groups is to permit group members to generate their own questions and issues. Thus an advantage of this approach is that it can allow participants to express information that the researchers who designed the questions overlooked.

As with case studies of individuals, focus-group research with groups of people is aimed at hypothesis generation rather than hypothesis testing. The hypotheses that develop from case studies and focus groups can then be tested with larger samples through correlational or experimental designs.

Evaluating Results of Studies of Sexuality

In the desire to improve our lives and relationships, we tend to be receptive to new information. In making decisions about whether to act on new information, we are wise to consider several issues. At the least, such factors as generalizability, potential side effects, temporary versus lasting effects, and **replication** of the results should be considered before we embrace a new discovery.

In evaluating a treatment, whether it involves a drug, psychotherapy, or other interventions, we should ask whether it applies to everyone under all conditions—that is, to what extent can we generalize the findings. A related issue is the extent to which we can generalize the results of research on animals to human populations. Researchers commonly test new drugs on nonhuman species such as rats and monkeys. Although many drugs have similar effects on humans and nonhumans, occasionally a drug will have a different effect on humans than it does on animals.

We should also investigate the possible side effects of a treatment, particularly those that may not appear right away. For example, millions of women adopted the pill within the first decade after it was marketed. Before making it widely available, the developers tested the pill and found that the immediate side effects were relatively minor and temporary. Unfortunately, it took far longer to discover that the pill could have more serious long-term effects for a small percentage of women, primarily those women who were already at risk for cardiovascular illness (see Chapter 8). Thus in making a decision about the use of a treatment, consumers should attempt to determine what is known about its short- and long-term risks.

Will a treatment that appears to solve a particular problem continue to be effective, or are there other factors responsible for a "quick fix" that may disappear in time? Central to this question are two phenomena: the effect of **placebos** and the effect of novelty.

In a variety of situations, a belief that something will help appears to contribute to a cure, known as the placebo effect. For example, when two partners spend time and money to avail themselves of a sex therapist to improve their sexual relationship, making a joint decision and setting aside time to focus on their relationship may be responsible for much of the benefit that they experience. If the couple's mutual commitment is the cause of the high cure rate reported by sex therapists, thousands of dollars could be saved, at least by some clients.

Novelty may also produce temporary effects. A person who has had various problems in his or her relationship may decide that the appropriate "treatment" is to find a new partner. In the new relationship, the person may describe the success of this solution: "Oh, he (she) is so warm and so much more capable of intimacy than _____. I didn't realize how great a relationship could be." The "treatment" (leaving the former partner and entering a new relationship) appears to be effective. Sometimes a conversation with this person six months later indicates, however, that the problems that riddled the previous relationship have emerged in the present one. The "treatment" had only a temporary effect. Before investing in a new treatment, then, we want to determine whether its effect is likely to be temporary or long lasting.

replication The practice of repeating a study with a different group of research participants to determine whether the results of previous research are reliable.

placebos Treatments or drugs that supposedly have some effect on people but that in reality should have no effect.

In conducting research, scientists generally have ideas—or theories—about why particular variables may be related to one another, for example, men's and women's preferences for particular characteristics in potential mates. We turn now to a description of the major theories that have guided scientists' investigations of human sexuality.

CONTEMPORARY EXPLANATIONS OF HUMAN SEXUALITY

copulation (kop-you-LAY-shun) Sexual intercourse involving insertion of the penis into the vagina.

What is sex? The amount of time we spend physically engaging in it—even for the most sexually active people—is minuscule compared to the amount of time we spend eating, bathing, sleeping, working, studying, and commuting.

Although most of us do not spend more than a tiny part of our lives directly engaging in sexual stimulation and **copulation,** we spend enormous amounts of time on quasi-sexual activities. We bathe, dress carefully, style our hair, and put cologne or shaving lotion on our skin in hopes of making ourselves appear more attractive. We notice interesting strangers and flirt with colleagues and classmates. And we think about sex. We may indulge in elaborate fantasies and mental rehearsals of potential interactions. Maybe we visualize running into someone in whom we are interested and then engaging in conversation and in physical contact at increasingly intimate levels. Sometimes the fantasy does not go the way we want it to, so we return to an earlier point in the fantasy to alter the script to our liking.

Part of this activity—the thoughts and fantasies—is an attempt to understand and explain sexual events to ourselves. We continue this process at the most personal and practical level as we try to make sexual decisions: "Will she think I'm not a man if I don't try to make love to her?" "Will he lose interest if I don't go to bed with him?"

We also try to understand and explain various aspects of sexuality at a more global level: "What effect would sex education beginning in kindergarten have on young children?" "What are the behavioral effects of viewing erotic materials?"

Theorists also try to understand and explain various aspects of sexuality. A *theory* is essentially a model of how something works. It is a tentative explanation that is not yet accepted as fact. Ideally, a theory leads to research questions that can be tested to see whether the evidence supports or refutes the theory.

Theories can become part of the belief systems of individuals and cultures. For example, the theory that women are dangerous sexual temptresses and inferior to men has dominated much of the history of Western civilization. In the twentieth century, Freud's theory about female sexuality has had a profound effect on the sex lives of millions of women and men. Accordingly, it is important to test theories whenever possible. Theories and the research that evolves from them provide us with the only reliable way of advancing knowledge about ourselves and our world.

In this section we examine four theoretical explanations of the function of sexuality in our lives. All four approaches have strengths and weaknesses. All four will undoubtedly continue to be refined and altered as we learn more about sexuality. At present, however, they provide us with the most useful vantage points available from which we can attempt to understand human sexuality.

Evolutionary Approaches

natural selection The process whereby species evolve as a result of variations in the reproductive success of their ancestors.

The origins of modern evolutionary theory can be traced back to the work of Charles Darwin. He proposed that living organisms evolved from one or more simple forms of life through a process called **natural selection.** Obviously, individuals in a population differ in the number and the characteristics of offspring they produce during their lifetimes. Individuals who produce a relatively large number of children are more likely to have their **genes,** the basic units of heredity, transmitted to future generations. However, according to evolutionary theorists, the effect of the sheer number of offspring is moderated by the characteristics of those offspring. They inherit characteristics from their parents that may be more or less adaptive, or useful, in the particular environmental conditions in which they live. Some of these characteristics—for example, hunting prowess, ability to search for and store food, and skill in attracting mates—increase the likelihood that the offspring will go on to produce children of their own. Thus adaptive characteristics are "selected" for continuation, producing **reproductive success,** a crucial concept in the theory of natural selection (see Figure 1.6).

Most contemporary evolutionists assume that the current characteristics of an organism exist because of their past usefulness in perpetuating the reproductive success of that organism's ancestors. Those organisms having greater reproductive success are considered to have greater **fitness.** Natural selection can favor us not only through our own reproductive success in transmitting our genes, but also through the fitness of other people who share our genes, such as our brothers and sisters. Natural selection therefore operates for the maximization of **inclusive fitness,** which involves both an individual's reproductive contribution to the gene pool of the next generation and that person's contribution in aiding the survival of kin, who pass on their shared genes (see Figure 1.7).

Figure 1.6
Reproductive Success? According to evolutionary theory, characteristics of the more reproductively successful organisms of a species are passed on to the next generation.

Figure 1.7
Families and Inclusive Fitness This family group illustrates one aspect of inclusive fitness—the bonds that relatives develop for their mutual well-being.

genes Part of DNA molecules, found in chromosomes of cells, that are responsible for the transmission of hereditary material from parents to offspring.

reproductive success The extent to which organisms are able to produce offspring who survive long enough to pass on their genes to successive generations.

fitness A measure of one's success in transmitting genes to the next generation (reproductive success).

inclusive fitness A measure of the total contribution of genes to the next generation by oneself and those with whom one shares genes, such as siblings and cousins.

REALITY or MYTH ? 4

gender (JEN-der) The social-psychological characteristics associated with being a male or a female in a particular culture.

ISSUES TO CONSIDER

To examine gender differences among your peers, you could ask a few sexually intimate couples whom you know to tell you who took the active role in initiating the first (a) date, (b) kiss, (c) necking, (d) petting, and (e) sexual stimulation to orgasm and/or ejaculation. If you find gender differences, how would you explain them?

Evolutionary theorists assume that sexual behaviors exist and are maintained because in the past they served the cause of reproduction. According to this perspective, many of our current sexual activities can be traced back to reproductive behaviors that are believed to have existed in early hunting and gathering groups. Scientists have used evolutionary theoretical analyses to try explaining a variety of human sexual behaviors. One of the more interesting hypotheses that has emerged from this framework concerns gender differences in sexuality.

GENDER DIFFERENCES IN SEXUALITY.

In a major analysis of the research on the relationship of **gender** to sexual attitudes and behaviors, Oliver and Hyde (1993) found a number of gender differences. One of the most pronounced differences between men and women emerged in attitudes toward casual sex. Compared to women, men held considerably more permissive attitudes regarding coitus between people in a casual relationship or in a dating relationship that did not involve commitment. This finding is quite consistent with evolutionary predictions, because during the time our species was evolving, women who conceived with uncommitted partners (i.e., single mothers) would usually have been less able to provide for their offspring from infancy to adulthood than would women who were impregnated by men committed to a long-term relationship with the woman and their children. In contrast, the survival of men's genes in successive generations would have been less endangered by the absence of commitment to a woman. What men might have lost in the survival of some of their offspring would have been compensated for by the large numbers of offspring that they sired.

In response to the question of gender differences, the evolutionary perspective has yielded an intriguing model called parental-investment theory. Specifically, Robert Trivers (1972) proposed that gender differences in the sexual behavior of a particular species are determined by fathers' versus mothers' amount of resources, time, and energy invested in their offspring.

Your mother and father committed various resources in rearing you. Who committed more? If your parents are typical of most in our culture, your mother invested a lot more than did your father (see Figure 1.8). After conception, she carried you for about nine months in her uterus. After giving birth to you, she fed you when you were too

Figure 1.8
Parental Investment From conception into adolescence, mothers typically invest more resources in their offspring than do fathers.

helpless to feed yourself. As you grew up, she took care of you to a greater extent than your father did. This does not mean that human males are lacking in capability for parental investment. But among most humans today, parental investment by women is greater than that by men.

Thus among species in which females invest more as parents and control reproductive success, males are at a disadvantage. Males must therefore try harder to succeed in passing on their genes. Whatever strategies and attributes males have that help them to succeed will be passed on. Characteristics that may render males less successful in competing against other males in attracting females, such as passivity and physical limitations, will tend to drop out of the gene pool.

Evolutionary theorists have been attacked for attempting to reduce complex social behavior to a genetic drama—**reductionism.** They are accused of painting a picture of humans as automatons driven by genetic codes. Evolutionary theorists, however, consider humans to be a species with an evolutionary history who are also influenced by current circumstances. They emphasize the psychological mechanisms arising from evolution that underlie human emotion, learning, and behavior (Allgeier & Wiederman, 1994; Buss, 1996; Tooby & Cosmides, 1992). In addition to sparking controversy over the accuracy of evolutionary explanations of gender differences in courtship strategies, mate selection, and other sexual behaviors, evolutionary approaches have generated a great deal of debate on political and moral grounds, a topic to which we return at the end of this section.

Evolutionary theorists, as we have seen, are concerned with how and why the early history of entire species determines what characteristics are transmitted through reproduction. Psychoanalytic theorists take a different perspective, however, emphasizing the influence of an individual's early experience on his or her subsequent development.

reductionism Explaining complex processes in terms of basic physical/chemical activities (for example, explaining human sexual desire solely in terms of hormonal activity).

Psychoanalytic Approaches

The creator of psychoanalytic theory, Sigmund Freud, utterly transformed beliefs about the influence of sexuality early in the life span when he argued that sexual experiences during infancy influence the development of adult personality. His ideas still shock and offend some people.

FREUD'S THEORY OF PERSONALITY DEVELOPMENT.

Freud believed that all human beings have two kinds of **instincts.** One kind—*eros,* the life instinct—operates to preserve or enhance the individual and species. The other kind—*thanatos,* the death instinct—motivates the organism to return to its original state of inorganic matter and is expressed in aggressive and destructive behavior. Freud assumed that each of the instincts had an accompanying energy source, pushing for release or expression. As part of the life instinct, he proposed a sexual instinct, and he named its accompanying energy source the *libido.* This instinct interested Freud the most. Unlike the need for food and water, the instinctive need for love and sex, according to Freud, can be **repressed** by the society or the individual. However, its energy source, the libido, remains. Freud spun his theory of personality development around the fate of the libido.

instincts As Freud used this term, biological excitations that lead to mental activity.

repression Not paying attention to thoughts or feelings because they are threatening.

THE ID, EGO, AND SUPEREGO.

Freud believed that the influence of libido on an individual's personality and behavior is determined by three subsystems in the mind: the id, ego, and superego. The **id** contains such instincts as hunger and sex. According to Freud, the id is present at birth and is not controlled by knowledge of reality or morality. The id seeks only to gratify instinctual drives and to enjoy the pleasure that results when tension aroused by instinctual needs is discharged. The id seeks immediate gratification without regard for moral or practical consequences.

id In psychoanalysis, the source of psychic energy derived from instinctive drives.

When we feel sexual tension or desire, we may spend hours imagining an encounter with a partner, but wishing does not provide one. To satisfy our sexual tensions, thirst, or hunger, we must be able to perceive and solve problems, organize and store knowledge, and initiate acts to achieve these goals. According to Freud, a second subsystem of the personality, the ego, develops out of the id to perform these functions.

ego In psychoanalysis, the rational level of personality.

The **ego** is shaped by contacts with the external world. It seeks to satisfy the demands of the id in light of the constraints of the real world. In working out a realistic strategy to fulfill our needs, the ego must try to satisfy three masters. It must deal with the id, which wants satisfaction of needs. It must take into account the demands of external reality, which prohibit many selfish behaviors. Finally, it must satisfy the last subsystem of personality to emerge, the superego.

superego In psychoanalysis, the level of personality corresponding to the conscience.

The **superego** develops initially from the learning of societal values, as taught by parents and other caretakers. As a child matures, the superego is also influenced by the child's own critical examination of different values. The superego includes what is called the conscience, which is concerned with whether a thought or behavior is good or bad, right or wrong.

 **? 5**

PSYCHOSEXUAL STAGES.

The unfolding of sexual energies from infancy on forms a central part of Freud's theory of personality development. He believed that early in life libido is channeled into certain body zones, which then become the center of eroticism (see Table 1.1). Each stage of development poses demands that must be met and conflicts that must be resolved. If conflicts are not resolved, fixation occurs, in which some libido remains invested in that stage, to be reflected in adult behavior. For instance, Freudians see smokers as partially fixated at the oral stage. Freud believed that much of adult personality was influenced by what went on in these early developmental stages.

Psychoanalytic theorists have taken many new directions since Freud did his original work. Most refinements of psychoanalytic theory, some of which are called object-relations theory, have stressed the adaptiveness of the ego and how we interact with others. For example, Nancy Chodorow (1978) pointed out that because infants—both boys and girls—generally have the most contact with their mothers, they initially

Table 1.1	**Freud's Psychosexual Stages**			
Age	**Psychosexual Stage**	**Erogenous Zone**	**Activities**	**Psychoanalytic Expectations**
0–1 yr.	Oral	Mouth	Sucking, biting, "taking things in"	Dependency on caretaker
2–3 yrs.	Anal	Anus	Expulsion and retention of feces	Clash of wills between child and parent; delay of gratification
4–5 yrs.	Phallic	Genitals	Playing with genitals	Oedipal complex, Electra complex, gender identity
6–12 yrs.	Latency	Genitals	Preference for same-gender playmates	Sublimation and repression of libido
13–20 yrs.	Puberty	Genitals	Dating, "practicing" for eventual mate selection	Flare-up of Oedipal conflict, usually reflected in a "crush" on older person
21–? yrs.	Genital	Genitals	Sexual intercourse	Mate selection, propagation of the species

identify and form intense relationships with their mothers. For girls, this identification is never completely severed, but boys must relinquish their identification with their mothers as they take on masculine roles. Chodorow maintained that this differing experience produces distinct coping strategies for males and females in dealing with the world. Specifically, women emphasize relationships *with* others, whereas men focus on their own individualism and independence *from* others (Gilligan, 1982).

Whatever the weaknesses or inaccuracies in psychoanalytic theory, some of its major hypotheses—for example, the concept of developmental stages and their importance for adult behavior and the concept of the unconscious—have been incorporated in one form or another into most current theories of personality.

Learning Approaches

The evolutionary and psychoanalytic theories that we have just described emphasize biological explanations of human sexual behavior. We turn now to an approach that focuses on the relationship of learning to our sexual behavior. The research presented throughout the text demonstrates that much of our sexual behavior—what we do; with whom we do it; when, where, and how we do it—is influenced by learning processes.

Learning theorists assume that most behavior, including sexual behavior, is strongly affected by learning processes. Many of the processes or "laws" of learning were formulated in the first half of the twentieth century, when a brand of psychology called **behaviorism** developed. The early behaviorists, among them John Watson (1878–1958), maintained that to be scientific, researchers must focus only on what is observable and measurable. Thus the early behaviorists studied overt behavior and disregarded mental events—thoughts, ideas, beliefs, and attitudes.

behaviorism A theoretical approach that emphasizes the importance of studying observable activity.

CONDITIONING.   Most students who have taken an introductory psychology course have learned about the concept of classical conditioning developed by Russian physiologist Ivan Pavlov (1849–1936). In the classic experiment, Pavlov presented dogs with food, an **unconditioned stimulus (UCS)** that caused them to salivate, salivation being an **unconditioned response (UCR)** to food. Pavlov sounded a buzzer at the same time that he gave the dogs the food; he repeated the conditioning until eventually the dogs would salivate at the sound of the buzzer alone. In terms of classical conditioning, the buzzer was a **conditioned stimulus (CS),** and the salivation in response to it was a **conditioned response (CR).** The dogs learned to salivate in response to a stimulus that previously had not elicited this response.

Researchers have employed classical conditioning to explain how people can come to be sexually aroused by a wide range of stimuli. You have undoubtedly experienced some classical conditioning of your own sexual arousal without fully recognizing it at the time. Have you ever felt arousal when smelling a particular cologne or perfume? If you have an erotic interest in someone who wears a specific brand, you may have noticed that the smell arouses you; that is, you shake, you feel short of breath, your pulse races, and your heart beats faster when you smell a scent that you associate with the person who attracts you.

unconditioned stimulus (UCS) A stimulus that evokes a response that is not dependent on prior learning.
unconditioned response (UCR) A stimulus-evoked response that is not dependent on experience or learning.
conditioned stimulus (CS) In classical conditioning, a stimulus that is paired with an unconditioned stimulus until it evokes a response that was previously associated with the unconditioned stimulus.
conditioned response (CR) An acquired response to a stimulus that did not originally evoke such a response.

OPERANT CONDITIONING.   Besides learning to respond to one stimulus because of its association with another stimulus to which we already have an unconditioned response, humans also learn to behave in particular ways as a function of whether their behaviors are rewarded, ignored, or punished. In the most general form, learning theory maintains that behavior is influenced by its consequences. Behavior followed by pleasurable consequences (positive reinforcement) is likely to recur and increase in frequency. Behavior associated with the removal of an aversive (or unpleasant) stimulus is also likely to recur and increase in frequency (negative reinforcement). Conversely, behavior that is not rewarded or is associated with an aversive stimulus (punishment) occurs at a diminished frequency or not at all. Upon removal of the aversive stimulus, the behavior may reappear or increase in frequency.

We learn many kinds of behavior through being rewarded, ignored, or punished for them. If an experience with another person—a conversation, a date, or sexual intimacy—is pleasurable, we are likely to try repeating the experience. We are less likely to repeat experiences that are not particularly pleasant or are punishing.

Other techniques—such as removing rewards in cases of undesirable behavior and rewarding responses that are often incompatible with undesirable behavior—are often more effective than punishment. In the case of children playing with their genitals, for example, parents can encourage a son or daughter to engage in that pleasurable activity in the privacy of the bedroom or at least not in the presence of people who might object, such as grandparents or neighbors. Interestingly, the work of many learning theorists supports some religious teachings stressing that acts of love (positive reinforcement) influence behavior more than does punishment.

In many studies little is said about the social context in which people were punished or what the punished people thought about it. Many students of sexual behavior consider these factors to be as important as conditioning principles. Concern with the influence of social and **cognitive** factors has led to extensions and revisions of the basic learning theories just outlined.

cognitive Related to the act or process of engaging in mental activity.

SOCIAL LEARNING THEORY. We learn most of our behavior in the context of our interactions with others. People need other people from the beginning of life to the end of it. Most of us can look at our own histories and see the central place of our interactions with particular people and the importance of our thoughts about them. In their early fervor to be scientific and to isolate behavior in the laboratory, behaviorists overlooked the significance of such social interactions and thoughts. Gradually, some behavioral scientists, known as social learning theorists, began to examine the influence of other people and of cognitions—observations, perceptions, ideas, beliefs, and attitudes—on sexual behavior.

Albert Bandura is one of the most influential of the social learning theorists. He argued that sex-related behavior can be learned, without the learner receiving any direct reinforcement, through observation of other people and events. This process is called **modeling.** Bandura (1986) would suggest, for example, that if we observed someone being rewarded or reinforced for engaging in premarital sex, we would be more likely to engage in this behavior. Similarly, if we observed someone being punished for practicing premarital sex, we would be less likely to have sex before marriage. In support of this hypothesis, Christopher, Johnson, and Roosa (1993) found that perceived peer sexual behavior was a strong predictor of early sexual involvement.

modeling Learning through observation of others.

Social learning theorists place significant emphasis on cognitions (Hogben & Byrne, 1998). Many current investigators of sexuality are guided by the general philosophy of social learning theory: that some combination of learning and cognitive principles will best explain sexual behavior. In attempting to explain sexual attitudes and behaviors in terms of cognition and complex social events, contemporary learning theorists have taken an approach similar to that of sex researchers trained in the discipline of sociology.

ISSUES TO CONSIDER

John has been forbidden by his parents to use "dirty" words. However, he has seen his father laugh affectionately when his mother occasionally swears. Based on learning principles, what is your expectation regarding John's future use of "taboo" words?

Sociological Approaches

In contrast to those scientists who take the evolutionary and psychoanalytic approaches, most sociologists concerned with sexuality believe that human sexual behavior is more readily understood through examination of **socialization** processes and cultural beliefs and norms rather than through study of biological development or individual learning experiences. According to John Gagnon and William Simon (1973, p. 9), without the complex psychosocial process of development experienced by humans, the physical acts involved in sexual activity would not be possible: "The very experience of excitement that seems to originate from hidden internal sources is in fact a learned process, and it is only our insistence on the myth of naturalness that hides these social components from us."

socialization The process of developing the skills needed to interact with others in one's culture.

The sociological perspective is similar to that taken by social learning theorists. However, social learning theorists tend to examine the socialization and conditioning of the individual; in contrast, sociologists take a broader view, looking at the relationship between beliefs and norms shared by members of a society to understand the sexual interactions of members of that group.

In addition, sociologists maintain that these individual learning experiences do not allow an adequate explanation for why people in one society differ so much in their sexual lifestyles from people in another society. For example, although all human females are capable biologically of experiencing great pleasure during sexual interaction, whether they do enjoy sexual relations varies from one culture to another and is related to the culture's perception of the importance of female sexual pleasure and of the purpose of sex. As discussed in "Across Cultures: A Polygynous African Tribe," the So women of Uganda do not enjoy sex but endure it because they want to conceive. In their culture genital touching is taboo, and orgasm is assumed to occur only in males (Allgeier, 1992). In contrast, the Mangaian people of Polynesia are encouraged from childhood on to learn as much as they can about how to give and receive sexual pleasure. Mangaian girls learn that women should be sexually active and responsive and should experience sexual relations with a number of men to find a spouse with whom they enjoy sex. Marshall (1971) estimated that women in this culture have three times as many orgasms as men.

 **? 6**

Ira Reiss (1986) hypothesized that in almost all societies (the So are an exception) genital stimulation and response usually lead to physical pleasure and self-disclosure. No matter how permissive most societies are about sexuality, they place importance on the potential for development of an interpersonal bond through the pleasure and disclosure characteristics of sexuality. Interpersonal bonding is universally emphasized because it is the basis of stable social relationships, the structural foundation of societies.

SCRIPTS.   To develop social stability, groups attempt to define what is proper behavior for a specific situation. Members of a particular society then have a set of social guidelines, or **scripts,** that they can adopt or alter to suit their purposes. On the individual level, scripts are cognitive plans that enable us to behave in an organized and predictable fashion.

scripts Largely unconscious, culturally determined mental plans that individuals use to organize and guide their behavior.

Our individual scripts are part of the cultural expectations about interactions between people. Just as actors have scripts to guide them through a play, we have our own scripts to guide us through various interactions. Just as actors learn their parts so thoroughly that they perform their roles without being conscious of the script, so do we perform much of our own scripted behavior as if it were second nature.

From the standpoint of script theory, there is little sexual interaction (or other behavior) that can truly be called spontaneous. Members of each culture share learned

Across Cultures

A Polygynous African Tribe

In 1969–1970 the anthropologist Charles Laughlin and I spent a year living with the So tribe in the semiarid mountains of northeastern Uganda in Africa (Allgeier, 1992; Laughlin & Allgeier, 1979). In this polygynous tribe, the number of cows and goats owned by a man is a measure of his wealth, and it is in cows and goats that he pays for his wives.

We spent several months informally observing the So, learning their language, and taking a census. I then conducted a series of interviews with a random sample of the tribal members to attempt to understand their sexual attitudes and behavior.

Following a general principle for studying sensitive topics, in the first interview I asked relatively innocuous questions to give the informant and me some time to become acquainted and feel at ease. In constructing the most intimate questions, I tried to avoid wording that would imply any value judgment.

There were some topics for which there were no So words. For instance, there was no term for *masturbation,* and although I was able to get the idea across to males through appropriate gesturing, the practice seemed to be totally unimaginable to females. Although adolescent males occasionally masturbated, it was taboo for married adult males to masturbate, because doing so constituted a "wasting of seed."

Love was another word for which no So term existed. There was *apudori* (sexual intercourse), and there were words for friendship, but no word for *love* per se. The So did not practice homosexuality, which fell into a category of behaviors (including adult masturbation, intercourse during menstruation, and bestiality) that they considered evidence of witchcraft. In addition, contraception was totally unknown to the So. My question "What can you do if you don't want to have any more children?" was greeted with the same sort of astonishment that you might express if someone asked, "What can you do if you no longer want your legs?"

The attitudes and experiences of men and women regarding intercourse differed strikingly. For men, intercourse was positive, both because they valued pro-

patterns that facilitate their sexual interaction. Inherent in script theory is the notion that scripts allow a sexual encounter to take place by providing the participants with a program for action. The script defines the situation, names the actors, and plots the sequence of events in a sexual interaction.

On the societal level, sexual scripts are the beliefs that people in a particular group share about what are good and bad sexual thoughts, feelings, and behaviors. These sexual scripts function as guideposts, describing the proper social circumstances in which sexual responses may occur. In a large and complex society such as our own, sexual scripts vary somewhat depending on social class and age group, but there is still much similarity in the sexual scripts across these groups. One such similarity has been the male control of resources in most cultures.

POWER, GENDER, AND THE RISE OF FEMINIST APPROACHES.

According to Reiss (1986), power is the ability to influence others and achieve one's objectives despite the opposition of others. Powerful people seek to obtain and retain their control over the valuable elements in their society. Insofar as sexuality is considered a valuable resource, powerful people seek to gain control of it. Men generally have had more power than women have had in almost all cultures. So according to Reiss, powerful men seek not only to obtain sexual satisfaction for themselves but also to control sexual access to those who are important to them, such as wives, daughters, and sisters. In his view, differences between the roles of men and women stem not from biological differences but from the degree of male control of key societal institutions.

Partly in response to this male dominance, Betty Friedan's (1963) book *The Feminine Mystique* and Germaine Greer's (1971) *The Female Eunuch* addressed issues that creation highly and because they enjoyed the activity itself. Those men who were married to more than one woman spent an equal amount of time with each wife, but they avoided a particular wife when she was menstruating. During intercourse they did not engage in any foreplay. Female breasts, which So women left exposed, had no erotic significance. And except for the incidental contact that occurs during vaginal penetration, to touch any portion of the vulva was forbidden.

In the absence of precoital stimulation, the negative attitude of So women toward sexual intercourse was not particularly surprising. I still have a vivid memory of one very beautiful middle-aged woman, with clenched teeth and hands, describing her first experience with intercourse. She said that it hurt badly—it burned—but that she got through it by telling herself repeatedly that she had to do this to get a baby and that she had to have a baby to get cows. When asked how she felt about sex now, she said that she wished her husband had enough cows to take a "little wife" but that it did not hurt as much now as it had at first. In no instance did a woman indicate ever having an orgasm; in fact, the So viewed orgasm as synonymous with ejaculation and as exclusively a male phenomenon. In exploring the total absence of female orgasm, I attempted to find out if So women were aware of having a clitoris. I described it and drew pictures of vulvas, but to no avail.

Over the years, I have considered at length these gender differences in sexual attitudes, attempting to find explanations. Perhaps the tribe's survival depended to some extent on these attitudes. In the face of disease and constant warfare with neighboring tribes, the tribe was in danger of extinction. Because females outnumbered males, the population could be maintained as long as women gave birth to as many children as possible. If women enjoyed sex, they might not want to share their husbands with other women. As it was, however, co-wives tended to have rather close relationships with one another. They did not compete for men; rather, they shared the responsibilities of raising their husband's children and providing him with food from their gardens. Were wives to value sexual intercourse other than for reproduction, they might resent the time their husbands spent with the others—three weeks out of four in the case of a man with four wives.

Source: E.R.A.

---

had largely been ignored by theorists and researchers—the role of female experience and thought. Their arguments have given rise to a larger number of scholars who view themselves as feminist theorists. In *Sexual Salvation,* Naomi McCormick (1994) summarized the range of feminist positions and their implications for how we view gender and sexuality. She described in detail two of the many feminist groups that she labeled "liberal feminists" and "radical feminists." The liberal approach emphasizes women's sexual pleasure and their freedom to explore beyond restrictive gender-role norms, whereas radical feminism concentrates on protecting women from danger and coercion. Radical feminism points to men, masculinity, and pornography targeted for heterosexual male audiences as the culprits in the subjugation (dominance) of women. Radical feminists believe that pornography is directly linked to male sexual violence and should be restricted.

Liberal feminists see motivation, rather than gender, as the major factor in antisocial sexual behavior. They do not support the suppression of pornography. Instead, woman-affirming erotica is proposed as an antidote to violent pornography. Liberal feminists perceive the sexual landscape as skewed toward a male or patriarchal direction that can be changed to produce more gender equality.

We will include feminist perspectives in appropriate sections in the text as we do with other theories. Our guiding principle is best stated by McCormick's (1994, p. 33) approach:

> As we move into the 21st century, it is time to make sexology holistic and woman-affirming. Too many years have been devoted to sexual bookkeeping, recording the frequency and variety of people's genital experiences. This distracts us from the more important aspects of sexuality, how we think and feel about intimacy.

ISSUES TO CONSIDER

Why do you think men have controlled the resources in most societies throughout history?

Political and moral reactions to particular theories can sometimes impede scientific understanding of human sexual behavior. As we'll see, all four approaches to sex have caused controversy.

Theories, Politics, and Morality

Confusion about the purpose of a theory is common among laypersons and not unknown among scientists. The goal of a theory is to present a model of the causes of human behavior. A theory is not intended to be a blueprint or set of directions for how we should behave, but rather a picture of why we do behave in particular ways. When Freud theorized that humans are capable of sexual feelings and motives from infancy on, the public and many of Freud's scientific colleagues were deeply offended. Some of their reactions resulted from a confusion of theory with advocacy. Freud was not advocating sexual experience for infants and children; instead, he was trying to understand factors that influence personality development, and he theorized that sexual energy was one of these factors that was present from birth onward.

This same confusion of theory and advocacy is apparent today in the passionate controversy surrounding evolutionary theory (Fairchild, 1991; Oyama, 1991). Questions of free will versus determinism (do we freely choose our behavior, or are we genetically programmed to respond in particular ways?), ethnic and gender discrimination, and religion are among the issues that have been raised by those who reject evolutionary approaches. Again, those scientists who propose evolutionary theories as explanations of human sexual behavior are not advocating superiority of males over females or of one ethnic group over another. Instead, these scientists are trying to understand how a widespread phenomenon—for example, that men generally *do* dominate women in most cultures—could have developed. Evolutionary theorists are also not suggesting that humans are forced by "inherited" characteristics to behave like robots responding to genetic programs. Evolutionary approaches explicitly recognize the ability to learn as an adaptive capacity. It is what enables us to evaluate the likely consequences of our behavioral choices.

Some of the criticisms of learning theory and sociological approaches also stem from a misunderstanding of the nature of a theory. The issue, again, is one of free will versus determinism. Most of us prefer to believe that we freely choose our behaviors. We may, by gaining knowledge, increase our ability to enhance our freedom of choice. But the research described throughout this book also demonstrates that our individual experiences and our cultural beliefs are quite predictive of how we behave. In subscribing to learning theories and sociological theories, researchers are not suggesting that we *should* be influenced by our individual reinforcement histories or by societal norms and beliefs, only that most of us *are* so influenced.

Another problem that has confronted scientists is opposition from those who see scientific theories as conflicting with religious morality. Religious and moral thinking is quite different, however, from scientific reasoning. Modern science is not a set of absolute truths; it is a method of inquiry—of testing hypotheses and building theories on the basis of data collected and verified according to standard procedures. Scientific theories are always tentative and subject to modification or rejection if they do not fit observable data. Most religions, in contrast, consist of absolute beliefs, which are not subject to empirical tests in scientific terms. As such, science and religion operate in different spheres of human experience.

Rather than judging theories in terms of politics, morality, or even the elusive quality of accuracy, scientists judge on the basis of usefulness. All four theories that we have reviewed, as well as the findings of research conducted to test them, have contributed to our understanding of human sexual behavior. We are all affected by our ancestral history (evolutionary theory), our childhood experiences (psychoanalytic theories), our socialization and conditioning (social learning theories), and our cultural expectations and beliefs (sociological theories). Rather than competing with one another, the four theories generally complement one another. The questions that arise from each theory demand analysis at different levels of abstraction. At present, it appears that the factors emphasized by each of the theoretical approaches combine to produce the complexities that are involved in our sexual interactions.

Summary of Major Points

1. The emergence of the scientific study of sexuality.

In the first half of the twentieth century, scientists began to conduct research on sexual attitudes and behaviors. Their pioneering efforts met with considerable opposition and harassment from those who believed that research on sexuality was immoral or unnecessary. Nevertheless, their courageous work laid the groundwork for what is now an active research field.

2. Research methods.

Research involves testing hypotheses about the relationship between operationally defined variables. A population is sampled, and members of the sample volunteer for research in which stimuli are manipulated or measured. The volunteers' responses are obtained and analyzed. In testing hypotheses about sexuality, researchers rely on one or more of the following approaches: surveys, interviews, direct observation, physiological measures, and case histories and focus groups. Each method has its advantages and disadvantages. More confidence may be placed in research results if the same findings are obtained using more than one of these methods.

3. Evaluating research results.

When experimental research involves the manipulation of the variables of interest and adequate control of other variables, it is possible to infer a cause-effect relationship between variables. When stimuli are measured but not manipulated, as in correlational research, causal inferences cannot be made. In making decisions based on research results, we should know the situations and populations to which results can be generalized. Before research results can be considered valid, they should be replicated with a variety of samples, locations, situations, and researchers.

4. The role of theory in understanding sexual behavior.

Sexual theories are explanatory models of the causes and/or consequences of various facets of sexual attitudes and behaviors. Theories lead to predictions about particular responses under specific conditions. Such predictions can then be tested by research. Research findings may support a theory or, if they do not, can lead to modification of the theory in an attempt to increase its accuracy.

5. Evolutionary approaches.

Evolutionary approaches trace the causes of much of contemporary sexual behavior back thousands of years to our distant ancestors. According to this view, modern sexual behaviors exist because they served the cause of reproductive success in the past. The characteristics of contemporary men and women, as well as their courtship patterns and sexual proclivities, evolved because they led to the reproductive success of their ancestors.

6. Psychoanalytic approaches.

To explain sexual behavior, the creator of psychoanalytic theory, Sigmund Freud, examined the history of the individual rather than the history of our species. Psychoanalytic theory has undergone many revisions and changes since Freud's day, but it still places heavy emphasis on early experience as a determinant of adult sexuality and personality.

7. Learning approaches.

Social learning theories, as the name implies, assume that most, if not all, sexual behavior is learned. Learning theorists have applied the principles of learning to the conditioning, maintenance, and elimination of sexual behaviors. By manipulating the reinforcements for a particular sexual act, learning theorists have been able to increase, reduce, or eliminate the performance of that act.

8. Sociological approaches.

Sociologists have attempted to explain how social institutions affect our sexual behavior. Because sexuality is a potent resource, the power structure of a society determines how male and female gender roles are defined. Inherent in the sociological approach is the idea that we must learn a complicated sequence of behaviors before a sexual or nonsexual interaction takes place. Thus sexual interaction is not spontaneous but rather is the result of scripts that we learn so thoroughly that we do not usually even think about them.

9. Feminist approaches.

Growing to some extent out of social learning and sociological approaches, there are a number of different feminist models that have been proposed to account for gender differences and similarities in gender roles and sexual behavior. The two most prominent—liberal feminism and radical feminism—have rather different underlying assumptions. Liberal feminists emphasize women's sexual pleasure and capacity for exploration beyond restrictive gender role norms. In contrast, radical feminists focus on strategies for protecting women from danger and sexual coercion and assume that men are inherently sexually aggressive.

10. The role of theories in society.

Confusion over the purpose of theory is common. A theory is an attempt to build a model or picture of what we do and why we do it. A theory of some aspect of sexual behavior is not a recommendation that we engage in or avoid that behavior. Nor is a theory an attempt to promote or advocate any particular moral or political stance. Each of the theoretical perspectives in this chapter is useful because each provides hypotheses about human sexual behavior that can be tested by researchers. People may argue about which theoretical approach is most accurate, but such arguments will probably never be resolved because each type of theory attempts to explain human sexual behavior from a different level of abstraction. In the real world, the multiple factors considered by multiple theories appear to interact in their impact on our sexual attitudes and behaviors.

CHECK YOUR KNOWLEDGE

1. The Kinsey group was (a) fully supported by professional colleagues, (b) criticized by many for using too small a sample size, (c) generally ignored and unknown in their day, (d) subjected to political harassment by McCarthy-era politicians. (p. 5)

2. The _____ variable is manipulated in an experiment: (a) control, (b) independent, (c) correlational, (d) dependent. (p. 8)

3. Sampling involves (a) separating volunteers from nonvolunteers, (b) obtaining complete data from every possible source, (c) measuring the presence of self-report bias, (d) obtaining a group of participants from the population to which we wish to generalize. (p. 9)

4. A theory is (a) a statement that has been proved, (b) a model of how one or more variables is (are) related to particular outcomes, (c) a meaningless generalization, (d) a blueprint for what ought to be. (p. 14)

5. Parental-investment theory has been used by evolutionary theorists to explain (a) women's dislike of sexual activity, (b) men's proclivity to rape, (c) gender differences in sexual behavior, (d) gender similarities in sexual behavior. (p. 16)

6. Freud (a) argued that sexuality was interwoven with all aspects of personality, (b) insisted that children be shielded against sexuality in all forms, (c) encouraged adults to act openly on their sexual desires, (d) located the id, ego, and superego in the brain. (pp. 17–18)

7. According to social learning theorists, sex-related behavior is most affected by (a) heredity, (b) observation of how other people act and are rewarded or punished, (c) social class, (d) social scripts. (p. 20)

8. According to script theory, sexual interactions result from (a) naturally occurring biological processes, (b) an innate drive to reproduce, (c) cognitive plans that enable people to behave in organized and predictable ways, (d) spontaneously occurring opportunities present in the environment. (pp. 21–22)

2

SEXUAL DIFFERENTIATION AND DEVELOPMENT

FERTILIZATION
Meeting of Sperm and Egg
Cell Division
Chromosomes and Genetic Inheritance
Sex Chromosomes and Genetic Sex

PRENATAL DEVELOPMENT

TYPICAL SEXUAL DIFFERENTIATION
Gonadal Sex
Hormonal Sex
Across Cultures: Aborting Female Fetuses as Population Control
Genital Sex
Highlight: The Major Sex Hormones

ATYPICAL SEXUAL DIFFERENTIATION
Sex Chromosome Abnormalities
Inconsistencies in Sexual Differentiation

DEVELOPMENT THROUGH THE REMAINDER OF PREGNANCY

SECONDARY SEXUAL CHARACTERISTICS
Female Maturation
Health: Meanings of Menarche
Male Maturation

SEXUAL DIFFERENTIATION AND GENDER IDENTITY
A Genital Accident
Ambiguous Genitals

SUMMARY OF MAJOR POINTS

CHECK YOUR KNOWLEDGE

1 The genetic sex of a child is determined by its mother.

2 By the eighth week of prenatal development, an embryo has a pair of gonads that will later become testes or ovaries.

3 Intersexuality refers to conditions caused by an inconsistency in sexual differentiation.

4 A fetus born five months after conception can survive outside its mother's uterus.

5 On average, males go through puberty at a later age than do females.

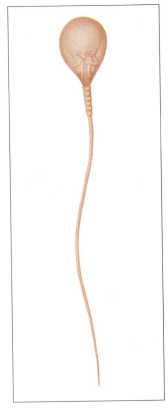

HOW can anyone know if a newborn baby is a boy or a girl? These are the responses of children aged 5 and older to this question, asked by Ronald and Juliette Goldman (1982, pp. 194–196) in their study of children's thinking about sexuality:

> *"Because mum dressed her in a dress. There's no other way to tell."*
>
> *"We began as girls and a penis grew later."*
>
> *"You can see it by the face, and if it cries a lot it's a boy."*
>
> *"Girls don't have dicky birds."*

In this chapter we describe the process of fertilization and the intricacies of genetic inheritance. We examine conception and prenatal development and then conclude the chapter with an overview of sexual differentiation.

FERTILIZATION

Although the origins of life on earth are still shrouded in mystery, we know a great deal about how individual humans begin life. Much of this knowledge is quite recent. As late as the eighteenth century, the scientific community was engaged in vigorous debate about whether a female's ovaries contained tiny embryos that were activated by male sperm or whether sperm contained preformed miniature human beings that began to grow after they had been deposited in a fertile womb (see Figure 2.1).

Even in this century some groups are unsure about how reproduction occurs. Some Australian Aborigine groups, for example, do not consider sexual intercourse to be particularly important in producing pregnancy. Rather, they see intercourse as an act of preparation for the reception of a spirit baby (Montagu, 1969). The Mehinaku of Brazil believe that pregnancy develops through repeated acts of intercourse that accumulate enough semen to form a baby (Gregor, 1985).

**Figure 2.1
An Early Theory of Conception** This drawing is from a seventeenth-century representation of a little man (homunculus) in the head of a sperm. At that time, some people believed that small, preformed humans were ejaculated from the penis into the womb, where they were housed and nourished until birth.

Meeting of Sperm and Egg

We now know that one of a woman's two ovaries releases an egg (ovum) about halfway through her monthly reproductive cycle in the process known as **ovulation.** The egg, about one-fourth the size of this dot (.), is the human body's largest type of cell. After

ovulation Release of an egg from the ovary.

29

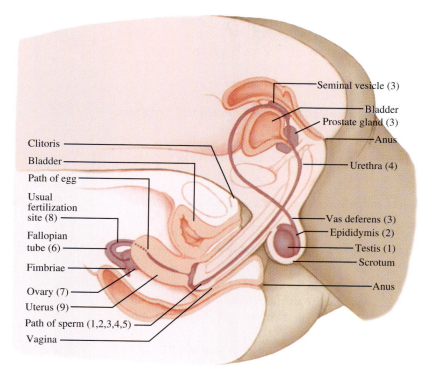

Sperm:

1. produced in the seminiferous tubules of the testes.
2. stored in epididymis.
3. during sexual arousal, travel through the vas and mix with seminal fluid from seminal vesicles and prostate.
4. released through urethra of penis during ejaculation.
5. deposited in the seminal pool of vagina, near cervix.
6. pass through cervix into uterus and fallopian tubes.

Egg:

7. produced by one of the ovaries.
8. fertilization site in upper third of fallopian tube.
9. site of implantation for developing zygote around 6th day.

Figure 2.2
Fertilization This drawing illustrates the journey of egg and sperm toward fertilization, which generally occurs in the upper third of the fallopian tube.

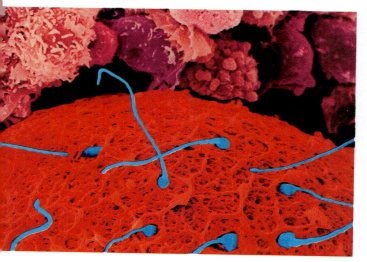

Figure 2.3
Sperm Penetrates Egg
Although numerous sperm surround an egg, only one sperm is able to penetrate it, at which point the egg is impenetrable to other sperm.

its release, the egg usually makes its way to the funnel-shaped end of the nearer fallopian tube.

Sperm are among the smallest cells in the body: Each sperm is only 1/600th of an inch from its head to its tail. Before reaching the upper third of the fallopian tube, where fertilization usually occurs (see Figure 2.2), sperm must make a lengthy journey, and most of them die en route.

The semen of fertile men who have not ejaculated in the previous 24 hours or so contains about 100 million to 400 million sperm. Because only one sperm normally penetrates an egg, such enormous numbers may seem rather wasteful. However, only 50 to 60 percent of the average man's sperm are **motile,** and some of these may be destroyed by the normally acidic secretions of the vagina. Others fail to get through the cervical mucus to enter the uterus. Of those entering the uterus, some head toward the fallopian tube that contains no egg. Each of these factors reduces the number of sperm that meet the egg.

After the remaining sperm (about two thousand) have reached the egg, they attach themselves to the membrane surrounding it (see Figure 2.3). As soon as one sperm has entered the egg, penetration by other sperm is generally impossible.

The fertilized ovum contains in its genes all the information needed to produce the estimated 100 trillion cells of an adult human. But to understand what happens after fertilization, we must first know something about the cellular structure of the human body.

Cell Division

The human body is composed of two structurally and functionally different types of cells. The sperm and ova are gametes, or **germ cells.** All other cells are **body cells.** Germ cells and body cells differ not only in function but also in the way they divide and in the number of **chromosomes** they contain.

Chromosomes—literally, "colored bodies"—are complex, threadlike bodies made up of two kinds of chemical material: deoxyribonucleic acid (DNA) and protein. They are found in the nucleus of every cell. All organisms possess chromosomes, which contain the genetic material that is passed on from generation to generation.

The human body develops and repairs itself through a complex process of cell division. Division of the somatic, or body, cells occurs through **mitosis,** a process that creates two new, identical cells. The replication process leads to two new cells that are exactly like the original parent cell and are called daughter cells. Mitosis is the process responsible for the development of the single cell that is the fertilized ovum into the trillions of cells that make up every adult human.

The gametes, or germ cells, divide by a different process, called **meiosis.** This results in the production of sperm in males and ova in females. In each case, however, the process produces daughter cells having half the number of chromosomes contained in the parent cell. That is, in the testes and ovaries a body cell with 46 chromosomes—23 pairs—divides in such a way that each daughter cell includes only one member of each pair of chromosomes. Thus mature egg and sperm cells contain only 23 single chromosomes rather than 23 chromosome pairs. When a sperm and an egg cell unite, the resulting **zygote** contains 46 chromosomes, arranged in two sets of 23, one set from the mother and the other set from the father. This process ensures that the amount of genetic material will not double with each generation, producing zygotes whose cell division becomes logistically impossible.

Chromosomes and Genetic Inheritance

Chromosomes carry the information that determines a person's inherited characteristics. Strung along the length of each chromosome like beads are thousands of segments called genes. These genes are the basic units of hereditary transmission. Genes are made up of the complex chemical **deoxyribonucleic acid (DNA),** which is the information-containing molecule that forms part of every organism. DNA acts as a blueprint for all cellular activity. It determines the makeup of every cell in our bodies, each of which contains an estimated one hundred thousand genes that determine our inherited characteristics.

Through a microscope, chromosomes can be distinguished as either **sex chromosomes** (chromosomes that determine whether an individual is female or male) or **autosomes** (chromosomes that do not determine a person's genetic sex). The 22 pairs of autosomes, which are similar in structure but of variable size, are responsible for the differentiation of cells that results in various characteristics of the body.

Sex Chromosomes and Genetic Sex

The twenty third pair of chromosomes in each cell of the human body is composed of the sex chromosomes, X and Y (see Figure 2.4, page 32). The X chromosome is about five times longer than the Y chromosome and contains at least one hundred genes.

motile Exhibiting or demonstrating the power of motion.

germ cells Sperm or egg cells.

body cells All the cells in the body except germ cells.

chromosomes The strands of deoxyribonucleic acid (DNA) and protein in the nucleus of each cell. They contain the genes that provide information vital for the duplication of cells and the transmission of inherited characteristics.

mitosis (my-TOE-sis) A form of cell division in which the nucleus divides into two daughter cells, each of which receives one nucleus and is an exact duplicate of the parent cell.

meiosis (my-OH-sis) Cell division leading to the formation of a zygote in which the number of chromosomes is reduced by half.

zygote (ZYE-goat) The developing organism from fertilization to implantation.

deoxyribonucleic acid (DNA) (dee-OX-see-RYE-boh-new-KLAY-ik) A chemically complex nucleic acid that is a principal element of genes.

sex chromosomes The pair of chromosomes that determines whether an individual is female or male.

autosomes The 22 pairs of chromosomes that are involved in general body development in humans.

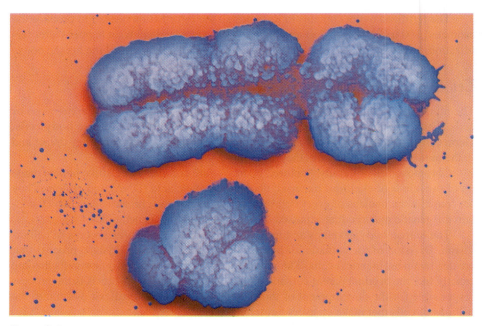

Figure 2.4
The X and Y Chromosomes The Y chromosome can be detected by its fluorescence when it is stained, as the top picture shows.

A female has two X chromosomes in each body cell; a male has an X and a Y chromosome in each body cell. Eggs therefore all carry X chromosomes, whereas a sperm may carry either an X or a Y. If a sperm with an X chromosome fertilizes an egg, the offspring will be female (XX). If a sperm with a Y chromosome fertilizes an egg, the offspring will be male (XY). The genetic sex of a child is thus determined by the father.

A female can apparently live with only one viable X chromosome, as males do, but there is no known case of a human being having no X chromosomes. Obviously humans can thrive in the absence of the Y chromosome, for females have none. If an embryo has more than two X chromosomes and lacks a Y, then female development takes place. If an embryo has more than one X chromosome and a Y chromosome, in a combination such as XXY, XXXY, or XXXXY, then development includes some male characteristics despite the presence of multiple female chromosomes. The gene sequence that determines male sexual differentiation exists on the Y chromosome (Lukusa, Fryns, & van den Berghe, 1992).

DOMINANCE AND RECESSIVENESS. In addition to carrying the genes that determine genetic sex and sex characteristics, the X and Y chromosomes carry a variety of other genes. All the genes located on these sex chromosomes are called sex-linked genes because inheritance of these genes is connected to inheritance of the sex of the individual. Studies of patterns of inheritance are based on this concept of **sex linkage**—that a person who inherits a chromosome also inherits the genes it carries. Thus males, who always inherit a Y chromosome, inherit other Y-linked characteristics, such as testes formation. Males also inherit an X chromosome, however, and they inherit with it characteristics that are X-linked, some of which are not related to sex characteristics.

Because we inherit a set of genes from each parent, our two sets of genes do not contain identical genetic information. One gene in each set is usually dominant over the other, in which case the dominant gene determines the person's inherited character-

sex linkage The connection between the sex chromosomes and the genes one inherits. When a person inherits a sex chromosome, he or she also inherits the genes it carries.

istic. For recessive genes to determine a person's characteristics, he or she must have either two recessive genes—one from each parent—or one recessive gene without a corresponding dominant gene. For example, brown eyes are dominant over blue eyes, and dark hair is dominant over blond hair. So for recessive genes to produce blue eyes, a person must have two recessive genes for blue eyes or one recessive gene for blue eyes without a corresponding dominant gene for brown eyes.

The latter condition usually occurs only in males because only when a person's sex chromosomes are X and Y (as in a male) does a chromosome normally lack an identical paired chromosome. In females both X chromosomes must carry a recessive gene before the characteristic controlled by the recessive gene is displayed. Because males can inherit recessive X-linked traits with only one recessive gene, they have more recessive X-linked traits. Thus males are more susceptible than females to a number of disorders carried by recessive genes, such as hemophilia and color blindness, even though the transmitters of such disorders are always females. There is evidence for more than 150 X-linked traits in humans, many of them disease related and recessive (McKusick & Amberger, 1993). Y-linked traits are comparatively few. We now consider the remarkable process of prenatal development following conception.

PRENATAL DEVELOPMENT

The nine months of pregnancy, called **gestation,** are conventionally described in terms of three trimesters. The first trimester includes the first through the third month, the second spans the fourth through the sixth month, and the third extends from the seventh through the ninth month.

After fertilization has occurred, the zygote begins a period of rapid cell division. It has entered the germinal stage, a period of time encompassing the first two weeks following conception. Within three days, continuing cell division produces a solid ball of cells. Meanwhile, the zygote has been moving down the fallopian tube toward the uterus and enters it at approximately this time (see Figure 2.5).

gestation The entire period of prenatal development from conception to birth.

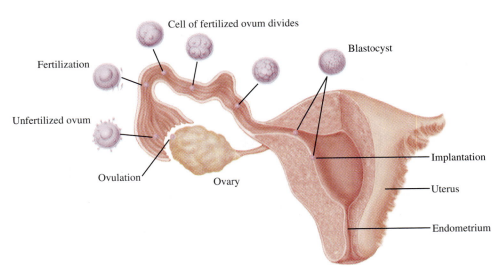

Figure 2.5
Fertilization and Migration The ovum is fertilized typically in the upper third of the fallopian tube, and numerous cell divisions take place before it implants in the uterine wall approximately five days later.

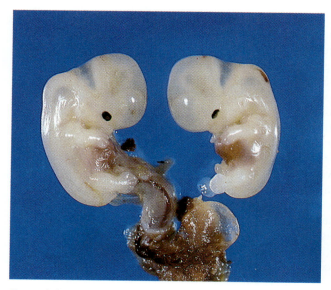

Figure 2.6
Eight-Week-Old Embryo (Twins) At eight weeks the embryo has the beginnings of both internal and external genitals. Fingernails, toenails, lips, nose, and ears have also begun to develop.

placenta The organ formed by the joining of the tissue of the uterine wall with that of the developing fetus; a major source of hormones during pregnancy.

embryo The unborn organism from the second to about the eighth week of pregnancy.

umbilical cord The connection of the fetus to the placenta, through which the fetus is nourished.

amniotic sac The pouch containing a watery fluid that envelops a developing fetus in the uterus.

On about the fourth day, after entering the uterine cavity, the mass of cells separates into two parts. The outer cell mass develops into the major part of the **placenta.** By the end of the fifth day, it is loosely implanted in the upper part of the uterus. After implantation, the developing inner cell mass is called an **embryo,** and by the end of the second week the embryo is usually firmly implanted in the uterus.

Meanwhile, the outer mass is developing into structures that nurture and protect the organism during its stay in the uterus. These include the placenta, the umbilical cord, and the amniotic sac. The placenta, which initially surrounds the fetus, subsequently moves to the side, but the placenta and the embryo remain connected by the **umbilical cord.** Through this passageway the placenta absorbs oxygen and nourishment from the mother's bloodstream and delivers body wastes from the embryo and transfers them to the mother. The placenta protects the embryo from a number of infections, although small viruses such as rubella (responsible for German measles) can pass through to the embryo. The placenta produces the hormones that support pregnancy and that later assist in preparation of the mother's breasts for lactation, the manufacture and secretion of milk. The **amniotic sac** is a fluid-filled space bounded by the amniotic membrane that encases the developing organism, cushioning it, giving it room to move, and ensuring that it does not permanently adhere to the uterine wall. The embryo's kidneys are the source of the fluid in the amniotic sac.

A critical embryonic stage begins with full implantation of the cell mass at the beginning of the second week of pregnancy and lasts until the end of the eighth week. It is a period of remarkable growth, during which the embryo develops its major organs, among them the eyes, which begin to form by 21 days.

At eight weeks the embryo is about an inch long. It has a recognizable brain and a heart that pumps blood through tiny arteries and veins. It has a stomach that produces digestive juices and a liver that manufactures blood cells. Its kidneys have already begun to function, and it has an endocrine system. The embryo now has limbs and a disproportionately large head with eyes, nose, ears, and mouth, although its eyelids have not yet formed (see Figure 2.6). By this time the embryo has begun to differentiate into a male or a female. We turn now to a description of that complex process.

TYPICAL SEXUAL DIFFERENTIATION

The process by which we differentiate into either males or females occurs in a series of stages during the development of the embryo and fetus and then again during puberty (see Table 2.1). Although the steps are usually predictable, variations can occur. We look first at the normal processes.

As described earlier, your genetic sex was determined at conception as a result of whether the sperm that your father contributed contained an X or a Y chromosome. If someone with "X-ray vision" had peered at you in your mother's womb six weeks after you were conceived, they could have seen your eyes and your major organs, but they would have been unable to tell whether you were a male or a female. Shortly after the sixth week, however, the process of sexual differentiation began, and it continued until

Table 2.1   Chronology of Sexual Differentiation

Prenatal Development

Characteristic	Source	Male Development	Female Development
Gonadal	Y chromosome	Testes	Ovaries
Internal sex organs	Androgens and Müllerian-inhibiting substance	Wolffian structures develop into ejaculatory duct and other reproductive structures; Müllerian structures degenerate	Wolffian structures degenerate; Müllerian structures develop into uterus, fallopian tubes, and other reproductive structures
External sex organs	Level of androgens	Scrotal sacs and penis	Labia and clitoris
Brain	Level of androgens	Masculine organization	Feminine organization

Pubescent Development

Characteristic	Source	Male Development	Female Development
Breasts	Pituitary growth hormone, estrogens, progestins		Growth of breasts (8–13 years)
Genitals	Pituitary growth hormone, testosterone	Growth of testes, scrotal sac (10–14 years); penis (11–15 years)	
Pubic hair	Testosterone in males; adrenal androgens in females	Growth of pubic hair (10–15 years)	Growth of pubic hair (8–14 years)
Menarche	Gonadotropin-releasing hormones, FSH, LH, estrogens, progestins		Onset of menstrual cycle (10–17 years)
Voice change	Testosterone	Growth of larynx, deepening of voice (11–15 years)	
Body hair	Testosterone in males; adrenal androgens in females	Growth of underarm and facial hair (12–17 years)	Growth of underarm hair (10–16 years)
Oil and sweat glands	Testosterone in males; adrenal androgens in females	Development of oil- and sweat-producing glands; acne (12–17 years)	Development of oil- and sweat-producing glands; acne when glands blocked (10–16 years)

about the twelfth or thirteenth week of gestation (see "Across Cultures: Aborting Female Fetuses as Population Control," page 37).

Gonadal Sex

At eight weeks the embryo, whether it is genetically male (XY) or female (XX), has a pair of gonads (which will become testes or ovaries) and the beginnings of external genitals. It also contains tissue that may eventually develop into female or male structures. If the tissue develops into female structures (the fallopian tubes, the uterus, and

 REALITY or MYTH ? **2**

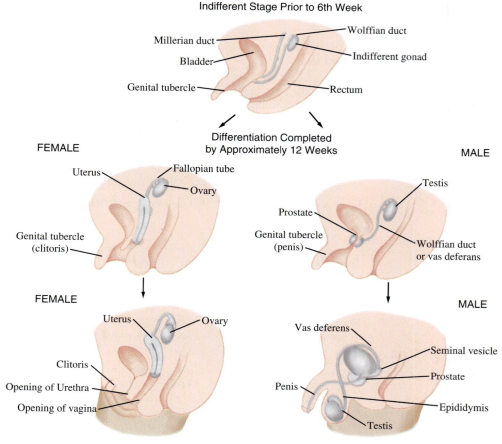

Indifferent Stage Prior to 6th Week

Millerian duct
Wolffian duct
Bladder
Indifferent gonad
Genital tubercle
Rectum

Differentiation Completed
by Approximately 12 Weeks

FEMALE
MALE

Uterus
Fallopian tube
Ovary
Testis
Prostate
Genital tubercle
(clitoris)
Genital tubercle
(penis)
Wolffian duct
or vas deferans

FEMALE
MALE

Uterus
Ovary
Vas deferens
Clitoris
Seminal vesicle
Opening of Urethra
Prostate
Penis
Opening of vagina
Epididymis
Testis

Figure 2.7
Internal Gender Differentiation This diagram shows differentiation of the internal sexual structures in a male or female direction. This gender differentiation occurs during the latter part of the first trimester of pregnancy.

Müllerian-duct system Fetal tissue that develops into the internal female reproductive structures if the fetus is genetically female.

Wolffian-duct system Fetal tissue that develops into the internal male reproductive structures if the fetus is genetically male.

the upper part of the vagina), it is called the **Müllerian-duct system.** The lower two-thirds of the vagina forms from the same tissue that gives rise to the urinary bladder and urethra. If the embryonic tissue develops into male structures, it produces the epididymis, vas deferens, seminal vesicles, and ejaculatory duct and is called the **Wolffian-duct system** (see Figure 2.7).

The location of the genes for the testes-determining factor is on the short arm of the Y chromosome (Lukusa et al., 1992). If no Y chromosome is present to issue these instructions, the embryo continues to grow for another few weeks before the outer part of the primitive gonads develops into ovaries packed with immature egg cells.

Hormonal Sex

The early development of the testes appears to be related to another embryonic phenomenon that provides a clue to how the process of sexual differentiation works. If the gonads are removed during the critical embryonic period, the embryo develops as a female, even if it is genetically (XY) male. Therefore, as John Money and Anke Ehrhardt (1972, p. 7) put it, "Nature's rule is, it would appear, that to masculinize, something must be added." This extra something consists of **testosterone** and **Müllerian-inhibiting substance (MIS).** When the primitive gonads differentiate as testes in the male, they begin to manufacture these two substances.

Testosterone promotes the development of the Wolffian ducts into the internal male reproductive structures, whereas MIS is responsible for curbing the growth of the Müllerian-duct system. Both of these substances must be present if normal development of the internal reproductive structures of the male is to occur. In normal male anatomical development, then, only one of the duct systems expands and develops. The development of the other system regresses, so that only traces of it remain in the body.

Because of the popular definition of **androgens** as male hormones and **estrogens** as female hormones, many people mistakenly assume that we produce one or the other, depending on whether we are male or female. In fact, both males and females secrete the same three kinds of sex hormones. In males the testes synthesize progesterone, one of a general class of feminizing hormones called **progestins;** testosterone (an androgen); and **estradiol** (an estrogen). Similarly, in females the ovaries secrete progesterone, androgens, and estrogen. Both males and females also secrete small amounts of all these hormones from the outer portion (cortex) of their adrenal glands (see "Highlight: The Major Sex Hormones," page 39).

Sexual differentiation depends on the relative amounts of these hormones in much the same way that the products of baking depend on the amounts of flour, sugar, salt, shortening, and other ingredients. Just as a cake is generally made with larger proportions of sugar and shortening, and bread results from higher proportions of flour and salt, the development of sexual anatomy is influenced by the relative proportions of androgens and estrogens secreted, as well as the numbers of cells that are responsive to these hormones. The proportion of androgens and estrogens varies somewhat among individuals, but as long as this variation falls within normal limits, it does not seem to affect the individual's gender identity or sexual functioning. The effects of differences in the levels of masculinizing and feminizing hormones on the developing brain are a subject of controversy.

testosterone The major natural androgen.

Müllerian-inhibiting substance (MIS) A hormone secreted by the fetal testes that inhibits the growth and development of the Müllerian-duct system.

androgens Generic term for hormones that promote development and functioning of the male reproductive system.

estrogens Generic term for hormones that promote development and functioning of the female reproductive system.

progestins Generic term for hormones that prepare the female reproductive system for pregnancy.

estradiol The major natural estrogen, secreted by the ovaries, testes, and placenta.

ISSUES TO CONSIDER

In describing fetal sex differentiation, Money and Ehrhardt concluded that "nature's rule is, it would appear, that to masculinize, something must be added." What is the evidence for their conclusion?

Genital Sex

genital tubercle A small protruding bud of fetal tissue that develops into either a penis or a clitoris.

labioscrotal swelling The fetal tissue that develops into either the scrotum in a male or the two outer vaginal lips in a female.

urogenital folds Folds or strips on each side of the genital tubercle of the fetus that fuse to form the urethral tube in a male or the inner vaginal lips in a female.

dihydrotestosterone (DHT) A hormone produced from testosterone that is responsible for the development of the external genitals of the male fetus.

phallus The penis.

Several weeks after the internal structures of the embryo have differentiated, with one set of potential reproductive organs beginning to develop and the other set beginning to atrophy, the external genitals start to differentiate (see Figure 2.8). Our external genitals are created from a small protruding bud of tissue called a **genital tubercle,** an opening with a small swelling called the **labioscrotal swelling,** and folds or strips of skin called the **urogenital folds** on each side of the tubercle. If testes are developing, testosterone begins circulating in the bloodstream. As we have seen, testosterone acts directly on the Wolffian ducts to cause differentiation of the vas deferens, epididymis, and seminal vesicles. For the development of the external male genitals, however, **dihydrotestosterone (DHT)** is produced by the metabolism of testosterone in cells within and outside the testes. DHT causes the elongation of the genital tubercle into the **phallus.** As the phallus grows, it pulls the urogenital folds forward, and they fuse with each other on the underside of the penis to form a urethral tube. The

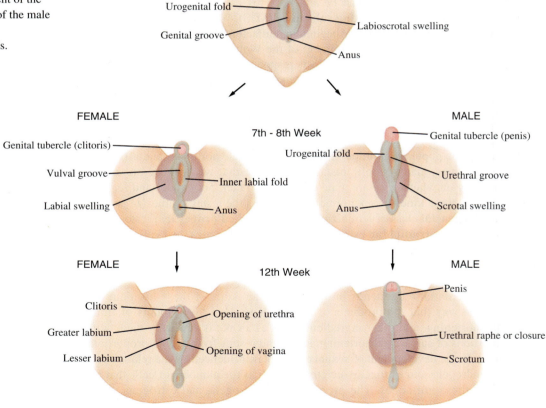

Figure 2.8
Differentiation of External Genitals After the internal reproductive structures of the fetus have differentiated, the external genitals differentiate in a male or female direction, as this figure shows.

The Major Sex Hormones

Androgens   The general name for masculinizing sex hormones; the two most common are testosterone and androstenedione. In males most of the androgen is produced in the testes; a small portion (about 5 percent) is produced by the adrenal glands. In females the ovaries and adrenal glands manufacture small amounts of androgen. Testosterone is considered to be the major biological determinant of sexual desire in men and women.

Estrogens   The general name for feminizing hormones that are secreted in the ovaries, testes, and placenta. Of the three major estrogens in humans, the most potent and abundant is estradiol. In both males and females, estradiol is metabolized within the body from progesterone of which the source is the steroidal substance cholesterol, from which the body derives all of its steroidal hormones. In females estrogens are important in maintaining the elasticity of the vagina and the texture and function of the breasts. They also contribute to the production of vaginal lubricant. In males the function of estrogens is unknown. Too much estrogen in males can result in diminished sexual desire, enlargement of the breasts, and difficulties with erection.

Progestins   The general name for hormones that prepare the reproductive organs for pregnancy. The most abundant of the progestins, progesterone, is produced by the corpus luteum of an ovary. Generally, progestins are active only in females because the hormones' effect is dependent on the previous action of estrogen. Males who receive estrogen and progesterone sequentially develop male mammary glands. Progesterone inhibits the flow of cervical mucus that occurs during ovulation, and it diminishes the thickness of the vaginal lining.

Follicle-stimulating hormone (FSH)   One of the gonadotropins (gonad changers) secreted by the pituitary gland. Beginning at puberty, FSH stimulates the production of sperm cells in the testes in males and prepares the ovary for ovulation in females.

Luteinizing hormone (LH)   Another gonadotropin that is produced by the pituitary. In females LH triggers ovulation, the release of an egg from the ovary. In males it is sometimes referred to as interstitial cell stimulating hormone because it stimulates the interstitial (Leydig) cells of the testes to manufacture testosterone.

Prolactin   A hormone produced by the pituitary gland that stimulates the production of milk in the breasts.

Oxytocin   A pituitary hormone that causes milk to flow from the glandular tissue of the breast to the nipple in response to a baby's sucking and induces strong contractions during childbirth. It is also released by males and females during the orgasmic phase of sexual response.

Vasoactive intestinal polypeptide   A peptide hormone involved in erection of the penis and vaginal blood flow during sexual arousal.

Gonadotropin-releasing hormone (GnRH)   A hormone produced by the hypothalamus that regulates the secretion of both follicle-stimulating hormone and luteinizing hormone by the pituitary. GnRH is also called luteinizing hormone-releasing factor.

Inhibin   A hormone produced by the testes that regulates sperm production by reducing the pituitary gland's secretion of FSH.

---

urethra connects to the bladder, prostate gland, and vas deferens. The two labioscrotal swellings fuse together to form a scrotum, which houses the testes when they eventually descend from the abdominal cavity, about eight months after conception.

The development of female external genitals needs no hormonal prompting; it occurs in the absence of androgens. In females the genital tubercle remains relatively small and becomes a clitoris. Instead of fusing, the urogenital folds of skin remain distinct and form the two inner vaginal lips and the clitoral hood. The two labioscrotal swellings also remain separate, forming the two outer vaginal lips. The opening develops a dividing wall of tissue that separates the vaginal entrance to the uterus from the urethra, which connects to the bladder.

We have been discussing normal development and sexual differentiation. However, much of our understanding of those normal processes has been produced by studies of atypical development, the topic to which we turn now.

ATYPICAL SEXUAL DIFFERENTIATION

E rrors in the process of sexual differentiation can occur at any stage of development. Abnormalities can be caused by defects in chromosomes, environmental threats to fetal development, inheritance of atypical sex chromosomes, abnormal differentiation of gonads, or alterations in the secretion or metabolism of sex hormones. Although there are many types of autosomal defects, we focus only on sex chromosome abnormalities.

Sex Chromosome Abnormalities

So far, more than 70 irregularities of the sex chromosomes have been identified (Levitan, 1988). Many of these result from abnormal combinations of sex chromosomes that cause a person to be neither an XX female nor an XY male. Some of the more common sex chromosome abnormalities are presented in Table 2.2.

The X chromosome appears to be crucial for survival. The genes on the Y chromosome are coded for "maleness" and little else. The presence of a single Y chromosome generally results in an individual having a male appearance, no matter how many X chromosomes that person has in his chromosomal makeup. Female development can occur without the presence of a second X, as in Turner's syndrome. But the absence of the second X reduces the likelihood of ovarian development and fertility.

In general, extra X chromosomes do not enhance feminine characteristics in females, but they may make males more like females. An extra Y chromosome, however, may increase height. In addition, the presence of extra X and Y chromosomes appears to be related to below-normal intelligence, although the intelligence of individuals with an extra Y chromosome is not as limited as that of persons with extra X chromosomes (Hoyenga & Hoyenga, 1993).

Inconsistencies in Sexual Differentiation

In addition to atypical sex chromosome patterns, another cause of atypical sexual differentiation is an error in the differentiation process during prenatal development. A discrepancy may occur between genetic sex and gonadal, hormonal, or genital sex. An inconsistency in the process of sexual differentiation results in a condition known as **intersexuality.** Intersex conditions also include birth defects of sex organs, accidents, and atypical changes in body structure at puberty.

intersexuality A condition in which a person is born with both male and female characteristics, such as an ovary on one side and a testis on the other, with an ovatestis on each side, or with ambiguous genitals.

SEXUAL DIFFERENTIATION IN GENETIC MALES.   We now briefly examine some of the conditions that can lead to problems in sexual differentiation in males. As we have seen, hormones are important in the determination of early sexual differentiation. Thus it may be reasonable to assume that atypical patterns of exposure to sex hormones might lead to atypical sexual differentiation. Numerous researchers have investigated this hypothesis.

Androgen Insensitivity Syndrome. Some XY people have a condition known as androgen insensitivity syndrome (AIS, sometimes called testicular feminization). The body secretes normal amounts of androgen, but the normal target cells are unresponsive to androgen. They do not have a normal androgen receptor gene on the X chromosome.

The Wolffian structures of an AIS fetus fail to develop into normal internal male structures (prostate, seminal vesicles, and vas deferens) because they are insensitive to androgen. The Müllerian-inhibiting substance, however, is usually produced, so the

Müllerian structures do not develop, either. Thus the fetus is born without a complete set of either male or female internal genital organs.

AIS individuals develop a normal clitoris and a short vagina. The vagina generally does not lead to a functional uterus, but occasionally a small structure regarded as a rudimentary uterus is present. Testes do not usually descend; if they do, they appear only as small lumps near the labia. (These small lumps are often misdiagnosed as hernias.) The undescended gonads (testes) do not produce viable sperm. Because people with this syndrome respond to the presence of female hormones, breast development and female pelvic changes occur at the onset of puberty. Menstruation does not occur, and the person with AIS cannot reproduce.

Table 2.2   Common Sex Chromosome Abnormalities

Syndrome	Makeup of Chromosomes	Incidence per Live Births	Characteristics	Treatment
Klinefelter's Syndrome	XXY; in rare cases an extra X occurs (XXXY).	1 in 1,000	Shrunken testes, breast development (gynecomastia) in about one-half of all cases, disproportionate arms and legs, elevated urinary gonadotropins, infertility in most cases, low levels of testosterone sometimes, increased likelihood of mental retardation	Administration of testosterone during adolescence often produces more masculine body contours and sexual characteristics in addition to increasing sexual drive.
XYY Syndrome	XYY	1 in 1,000	Genital irregularities, decreased fertility, increased likelihood of mental retardation	None
Turner's Syndrome	XO	1 in 5,000*	Short stature (4 to 5 ft), loose or weblike skin around the neck, a broad and "shieldlike" chest with the nipples widely spaced, nonfunctional ovaries, no menstruation or development of adult breasts, infertility in almost all cases	Administration of estrogen and progesterone can induce menstruation and development of the breasts, external genitals, and pubic hair. Androgen administered during puberty can help the child attain a greater adult height.
Triple-X Syndrome	XXX	1 in 1,000	Almost no major abnormalities, though these women are likely to be less fertile than XX females; higher incidence of mental disturbance than among XX females	None

*This figure is not an accurate indicator of the incidence of the condition. About one-tenth of all pregnancies that end in spontaneous abortion are XO—although this is a conservative estimate because many embryos with Turner's syndrome and other atypical chromosomal patterns are spontaneously aborted, at times before the woman is even aware she is pregnant.

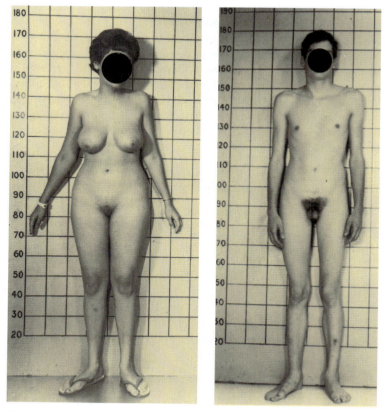

Figure 2.9
Androgen Insensitivity Syndrome The development of genetic males with this abnormality is influenced solely by the secretion of estrogen during both the prenatal period and at puberty since their cells are unresponsive to the testosterone that they secrete. The individual in the photograph on the right has had his breasts and testes surgically removed. His penis remains very small despite surgery, and erection is impossible for him.

Sexual activity and orgasm can occur in AIS individuals. Because their genitals appear to be female, they are typically reared as females from birth, and they develop feminine identities. Minor surgery is sometimes needed to lengthen the upper vagina for satisfactory sexual intercourse. If testes are discovered, they are generally surgically removed during childhood or adolescence because leaving the testes in place increases the risk of cancer. These individuals then take estrogen supplements to replace the estrogen formerly secreted by the testes.

Occasionally, an individual with AIS has a phallus large enough to cause him to be identified as a male at birth. When he reaches puberty, however, he begins to develop breasts and lacks masculine body traits (see Figure 2.9). His penis may not have the ability to become erect, and his prostate gland may not produce ejaculatory fluid. Surgery can complete the fusion of his scrotum and bring his sterile testes down into it, but it cannot make his penis grow. His pubescent breasts can be surgically removed, but masculine secondary sexual characteristics cannot be created. Giving him extra doses of testosterone is useless: He is producing all that he needs, but his body cells cannot use it. People with AIS tend to have bodies that appear female, and they have difficult sex lives.

ISSUES TO CONSIDER

If you were (or are) a parent, how would you respond to the news that physicians have determined that your son has androgen insensitivity syndrome?

Borderline Androgen Insensitivity Syndrome. Individuals with a condition known as borderline androgen insensitivity syndrome can make partial use of testosterone. The infant is born with a "penis" only slightly larger than a clitoris and a urethra located in the peritoneal area rather than in the penis. His scrotum is partially unfused, and the testes can be felt as lumps in the groin. The usual solution is for this child to be reared as a female. Surgery can reduce the size of the penis and separate the scrotum to open and deepen the vagina. Female hormones (estrogen) can be administered to produce the development of breasts and other feminine characteristics. For the individual with AIS, then, the possession of an XY chromosome pattern and testes does not always mean being "male."

Dihydrotestosterone-Deficiency Syndrome. DHT-deficiency syndrome is a genetic disorder that prevents the prenatal conversion of testosterone into DHT. Males with DHT-deficiency syndrome lack an enzyme (5-alpha reductase) that is necessary for this conversion. As described earlier, DHT stimulates the development of the external male genitals. Thus at birth males with DHT-deficiency syndrome do not have identifiably male genitals.

Researchers studied 33 genetically male inhabitants of an isolated village in the Dominican Republic who had the enzyme deficiency (Imperato-McGinley, Guerrero, Gautier, & Peterson, 1974; Imperato-McGinley et al., 1982). At birth these males had genitals that either were ambiguous or resembled those of females. At puberty, however, they experienced an increase in muscle mass, growth of the phallus and scrotum, and deepening of the voice. Nineteen of the males studied by the researchers had been brought up as females to the age of puberty. Of these, adequate information could be obtained on 18. Of the 18, 16 gradually adopted a masculine gender identity and erotic interest in women.

Imperato-McGinley and her colleagues hypothesized that the increase in testosterone at puberty masculinized not only the body but also the mind, including the sex drive. Thus nature seems to have triumphed over nurture among these boys. As you might expect, however, this explanation is oversimplified and underestimates some important psychosocial factors. Although these males lived as girls, they had been stigmatized as freaks. At age 12 they were called *huevodoces,* which translates literally as "two eggs" ("eggs" meaning testicles). They were also known as *machihembra,* which translates roughly to "macho miss," with the implication that they were half-girl, half-boy freaks. In their traditional Hispanic village culture, there was no possibility of their becoming wives or mothers, nor was there any other feminine role for them that would not make them an economic liability to their families. The only real alternative was to adapt as best they could to being males.

The foregoing discussion of DHT-deficiency syndrome illustrates that gender identity and sexual orientation cannot be ascribed to any one biological or psychosocial variable. The "females" would not have changed to "males" if their bodies had not failed them at puberty. After their bodies no longer supported a feminine identity, cultural expectations and social conditions helped to create their gender-identity change.

SEXUAL DIFFERENTIATION IN GENETIC FEMALES.

Prenatal exposure to excess androgen has the effect of masculinizing genetic females. Researchers have identified three sources of such masculinization: (1) malfunction of fetal adrenal glands, (2) administration of hormones to pregnant women, and (3) ovarian tumors during pregnancy.

Congenital Adrenal Hyperplasia. A condition known as congenital adrenal hyperplasia (CAH) is a genetically transmitted malfunction of the adrenal glands. The fetus

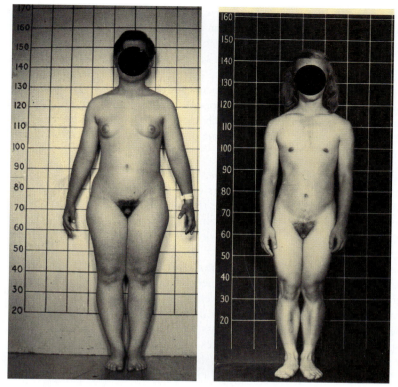

Figure 2.10
Congenital Adrenal Hyperplasia (CAH) The 13-year-old on the left was reared as a boy. His penis needed no surgery, but he received masculinizing hormones. The photo on the right shows a 12-year-old genetic female who was reared as a girl. Her genitals were later surgically feminized, and she was given feminizing hormones.

with this condition secretes too much adrenal androgen. Normally, the adrenal glands secrete both cortisol and androgens (cortisol is related to androgen levels in the body). The adrenal glands of CAH females, however, fail to synthesize cortisol and instead secrete excess androgens (Diamond, 1996a).[1]

The release of extra androgens during the critical period for differentiation of the external genitals (about three months after conception) leads to masculinization of the external genitals. The vagina may not be open, and the clitoris is often enlarged. The surge in androgen comes too late in development to affect the internal organs, so the ovaries, fallopian tubes, and uterus are normal (Zucker & Bradley, 1995). If it is realized at birth that the masculinized baby is really a female, her external genitals can be surgically altered shortly after birth. In addition, she can be given cortisone to reduce the output of androgens from the adrenal glands. Under these conditions, the child will be relatively well adjusted and undergo the typical sexual differentiation associated with puberty (Zucker, 1996). If the problem is not corrected by cortisone injections from infancy onward, however, the excessive androgen secretion continues to masculinize the child after birth and at puberty (see Figure 2.10).

---

[1]Males can also inherit CAH, but it is not detected except during diagnoses of illnesses that some males experience from malfunctioning of the adrenal glands.

Changes in Maternal Hormone Levels. Masculinization of the external genitals of genetic females may also result from the mother receiving hormones called progestins during pregnancy (Ehrhardt, Meyer-Bahlburg, Feldman, & Ince, 1984; Reinisch, Ziemba-Davis, & Sanders, 1991). Progestins were at one time given to women who were at risk of miscarriage to help them maintain their pregnancies. Progestins, whether natural or synthetic, are biochemically similar to androgens and act on the body in similar ways. Follow-up studies of baby girls born to women who took progestins during their pregnancies have shown that the masculinizing effects of the hormones were limited to the prenatal period. After the babies were born, the masculinizing influence ended.

At birth the appearance of babies affected by progestins varied, depending on the strength of the masculinizing hormone. Some looked female, some looked male, and some looked ambiguous. Their internal reproductive organs, however, developed normally. Thus babies recognized as females and given adequate surgical and hormonal treatment developed normally and were capable of reproduction.

The fate of genetic females with progestin-induced masculinized external genitals provides an example of the interaction of biological, psychological, and social factors in the formation of gender identity. When the effect of the progestin is pronounced, females may be born with a clitoris the size of a penis and with labia that have fused and give the appearance of a scrotum. The "penis" may even contain the urethral tube. Under these circumstances, the pronouncement at birth that it's a boy is quite understandable. The fact that the newborn's "scrotum" is empty would not necessarily raise questions because in 2 percent of all males the testes do not descend into the scrotum until after birth. At puberty, however, the child's ovaries secrete normal amounts of estrogen, which elicits menarche (first menstruation) and the beginnings of female body contours. By this time, of course, the genetic female has lived a dozen or more years under the assumption that she is a male, and the discovery of her internal femininity, not to mention the enlargement of breasts, can be a shock. After passing so many years with a male gender identity, the person may choose to have the female internal organs (ovaries and uterus) removed surgically. At the same time, administration of androgen helps to masculinize the body, and artificial testes can be inserted into the scrotum, although no sperm will be produced.

The effects of excess estrogen on human genetic females are not clear. There appear to be no effects on sexual differentiation of the genitals. There also seems to be little or no effect on gender-role behavior (Ehrhardt & Meyer-Bahlburg, 1981; Lish, Meyer-Bahlburg, Ehrhardt, Travis, & Veridian, 1992).

DEVELOPMENT THROUGH THE REMAINDER OF PREGNANCY

At about the beginning of the ninth week of pregnancy, bone cells appear, and the embryo enters the fetal stage. The embryo is called a **fetus** from this point until birth. These bone cells gradually begin to replace the cartilage cells that formed the initial embryonic skeleton, although cartilage continues to make up the soft parts of the nose and ears of an adult.

Only a few new structures appear during the fetal period. Development primarily involves the growth and maturation of tissues and organs that began to form during the embryonic stage. This delicate growth continues as the fetus moves month by month toward the point of birth.

fetus The unborn organism from the ninth week until birth.

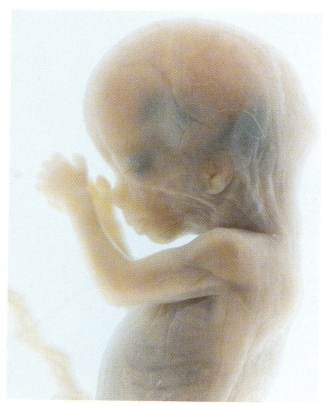

Figure 2.11
A Five-Month-Old Fetus
Weighing only about half a pound, this fetus could not survive outside the uterine environment.

 **REALITY** or MYTH ? **4**

The fetus is protected from the outside world by the fluid-filled amniotic sac. The amniotic liquid provides a stable, buffered environment, and the fetus floats in a state of relative weightlessness.

The fourth month begins a period characterized by rapid body growth. The umbilical cord is as long as the fetus and continues to grow with it. Skeletal bones are hardening; X-rays (taken only for diagnostic reasons) clearly show skeletal bones by the beginning of the sixteenth week. The legs are well developed, and the ears stand out from the head. A fetus at this age can suck its thumb.

By the time a fetus is five months old, it appears in many ways to be a fully developed human being. If it were to be taken from its protective environment, however, the fetus would not survive. Only about 10 inches long and weighing about half a pound, it has lungs that are well formed but not yet ready to function, and its digestive system cannot yet process food (see Figure 2.11).

At six months the fetus has begun to develop a padding of fat beneath its skin. Its skin is somewhat wrinkled and is pink to red in color because blood in the capillaries has become visible. It can cry and make a fist with a strong grip. Fingernails are present, and all organs are fairly well developed. The fetus that is born prematurely at this point, however, often dies within a few days because of the functional immaturity of its respiratory system.

At seven months the fetus could live if born prematurely. Its potential for survival, however, is still low because of the continuing likelihood of respiratory difficulties. A premature infant weighing at least three and a half pounds has a fairly good chance of survival if intensive medical care is provided. A fetus born at this point would probably have to live in an incubator until its weight increased to five pounds.

The fetal nervous system has developed to the point at which the fetus can sustain rhythmic breathing movements and control its body temperature. Eyes are open, and eyelashes are present. From this point on, the fetus is aware of events outside its mother's body. It responds to loud sounds as well as to the reaction of its mother's heart to such sounds.

At eight months layers of fat continue to develop and smooth out the skin. The fat helps the fetus adjust to the temperature variations that it will experience after leaving the uterus. Toenails are now present. The fetus is 18 to 20 inches long, and it weighs between five and seven pounds.

At nine months most fetuses are plump and crowd the uterus. The reddish color of the skin is fading. The chest is prominent, and the mammary glands protrude in both males and females because they are affected by the hormones that are preparing the mother's breasts to secrete milk. In males the testes have usually descended from the abdominal cavity to the scrotum.

During the ninth month the fetus usually acquires some antibodies from its mother's bloodstream. These provide the fetus with temporary immunity against whatever agents (bacteria and viruses, for example) from which its mother is protected. This is important because the newborn's immune system is not yet fully functional. It is now ready for birth, but we will save the description of that remarkable event until Chapter 7.

SECONDARY SEXUAL CHARACTERISTICS

After the period from the sixth to the twelfth week of gestation, sexual differentiation remains relatively inactive until around the age of 9 or 10, when the first signs of puberty occur—the growth of pubic hair and the formation of breast buds. The age at which puberty begins varies from one person to the next. Menstruation starts for some girls at the age of 10 or 11 but does not begin for others until they are 15 or 16. Similarly, although the onset of sexual maturation occurs on the average a couple of years later in boys than it does in girls, boys vary considerably in the age at which the process of sexual maturation begins.

Puberty represents another major biological event in our development as a male or a female. At puberty both males and females begin to grow hair around their genitals and, somewhat later, under the arms. Both discover that their developing sweat glands emit relatively strong odors. For the first time, both become capable of releasing mature germ cells (eggs or sperm). And both discover themselves suddenly, and involuntarily, emitting fluid from their bodies—menstrual flow in the case of females and semen in the case of males.

Offsetting these developmental similarities are a number of differences. First, whereas males are totally unaware of the reproductive processes of sperm production and maturation taking place in their bodies, females are dramatically reminded of their reproductive capacity through the regular appearance of their menstrual periods.

Second, the role of hormones in the reproductive capacities is different for males and females. Prior to the onset of puberty, equal levels of estrogen (secreted by the adrenal glands) are found in the urine of boys and girls. One of the first indicators of puberty in females is an increase in the production of estrogen. Although both genders manufacture the same three major hormones—estrogens, progestins, and androgens—after they have reached puberty, the average female produces more of the first two, and the average male manufactures more of the third. Thus the reproductive capacities of women are influenced by the interactions and fluctuations of these major hormones, which, together with other hormones secreted by the brain and the adrenal glands, produce the characteristic monthly cycle. In contrast, the reproductive capacity of males is relatively acyclic (stable). The extent to which men experience cycles is a matter of debate, but any cycles that males may experience are less obvious and dramatic than are the cycles of females.

Female Maturation

Between the ages of 8 and 14, the ovaries begin to secrete estrogen and the follicles in the ovaries grow. At the same time, the uterus enlarges. The formerly convoluted fallopian tubes mature and increase in both length and width, becoming straighter in the process. The vagina and clitoris also grow, and the fine downy hair on the vulva is gradually replaced with a few coarse little hairs. At about the same time, the breasts start to protrude a bit, mainly right around the nipples. The areola and labia also increase in size. Estrogen plays an extremely important role in most of these specific changes, as well as in the spurt of general body growth and the widening of the pelvic girdle. Many other hormones, either in interaction with estrogen or on their own, also stimulate the differentiation and growth of the pubescent female.

Several years after the onset of these initial, relatively subtle signs of puberty, menarche—the first menstrual period—occurs (see "Highlight: Meanings of Menarche," page 48). Adolescent girls tend to be shy about this event, often using euphemisms for menstruation. Although the average age of menarche is 12½, the point at

HIGHLIGHT

Meanings of Menarche

My mother had described menstruation to me and had bought me some sanitary napkins and a belt, and from the time I was about 12, I waited in anticipation for it to appear. Finally, in the middle of my thirteenth year (I can still remember the exact date), I went to the bathroom and discovered, to my surprise, some blood on the toilet paper. I went racing out of the bathroom, yelling, "I'm a woman, I'm a woman!" at the top of my lungs, only to discover, much to my embarrassment, that my mother had gone out. In response to my father's inquiries, I muttered "Never mind" and waited impatiently for my mother to return so that I could tell her the wonderful news. My irrational sense of pride with myself each month my period began didn't finally diminish until after I'd had several children.

I was in the eighth grade when I got my first period. Some of my friends had already started their period, and I was kind of apprehensively awaiting mine. The day it started, my mom was flat on her back with a bad case of the flu, and my dad and brother were avidly watching a football game.

I can remember trying to figure out how the pad fit on the sanitary napkin belt. I was so scared I almost cried. I wanted to talk to my mom, but I was afraid to because she was sick. So I put on the bulky pad, and I remember being very self-conscious, thinking that everyone noticed.

Mom asked me the next day if I had my period. She had noticed a napkin as she emptied the trash. She started telling me horror stories of the bad cases of cramps she used to get. I wondered if the dull aches I felt were cramps. I don't think I thought even once that they were cramps before that.

I was bitter for probably about a year because I couldn't understand why women had to go through this torture. I couldn't understand why I had to tell my friends that I couldn't go swimming because I was "ragging it." Finally, I said, "Mom, will you please let me try tampons?" She was a rough case, but I finally convinced her. She thought tampons were nothing but trouble. It turned out that they made all the difference in the world. That dreaded five days was now just like the rest of the month.

The feelings I had the day I got my first period are clear to me. When I saw the blood on my underpants while in the bathroom at school, I felt scared. Then a surge of warmth ran all through me, and I caught myself smiling alone in the bathroom stall. I went to find my best friend. She went with me to the nurse's office. The nurse's scratchy voice seemed extra loud that day when she asked me if I wore tampons or napkins. I said quietly, "I don't know, this is my first time." She got me a belted napkin and went on explaining how to use it for what seemed like an eternity while I turned crimson. After that, I called my mom and said, "Guess what? I got my period!"

She shared and even increased my enthusiasm as she congratulated me and said, "We'll have to celebrate tonight!" When my family was all seated around the dinner table that night, mom brought out a bottle of champagne and toasted me, saying, "You're a woman. Congratulations!" I felt a little embarrassed and I'm sure I blushed, but more than that I felt special, as if in that day I had matured years. I am especially thankful for my mother's response of delight and enthusiasm, which made my coming into womanhood as special and wonderful as it should be.

Source: Authors' files.

---

which the first menstruation begins ranges widely from about 9 to 17 years. Biologically, puberty is considered to be precocious (unusually early) if its presence is detected before age 8 in females and is considered to be delayed if no breast growth has occurred by age 14, or if no skeletal growth spurt has appeared by age 15.

Menstruation can be quite erratic after the first period. Within a few years, however, the interval tends to become fairly regular, with menstruation appearing every 23 to 32 days or so. Over the course of approximately 35 years of reproductive capacity, women will menstruate about 420 times, minus 9 or 10 menstrual periods per birth. Such a repetitive event becomes routine for most women, and they take menstrual periods in stride.

Male Maturation

For males, the onset of puberty arrives later on average than for females. Male puberty is considered to be precocious if it occurs before age 10 and delayed if it has not begun by age 15. The pituitary gland and the hypothalamus begin secreting follicle-stimulating hormone (FSH) and luteinizing hormone (LH) (sometimes called interstitial-cell stimulating hormone) just as they do in females. The LH stimulates the interstitial cells in the testicles to manufacture increased levels of testosterone. FSH elicits the production of sperm cells in the seminiferous tubules and causes the various other sexual structures to increase in size.

Externally, the testes and penis begin to grow, pubic hair gradually replaces the softer body hair around the genitals, and height and muscular strength increase. Several years later hair grows under the arms and on the face, although the coarse hair that characterizes the adult beard is not in evidence until several years after soft, downy hair first appears on the upper lip. Although a young man may take pleasure in these effects of testosterone, he does not welcome another common symptom of male pubescence, acne. These skin eruptions are partially the result of the influence of testosterone. Secretion of that hormone elicits a dramatic increase in the production of oil-releasing glands in the skin. Sebum, the oil manufactured by these glands, acts as a lubricant and can irritate and block the hair follicles, causing redness and blackheads. Because acne is primarily due to the pubescent rise in adrenal androgens, it is less common in females, who secrete lower levels of these androgens. Testosterone also stimulates the growth of the larynx; the adolescent boy's voice begins to break unpredictably at about 13 or 14, becoming the reliably deeper voice of an adult male at about 15 or 16. The areolae double in diameter, and marked breast enlargement occurs in the majority of boys, diminishing within a year or so.

Just as pubescent girls begin to menstruate, pubescent boys start to experience **nocturnal emissions;** that is, while asleep they expel semen containing sperm. Although they are capable of orgasm from birth on, the ability to ejaculate semen does not develop until the testes enlarge at puberty.

All these changes produce the capacity for normal anatomical and physiological sexual functioning. But what is the experience of development for those who are intersexual?

nocturnal emission Ejaculation of semen during sleep.

SEXUAL DIFFERENTIATION AND GENDER IDENTITY

The earlier overview of the disorders associated with atypical hormone exposure indicates that the sex hormones, particularly the androgens, have an enormous influence on anatomical differentiation in a male or a female direction during prenatal development. However, the development of gender identity stems from the interaction of physiological factors and environmental influences. Milton Diamond (1997) has reviewed a number of cases in which individuals, because of accidents to their genitals or because they were born with ambiguous genitals, were assigned a gender they later rejected.

A Genital Accident

To back up a bit, in the early 1960s two male (XY) twins were circumcised when they were 8 months old. The circumcision (removal of the foreskin of the penis) went fine with one of the twins. However, the other twin, John (pseudonym), had his penis burned beyond repair during his circumcision. The parents and local medical personnel consulted with authorities and ended up taking the advice of John Money and his associates at Johns Hopkins University. Believing that people are psychosexually neutral at birth, Money and his colleagues recommended that John be raised as a girl. When John was 17 months old, he was surgically reassigned as a female. His testes were removed, and physicians began to construct a vulva. John, now Joan (pseudonym), was treated as a girl by her parents, family, and all professionals associated with the case. Her reassignment as a girl was described as highly successful (Money & Ehrhardt, 1972; Money & Tucker, 1975).

However, in the late 1970s the British Broadcasting Company (BBC) decided to produce a follow-up on Joan's life. As described by Diamond (1982, 1997), independent psychiatrists obtained by the BBC to interview Joan reached a very different conclusion. In spite of Joan's rearing from infancy on as a girl, she did not feel like a girl. She preferred to play with boys and to engage in typical boys' activities. She avoided the typical activities and interests of girls. She had been given estrogen therapy by her physician, which produced breast development and rounded hips. Her preference for male behaviors continued, however, and when she was 14, she rebelled at living as a girl, although she was unaware of her history. She told her physician that "I suspected I was a boy since the second grade" (Diamond, 1997, p. 200).

Subsequently, Joan, the clinical team involved in her treatment, and her family discussed Joan's desire to live as a male. When she switched to living as John, finally finding out about his history provided him with relief, as it confirmed what he had believed all along. John's parents felt guilty about their participation in the original sex reassignment, but they and John have reconciled. John subsequently obtained a mastectomy and a surgically created penis and lives as a male. Although he had been approached romantically by boys and men when he was living as a girl, he had always rejected them. In contrast, he was very erotically interested in girls and women. At age 25 he married a woman several years older than he and adopted her children.

Ambiguous Genitals

Working with members of the Intersex Society of North America (ISNA), a peer support group for intersexuals and their families, Diamond (1997) described several cases of individuals born with both male and female characteristics. Samantha (pseudonym) was described as a girl at birth, but began to grow the bud of a penis at the age of 5. She was raised as a girl but failed to begin menstruation or breast development. During puberty her voice deepened, she began growing thicker body hair, and she was shaving by age 15. Her physician prescribed oral contraceptives to counteract hair growth and stimulate menstruation and breast growth. Samantha (now Sam) noted that the physician did not give her a physical examination or discuss her situation with her. The oral contraceptives did stimulate cyclic bleeding, but she was disgusted by menstruation.

When she was 18, she had her first (brief) sexual experience with another person. Her male partner "found the vagina she herself never previously investigated. The session was brief, and her partner did not mention anything notable. Sam recalled enjoying the reification of her female self and her ability to attract a man she found handsome but reported feeling it was actually more of what she imagined a homosexual encounter might be like" (Diamond, 1997, p. 201).

Sam left home to live by herself for the first time when she was 23. She sought a medical examination to resolve the male-female questions she had. She was diagnosed an XX true **hermaphrodite** with ambiguous genitals. At 28 she discussed the situation

hermaphroditism A condition in which a person is born with both male and female characteristics, such as an ovary on one side and a testis on the other.

with a counselor, who suggested that Samantha might be happier living as a male. Sam, now in his late 40s, said:

> *After years spent wandering in an emotional quagmire and living an agonizing lie I made the mammoth switch to becoming a man. I did it cold turkey, almost overnight. I just stopped taking the estrogens and let my beard grow in. I imme- diately gave away everything that was female. And I never looked back. . . . And when I got my brand new male birth certificate from the court (after prolonged legal wrangling) it was the happiest moment of my life. Now I don't think of how to behave. My maleness just comes naturally. (Diamond, 1997, p. 202)*

Sam now describes himself as a bisexual male seeking another person with whom to share his life. To prevent any possibility of getting pregnant, Sam had a tubal liga- tion (female sterilization). He takes androgens and believes his decision to live as a male was correct and psychologically necessary.

In another case with a similar diagnosis, Bill (pseudonym) was born with an en- larged clitoris and apparently normal genitals and reproductive organs. He was initially diagnosed as a male pseudohermaphrodite and assigned to be raised as a boy. However, at 18 months of age he was diagnosed as a true hermaphrodite, and Bill was reassigned as a girl. Billie's clitoris and inner vaginal lips were removed. Although she was not told why, at age 8 the testicular portions of her gonads were surgically removed. When Billie was about 10, her mother told her that her clitoris had been removed but not why or what her clitoris was. She was taken to a psychiatrist because she was supposedly "incorrigible." The psychiatrist reinforced her femaleness (with no discussion of doubt), and Billie entered adolescence no longer doubting her assignment as a female, although her interests were more stereotypically masculine (e.g., electronics, construc- tion) than feminine (e.g., cooking, dresses).

She began normal menstruation and breast development during puberty, but did not date while she was a teenager. She spent time with boys because of shared inter- ests, not because of erotic interest. She tried to masturbate during puberty, but her geni- tals were not sensitive to touch. Years later, when she was 22 she finally convinced a physician to obtain her old hospital records and finally learned her true diagnosis.

Billie went through many years of great emotional crisis before finally coming to terms with her situation:

> *She continued to live as a woman reinforced by a female body with breasts and menstruation. Moreover, she now took pride in her differences. She found strength in identifying as an intersexed person with male and female aspects that meld in ways that she felt appropriate. This acceptance of her hermaphro- ditism, however, has not come easily. It required coming to grips with feelings of shame and inadequacy. It still requires living with a great deal of anger over the surgical loss of her clitoris and associated erotic sensitivity. Billie would have preferred the opportunity to participate in deciding her future as a male or female. . . . Angry over loss of her genital sensitivity, Billie is adamantly against the nonconsensual enforcement of either gender with accompanying genital surgery on infants. Billie is now a professional woman active in the In- tersex Society of North America (ISNA). (Diamond, 1997, p. 203)*

There is intense disagreement among researchers and health care professionals re- garding how to respond to intersexed infants. Some, following the lead of John Money, adhere to the belief that intersexed infants should be unambiguously assigned to one or the other gender at as early an age as possible—preferably before the emergence of

ISSUES TO CONSIDER

Diamond (1997) has argued that surgery should not be done on intersexed children until they are old enough to understand the possible risks and benefits and give informed consent. What do you think?

gender identity in the second year of life. Others, agreeing with the position taken by ISNA members, think that performing surgery on infants and children too young to give their informed consent to the procedures invades their rights as humans to make such decisions when they are old enough to consider the costs and benefits of such surgical invasions, or to choose to remain as intersexed individuals with their own identity.

For the sake of those dealing with ambiguous genitals, we hope that considerably more is learned about these conditions in the next few years. See the Appendix for the address of ISNA. In the next chapter we focus on the sexual anatomy and physiology of men and women who have experienced more typical development.

SUMMARY OF MAJOR POINTS

1. Fertilization.

Fertilization depends on the depositing of a large number of viable sperm in the vagina around the time of ovulation. Many sperm are lost in the journey from the vagina to the fallopian tube containing the mature egg (ovum). For fertilization to occur, a large number of sperm must attach themselves to the egg, where they secrete an enzyme that helps to dissolve cellular material on the outside of the ovum, permitting one sperm to penetrate it.

2. Creation of a zygote.

The genetic sex of the fetus is determined immediately upon fertilization. The egg contains 22 autosomes (chromosomes that determine body characteristics) and one X chromosome. The sperm contains 22 autosomes and either one X chromosome or one Y chromosome. The combination of the X chromosome from the egg and an X chromosome from the sperm results in a genetic female (XX); the combination of the X chromosome from the egg and a Y chromosome from the sperm results in a genetic male (XY).

3. Sexual differentiation.

Genetic sex is determined by the combination of sex chromosomes (XX or XY), which occurs at fertilization. Sexual differentiation of the fetus begins about six weeks after conception, at the onset of the fetal stage. If the fetus carries a Y chromosome, this chromosome signals the development of gonads into testes rather than into ovaries. The testes then secrete testosterone, which masculinizes first the internal and then the external genital organs. The testes also secrete Müllerian-inhibiting substance, which inhibits the development of female sexual and reproductive structures. In the absence of testosterone or MIS, the fetus differentiates in a female direction, regardless of genetic gender. This finding suggests that the basic human form is female and that substances must be added to produce a male.

4. Atypical sexual differentiation.

Observations of individuals who have experienced atypical sexual differentiation have enhanced our understanding of fetal differentiation into a male or a female. Possession of at least one X chromosome appears to be crucial for survival, whereas possession of the Y chromosome seems to be important for maleness but not for life. Regardless of genetic sex, exposure to androgens during the early fetal period masculinizes a fetus. In the absence of androgens, or if the fetus is unable to respond to them, it differentiates in a feminine direction.

5. Development during the fetal stage.

The developing human is called a fetus when its bone cells, replacing cartilage cells, begin to appear, approximately two months after conception. From this point on development consists primarily of the growth and maturation of organs and structures that appeared during the embryonic stage.

6. Sexual and reproductive maturation.

As young people move into their second decade, hormonal processes within their bodies stimulate the changes associated with puberty. Females generally enter puberty at an earlier age than do males. The most obvious physical sign of girls' maturation is menarche, and of boys' maturation, nocturnal emission.

7. Sexual differentiation and gender identity.

For those born with ambiguous genitals or who experience a genital accident, the course of development to adulthood can be considerably more difficult than it is for those with unambiguously male or female genital and reproductive organs. We do not know to what extent the difficulties experienced by such intersexual people stem from interventions performed by well-meaning caretakers and professionals rather than from the intersexual condition itself.

CHECK YOUR KNOWLEDGE

1. Sperm are (a) miniature, preformed human beings that need to be united with an egg (ovum) to survive and develop; (b) among the largest cells in the human body; (c) produced by the endometrium; (d) among the smallest cells in the human body. **(p. 30)**

2. By the process known as mitosis, (a) the zygote is formed; (b) the genetic sex of an embryo is determined; (c) body cells divide, creating two new, identical cells; (d) genes are arranged in place on chromosomes. **(p. 31)**

3. Dominant genes are those that (a) are located on the male Y chromosome, (b) are located on the female Y chromosome, (c) survive the perilous journey down the fallopian tubes, (d) determine a person's inherited characteristics. **(p. 32)**

4. Which of the following is true about the ovum? (a) It is fertilized by the sperm in the vagina; (b) It becomes implanted in the uterine wall within 24 hours after it is fertilized; (c) It is the largest cell in the human body; (d) It releases cervical mucus after being fertilized. **(p. 29)**

5. Chromosomal sex is (a) not understood by modern science, (b) determined in the second trimester of pregnancy, (c) determined at conception, (d) linked to the inheritance of a dominant gene. **(p. 31)**

6. The external male and female genitals begin to differentiate (a) at the moment of fertilization, (b) after the internal structures of the embryo have differentiated, (c) at birth, (d) during the eighth month of pregnancy. **(p. 38)**

7. The onset of puberty and reproductive maturity, (a) begins earlier in boys than in girls, (b) shows much greater variability in timing of onset in boys than in girls, (c) is much more apparent to girls than it is to boys, (d) results in much greater variability in the cycles of hormone secretion in boys than in girls. **(p. 47)**

8. In the case of children born with ambiguous genitalia, (a) genital surgery should be provided before they are 2 years old and have developed a firm gender identity, (b) health care professionals should prescribe small levels of hormone treatments in infancy and childhood and larger amounts at puberty, (c) no action should be taken until they are old enough to understand their condition so they can decide what they want to do, (d) research has yet to determine what approach is most likely to produce satisfactory results for such people. **(p. 51)**

3

SEXUAL ANATOMY AND PHYSIOLOGY

SEXUAL ANATOMY
The Male Sexual System
Health: Testes Self-Examination
The Female Sexual System
Across Cultures: Female Circumcision
Health: Kegel Exercises
Health: Breast Self-Examination

HORMONES AND THE ENDOCRINE SYSTEM
The Endocrine Glands
The Effects of Hormones
The Menstrual Cycle

THE NERVOUS SYSTEM
The Sympathetic and Parasympathetic Nervous Systems
The Central Nervous System

SUMMARY OF MAJOR POINTS

CHECK YOUR KNOWLEDGE

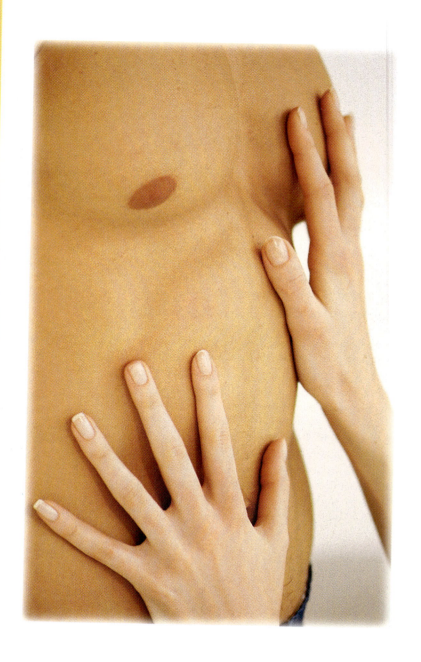

REALITY or MYTH ?

1 Cancer of a testicle usually results in erectile dysfunction.

2 Male circumcision is now common in all societies that have been studied.

3 The area most sensitive to sexual stimulation in women is the clitoris.

4 The ovaries are the only source of estrogen in females.

5 Ejaculation or orgasm can be influenced by our thoughts.

SEXUAL arousal involves the body in a concert of responses that usually culminates in a coordinated climax far more intricate than that achieved by the conductor and members of an orchestra. Sexual response is influenced by the interactions of the sexual organs, the endocrine system, the brain and the nervous system, childhood socialization processes, previous sexual experience, and the immediate situation. In this chapter we focus on the first three variables: the sexual organs, the endocrine system, and the nervous system. We also explore the effects of certain illnesses on sexual functioning.

SEXUAL ANATOMY

The entire body participates in sexual response. In this section we describe the anatomy of the genitals—those parts of the body most closely identified with sexual response.

The Male Sexual System

The male sexual system consists of a pair of testes, which produce sperm and sex hormones; a network of ducts that transport sperm from the testes to the outside world; a number of glands that produce seminal fluid; and the penis, which delivers the semen (see Figure 3.1, page 56).

THE TESTES. The word **testes** (singular, *testis*) comes from the Latin word for "to testify" or "to witness." Instead of placing hands on a Bible, as is customary today, the early Romans placed their hands over their testes when taking an oath. The fact that women do not have testes did not pose a problem because Roman women were not considered important enough to take oaths.

A popular slang term for the testes, *balls,* suggests that they are round in shape. Actually they are oval, or egg-shaped, organs, located in a saclike structure called the **scrotum.** The scrotum helps to maintain the temperature necessary for the production of viable sperm. Normal scrotal temperature is about five and a half degrees lower than normal core body temperature. Within the scrotum, each testis is suspended at the end of a cord called the **spermatic cord.** The cord contains blood vessels, nerves, a sperm duct called the vas deferens, and the thin **cremaster muscle,** which encircles each testis and raises it closer to the body in response to cold, fear, anger, or sexual arousal (see "Health: Testes Self-Examination," page 57).

testes (TES-tees) Two small oval organs located in the scrotum that produce mature sperm and sex hormones.
scrotum (SCROH-tum) Sac that contains the testes.
spermatic cord (spur-MAH-tik) Cord that suspends the testes and contains the vas deferens, blood vessels, nerves, and cremaster muscle.
cremaster muscle (CRE-mah-ster) Muscle that runs from the testes into the spermatic cord and controls the proximity of the testes to the body.

55

Figure 3.1
The Male Genital System

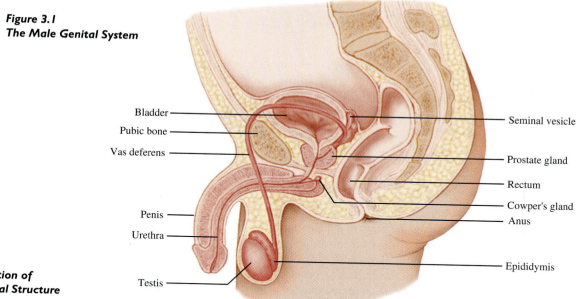

Bladder

Pubic bone

Vas deferens

Penis

Urethra

Testis

Seminal vesicle

Prostate gland

Rectum

Cowper's gland

Anus

Epididymis

Figure 3.2
**Cross-Section of
the Internal Structure
of a Testis**

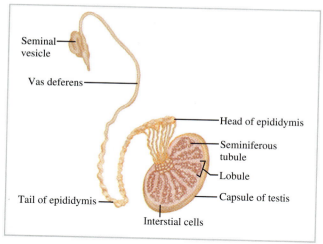

Seminal vesicle

Vas deferens

Tail of epididymis

Interstial cells

Head of epididymis

Seminiferous tubule

Lobule

Capsule of testis

seminiferous tubules (sem-ih-NIF-er-us) Long, thin, tightly coiled tubes, located in the testes, that produce sperm.

interstitial cells Cells in the spaces between the seminiferous tubules that secrete hormones.

epididymis (ep-ih-DIH-dih-mis) Tightly coiled tubules, located at the top of the testes, in which sperm are stored.

Each testis contains **seminiferous tubules** and **interstitial cells** (also called Leydig cells). Sperm are produced within the seminiferous ("seed-bearing") tubules. Hundreds of these tubules lie tightly coiled within each testis, and each tubule is between one and three feet long (see Figure 3.2). The interstitial cells, which are located in the connective tissue between the seminiferous tubules, synthesize and secrete sex hormones. About 95 percent of the testosterone manufactured by the body comes from testicular interstitial cells; the remainder comes from the adrenal glands. Interstitial cells also produce small amounts of estrogen, a feminizing hormone.

Sperm pass out of the seminiferous tubules and into the **epididymis,** which lies adjacent to the back portion of each testis. It is in the tightly coiled tubules that make up the epididymis that sperm become functionally mature and then are stored until they are ejaculated from the body. The smooth muscle of the wall of the epididymal tubules contracts when a male ejaculates. These contractions move the sperm out of the epididymis and into the vas deferens for transport to the urethra.

THE MALE GENITAL DUCTS.   The ducts of the male genital organs include the vasa deferentia, the ejaculatory ducts, and the urethra. The *vasa deferentia* (singular, **vas deferens**) consist of two slender ducts or tubes, one from each epididymis. These run from the epididymis into the abdominal cavity and join with the duct from the seminal vesicles at the back of the urinary bladder to form the ejaculatory ducts. Sperm travel through each vas deferens to the ejaculatory duct, where they receive fluid from the seminal vesicles.

Testes Self-Examination

About 4 out of every 100,000 U.S. men will develop cancer of the testes. Testicular cancer strikes at a younger age than do most other cancers, usually afflicting men between the ages of 20 and 35. The American Cancer Society estimated that 7,000 new cases of testicular cancer would develop in 1996, but expected only 350 deaths. Risk of developing this cancer increases to 11–15 percent in men whose testes either do not descend or descend after the age of six.

Because self-examination is helpful in detecting testicular cancer, men should examine themselves monthly. In this procedure, each testis is rolled between the thumb, which is placed on the top of the testis, and the index and middle fingers, which are positioned on the underside of the testis.

If a man discovers a hard lump, he should see a doctor immediately, even though the lump may not be cancerous. With early detection and treatment, testicular cancer is highly curable. Delayed treatment, however, increases the risk of the cancer spreading to other parts of the body. Treatment generally involves removal of the diseased testis. Sexual functioning and fertility usually remain unimpaired because the other testis can manufacture enough androgen and sperm to compensate for the missing testis.

REALITY or **MYTH** ? **I**

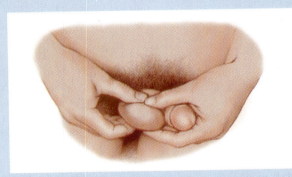

Self-Examination of Testes

The **ejaculatory ducts** enter the **prostate gland,** where fluid from the prostate and the seminal vesicles combines with sperm to produce the semen that enters the urethra. The **urethra** has two functions in the male: It conveys both urine and semen.

GLANDS PRODUCING SEMINAL FLUID. Despite the presence of 200 million to 400 million sperm in the average ejaculate, sperm account for only about 1 percent of the total volume of **semen.** Secretions from the epididymis contribute a small amount of fluid, but most of the teaspoonful of semen in the average ejaculate comes from the seminal vesicles, the prostate gland, and the Cowper's glands.

The **seminal vesicles** are two saclike structures on either side of the bladder. At their base are two straight, narrow ducts that enter into the ejaculatory duct. The seminal vesicles secrete a fluid that not only provides sperm with energy in the form of fructose (a sugar) but also neutralizes the normal acidity of the female's vagina, which can be fatal to sperm.

The prostate gland, which surrounds the urethra at the base of the urinary bladder, is about the size of a large walnut. At the moment of ejaculation, it expels its alkaline fluid into the urethra just below the urinary bladder. During ejaculation the nervous system coordinates the closing of sphincter muscles where the urethra leaves the urinary bladder, allowing semen to pass through the urethra without mixing with urine.

The majority of men beyond their mid-forties experience enlargement of the prostate that can cause problems with urination. This condition is usually benign, but in some cases it can become cancerous. In 1996, about 317,000 new cases of prostate cancer were diagnosed, and in that same year about 41,000 died from the disease (American Cancer Society, 1996). Prostate cancer may be detected through laboratory

vas deferens (VAS DEH-fur-renz) Slender duct through which sperm are transported from each testis to the ejaculatory duct at the base of the urethra.

ejaculatory ducts (ee-JAK-u-la-TOR-ee) Tubelike passageways that carry semen from the prostate gland to the urethra.

prostate gland Gland located at the base of the male bladder that supplies most of the seminal fluid.

urethra (ur-REE-thrah) Duct or tube through which urine and ejaculate leave the body.

semen (SEE-men) Milky-white alkaline fluid containing sperm; a product of fluids from the epididymis, seminal vesicles, prostate, and Cowper's glands, combined with sperm from the testes.

seminal vesicles (SEM-ih-nal VES-ih-kelz) Two saclike organs lying on either side of the prostate that deposit fluid into the ejaculatory ducts to contribute to semen.

Cowper's glands (COW-perz) Two small glands that secrete a clear alkaline fluid into the urethra during sexual arousal.

tests and rectal exams. A variety of treatments are available, and the five-year survival rate is more than 80 percent.

The **Cowper's glands,** each about the size of a pea, flank the urethra and empty into it through tiny ducts. During sexual arousal these glands secrete a clear, slippery fluid, a drop of which usually appears at the tip of the penis prior to ejaculation. This alkaline fluid helps to neutralize the acidic effects of urine in the urethra, making the urethra more hospitable to the passage of sperm. The fluid sometimes contains small numbers of sperm, particularly when a couple engages in coitus a second time without the male's having urinated. In such a case, any sperm remaining in the urethra from the previous ejaculation are likely to be carried out of the penis in the fluid secreted from the Cowper's glands during sexual arousal. People who have been practicing withdrawal to avoid conception may be surprised to learn that sperm can be carried into the vagina by this fluid before ejaculation, sometimes causing pregnancy to occur even if the man avoids ejaculating into the woman's vagina.

penis (PEE-nis) The male sexual organ.

corpora cavernosa (COR-por-uh kah-vur-NOH-sah) Two columns within the penis that contain small cavities capable of filling with blood to produce an erection.

THE PENIS.   The human **penis** consists of three parallel cylinders of spongy tissue that provide the penis with its capacity to become erect (see Figure 3.3). Two of these cylinders are called the cavernous bodies, or **corpora cavernosa.** If the penis is held straight out, the third cylinder, the **corpus spongiosum,** can be felt on the underside of the penis. It surrounds the urethra.

Each of these cylinders contains tissue with irregular cavities, or spaces. These spaces do not have much blood in them when the penis is flaccid, or soft. When a male becomes sexually aroused, however, the blood vessels dilate (open up), and the cavities become engorged with blood. This engorgement produces the rigidity and stiffness of an erection, known in slang as a "hard-on."

The end of the corpus spongiosum enters the **glans** at the tip of the penis. The glans is more sensitive to stimulation than the rest of the penis because it contains abundant sense receptors to pressure and touch. The most sensitive parts of the glans are the **corona,** or rim, and the **frenulum,** a strip of skin on the underside where the glans meets the body of the penis. At the time of birth, the penis has a fold of skin called the foreskin, or prepuce. More than 60 percent of American males and about 50 percent of Canadian males have their foreskin surgically removed through circumcision within a few days of birth (Niku, Stock, & Kaplan, 1995). This practice is very uncommon in northern Europe, Central and South America, and Asia.

When flaccid, the average penis is about 10 cm (3.9 in) in length and about 9.5 cm (3.75 in) in circumference. An erect penis is about 16 cm (6.3 in) in length and about 12 cm (4.85 in) in circumference (Jamison & Gebhard, 1988). Wardell Pomeroy (1972) reported that the largest penis he and his associates encountered in their research was 10 inches long when erect. The smallest erect penis was 1 inch long. Medical literature contains reports of men whose penises do not exceed 1 cm when erect. This

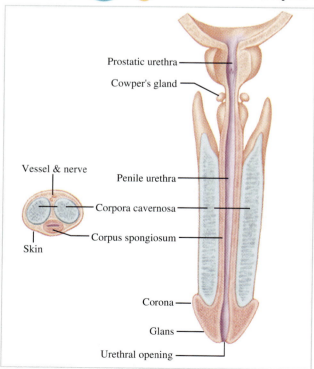

Prostatic urethra

Cowper's gland

Vessel & nerve

Penile urethra

Corpora cavernosa

Corpus spongiosum

Skin

Corona

Glans

Urethral opening

Figure 3.3
The Internal Structure of the Circumcised Penis
A cross-section and a longitudinal section are shown.

condition, sometimes called micropenis, usually results from inadequate levels of masculinizing hormones during early development.

Penis size tends to be of great concern to many people because size is commonly equated with sexual prowess. Among adolescent women, rumors circulate that you can tell the length of a man's penis by his height or by the length of his foot, nose, or thumb. Research has not demonstrated a relationship between penis length and the proportions of any other part of a man's body. In addition, smaller flaccid penises undergo greater increases in size during erection than do larger flaccid penises (Jamison & Gebhard, 1988).

As far as the issue of sexual prowess is concerned, it is important to realize that various characteristics of female sexual anatomy make penis length irrelevant to the physiological arousal of most women. For many women, stimulation of the vagina is less effective for sexual arousal than is stimulation of the clitoris. Further, the vagina is an extraordinarily elastic organ. Although it expands to accommodate the passage of babies, which are far larger than the biggest penis, it is quite small in its nonaroused state.

Some people have speculated that long penises may be more psychologically arousing than shorter penises. So far, only one study has examined the influence of penis length on erotic arousal (Fisher, Branscombe, & Lemery, 1983). Although volunteers were clearly aroused by the erotic stories they were given to read, their arousal did not vary as a function of the length of the penises described in the stories. The answer to the question posed by the researchers in the title of their study—"The Bigger the Better?"—seems to be no.

The Female Sexual System

The female sexual system consists of a pair of ovaries, a pair of fallopian tubes, a uterus (or womb), vagina, clitoris, and vulva (see Figure 3.4). The female has at least two areas of intense erotic sensation. One area is the clitoris, which is located externally at the top of the vulva, where the inner lips meet. The inner lips and the entrance to the

corpus spongiosum (COR-puhs spun-jee-OH-sum) A column of spongy tissue within the penis that surrounds the urethra and is capable of blood engorgement during sexual arousal.
glans The sensitive tip of the penis or clitoris.
corona (cor-OH-nah) The sensitive rim of the glans.
frenulum (FREN-yu-lum) A small piece of skin on the underside of the male glans where the glans meets the body of the penis.

REALITY or MYTH ? 3

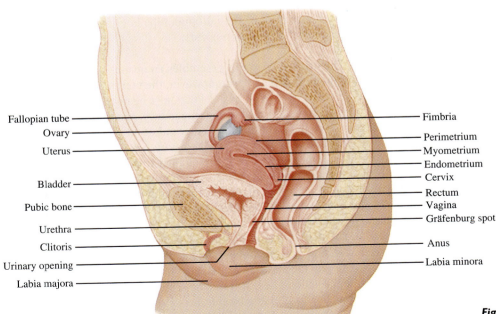

Fallopian tube

Ovary

Uterus

Bladder

Pubic bone

Urethra

Clitoris

Urinary opening

Labia majora

Fimbria

Perimetrium

Myometrium

Endometrium

Cervix

Rectum

Vagina

Gräfenburg spot

Anus

Labia minora

Figure 3.4
The Female Genital System

vagina are also sensitive in some women, as are the breasts and nipples. A second area, known as the Gräfenberg spot, is located at the base of the bladder and can be accessed by stimulation of the anterior wall (the top wall if the woman is lying on her back) of the vagina.

ovaries (OH-vah-rees) Two small organs that produce eggs and hormones, located above and to each side of the uterus.

THE OVARIES.
The **ovaries** are flattened, egg-shaped organs located in the pelvic cavity. They lie nestled in the curve of the fallopian tubes. The ovaries are similar to the testes: Both develop from similar tissue within a few months after conception, both produce reproductive cells (eggs or sperm), and both secrete hormones. The principal hormones secreted by the ovaries are the feminizing estrogens and progesterone. The ovaries also secrete smaller amounts of masculinizing hormones, one of which is testosterone. To give you an idea of how potent these hormones are, consider that a woman produces only two tablespoons of these hormones during her entire life span.

follicles (FALL-ih-kulz) In the ovary, sacs of estrogen-secreting cells that contain an egg.

The ova (singular, *ovum*), or eggs, are found near the surface of the ovary. Each ovum is encircled by clusters of nutrients and hormone-secreting cells. These bundles (ovum, nutrients, and hormone-secreting cells) are called ovarian **follicles.** The number of ovarian follicles present in both ovaries at birth ranges from four hundred thousand to five hundred thousand. During a woman's lifetime, however, no more than four hundred to five hundred ova are released through ovulation. Generally, one ovum is discharged from its follicle every month from puberty until menopause, except during pregnancy or in some women while they are breast-feeding.

fallopian tube (fah-LOW-pee-an) Tube through which eggs (ova) are transported from the ovaries to the uterus.

THE FALLOPIAN TUBES.
Each **fallopian tube** is about four inches long. The end of the fallopian tube nearest the ovary is not directly connected to the ovary but opens into the abdominal cavity. The other end of each tube is connected to the uterus.

When an ovum is released from an ovary, it is propelled into the near fallopian tube by thin, hairlike structures that line the opening of the fallopian tube. After the ovum is in the fallopian tube, tiny hairlike structures called *cilia* help transport it toward the uterus. The cilia sweep in the direction of the uterus, acting as tiny fingers that aid the ovum in its movement. Contractions of the fallopian tube itself also help to propel the ovum. The upper third of the fallopian tube is typically the site of the union between egg and sperm if fertilization occurs.

uterus (YOU-tur-us) The place where a fertilized egg is implanted and the fetus develops during gestation.

THE UTERUS.
The **uterus,** or womb, resembles an upside-down pear (see Figure 3.5). In contrast to the thin-skinned pear, however, the uterus has thick, muscular walls. It is suspended in the pelvic cavity by a collection of ligaments, which allow it to shift and contract in response to sexual tension, pregnancy, and the filling of the urinary bladder or rectum. The uterine walls are composed of three layers of tissue. The most internal layer—the one that lines the uterine cavity—is the **endometrium.** The inner two-thirds of the endometrium are shed during menstruation. The middle layer of the uterine wall is the **myometrium,** a thick layer of smooth muscle. The myometrium is responsible for the contractions of the uterus that occur during sexual tension, orgasm, childbirth, and menstruation. The external surface of the uterus is covered by a thin membrane, the **perimetrium.**

endometrium (en-doe-MEE-tree-um) The lining of the uterus, part of which is shed during menstruation.
myometrium (MY-oh-MEE-tree-um) The smooth muscle layer of the uterine wall.
perimetrium (pehr-ih-MEE-tree-um) The thin connective tissue membrane covering the outside of the uterus.

The lower end of the uterus extends into the vagina and is called the **cervix** (neck). It contains glands that secrete varying amounts of mucus. The presence of this mucus, which plugs the opening into the uterus, may explain why male ejaculate contains millions of sperm. Despite the action of enzymes in the semen that digest the cervical mucus, the cervix still creates a formidable barrier. It is more likely to be penetrated by sperm at ovulation when the mucus is thinner.

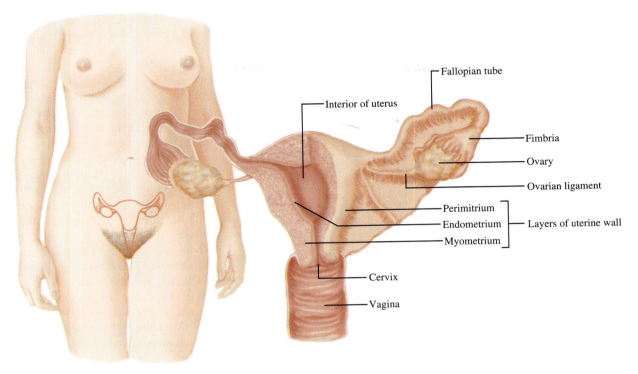

Interior of uterus

Fallopian tube

Fimbria

Ovary

Ovarian ligament

Perimitrium

Endometrium

Myometrium

Layers of uterine wall

Cervix

Vagina

Figure 3.5
The Internal Female Reproductive System Parts of the uterus and vagina are cut away in this illustration.

To improve the chances of early detection of cancer of the cervix, women should get a PAP test done at least once a year beginning in their late teens or at the point when they become sexually active. Overall, the death rate for uterine cancer has decreased more than 70 percent in the past 40 years. This dramatic decline is attributable to early detection through the PAP test and regular checkups. If cervical cancer is diagnosed and treated early, before it has spread beyond the cervix, the five-year survival rate is 90 percent (American Cancer Society, 1996). Treatment depends on the stage at which the cancer is discovered. It may involve **hysterectomy** followed by radiation, or, if the disease is detected early, destruction of the cancerous cells through extreme cold (cryotherapy) or extreme heat (electrocoagulation).

THE VAGINA.   The **vagina** is a thin-walled muscular tube that extends from the uterus to the external opening in the vulva. The vagina is a passageway that increases in length and width during sexual arousal and childbirth. The vaginal walls contain many small blood vessels that become engorged with blood during sexual excitement, in a process similar to that leading to erection in the male. The pressure from this congestion causes small droplets of the colorless, fluid portion of the blood to ooze through the vaginal walls. These droplets appear as beads on the internal surface of the vaginal walls, and they coalesce into a layer of shiny **lubricant** that coats the walls.

The walls of the vagina, particularly the inner two-thirds, contain few touch and pressure receptors, making it relatively insensitive to erotic stimulation. If the vagina were more sexually sensitive, childbirth would be more painful than it is for the delivering mother.

cervix (SIR-vix) The lower end of the uterus that opens into the vagina.

hysterectomy Surgical removal of the uterus.

vagina (vah-JYE-nah) The female's muscular tube that extends from the uterus to the vulva.

lubricant A shiny slippery fluid secreted through the walls of the vagina during sexual arousal.

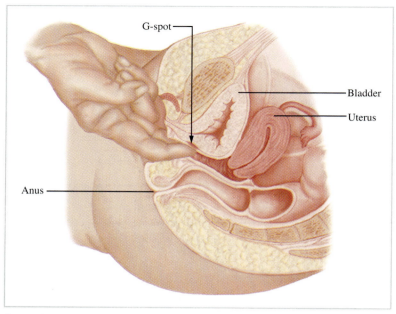

Figure 3.6
The Gräfenberg Spot

THE GRÄFENBERG SPOT. The **Gräfenberg spot,** or G-spot, provides the exception to the general rule that the vagina is erotically insensitive. The Gräfenberg spot is accessed through the anterior wall (the upper wall nearest the urethra) of the vagina, about halfway between the pubic bone and the cervix (see Figure 3.6). It varies from about the size of a dime to a half dollar. Coital positions in which the penis hits the spot, such as woman above or rear entry, as well as stimulation of the spot with the fingers, may produce intense erotic pleasure (Perry & Whipple, 1982).

There is conflicting evidence on the location of the Gräfenberg spot. As we see in Chapter 5, some researchers maintain that the entire front wall of the vagina, not just a single spot, is erotically sensitive. We should also note that not all women who have been studied report erotic feelings in response to stimulation in this area (Whipple, 1994).

THE VULVA. The **vulva,** which includes all the external genitals of the female, is shown in Figure 3.7. The major external female genitals are the mons pubis, the outer and inner lips, the clitoris, and the vaginal opening.

The **mons pubis,** or mons veneris ("mound of Venus"), is essentially a cushion of fatty tissue covered by pubic hair. The mons has more touch receptors than does the clitoris, but fewer pressure receptors. Stimulation of the mons can produce intense sexual excitement and can even trigger orgasm in some women.

Figure 3.7
The Vulva The external genitals of the female, collectively referred to as the vulva, are shown.

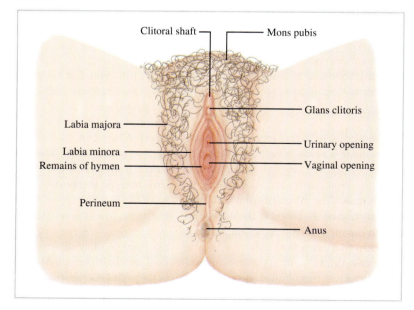

The **outer lips** (*labia majora*) are the outermost, hair-covered folds of skin that envelop the external genitals. They merge with the other body skin in the back, near the anus. In the front, they come together a small distance above the clitoris. The outer lips are similar to the skin of the scrotum in the male. During sexual stimulation the outer lips flatten and expose the inner lips as well as the vaginal opening.

The **inner lips** (*labia minora*) are the second, inner covering of the vaginal opening. The minor (inner) lips are thinner than the major (outer) lips and are hairless. During sexual stimulation these layers of skin become engorged with blood and turn from their customary pink to a dark red. The minor lips enclose both the vaginal and urethral openings, as well as the ducts of the Bartholin's glands. The Bartholin's glands correspond to the Cowper's glands in the male, but their function is not known.

The **clitoris** is the only part of the human external sexual anatomy that appears to have a purely sexual function; all of the other structures also have reproductive functions. At the top of the vulva, the inner lips come together to form the clitoral hood, also known as the prepuce or foreskin of the clitoris. Anatomically, the hood is similar to the foreskin of the penis. The minor lips, which closely surround the vagina, are stretched back and forth during intercourse as the penis thrusts in and out. The minor lips, in turn, tug on the clitoral hood, providing stimulation that may elicit orgasm. Alternatively, the clitoris may be stimulated manually or orally.

The clitoris develops out of tissue similar to that which forms the penis in the male. Like the penis, the clitoris contains two corpora cavernosa. Unlike the penis, the clitoris is physically separated from the urethra and does not contain the corpus spongiosum. It does, however, have a swelling at its tip—the glans—similar to the male penile glans. During sexual excitement the clitoris becomes engorged with blood, increasing in diameter and remaining enlarged during sexual stimulation. The clitoris is permeated with sensory receptors and has more pressure receptors than the penis (Levin, 1992).

Just as most North Americans consider the circumcision of male infants normal, some 40 countries, mostly in Africa, consider female circumcision natural. This practice, also described as female sexual mutilation, can involve removal of the clitoris and sometimes the inner vaginal lips (see "Across Cultures: Female Circumcision," page 64).

Most newborn girls have a ring or fold of connective tissue at the vaginal opening. This tissue is the **hymen,** commonly called the "cherry" in slang. The hymen varies in size, in shape, and in the extent to which it blocks the vaginal opening. Some females are born without hymens. Contrary to popular belief, the presence or absence of the hymen is not a reliable indicator of whether a woman has had sexual intercourse. The hymen may be ruptured during bicycle or horseback riding, vigorous exercise, or insertion of menstrual tampons. And the hymens of some sexually active women remain intact until they go through childbirth.

Another common belief is that first intercourse for a woman is painful because of the rupture of the hymen. This may be the case for a woman with a particularly thick hymen that blocks most of the vaginal entrance. Other women, however, experience first intercourse and the rupturing of the hymen, if it is intact, without any pain. The example of one of our students is rather typical:

> *After he came, the man I had sex with for the first time accused me of lying about being a virgin. He said that if I were a virgin, it would have hurt and there would have been some bleeding when my cherry was broken. Actually, I didn't feel much of anything physically—no pain, and no particular pleasure. What I did feel was disappointment that sex wasn't any big deal, and anger over his accusation.*

Because of the myth that an intact hymen indicates virginity, many men have attached a lot of importance to the tissue, and many women have expended a lot of energy to demonstrate its existence. To this day, physicians are asked to sew in hymens for women without them. Some of these women are hymenless virgins, whereas others are sexually experienced women who wish to convince a future partner that they are inexperienced. Despite all the concern about this little piece of tissue, its purpose or function is not known.

Gräfenberg spot (GRAY-fen-berg) Also known as the G-spot; an area of sensitivity accessed through the upper wall of the vagina.

vulva (VULL-vah) External female genitals, including the mons pubis, outer and inner lips, clitoris, and vaginal opening.

mons pubis In adult females, cushion of fatty tissue above the labia that is covered by pubic hair.

outer lips The hair-covered lips that enfold the inner lips, clitoris, and vaginal entrance.

inner lips The hairless lips between the outer lips that enclose the clitoris and vaginal opening.

clitoris (CLIH-tor-iss) Small, highly sensitive erectile tissue located just above the point where the minor lips converge at the top of the vulva; only known function is to provide female sexual pleasure.

hymen (HYE-men) Layer of tissue that partially covers the vaginal entrance of most females at birth.

Female Circumcision

In the Sudan, a procedure known as Pharaonic circumcision involves removal not only of the entire clitoris but also of the inner and all except the outer layers of the vaginal lips. The remaining skin is then sewn together, leaving a vaginal opening that is the circumference of a matchstick. Following surgery, females must pass urine and menstrual discharge through this small opening.

Hanny Lightfoot-Klein (1989) observed and conducted interviews with Sudanese women, doctors, historians, midwives, and religious leaders in an attempt to understand the contemporary rationale for and effects of this practice. More than 90 percent of the 300 women in her sample had been Pharaonically circumcised. The exceptions were from upper-class, educated families.

Female circumcisions are generally performed by trained midwives in cities or towns and by untrained women in villages on girls between 4 and 8 years old. Of the women interviewed by Lightfoot-Klein, more than half had been circumcised without any form of anesthesia. Immediate complications included infection, hemorrhage, shock, septicemia (bloodstream infection), tetanus (acute bacterial infection causing spasmodic muscle contractions), urine retention, trauma to adjacent tissues, and emotional trauma. No count of fatalities from the procedure could be obtained, but some Sudanese doctors estimated that in regions where antibiotics are unavailable, one-third of the females who are circumcised die from the procedure. Nearly all of the women reported urinary and menstrual problems until their labia were "opened" at marriage. Pharaonically circumcised virgins described taking an average of 10 to 15 minutes to urinate, with urine emerging drop by drop, and some women in Lightfoot-Klein's sample reported needing two hours to empty their bladders. As would be expected, urinary-tract and kidney infections were common. In addition, the small opening often blocked menstrual flow almost completely, producing a buildup of clotted blood that often could be removed only by surgery.

When a Pharaonically circumcised woman marries, her husband is expected to open the sewn-up entrance, which is usually difficult to do. The scars are often so extensive and hardened that even surgical scissors cannot cut through the tissue. The women reported going through extreme suffering during a process of gradual penetration that lasted an average of two and a half months. Tearing of surrounding tissues, hemorrhage, infections, and psychic trauma were common. Of the women Lightfoot-Klein interviewed, 15 percent reported that penetration was impossible. Other women had had midwives cut their labia with knives, but they did so secretly because of the belief that the necessity for this surgery demonstrated a husband's lack of potency. In addition, almost all Sudanese women who became pregnant required surgery during labor to permit their infant to be born because the circumcision scar prevents normal dilation. Following childbirth, almost all women had their labia sewn together again.

In view of this account, you might find it surprising that 90 percent of the women Lightfoot-Klein interviewed said that they had experienced orgasm during sexual relations. Her findings call into question the emphasis placed on the central role of the clitoris by Western experts (see Chapter 7). Despite the formidable obstacles, including removal of the clitoris and cultural prohibitions against female enjoyment of sexuality, most Sudanese women apparently retain their ability to have pleasure and orgasm during sexual relations.

In 1946 British rulers of the Sudan passed a law that made all forms of female sexual mutilation illegal. In reaction to this colonial interference, many Sudanese promptly Pharaonized their daughters. In the mid-1970s, the Sudanese passed a law against surgically altering the labia, but removal of the clitoris remains legal.

Although the pelvic muscles and breasts are not part of the female genitals, both are important in sexual arousal. We therefore turn to a description of their sexual functions.

pubococcygeus muscle (PC muscle) (pew-bow-cawk-SEE-gee-us) The muscle that surrounds the vaginal entrance and walls.

THE PELVIC MUSCLES. A ring of muscles surrounds the vaginal opening. One of these muscles, the **pubococcygeus muscle (PC muscle),** is important in female orgasmic response. The PC muscle is a slinglike band of muscle fibers that forms part of the floor of the pelvic cavity and partially supports the uterus, part of the vagina, the

Health

Kegel Exercises

Kegel exercises, named for the physician, Arnold Kegel (1952), who devised them, promote healthy muscle tone in the vagina and urethra and can be practiced by both men and women. In addition to increasing awareness of the location of the pubococcygeal (PC) muscle, which is active during orgasm, exercise for the purpose of toning this muscle may also reduce stress incontinence (involuntary passage of urine upon, for example, sneezing or being tickled), aid women who have recently given birth to restore the vagina to its former tone, and benefit men following surgery for prostate cancer.

You are probably already aware of your PC muscle, although you may not have consciously thought about it. If you have ever urgently needed to urinate or defecate while in the midst of a phone call, you perhaps recall contracting your PC muscle until you could get to a bathroom. The next time you are urinating, you can identify your PC muscle by stopping the flow of urine midstream. The muscle you contracted to halt urination is the PC muscle. Having identified it, you can exercise it in a variety of ways—even in such public situations as sitting in class or waiting in a grocery store line.

One exercise requires contracting the PC muscle for three seconds, then relaxing it for three seconds, and finally contracting it again. Barbach (1976) suggested doing 10 three-second squeezes at three different times daily. Although the "workout" sounds simple (you can try it as you read this), initially it may be difficult to hold the contraction for three whole seconds, so you may want to start with one or two seconds and gradually lengthen the contraction time as your PC muscle gets stronger.

Another exercise consists of contracting and releasing the PC muscle as quickly as possible, aiming for a sequence of 10 contraction-release cycles three times a day. A woman may also exercise her PC muscle by pretending that she is trying to pull something into and then push something out of her vagina, again holding each effort for three seconds. Barbach (1976) recommended slowly increasing the number in each series of exercises until you can do 20 repeats of every exercise in succession three times a day. As with any other exercise that you are just beginning, you may feel some tightness or stiffness at first, but with continued practice, the exercise will feel comfortable and can be done with ease.

urinary bladder, the urethra, and the rectum. If this muscle is not taut, the uterus and vagina can sag, allowing leaking of urine from the urethra (that is, urinary incontinence). Some time ago, Arnold Kegel (1952) suggested that sexual responsiveness could be increased through exercise of this muscle. See "Health: Kegel Exercises" for directions for doing these exercises.

THE BREASTS. The breasts are fatty appendages that play an important role in sexual arousal for many women and men. A few women have orgasm solely through stimulation of their nipples and breasts, and some can experience arousal while breast-feeding.

Embedded in the fatty breast tissue are secreting glands that have the potential to produce milk. The nipples contain erectile tissue and can become erect in response to sexual stimulation or cool temperatures. The sensitivity of the nerve fibers in the breasts is associated with hormonal levels that fluctuate with pregnancy and the menstrual cycle. Women should carefully examine their breasts on a monthly basis for lumps (see "Health: Breast Self-Examination," pages 66–67).

Just as men experience concern over penis size, many women worry about the shape and size of their breasts. The fact that the number of nerve endings does not vary with breast size suggests that small-breasted women would be more erotically stimulated by the fondling of a particular amount of breast tissue than would large-breasted women.

ISSUES TO CONSIDER

Female circumcision is practiced in more than 40 countries in the world for religious and cultural reasons. Do you think that this tradition should be accepted out of respect for cultural traditions or discouraged out of concern for its effects on female genitals?

Breast Self-Examination

One in eight U.S. women gets breast cancer during her lifetime, and 184,000 new cases were estimated for 1996, with 1,000 of these expected in men. Killing 46,000 women (and 300 men) in 1996, breast cancer is the second leading cause of cancer deaths among women. With early detection and treatment, 93 percent of women with localized breast cancer survive for at least five years after treatment (American Cancer Society, 1996). If the cancer is noninvasive, the survival rate is almost 100 percent, and even when the cancer is invasive and has spread, the survival rate is 71 percent. At age 20 women should begin engaging in monthly breast self-examinations (BSEs). They increase the likelihood that women will detect cancerous lumps before they have spread beyond the readily treatable stage. (Nevertheless, 80 percent of breast lumps are nonmalignant.) Early detection of a lump through a monthly BSE improves a woman's chance of survival. Because most breast lumps are painless, some time may elapse before a woman detects a lump unless she performs BSEs routinely. More than 90 percent of all breast cancers are self-diagnosed.

1. Before a Mirror

Facing the mirror, inspect your breasts with arms at your sides. Next, raise your arms high overhead. Look for changes in the contour of each breast: a swelling, dimpling of skin, or changes in the nipple. Left and right breast will not exactly match; few women's breasts do. Then rest your palms on your hips and press down firmly to flex your chest muscles. Again, look for changes and irregularities. Regular inspection reveals what is normal for you and will give you confidence in your examination.

2. In the Shower

Examine your breasts during your bath or shower because your hands will glide more easily over wet than dry skin. Hold your fingers flat, and move them gently over every part of each breast. Use the right hand to examine the left breast and the left hand for the right breast. Check for any lump, hard knot, or thickening.

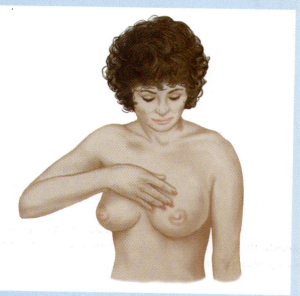

3. Lying Down

To examine your right breast, put a pillow or folded towel under your right shoulder. Place your right hand behind your back; adopting this position distributes breast tissue more evenly on the chest. With the left hand, fingers flat, press gently in small circular motions around an imaginary clock face. Begin at the outermost top of your right breast for twelve o'clock, then move to one o'clock and so on around the circle back to twelve. (A ridge of firm tissue in the lower curve of each breast is normal.) Then move one inch inward, toward the nipple. Keep circling to examine every part of your breast, including the nipple. A thorough inspection will require at least three more circles. Now slowly repeat the procedure on your left breast with a pillow under your left shoulder and your left hand behind your head. Notice how your breast structure feels. Finally, squeeze the nipple of each breast gently between the thumb and index finger. Immediately report any discharge, clear or bloody, to your doctor.

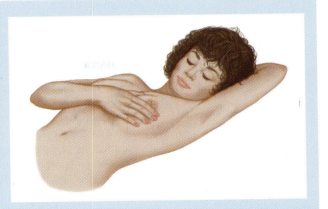

Periodic self-examination of the breasts is recommended for men as well as for women. Most lumps are benign, but if one is discovered, it is best to see a physician for a more thorough examination.

Source: American Cancer Society.

However, responsiveness to the stimulation of breasts—by both the receiver and the giver—is generally related far more to learning than to the size or shape of the breasts.

HORMONES AND THE ENDOCRINE SYSTEM

The body has two kinds of glands: **endocrine** or ductless **glands** that secrete hormones directly into the bloodstream, and exocrine glands. Exocrine glands secrete substances into ducts that empty into body cavities and other body surfaces. Sweat glands, salivary glands, mammary glands, and digestive glands are examples of exocrine glands.

endocrine glands (EN-doe-crin) Ductless glands that discharge their products directly into the bloodstream.

The Endocrine Glands

The term **hormone** derives from the Greek word meaning "to activate." Hormones are carried by the blood throughout the entire body. The internal organs, the glands, and the central nervous system (CNS) can be affected by any hormones for which they have receptors. Six endocrine glands are directly involved in sexual functioning: the adrenal glands, the pituitary gland, the hypothalamus, the testes, the ovaries, and, when pregnancy occurs, the placenta.

hormone (HOR-mohn) Internal secretion of an endocrine gland that is distributed via the bloodstream.

THE ADRENAL GLANDS. The adrenal glands lie on top of the kidneys and are composed of two sections, the outer cortex and the inner medulla. The outer cortex secretes androgens (masculinizing hormones) and estrogens (feminizing

REALITY or MYTH ? **4**

hormones), along with other steroid hormones that are only indirectly related to sexual function.

THE PITUITARY GLAND.
The pituitary is a pea-sized gland attached to the base of the brain and functionally connected to the hypothalamus by a system of blood vessels and nerve fibers. The pituitary gland is largely controlled by the hypothalamus. It secretes many different hormones, some of which stimulate the other endocrine glands to produce their hormones.

One of the pituitary hormones, growth hormone, stimulates the development and maturation of various body tissues. Two other pituitary hormones, **gonadotropins** (which means "gonad changers"), stimulate the gonads (ovaries and testes). One of the gonadotropins is **follicle-stimulating hormone (FSH),** which induces the ovarian follicles to mature. In the male FSH stimulates sperm production in the testes beginning at puberty. The other gonadotropin is **luteinizing hormone (LH),** which stimulates the female to ovulate and the male to secrete androgen from his testes.

Prolactin and oxytocin are two other hormones that come from the pituitary gland. Both are important in the production of breast milk. Prolactin stimulates the mammary glands in the breasts to manufacture milk, and oxytocin causes the release of milk from the glands, so that it is available to the sucking infant.

Oxytocin is also released by males and females during the orgasmic phase of sexual response (Carmichael, Walburton, Dixen, & Davidson, 1994). It may play a role in sperm transport in males as it contracts smooth muscles. In females it stimulates uterine contractions that may also facilitate sperm transport (Carter, 1992).

THE HYPOTHALAMUS.
As noted earlier, the functioning of the pituitary gland is under the direct control of the central nervous system through a network of blood vessels that links the pituitary with the hypothalamus. Some of the cells of the hypothalamus secrete substances that directly control the synthesis and storage of pituitary hormones. For example, cells of the hypothalamus secrete gonadotropin-releasing hormone (GnRH) through the system of blood vessels, prompting the pituitary to release gonadotropins, which in turn affect the activities of the gonads and their discharge of sex hormones.

Two of the other endocrine glands directly involved in sexual functioning, the ovaries and the testes, were discussed earlier in this chapter. Both the ovaries and the testes reach maturity during puberty through the action of the sex hormones.

The Effects of Hormones

The hypothalamus, pituitary, and gonads operate in continuous feedback loops in which specific glands monitor levels of hormones and secrete substances that regulate the release of hormones from other glands. For example, the hypothalamus is sensitive to varying levels of circulating sex hormones. It monitors the levels of various hormones in the body and responds by either increasing or decreasing the rate of secretion of hormones or releasing factors. If the level of a particular hormone becomes too low, gonadotropins are discharged by the pituitary until the gonads produce enough sex hormone to signal a stop to gonadotropin secretion. Thus the brain, pituitary, and gonads interact continuously. Changes in one system lead to alterations in the other systems.

Hormones also affect the sex centers of the brain. In most female mammals estrogen influences sexual attraction and receptivity, but in human females the estrogen

gonadotropins (goh-NAH-doe-TROE-pinz) Chemicals produced by the pituitary gland that stimulate the gonads.
follicle-stimulating hormone (FSH) A gonadotropin that induces maturation of ovarian follicles in females and sperm production in males.
luteinizing hormone (LH) A gonadotropin that stimulates female ovulation and male androgen secretion.

level, if within the normal range, does not appear to affect sexual desire. Excessive estrogen, however, seems to reduce sexual desire in both men and women. Testosterone is evidently the hormone that plays the major role in the sexual desire of both males and females: When it is not present, there is little sexual desire. However, research indicates that GnRH may enhance sexual desire in the absence of testosterone or in cases where testosterone is ineffective (Dornan & Malsbury, 1989).

The major difference between male and female sex-hormone secretion lies in the pattern of secretion. Females secrete estrogen in a cyclic pattern, resulting in the monthly rhythm of the menstrual cycle. Males secrete testosterone in a daily cycle, with the level rising during the night and reaching its peak in the early morning hours (Hoyenga & Hoyenga, 1993).

The Menstrual Cycle

Most of the time, we go about our lives unaware of the efficient performance of our endocrine glands and of the effects of the hormones they secrete. One of the most dramatic demonstrations of the complex relationships between the activities of these glands, however, appears with the onset of the menstrual cycle in females. Most women can describe where they were and what they were doing at **menarche.**

The menstrual cycle involves a highly intricate set of interactions of physiological processes, some of the details of which are beyond the scope of this book. The menstrual cycle can be conceptualized as a series of five overlapping processes: the **follicular phase, ovulation,** the **luteal phase,** the **premenstrual phase,** and **menstruation.** The complete cycle generally ranges from 23 to 32 days in length. A cycle longer than 32 days or shorter than 23 days is considered irregular. Each phase of the cycle is controlled by fluctuations in the kind and amount of hormones secreted into the bloodstream from the ovaries, the pituitary, and the brain (see Figure 3.8 on page 70).

THE FOLLICULAR PHASE.   The follicular phase lasts from 7 to 19 days and is controlled by sensitivity of the ovary to FSH. At about the time menstruation (uterine discharge) begins, the production of estrogen and progesterone drops. The low levels of these hormones bring about an increase in ovarian sensitivity to FSH. FSH causes 6 to 12 follicles to start growing within the ovaries—the phenomenon from which the follicular phase gets its name. Normally, only one of these follicles reaches the mature stage.

As the follicle grows, its cells secrete estrogen. After several days the estrogen level in the blood reaches the point of creating a relative insensitivity of the ovary to FSH. High levels of estrogen prompt the hypothalamus to release GnRH, which stimulates a surge in production of LH shown in Figure 3.8.

OVULATION.   About 18 hours after the LH surge, the mature follicle in the ovary ruptures and releases the developing ovum. This process is called ovulation. The ovum enters the fallopian tube, where it may be fertilized by a sperm. Some women are able to feel the rupturing of the follicle releasing the ovum from the ovary as a sharp twinge. But most women must rely on other methods to determine the date of ovulation (see Chapter 7).

THE LUTEAL PHASE.   The luteal phase lasts from eight to ten days. Following ovulation, the ruptured follicle, known in its empty state as the **corpus luteum** ("yellow body"), secretes progesterone, starting the luteal phase. Progesterone stimulates the growth of the endometrium (uterine lining) in preparation for the egg if it is fertilized.

menarche (MEN-ark) The first menstrual period.
follicular phase Menstrual-cycle phase during which FSH stimulates the growth of the ovarian follicles.
ovulation The release of a mature egg from an ovary.
luteal phase Menstrual-cycle stage following ovulation during which growth of the uterine lining is stimulated by secretion of progesterone from the corpus luteum.
premenstrual phase The six days prior to menstruation, when the corpus luteum begins to disintegrate if the egg has not been fertilized.
menstruation The sloughing of the uterus's endometrial lining, which is discharged through the vaginal opening.

corpus luteum (COR-pus LOO-tee-um) The cell mass that remains after a follicle has released an egg; it secretes progesterone and estrogen.

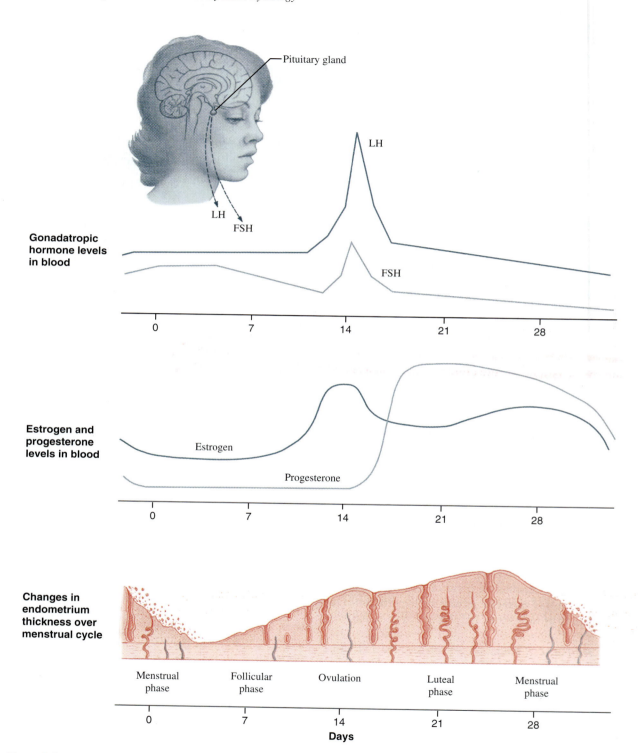

Figure 3.8
The Menstrual Cycle and Hormonal Fluctuations This figure shows the cyclical secretion of LH, FSH, estrogen, and progesterone during the menstrual cycle. Changes in the endometrial thickness are also shown.

THE PREMENSTRUAL PHASE.   In the absence of fertilization, the corpus luteum begins to disintegrate, producing a decrease in the levels of both progesterone and estrogen. Women vary in their awareness of the premenstrual phase, which lasts approximately from four to six days. Some experience a sense of heaviness or aching in the pelvic area and at times some depression.

MENSTRUATION.   The disintegration and discharge of part of the endometrium—menstruation—goes on for about three to seven days. This part of the menstrual cycle results from a decrease in progesterone and estrogen. The lining of the uterus, containing blood, nutrients, and mucus, is discharged through the cervix and vagina to the vaginal opening.

In describing the menstrual cycle, we started with the follicular phase, as if the menstrual cycle proceeded in a linear fashion, with the follicular phase representing the first phase and menstruation representing the last phase. The menstrual cycle is continuous, however, and thus is more accurately represented by a set of overlapping circles than by a line with a beginning and an end. For instance, before the end of the premenstrual phase, the follicular phase begins again, with prompting of the growth of follicles in the ovary opposite the one that released a follicle the previous month.

Although the menstrual cycle does not really begin with any one phase, the first day on which menstrual blood appears is counted as day one of the cycle simply because this is the easiest way to keep track of the phases. Monitoring the menstrual cycle is useful for purposes of becoming pregnant, avoiding pregnancy, or determining whether one's cycle has suddenly changed (a circumstance that might indicate either pregnancy or disease).

The complex relationship between the sexual organs and the endocrine system cannot be fully understood without a consideration of the nervous system. It coordinates the menstrual cycle as well as other sexual and reproductive events.

THE NERVOUS SYSTEM

As you read this text, you are probably not paying much attention to such life-sustaining activities as breathing, the pumping of blood by your heart, and the activity of your digestive system. Such bodily functions are controlled by nerves that extend to every organ in the body.

We can divide the nervous system into a number of different components. The peripheral nervous system and the central nervous system are the two major components. The central nervous system includes the brain and spinal cord. The peripheral nervous system includes the nerves that provide input to and output from the sense organs, muscles, glands, and internal organs outside the central nervous system.

Many bodily functions are directed by the autonomic portion of the peripheral nervous system. The autonomic nervous system derives its name from its independent control of involuntary functions.

The Sympathetic and Parasympathetic Nervous Systems

Sexual functioning is intricately tied to the subdivisions of the autonomic nervous system: the sympathetic and parasympathetic systems. These two systems differ from each other in both structure and function. Although they affect many of the same organs, they usually act in an antagonistic manner.

The sympathetic nervous system prepares the body to deal with emergency situations. It prepares us for "fight or flight." The system speeds up the heart, sends blood to the muscles, and releases sugar from the liver for quick energy. It can be activated by threat or by sexual arousal.

In contrast, the parasympathetic nervous system predominates when we are relaxed and inactive or when an emergency has passed. The parasympathetic system carries out a variety of maintenance needs. It promotes digestion, provides for the elimination of wastes, directs tissue repair, and generally restores the supply of body energy.

In sexual arousal, the two systems take turns in influencing sexual response. The system primarily involved in periods of relaxation is also responsible for initial sexual arousal. In males, for example, initial arousal and penile erection primarily result from the firing of the parasympathetic nerves, which causes the arteries in the penis to dilate, so that blood can rush in. The sympathetic nervous system, which figures in intense arousal, then becomes dominant. It appears likely that sympathetic nerve fibers close off valves in the penis, thus reducing the flow of blood out of the penis (Batra & Lue, 1990).

Ejaculation is also carried out primarily by the sympathetic nervous system, with some help from nerve fibers that are partially under voluntary control. Ejaculation of semen consists of two phases: emission and expulsion. During the emission phase, seminal fluid and the glandular secretions of the prostate are moved by muscular contractions from the epididymis through the vas deferens to the base of the penis. This movement is under the control of the sympathetic nervous system. After emission, nerves more responsive to voluntary control produce the muscular contractions that propel semen out of the penis. This event, known as the expulsion phase, also involves movements of the pelvic muscles and other portions of the body. Shortly after ejaculation, the penis begins to become flaccid. The action of the sympathetic nerves accompanying ejaculation constricts the arteries—vessels that carry blood from the heart—in the penis. The accumulated blood then flows out of the penis through veins—vessels that carry blood to the heart.

Little research has centered on the working of the sympathetic and parasympathetic nervous systems in female sexual arousal. It has been assumed that the swelling of various parts of the female vulva and vagina and subsequent lubrication lie primarily under the control of the parasympathetic nervous system. The sympathetic nervous system becomes dominant at orgasm (Levin, 1992).

The fact that anxiety or fear is common to most sexual dysfunctions can be explained in terms of the different roles of the sympathetic and parasympathetic nervous systems. Anxiety or fear activates the sympathetic nervous system, which can interfere with the functioning of the parasympathetic nervous system by blocking the relaxation needed for initial sexual arousal (erection, lubrication).

The Central Nervous System

The central nervous system (CNS) coordinates all bodily functions and behavior. It is the processing unit for all components of the nervous system.

Networks of nerves within the CNS are organized into hierarchical schemes to serve certain functions; that is, higher centers exert control over lower ones. Such human sexual responses as ejaculation, erection, and vaginal lubrication are influenced by reflex centers located in the lower centers. Anatomically, these functions are controlled by nerves located toward the lower end of the spinal column. These reflex centers controlled the same processes in our primate vertebrate ancestors (animals with segmented spinal columns). As the human brain evolved, these reflex centers were influenced and modified by higher centers located in the brain.

Some of our reflexes—for example, ejaculation and orgasm—can be influenced by our thought processes and can therefore be brought under some degree of voluntary control. Other reflexes operate on an involuntary basis. For instance, we usually cannot decide to produce an erection of the nipples or penis. We cannot simply choose to make our genitals fill with blood (vasocongestion) to produce erection or vaginal lubrication. Many "higher-brain" factors do affect the lower reflex centers, however, and thus can influence sexual response, regardless of whether the particular response is voluntary or involuntary.

Among these factors are various thought processes in the brain. Although we cannot directly command our genitals to respond sexually, we can think about, or discuss with a partner, erotic situations that may, in turn, produce erection or lubrication. Alternatively, sexual response can be inhibited by thoughts of pregnancy, punishment, or interruption. In fact, one of the strategies used by some men who ejaculate sooner than they want to is to focus on nonerotic thoughts or tasks (for example, mental arithmetic or unpleasant situations) to try forestalling ejaculation.

THE SPINAL CORD.

The spinal cord is crucial in sexual response. It is a thick cable of nerves that extends through the interior of the bony spinal column to and from the brain. The spinal cord carries nerve fibers in both directions—up the cord to the brain, where sensations are actually felt, and down the cord to muscles and other organs, where actions are carried out. The brain and spinal cord thus work together as an integrated unit.

The spinal cord is divided into segments and numbered relative to the spinal vertebrae (see Figure 3.9). Different segments are associated with specific functions. For instance, when a man's genitals are touched erotically, spinal cord segments S2, S3, and S4 (the S stands for sacral segment) produce a reflexive response.

A second penile erection center is located higher in the spinal cord, in segments T11 through L2 (T stands for thoracic, and L stands for lumbar), which are part of the sympathetic nervous system. This center is affected by brain activity such as thinking or fantasizing about sex.

Responses involved in ejaculation also have dual locations on the spinal cord. The first phase of ejaculation, seminal emission, is triggered by the sympathetic segment of the spinal cord (segments T11 through L2). The second phase of ejaculation, expulsion, is triggered by segments S2 through S4. Men whose spinal cords have been severed may be able to respond to stimulation of the penis with ejaculation, although they feel no genital sensation when it occurs; that is, ejaculation can occur without erection, just as erection can occur without ejaculation.

In the erotic response of males, two nerves running from the genitals to segments S2 through S4 of the spinal cord appear to be important. One of these, the **pudendal nerve,** transmits sensations arising from stimulation of the surface of the penis. The other, the **pelvic nerve,** relays sensations of sexual tension from within the corpora cavernosa and corpus spongiosum inside the penis. Because a reflex center higher up in the spinal cord mediates these sexual responses and transmits them to the brain, these involuntary reflexes may be modified by specific learned experiences or emotional states.

THE BRAIN.

Some people have been taught that sexual response involves animalistic drives. All levels of the brain, however, from the lower centers that we share with our animal ancestors to the distinctly human portions, are involved in human

REALITY or MYTH ? 5

Figure 3.9
The Spinal Cord and Sexual Response The spinal cord is intimately involved in sexual response. Different portions of the spine transmit sensory and mental stimulation.

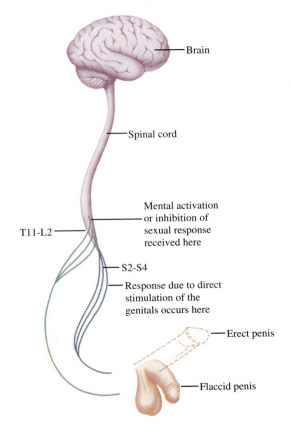

Brain

Spinal cord

T11-L2 — Mental activation or inhibition of sexual response received here

S2-S4 — Response due to direct stimulation of the genitals occurs here

Erect penis

Flaccid penis

pudendal nerve (poo-DEN-dal) Nerve that passes from the external genitals through spinal cord segments S2 through S4 and that transmits sensations from the genitals.

pelvic nerve The parasympathetic nerve involved in involuntary sexual responses of the genitals.

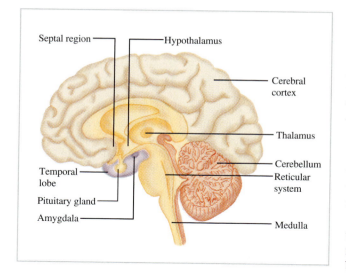

Septal region — Hypothalamus

Cerebral cortex

Thalamus

Cerebellum
Reticular system

Temporal lobe

Pituitary gland

Amygdala

Medulla

Figure 3.10
Side View of the Human Brain Most of the structures and processes affecting sexual behavior are centered in the forebrain. The medulla is part of the hindbrain, and the reticular activating system extends from the hindbrain through the midbrain and into the forebrain. The remaining structures shown here are part of the forebrain.

sexual behavior. We focus here on those shown to have the most direct effects on sexual behavior. The major portions of the brain are the hindbrain, the midbrain, and the forebrain (see Figure 3.10).

The hindbrain is believed to be the earliest part of the brain to have evolved because it is found in even the most primitive vertebrates. In humans it is located at the base of the skull where the spinal cord emerges from the spinal column, and it forms the lower part of the brain.

The midbrain, as the name implies, lies between the base of the brain and the top of the brain (forebrain). It contains cell bodies that either trigger immediate responses or relay information to more complex parts of the brain.

The forebrain contains a number of structures that are important for sexual functioning, including the thalamus, the hypothalamus, and the cerebrum. The **thalamus** acts as a relay station sending incoming messages from the sense organs to the outer layer of the cerebrum. The nerve pathways involved in transmitting and relaying tactile information to the forebrain are also involved in ejaculation. Stimulation of certain areas in the thalamus, and along a nerve tract that enters the thalamus, produces ejaculation.

thalamus (THAL-uh-mus)
The major brain center involved in the transmission of sensory impulses to the cerebral cortex.

amygdala (Uh-MIG-duh-la)
Brain center involved in the regulation of sexual motivation.

The **amygdala** is a complex collection of cell groups adjacent to the temporal lobe. The amygdala is thought to play an important role in the regulation of a number of primary emotional states, including sexual arousal. Among these roles, it appears that the amygdala interprets sensory information for its emotional significance. Is the stimulus punishing or rewarding? Damage to the amygdala is associated with hyposexuality (low levels of sexual interest), which results from the inability to appreciate the significance of sensory stimuli (LeVay, 1993).

The hypothalamus, although only about the size of a marble, contains cells that regulate body temperature, eating, drinking, and sexual behavior. Parts of the hypothalamus are important in the control of milk production and the reproductive cycles in females and can affect the manufacture of masculinizing hormones. As noted earlier, the hypothalamus is connected to the pituitary gland, which is involved in the production of sex hormones. The hypothalamus also plays a role in erection and in orgasmic response. The fact that damage to the hypothalamic regions of the human brain can produce either extreme sexual desire or loss of interest in sex suggests the existence of a region that regulates sexual behavior.

The hypothalamus contains both pleasure and pain centers that are probably intimately connected with sexual response. Experiments with the pleasure centers in the brain were first described by Olds and Milner in 1954. Rats were given access to a lever that could deliver a brief pulse of electric current to a thin wire electrode implanted in the brain. If the electrode tip was in one of the so-called pleasure centers of the brain, the rats repeatedly pressed the lever. They chose to stimulate their brains in preference to eating, drinking, and other activities. One rat pressed the lever as often as five thousand times an hour.

Research has indicated that the cells of the pleasure center respond to endorphins, a special class of molecules manufactured by brain cells. These molecules act on brain cells in much the same way as do morphine and other opiates, producing euphoria and alleviating pain.

Close to these pleasure centers are systems that, if stimulated, produce unpleasant feelings. These pain centers are crucial to our survival, and it makes evolutionary sense that they take priority over areas associated with pleasure. Attending to sexual desire, rather than to a threat, would leave us vulnerable. Thus the pain centers of the brain inhibit sexual desire when we experience physical harm, anticipate danger, or undergo severe stress (Dornan & Malsbury, 1989).

The most recently evolved and physically prominent part of the human brain is the **cerebrum,** which balloons out over the rest of the brain. The surface layer of the cerebrum is called the cerebral cortex. The cerebrum is divided into two nearly symmetrical halves, called the cerebral hemispheres. Each of the cerebral hemispheres is, in turn, divided into four sections, or lobes.

The cerebral cortex is at the top of the hierarchical scheme of the nervous system and is involved in the complex functions of perception, learning, thinking, and language. Thus it can facilitate or inhibit the sexual response systems found lower in the CNS. Erotic fantasies, daydreams, and memories of pleasant sexual experiences are processed by the cortex and can produce arousal.

Some systems within the brain are not limited to one area of the brain, such as the hindbrain, midbrain, and forebrain. One such system is called the **reticular activating system (RAS),** which is the arousal center of the brain. Beginning in the hindbrain, the RAS extends through the midbrain and sends its fibers up to the forebrain. When the RAS is stimulated, a person seems to become receptive to sexual stimulation. People have reported experiencing relatively long periods of sexual stimulation under the influence of drugs such as cocaine and amphetamines, which affect the RAS (Rosen, 1991).

The **limbic system** is another example of a functional entity within the brain that is not confined to just one area. It consists of a ring of structures in the center of each cerebral hemisphere. The limbic system includes the amygdala, hypothalamus, part of the thalamus, and several other forebrain structures that lie inside the cortex. The limbic system also contains nerve fibers that connect it to the hindbrain. Stimulation of parts of the limbic system in male animals produces erection, mounting, and grooming behavior; pleasure centers have been found near these sites. Stimulation of other parts of the limbic system provokes aggressive behavior.

The limbic system is also involved in the sense of smell in most species, including humans. The close relationship between arousal and smell in some animals reinforces the idea that the limbic system is connected to sexual response. When dogs or cats are in heat, they secrete substances called **pheromones** that sexually stimulate members of the other sex of their species when they are detected through the sense of smell. Researchers have proposed that humans also secrete pheromones. So far, the only evidence for any impact of pheromones on humans is that the menstrual cycles of women living in close proximity may become synchronized (McClintock, 1971; Haynes, 1994). The mechanism producing this synchrony is unknown, but when women in one study were exposed to the underarm odor of a female stranger, their menstrual cycles became synchronized with that of the stranger (Preti, Cutler, Garcia, Huggins, & Lawley, 1986), a development suggesting that pheromones secreted by glands under the arms may be partially responsible.

In Chapters 2 and 3 we have emphasized the biological bases of sexual development and function. Although our biological capacities are crucial for human sexual activity, it is interwoven with the texture of human experience. We turn to this experience in Chapter 4 as we explore the many ways in which humans assign meaning to their sexuality and communicate their feelings.

cerebrum (ser-REE-brum) The surface layer of cell bodies that constitutes the bulk of the human brain.

reticular activating system (RAS) The system of nerve paths within the brain that is involved in arousal.

limbic system The set of structures around the midbrain involved in regulating emotional and motivational behaviors.

pheromones (FARE-oh-mohnz) Externally secreted chemical substances to which other members of the same species respond.

SUMMARY OF MAJOR POINTS

1. The structural similarity of males and females.

Both males and females have gonads (ovaries or testes) that secrete sex hormones and produce reproductive cells (eggs or sperm). The hormones are released into the bloodstream, and the reproductive cells are transported through a system of ducts: the fallopian tubes in the female or the vasa deferentia in the male. For females, stimulation of the clitoris and of the Gräfenberg spot produces intense arousal. For males, penile stimulation triggers the most intense sexual arousal.

2. Hormones and sexuality.

The hormone-secreting endocrine glands also influence sexual behavior. These glands—the adrenals, pituitary, ovaries, and testes—secrete hormones into the bloodstream. The hormones, in turn, affect the nervous system and influence the secretion of hormones from other endocrine glands. Hormone secretion in females of reproductive age fluctuates in a monthly cycle. Testosterone levels fluctuate daily in males.

3. The menstrual cycle.

One effect of the cyclical pattern of hormone secretion in females is the menstrual cycle. This cycle consists of a continuous series of overlapping processes. During the follicular phase, ovarian follicles ripen and mature. At ovulation a follicle ruptures from the ovary and an egg is released from the follicle. The ruptured follicle, known in its empty state as the corpus luteum, secretes the progesterone that stimulates the growth of the uterine lining during the luteal phase. In the absence of fertilization, the egg fails to implant in the uterine lining, which then begins to disintegrate during the premenstrual phase. The uterine lining is discharged from the body during menstruation.

4. Sexual response and the nervous system.

The responsiveness of the genitals to sexual stimulation is mediated by the nervous system. The parasympathetic nervous system is predominant in initial arousal: erection in males and vaginal lubrication in females. The sympathetic nervous system is more active during emission in males and during orgasm in females. Psychological responses such as fear, anxiety, stress, and fatigue can inhibit nervous system responses and thus inhibit sexual feelings and processes.

5. The contribution of the brain and spinal cord to sexual response.

Some people believe that sexuality stems from animalistic drives. The entire brain, however, from those centers that we share with our animal ancestors to the distinctly human portions, is involved in human sexual behavior. Supplementing the roles played by the thalamus, hypothalamus, and limbic system, the cerebrum can aid sexual response through erotic fantasies and pleasant memories or can inhibit response through negative learning and painful memories. Arousal can occur through genital stimulation and is transmitted via the spinal cord to the brain. Conversely, erotic or painful mental events processed by the brain can result in the transmission through the spinal cord of messages that either enhance or inhibit genital response.

CHECK YOUR KNOWLEDGE

1. Penis length is primarily important only to (a) the extent of female sexual arousal, (b) the depth of vaginal penetration, (c) male sexual performance, (d) male sexual arousal. (p. 59)

2. The epididymis is (a) part of the uterine wall, (b) on the frenulum of the penis, (c) a storage area for sperm, (d) a major producer of testosterone. (p. 56)

3. Intense sexual sensitivity in females is concentrated in the (a) cervix, (b) clitoris, (c) uterus, (d) labia. (p. 59)

4. The Gräfenberg spot is (a) located on the cervix, (b) a center of female sexual sensitivity, (c) a possible but controversial center of male sexual sensitivity, (d) now established to be nonexistent. (pp. 60, 62)

5. Anatomically, the clitoris is most akin to the (a) lips, (b) tongue, (c) penis, (d) prostate. (p. 63)

6. Menarche is (a) one of the female sex hormones, (b) the phase of the menstrual cycle in which the ovum (egg) can be fertilized, (c) the first menstrual period, (d) the diminishing of the menstrual flow around the time of menopause. (p. 69)

7. Ovulation is the phase of the menstrual cycle in which the ovum (egg) is (a) produced, (b) released from the ovary, (c) moved from the fallopian tube to the uterus, (d) expelled from the uterus. (p. 69)

8. The testes and ovaries are (a) similar in function in that both produce germ cells and hormones, (b) different in that the ovaries lie just outside the body in the base of the labia whereas the testes reside inside the pelvic cavity, (c) different in that the ovaries reside inside the pelvic cavity whereas the testes lie in the base of the penis, (d) similar in that they both produce the largest cells in the human body. (p. 60)

4

AROUSAL AND COMMUNICATION

LEARNING TO BE AROUSED
Models of Arousal
The Two-Stage Model of Sexual Arousal
The Purposes of Sexual Arousal

SOURCES OF AROUSAL
Touch
Smell
Sight
Hearing
Fantasy and Sexual Arousal
Attitudes Toward Sexuality
Highlight: Do You Feel Guilty About Your Sexual Feelings?
Gender Differences and Similarities in Arousal

COMMUNICATION ABOUT SEXUALITY
Socialization for Communicating About Sex
Gender Differences in the Communication of Feelings
Interpersonal Communication and Sexual Intimacy
Enhancing Interpersonal Communication
Informed Consent and Sexual Intimacy
The Management of Sexual Feelings and Behavior
Highlight: Negotiating a Sexual Relationship
Honoring Agreements

SUMMARY OF MAJOR POINTS

CHECK YOUR KNOWLEDGE

REALITY or MYTH ?

1 Women are primarily interested in sex only when they are fertile.

2 Many women employ fantasies to increase their sexual arousal during sexual intercourse with a partner.

3 Women who feel guilty about sexuality are more likely to use contraception than are those who do not feel guilty.

4 Most children receive the majority of their sex education from parents.

5 Contrary to stereotypes that men do all the initiating, women also initiate romantic relationships.

6 Initially saying no when one is willing to become sexually intimate is known as the "token no."

*Maybe I'll see him at the party Friday night and be able to talk to him. . . .
We'll get into a good conversation, get hungry for pizza and decide to go pick
up some, and then get stuck in a snowstorm and have to leave the car. And then
we'll walk back to my apartment. He'll come in and take off his coat, and I'll
put some music on. He'll say, "Do you want to dance?"—I wonder if he likes
to dance. We'll start dancing, and he'll nuzzle my neck. We'll kiss, and then
sit down on the couch. He'll start to play with my breasts slowly and gently,
and . . . he'll start to take my clothes off and I'll ask him if he wants to take a
shower, and . . .*

IN the previous two chapters, we examined the process by which humans differentiate into males or females. We develop male or female anatomies, and we secrete masculinizing and feminizing hormones at some point around the beginning of our second decade of life. We then typically have sexual **fantasies** and feel sexual arousal. We mentally construct sequences of events leading to romantic and sexual interaction, such as the fantasy in the preceding vignette, and we experience sexual arousal in connection with our fantasies. Before we can decide whether to express some of our fantasies and feelings with a potential partner, we first need to be able to communicate, both verbally and nonverbally, with other people.

In this chapter we describe the process by which we learn to feel sexually aroused and the purposes of sexual arousal. The impact of our senses and our thoughts on sexual arousal is examined. We then turn to the interpersonal communication of arousal and consider individual differences in reactions to arousal. For example, some people respond to feelings of arousal with happiness and pleasure, whereas others feel embarrassment and guilt. Finally, we discuss the importance of being able to communicate clearly with each other if we are to have satisfying relationships, and we consider some practical issues relevant to the management of fantasy and arousal.

fantasies Usually pleasant mental images unrestrained by the realities of the external world.

LEARNING TO BE AROUSED

The capacities for language and sexual arousal are both innate; however, just as the specific language that we speak is learned, the specific objects and acts that we find sexually arousing appear to be—for the most part—conditioned by our culture and our own experiences (see Figure 4.1). For example, if a man or woman with a nickel-sized hole in the lower lip, out of which tobacco juice and saliva were dribbling, walked up to you enticingly, would you feel sexual attraction? You might if you had been reared among the So of northeastern Uganda. And within a culture, the specific stimuli that are paired with arousal vary from one time period to the next. For example, sometimes big breasts are fashionable, whereas at other times in the same culture, people may respond erotically to small, delicately formed breasts.

Figure 4.1
What Is Attractive?
What is considered sexually attractive varies across cultures, subcultures, and historical periods.

If you watch a ten-year-old movie on late-night television, you might remember wearing styles similar to those of the actors and considering those fashions attractive at the time. The hairstyles and hem lengths probably look silly now, however, because you have learned to find current styles attractive.

Both of these examples demonstrate culturally shared ideas about what is arousing. When everyone around us seems to share the same general perceptions about what is attractive, it is easy to assume that there is something natural about being attracted to particular types of stimuli. Our own unique experiences, however, can lead us to respond sexually to particular experiences that do not have any erotic significance for our friends.

What would happen if you showed the drawing in Figure 4.2 to friends, parents, grandparents, and members of the clergy and asked them for their reactions? It is likely that their responses would vary and that the variations would be a function of their age, gender, and moral beliefs. The picture would probably be meaningless to a 2-year-old or 3-year-old child. A child that age would be unlikely to perceive the picture as either erotic or disgusting. (We are *not* suggesting that you show this picture to young children, however.) The point is that we *learn* to interpret certain pictures, objects, and parts of people's bodies as sexually arousing. We go through a long period of training during childhood and adolescence. Depending on our generation, culture, socioeconomic status, unique experiences, and momentary feelings, we learn to feel aroused, unaffected, or disgusted by particular body types, pictures, objects, sensations, and situations.

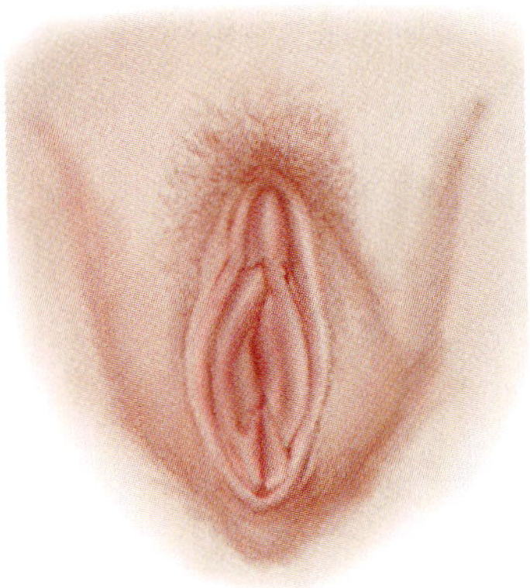

Figure 4.2
What Is Your Response?
Most of our erotic responses are learned. Depending on training, adults might respond to this drawing with arousal, indifference, or disgust, but it would be meaningless to a 3-year-old.

Models of Arousal

If you have ever felt intense erotic attraction toward someone, the experience probably defied easy explanation. You might say that you simply "fell in love." The language that we use in describing our intense arousal often places responsibility for our feelings outside ourselves. This tendency to attribute our feelings to some force beyond our control is so thoroughly ingrained in our culture that it is difficult to imagine thinking otherwise. In fact, however, sexual arousal is a complex set of responses by an individual. Even something that is commonly assumed to evoke unconditioned (that is, unlearned or involuntary) responses—such as having our genitals stroked—does not necessarily elicit sexual arousal.

Looking back on your own experiences, you may recall feeling arousal and attraction toward people who rewarded you (operant conditioning) and toward stimuli associated with those people (classical conditioning). You may have had other experiences, however, that do not fit neatly into the classical and/or operant conditioning models. What about the situation in which you feel respect and admiration for one person who is good to you, and yet your sexual arousal and attraction are directed toward someone not nearly so kind or admirable? In fact, you may be most aware of your arousal and desire for this person at times when you are feeling jealousy, an emotion that is not pleasant or rewarding. How does this kind of feeling develop?

ISSUES TO CONSIDER

How would you explain your sexual arousal to another person?

The Two-Stage Model of Sexual Arousal

Noting that people sometimes feel attracted to and aroused by others who apparently provide them with more pain than pleasure, Ellen Berscheid and Elaine Walster (1978) proposed that simple conditioning models may not be adequate to explain all instances of intense attraction. They argued that the experience of love—perhaps **lust** would be a more accurate word—may result from a two-stage process. First, we feel physiological arousal and the responses that accompany it, such as a racing heart and pulse, sweating

lust   Intense sexual desire.

palms, and heavy breathing. Second, in our desire to understand the source of the arousal, we search for an explanation—a label—for the arousal.

Berscheid and Walster (1978) proposed that under some conditions, we may experience physiological arousal and conclude that we are feeling love or sexual attraction. If the arousal occurs in the context of sexual intimacy with an appropriate object of our love, this conclusion seems logical. However, Berscheid and Walster suggested that *any* source of arousal can, under certain conditions, increase the likelihood that we will label our feelings love or attraction. For example, physical arousal from such sources as exercise could be mistaken for attraction to another person.

On the basis of experiments examining the influences of arousal on attraction, Berscheid and Walster (1978) concluded that under the appropriate circumstances, arousal—regardless of its source—increases the likelihood that one person will be attracted to another. Their analysis may help to explain why someone is attracted to another person when, to outside observers, there seems to be no logical reason for the attraction.

The Purposes of Sexual Arousal

Cultural beliefs about the goodness or badness of sexual feelings affect individuals' responses to sexual stimulation. From childhood on, some people are taught that sexual arousal is bad or sinful and should be avoided or controlled except for purposes of reproduction. Others learn that their capacity for sexual arousal and expression is an enjoyable, healthy, and positive aspect of being alive. Most people receive mixed messages about sexuality, leading to confusion and doubts about their own sexual experiences and desires.

Comparing our species with others helps us to understand the functions of human sexual arousal. If the only purpose of sexual arousal is to reproduce, it would make more sense for human females to be uninterested in sexual interaction except when they are fertile. In fact, the females of most species are receptive to sexual interaction only when they are fertile. In contrast, human females, though fertile only one-seventh of the time, are continuously capable of strong sexual interest and arousal (Meuwissen & Over, 1992). Indeed, most human females report sexual arousal and behavior long after they cease menstruating and are no longer able to reproduce.

The fact that human females eagerly engage in sexual intimacy at times when they are not fertile leads to an enhancement and lengthening of the period of sexual attraction. This was an evolutionary adaptation that made sense for the survival of our early ancestors' offspring. Human infants take nine months to mature in the uterus and many more years to develop to the point of self-sufficiency and reproductive maturity. Presumably, until recently in our evolution, it would have been difficult for a single parent to rear offspring to the point of reproductive maturity; forming a strong bond with a companion who would help to provide sustenance and support for the offspring would improve the child's chances of survival. The offspring of those early humans who felt continuing attraction toward each other may therefore have been more likely to survive than those whose parents were less sexually attached to each other.

Sexual arousal, then, can form the basis of a continuing bond. It can be disruptive of bonding, however, when it promotes attraction to persons outside the bond. Sexual arousal can lead to short-term, pleasure-oriented encounters or to nothing at all. The many purposes of sexual arousal depend on how the individual has learned to interpret and perceive his or her arousal.

SOURCES OF AROUSAL

Our senses are an intimate part of our sexuality. Touch, smell, sight, and hearing can all be sources of erotic arousal as a wide variety of sensory stimuli come to be associated with the pleasure of sexual experience. In this section we examine the role of the senses in arousal.

Touch

Our tactile capacities (that is, our ability to receive sensory stimulation from touch and pressure receptors) are intricately involved in sexual arousal. Our bodies—particularly our genitals—are richly endowed with receptors for touch and pressure. Because these receptors are distributed unevenly, some parts of the body are more sensitive than others. The most erotically sensitive areas are called **erogenous zones.** Many areas besides the genitals can be erotically sensitive to touch: the mouth, ears, buttocks, palms of the hands, fingers, abdomen, inner thighs, soles of the feet, and toes, for example.

erogenous zones Areas of the body that are erotically sensitive to tactile stimulation.

Touch is the only type of stimulation that can elicit a reflexive response that is independent of higher-brain centers. For example, men with spinal cord injuries that prevent impulses from reaching the brain but leave the sexual centers in the lower spinal cord intact are able to respond with an erection when their genitals or inner thighs are touched.

The erotic aspects of touching must be understood in the broader context of the fundamental human need for bodily contact, a need that is apparent from infancy. Of all our senses, neural pathways underlying skin sensation and responses to body stimulation are the first to develop. Touch is crucial in the fulfillment of the basic needs for affection, security, and love and in the development of our capacity to give affection (Hatfield, 1994).

Smell

As you read in Chapter 3, many species rely heavily on chemical attractants in their sexual interactions. Such attractants are loosely categorized as pheromones. There are numerous examples of the importance of pheromones in regulating the behavior of nonhuman organisms.

Interest in searching for human pheromones has grown since it was discovered that female rhesus monkeys secrete fatty acids called copulins, which seem to have an aphrodisiac effect on males. It appears, too, that human females vaginally secrete copulins, which may have some effect on sexual desire. Smelling copulins may stimulate the desire for sexual activity among some couples, although for other couples sexual desire seems to be unaffected by copulins (Morris & Udry, 1978).

It is interesting in this regard that most people in our culture believe that the secretory odors of bodily areas as diverse as the mouth, underarms, genitals, and feet are unpleasant or downright disgusting. Adolescents use the comment "He sniffs bicycle seats" as an insult, implying that someone who would deliberately expose himself to such an odor is perverted. You, too, may think that an aversion to the odor of bodily secretions is natural. The deodorant industry spends millions of dollars attempting to convince us so. The ads assure us that if we buy underarm and vaginal deodorants, we will be free of worries about these unpleasant and embarrassing smells. Many vaginal deodorants on the market are harmful to the delicate genital tissues. Furthermore, they are unnecessary; regular bathing with soap and water is sufficient to eliminate old bacteria that produce strong odors. Young children do not appear to be troubled by the smell of bodily secretions, and cross-cultural data suggest that not all adults characterize bodily odors as offensive. Thus in all likelihood our response to such smells is learned rather than innate.

Sight

As with the sense of smell, the extent to which our sexual responses are affected by inborn versus learned reactions to what we see is not clear. We do know that what we consider visually attractive is heavily influenced by our training. What we do not know is whether humans as a species have any innate preferences for specific visual sights as erotic stimuli.

Evolutionary theorists have suggested that human males are inherently attracted by females' complexions, which are seen as windows into their general health and reproductive fitness. Another indicator of reproductive fitness is a woman's waist-to-hip ratio (WHR) (see Figure 4.3). The lower the female WHR (waist is smaller than hips), the more attractive both men and women rate female figures (Singh, 1994). Females may place more importance on males' physical stamina, which might serve as an indication that a male may be a good provider. In an examination of what college students rate as important in judging male and female physical attractiveness, Franzoi and Herzog (1987) found generally that men stressed those parts of women's bodies directly related to sexuality and women emphasized men's physical condition or endurance. Franzoi and Herzog (p. 29) suggested that men are "socialized to perceive women as sexual providers, whereas women may be taught

Figure 4.3 Waist-to-Hip Ratios The smaller the female's waist is in relation to the hips, the more sexually attractive males perceive her to be.

to perceive men as material providers." David Buss and his colleagues (1989) found that across cultures men placed more stress on a potential mate's physical attractiveness than did women, whereas women rated financial prospects, ambitiousness, and industriousness as more central in their choice of a mate than did men (see Chapter 16). Thus sight seems to play a more central role for men than for women in the evaluation of attractiveness.

Hearing

Touch, smell, and sight are the senses most strongly implicated in sexual arousal, but hearing can also come into play. The sensuous rhythms associated with certain types of music and poetry can raise our level of sexual arousal and thus are often used to enhance sexual excitement. We may also learn to respond sexually to the tone and rhythm of a person's voice or to the kind of language used by a partner. The particular terms or phrases that arouse us vary from one person to another. For example, some individuals are turned on by explicit sexual words, whereas others are excited by gentle romantic whispers of endearment.

Generating sounds during sexual interaction is widespread among primates and humans, but little attention has been paid to its significance. Groans, moans, sighs, and screams and logical, directive vocalizations can provide information about pleasure, reactions to sexual stimulation, and orgasm (Wiederman, Allgeier, & Weiner, 1992). Many of these sounds can be highly arousing to men and women and may facilitate orgasm. In addition, commercial telephone sex produced mainly for the male market relies exclusively on sounds and vocalization to arouse the listener sexually.

Fantasy and Sexual Arousal

One of the most intriguing aspects of being human is the ability to fantasize. In our minds we can recall and refashion past experiences, anticipate and rehearse future events, and create unique scenes that are neither likely nor desired in reality. People may imagine receiving recognition for scholastic or athletic achievements or appreciation for their acts of generosity. They may imagine failing, perhaps on tests or in job interviews.

Similarly, sexual fantasies may involve either pleasant events, such as sexual or romantic interest from a person toward whom we are attracted, or unpleasant occurrences, such as rejection by a desired partner. Erotic fantasies can give both intensity and direction to sexual goals, and they may be a major influence on sexual identity and orientation. Many scholars believe that early adolescence is a critical period in the formation of sexual attitudes and behavior (Byrne, 1977; Money, 1991; Storms, 1980, 1981). Surveys on adolescent sexual fantasies indicate that they begin shortly after the onset of sexual arousal. For boys, this is around 11½ years and for girls about one to two years later (Gold & Gold, 1991; Knoth, Boyd, & Singer, 1988). At first, these fantasies tend to be about familiar persons, such as a teacher or an older acquaintance, or situations, such as dates. By late adolescence, most people have developed fantasies with well-defined, specific, erotic scripts that often involve daring, unconventional themes such as engaging in group sex, being caught or observed having sex, and having sex with strangers.

Gender differences are present from the beginning of sexual fantasy life. In general, males' fantasies contain visual images, physical characteristics, active and explicit sexual behavior, and interchangeable partners. Compared to males, females' fantasies are more concerned with emotional involvement, romance, committed partners in a caring relationship, and touching. Females' fantasies are also more complex and vivid (Alfonso, Allison, & Dunn, 1992; Ellis & Symons, 1990; Gold & Gold, 1991). Males tend to report more frequent sexual fantasies than do females. These gender differences in sexual fantasy are consistent with traditional societal definitions of gender roles in Western cultures.

Most people fantasize when they are engaged in nonsexual activities such as washing dishes, and the majority of individuals report employing sexual fantasies while they are masturbating or involved in sexual interactions with others (Cado & Leitenberg, 1990; Lunde, Larsen, Fog, & Garde, 1991; Pelletier & Herold, 1988). For both men and women, sexual fantasies decrease but do not disappear as they advance from adolescence to old age (Purifoy, Grodsky, & Giambra, 1992).

FANTASIES: HEALTHY OR DEVIANT?
Sigmund Freud theorized that sexual fantasies represented wishes or unfilled needs. Basically, he believed that sexual fantasies were signs of sexual frustration and emotional immaturity. In the beginning of the twentieth century, his thinking was reflected in the beliefs of many clinicians and psychoanalytic theorists.

More recently, clinicians have emphasized the positive contributions of fantasy to sexual interaction (Heiman & LoPiccolo, 1988; Leiblum, Pervin, & Campbell, 1989). This change may be welcome news to the majority of North Americans who fantasize during masturbation and coitus but who may experience guilt over their thoughts (Cado & Leitenberg, 1990; Davidson & Hoffman, 1986).

Guilt reactions to fantasies, particularly when they occur during intercourse, are related to beliefs that such fantasies are deviant and negatively related to sexual adjustment. In fact, Cado and Leitenberg (1990) found that those people who reported feeling most guilty about having fantasies during intercourse were more sexually dissatisfied and had more frequent sexual problems than did those individuals who felt less guilty.

Perhaps the reason that sexual fantasies have been regarded historically with fear and guilt lies in the Christian belief that thinking about something is the same as doing it, in which case thinking about having sex with someone other than a marital partner is as much a sin as having sex with the person. This lack of distinction between thought and behavior continues to color opinion about sexual fantasy.

It is important to recognize the difference between fantasy and reality. Fantasizing about socially unacceptable behavior is not the same as engaging in it. We may have numerous fantasies in the course of a day that we never act out. Although relatively little research is available on the various functions that fantasy can fulfill, some of the more common of these functions can be identified.

THE FUNCTIONS OF FANTASY.
At different times and at different stages in a relationship, the same person can have fantasies for different reasons. Many of us have felt attraction to someone with whom we have been casually acquainted. In the desire to change the relationship from a friendship to a romance, one or both people may imagine conversations and interactions leading to increasingly intimate emotional and physical contact. An example of such an extended fantasy appeared at the beginning of this chapter. These imaginary encounters permit us to rehearse ways of approaching the other person, to consider his or her likely responses, and even to make ourselves aware of the long-term consequences of the various behaviors that we envision ourselves try-

ing. The utility of such rehearsal fantasies is that we can select the one that feels most comfortable and that seems most likely to lead to the outcome we desire.

Some fantasies involve imagined events that the person has no desire to experience in reality, such as sadomasochistic activities or rape. Such fantasies may be either solitary or shared with a partner. It is particularly important to realize that this kind of fantasy does not in and of itself indicate that the fantasizer actually wants to be the helpless victim of an aggressor.

Finally, individuals may use fantasy either to enhance or to intensify sexual intimacy in a relationship of long duration. For example, in numerous studies a majority of the women reported having fantasies during sexual intercourse with their husbands or partners (Crepault, Abraham, Porto, & Couture, 1977; Lunde et al., 1991; Pelletier & Herold, 1988). They often employed these fantasies to enhance their sexual arousal and to help to trigger orgasm (Davidson & Hoffman, 1986; Lunde et al., 1991). The use of fantasies for this purpose appears to be positively related to orgasmic capacity and sexual satisfaction for women, but this relationship is less clear in men (Alfonso et al., 1992; Arndt, Foehl, & Good, 1985; Purifoy et al., 1992). In other words, fantasies are not necessarily compensations for an unrewarding sexual existence. Such fantasies may be enjoyed without the knowledge of the other partner, or they may be shared and enacted with a partner, as described in the book *Shared Intimacies* (Barbach & Levine, 1980, pp. 85–86):

> *Once we were traveling out of the country and we decided to act out a fantasy of mine. I went down to the hotel bookstore and Murray came down and acted as if we were strangers and picked me up. We just started talking, asking each other our names and where we were from. Then he invited me back to the room and it was as if we hardly knew each other and were having sex for the first time.*

> *We decided to act out our own fantasy, to make up our own film, so to speak. . . . It was weird because when we walked in the door, we felt like these other people. . . . Then it became obvious to both of us, these two new people, that there was an interest and a desire to continue from that point on. We undressed each other and explored each other's bodies and the whole time it was nonverbal. . . . We made love to each other, and held each other afterward. Then we just went to sleep. The next morning, we were back to ourselves.*

These two fantasies, the first by a 35-year-old woman and her husband, and the second by a 34-year-old woman and her female lover, show how sharing fantasies can provide both partners with pleasure. But a word of caution is in order. When two people know each other well, are secure in their relationship, and have agreed that the sharing of fantasies is fun and a source of pleasure, mutual disclosures can enrich a relationship. However, the disclosure of fantasies under other conditions can evoke pain in a mate, who may conclude that the partner finds him or her unsatisfying or who may come to feel inadequate in the face of a lover's desires that he or she can never fulfill. In deciding whether to share fantasies with a loved partner, consider your reasons as well as the potential effect of doing so.

Attitudes Toward Sexuality

Negative attitudes about sexuality may also be associated with difficulties in relationships in both the sexual and the nonsexual realms. Several different measures have been developed to assess attitudes about sexuality, including the Sexual Opinion Survey and the Sex Guilt Scale.

REALITY or MYTH ? **2**

ISSUES TO CONSIDER

How would you react to the revelation from a steady sexual partner that he or she often had fantasies while you were having sex together?

erotophobic Having a negative emotional response to sexual feelings and experiences.

erotophilic Having a positive emotional response to sexual feelings and experiences.

EROTOPHILIA AND EROTOPHOBIA.

To measure emotional responses to sexuality, Donn Byrne and his colleagues (Byrne, Fisher, Lamberth, & Mitchell, 1974) developed the 21-item Sexual Opinion Survey (SOS). Responses to the survey can range from primarily negative (when a respondent is **erotophobic**) to primarily positive (when a respondent is **erotophilic**). Items in the survey include the following: "Swimming in the nude with a member of the opposite sex would be an exciting experience" (positive); "If people knew that I was interested in oral sex, I would be embarrassed" (negative); "Thoughts that I may have homosexual tendencies would not worry me at all" (positive). Erotophilia-erotophobia is thought to be learned in childhood and adolescence through experiences associating sexual cues with positive or negative emotional states.

SOS scores are predictive of a wide range of sexual attitudes and behaviors among North American students, as well as among university graduates from India and Hong Kong. In most studies females have tended to be more erotophobic than are males. This gender difference may stem from females' greater exposure than males to negative messages about sexuality. As might be expected, erotophobic students reported more parental strictness about sex than did erotophilic students. Compared to erotophilic parents, erotophobic parents reported having given their children less information about sex. And the college students' early experiences appear to be related to differences in their sexual and contraceptive behaviors. Erotophilic college students reported more past sexual experience, more frequent masturbation, and more sexual partners than did erotophobic students. Furthermore, use of contraception was both more common and more consistent among erotophilic students than among their erotophobic peers.

A number of other behaviors are associated with erotophilia-erotophobia. Erotophilic people, compared to those who are erotophobic, have more positive reactions to erotic material, think about sex more often, draw more explicit and more detailed nude figures, and create more explicit and positively toned erotic fantasies (Byrne & Schulte, 1990; Fisher, Byrne, White, & Kelley, 1988).

sex guilt Sense of guilt resulting from the violation of personal standards of proper sexual behavior.

SEX GUILT.

Among the emotions that can become associated with sexual arousal is guilt. **Sex guilt** is the fear that we will feel badly if we violate or think we will violate standards of proper sexual conduct (Mosher, 1966, 1988). Psychologist Donald Mosher constructed a measure of sex guilt in 1966 that was revised in 1988. The measure has been widely used in the investigation of various sexual issues. For a sample of the items in the revised Mosher Guilt Inventory, see "Highlight: Do You Feel Guilty About Your Sexual Feelings?" on page 90. Mosher assumed that individuals who feel guilty about their sexual responses were scolded and punished during their childhood for interest in sexual matters to a greater extent than were people who respond to their sexual feelings with acceptance and enjoyment (see Figure 4.4).

For example, imagine a 3-year-old girl playing idly with her vulva while watching "Sesame Street" on television. Her parents might scold her, slap her hand, or order her to stop. One isolated incident would probably have little effect on the extent to which the child will associate guilt and anxiety with sexuality in her adulthood. The parent who spanks a 3-year-old for casually playing with herself, however, is probably also likely to punish the girl for other activities that the parent interprets as sexual—for example, playing doctor, asking questions about genitals, or telling sexual jokes. Over time the child absorbs the message that sex is bad, dirty, and sinful and the person who shows too much curiosity or interest about sexuality is equally bad, dirty, and sinful.

To protect children from the unwanted consequences of sexual intimacy, such as unintended pregnancy and sexually transmitted diseases (STDs), parents may discourage children from having anything to do with sex. The problem with such discourage-

Figure 4.4
Parental Responses to Self-Exploration Although many parents take a dim view of their toddlers' self-exploration and genital stimulation, this mother grins while watching her son playing with his genitals.

ment is that long-term association of sex with anxiety and guilt is linked to the development of certain undesirable characteristics. Indeed, several studies have found that people high in sex guilt operate at lower levels of moral reasoning than do people with less sex guilt. For example, Gerrard and Gibbons (1982) studied the relationship among sexual experience (not necessarily intercourse), sex guilt, and sexual moral reasoning. Their findings indicated that experience is important in the development of sexual morality and that people high in sex guilt tend to avoid sexual experience, thus hindering their development of sexual morality. Based on research with female college students, Meg Gerrard (1987) concluded that, although sex guilt did not necessarily keep women from having sexual intercourse, it did appear to inhibit the use of effective contraceptives.

Extensive research on sex guilt after childhood demonstrates the influence of conditioned or learned responses on our capacity for sexual arousal and pleasure. Dennis Cannon (1987, p. 9) summarized the research on the relationship of sex guilt to other variables. Based on these studies, he characterized a "sexually guilty" person as

> *devout and constant in religious beliefs, who subscribes to higher authority, believes in myths about sex, may use denial in dealing with feelings about sex, is less sexually active, is more offended and disgusted by explicit sexual material, less tolerant of variations in others' sexual behavior, at a lower level in Kohlberg's stages of moral reasoning, and who holds traditional views of what males' and females' sexual roles should be.*

Do You Feel Guilty About Your Sexual Feelings?

The following statements are a sample of items from Mosher's (1988) revised measure of sex guilt. Respondents are instructed to rate each item on a 7-point scale from 0 (not at all true) to 6 (extremely true).

Masturbation

1. is wrong and will ruin you.
2. helps you feel eased and relaxed.

Sex relations before marriage

3. should be permitted.
4. are wrong and immoral.

When I have sexual desires

5. I enjoy them like all healthy human beings.
6. I fight them, for I must have complete control of my body.

In my childhood, sex play

7. was considered immature and ridiculous.
8. was indulged in.

Unusual sex practices

9. are awful and unthinkable.
10. are all right if both partners agree.

Rather than rearing offspring to feel guilty about sex, parents might emphasize effective communication skills and the importance of open discussion about sexual functions and feelings. Building children's sexual knowledge and confidence will more adequately prepare them for dealing with their emerging sexual feelings in a healthy manner than will instilling guilt.

Studies of sex guilt have consistently yielded this finding: Females score higher on measures of sex guilt than do males. Is there something in the biology of females that makes them more susceptible than males to anxiety and guilt over sexuality? Probably not. The explanation probably lies in the fact that daughters, not sons, can become pregnant, and so parents may be more restrictive in training their daughters than in training their sons.

Gender Differences and Similarities in Arousal

As we will see in Chapter 5, females are less likely to engage in self-stimulation than are their male counterparts, and they generally respond more slowly during sexual interaction. An examination of research on the conditions under which males and females respond to erotic material suggests that different cultural expectations for men and women contribute heavily to the observed gender differences.

A great deal of survey research has supported the assumption that men are more interested in, and more responsive to, sexual cues than are women. However, experimental studies conducted during the past decade have indicated that men and women respond similarly to erotic stimuli such as sexually explicit stories and pictures and X-rated films. Why does survey research find gender differences that experimental research does not?

In the survey method men and women are asked to report their past and present levels of arousal to erotic material, how often they purchase or seek such material, and so forth. In our culture interest in sex is considered more appropriate for men than for women. Thus in responding to surveys, men may accurately estimate, or even overestimate, their interest in erotica, whereas women may underestimate theirs in an attempt to present themselves in a socially desirable light.

How have the experimental studies differed from the survey methods? Volunteers for experimental research on erotica are exposed to sexual stimuli. Their responses are then measured through self-reports, physiological recordings of their genital responses, or both. These physiological measures generally demonstrate little or no difference in arousal between men and women when they are exposed to erotica. As William Fisher (1983) pointed out, compared with men, women have been trained over a long period of time to avoid erotic material and to show less interest in sex. But when men and women are exposed to sexual stimuli, women are as capable of arousal as are men.

The differences produced by the two research approaches are exemplified by Julia Heiman's (1975) study of responses to erotic audiotapes. She found that males and females did not differ when their arousal was assessed by physiologic measures. When self-reports of arousal were compared, however, several male-female differences emerged. First, on average, males reported greater arousal than did females. Second, whereas the arousal reported by males matched the arousal indicated by their physiologic recordings, females' reports did not always reflect the physiologically measured arousal. In fact, in about half the cases females reported either no arousal at all or less arousal than was indicated by the devices attached to their bodies.

Why did many of the women in Heiman's study fail to perceive their own arousal? When we first read her study, that question intrigued us, so we asked students in our human sexuality classes to recall the first time they could remember having the kind of feeling that they would now label as sexual arousal. We asked them to write down their thoughts on the reasons for their physical responses at that time.

In general, the men attributed their erections, pre-ejaculatory emissions, and so forth to having been aroused either by their thoughts about, or their interaction with, another person. About half the women drew similar conclusions about their vaginal lubrication and "tingling" genital feelings. But the other half of the women gave various other explanations. Many thought the vaginal lubrication had been just another variation in their menstrual cycle that they had not noticed before. Several women attributed the lubrication to a "clear period," and a sizable number reported that they thought they might have had a vaginal infection. One woman wrote that she had asked her mother whether she should see a doctor or get some medicine.

Biological differences in the extent to which physical changes associated with sexual arousal are readily observable may also account for some of these gender differences. Although arousal produces vasocongestion (blood engorgement) in both men and women, women are sometimes unaware of the lubrication of their vaginas, whereas erect penises call attention to themselves.

This biological difference in the effects of vasocongestion is enhanced, in turn, by cultural expectations. Men are encouraged to be sexually active, whereas women are generally discouraged from seeking sexual stimulation and satisfaction. Men are trained to be sexual responders, and women learn to be sexual stimuli. In summary, anatomical differences and learned psychological differences between males and females may interact to produce differences in the tendencies of men and women to report arousal. When physiological arousal is directly measured, however, the gender differences are reduced or eliminated (Heiman, 1977). Some stereotypes about gender differences in sexual behavior may be less accurate than is commonly believed.

COMMUNICATION ABOUT SEXUALITY

In the preceding section we considered the communication of fantasies with a loved one. In this section we broaden the discussion to include the development of communication skills relating to sexuality. Communicating sexual feelings to a potential or actual partner requires care and practice. For people who have learned to associate their sexual feelings with shame or sin, sharing sexual feelings can also take courage. We discuss socialization practices that increase or reduce the likelihood that we can communicate our sexual feelings effectively. Traditionally, males and females are given different messages about discussing their feelings, and we examine how that may relate to communication. Finally, we focus on methods of enhancing interpersonal communication, especially relating to sexual issues.

Socialization for Communicating About Sex

We are constantly bombarded with the message that sexiness is an attractive quality; indeed, our media stars get a great deal of money and adulation for projecting "sexy" images. But just like the rest of us, stars have private lives in which they need to communicate and negotiate their desires with their partners. Unfortunately, many of us—private citizens and media stars alike—are given little training in communication skills.

Few members of our culture are given labels for sexual feelings during infancy, childhood, or adolescence. Furthermore, if we fondled our genitals during infancy and childhood, most of us not only learned no label for that activity but also may have been punished for our behavior. If, instead, we were taught sexual labels and encouraged to communicate our feelings, such training might reduce or prevent sexual problems later in life.

Although students enrolled in a human sexuality course tend to be more liberal and knowledgeable about sex—even when they begin the class—than those enrolled in other classes at the same academic level, these well-informed students typically received little of their information from their parents. For example, only 14 percent of students enrolled in our sexuality course in 1996 had heard the word *clitoris* from their mothers, and only 3 percent (all men) had heard the word from their fathers. The word *penis* had been used by 20 percent of the students' mothers and 55 percent of their fathers.

We have also asked our students to indicate their most accurate source of information regarding the reproductive and passionate aspects of sexuality. Opponents of public school sex education assert that children should receive information about sexuality from their families rather than from teachers. As Table 4.1 shows, however, students clearly perceived their parents as providing little information about the reproductive aspects of sex and even less about its passionate aspects. These findings about our own students are consistent with other research in the past two decades (Allgeier, 1983; Gebhard, 1977).

This discrepancy in the likelihood of hearing the word *clitoris* versus the word *penis* from parents might be partially explained by the fact that the penis can be seen more easily than the clitoris. Another possible explanation is that every other organ of the body can be described as having some separate, societally approved function. To describe clitoral function, however, parents or teachers must introduce the concept of sexual arousal and pleasure. Other parts of the body (nose, mouth, penis, rectum, vagina) may also be associated with sexual pleasure, but parents can provide an explanation of what those organs do without ever mentioning sexual pleasure. Parental reluctance to acknowledge the pleasurable sensations that many children experience may explain parents' failure to discuss the clitoris when describing sexual anatomy to children.

| Table 4.1 | Sources of Information About Sexuality | |

We asked our sexuality course students to indicate their most accurate source of information regarding the reproductive aspects of sexuality, such as fertilization and pregnancy, and the passionate aspects, such as arousal, lubrication, erection, and orgasm. Their responses are presented in this table.

Source	Reproductive Aspects (%)	Passionate Aspects (%)
Mother	22	0
Father	1	0
Sibling	1	5
Friends	7	25
Boyfriend/Girlfriend	0	22
Books/Magazines	11	32
School	47	11
Doctor	3	0
Church	0	0
Other	3	0

Not only do we often ignore the function of the clitoris, but we also have few ways of referring to it. Although we have many slang terms for the penis (*prick, bone, dick, tool, peter,* and *thing,* to name a few), there are few slang terms for the clitoris beyond the shortened form *clit.* In our informal search among students, friends, and colleagues, we have encountered only three other slang terms for the clitoris—*joy button, magic button,* and (ironically, given that the clitoris is part of the female anatomy) *little man in a boat.* There is a similar discrepancy in the number of slang terms for male ejaculate and vaginal lubrication. How many expressions have you heard for each?

What if our parents did, however, acknowledge that we have sexual feelings and that there are words—labels—for these feelings: *arousal, interest, curiosity?* We might then be given permission to talk freely about our own sexual feelings. But that parental acknowledgment rarely occurs in our society. So we enter adolescence with an inadequate vocabulary and, in most cases, without an environment conducive to open discussions with our parents. Thus the people who presumably care about us the most at that point in our lives avoid giving us the opportunity to "rehearse" later discussion of sexual feelings.

Those parents who avoid discussion of sexual topics may do so because of fears that such conversations will encourage their offspring to engage in early sexual exploration. To examine the relationship of parental attitudes, extent of family communication, and adolescent sexual activity, Terri Fisher (1987, 1988, 1989a, 1989b, 1993) conducted a series of studies in which information was gathered from adolescents and their parents. She found that among parents with relatively permissive attitudes, family discussions of sex were related to a greater likelihood of females engaging in premarital sexual behavior. One could argue that permissive families produce more sexually active adolescents. It is also plausible, however, that sexually active young women find it easier to discuss their sexual experiences and feelings with relatively permissive parents than do sexually active women with more restrictive parents. Fisher also found that males who had discussed sex with their parents, and males with sexually liberal

ISSUES TO CONSIDER

Where did you first get information about the reproductive aspects of sexuality? The passionate aspects of sexuality?

parents, had more accurate sexual information and were more likely to report using contraception.

Gender Differences in the Communication of Feelings

Despite overall societal restrictions on parent-child communication about sex, there are differences in the extent to which it is acceptable for males versus females to talk about feelings versus sex. In most families it is more acceptable for girls than for boys to talk about their positive or depressed emotions (the so-called tender feelings), and more acceptable for boys than for girls to talk about hostile feelings, such as anger and aggression, and sexual interests.

We are not suggesting that these differences in communication styles are inherent aspects of being male or female. Instead, the tendency in our culture for males to suppress their feelings or to give only minimal information about their emotions, and for females to provide more detail than males about their fears and hopes, presumably stems from the differences in training to become a "man" or a "woman." When people subsequently attempt to establish heterosexual relationships, these gender differences in the content and style of communication of feelings may magnify the difficulty of resolving the inevitable problems that emerge in ongoing relationships.

When the focus is on *sexual* feelings, the gender-role expectations are different. A stereotypic part of being masculine in our culture involves intense interest in obtaining sexual experience, for example, "scoring." In contrast, many adolescent women fear that communicating about their sexual desires in general, or their preferences for specific kinds of stimulation in particular, signals that they are immoral, dirty, or "experienced." Another concern that women may have is that sexual requests may threaten their partners' feelings of prowess. Regardless of the source, such reluctance to communicate may result in sexual dysfunctions and/or date rape (see Chapters 6 and 14).

Interpersonal Communication and Sexual Intimacy

Based on 900 hours of observation conducted in bar settings, Timothy Perper (1985) concluded that it is often women, not men, who determine the outcome of a casual contact in a singles' bar. Perper observed a fairly standard sequence of events between couples in their initial interaction: approach, talk, turn, touch, and synchronization of body movements and posture. Initially, synchronization involves only arm and head movements, but it progresses to such complex, simultaneous movements as drinking in unison, and it can end in full-body synchronization. Either person in a potential courtship can escalate the situation by making an overture that, if accepted, raises the level of intimacy between the two people. If the overture is not accepted or responded to, the interaction de-escalates—for example, one person may look away while the other is talking.

Perper observed that more than half the time the woman initiated the courtship sequence by signaling or approaching the man. Women, Perper found, have a much clearer understanding of courtship strategies than do men; he estimated that 90 percent of men cannot accurately describe the courtship sequence, even though most of them can enact it with a female initiator. A woman's ability to initiate and escalate a romantic and/or sexual interaction is called **proceptivity.** In proceptive behavior, a woman must first choose a man in whom she is interested. If a man responds with interest to a woman's proceptive behavior, a "power transition" may occur in which he initiates overt sexual behavior. Perper hypothesized that couples pass through a transition state

proceptivity The initiation and escalation of a sexual interaction with another person.

that begins with proceptivity and ends with both people being sexually aroused; the man then initiates sexual foreplay.

There is further evidence that women take an active role in courtship (Moore, 1985; McCormick & Jones, 1989; O'Sullivan & Byers, 1992). Monica Moore (1985) observed more than 200 women in diverse settings and coded their nonverbal behaviors. For example, Moore described several different kinds of glances that she observed women using (see Figure 4.5). With the room-encompassing glance a woman scans an entire room in not more than five or ten seconds without making eye contact with anyone. With the short, darting glance a woman gazes at a man but looks away within three seconds. With the gaze fixate a woman makes eye contact for more than three seconds; sometimes her glance is returned. Moore also frequently witnessed such behaviors as smiling and laughing, and tossing, touching, or twisting the hair; but she observed coy smiles and giggles less commonly. A woman's signaling gestures included hiking her skirt slightly and touching various parts of her own body or the potential partner's body. Two behaviors involved whole-body movement: parade and approach. In the parade a woman walks across the room with an exaggerated swing of her hips, her stomach held in, her head held high, and her back arched, so that her breasts are pushed out. In approach behavior a woman positions herself within two feet of a man, after which the two usually talk.

Figure 4.5
Women's Nonverbal Signaling Notice the use of "gaze fixate," which the woman is directing at this man.

Moore found a strong correlation (.89) between the number of solicitations or displays that women gave to men and the likelihood of men approaching the women. Moore concluded that women are able to determine when and where they interact with potential partners by exhibiting or withholding displays and solicitations. She theorized that because women can successfully elicit numerous male approaches, they can choose from a variety of available men. Moore also noted that sometimes it took several signals by a particular woman before a man would approach and that a man was generally reluctant to approach if he had not been signaled that the woman would accept his advances.

How do women develop their repertoire of signals? To address that question, Moore (1995) observed junior high school girls' signaling. They displayed a smaller number of signals to junior high school boys, but the signals they employed were more exaggerated than those employed by adult women. For example, the hair toss was considerably more dramatic than that displayed by women. In addition, they appeared to mimic the signaling behavior of the dominant girls in their group. Interestingly, the boys were far less likely to approach these girls than were men to approach women who engaged in the more subtle but wider range of signals. Perhaps these displays by the girls were rehearsals for later behaviors that would be more effective in eliciting male interest.

Thus recent research bears out what many women already know: Women use a wide repertoire of signals and displays to attract men. If a man responds to a woman's initiations, the courtship dance begins. If both partners respond to each other, there follows an escalation of intimacy and eventually a power transition in which the man assumes responsibility for initiating sexual intimacy.

ISSUES TO CONSIDER

Have you ever tried to matchmake—that is, to set up a relationship between two friends of yours who did not know each other? Have you ever watched a woman attempt to develop a relationship with a man to whom she is attracted? What do you think are the most important factors influencing these interactions?

We have considered situations in which two people respond to each other's initiations. Courtship does not always proceed so smoothly, however. Two problems may arise. First, at any point in the sequence one person may reject the other's advances. Second, one person may misinterpret the other's verbal or nonverbal communication.

Enhancing Interpersonal Communication

During infancy and early childhood, we are provided with labels to help us distinguish and communicate our desires for hunger versus holding. Many of us, however, are not given labels to help us distinguish, as we advance into adolescence and adulthood, between desire for cuddling and desire for coitus or for cunnilingus or fellatio (oral stimulation of the female or male genitals). Negative cultural connotations associated with desire for various forms of sexual stimulation, or the fear that specific sexual requests will upset a partner, can make it difficult for us to say to a mate, "You know, I'd really enjoy giving (or receiving) oral sex," or to say, "Right now, I'm feeling very tense about my final exams, and I'd just like you to cuddle me."

How can we improve interpersonal communication about our personal and/or sexual feelings? What can we do to increase the likelihood of honestly relating our feelings to potential or actual partners? At the outset, as noted earlier, we need a vocabulary to use and permission to use it from those whom we admire: our parents, teachers, peers, and partners. Once we have a sexual vocabulary and feel free to use it, we need to communicate—verbally and nonverbally—what we want from potential or actual sexual partners.

Even with the best intentions, it is sometimes difficult for a man to interpret a woman's signals, and vice versa, in the complex world of sexual interactions. Men's difficulties in evaluating a woman's desire may be magnified by the fact that in our society it is still considered the man's prerogative to initiate sexual intimacy, whereas women are expected to be the "gatekeepers"—that is, to take responsibility for setting the limits on the extent of sexual intimacy. In several surveys of students' misperceptions in natural settings, 72 percent of women and 60 percent of men reported having had their friendliness misperceived as a sexual invitation (Abbey, 1987). Misperceptions were most common by casual friends or acquaintances and less common by strangers or close friends. When students in Antonia Abbey's (1987) surveys were asked to describe their experiences with misperceiving the intentions of potential partners, men and women were equally likely to report having misperceived someone else's friendliness as indicating sexual interest (40 percent). For example, one woman wrote: "Since I liked him I took everything he did as a hint, and he was very attentive and nice to me. However, the next day he acted as though he had never seen me before in my life" (pp. 189–190).

We noted earlier that women appear to select men and to signal their interest in getting to know them better. A signaling of interest is simply that; it does not necessarily mean that a woman is ready to have sex with the man. Women appear to be signaling a desire to get to know the man better and then deciding whether they want to develop a relationship with him; that is, women may perceive the process as involving a series of steps, with each decision dependent on previous interactions.

Misperceptions may occur because the behaviors that are misperceived can have ambiguous meanings. You may engage in a smiling conversation with someone and leave a party with him or her because you feel sexually attracted or merely because you are interested in the topic being discussed and are tired of the smoke and noise at the party.

Thus difficulties may arise in an individual's interpretations of others' intentions and behavior. Because of women's socialization in our culture, and perhaps because of the gender differences in mate-selection strategies discussed earlier, most women want to spend some time getting to know a man before deciding whether to become sexually intimate. Even if a woman desires intimacy fairly early in the relationship, she risks the stereotype that a woman who does so is "easy" or has "rocking-chair heels" (that is, if a man pushes her slightly, she will immediately lie down for him).

Therefore, if the woman is interested in further interaction with the man, she is confronted with a dilemma: She needs to communicate interest but probably wants to avoid giving him the impression that she is sexually available to anyone who approaches her. If the man is interested in pursuing the relationship, he faces the problem of deciphering her intentions.

The man's difficulties in trying to infer the woman's intentions are also increased by the woman's use of what is known as the "token no"—initially saying no when she is willing to become sexually intimate. For example, in Muehlenhard and Hollabaugh's (1988) study almost 40 percent of the women reported refusing sexual intercourse when they wanted to have coitus.

Their explanations for saying no when they really meant yes are instructive. Muehlenhard and Hollabaugh (1988) isolated three major categories of reasons for the use of the token no. The first involved "practical reasons," which included the fear of appearing promiscuous, the belief that sex was inappropriate in the relationship (because he was a boss or coworker or because she or the man was involved in another relationship), uncertainty about the potential partner's feelings for her, fear of getting pregnant or contracting a sexually transmitted disease, and inappropriateness of the physical setting for a sexual interaction. The second category was labeled "inhibition-related reasons" and included emotional, religious, and moral reasons; the woman's fear of physical discomfort; and self-consciousness or embarrassment about her body. The third category, "manipulative reasons," included game playing, anger with the partner, and a desire to be in control.

Individual differences among the women were also related to the probability of their use of the token no. Those who say no when they want to say yes to sex are at intermediate levels of traditionalism in their sexual attitudes. They are more likely to believe that token resistance is a common behavior among women, that male-female relationships are adversarial, that it is acceptable for men to use physical force in obtaining sex, and that women enjoy sex more when men resort to force in sexual relationships. These findings do not sit well with those who endorse egalitarian relationships between men and women or between sexual partners of the same gender, but use of the token no is common among heterosexual women and men. Research is needed to see if gay and lesbian people use the token no.

Informed Consent and Sexual Intimacy

Clearly, men and women have difficulty communicating their sexual intentions to each other, in part because of their fear of what their potential partners will think about them (for example, a man's worries that he will not be seen as masculine if he refuses an opportunity for sex, or a woman's apprehensions that she will be perceived as easy if she agrees to have sex too readily). In this section we propose what should not be a radical model of communication but nevertheless is, given contemporary stereotypes about sexual communication. In this model we recommend that people be direct with each other about what they want. This directness should apply equally to the initial phases of courtship and to specific acts and timing after two people have become sexually involved. In Chapter 1 we introduced the concept of informed consent in the context of research. This concept is also useful for couples who are negotiating their sexual relationships.

The process of obtaining informed consent for sexual intimacy involves several steps. Until you have tried the technique, you may react to what follows with "Aargh—this will ruin the spontaneity and turn off my partner." Nothing could be further from the truth. Regardless of your ultimate decision to have or to avoid sex with a potential partner, the *process* of engaging in informed consent is arousing and fun. See "Highlight: Negotiating a Sexual Relationship" on page 100 for a sample interaction.

Here are some of the issues that you must consider in seeking to obtain informed consent for sexual intimacy.

1. What are the conditions under which you and your partner are comfortable with increased sexual intimacy? How well do you believe you should know each other? What level of relationship is needed before you become sexually intimate—mutual attraction? dating each other exclusively? engagement? marriage? Two partners may view each other as an "S.O.," but "S.O." may stand for "significant other" to one and "sex object" to the other. This is not to suggest that sex is appropriate only under conditions of strong commitment. Instead, it is important that each person understand his or her own motivations for the sexual interaction.

2. If you do not wish to conceive a child, how will you reduce the likelihood of conception, especially given that no contraceptive is 100 percent effective? What will you do in the event that pregnancy occurs?

3. How will you reduce the risk of contracting or transmitting a sexually transmitted disease? If one or both of you have had multiple sexual partners in the past, have you been screened to confirm that you do not currently have an STD? Testing is important because STDs do not necessarily have symptoms in their early, most treatable stages; one of you may have an STD without being aware of it.

4. What are your beliefs about sexual exclusivity? Two people may assume that if they become sexually intimate with each other, they will not engage in sex with others until or unless the current relationship ends. Based on responses from our students, many do not even discuss the issue. If both assume that they will be sexually exclusive, fine. But if that is not the case, then both people need to be aware of their potential differences in beliefs about exclusivity before making a decision to become intimate.

Several other issues come into play in the process of obtaining informed consent, and these are discussed throughout the text. The main point is that it is important to discuss your intentions, feelings, and motives with a partner, preferably before becoming physically intimate. Such discussions will reduce the likelihood of disappointment and feelings of degradation or abuse.

In a couple's discussions either prior to or after sexual intimacy, a general format taught in communication skills classes can be helpful in clarifying feelings, resolving problems, and preventing arguments. The format centers on taking responsibility for your own feelings and behavior and realizing that neither you nor your partner can read minds. At the practical level, people who are skilled in this method of communicating use what are called "I feel" messages and then describe the other person's behavior, while avoiding the attribution of motives or intentions to the other person.

For example, assume that Kim and Chris are lovers but have not discussed the issue of sexual exclusivity. Kim is upset with Chris after discovering that Chris is having sexual relations with someone else, while Kim assumed that they would have sex only with each other. In the attempt to resolve the issue, Kim has the following discussion with Chris.

> **KIM:** "Chris, I'm feeling really hurt that you had sex with Fran. I thought that when we got involved, you wouldn't be intimate with anyone else." [Note that Kim avoids words like cheating and makes no attributions about Chris's motives: for example, "You don't love me."]

> **CHRIS:** "Oh, Kim, I'm sorry that you're feeling hurt. Because we never discussed it, I didn't realize that you assumed we'd see only each other. I guess we'd better talk about this; I really care about you." [Note that Chris does not put Kim down or make accusations about control issues.]

> **KIM:** "I really care about you, too, and I want us to give our relationship a chance to see where it goes. If you want to see other people, that's your right, but I want us to date just each other." [Note that while Kim acknowledges Chris's freedom to make his/her own choices, Kim also values his/her own desires.]

Chris may have assumed all along that Kim was also seeing other people. Chris may in fact be quite happy to agree to a monogamous relationship with Kim. Alternatively, Chris may not want to be confined to one person at this point. In any event, if each partner can communicate using "I feel . . . about your behavior, and I want . . ." without making attributions about the other's motives, the two of them are more likely to be able to resolve differences or, conversely, to discover that their desires are so different that they perhaps should not continue their intimate relationship.

The Management of Sexual Feelings and Behavior

Regardless of whether we are single or involved in an ongoing, committed relationship, most of us feel sexually attracted to different people throughout our lives. Attraction and sexual arousal are feelings, and as such they do not necessarily require any action or guilt. If we decide not to act on them, we can simply enjoy them. These feelings can be intense, however, and if we are moved to express them, we are wise to rely on rationality in our decision making.

As noted earlier, women, to a greater extent than men, have been socialized to be sexual gatekeepers. Societal expectations may be such a source of emotional conflict that a woman will justify an affair with the claim that she could not resist her feelings of attraction to a particular person. The tendency to attribute one's behavior to a force greater than one's will—"I just couldn't help myself"—is not unique to women. Both men and women indulge in rationalizations of helplessness in a sexual encounter, such as "I got carried away," "I was drunk," "I thought I was in love," "I thought she/he loved me." The fact is that humans generally *are* capable of controlling their behavior. People who truly cannot help acting on "irresistible" impulses tend to end up in institutions—jails or mental hospitals.

In the next section we focus on people who are committed to a primary relationship but feel attraction to someone outside the relationship. It is wise for people who feel commitment to a primary relationship—marital or otherwise—to reach agreements on how they will handle the (inevitable) attraction to people who are outside the relationship. Keep in mind that there is no guarantee that either partner will be able to live up to any agreement.

ISSUES TO CONSIDER

What are the consequences of women's traditional role in Western culture as gatekeepers who set limits on the extent of sexual intimacy? What social, cultural, religious, and biological factors might account for this role? What conditions might change it?

HIGHLIGHT

Negotiating a Sexual Relationship

Tom and Becky were introduced to each other by a mutual friend at a party about two weeks before the beginning of summer vacation. They talked for about half an hour, but Becky said that she needed to leave the party early because she had to finish a term paper. Tom asked if he could give her a call, and Becky gave him her phone number.

They went out several times before the end of the semester and discovered that they had a lot in common, including the fact that they were both enrolled in the same class on human sexuality. One evening they stayed up very late talking at Becky's place. It turned out that they each had partners back in their hometowns, and despite their mutual attraction, they avoided any physical intimacy. But when Tom got ready to go, Becky walked him to the door, and they embraced. Both acknowledged that they were sorry that vacation was beginning after finals the next week because their homes were several hundred miles apart and both had summer jobs back home.

Over the summer they had several long distance phone conversations, and both eagerly anticipated their reunion in the fall. As soon as Tom arrived back at college in the fall, he called Becky to invite her out. She agreed, and he picked her up late that afternoon. They greeted each other rather shyly and went to a local college bar. They each ordered a beer and compared notes on their course schedules.

BECKY: You know, it's hard to believe that we knew each other for only two weeks before summer break.

TOM: Yeah, I've really been looking forward to seeing you again. What happened with your old boyfriend back home?

BECKY: Uh, well, I went out with him once after I got home, but I didn't have the same feelings about him. We just didn't seem to have that much in common anymore.

TOM: I have to admit that I'm glad to hear that. I saw my old girlfriend, but after I met you, she just didn't seem that interesting, so I broke it off.

BECKY (smiling and reaching out for his hand): Well, it's been an eventful summer for both of us!

TOM (grinning): Yeah! I think we should go out for dinner to celebrate. [They go to a Mexican restaurant, order margaritas and dinners, and then sit just gazing at each other.]

TOM: Boy, you know I'd just like to take you back to my apartment right now. My roommate won't be coming in for a few days yet.

BECKY: I'd love to go, but I think we should talk about some things over dinner. Sounds like you aren't involved with anyone right now.

Honoring Agreements

Regardless of what agreements you and your partner make, there will be times when you feel sexual arousal toward someone outside your primary relationship. Let us assume that the feelings you experience are ones that you believe you should not actualize (express behaviorally) with the other person. The trick is to give yourself time to think about the strong attraction you feel and what you are comfortable doing and not doing about it. That is not always easy; a chance meeting, a long-term friendship, or an effective working relationship with a classmate or with a colleague can suddenly (sometimes it seems as if it takes only a few seconds) turn into a potential romance. There you are, minding your own business, having a conversation with a person whom we will call Tracy. All of a sudden, you see Tracy differently. You may start shaking or perspiring, and you may wonder what is wrong. The situation can be particularly difficult if the shift in feelings is reciprocal, that is, if Tracy also sees you in a new light. What do you do?

First, get away from Tracy as quickly as you can to give yourself time to think. Then try to decide whether increased involvement with Tracy is consistent with, or a violation of, your agreement with your primary partner. If an affair with Tracy would be acceptable in the context of your agreement with your partner, and if you feel comfortable with your partner and see Tracy as primarily a supplement, rather than as a potential replacement, then—provided that you and Tracy are each aware of the other's motives and goals—an affair might be mutually satisfying.

TOM (with a big smile): Well, present company excepted.

BECKY (smiling and tracing a circle on the back of Tom's hand): Well, yeah. Uhhh . . . did you and your old girlfriend get together this summer? I mean . . .

TOM: You mean did we have sex?

BECKY: Well, yeah.

TOM: No. I guess after I met you, I just wasn't interested in her or anyone else.

BECKY: Well, gee. The same thing happened to me. We kissed and stuff, but I didn't feel about him the way I used to, so I didn't want to make love. Also, the previous summer I'd been on the pill, but I went off it last fall and haven't started taking it again.

TOM: Yeah, I was wondering about that—birth control, I mean.

BECKY: You know, after taking that sex class, I wonder if condoms might be better? The prof said we should all get ourselves tested for STDs. I've had only two partners, Bob and then—real briefly [she smiled]—a guy I went to senior prom with in high school, and I don't think I've got anything. But I don't know how many people you've been with.

TOM: Uh, I . . . fooled around quite a bit in high school until I got involved with my girlfriend, but I haven't been with anyone since her. But if you want to go get tested, we could go together. The prof said that Planned Parenthood gives screening tests for both guys and girls.

BECKY (gazing at Tom): Yeah, that would be good. But I'd also like to go back to your apartment as long as your roommate isn't in yet. Do you have any condoms? I don't think I want to rely on them for long for contraception, but . . . well, just in case we get carried away.

TOM (with a big grin on his face): No, I don't have any, but there's a drugstore down the street from my place. How about we go shopping after dinner? We don't have to use them tonight, but it might take awhile to get an appointment at PP and then get the results.

BECKY: Hey, I like shopping! [Becky smiles warmly at him.]

Their dinners arrived. They weren't particularly hungry at that point—for dinner, anyway—so they ate a bit and then asked their server to bring them boxes, so that they could take their dinner home with them. They went shopping, then back to Tom's apartment. Later that evening they reheated their food and had a midnight snack. They congratulated each other on their responsible behavior, and they had every right to be proud of themselves!

If you decide that you are not going to get involved in an affair with Tracy, with whom you already have an ongoing friendship, what do you do about your feelings of sexual arousal? You can enjoy the feelings and fantasies, but your behavior must be consistent with your decision rather than with your fantasies. From a practical standpoint, here are three guidelines that you might apply to your situation with Tracy.

1. *Avoid any location (your apartment, a hotel room, a classroom) where only the two of you will be present.*

2. *Avoid drinking alcohol or using other intoxicants when you are with Tracy.*

3. *Learn from your feelings and fantasies.* Are there some aspects of your relationship with Tracy that you could infuse into your primary relationship? Revitalizing your primary relationship may reduce the intensity of your attraction to Tracy, so that you can resume the pleasure of your friendship without fear that you will violate your decisions about sexual intimacy.

In this chapter we have examined sexual fantasies, arousal, and communication and their roles in sexual intimacy. In the next chapter we explore the variety of sexual behaviors that intimate partners enjoy.

ISSUES TO CONSIDER

Assume that you are in a committed relationship but are feeling attracted to someone else. Based on advice given in this chapter, how would you handle the situation?

SUMMARY OF MAJOR POINTS

1. The conditioning of arousal.

Our capacity for sexual arousal is part of our biological heritage, but the specific objects, acts, situations, and people whom we find arousing are influenced by societal norms and by our own unique experiences. We learn to respond sexually to particular external stimuli through association of those stimuli with arousal (classical conditioning) and through sexually rewarding or punishing experiences involving those stimuli (operant conditioning). Some evidence supports the hypothesis that any source of arousal, whether positive or negative, can lead to heightened attraction to a person who is associated with that arousal.

2. Sexual arousal and our sensory capabilities.

Almost all of our senses come into play when we are sexually stimulated. Touch, smell, and sight are all important in sexual arousal. We learn to consider particular kinds or locations of tactile contact, particular smells, and certain sights to be erotic. Because these associations are unique to each individual, the specific touches, sights, smells, and sounds that arouse one person do not necessarily arouse another.

3. Variations in response to sexual arousal.

Just as we learn to associate sexual responses with different stimuli, we learn different attitudes toward the process of sexual arousal. Some of us are taught that sexual arousal is a healthy, normal, enjoyable process, whereas others learn to feel guilty about feeling sexy. These attitudes are instilled over a long time, from an early age, and are consistently related to our capacity to respond sexually in a variety of situations. Females are more frequently taught to view their sexuality negatively than are males, and the average female feels guiltier about sexual feelings and behavior than does the average male. When responses are physiologically measured, however, males and females do not differ in their arousal by erotic material.

4. Fantasy and sexual arousal.

Just as learned attitudes toward sexual arousal vary, so do reactions to the capacity to have fantasies. They provide us with a way to rehearse future events and to try out different alternatives in our minds. They can also embellish our own experiences, enhance our relationships, and entertain us. Traditional Christianity's emphasis on the importance of purity in thoughts and motives as well as in actions may be responsible for the negative reactions that some people have toward their fantasies. Imagination and reality are not the same thing, and it is only when an individual confuses them, or uses fantasy as a substitute for relations with others, that any problem with fantasy arises. Fantasies of arousal can be acted out with a willing partner under certain conditions. When we experience sexual arousal that we would rather not act on, we must take practical steps to manage our behavior.

5. Communication and sexual feelings.

In making wise decisions about whether to act on sexual feelings, we should be aware of, and discuss, our sexual policies with potential partners. Open communication enhances the likelihood that our interactions with others will be pleasurable and satisfying.

CHECK YOUR KNOWLEDGE

1. The capacity for sexual arousal is (a) inborn, (b) learned from peers, (c) acquired by experience, (d) acquired from one's specific culture. **(p. 80)**

2. The two-stage model of sexual arousal involves (a) the pairing of a previously neutral stimulus with a stimulus that can evoke sexual arousal; (b) the feeling of sexual arousal, followed by reward, punishment, or lack of attention; (c) the awareness of physiological arousal, followed by the search for a cognitive label; (d) the awareness of a cognitive label, followed by the sensation of physiological arousal. **(pp. 81–82)**

3. Which of the following statements about our sense of touch is true? (a) Touch is the only type of stimulation that can produce a reflexive response that is independent of higher brain centers. (b) Receptors for touch and pressure are evenly distributed throughout the body. (c) Being touched and cuddled during infancy is unnecessary for the development of the capacity to give affection. (d) The areas where touch receptors are most highly concentrated are called the pheromonic zones. **(p. 83)**

4. Evidence suggests that human evaluation of bodily odors as pleasant or unpleasant is (a) innate, (b) learned, (c) similar to that of animals, (d) an instinctive defense against harmful substances. **(p. 84)**

5. Research on the conditions under which men and women respond to erotic materials suggests that (a) there are no significant gender differences in sexual responses to erotic stimuli, (b) observed gender differences in response to erotic materials reflect basic biological gender differences, (c) women are rarely aroused by such materials, (d) differing cultural expectations for men and women are strongly related to the observed gender differences. **(p. 91)**

6. Informed consent about sexual behavior refers to (a) never engaging in atypical sexual behavior, (b) following all federal guidelines concerning sexual behavior, (c) engaging in sexual behavior that is acceptable to everyone involved, (d) accepting your own sexual impulses as normal. **(p. 98)**

7. When disagreements arise between you and your partner, your best course of action is to (a) confront your partner directly, describing his or her motivations for the behavior; (b) describe your partner's behavior and your feelings about it; (c) do the same thing to your partner that he or she did to offend you; (d) see your family physician. **(p. 99)**

8. Women who say no when they want to say yes to a sexual invitation are likely (a) to believe that it is unacceptable for men to use physical force in obtaining sex, (b) to dislike men's use of force to obtain sex, (c) to believe that male-female relationships are marked by conflict, (d) to believe that most women rarely use token resistance. **(p. 97)**

5

SEXUAL BEHAVIOR

SOURCES OF SEXUAL PLEASURE
Nocturnal Orgasm
Masturbation
Highlight: Mark Twain on Masturbation
Mutual Masturbation
Oral Sex
"Foreplay" and Coitus
Coitus and Coital Positions
Anal Sex
Frequency of Coitus and Number of Sexual Partners
Sexual Satisfaction and Enjoyment
Simultaneous Orgasm: A Note

SEXUAL RESPONSES
Sexual Desire
Excitement/Plateau
Orgasm
Resolution
Highlight: Physical Reactions During Sexual Response
Patterns of Sexual Response
Highlight: Whose Is It?
Normal Variations

VARIETIES OF ORGASM
Female Orgasm: Different Types?
Research on Female Ejaculation
The Consistency of Female Orgasm
The Consistency of Male Orgasm
Multiple Orgasms in Females
Multiple Orgasms in Males

SUMMARY OF MAJOR POINTS

CHECK YOUR KNOWLEDGE

REALITY or MYTH ?

1 Nocturnal emissions, or "wet dreams," often are a sign of sexual problems.

2 Masturbation by a married person is almost always related to marital problems.

3 Oral-genital sex is illegal in a number of states in the United States.

4 There have been no consistent differences among ethnic groups in reported frequency of sex or in numbers of sexual partners.

5 If two people are engaging in effective sexual stimulation, they should experience simultaneous orgasm.

6 A person cannot be physically satisfied with sexual activity if she or he does not have orgasm.

Because we can't live together right now and are often separated, we masturbate together by talking on the telephone, which is just out of sight! We talk to each other late in the evening because both of us are very busy during the day and sometimes we'll be on the phone almost all night talking each other into coming, . . . and then we become more intimate and feel closer.

To me, good sex means being able to give and also being able to take. When I'm with a man who doesn't like to take, who's unwilling to just lie back and let me give to him, a man who needs to be in charge all the time, I lose interest.

The most important breakthrough in my sex life was when I learned it was all right for me to touch my own clitoris during intercourse. Since I've started doing that, I almost always have orgasms, and I have come to believe that this is just the way I am and that there's nothing wrong with it. Because I believe that, my partners have accepted it without any difficulty.

The relationship is what has always mattered to me. I never went to bed just to be going to bed or because he was "Joe Blow." It had to be with a person who had some depth and warmth. I didn't have to be in love necessarily, but we had to be able to communicate well. For me, good sex comes from good communication. (Barbach & Levine, 1980, pp. 11, 91–92)

As the foregoing quotations of different individuals from the book *Shared Intimacies* illustrate, there is a great deal of diversity in what people find sexually pleasurable. In our culture, however, the popular perception is that in heterosexual intercourse the woman lies on her back and the man lies on top of her. After they have engaged in enough foreplay to elicit vaginal lubrication, he inserts his erect penis into her vagina and moves it in and out until he is stimulated to ejaculation. She may or may not have an orgasm. This method works well for purposes of procreation, but it represents a rather rigid, stereotyped view of sexual intimacy, and the extent to which it provides sexual pleasure varies from one person to the next and, for some individuals, from one sexual encounter to the next.

In this chapter we consider what humans do sexually to stimulate themselves and others. Effective sexual stimulation evokes a relatively predictable pattern of bodily responses, which we review. We also examine researchers' varying views on what actually happens in the human sexual response cycle, and we examine the similarities and differences in male and female orgasmic patterns.

SOURCES OF SEXUAL PLEASURE

Our focus in examining what humans do to produce sexual sensation and response is behaviorally oriented. Remember, however, as we emphasized in the last chapter, that people's sexual actions and responses are strongly associated with their thoughts, feelings, and fantasies.

Sexual behavior among the majority of heterosexual Americans follows a general script (DeLamater & MacCorquodale, 1979; Laumann et al., 1994; Simon & Gagnon, 1987). Gay people engage in the same general activities with the obvious exception of vaginal intercourse. The scenario starts with kissing and eventually leads to the male touching the female breast while covered by clothing and then under clothing. The next step in the script involves caressing of the female's genitals by the male, followed by the female's fondling of the male's penis. This is usually followed by genital contact and vaginal intercourse, although some couples engage in oral-genital stimulation prior to or instead of vaginal intercourse. Various factors may slightly alter the script, but the order of events usually unfolds in this manner. Before focusing on sexual activities involving a partner, we begin with solitary sexual experiences.

Nocturnal Orgasm

wet dream Slang phrase for orgasm and/or ejaculation while asleep.

Nocturnal orgasm refers to the sexual arousal and response that occur while a person is sleeping. It is experienced by both males and females and is often accompanied by erotic dreams—thus the popular term **wet dream** for ejaculation during sleep. Almost all men and 70 percent of women who participated in the Kinsey et al. (1948, 1953) studies reported having sexual dreams. Nocturnal orgasms were reported by 90 percent of the men but by less than 40 percent of the women.

The Kinsey group (1948, 1953) found that men reported the highest frequency of nocturnal orgasm during their late adolescence and early 20s. In contrast, women reported the highest frequency of nocturnal orgasm during their 40s. Among women who experienced nocturnal orgasm, the frequency was about three or four per year, whereas men reported having three to eleven nocturnal orgasms a year. About 5 percent of men and 1 percent of women averaged one nocturnal orgasm a week.

Barbara Wells (1986) found evidence that the percentage of young women reporting nocturnal orgasms may be increasing. Of 245 undergraduate and graduate women she surveyed, 37 percent had experienced nocturnal orgasms. In contrast, only 8 percent of the women in the Kinsey group sample (1953) had nocturnal orgasm by the time they were 20 years old. Liberal sexual attitudes as well as positive feelings about and knowledge of nocturnal orgasm were strongly related to experiencing orgasm while sleeping.

Why do people have orgasms while they sleep? One common belief is that nocturnal orgasm fulfills a compensatory function; that is, if sexually mature adults have a decrease in sexual outlets during their waking hours, they will experience a corresponding increase in nocturnal orgasms. This hypothesis has not been supported, however; the available research has found no relationship between the frequency of sexual release while people were awake and the frequency of nocturnal orgasm (Burg, 1988; Kinsey et al., 1948). Whatever the function of nocturnal orgasms, they should be enjoyed as much as other sexual activities because for most of us they are few and far between.

REALITY or **MYTH** ? **1**

Masturbation

Masturbation is a common form of sexual outlet for the majority of North Americans and Europeans (Breakwell & Fife-Schaw, 1992; Clement, 1990; Leitenberg, Detzer, & Srebnik, 1993) (see Table 5.1). Clement, Schmidt, and Kruse (1984) found masturbation to be the first sexual experience among the majority of a sample of German students (66 percent of women and 90 percent of men). More men than women masturbate, and of those who do, men masturbate more frequently than do women (Laumann et al., 1994; Oliver & Hyde, 1993). In one study of U.S. university students, nearly twice as many men as women reported ever having masturbated. Of those who masturbated, men reported doing so almost three times more frequently than did women (Leitenberg et al., 1993).

The more formal education people have, the more likely they are to masturbate frequently. They are also more likely to report pleasure from masturbation (Laumann et al., 1994). There is also an interaction between education and ethnicity, with Black men and women reporting less masturbation than do Whites. For example, Black men were almost twice as likely to report not masturbating in the past year than were White men (Laumann et al., 1994).

Masturbation is sometimes called **autoeroticism,** or the seeking of pleasure with oneself. In this section we focus on solitary masturbation—stimulation of the genitals when no one else is present. A person also may engage in self-stimulation in the presence of a partner; or partners may masturbate each other. Throughout history attitudes toward this pleasurable practice have been riddled with misconceptions, guilt, and fear. These traditional biases continue to have an impact on many people (see Figure 5.1, page 108).

In the eighteenth century Simon André Tissot (1728–1797) theorized that semen was important for healthy bodily functioning and that wasting it through sexual activity

ISSUES TO CONSIDER

Why do you think that men masturbate more frequently than women?

autoeroticism Sexual stimulation of oneself.

Table 5.1	**Prevalence of Self-Stimulation**

Results of surveys by the Kinsey group and Hunt and research conducted by Janus and Janus (1993) show that the proportion of people who report engaging in masturbation has remained about the same for males and females, with slight variations that probably stem from methodological differences.*

	Kinsey group (1938–1949)	**Hunt (1972)**	**Janus & Janus (1988–1992)**
Males	92%	94%	81%
Females	62%	63%	72%

*In a national probability sample of Americans, more than 60 percent of men and almost 50 percent of women reported masturbating in the past year (Laumann et al., 1994).

Figure 5.1
Supposed Effects of Masturbation This nineteenth century picture shows the supposed fate of a masturbator. In addition to insanity, masturbation was thought to cause a variety of physical disorders, among them epilepsy, poor eyesight, and loss of memory.

would weaken the body and produce illness. Fear of masturbation and of its supposed harmful effects was rampant in the nineteenth century, creating some extreme "treatments" for this practice, although some individuals did not take these ideas seriously (see "Highlight: Mark Twain on Masturbation," page 110).

The catastrophic consequences of self-stimulation could not, according to Shannon (1913), be avoided by having someone else stimulate the genitals. He wrote that married people who manually brought each other to orgasm risked all the same physical and mental afflictions as solitary masturbators and thereby, of course, shortened their lives. Barraged by such pronouncements from medical and religious authorities, a person who masturbated could easily conclude that he or she was on the road to weak character development from a medical point of view or on the road to hell from a religious point of view. These writers would probably be terribly concerned about the threat to our species posed by such contemporary books as Betty Dodson's *Sex for One: The Joys of Self-Loving* (1987), which encourage self-stimulation as part of healthy sexuality. Furthermore, masturbation training has become part of the therapeutic techniques used in treating certain sexual dysfunctions. The more often people masturbate, the more likely they are to experience orgasm during this activity (Laumann et al., 1994).

Beginning in the twentieth century, the connection between masturbation and illness became more difficult to defend. Concern shifted to particular aspects of masturbation. One controversy centered on the definition of "excessive" masturbation. Unfortunately for the masturbator, these "authorities" never concretely defined what was too much, normal, or too little. Harold Leitenberg et al. (1993) found that the university men in their sample reported masturbating once a week and the women reported doing so once a month.

Roughly half of men and women who reported masturbating said that they felt guilty afterward (Laumann et al., 1994). However, early masturbation experience appears to be unrelated to sexual adjustment in young adulthood (Leitenberg et al., 1993).

The conditions under which masturbation occurs also affect attitudes about self-stimulation. For example, masturbation may be condoned in cases in which a person has no partner but considered inappropriate if a person has a spouse or regular partner. Even though cohabiting individuals and young married respondents reported comparatively high rates of both partnered and solitary sexual stimulation, these beliefs persist (Laumann et al., 1994). Perhaps they are maintained by our culture's view that a person's sexuality belongs to his or her sexual partner. From this perspective, to masturbate when an appropriate partner is available is to violate that partner's property rights. Or perhaps people assume that something is lacking in a couple's sexual relationship if one or both partners engage in solitary masturbation. In one study of married women, however, those who reported having masturbated to orgasm had higher self-esteem, more orgasms with their spouses, greater sexual desire, and greater marital and sexual satisfaction than married women who did not masturbate to orgasm (Hurlbert & Whittaker, 1991).

The most frequent reasons that people say they masturbate are to relieve sexual tension, achieve physical pleasure because of no available partner, and relaxation (Laumann et al., 1994). Thus self-stimulation can provide sexual release when a partner is not available or when you are feeling sexually aroused by someone with whom sexual intimacy is impossible or inappropriate. It is also pleasurable—you can be good to yourself physically after having a bad day or reward yourself for spending hours on chores. Finally, knowing how to make yourself feel good gives you self-knowledge—information that you can share with another person.

ISSUES TO CONSIDER

If you learned that your steady partner engaged in masturbation, how would you react? Why?

MALE METHODS.   When masturbating, men tend to focus on stimulation of the penis. It may be rubbed against the body with one or both hands, or it may be rolled between the palms of the hands as they move up and down the shaft of the penis. Some men reach orgasm by lying on a pillow and thrusting against it. However, the majority of the 312 men who masturbated while being observed by William Masters and Virginia Johnson (1966) moved their hands up and down the shaft of their penises (see Figure 5.2). The stroking of the penis can vary from a light touch to a strong grip, as

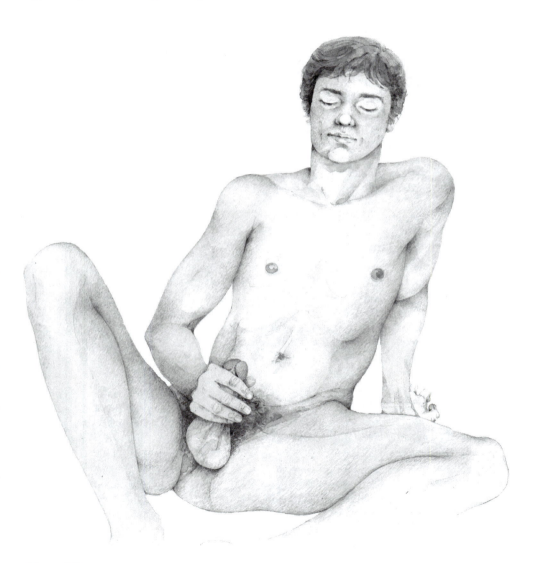

Figure 5.2
Male Masturbation Although we are all unique in what pleases us sexually, there are some general differences between the self-stimulation methods used by males and those used by females.

HIGHLIGHT

Mark Twain on Masturbation

Mark Twain delivered the following musings at a private club in Paris in 1879. The material was considered so scandalous that it was not published until many years later.

Homer in the second book of the Iliad, *says with fine enthusiasm, "Give me masturbation or give me death!" Caesar, in his* Commentaries, *says "To the lonely it is company; to the forsaken it is a friend; to the aged and to the impotent it is a benefactor; they that are penniless are yet rich, in that they still have this majestic diversion." In another place this experienced observer has said, "There are times when I prefer it to sodomy." Robinson*

Crusoe says, "I cannot describe what I owe to this gentle art." Queen Elizabeth said, "It is the bulwark of Virginity." Cetewayo, the Zulu hero, remarked, "A jerk in the hand is worth two in the bush." The immortal Franklin has said, "Masturbation is the mother of invention." He also said, "Masturbation is the best policy." Michelangelo and all the other old masters—Old Masters, I will remark, is an abbreviation, a contraction—have used similar language. Michelangelo said to Pope Julius II, "Self-negation is noble, self-culture is beneficial, self-possession is manly, but to the truly grand and inspiring soul they are poor and tame compared to self-abuse."

well as from a leisurely speed to a more rapid movement. As males approach ejaculation, they tend to increase the speed of stimulation to the penis. When they begin to ejaculate, however, most men decrease or stop penile stimulation abruptly, reporting that continued intense stimulation of the glans is unpleasant (Masters & Johnson, 1966).

Aside from a minute amount of fluid, produced by the Cowper's glands, that appears at the opening of the urethra, there is no natural lubrication of the external skin of the penis. Therefore, some men use saliva, oil, cream, or soap (during a shower or bath) to allow the hand to glide smoothly over their penises. A vibrator may also be used to stimulate the penis. Some men stimulate their nipples or anus with one hand while rubbing their penis with the other hand.

Many males are completely oriented toward orgasm in their masturbatory techniques. The average man reported to the Kinsey group (1948) that he ejaculated after stimulating himself for two or three minutes. Some men reported a more leisurely pattern of self-stimulation; a few men reported ejaculating within 30 seconds of the onset of masturbation. This efficiency is useful if one has an appointment to keep, but it may be poor preparation for shared sex; racing through one's sexual response is not generally conducive to mutual pleasure.

FEMALE METHODS.   In contrast to males, females vary considerably in the methods they use to stimulate themselves. Masters and Johnson (1966) found that no two of their female research volunteers masturbated in quite the same way. Stimulation of the clitoral shaft, clitoral area, and mons with a hand or an object is the method that women most commonly employ (see Figure 5.3). For direct stimulation, making a circular motion around the clitoral shaft and glans and rubbing up and down one side of the clitoris are popular methods. Pulling on the inner lips causes the loose skin covering the clitoral glans to slide back and forth, creating a sensation that can be quite sexually arousing. Clitoral stimulation can also be accompanied by moving the fingers in and out of the vagina. Vaginal penetration alone, however, is not frequently used by women as a masturbatory technique. Masters and Johnson (1966) reported that most women in their research preferred to stimulate the entire mons area rather than concentrate exclusively on the clitoris. The clitoral glans is sensitive, and direct stimulation for an extended period of time can be irritating.

Figure 5.3
Female Masturbation

Other masturbatory techniques that women use include pelvic thrusting, squeezing and contracting the thigh muscles, inserting objects into the vagina, stimulating the breasts, and fantasizing. Pelvic thrusting of the genitals against a bed, pillow, clothing, or other objects produces direct stimulation of the vulval area as well as increasing muscular tension through contraction of the thigh and gluteal muscles. This technique spreads stimulation over a wide area. For some women, pressing the thigh muscles together, usually with their legs crossed, applies steady, rhythmic pressure on the genitals.

Some women also masturbate by using a vibrator. Vibrators, which may be purchased in a variety of sizes and shapes (see Figure 5.4, page 112), are usually battery operated or electric. Some vibrator kits have a number of different accessories and provide a choice of several vibration speeds. Vibrators should not be lent to other people because of the potential for passing on infections and sexually transmitted diseases.

A small percentage of women report that they can reach orgasm through breast and/or nipple stimulation alone (Kinsey et al., 1953; Masters & Johnson, 1966). Usually,

Figure 5.4
Examples of Various Vibrators Nearly all the vibrators in this photo support the male notion that women use vibrators as surrogate penises. Although this is true for some women, most others use a smaller device intended not for insertion in the vagina but for stimulation of the clitoris. The small device at top center (beside the red-and-white vibrator) appears to be one of the latter type.

however, women who stimulate their breasts during masturbation (about 1 in 10 of Kinsey's respondents) do so in combination with stimulation of the clitoral area. About 2 percent of Kinsey's respondents claimed that they could reach orgasm through erotic fantasy with no direct stimulation of the genitals—a real tribute to the powers of the mind. This phenomenon has been measured by self-report and physiological indices in lab settings where 7 out of 10 women had orgasm relying only on fantasy (Whipple, Ogden, & Komisaruk, 1992). Breast stimulation or fantasy alone is rarely used by women, however, and even less commonly by men.

Masters and Johnson (1966) observed an interesting gender difference in the process of self-stimulation. Most women prefer continued stimulation of the clitoral shaft or mons area during orgasm. In contrast, men typically slow down or stop manual stimulation during orgasm. This gender difference appears to be true of coital orgasm as well and thus has implications for sexual interaction.

Female sexual response is not much slower than male response during masturbation: a little less than four minutes after the beginning of self-stimulation (Kinsey et al., 1953). Some women have an orgasm in less than 30 seconds. The relatively small difference between male and female patterns of response becomes larger during stimulation through sexual intercourse. It takes the average woman longer than the average man to have orgasm during coitus because there is usually not as much direct stimulation of the clitoral area as there is during masturbation.

Mutual Masturbation

Mutual caressing of the breasts and genitals is widely practiced in our culture. More than 90 percent of men and women report manually stimulating the genitals of their

Figure 5.5
Tribadism

sexual partners (Breakwell & Fife-Schaw, 1992; Kinsey et al., 1948, 1953). Manual stimulation of a partner's genitals can serve as a prelude to oral sex or sexual intercourse, or it can be the means of achieving orgasm for one or both partners. Couples who have considerable experience with solitary masturbation can give each other information and guidance about what techniques are most pleasing.

Mutual masturbation provides a satisfying and pleasurable form of sexual intimacy and release for many couples. If birth control is unavailable and a heterosexual couple wants to have sex, it offers one of several enjoyable alternatives to sexual intercourse. Mutual masturbation is also one of the most common techniques that gay and lesbian couples use during sexual intimacy.

The two women shown in Figure 5.5 are engaging in **tribadism.** They are rubbing against one another for clitoral stimulation.

tribadism Sexual activity in which one woman lies on top of another and moves rhythmically for clitoral stimulation.

Oral Sex

KISSING.   Kissing—mouth-to-mouth contact—is usually the first step in sexual interactions in Western cultures. Among other cultures and species, however, deep kissing for the purpose of erotic arousal is relatively rare. Although all human cultures use some form of mouth or nose contact to indicate greeting and affection, in many societies people do not include kissing in their erotic interactions.

The pleasure that lovers obtain from kissing may be partially due to the fact that all the senses can be stimulated during that activity. The lips, mouth, and tongue are among the most exquisitely sensitive parts of the body. Indeed, 5 of the 12 cranial nerves that affect brain functions are involved in a kiss. Kissing also involves our senses of hearing and sight. We may be aroused by the associated sounds of sucking and licking, and we may be affected by the sight of a partner's lips and tongue.

ORAL-GENITAL SEX.   Although deep kissing is relatively uncommon across cultures, kissing or licking of other parts of the body—including the genitals—is widely documented in many societies. Historically, North Americans have held negative attitudes toward oral-genital sex. It has been, and remains, illegal in a number of states.

Attitudes toward oral-genital sex have changed rapidly in this century. Acceptance of oral sex has increased significantly among married couples and for some is a favored means to orgasm (Hurlbert & Whittaker, 1991; Janus & Janus, 1993) (see Table 5.2). The incidence of oral sex is also rising among adolescents, particularly among those with coital experience, partly because it eliminates worries about birth control for heterosexuals (Billy, Tanfer, Grady, & Klepinger, 1993; Whitley, 1989).

There appear to be ethnic differences in giving and receiving oral sex. In a nationally representative sample, more White men performed (81 percent) and received (81 percent) oral sex than did Black men (50 percent performed and 66 percent received oral sex) (Laumann et al., 1994). More White women performed (68 percent) and received (73 percent) oral sex than did Black women (34 percent performing and 49 percent receiving). Hispanic men and women engaging in oral sex fell roughly midway between the percentages reported by Blacks and Whites. As we saw with masturbation, the higher the educational level was, the more likely it was that an individual had engaged in oral sex (Laumann et al., 1994).

There are many ways of having oral sex. Partners may stimulate each other's genitals with their mouths before sexual intercourse or orally caress each other to mutual orgasm. Depending on preference, a person can swallow the semen or stop orally stimulating the penis just before ejaculation and move slightly away.

Partners can perform **cunnilingus** and **fellatio** using a variety of positions. Some partners like to take turns, bringing each other to orgasm in sequence. Others prefer to stimulate each other orally at the same time (see Figure 5.6). Simultaneous oral stimu-

REALITY or *MYTH* ? **3**

ISSUES TO CONSIDER

The higher the educational level, the more likely it is that a person has engaged in oral sex. How would you explain this relationship?

cunnilingus (KUN-nih-LING-gus) Oral stimulation of the female genitals.

fellatio (fell-LAY-she-oh) Oral stimulation of the male genitals.

Table 5.2 Prevalence of Oral Sex				
The proportion of people who reported engaging in oral sex increased from the 1930s to the 1990s.				
	Kinsey* group (1938–1949)	**Hunt* (1972)**	**Laumann et al. (1992)**
Fellatio			
Males	59–61%	54–61%	78%
Females	46–52%	52–72%	68%
Cunnilingus			
Males	16–51%	55–66%	77%
Females	50–58%	58–72%	73%

*The Kinsey and Hunt figures included only married people.

Figure 5.6
Mutual Oral-Genital Stimulation

lation is known popularly as "69." Many couples enjoy having other parts of their bodies kissed and licked during sexual intimacy. For some partners, the sexual repertoire includes **analingus,** the oral stimulation of the sensitive tissue around the anus. It is important for both heterosexual and homosexual couples to realize, however, that HIV can be transmitted during oral stimulation of the genitals (see Chapter 13). Small fissures in the gums, genitals, or anus may permit transmission of the virus from an infected person to the bloodstream of a noninfected person. Thus unless a couple is monogamous, partners should make sure that they are both free of HIV before engaging in oral sex or analingus.

analingus (A-nil-LING-gus) Oral stimulation of the tissues surrounding the anus.

In cunnilingus a woman's partner can caress and separate her vaginal lips with the hands or tongue. The clitoris can be licked, sucked, or gently nibbled, although too much direct stimulation may be uncomfortable because the clitoris is extremely sensitive. Having the side of the clitoral shaft massaged or rapidly flicked by the tongue is generally quite pleasurable for women.

Oral stimulation of a man's genitals can also provide deep pleasure. The most sensitive parts of the penis are the glans, or tip, and the frenulum on the underside of the glans. Having these areas licked or sucked is quite pleasurable. The testes can also be taken gently into the mouth and sucked or licked. The head and shaft of the penis can be sucked slowly or rapidly while the penis is held and the scrotum is caressed.

These are some of the more common means of oral stimulation. As with other forms of sexual intimacy, people need to be sensitive to the likes and dislikes of their partners when giving and receiving oral stimulation.

"Foreplay" and Coitus

The term **foreplay** usually refers to activities, such as kissing, manual caressing of the genitals, and oral sex, that are seen as a prelude to intercourse. The term reflects the long-ingrained belief in our culture that "having sex" is an experience that must

foreplay Term used by some people to refer to sexual behavior occurring before intercourse.

culminate in coitus and male orgasm, or else it isn't really sex. Rather than being viewed as pleasures and ends in themselves, mutual caressing, kissing, and oral sex are often seen as necessary tasks on the way to achieving coital orgasm.

Given this belief, how much time do partners spend in stimulating each other before and during sexual intercourse? The average duration of foreplay appears to be about 12 to 15 minutes (Fisher, 1973; Hunt, 1974). In more recent research, women indicated that they preferred an average of about 17 minutes of foreplay prior to penile penetration (Darling, Davidson, & Cox, 1991). Thus there may be a discrepancy of 2 to 5 minutes between what women desire and what they get.

After penile insertion, women seem to require an average of about 8 minutes to experience orgasm, although the preferred length of intercourse after penile insertion was about 11 minutes (Darling et al., 1991; Fisher, 1973). It should be noted that there was a wide range in the length of time women needed to experience orgasm, with some requiring just 1 minute and others needing about 30 minutes.

For men, the average time from insertion to orgasm was about 10 to 11 minutes (Darling et al., 1991; Hunt, 1974). This longer duration to orgasm for men than for women is interesting in that women in the Fisher study estimated that it took them 40 percent to 80 percent more time to attain orgasm than it did their partners. Some of this discrepancy is undoubtedly due to different sampling and methodological techniques used in these studies. However, women who experienced orgasm after their partner reported less sexual satisfaction than did women who had orgasm before or simultaneously with their partner (Darling et al., 1991). Although women prefer more time spent in sexual foreplay and in sexual intercourse, research on men's preferences is lacking.

Having reported these data on time spent in "foreplay" and intercourse, we want to caution readers not to focus too heavily on timing as an index of sexual pleasure. We know one couple who ended up in therapy because the husband was experiencing difficulty getting an erection. It turned out that his wife—a very busy woman—was in the habit of keeping a stopwatch by their bed to time how long it took him to reach orgasm!

Coitus and Coital Positions

Nonhuman species rely almost entirely on rear entry as their main position during sexual interaction, although porpoises use a face-to-face position while swimming. In contrast, humans employ a wide range of positions during sexual activity, and the popularity of various positions differs from one culture to another. The typical coital position used in a particular culture appears to be correlated with the social status of females (Beigel, 1953). For example, among several American Indian tribes and among groups in the South Pacific, where females enjoy high status, the woman-above position is most popular, and sexual satisfaction is considered at least as important for women as it is for men. The cross-cultural association between female status and coital position is especially interesting in light of two studies in our own culture. Although Masters and Johnson (1966) found that the woman's sexual response develops more rapidly and with greater intensity in the face-to-face, woman-above position than in any other coital position, the Kinsey group (1948, p. 578) concluded that "nearly all coitus in our English-American culture occurs with the partners lying face to face, with the male above the female. There may be as much as 70% of the population which has never attempted to use any other position in intercourse."

This man-above position remains quite popular, but many couples now vary the positions they use during sexual intercourse (see Table 5.3). Although different coital positions can produce different physical sensations, any position in which the penis

Table 5.3   Prevalence of Coital Positions

The Kinsey and Hunt surveys showed the following trends among married people in use of coital positions.

	Kinsey Group (1938–1949)	Hunt Study (1972)
Female-above position	33%	75%
Side-by-side position	25%	50%
Rear-entry (vaginally) position	10%	40%
Sitting position	8%	25%

penetrates the vagina can result in conception, so couples who do not want to conceive should use a reliable contraceptive when they have coitus of any kind.

FACE TO FACE, MAN ABOVE.   In the face-to-face, man-above position, a woman usually lies on her back with her legs apart and her knees slightly bent (see Figure 5.7). A man lies on top of her with his legs between hers, and he supports most of his weight with his elbows and knees.

Because the partners are face to face, they can communicate their feelings by continued erotic kissing, eye contact, and facial expressions. The penis can be inserted into the vagina as the partners move their bodies together, or it can be directed by hand. After insertion of the penis, the man has more control of body movement than does the woman, whose pelvic movements are restricted by the pressure of his weight. Such

Figure 5.7
Face-to-Face, Man-Above Coital Position

limitation of the woman's pelvic movement can be a drawback of this position. When a man is considerably heavier than a woman, another coital position may permit greater participation from the woman. In the man-above position, however, a woman can enhance her capacity to move in pleasurable ways by pulling her legs up toward her shoulders or by placing them on the man's shoulders. She can also entwine her legs around his back and lock her feet together. These actions can be supplemented by placement of a pillow under her lower back, which increases the contact between a woman's clitoris and her partner's body. By changing the position of her legs, a woman can then more easily coordinate the movement of her pelvis with the man's coital thrusts, as well as maintain the kind of stimulation to her clitoral area that will result in orgasm.

A disadvantage of the face-to-face, man-above position is that a man's hands are not free to stimulate his partner. For couples who desire this pleasure, the coital position that follows is recommended.

FACE TO FACE, WOMAN ABOVE.

In the face-to-face, woman-above position, a man lies on his back with a woman kneeling over him, her knees positioned on either side of his body. She can lean her upper body forward and guide his penis into her vagina as she moves down on it. She can then either sit upright or lie on top of her partner, depending on how much body contact she wants (see Figure 5.8). If she remains sitting or kneeling, he can readily caress her breasts and face.

Figure 5.8
Face-to-Face, Woman-Above Coital Position

The advantages of this position for women are similar to the advantages of the man-above position for men. Positioned above her partner, a woman has better control over coital movement and depth of penetration, and either she or her partner can manually stimulate her clitoris. Men often experience less sexual intensity in this position, and this may be desirable if the woman is typically slower to respond than the man or if the man ejaculates more quickly than he wishes. Furthermore, when a man wants to prolong the pleasure of arousal, leisurely lovemaking may be easier for him in this position than in the man-above position, in which he is likely to reach orgasm faster.

The woman-above position is not desirable on those occasions when a man wants to take primary responsibility for sexual movement. In addition, the position may put some men in a passive or subordinate role that makes them psychologically uncomfortable. Thus a person who wishes to try the woman-above or any other coital position should ask his or her partner's feelings about it rather than simply assuming that the partner has the same desires.

FACE TO FACE, SIDE BY SIDE.   The side-by-side variation of the face-to-face position offers both partners the opportunity to control their own body movements during coitus (see Figure 5.9). The partners can lie in several different positions, all of which eliminate weight on either partner. These positions allow a lot of body contact and free the hands for caressing and touching. The side-by-side positions are particularly useful for overweight people and for women in the later stage of pregnancy, when man-above and woman-above positions may both be uncomfortable because of the woman's enlarged abdomen.

Figure 5.9
Face-to-Face, Side-by-Side Coital Position

Partners may begin in the man-above position and then roll onto their sides with the penis inserted in the vagina. In this position penetration tends to be shallow, and movements may be somewhat restricted or less vigorous. Depending on partners' preferences at a particular time, the more gentle movement can be either an advantage or a disadvantage. They might choose this position, for example, when they want to prolong playful and intimate sexual relations before orgasm.

REAR ENTRY.   This approach involves vaginal intercourse in which the male positions himself behind the woman. Rear-entry coitus does not mean anal sex, with which it is sometimes confused. Because rear entry is the most prevalent coital position among nonhuman species, some people believe that the position is degrading or animalistic. This idea is unfortunate because there are advantages to rear-entry positions. For example, they allow a man more access to a woman's body. If both of them are lying on their sides, the man can caress the woman's breasts, most of her upper body, and her abdomen, clitoris, buttocks, and back. In fact, stimulation of the clitoris is easier in rear-entry than in any other coital position. In addition, stimulation of the Gräfenberg

Figure 5.10
Scissors Position

spot by the thrusting of the penis against the anterior wall of the vagina is more likely in rear-entry than in the face-to-face positions.

Rear entry can be accomplished with a woman lying on her stomach or kneeling. The man faces her back and inserts his penis into her vagina. Alternatively, the woman can sit on the man's lap, facing away, or the man can enter the woman while both are standing up, although it may be necessary for the woman to stand on a stool if the man is considerably taller than she is.

A variation of this position, known as the "scissors position," permits a woman to vary her pelvic thrusting with more ease while allowing a man greater ejaculatory control. To use the scissors position, the partners may begin with both the woman and the man lying on their left sides, with the woman's back to the man. She then rolls partially onto her back, putting her right leg over the man's legs, so that his penis can enter her vagina. For ease of entry, their heads and upper bodies should be at some distance from each other so that their bodies resemble a pair of open scissors. This position allows the man to caress the woman's genitals or breasts easily. The ease with which the partners may caress and look at each other contributes to the intimacy of this position (see Figure 5.10).

Rear-entry positions can be less physically demanding than other positions. They can be used during the third trimester of pregnancy or during illnesses that limit physical activity.

Anal Sex

Anal sex involves the stimulation of the anus by a partner. The stimulation may involve fingers, the tongue, a penis, or an object. The anus is rich in nerve endings and is involved in sexual response regardless of whether it is directly or indirectly stimulated. The anus does not produce much lubrication, but lubrication can be supplied through the use of a sterile, water-soluble product such as K-Y jelly. Vaseline and other petroleum-based lubricants should not be used in the anus or the vagina because they tend to accumulate and are not as easily discharged as are water-soluble lubricants.

The anal sphincter muscle responds to initial penetration with a contraction that may be uncomfortable. The spasm usually relaxes within 15 to 30 seconds in a person who is familiar with anal intercourse (Masters & Johnson, 1979). In a tense, inexperienced person, the spasm may last for a minute or longer, but the discomfort usually disappears.

Like masturbation, oral stimulation, and coital position variations, anal sex apparently became more prevalent in the past 50 years. Even with the advent of AIDS and the urgent need for safer-sex practices, there has not been a marked decline in anal sex in the United States, as can be seen in Table 5.4.

Table 5.4 Prevalence of Anal Intercourse		
These studies of percentage of people engaging in anal intercourse are difficult to compare because researchers asked questions in different ways.		
Kinsey group (1938–1949)	**Hunt (1972)**	**Laumann et al. (1992)**
Never tried: 89%	Under age 25: 25%	
Tried unsuccessfully: 3%	At ages 25–34: 25%	Males 18–59: 26%
Have experienced: 8%	At ages 35–44: 14%	Females 18–59: 20%

As with oral sex, there appear to be ethnic differences in the likelihood of people engaging in anal sex (Laumann et al., 1994). The patterns are complicated among men and women. Hispanic men report the most experience with anal intercourse (34 percent), and Black women report the least experience (10 percent).

If partners choose to engage in anal sex despite the risk of AIDS, a lubricated condom should be worn, and penile penetration of the anus should be carried out gradually and gently. The penis should never be inserted into the vagina or mouth after anal penetration unless it has been washed. The anus contains bacteria that can cause infection.

Frequency of Coitus and Number of Sexual Partners

Concern about what is a "normal" or average number of sexual contacts often surfaces in our sexuality classes. Most of these questions involve sexual intercourse. In addition to frequency, the number of sexual partners people have has become a mounting concern with the threat of AIDS as well as other sexually transmitted diseases.

The average American couple has coitus about one to three times a week in their early 20s, with the frequency declining to about once a week or less for those aged 45 and older (Blumstein & Schwartz, 1983; Hunt, 1974; Smith, 1991). These figures give us rough estimates for the total sample but do not give us a true notion of the variability in sexual activity among Americans. For example, 22 percent of Smith's (1991) national sample reported total abstinence in the past year, whereas Billy, Tanfer, Grady, and Klepinger (1993) found a few men in their national sample who reported having vaginal intercourse more than 22 times a week! Thus there is no "gold standard" against which we can measure the "appropriate" frequency of sexual activity. There is simply a great deal of variability among couples and for a given couple over different time periods. As we discuss in the next chapter, however, lack of, or very little, sexual activity is often associated with relationships characterized by friction and strain.

Regarding the number of sexual partners, Smith (1991) found an average of seven partners since age 18, although men reported considerably more partners (12) than did women (three), which he believed stemmed from men overreporting and women underreporting. When the 12 to 18 months prior to data collection were considered, the number of partners was a little over one. As might be expected from the decrease in frequency of sexual activity with age, the number of sexual partners also declined with age. As with frequency of sexual activity, there is a great deal of variability among individuals in their reported number of sexual partners. In the Laumann et al. (1994) and Billy et al. (1993) studies, 17 percent and 23 percent, respectively, of the men had twenty or more coital partners, and a few men reported more than nine hundred lifetime coital sex partners. Only 3 percent of women reported 21 or more partners since age 18 (Laumann et al., 1994). No consistent ethnic or social differences emerged in self-reported frequency of sex or numbers of sexual partners (Billy et al., 1993; Laumann et al., 1994; Smith, 1991).

Sexual Satisfaction and Enjoyment

The preceding descriptions of the various types of sexual stimulation are by no means exhaustive. The possibilities are limited only by imagination, body build, energy level, and agility. Some couples may find a particular position or stimulation technique so satisfying that they have little interest in exploring others. If they do not find their pattern monotonous, there is no compelling reason that they should experiment. Partners who feel that their sexual interaction has become automatic may be able to add zest and intensity to their lovemaking by trying alternative ways of giving pleasure to each other.

It is important to keep in mind that the physical expression of our sexuality takes place in the context of daily life. Sexual intimacy can provide a break from a demanding schedule in the form of experiences ranging from simple physical release to the communication of intensely felt affection and connection. Perhaps the ultimate measure of sexual satisfaction is the quality of the period of time following orgasm. At its best, it is a time of mutual relaxation and shared intimacy, a time when we may be more open than usual to new ideas and suggestions. This aftermath can provide an opportunity to talk about and reflect on matters not directly related to mundane daily tasks. At other times, we may feel energized by sexual interaction, ready to return to work or other activities with renewed vigor.

Sexual intimacy, then, can have different purposes. Release from tension, the sense of intense union, or the expression of affection can be part of any sexual contact that is more than just momentary. Sometimes a source of ecstasy, sometimes mediocre or rather disappointing, the experience of sexual contact can fluctuate a great deal. If we accept these variations and do not focus on any one episode as the main determinant of the quality of our sexuality, we can enjoy the diversity.

Simultaneous Orgasm: A Note

In the section on masturbation we noted that most men slow down or stop manual stimulation of the penis during orgasm. In contrast, women generally prefer continued stimulation of the clitoris or mons during orgasm. This difference is consistent with the observation that most men attempt deep vaginal penetration with little further thrusting at the onset of ejaculation during coitus, whereas the typical woman prefers continued male thrusting during her orgasm (Masters & Johnson, 1966). Because of this difference in the typical response styles of men and women, simultaneous orgasm can be difficult to obtain. In a study of female nurses, only 17 percent of the sample experienced orgasm at about the same time as their partner (Darling et al., 1991). Because women can continue coitus indefinitely before and/or after orgasm, whereas men's erections generally subside after ejaculation, an approach to orgasm that emphasizes "ladies first" may be most satisfying for many couples. For example, if a woman finds it easier to have an orgasm in the woman-above position, a couple can employ this position until the woman has orgasm. At that point, the couple can move into whatever position the man finds most stimulating.

REALITY or MYTH ? 5

Another kind of satisfying experience may provide a useful model for many couples: a massage. Having your body massaged allows another person to give you pleasure, while you simply relax and let your feelings emerge. It can also be rewarding to take the active role, arousing great pleasure in your partner. Regardless of what positions and techniques couples use in their sexual interaction, their bodies tend to respond in one of just a few relatively predictable patterns of physical response.

Preoccupation with the attempt to achieve simultaneous orgasm can detract from what might otherwise be a pleasurable experience. An exception to this generalization is when a couple is "swept away" with the emotional intensity of the interaction, a typical situation during the early stages of a sexual relationship or during the periodic renewal of intensely passionate feelings that can occur in long-term relationships. These conditions can lead to simultaneous orgasm that has little to do with sexual technique.

ISSUES TO CONSIDER

How would you deal with a partner who insisted on having simultaneous orgasm in all your sexual encounters?

SEXUAL RESPONSES

Prior to Masters and Johnson's (1966) work, men and women were believed to be different in their sexual responses. Common "wisdom" held that men had easily triggered sexual drives, whereas women's responses needed careful nurturing through long periods of courtship and foreplay. In addition, men were thought to reach orgasm readily and quickly. In contrast, orgasm for women was perceived by those who believed in its existence as a highly elusive response. Furthermore, it was thought that men could ejaculate and that women could not. The extent to which these perceived differences resulted from differences in cultural training rather than (or in addition to) differences in physiology was seldom considered.

In focusing on biological capacities, Masters and Johnson emphasized the similarities, rather than the differences, in the sexual responses of men and women. They found that most of the bodily changes that occurred in the sexual response cycles of both men and women were attributable to two major alterations in the genital organs: vasocongestion and muscle tension.

Vasocongestion, or blood engorgement, is the process by which various parts of the body (primarily the genitals and breasts) become filled with blood during sexual excitement. **Muscle tension** refers to involuntary contractions of muscles during sexual response. Masters and Johnson's physiological recordings of the contractions of orgasm showed that one occurred every eight-tenths of a second in males—precisely the same interval as was recorded between the orgasmic contractions in females.

Masters and Johnson concluded that there were only two major differences between the sexual responses of men and women. First, men could ejaculate and women could not. Second, women were capable of having a series of orgasms within a short period of time, and men were not. More recent research has suggested that even these differences may not be absolute. As you will see later, some men are capable of multiple orgasms, and some women appear to ejaculate a fluid at orgasm.

We turn now to the phases of the sexual response cycle (desire, excitement, orgasm) as described by Kaplan (1974, 1979) and Masters and Johnson (1966). It is important to remember that these are descriptions of physiological changes, with little attention paid to the psychological states that accompany them.

vasocongestion Engorgement with blood.

muscle tension Involuntary contractions of muscles during sexual response.

Sexual Desire

Helen Singer Kaplan (1974, 1979) was one of the first sexual scientists who emphasized the importance of sexual desire in the sexual response cycle (SRC). She believed that desire was interconnected with the other phases of sexual response but also separate in terms of the biological systems that underlie them. Most of us have a pretty good understanding of the subjective experience of sexual desire.

Distinguishing sexual desire as a separate phase in the SRC has important implications for sexual dysfunctions and their treatment, discussed in Chapter 6. For now, we will simply let Kaplan (1979, p. 10) describe the desire phase of sexual response:

Sexual desire or libido is experienced as specific sensations which move the individual to seek out, or become receptive to, sexual experiences. These sensations are produced by the physical activation of a specific neural system in the brain. When this system is active a person is "horny"; he may feel genital sensations or he may feel vaguely sexy, interested in sex, open to sex, or even just restless. These sensations cease after sexual gratification, i.e., orgasm.

Excitement/Plateau

A summary of responses during the SRC is presented in "Highlight: Physical Reactions During Sexual Response," on page 127. In the excitement phase, the penis begins to become erect. This swelling is due entirely to vasocongestion—the filling of the three spongy columns of the penis (the two corpora cavernosa and the corpus spongiosum) with blood. Arteries carrying blood into the penis dilate, allowing blood to engorge the spongy tissues.

During the plateau phase, the erection of the penis becomes more stable; that is, a man is less likely to lose his erection in the face of such distractions as ringing phones or nonerotic thoughts. This stability may be related to a further engorgement of the penis with blood, which has the effect of constricting the three veins that carry blood out of the penis. In addition to swelling the penis, vasocongestion affects the testes, increasing their size by about 50 percent.

Erotic excitement produces vasocongestion in the female genitals, as in the male genitals. Whereas engorgement of the penis results in erection, engorgement of the inner lips, clitoris, and vaginal walls with blood produces a slippery, clear fluid—vaginal lubrication—on the vaginal walls. As the vaginal walls swell with blood, the inner two-thirds of the vagina widens and lengthens in what is called the tenting effect (see Figure 5.11). The clitoris becomes congested with blood and increases in diameter. It remains enlarged during the plateau and orgasm phases. The outer lips, which touch when the woman is not aroused, now flatten and move apart to leave the swollen inner lips, clitoris, and vaginal entrance exposed.

The enlarged clitoris retracts beneath the clitoral hood during the plateau phase and cannot be seen again until after orgasm. However, it can continue to receive stimulation through manual or oral movements on the clitoral hood. Thrusting of the penis in the vagina can also stimulate the clitoris, as pressure of the penis on the inner lips pulls the clitoral hood back and forth.

**Figure 5.11
Muscular Contractions
of Female Orgasm**

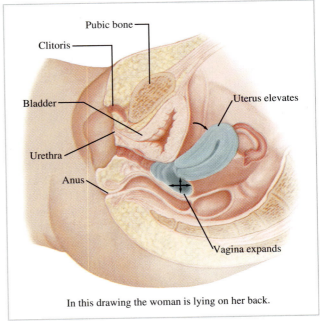

Pubic bone

Clitoris

Bladder

Urethra

Anus

Uterus elevates

Vagina expands

In this drawing the woman is lying on her back.

Orgasm

The orgasm phase actually occurs in two stages for the male, both of which involve contractions of the muscles associated with the internal sex organs. The first stage, **emission,** takes two or three seconds. During emission, sperm and fluid are expelled from the vas deferens, seminal vesicles, and prostate gland into the base of the urethra near the prostate. As seminal fluid collects there and the urethra expands, men have the feeling that they are about to ejaculate ("ejaculatory inevitability"), but semen is not yet expelled from the urethra.

The second stage, **ejaculation,** involves expulsion of the semen by means of muscle contractions. There is also a contraction of the neck of the bladder, which prevents semen from flowing into the bladder. The semen is propelled by the muscular contractions of orgasm into the portion of the urethra within the penis and then expelled from the urethral opening in the glans (see Figure 5.12). These orgasmic contractions

emission Propulsion of sperm and fluid to the base of the urethra during orgasm.

ejaculation Expulsion of seminal fluid out of the urethra during orgasm.

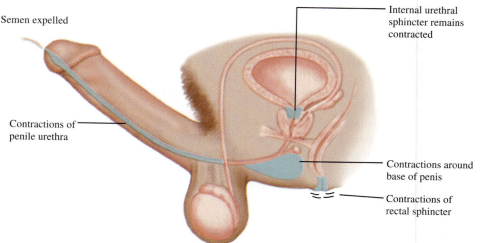

Semen expelled

Internal urethral
sphincter remains
contracted

Contractions of
penile urethra

Contractions around
base of penis

Contractions of
rectal sphincter

Figure 5.12
Ejaculation Stage of Male Orgasm

occur four or five times, at intervals of eight-tenths of a second. Simultaneously, muscles within the anus contract because both sets of muscles share a common nerve supply.

As a woman approaches orgasm, the outer third of the vagina becomes constricted through blood engorgement. This constriction forms a narrow tube. The muscular contractions associated with orgasm occur in the vagina, uterus, and fallopian tubes (refer to Figure 5.11). Most women, however, subjectively experience the contractions in the outer third of the vagina as the most intense. Muscular contractions often occur in many other parts of the body as well.

Resolution

refractory period Period
of time following ejaculation
during which nerves cannot
respond to further stimulation.

After ejaculation the resolution phase begins in the male. This process restores the genital organs and tissues to their pre-excitement phase as the blood that filled the penis flows back into the veins. After this phase most men experience a **refractory period**— that is, a period of time following ejaculation during which nerves cannot respond to further stimulation. Most of us have experienced refractory periods in other contexts. For example, when a flashbulb is used to take our picture, most of us are momentarily blinded because the nerves in our eyes are temporarily unable to respond to the stimulation of light. Similarly, for many men further erotic stimulation for a period of time following ejaculation provokes no response and may even be unpleasant. Masters and Johnson (1966) described the male refractory period as lasting between 30 and 90 minutes. However, some men are not able to become erect again for a considerably longer interval. Other men can have multiple orgasms; that is, they do not experience the typical refractory period.

During the resolution phase, the female body returns to its pre-excitement state. With continued stimulation, however, some women have additional orgasms with little intervening time; that is, females do not have the refractory period characteristic of males. In about 30 percent to 40 percent of men and women, a sweating reaction occurs during resolution.

Physical Reactions During Sexual Response

Excitement/Plateau

Engorgement of penis with blood

Increase in length and diameter of penis

Engorgement of vaginal walls and inner lips with blood

Onset of vaginal lubrication

Flattening of outer lips and their retraction from the vaginal entrance

Lengthening and expansion of inner two-thirds of the vagina

Initial slight swelling of the clitoris followed by retraction of the clitoris until it is completely covered by the clitoral hood and decreases about 50 percent in length

Swelling, elevation, and rotation of testes

Erection of nipples (less common among males)

Size increase of female breasts

Appearance of a "sex flush," a rosy, measles-like rash over the chest, neck, face, shoulders, arms, and thighs

Increase in heart rate and blood pressure

Increase in muscle tension

Secretion of fluid by Cowper's glands

Increase in respiration

Orgasm

Contractions beginning as far back as the testes and continuing through the epididymis, vas deferens, seminal vesicles, prostate gland, urethra, and penis

Beginning of strong muscle contractions in outer third of vagina, with first contractions lasting for 2 to 4 seconds and later contractions lasting from 3 to 15 seconds, occurring at 0.8-second intervals

Contraction of uterus

Occurrence of three or four powerful ejaculatory contractions at 0.8-second intervals, followed by two to four slower contractions of the anal sphincter

Slight expansion of inner two-thirds of the vagina

Testes at their maximum elevation

Sex flush at its peak

Heart rate up to 160–180 beats a minute

Respiration up to 40 breaths a minute

General loss of voluntary muscle or motor control

Note: During the resolution phase, the body returns to its pre-excitement state.

Patterns of Sexual Response

Major differences in the patterns of sexual response among males mainly involve the length of various phases rather than the intensity of response. In contrast, among females, Masters and Johnson (1966) concluded that there is a wide range of intensity. Also, a particular woman may respond with different patterns at various times, depending on her past experiences and the effectiveness of stimulation.

Masters and Johnson observed three typical patterns of sexual response in their female volunteers. In pattern A, a female proceeds through the entire response cycle into one or more orgasms without interruption. This pattern is the typical multiple-orgasm response, with orgasms occurring far enough apart that they are distinguishable from one another. In pattern B, there is a gradual increase in arousal and a fluctuating plateau phase, with small surges toward orgasm followed by a relatively slow return to the physiological state of prearousal. This pattern seems to occur in young or sexually inexperienced women, who may not be sure that they have experienced orgasm. In pattern C, there is a single orgasm of extreme intensity with little time spent in the plateau phase. Women report feelings of great release and gratification with this pattern.

Despite gender differences at the physiological level, the subjective feelings of men and women during intense sexual response may be similar (see "Highlight: Whose Is It?" on page 128).

HIGHLIGHT

Whose Is It?

Some of the following descriptions of excitement and orgasm were written by women and some by men (Vance & Wagner, 1976). Can you tell the gender of the author of each description? For the answers, see page 129.

1. I think that there are a variety of orgasms that I experience. I have noted a shallow "orgasm" which consists of a brief period that is characterized by an urge to thrust but which passes quickly. On the other hand, I have also experienced what I call a hard climax, characterized by a mounting, building tension and strong thrusting movements which increase in strength and frequency until the tension is relieved.

2. It is a very pleasurable sensation. All my tensions have really built to a peak and are suddenly released. It feels like a great upheaval; like all of the organs in the stomach area have turned over. It is extremely pleasurable.

3. Tension builds to an extremely high level—muscles are tense, etc. There is a sudden expanding feeling in the pelvis and muscle spasms throughout the body followed by release of tension. Muscles relax and consciousness returns.

4. Orgasm gives me a feeling of unobstructed intensity of satisfaction. Accompanied with the emotional feeling and love one has for another, the reality of the sex drive, and our culturally conditioned status on sex, an orgasm is the only experience that sends my whole body and mind into a state of beautiful oblivion.

5. Physical tension and excitement climaxing and then a feeling of sighing, a release of tension-like feeling.

6. An orgasm is a very quick release of sexual tension which results in a kind of flash of pleasure.

Normal Variations

In examining the patterns of sexual response, we must remember that they represent the typical patterns that Masters and Johnson found in their volunteers. Some people are tempted to measure themselves against such patterns. If their own responses do not generally match one of these patterns, they may conclude that there is something wrong with them, ignoring the fact that there are variations from one person to the next and from one sexual episode to the next. There are two reasons that we may be tempted to place undue importance on such patterns in evaluating our own sexual responses.

First, until recently there was little research on sexual response. We had no authorities to provide us with information or bases for comparing our own feelings and responses to those of other people. Second, although we are encouraged to ask parents, friends, and teachers about a variety of matters, including facts pertaining to reproduction, a cultural taboo has prevailed against "comparing notes" or seeking information about sexual pleasure, a circumstance that may make us overly receptive to recent research and information on the topic. It is fascinating, for instance, that each of the volumes by Masters and Johnson (1966, 1970) has sold well, even though the writing is quite technical and thus difficult for the average person to understand.

These two factors—the absence of research on sexual response until recently and the taboo against sharing information with our relatives and friends—have conspired to make us overly vulnerable and insecure about our own sexual feelings and responses. In our eating habits, we do not generally worry that we sometimes enjoy wolfing down a hamburger but at other times love the ritual of a seven-course meal. Nor are we upset when we have no appetite for either potato chips or chateaubriand. We realize that what is important is whether we feel good while having a particular meal, not whether we conform to the average American's typical pattern of eating an average of seven hundred calories per meal in an average of 17.3 minutes. Yet we may become overly concerned about going from the sexual excitement phase through plateau to orgasm in the space of five minutes or less or responding slowly during sexual intimacy, lingering over each phase. At times like this, we should remember that the measure of sexual health is not the extent to which we conform to some average pattern, but whether the process feels good and is satisfying to us and to our partners.

Orgasm consistently draws more attention, rightly or wrongly, than any other sexual response, both by the public and the sex-research community. In the following section, we present some of the current research on this human phenomenon.

ISSUES TO CONSIDER

How do you know your sexual life is "normal"? How could you find out?

VARIETIES OF ORGASM

Females show greater variability in their sexual response patterns than do males. It appears, however, that the personal or subjective experience of orgasm does not differ between men and women. In the previous "Highlight" we presented some descriptions of orgasm written by men and women who participated in Vance and Wagner's (1976) study. These researchers obtained 48 such descriptions. After removing obvious gender cues, they presented these descriptions to physicians, psychologists, and medical students and asked them to judge whether each had been written by a male or a female. The fact that these professionals could not accurately judge the samples suggests that the experience of orgasm is quite similar for females and males. How did you do? The first three quotes in the "Highlight" were written by women and the last three by men.

Female Orgasm: Different Types?

For decades psychoanalysts believed that adult women should respond orgasmically to penile thrusting in the vagina. They described women who obtained orgasm primarily from clitoral stimulation as being fixated at the phallic stage of childhood, as suffering from penis envy, and as having failed to develop "normal" adult female patterns of sexual response. It was in an atmosphere of general acceptance of that point of view that Masters and Johnson (1966) published one of their most influential findings. Specifically, they reported that for a woman the site of effective stimulation for orgasm is the clitoris, with orgasmic contractions then occurring in the vagina. Their conclusion helped deal the death blow to the idea that there was a clitoral orgasm that was distinct from a vaginal orgasm. Their physiological recordings of responses at the outer portion of the vagina indicated that the same orgasmic response occurred regardless of the site of stimulation.

Masters and Johnson did not focus on psychological reactions to orgasms or compare orgasms produced during coitus with those produced by clitoral stimulation alone. Other studies, however, have indicated that women do make subjective distinctions between masturbatory and coital orgasms (Bentler & Peeler, 1979; Singer & Singer, 1978). Women in one study described vaginally induced orgasms as "more internal," "fuller, but not stronger," and "more subtle" than orgasms resulting from clitoral stimulation (Butler, 1976).

Perhaps the most well-developed criticism of Masters and Johnson's work on orgasm came from Singer and Singer (1978). The latter took issue with the conclusion that all orgasms are physiologically the same regardless of the type or site of stimulation. The Singers favored a broader definition of orgasm that includes emotional satisfaction as well as physiological changes. Accordingly, they described three types of female orgasm.

The first type is the vulval orgasm, which can be induced by coital or noncoital stimulation and does not have a refractory period following it. This orgasm is the type measured by Masters and Johnson (1966). It is characterized by involuntary rhythmic contractions of the outer third of the vagina. In contrast, a uterine orgasm is characterized by a gasping type of breathing that culminates in involuntary breath-holding. The breath is explosively exhaled at orgasm, and the orgasm is followed by a feeling of relaxation and sexual satiation. This response seems to occur upon repeated deep stimulation involving penis-cervix contact that displaces the uterus and causes stimulation of the membrane lining the abdominal cavity. This type of orgasm is followed by a refractory period. The third type of orgasm, which combines elements of the other two types, is called a blended orgasm. It is felt as being deeper than a vulval orgasm and is characterized by both breath-holding and contractions of the orgasmic platform.

It is possible that orgasm resulting from clitoral stimulation corresponds to what Singer and Singer (1978) call vulval orgasm. The uterine orgasm described by the Singers may correspond to orgasm produced by vaginal-wall stimulation. Finally, the blended orgasm they describe may result from simultaneous stimulation of the clitoris and the vaginal wall. Researchers continue to study possible variations in female orgasm as well as the physical response systems associated with them. In addition to watching for the results of their findings, you may want to note interpretations of the significance of different kinds of orgasms. We hope that there will be no return to the practice of attributing moral and emotional superiority to any particular orgasmic pattern.

Research on Female Ejaculation

Some women have reported that stimulation of the anterior wall of the vagina produces enlargement of the Gräfenberg spot at the base of the bladder. A number of these women described expulsion of a clear to milky-white fluid from the urethra at orgasm (Belzer, 1981).

At this time there is no basis for accurately estimating the incidence of female ejaculation. Nor do we know the source of the ejaculate, although some researchers have suggested the presence of a rudimentary prostate gland at the base of the bladder (Sevely & Bennett, 1978; Zaviacic & Whipple, 1993). Considerably more investigation is needed before researchers can reach firm conclusions about the function of female ejaculation.

The Consistency of Female Orgasm

Although most women are capable of experiencing orgasm, some women do so inconsistently, and others do not have orgasms at all. Kinsey et al. (1953) reported that 10 percent of married American women and 30 percent of sexually active unmarried women had never experienced orgasm.

In the Laumann et al. (1994) study, only 29 percent of the women reported that they always had an orgasm during sexual activity with a partner. Nevertheless, 40 percent claimed to be extremely physically satisfied with their partner, and 39 percent were extremely emotionally satisfied with their partner. It should be noted that some women who did not experience orgasm nevertheless reported their sexual activity as quite pleasurable.

Many women who do not experience orgasm consistently, however, may feel pressured to meet their partner's and society's expectations that people should have at least one orgasm during each sexual encounter. Some pretend to have orgasms in their desire to please their partners. In a sample of 805 professional nurses, 58 percent reported that they had pretended at some point to have orgasm during sexual intercourse (Darling & Davidson, 1986). In a study of more than two hundred college women, about one-quarter had not yet experienced intercourse (Wiederman, 1997). Of those women who had had coitus, slightly more than one-half reported having pretended having orgasm. How do you think the pretenders differed from the nonpretenders? It may surprise you to learn that compared to the nonpretenders, the pretenders had more liberal sexual attitudes, higher sexual esteem, began coitus at a younger age (just under age 16 versus just over 16½), and perceived themselves to be more facially attractive! The pretenders also reported a greater number of intercourse and oral sex partners.

Although some women may attempt to soothe the egos of their partners by pretending orgasm, they may actually be providing misleading feedback to their partners. This sexual deception could lead the partner into thinking everything is going well in the couple's lovemaking rather than looking for other approaches that might be more satisfying to the woman.

The Consistency of Male Orgasm

The Kinsey group (1948) did not present detailed data on the consistency of male orgasm because they assumed that married men had orgasms almost 100 percent of the time. However, 25 percent of men in the Laumann et al. (1994) study indicated that they did not always have an orgasm during sexual activity with their partner. Men as well as women can pretend orgasm, although there has been no systematic research on men faking orgasm.

Multiple Orgasms in Females

One of the most frequently quoted findings of Masters and Johnson (1966) is their report of multiorgasmic responses among some of their female volunteers. More recently, Darling, Davidson, and Jennings's (1991) survey of nurses indicated that almost 43 percent usually experienced multiple orgasms during some form of sexual activity. However, it was Masters and Johnson's (1966) report of physiological recordings of multiple orgasm in women that prompted contemporary interest in the phenomenon. Their research indicated that most women are capable of having multiple orgasms if they are adequately stimulated.

Some writers have interpreted women's capacity for multiple orgasm as an indication that women are "more sexual" than men (Sherfey, 1972). Others have assumed that multiorgasmic women are sexually superior to women who have one orgasm or who do not have orgasms at all. Most of this reasoning could be dismissed as downright silly if it did not adversely affect the sexual lives of many women and men. The multiple-orgasm response is not the zenith of sexual activity. Many women who are able to have multiple orgasms often prefer to experience just one intense uterine orgasm (Singer & Singer, 1978). Some women enjoy alternating their sexual patterns, so that they experience multiple orgasms some of the time and one orgasm at other times. Sometimes they may experience no orgasm at all during lovemaking.

Multiple Orgasms in Males

Masters and Johnson (1966) found a few men below age 30 who experienced repeated orgasm and ejaculation without the refractory period that is characteristic of most men. These individuals were called multiejaculatory because the repeated orgasms were each accompanied by ejaculation.

More recently there is evidence that some men can experience two or more orgasms before or following ejaculation (Dunn & Trost, 1989; Robbins & Jensen, 1978).

These men reported having an average of 2 to 16 orgasms per sexual encounter, and one of the individuals in Robbins and Jensen's study reported as many as 30 orgasms in a one-hour period (confirmed by physiological measures). After an orgasm the degree of penile engorgement decreased, but his penis remained fully erect, and the resolution phase did not occur.

Some of the men in the Dunn and Trost (1989) study thought that they had always been multiorgasmic and that their experience was "natural," whereas others reported learning to inhibit or control ejaculation until the final orgasm. It is widely believed that men are capable of only a single orgasm and ejaculation. As men become more aware of the possibility of multiple orgasm, it will be interesting to see whether the percentage of men experiencing it, which is presumably small, increases. For those who are interested, William Hartman and Marilyn Fithian's (1984) book *Any Man Can* provides detailed instructions for learning how to have multiple orgasms.

The techniques that elicit sexual responses obviously do not develop in a social vacuum. Our personal histories and the social situations in which we interact are strongly related to our patterns of sexual arousal. In Chapter 6 we examine some ways in which learning and feelings, as well as medical problems, may interfere with sexual arousal and response.

Summary of major points

1. Autoeroticism and sexual learning.

Self-stimulation can provide useful training for sexual interaction with a partner, as well as being pleasurable in its own right. Women show more variety in the kinds of stimulation they use during masturbation than do men. Women tend to prefer continued self-stimulation during orgasm, whereas men usually stop stimulation or move their hands more slowly as they begin to have an orgasm.

2. Mutual sexual stimulation.

Almost any part of the body can be employed in stimulating another person, but the hands, mouth, genitals, and, to a lesser extent, the anus generally are used most often during sexual interaction. A couple can engage in coitus in a variety of positions, each of which provides somewhat different possibilities for stimulation. The choice of positions and stimulation techniques during sexual interaction should be guided by personal preference and pleasure; no one way is necessarily superior or inferior to any other.

3. Response of the body during sexual stimulation.

The sexual response cycle includes desire, excitement, and orgasm. Desire involves awareness of wanting sexual stimulation. During excitement, vasocongestion produces erection and vaginal lubrication accompanied by mounting muscle tension. Orgasm involves spasm contractions and tension reduction and is followed by resolution—a return to the pre-excitement state.

4. Varieties of orgasmic experience in women.

Recent evidence indicates that women are capable of having diverse orgasmic experiences, depending on the site of stimulation. Both clitoral stimulation and deep pressure on the vaginal walls can produce intense pleasure for women. Preliminary data suggest that some women ejaculate fluid from the urethra. The range of responses to sexual stimulation from one woman to the next is quite large, and individual women respond differently from one sexual encounter to the next. Some women rarely have an orgasm, others have a series of orgasms during sexual stimulation, and still others experience a single, intense orgasmic release.

5. Varieties of orgasmic experience in men.

Compared with women, men appear to show fewer individual differences in response to sexual stimulation. In general, sexual contact leads quite reliably to a single orgasm, followed by a refractory period during which the nerves do not respond to further stimulation. A few men, however, have trained themselves to have multiple orgasms by preventing full ejaculation until the final time they have orgasm in a particular sexual encounter.

CHECK YOUR KNOWLEDGE

1. Studies of sexual behavior have established that most couples (a) find it difficult to have simultaneous orgasm, (b) find the quest for simultaneous orgasm deeply satisfying even if they rarely achieve it, (c) experience simultaneous orgasm with increasing frequency as their relationship develops, (d) have simultaneous orgasm with decreasing frequency as a result of aging. **(p. 123)**

2. During the excitement phase, (a) women vaginally lubricate and men ejaculate, (b) the clitoris expands in diameter and the penis increases in length and diameter, (c) the heart rate remains stable in both genders, (d) muscular tension increases in men and decreases in women. **(pp. 125, 127)**

3. Which of the following is most likely true? (a) Males show greater variability in sexual response than do females; (b) the personal or subjective experience of orgasm does not differ between men and women; (c) anal sex is almost nonexistent among heterosexuals since the advent of AIDS; (d) White men report engaging in anal sex more frequently than do men from other ethnic groups. **(pp. 127–128)**

4. Research by Masters and Johnson established that (a) stimulation of the Gräfenberg spot produces female ejaculation, (b) the physiological responses during orgasm produced by vaginal stimulation do not differ from those produced by clitoral stimulation, (c) primate females do not experience orgasm, (d) vaginal stimulation is the most effective way of triggering female orgasm. **(p. 129)**

5. Multiple orgasm is apparently (a) possible for both men and women, (b) impossible for men but possible for women, (c) generally regarded as the peak of sexual experience for all women capable of experiencing it, (d) a myth. **(pp. 131–132)**

6. Deep kissing is (a) a universal human behavior, (b) unknown in the United States before the Great Depression of the 1930s, (c) relatively uncommon across most cultures, (d) a sign of friendship among most Inuit groups. **(p. 113)**

7. The coital position that is likely to be most comfortable for people who are overweight or women who are in advanced stages of pregnancy is (a) man-above, face-to-face; (b) woman-above, face-to-face; (c) face-to-face, side-by-side; (d) man-above, rear entry. **(p. 119)**

8. Vaginal lubrication during sexual excitement is caused by (a) vasocongestion of the vaginal walls, (b) secretions of the Bartholin's glands, (c) contractions of the outer third of the vagina, (d) stimulation of the Gräfenberg spot. **(p. 125)**

6

SEXUAL DYSFUNCTION AND THERAPY

SEXUAL DYSFUNCTION: CONTRIBUTING FACTORS

Biological Factors

Psychosocial Factors

Health: Disorders, Diseases, and Other Factors That Can Affect Sexual Functioning

Health: Excessive Sexual Desire

TYPES OF SEXUAL DYSFUNCTION

Sexual Desire Disorders

Sexual Arousal Disorders

Orgasm Disorders

Sexual Pain Disorders

SEX THERAPY

Masters and Johnson's Approach

Kaplan's Approach

Treatment of Sexual Dysfunctions

Health: A Treatment Program for Orgasmically Inhibited Women

Qualifications and Ethics of Therapists

SUMMARY OF MAJOR POINTS

CHECK YOUR KNOWLEDGE

REALITY or MYTH ?

1 Hypoactive sexual desire is caused by abnormally low levels of estrogen.

2 Nymphomania is the most common female sexual dysfunction.

3 Premature ejaculation refers to ejaculation before the man wants it to occur.

4 Masters and Johnson developed the most successful approach to sex therapy.

5 In sex therapy one therapist (of either gender) working alone is as effective as two (a man and a woman) working together.

6 Before sex therapists advertise their services, they must obtain licenses certifying their competence.

BOB and Elaine have been cuddling on the couch, drinking wine, and watching the late movie on television. Elaine starts fondling Bob's penis, but it does not get erect, although Bob wants to have intercourse. Across town Sally and Don returned from the ballgame more than an hour ago and immediately took off their clothes and went to bed. They have been kissing and caressing pretty much steadily since then, but Sally's vagina has remained dry. Meanwhile, next door their neighbors, Mary and Lisa, are both excited and wet, and Mary has come several times. Lisa wants badly to have an orgasm, too, but no matter what she and Mary do, she cannot quite come.

Does Bob have erectile dysfunction? Is Sally the victim of inhibited sexual excitement? What about Lisa—does she have orgasmic dysfunction? Yes, all three are sexually dysfunctional for the moment; that is, they are not responding sexually in the way that they want. Whether they would be diagnosed as having sexual dysfunctions would depend on the frequency of their inability to respond sexually and how they feel about it.

The diagnoses would also depend greatly on the beliefs of the particular clinicians whom they saw if they decided to seek help. Professionals do not always agree with one another on the sources of, and solutions to, sexual problems, as you will see. In this chapter we examine common dysfunctions and their treatments. We also consider the issue of sexual interaction between therapist and client and some other sources of controversy among therapists who treat sexual dysfunction.

SEXUAL DYSFUNCTION: CONTRIBUTING FACTORS

There was little systematic survey information on the frequency of sexual dysfunction in this country until the Laumann et al. (1994) study. In this research, respondents indicating that they had experienced a sexual problem in the past year varied from roughly 5 percent to 25 percent depending on the disorder, with the exception that about one–third of women reported lacking interest in sex for a period of several months or more (see Table 6.1, page 136).

Table 6.1 Estimates of Sexual Dysfunctions		
Dysfunctions	**National Probability Sample[a]**	**Clinical Samples[b]**
Sexual Dysfunctions of Men		
Climax too early	28%	15–46%
Anxiety about performance	17%	—
Lacked interest in sex	16%	32–60%
Unable to keep an erection	10%	36–53%
Unable to have orgasm	8%	3–8%
Sex not pleasurable	8%	—
Pain during sex	3%	—
Sexual Dysfunctions of Women		
Lacked interest in sex	33%	37–70%
Unable to have orgasm	24%	18–76%
Sex not pleasurable	21%	—
Had trouble lubricating	19%	14–62%
Pain during sex	14%	5–18%
Anxiety about performance	12%	—
Climax too early	10%	—

[a]Proportion reporting experience in the previous 12 months (Laumann et al., 1994).
[b]Proportion reporting problem in clinical settings (Spector & Carey, 1990).

Most factors that impair sexual functioning are classified as either biological or psychosocial in origin. Although we make use of this convenient division, it does not reflect the complex interactions of biological, psychological, and social factors that produce sexual dysfunctions—a fact that we discuss further at the end of this section.

Biological Factors

In general, any disease or surgery that affects the reflex centers in the spinal cord and the nerves that serve them can result in sexual impairment. Many of the drugs used to treat particular mental and physical conditions can reduce responsiveness. Raul Schiavi (1994) described a variety of medical conditions that can influence sexual functioning. See "Health: Disorders, Diseases, and Other Factors That Can Affect Sexual Functioning."

Psychosocial Factors

Many sexual difficulties result from psychosocial factors, but there is little consensus on the nature of these factors. Those professionals influenced by psychoanalytic theory look to critical childhood experiences to explain sexual dysfunction. The underlying assumption is that specific incidents in one's childhood exert a subconscious influence on one's adult behavior. In contrast, other therapists and researchers assume that the causes of sexual problems can be found in a couple's immediate situation. Communication difficulties, sexual misinformation, conflicted relationships, and

Health

Disorders, Diseases, and Other Factors That Can Affect Sexual Functioning

Neurological disorders affect the sex centers of the brain and the spinal cord structures that serve the genital reflexes. Head injuries, strokes, multiple sclerosis, tumors, and Parkinsonism are examples of such disorders.

Endocrine disorders affect the body's hormonal balance. Any problem that results in lowered testosterone levels may alter sexual response. Diabetes, thyroid disorders, and kidney disease are examples of endocrine disorders.

Cardiovascular disorders affect the circulatory system. Cardiac disease, hypertension, and atheroscle-rosis are some vascular disorders that can impair sexual functioning.

Debilitating illnesses, such as lung disease and advanced stages of cancer, produce general ill health that can reduce sexual responsiveness.

Drugs, such as tranquilizers, antipsychotics, and antidepressants, used to treat emotional problems can cause sexual dysfunction. Alcohol, heroin, and barbiturate abuse can have the same result. Drugs that are frequently prescribed for the treatment of high blood pressure may periodically cause sexual dysfunction.

faulty learning are some of the immediate factors seen as crucial in the development of dysfunctions.

Sexual dysfunctions can be related to both recent experiences *and* childhood events. Although we categorize factors related to dysfunction as either past or current, keep in mind that recent and remote factors often interact to produce sexual difficulties.

PAST EXPERIENCES AND SEXUAL DYSFUNCTIONS.

Our experiences with our bodies and with sexuality begin in infancy. Deprivation of physical contact and love can blunt our emotional growth and our potential for sexual expression (Hatfield, 1994). Although most of our early experiences take place within a family, the nature and quality of those experiences can also depend on the larger social context that encompasses a family. For example, some cultures are extremely restrictive about eroticism; others are relatively permissive. The restrictiveness of a culture is linked to the incidence of difficulties in a man's getting or maintaining an erection. In an examination of 30 preindustrial and industrializing countries, Welch and Kartub (1978) found that the more restrictive a society was regarding such behaviors as premarital, marital, and extramarital sex, the greater was the number of reported problems with erectile functioning.

In addition to the sexual restrictiveness of a specific culture and family background, traumatic childhood events have also been implicated in sexual dysfunction (Beitchman et al., 1992). Rape, parental discovery of sexual activity, and incestuous experiences are examples of events that can bring about a sexual dysfunction.

Many sexual problems originate in myths and misinformation that individuals are exposed to at a fairly young age. These mistaken ideas can lead to misguided or ineffective attempts at sexual interaction that leave the individual feeling depressed and incompetent. Several botched sexual experiences can result in the avoidance of future sexual contact.

The differences between the backgrounds of people with healthy sexual responses and those of people with sexual dysfunctions should not lead you to believe that being brought up in a sexually restrictive environment is sufficient by itself to cause sexual dysfunction. Many people with adequate sexual functioning have family and cultural backgrounds that are similar to those of people with sexual dysfunctions (Heiman,

ISSUES TO CONSIDER

Why do you think societies regulate sexuality?

Gladue, Roberts, & LoPiccolo, 1986). Factors such as the ones described in the next section are also related to the development of dysfunctions and may interact with the more remote factors that we have just discussed.

CURRENT SOURCES OF SEXUAL DYSFUNCTION.   The most frequent contributors to current sources of dysfunction are (a) anxiety, perhaps over sexual performance, and ideas that interfere with sexual arousal; (b) inadequate information about sexuality that leads to ineffective sexual behavior; (c) failures in communication; and (d) stress (Cranston-Cuebas & Barlow, 1990; Masters & Johnson, 1970; Morokoff & Gillilland, 1993). Anxiety and thoughts about sex can interact in complex ways (see "Health: Excessive Sexual Desire").

Anxiety.   Helen Singer Kaplan (1974) and William Masters and Virginia Johnson (1970) concluded that anxiety about sexual performance is the most important immediate cause of sexual dysfunction. Concerns about performance consist of an emotional component (performance anxiety) and a cognitive component (a person's evaluation of his or her sexual performance). Anxiety over sexual performance usually involves the fear of failure. After a person has experienced the inability to have or maintain an erection or vaginal lubrication, he or she may become obsessed with failing again. This fear of failure can start a vicious cycle in which the person does fail again because of fear.

spectating Evaluating one's own sexual performance rather than involving oneself in the sexual experience with one's partner.

Spectating refers to a person inspecting and monitoring his or her own sexual activity rather than becoming immersed in the sexual experience. The person becomes a spectator rather than a participant, monitoring his or her own behavior and the partner's response. A man may worry: "Is my erection firm enough?" "Is my partner being satisfied?" A woman may engage in the same sort of judgmental viewing: "Am I wet enough for him?" "Is my partner getting tired of rubbing my clitoris?" "Should I change the rhythm of my movement?" "Will I come?" People who become absorbed in such self-questioning cannot suspend distracting thoughts and lose themselves in the erotic experience. Such interruption of the unfolding of sexual feeling and autonomic functioning leads to problems with arousal and/or orgasm.

The relationship between anxiety and sexual dysfunction is not simple, however. In some circumstances anxiety appears to facilitate sexual response. In a series of carefully designed experiments, David Barlow and his colleagues (summarized in Cranston-Cuebas & Barlow, 1990) compared men who were functioning well sexually ("functional") to men who had sexual difficulties—in particular, inability to develop and maintain an erection ("dysfunctional"). These two groups responded very differently while watching erotic films. Anxiety produced by the threat of being given a painful electric shock often *increased* sexual response of functional men but *decreased* the sexual response of dysfunctional men.

Functional men and dysfunctional men react differently to their motivational states and use different cognitive processes to understand them. Dysfunctional men have an expectation that they must match some idealized image of sexual performance; fearing that they may fail, they feel anxiety. This anxiety leads them to become preoccupied with nonerotic thoughts—for example, "Am I losing my erection?" In addition, dysfunctional men experience this anxiety as negative arousal. Functional men perceive their increased arousal as sexual excitement.

This analysis of sexual dysfunction is promising, but it has been done primarily with men. It also does not tell us how these men developed different ways of perceiving emotional states or why they interpreted their arousal in different ways.

Misinformation.   Some couples who seek help for sexual dysfunctions reveal a lack of knowledge about their bodies and sexual functioning that leads to ineffective

Health

Excessive Sexual Desire

The client was a 26-year-old male who was referred for therapy by his parole officer. He was living in a halfway house after having been released from prison following conviction for automobile theft. While in prison he had been raped many times and had been involved in several stabbing incidents, one of which had led to another inmate's death.

His sexual behavior was problematic. Staff at the halfway house reported that he often masturbated in public and had been accused of exhibitionism. The homosexual prison rapes had traumatized him, and he felt his sexual behavior had changed drastically. He had had several sexual experiences with different women since his release from prison and was steadily dating a woman 15 years older than he was. All his sexual episodes involved rather long bouts of intercourse in which he had orgasm 10 or 15 times. He reported that the women all commented positively on his sexual prowess.

Closer questioning revealed that the client experienced little relief or relaxation after orgasm. He also claimed that he masturbated from 8 to 20 times a day. Whenever he began to feel tense, he would "jack off." The client had an obsessive-compulsive reaction. His short stature (five feet three inches) and the prison rapes had led to obsessive fears that he was not masculine and possibly gay. This fear created anxiety that he could reduce temporarily by compulsive sexual behavior, which reassured him. Without the ritual of sex, his anxieties would overwhelm him and drive him "crazy."

Source: Authors' files.

---

sexual behavior. They may not know where the clitoris is or may not be aware of its erotic potential. If ignorant of a woman's sexual response, a man may not engage in sufficient stimulation to arouse his partner. Because of her own socialization, the woman may be too naive or embarrassed to tell him what feels good. Thus she may be inadequately lubricated for intercourse and may consequently experience it as painful.

The abundance of sexual misinformation in our culture can also contribute to sexual problems. Men may succumb to the myth that they should always be ready to engage in genital sex with regularity, enthusiasm, and efficiency, regardless of their mood and the situation. When they experience temporary fluctuations in desire or when their sexual response is diminished by fatigue, they may react with great alarm and subsequently become obsessed with "failing" again. Women may succumb to the myth that they should be interested in sex only when their partners are or that they should reach orgasm only through stimulation of the vagina in intercourse—and then they wonder why they experience difficulties with orgasm.

Communication Difficulties. A substantial number of sexual problems could be resolved if people felt free to communicate with their sexual partners or friends about their sexual feelings. The notion that sex is something people do not and should not talk about is directly associated with sexual problems. This attitude assumes that we are mind readers and should know each other's sexual feelings. At an initial therapy session, one or both members of a sexually troubled couple often make such statements as, "Gee, I never knew you felt that way," or "I never tried to do that because I thought you wouldn't like it." Some of these couples might have saved themselves time and money if they had learned to communicate effectively by giving information about their sexual feelings and asking about their partner's feelings. Many people have difficulty telling their sex partner directly about their feelings and responses, but they must learn to do so if the other person is to find out whether he or she is providing pleasure. Talking about sex involves revealing our innermost private feelings, but

ISSUES TO CONSIDER

Why do you think sexual dysfunction occurs in our culture?

Figure 6.1
The Importance of Trust

taking this risk can lead to more intimate and satisfying sexual relationships. Such open communication can also develop a sense of trust.

Trust is central to any personal relationship, particularly one that involves sexuality. A couple's progression into intimate behavior can be a complicated ritual as each person tries to determine the other's intentions and trustworthiness (see Figure 6.1). Traditionally, the complications have often revolved around women's feelings of being used as sexual objects. However, being used is a concern for men as well. Uncertainty about commitment to a relationship, whether heterosexual or homosexual, can lead to mixed sexual feelings and behavior that fosters sexual problems. Fear of sexually transmitted diseases and concerns about birth control and pregnancy can also inhibit pleasurable sexual relations.

Sexual dysfunctions are often related to nonsexual problems that are not discussed openly in a relationship. Money worries, conflicts involving dominance, decision-making controversies, or problems in expressing affection are a few of the difficulties that can manifest as sexual problems. For instance, women who feel that their partners are not affectionate except when making love may express their resentment by not becoming aroused or orgasmic. Their partners then cannot have the satisfaction of bringing them sexual pleasure.

Many romantic relationships are as much about power and control as they are about love and sex. Some people feel that one partner dominates the relationship and makes most of the important decisions. Their resentment toward the partner may result in an inability to release themselves to the pleasure of sex because doing so would be seen as another sign of dependency. Similarly, they may make themselves sexually unavailable to demonstrate that they have the power to control sexual activity in the relationship. Thus the bed can become a battleground on which combatants vie for the upper hand in a relationship.

stress Physical, emotional, or mental strain or tension.

Stress.   The diagnosis of causes of sexual dysfunction as biological *or* psychosocial obscures the complex interactions between our minds and our bodies. Sexual dysfunctions are almost always the result of **stress** originating from biological and psychosocial sources. Whatever the cause(s), stress can disrupt sexual functioning, decrease testosterone and luteinizing hormone levels, and lower sexual drive (Morokoff & Gillilland, 1993).

Some diseases or psychological factors may be severe enough to disrupt sexual functioning directly. In other cases a physical illness may make an individual vulnerable to psychological factors, such as depression and anxiety, that result in sexual dysfunction. Schumacher and Lloyd (1981, p. 49) postulated the following relationship between stress and sexual dysfunction:

> *In the hierarchy of systems of the body, sexual function has a low status since it does not appear essential for the individual's life or health. Therefore when the body is under threat from physical and/or psychological stress, sexual functions may be sacrificed to foster the systems that are more important for survival or health.*

A severe emotional state such as clinical depression brought about by a psychosocial factor (rejection or loss of a job or partner, for example) can impair sexual functioning by affecting the nervous and endocrine systems (Morokoff & Gillilland, 1993). Thus biology and psychology are delicately intertwined, influencing each other in many ways. To arrive at a complete understanding of a sexual dysfunction, we must attempt to understand the relative contribution of these factors to the different types of sexual dysfunctions.

TYPES OF SEXUAL DYSFUNCTION

Psychosexual disorders were listed for the first time in 1980, in the third edition of the American Psychiatric Association's *Diagnostic and Statistical Manual DSM-III* (1980), a handbook used by almost all mental health professionals. The *DSM-IV* (American Psychiatric Association, 1994) classifies sexual dysfunctions as primary or secondary. A primary dysfunction occurs when an individual has never experienced one of the phases of the sexual response cycle. A secondary dysfunction refers to a situation in which a person has been able to respond in the past to one of the phases but is not responsive at the current time.

It is important to remember that many people do not fit neatly into any of the diagnostic categories we are about to describe. In one study almost half the patients seeking treatment had a sexual problem in more than one area. Thus in many cases, problems with desire, excitement, and orgasm overlap (Segraves & Segraves, 1991).

In addition, the classification of psychosexual disorders in the *DSM-IV* has led to the increasing medicalization of sexual problems, which allows individuals to avoid examining their own attitudes and experiences that could have contributed to their dysfunction. If the source of the problem is "medical," then people may not see the need to take responsibility for their problems. If the problem is a lack of desire, the medical diagnosis can be used as a rationale to continue avoiding sexual activity.

Sexual Desire Disorders

Deciding whether a given response should be considered a dysfunction is particularly problematic in the case of desire disorders, where the variable is the amount of sexual interest. What is a "normal" level of sexual desire? In our culture men are expected to want sex more frequently than are women. Thus gender-role expectations are related to our beliefs about what constitutes "normal" levels of sexual desire.

HYPOACTIVE SEXUAL DESIRE AND SEXUAL AVERSION.   The *DSM-IV* divides desire disorders into two categories: hypoactive sexual desire disorders and sexual aversion disorders. The first of these, **hypoactive sexual desire disorder,** is defined as deficient or absent sexual fantasies and desire for sexual activity with anyone. The judgment of deficiency or absence is made by the clinician, taking into account factors that affect sexual functioning such as age, sex, and the context of the person's life. The deficiency may be selective: A person may experience erection or lubrication and orgasm but derive little pleasure from the physical feelings. In other cases the individual's desire is at such a low ebb that he or she has no interest in self-stimulation or in participation in sexual interaction that might lead to arousal. For example, a young man whom we know told us about his strong romantic attraction to another man but said that he felt inhibited about trying to develop the

hypoactive sexual desire disorder Deficient or absent sexual fantasies and desire for sexual activity with anyone.

relationship because, although his feelings of love had previously been directed toward men, rather than women, he experienced very little desire for sexual interaction. Some people can be described as asexual; that is, they do not experience desire for any kind of sexual activity. This is not considered a dysfunction if the individual is satisfied with not engaging in sexual activity.

The sources of sexual desire disorders have not been well clarified. Most current knowledge of the causes of low sexual desire is based on clients who are seen in therapy and thus must be viewed with caution until more objective research has been conducted using nonclinical samples. With that caveat in mind, low sexual desire has been associated with such factors as anxiety, religious orthodoxy, depression, **habituation** to a sexual partner, fear of loss of control over sexual urges, sexual assault, medication side effects, marital conflict, and fear of closeness (Letourneau & O'Donohue, 1993; LoPiccolo & Friedman, 1988).

Comparisons of women experiencing inhibited sexual desire with women expressing normal sexual desire revealed no differences in psychological adjustment or hormonal levels (Letourneau & O'Donohue, 1993; Stuart, Hammond, & Pett, 1987). Women with inhibited sexual desire did report significantly greater dissatisfaction with their marital relationship than did other women. Depression may play a crucial role in hypoactive sexual desire; women with inhibited sexual desire reported twice as many depressive episodes as did women with normal sexual desire (Schreiner-Engel & Schiavi, 1986). Additional research is needed, however, to determine whether depression leads to low sexual desire, low desire produces depression, or other factors mediate this relationship.

In the general population 16 percent of men and 33 percent of women aged 18 to 59 (refer to Table 6.1) reported that they lacked interest in sex for a period of several months or more in the year before they were interviewed (Laumann et al., 1994). The suppression of sexual desire is, of course, not dysfunctional in and of itself. Most of us learn scripts to suppress sexual desire for inappropriate partners, such as parents, close relatives, and children, and in inappropriate situations.

Alcohol and marijuana may act to release suppressed sexual desire, but this release is usually only temporary. A person who experiences an intense sexual desire for someone after drinking alcohol or smoking marijuana may not feel the same way after the drug wears off—a situation colloquially called "beer goggles." Awakening in the morning with their inhibitions back, some people who have acted on the desires unleashed while they were "high" then wonder how they ever found the person lying next to them sexually desirable.

Sexual aversion disorder is a persistent aversion to almost all genital sexual contact with a partner. Whereas individuals displaying hypoactive sexual desire are often indifferent about sexual interaction, sexual aversion reflects fear, disgust, or anxiety about sexual contact with a partner. An individual with sexual aversion disorder may still engage in autosexual behaviors such as masturbation and fantasy, while avoiding interpersonal sexual behavior.

People with sexual aversion disorder tend to experience anxiety and sometimes hostility toward their partners. When they anticipate sex with their partners, their feelings of anxiety or hostility suppress any initial stirrings of erotic sensation. Eventually, they block sexual arousal at its earliest stage and avoid the anxiety associated with sexual expression. Childhood sexual abuse and adult rape have been found to be related to sexual aversion (Gold & Gold, 1993).

EXCESSIVE SEXUAL DESIRE.
Excessive sexual desire, which has also been called hyperactive desire, sexual compulsion, or sexual addiction, has received consid-

---

habituation A decrease in sexual arousal in response to repeated and/or long-term exposure to the same stimulus (e.g., a sexual partner of long duration).

REALITY or **MYTH** ? **l**

sexual aversion disorder Extreme dislike and avoidance of genital sexual contact with a partner.

erable publicity in the popular media. Despite this attention, clinicians and therapists seldom encounter individuals with excessive sexual desire. Although people with enormous sexual appetites are fairly common in erotic literature and films, **nymphomania** in women and **satyriasis** in men appear to be rarities in real life. Donald Symons (1979, p. 92) suggested that the "sexually insatiable woman is to be found primarily, if not exclusively, in the ideology of feminism, the hopes of boys and the fears of men."

Excessive sexual desire is often associated with paraphilias (see Chapter 15) and/or with an **obsessive-compulsive reaction,** such as the one described earlier in "Health: Excessive Sexual Desire," page 139. In obsessive-compulsive states, the individual becomes preoccupied with sexuality. Masturbation and/or sexual interaction with a partner may occur five or ten times a day. The sexual activity is used to reduce the anxiety and tension resulting from obsessive thoughts about sex or other aspects of the person's life.

Sexual Arousal Disorders

Some people feel deep sexual desire and want to make love with their partners but experience little or no physical response (erection or vaginal lubrication and swelling) to sexual stimulation. **Sexual arousal disorders** are diagnosed when there is recurrent or persistent failure by a woman to attain or maintain the lubrication and swelling response or by a man to attain erection during sexual activity. Such a diagnosis is made only when the clinician is sure that the difficulty does not stem from physical disorders or medication and when the amount of sexual stimulation provided should be adequate to produce vasocongestion. Sometimes failure to respond results from insufficient stimulation rather than from inhibition of excitement.

Sexual arousal disorders were formerly called frigidity in women and impotency in men. Both terms are degrading and sound more like complaints than clinical disorders. They suggest rigid and distant women and ineffectual and helpless men. We have known men who employ the term *frigid* to describe any woman who refuses to have sex with them. In contrast, the phrase *sexual arousal disorder* is descriptive without being demeaning.

It is important to realize that occasional nonresponsiveness during sexual interaction is common. Many men have experienced sexual arousal and a desire for interaction when they have had too much to drink, only to find that, although the mind was willing, the genitals were unresponsive. Women who smoke marijuana may also notice a diminishing of vaginal lubrication (along with a sense of dryness in the mouth and nose). Similarly, fatigue, stress, and minor irritations with one's partner can temporarily interfere with sexual response. Such occasional nonresponsiveness can become problematic if people fear that they may not be able to respond sexually in the future. This fear of failure can create anxiety about sexual performance, which can lead in turn to future problems in responding. If the individual instead accepts the fact that occasional inability to respond sexually is normal, dysfunctions are less likely to arise.

Women's reactions to an inability to respond to erotic stimulation show a much greater variation than do men's. Most men react to **erectile dysfunction** as if it were a disaster, whereas women's responses range from anxiety or distress to casual acceptance of the difficulty. To some extent, cultural expectations are responsible for these differences. In most cultures men are expected to be sexually active and to perform satisfactorily. Women are not generally subjected to the same performance pressures and in some cultures are not expected to be sexually responsive. In addition, differences in anatomy and physiology make it more difficult for men to cover up and compensate for a dysfunction. A limp penis is difficult to hide and to use in a sexual interaction,

nymphomania Excessive and uncontrollable sexual desire in women.

satyriasis (SAH-ter-RYE-uh-sis) Excessive and uncontrollable sexual desire in men.

obsessive-compulsive reaction Engaging in compulsive behaviors in reaction to persistent or obsessive thoughts.

sexual arousal disorders Failures to attain or maintain erection or vaginal lubrication and swelling despite adequate stimulation.

erectile dysfunction Recurrent and persistent inability to attain or maintain a firm erection despite adequate stimulation.

whereas a dry vagina is more easily hidden and, with the aid of a lubricant, can even accommodate sexual intercourse.

Erectile dysfunction is generally the most common complaint among men who seek sex therapy. In more representative samples, however, about 10 percent of men report experiencing erectile dysfunction (Laumann et al., 1994). Some men with erectile dysfunction never have more than a partial erection during sexual activity. Others become erect, only to lose firmness when they attempt to have intercourse. Some men have erection problems with one partner but not with another.

Ruling out medical difficulties as a major cause is easier with erectile dysfunction than with most other dysfunctions. During an average night a male will have three to five erections during the stage of sleep called rapid eye movement sleep, which is highly correlated with dreaming. If a procedure called the nocturnal penile tumescence test in a sophisticated sleep laboratory reveals that a male does not have these erections or that they are impaired, the source of his problem is likely to be physical. But simply asking men whether they have early-morning erections—the so-called "piss hard-on"—is just as predictive of biological impairment as are the fairly sophisticated and expensive biological measures. Men who report that they do not have morning erections usually have biological or medical problems (Gordon & Carey, 1995; Segraves, Segraves, & Schoenberg, 1987).

Most men who experience problems with erection after a period of normal responsiveness respond well to treatment. The prognosis is not so good for men who have never been able to attain or maintain an erection with a partner (Hawton, 1992).

priapism (PRE-uh-PIZ-um) Prolonged and painful erection without sexual desire.

A rare condition that seems to be the opposite condition of erectile dysfunction is **priapism,** or prolonged erection without sexual desire. This condition can result from damage to the valves in the corpus cavernosa that regulate the flow of blood, as well as from infection, tumors, cocaine and heroin use, and some medications. Untreated, it can lead to destruction of the spongy tissue of the penis from the coagulation of blood, resulting in permanent erectile dysfunction.

About 20 percent of women aged 18 to 59 in the general population reported trouble lubricating in the past year (Laumann et al., 1994). Often the problem stems from the combination of widespread ignorance in our culture regarding women's sexual anatomy and the socialization of women to attend more to others' needs than to their own. We consider the issue of women's difficulties with orgasm in the next section.

Orgasm Disorders

Some people have orgasms within minutes of sexual interaction. Others engage in sexual stimulation for an hour or more before having orgasm. And some people do not have orgasm at all. Nowhere is the problem of defining sexual dysfunction more evident. In fact, except in extreme cases involving orgasm within seconds or no orgasm at all, the main difficulty is a difference in the speed of the partners' responsiveness rather than any dysfunction.

The fact that one person responds quickly and his or her partner responds more slowly does not necessarily imply that either is dysfunctional. As noted in Chapter 5, orgasm need not and generally does not occur simultaneously for a couple. This implies not that there is no such thing as an orgasmic dysfunction or ejaculation problem, but that differences between two people are not necessarily problematic or indicative of sexual dysfunction.

 **? 3**

PREMATURE EJACULATION.   Perhaps the most useful definition of **premature ejaculation** is ejaculation before the man wants it to occur. Speed of ejaculation is related to age (older men have fewer problems with ejaculatory control than do younger men, particularly adolescents), sexual inexperience, and novelty of the sexual partner.

The diagnosis of premature ejaculation is not appropriate unless the speed of a man's ejaculation becomes a regular, unwanted aspect of a couple's sexual activity. Ejaculation is a reflex that is difficult to control once it has been activated. The key to learning control is to recognize those signals that occur just before ejaculation—an awareness that can be difficult for young, inexperienced men. Roughly 30 percent of men report that they ejaculate more rapidly than they would like. Some men who continue to have problems with premature ejaculation after they have become sexually experienced may be hypersensitive to penile arousal and predisposed to early ejaculation (Grenier & Byers, 1995; Strassberg, Mahoney, Schangaard, & Hale, 1990).

premature ejaculation
Ejaculation before the man wants it to occur.

INHIBITED MALE ORGASM. In clinical studies inhibited male orgasm (also known as retarded ejaculation or ejaculatory incompetence) accounts for about 3 to 8 percent of men seeking treatment, and this rarer form of sexual dysfunction has been found to occur in about 3 to 10 percent of men in nonclinical samples (Laumann et al., 1994; Spector & Carey, 1990; refer to Table 6.1). The inhibition of orgasm may include delayed ejaculation or a total inability to ejaculate despite adequate periods of sexual excitement. As with the other dysfunctions, a diagnosis of inhibited male orgasm is not made when the problem stems from medication or some physical disorder.

Interestingly, many men diagnosed as having inhibited ejaculation sustain erections far beyond the ordinary range during coitus, and their wives are often multiorgasmic (Apfelbaum, 1989). Many of these men say that they prefer masturbation over intercourse, even though they continue to produce an erect penis for coitus with their partner. It also appears that some men may condition themselves to patterns of stimulation and ejaculation that are different from the stimulation provided by coitus. Jay Mann (1977) reported examples of masturbation techniques that include stroking the urethral opening with a throat swab and striking the shaft of the penis forcefully with the heel of the hand. It is understandable that men accustomed to such stimulation might not be able to have orgasm during coitus.

Clinicians have identified various factors associated with inhibited orgasm. Religious orthodoxy, fear of creating a pregnancy, negative feelings toward the sexual partner, maternal dominance, hostility, aggression, and fears of abandonment have been related to the development of this condition (Dekker, 1993). Men who have lost the capacity to ejaculate after a period of normal functioning often report that a stressful event preceded the problem.

In a physical condition known as **retrograde ejaculation** the usual expulsion of ejaculate through the urethra is reversed. The neck of the bladder does not contract, allowing the semen to flow into the bladder rather than out through the urethral opening in the penis. The condition usually results from surgery involving the genitourinary system or can be a side effect of some medications.

retrograde ejaculation A condition in which the base of the bladder does not contract during ejaculation, resulting in semen discharging into the man's bladder.

INHIBITED FEMALE ORGASM. Some women suffer from inhibited orgasm, a condition that prevents them from having orgasm despite adequate sexual stimulation. Difficulty with orgasm is one of the most common sexual concerns among women (refer to Table 6.1, page 136).

Women with this dysfunction may look forward to sex, and many experience high levels of sexual excitement with vaginal swelling and lubrication, but they are usually unable to have orgasm. Sexual arousal causes congestion of the pelvic blood vessels, and without orgasm, the congested blood remains for a while (analogous to the congestion in the testes associated with the absence of orgasmic release in highly aroused

ISSUES TO CONSIDER
If a woman does not consistently experience orgasm during sexual intercourse, should she seek sex therapy?

Table 6.2 Factors Inhibiting Women's Orgasm During Coitus	
Factors	**Percent**
Lack of foreplay	63.8
Fatigue	53.6
Preoccupation with nonsexual thoughts	45.5
Ejaculation too soon after intromission*	43.1
Conflicts between partners unrelated to intromission	34.6
Lack of interest or foreplay by partner	24.3
Lack of adequate vaginal lubrication	23.7
Lack of tenderness by partner	22.7
Lack of privacy for intromission	20.3
Overindulgence in alcohol	16.3
Desire to perform well after intromission	14.9
Difficulty with sexual arousal with partner	14.3
Painful sexual intercourse	12.0
Overeating	10.3

*Insertion of the penis into the vagina.

Source: Adapted from Darling et al.'s (1991) study of more than 700 nurses, p. 11.

men). Consistent arousal in women without orgasmic release can result in cramps, backache, irritation, and chafing.

Inhibited female orgasm may arise from guilt-producing thoughts. Kelly, Strassberg, and Kircher (1990) compared the sexual activities reported by orgasmic women with the sexual experiences of women who seldom had orgasms. The relatively nonorgasmic women described more negative attitudes toward masturbation, greater sex guilt and endorsement of sex myths, and more discomfort over communicating with their partners about sexual activities involving direct clitoral stimulation than did the women who experienced orgasm more consistently.

In keeping with the view that sexual dysfunction is a problem only when it persistently interferes with personal satisfaction, only those women who wish to have orgasm during coitus but cannot do so should seek treatment. It is debatable whether a dysfunction exists when a woman does not have orgasm during coitus but does climax during other kinds of stimulation—oral or manual stimulation, for example. Calling this pattern a sexual dysfunction and assuming that it requires sex therapy would dictate treatment for a large number of women, given that fewer than 50 percent of women consistently have orgasm during coitus, as discussed in Chapter 5. Darling et al. (1991) asked more than seven hundred nurses to report the factors they believed inhibited them from having orgasm during coitus, and the women's responses are shown in Table 6.2. Many therapists no longer consider a woman dysfunctional unless she suffers from primary orgasmic dysfunction and then only if she perceives it as a problem.

Sexual Pain Disorders

Sexual pain disorders include dyspareunia, which can be experienced by males and females, and vaginismus, which is exclusively a female complaint.

dyspareunia (DIS-par-OO-nee-ah) Recurrent and persistent pain associated with intercourse for a woman or man.

DYSPAREUNIA (PAINFUL INTERCOURSE).   **Dyspareunia** is the technical term for recurrent and persistent genital pain in either a male or female before, during, or after sexual intercourse. In women repeated dyspareunia is likely to result in vaginismus. The pain may be experienced as repeated, intense discomfort; momentary sharp sensations of varying intensity; or intermittent twinges and/or aching sensations. Dyspareunia in men appears to be much less common than painful intercourse in women (refer to Table 6.1). In these cases men may experience pain in the testes and/or the glans after ejaculation.

A wide variety of diseases and disorders of the external and internal sex organs and their surrounding structures can make intercourse painful for men and women. When physical disorders have been ruled out, psychological factors are assumed to be the cause. Arnold Lazarus (1989) reviewed 20 cases of female dyspareunia that he had treated and noted that almost half these women reported they were involved in unhappy relationships. Lazarus (1989, p. 91) speculated that after ruling out biological factors, he would not be surprised if "about half the women who suffer from dyspareunia are simply having sexual intercourse with the wrong man!"

VAGINISMUS.   **Vaginismus** refers to the involuntary spasm of the pelvic muscles surrounding the outer third of the vagina. Women who experience these spasms of the pubococcygeus (PC) and related muscles cannot have intercourse but may be quite capable of becoming sexually aroused, lubricating, and experiencing orgasm (Beck, 1993). The partner of a woman with this dysfunction who tries to have intercourse with her may have the sensation that his penis is hitting a rigid wall about an inch inside her vagina. Vaginismus rates have ranged from 12 to 17 percent of the women treated at sex-therapy clinics (Spector & Carey, 1990).

The vaginismus spasm can be triggered by anticipated penetration of the vagina. Vaginismus can be a source of dyspareunia, just as recurrent dyspareunia can precede vaginismus.

Among the events triggering vaginismus are rape, abortion, painful gynecological exams, pelvic inflammatory disease, and accidents producing vaginal injury. Other factors in women's histories related to vaginismus include vaginal surgery, problems stemming from episiotomies (surgical incision of the vagina in preparation for childbirth, see Chapter 7), vaginal infections, constipation, and pelvic congestion (Beck, 1993). Imagined rapes and general fears about men and vaginal penetration are also associated with vaginismus in some women. Regardless of the source of the difficulty, the contractions of vaginismus cannot be controlled by the woman. Attempts at vaginal penetration produce pain and anxiety, and the woman may try to avoid the possibility of such pain by avoiding sexual encounters.

Treatment ranges from the medical correction of physical problems to the use of psychotherapy, although it is sometimes difficult to determine the precise source(s) of the vaginismus (Beck, 1993; Hawton, 1992). Relaxation training and gradual insertion of successively bigger dilators into the vagina appear to be very effective in curing vaginismus. It is very important, however, that the woman (rather than a therapist or her partner) control the pace of treatment and the size of the dilator (LoPiccolo & Stock, 1986).

From the foregoing review of sexual dysfunctions, it should be clear that whatever the original source (biological and/or psychosocial) of a person's inability to respond as he or she wishes, the problem may be aggravated by the development of fear of failure in future sexual contacts. Such fear can produce self-fulfilling prophecies; that is, an intense focus on whether a person will respond adequately can reduce the likelihood that healthy sexual feelings and responses will unfold. No matter what particular treatment procedures sex therapists use, they should also identify and attempt to eliminate both clients' fears of sexual inadequacy and their tendency to engage in distracting and maladaptive thoughts during sexual intimacy.

vaginismus (VAH-jih-NIS-mus) Involuntary spasms of the pelvic muscles surrounding the outer third of the vagina.

SEX THERAPY

Until the 1960s the predominant approach to the treatment of sexual dysfunction was psychoanalysis. Sexual problems were viewed as symptoms of emotional conflict originating in childhood. The sexual difficulties or symptoms would persist, the analysts claimed, unless the conflict could be resolved and the personality of the individual restructured. The trouble with this approach is that the sexual difficulties may persist even after the client understands or gains insight into the origin of the problem. In addition, psychoanalytic therapy can be time-consuming and expensive.

Cognitive-behavioral psychologists have long taken issue with the psychoanalytic approach. They believe that a person can be emotionally healthy and still have sexual difficulties. Maladaptive sexual functioning is learned, they believe, and it can be unlearned without extensive probing into a client's past. Cognitive-behavioral approaches deal directly with sexual dysfunction by using techniques designed to overcome anxiety and to change self-defeating thought patterns. Behavioral therapies were first applied to sexual problems in the 1950s. The behavioral approach was later used by Masters and Johnson (1970). Although sexual dysfunctions have also been treated by a wide array of different psychotherapies, in this section we concentrate on the most commonly used techniques in sex therapy.

Masters and Johnson's Approach

The treatment program developed by Masters and Johnson is a two-week process. It is conducted by a man and a woman. Each partner in the couple seeking treatment is given a thorough medical examination and is interviewed by the therapist of the same gender. This interview is followed by an interview with the other therapist. All four people (the couple and the two therapists) then discuss treatment goals.

Masters and Johnson recommended the use of both a male and a female therapist to provide a "friend-in-court" for the client of the same gender. They stressed the treatment of specific symptoms rather than extensive psychotherapy aimed at determining potential underlying, unconscious sources of difficulty.

One of the most impressive aspects of Masters and Johnson's (1970) therapeutic approach with more than five hundred couples and individuals without partners was the overall "failure rate" of 18.9 percent. Put another way, they reported success in treating more than 80 percent of their clients who experienced various types of sexual dysfunction (Kolodny, 1981). Of the successful clients who could be found five years later (313 couples), only 5.1 percent reported recurrence of the dysfunctions for which they had obtained treatment. The therapeutic community was quite impressed with the success of Masters and Johnson's approach, and for years other therapists used modified versions of many of their methods.

 ? 4 Gradually, however, outcome statistics reported from clinical practice revealed overall improvement in only about two-thirds of the cases. The improvements obtained from controlled treatment studies have all been more modest than the proportions reported by Masters and Johnson (Grenier & Byers, 1995; Hawton, 1992). Do these findings indicate that the only reliable source of sex therapy is Masters and Johnson? Probably not. Instead, differences between the failure rates reported by Masters and Johnson and those reported by other sex therapists and researchers are probably due to a combination of factors other than Masters and Johnson's skill as therapists. Among these factors are methodological problems, increasing sexual knowledge among North Americans, and changing characteristics of clients.

Bernard Zilbergeld and Michael Evans (1980) noted that Masters and Johnson's research methodology was quite vague and that they may have been lenient in their judgments of what constituted a successful outcome. Another factor in Masters and Johnson's reported success rates may have been that 90 percent of their clients traveled to St. Louis from other parts of the country. Having left behind the routine and cares of their daily lives and making the commitment of time and money to improve their relationships, these couples were likely candidates for rekindling sexual interest and changing their sexual attitudes and behavior.

In addition, many of the problems experienced by Masters and Johnson's clients stemmed from misinformation and ignorance; people in the 1950s and 1960s did not have the easy access to information about sexuality that we have today. In fact, the seemingly endless stream of sex manuals now being published has provoked countless satires. Clients who simply lack information today may be "curing" themselves instead of seeking professional treatment. The caseloads of sex therapists today may include a greater proportion of clients with sexual difficulties resulting from deeply rooted emotional problems or from conflicts within their relationships. These kinds of sexual problems are often difficult to treat. This factor would, of course, result in lower success rates and higher relapse rates.

Another question that must be addressed in the evaluation of any sex therapy is whether the treatment yields sustained change over the years. There is very little available research on this subject. Summarizing what is known, Hawton (1992) reported that the successful short-term results of sex therapy for erectile dysfunction were maintained in the long term (one to six years), whereas those for premature ejaculation were less permanent. Men with low sexual desire had a fairly poor response to treatment in the short and long term. Sex therapy for vaginismus was highly effective in the short and long term, whereas the long-term results of treatment for low sexual desire in women were fairly poor. Interestingly, there was improvement in the way a number of clients *felt* about their sexuality, despite the fact that some had returned to pretreatment dysfunctions in sexual behavior. If these clients had received occasional clinical "booster" sessions over the years, their post-treatment improvement would perhaps have been maintained through preventive measures (McCarthy, 1993).

Kaplan's Approach

Helen Singer Kaplan developed an approach to sex therapy that combined some of the insights and techniques of psychoanalysis with behavioral methods. Her approach began at the "surface" level, or behavioral level, and probed more deeply into emotional conflicts only if necessary.

Many sexual difficulties stem from superficial causes. If a sexual difficulty is rooted in a lack of knowledge, for example, information and instruction may be all that are needed to treat it. If the trouble is of recent origin, a series of guided sexual tasks may be enough to change patterns of response. If deep-seated emotional problems exist, however, the therapist may use more analytic approaches to help clients obtain insight into the less conscious aspects of their personality. This last approach has been designated as psychosexual therapy to distinguish it from sex therapy.

 **?** **5**

Kaplan questioned Masters and Johnson's use of two therapists. Research, too, has indicated that the effectiveness of a treatment is not enhanced by the assignment of two therapists instead of one or by the employment of a therapist who is of the same gender as the dysfunctional member of the couple being treated (Hawton, 1992; LoPiccolo, Heiman, Hogan, & Roberts, 1985). The involvement of two trained professionals is, of course, also twice as expensive as the use of one.

Treatment of Sexual Dysfunctions

In this section we consider some of the more common treatments used in sex therapy. Caird and Wincze (1977) suggested that most behavioral treatment programs include three general components:

Education: The client and/or partner receives instruction in communication skills, sexual techniques, and the anatomy and physiology of sexual functioning.

Redirection of sexual behavior: The client's focus of attention is redirected from self-monitoring to giving pleasure to the partner.

Graded sexual exposure: Anxiety about sexual performance is reduced through gradual exposure to the anxiety-evoking situation. Exposure may be brought about through a series of relaxation exercises or through homework exercises with a partner.

When problems are based on relationship conflicts or serious individual disturbances, behavioral approaches may not be effective because they require both partners' active cooperation. Individual psychotherapy may be more likely to resolve individual disturbances, and communication skills training may be helpful for relationship conflicts. This is the case for gay and lesbian couples and heterosexual couples.

NONDEMAND PLEASURING AND SENSATE FOCUS.

In exercises involving nondemand sensate focus, the clients initially avoid sexual intercourse. In fact, couples are forbidden to engage in any sexual activity until the therapist instructs them to do so. Over the course of treatment, they receive homework assignments that gradually increase their range of sexual behaviors. Initially, only kissing, hugging, and body massage may be allowed.

The partners are instructed to take turns in the roles of giver and receiver as they touch and caress each other's body. When playing the role of giver, the person explores, touches, and caresses the receiver's body. In applying this technique, called **nondemand pleasuring,** the giver does not attempt to arouse the receiver sexually. In an exercise called **sensate focus,** the receiver concentrates on the sensations evoked by the giver's touch on various parts of the body. In these exercises the giver's responsibility is to provide pleasure and to be aware of his or her own pleasure in touching. The receiver's role is to prevent or end any stimulation that is uncomfortable or irritating by either telling or showing the partner his or her feelings.

Men and women with sexual excitement difficulties may find that taking a turn as the receiver helps to counteract any guilt they have learned about receiving sexual attention. Because they are not expected to do anything but receive the pleasure and give feedback when appropriate, the exercise may help them focus on their own erotic sensations.

The next step is to engage in nondemand breast and genital caressing while avoiding orgasm-oriented stimulation. Masters and Johnson (1970) recommended the position shown in Figure 6.2 for this phase because it allows easy access to the breasts and vulva when the woman is in the receiving role. It also allows the receiver to place his or her hand over the partner's hand to provide guidance to the kind of stimulation that is most pleasurable. If the partner of the person who is experiencing sexual difficulty becomes highly aroused during this exercise, that partner may be brought to orgasm orally or manually *after* completion of the exercise.

Other sexual behaviors are gradually added to the clients' homework. Successive assignments may include nongenital body massage, breast and genital touching, simultaneous masturbation, penile insertion with no movement, mutual genital manipulation to orgasm, and, finally, intercourse.

After the partners reach a sufficient level of arousal through sensate focus and nondemand pleasuring, they proceed to nondemand coitus. If the woman has had problems involving either excitement or orgasm, she is instructed to initiate sexual intercourse when she feels ready. Masters and Johnson (1970) recommended the woman-above position because it gives the woman more control over both insertion of the penis and intensity and frequency of thrusting. Her partner is typically advised to thrust slowly rather than forcefully. Usually the couple is counseled to disengage several times during coitus and to perform the nondemand genital stimulation exercises. Throughout these exercises the woman is encouraged to remain relaxed and to indulge in arousing fantasies. The couple can thus learn to enjoy sexual pleasure without worrying about performing later.

---

nondemand pleasuring Partners taking turns in exploring and caressing each other's bodies without attempting to arouse their partner sexually.
sensate focus Concentration on sensations produced by touching.

Figure 6.2
Nondemand Pleasuring This position, which allows easy access to the breasts and vulva, is often used in exercises designed to relieve sexual problems.

MASTURBATION TRAINING.   Most treatment programs for orgasmically inhibited women include training in masturbation, particularly if the woman has never had an orgasm. A treatment program for such women is presented in "Health: A Treatment Program for Orgasmically Inhibited Women" on page 152. This approach, which is used mainly in cases of primary orgasmic dysfunction, encourages women to learn about their bodies and relax to the point where they can experience orgasm.

Women with secondary orgasmic dysfunction usually do not require such an extensive and involved approach. Nondemand sensate focus exercises combined with techniques to heighten arousal are often effective in treating secondary inhibited orgasm. Kaplan (1974) claimed that sexual arousal can be enhanced by having a man penetrate his partner slowly and then withdraw after a brief period, engaging in sexual foreplay before reentering with slow, teasing thrusts.

A Treatment Program for Orgasmically Inhibited Women

The psychologist Joseph LoPiccolo and his colleagues (Heiman & LoPiccolo, 1988; LoPiccolo & Lobitz, 1972) developed a treatment program for orgasmically inhibited women that involves four major components.

1. Masturbation Training

    a. The woman is instructed to take a warm bath and examine her genitals with a mirror. Diagrams are used to aid her in identifying her muscles and genital organs. Pubococcygeal muscle exercises are begun.

    b. The client is instructed to explore her genitals by touch.

    c. The client continues tactile and visual exploration in an effort to locate pleasure-sensitive areas.

    d. The woman manually stimulates the pleasure-producing areas while using a sterile lubricant.

    e. If orgasm has not occurred by this time, the client is instructed to purchase a vibrator and use it to reach orgasm, placing it on her mons pubis near her clitoris.

2. Skill Training for the Partner

    a. The partner observes the woman's masturbation to learn what is pleasurable for her. Various aspects of sensate focus exercises are begun.

    b. The partner masturbates the woman to orgasm.

    c. Manual stimulation is combined with intercourse.

3. Disinhibition of Arousal: Some women may not be able to reach orgasm with their partner because they are embarrassed about showing intense arousal or fear losing self-control. These women are asked to role-play a grossly exaggerated orgasm, with violent convulsions, screaming, and other extreme behavior. Repeated performances in the company of the partner usually result in amusement and, eventually, boredom.

4. Practice of Orgasmic Behaviors: Actions such as pelvic thrusting, pointing the toes, tensing the thigh muscles, holding the breath, pushing down with the diaphragm, and throwing back the head often occur involuntarily during intense orgasm. If the woman practices these behaviors voluntarily when she is experiencing sexual arousal, they may trigger orgasm.

---

squeeze technique A treatment for premature ejaculation in which a man signals his partner to apply manual pressure to his penis to delay ejaculation.

THE SQUEEZE TECHNIQUE. The approach most commonly employed for premature ejaculation is the **squeeze technique** (Masters & Johnson, 1970). The partner circles the tip of the penis with the hand, as shown in Figure 6.3. The thumb is placed against the frenulum on the underside of the penis, while the fingers are placed on either side of the coronal ridge on the upper side of the penis. When the man signals that he is approaching ejaculation, his partner applies fairly strong pressure for 3 to 5 seconds and then stops with a sudden release. The partner stimulates his penis again after the sensations of impending ejaculation diminish, usually within 20 to 30 seconds. Typically, the man is told that he should not try to control his ejaculation but should rely instead on the squeeze technique. The entire process is usually carried out three to four times per session before ejaculation is allowed.

Some couples prefer to apply the squeeze technique at the base of the penis rather than the tip. This variation has the advantage of being easier to do during intercourse, but for some couples it does not work. In this procedure the penis must be grasped as close as possible to its base.

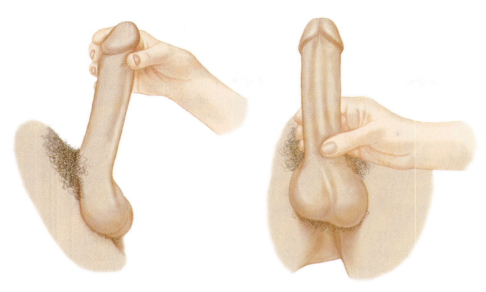

Figure 6.3
The Squeeze Technique The squeeze technique, which can be applied either at the corona (left) or at the base of the penis (right), is useful for the treatment of premature ejaculation.

The next step is to apply a water-soluble lubricant, such as K-Y jelly, to the hand and then stimulate the penis to approximate more closely the sensations experienced during vaginal intercourse. The squeeze technique is then applied again. If this step is successfully completed, the partners can move on to further sexual interaction. If the man does not feel close to orgasm, his partner can start to provide further stimulation. When he signals that he feels the sensations of impending orgasm, his partner withdraws from contact and applies the squeeze technique. The process is repeated after the urge to ejaculate diminishes. The man is usually not permitted to ejaculate until the squeeze technique has been applied three or four times or until his partner experiences orgasm. From this point the couple often progresses to side-by-side coitus, using the squeeze technique as needed. The final step is coitus in the man-above position. After satisfactory coitus with the man on top, the choice of sexual positions and techniques is left up to them.

Having tried the side-by-side position, couples treated by Masters and Johnson (1970) continued to use it 75 percent of the time, even after having had success with the man-above position. Success in gaining ejaculatory control using the squeeze technique is around 60 percent (Grenier & Byers, 1995).

GROUP THERAPY AND SYSTEMATIC DESENSITIZATION.   Numerous other therapy formats and techniques are sometimes used in conjunction with the foregoing approaches to treatment of sexual dysfunctions. For example, for women who have primary or secondary orgasmic dysfunction, group therapy is less expensive than individual therapy (LoPiccolo & Stock, 1986; McCabe & Delany, 1992).

Systematic desensitization involves learning a series of muscle relaxation exercises. The client and therapist then construct a set of imaginative anxiety-provoking scenes that go from the least to the most anxiety producing. Gradually, the client attempts to replace anxiety to the imagined scene with a relaxation response. After clients can imagine the last scene without anxiety, they attempt to transfer what they have learned to real-life situations.

systematic desensitization A behavior therapy in which deep relaxation is used to reduce anxiety associated with certain situations.

sexual surrogate A member of a sex-therapy team whose role is to have sexual interactions with a client as part of the therapy.

SEXUAL SURROGATES.   Most sexual therapies include homework assignments that require a cooperative partner. In attempting to meet the needs of the dysfunctional client who has no steady partner, some therapists have used "bodywork therapy" in which the client and a **sexual surrogate,** with the direction of a therapist, may engage in private sexual activity as part of the treatment (Apfelbaum, 1984).

Most professionals view sexual contact between clients and therapists as unethical. Masters and Johnson (1970) attempted to solve this problem by employing sexual surrogates. They reported that the participation of a cooperative and skilled surrogate who had no prior association with the client was as effective as the participation of marital partners in the treatment of sexual difficulties. But Masters and Johnson discontinued the controversial practice, as have many other therapists, because the use of sexual surrogates is very controversial. In most clinics that treat sexual dysfunctions, the use of sexual surrogates has been abandoned (Leiblum & Rosen, 1989).

OTHER TREATMENT APPROACHES.   Various approaches involving surgery, hormones, and drugs have been used in the attempt to treat sexual dysfunctions. The fact that most of these treatments have been developed for male sexual difficulties probably reflects our culture's emphasis on male sexual performance. In general, before permitting these kinds of treatments, the client should make sure that no other type of treatment is effective for him and obtain a second opinion.

Surgical procedures, including implants, have been used in the treatment of erectile dysfunction. There are two basic types of plastic or silicone implants. One is a semirigid rod that keeps the penis in a constant state of erection but can be bent for concealment under clothing. The other type of silicone or plastic (polyurethane) implant, an inflatable device (see Figure 6.4), is implanted under the skin of the penis, and erection is achieved by the man pressing a pump implanted in the scrotum. The pump forces fluid from a reservoir put under the abdominal muscles into the cylinders implanted in the penis. Complications of this method include infection and mechanical

prosthesis Artificial replacement for a body part.

failure. Follow-up studies of **prosthesis** recipients and their partners have indicated that they were generally satisfied with the choice to have the surgery (Graber, 1993). No differences in satisfaction have been reported between men who received the inflatable or the semirigid prostheses (Tiefer & Melman, 1989). Most men who have implants can still experience ejaculation and orgasm unless there has been previous neurological damage (Krane, 1986; McCarthy & McMillan, 1990).

The vacuum pump has been used to treat erectile difficulties. The penis is inserted into an acrylic tube while a hand-held vacuum pump draws blood into erectile tissue. A rubber band holds the blood in place for 30 minutes.

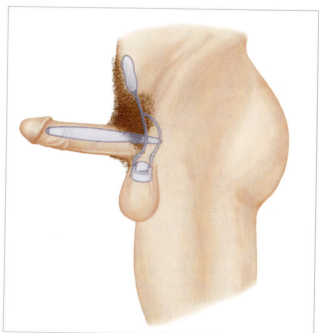

Figure 6.4
Inflatable Penile Prosthesis This drawing shows an inflatable penile prosthesis. With most inflatable penile prostheses, a reservoir of fluid is implanted under the abdominal muscles, and an attached pump is embedded in either the abdominal cavity or the scrotum. A man presses the pump to force fluid into cylinders in his prosthesis when he wishes to have an erection. A release valve allows the fluid to return to the abdominal reservoir.

A diversity of surgical techniques, including microsurgery, have been developed to increase blood flow to the penises of men with erectile dysfunction. The surgery is similar in principle to bypass surgery for heart patients with blocked arteries. The blocked arteries are bypassed through grafts that allow for a greater blood supply to the penis. This procedure appears promising, but results so far have been quite variable, and the procedure appears suited for only a small percentage of men who have erectile dysfunction (Graber, 1993; Tiefer & Melman, 1989).

Hormones have also been used for years to treat erectile dysfunction. If the problem is not due to hormone deficiency, however, hormones can increase sexual arousability without improving performance, which can result in further deterioration of the client's condition (Rosen & Ashton, 1993; Segraves, 1988). Hormone treatment also increases the risk of coronary thrombosis, atherosclerosis, and cancer of the prostate.

DRUGS.   Drugs are sometimes used to alleviate some of the symptoms associated with the dysfunctions. As noted earlier, anxiety plays a large role in the development of sexual dysfunction in both women and men. Physicians may attempt to treat some dysfunctions through the prescription of minor tranquilizers, such as Librium or Valium, that reduce anxiety. Some individuals with a sexual dysfunction have reported improvement after treatment with antidepressant medications (Crenshaw & Goldberg, 1996). Although their frequency of sexual behavior did not increase significantly, their satisfaction with their own sexuality did.

A new drug, sildenafil, which still needs to be approved by the Food and Drug Administration, is taken orally. It is thought to work by blocking an enzyme that allows blood to flow out of the penis. Unlike other treatments, the pill doesn't work without the person first experiencing sexual arousal (Rosen, 1996).

A number of drugs can create pharmacological erection through injection into the penis by relaxing the smooth muscle of the corpora cavernosa (Wagner & Kaplan, 1993). They appear to be most useful for men with irreversible biological erectile dysfunction. The client can be taught to inject the drug himself. Erection usually occurs within 10 minutes and lasts about two hours. There is some risk with this treatment, as it has a number of side effects.

Self-help groups offer support to individuals affected by erectile dysfunction. Bruce MacKensie, who received an inflatable penile implant in 1981, and his wife, Eileen, were cofounders of Impotents Anonymous in 1983. There are also groups for partners of men with erectile dysfunctions (see Appendix). We have tried to locate corresponding self-help groups for nonorgasmic women, but to the best of our knowledge no such nationwide groups exist.

Qualifications and Ethics of Therapists

One of the challenges faced by individuals experiencing sexual problems is finding a qualified therapist. There are a considerable number of people who call themselves sex therapists, but have little training or competence.

How can you find out whether a therapist is qualified? Most qualified sex therapists make themselves and their credentials known to other professionals in the community. There is no legislative control of the title "sex therapist" in many states, and so the appearance of the title in the phone book does not testify to an individual's skills. In all states, however, licensing laws control who can be listed as a psychologist or physician. The American Association for Sex Educators, Counselors, and Therapists certifies individual sex therapists (see Appendix). Before expending a lot of time and money in therapy, however, try to identify what your goals are, and discuss these with a potential sex therapist to see if you are in general agreement. For example, gay or lesbian couples who

ISSUES TO CONSIDER

Your friends are seeking a sex therapist, know that you're taking a human sexuality course, and ask your opinion on finding a qualified professional. What advice would you give them?

experience sexual difficulties may seek help from a therapist only to discover that the therapist has an implicit belief that the "problem" is that they are trying to have a committed sexual relationship with a person of the same gender and the "solution" is for them to separate and find a partner of the other gender. A therapist with this value system in not likely to be able to provide the help that the gay or lesbian couple needs in resolving sexual difficulties. The same problems can emerge if a couple (or individual) differs from a therapist regarding appropriate roles for men versus women. Thus people should ask a potential therapist about his or her values and assumptions.

SUMMARY OF MAJOR POINTS

1. Stress and sexual dysfunctions.

Problems in sexual response are associated with a variety of physical and psychological stresses, including long- or short-term medical conditions, fatigue or illness, anxiety, a disproportionately heavy focus on performance evaluation, ignorance about sexuality, and relationships dominated by conflict or inadequate communication.

2. Specific types of sexual dysfunction.

Levels of desire and responsiveness normally vary from one individual to the next and from one time to the next. When an individual is bothered by consistent failure to respond in the way he or she wishes, however, it may be appropriate to seek professional help. A person can experience difficulty during any phase of a sexual interaction. The individual may feel little or no desire for sexual relations or may be obsessed with the desire for sexual stimulation. If a person's level of desire is consistently different from that of his or her partner, therapy can be used to resolve the discrepancy. Alternatively, an individual may feel deep desire for sexual relations but have difficulty becoming excited or aroused. Difficulty obtaining orgasm is reported to be a problem by a higher proportion of women than of men. Finally, an individual may respond quickly or slowly to sexual stimulation. When a person's pattern of desires is consistently different from that of his or her partner and from the way the person wishes to respond, sex therapy may help the couple.

3. Major approaches to sex therapy.

Masters and Johnson's approach, which stresses the learned nature of many sexual responses, focuses on the development of more satisfying patterns of response. Kaplan included a similar approach in her therapeutic treatment but distinguished between specific maladaptive sexual responses and more general sources of difficulty, including personal conflicts and unresolved problems between a couple, which may require more prolonged and in-depth treatment.

4. Effectiveness of sex therapy.

Masters and Johnson reported higher success rates than many contemporary sex therapists typically experience. Although it is possible that they employed superior techniques, it is likely that several other factors explain this difference.

5. Treatment of sexual dysfunctions.

Sex therapists use various techniques to help people have more satisfying sexual experiences. These include systematic desensitization, nondemand pleasuring, sensate focus, masturbation training, and the squeeze technique, in addition to psychotherapy.

6. Controversies surrounding sex therapy. The use of client-therapist sexual contact, the employment of sexual surrogates, and the basis for providing sex therapists with credentials to practice are among the issues currently debated by therapists. Sexual contact between therapist and client is unethical and usually has negative effects on the client. There is no evidence regarding the effectiveness of sexual surrogates in treating sexual dysfunction, and few therapists employ them because of the additional expense. Most sex therapists have licenses to practice as psychologists, physicians, social workers, or counselors.

CHECK YOUR KNOWLEDGE

1. According to recent research, which of the following statements is most likely to be true? (a) Most sexual dysfunctions result from psychological factors alone. (b) Freud's theory that critical childhood experiences explain sexual dysfunctions has now been supported. (c) Most sexual difficulties stem from brain dysfunction. (d) Anxiety about sex and performance is probably the most important immediate cause of sexual dysfunctions. **(p. 138)**

2. Excessive sexual desire is (a) the most frequent sexual problem reported by men, (b) the most frequent sexual problem reported by women, (c) primarily a lesbian sexual dysfunction, (d) an infrequently reported sexual dysfunction. **(p. 143)**

3. Vaginismus is (a) a condition involving the involuntary contraction of the PC muscle surrounding the outer third of the vagina; (b) a condition involving lack of muscle tone in the vagina; (c) correlated with such factors as rape, abortion, painful gynecological exams, pelvic inflammatory disease, accidents, and general fears about men and/or rape; (d) rarely cured by therapy. **(p. 147)**

4. Vaginal lubrication is (a) never a problem during sexual interaction among college-educated women, (b) necessary for conceiving a child, (c) related to priapism, (d) a problem for as many as one in five women each year. **(p. 146)**

5. Nondemand pleasuring is a therapeutic approach involving (a) sexual intercourse in a relaxed, low-anxiety environment; (b) mutual masturbation; (c) the giver's deliberate avoidance of attempts to arouse the receiver sexually; (d) use of the squeeze technique. **(p. 150)**

6. The use of implants to correct male erectile dysfunctions is (a) completely impractical and unsafe, (b) painful, (c) almost always a failure, (d) now generally effective but should be used only if all other approaches have failed. **(p. 154)**

7. _____ contended that one sex therapist is as effective for a couple as having a man and a woman therapy team and that sex therapy sometimes requires in-depth probing of emotional conflicts: (a) Masters and Johnson, (b) Kaplan, (c) Apfelbaum, (d) Bullough and Bullough. **(p. 149)**

8. Masturbation training is often used (a) in the treatment of orgasmically inhibited women; (b) in the treatment of excessive sexual desire; (c) in the treatment of infertile men; (d) to calm prisoners in maximum security institutions. **(p. 151)**

7

PREGNANCY AND BIRTH

PREGNANCY
Early Symptoms of Pregnancy
Health: The Inability to Conceive
Threats to Fetal Development
Stages of Pregnancy
Health: Tests for Identifying Fetal Abnormalities
Sex During Pregnancy

LABOR AND BIRTH
Preparation for Childbirth
Highlight: A Personal Account of Childbirth
Labor for Childbirth

POSTPARTUM EVENTS AND DECISIONS
Feeding
Health: Possible Birth Complications
Circumcision
Postpartum Adjustment
Postpartum Sexual Expression

SUMMARY OF MAJOR POINTS

CHECK YOUR KNOWLEDGE

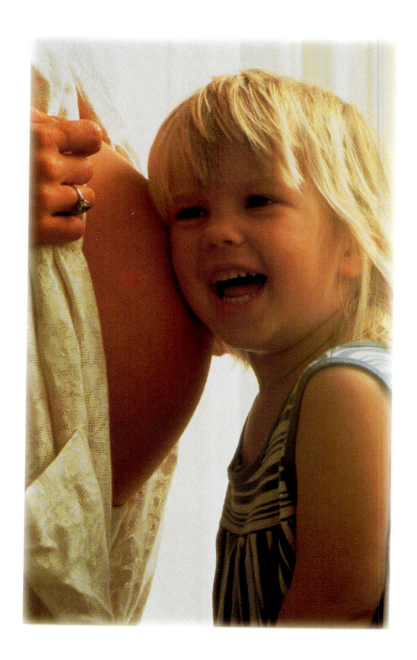

REALITY or MYTH ?

1 Most pregnancy tests are based on detection of human chorionic gonadotropin (HCG) in women's blood or urine.

2 The average woman gains 20 to 30 pounds during pregnancy.

3 Shaving of the laboring mother's pubic hair is required in all North American hospitals.

4 Women can become sexually aroused while breast-feeding an infant.

5 Most women experience health problems in the first two weeks after giving birth.

6 Most couples begin engaging in sexual intercourse in the first month after birth.

To impregnate and to become pregnant signify to the individual a kind of categorical maturity as human beings; the natural consequence of sexual intercourse fixes more permanently and obviously the private experience of love-making and the status of adulthood, of being grown up. (Rainwater & Weinstein, 1960, pp. 81–82)

IN this chapter we present the processes of pregnancy and birth. Sexual intercourse during pregnancy, preparation for childbirth, normal birth, and some of the controversies regarding medical and hospital childbirth policies are reviewed. We discuss such **postpartum** issues as depression, breast-feeding, circumcision, and sexual intimacy between the new parents.

postpartum (post-PAR-tum) Relating to the time immediately following birth.

PREGNANCY

Even though millions of women give birth each year, there is a tendency for women, particularly with their first pregnancies, to feel that they are doing something uniquely remarkable—and indeed they are.

Early Symptoms of Pregnancy

A few women—especially those who have been pregnant before and those who are actively trying to conceive—suspect pregnancy within 10 days or so of conceiving. They may recognize heaviness in the abdomen and breasts, and the nipples may feel a bit irritated. For most women, however, the first real indication of pregnancy is the absence of menstruation about two weeks after conception.

As soon as a woman believes that she is pregnant, she should obtain a pregnancy test. Early diagnosis of pregnancy is important for a number of reasons. First, pregnant women should avoid most drugs and exposure to certain diseases (see Table 7.1, page 160). Second, some potentially dangerous medical conditions, if identified early on, can be corrected, drastically improving the chances of a positive outcome for both woman and baby. Third, occasionally a woman can have symptoms of pregnancy,

Table 7.1   Factors That May Affect the Fetus

Drugs

Alcohol	Small head size, defective joints, congenital heart defects, mental retardation
Nicotine	Spontaneous abortion, prematurity, low birth weight, stillbirth, nicotine dependency at birth
Vitamin A (excessive doses)	Cleft palate, neural tube defects
Aspirin (moderate use)	Relatively safe until third trimester; use then may prolong labor and lengthen clotting time for both mother and baby, increasing the risk of hemorrhage
Tetracycline	Bone and tooth damage, discolored teeth
Heroin	Spontaneous abortion, low birth weight, fetal addiction and withdrawal, respiratory depression
Methadone	Low birth weight, respiratory depression, mild degrees of mental retardation
Marijuana	Reduced fetal growth rate, overall risk of congenital malformations, limb deficiencies
Cocaine	Neonatal intoxication

Diseases or Medical Conditions

Rubella virus	Infant deafness, blindness, cataracts, heart malformations
Diabetes	Spontaneous abortion, maternal toxemia, stillbirths, abnormally large fetus, respiratory difficulties
Syphilis	Spontaneous abortion, prematurity, stillbirth, syphilitic infant
Herpes, type II	Spontaneous abortion, prematurity, stillbirth, neonatal herpes infection, congenital abnormalities
AIDS	Postnatal death from opportunistic infections
Radiation	Microcephaly, mental retardation, skeletal malformations

Hormones

Androgens	Female offspring: masculinization of internal and/or external genitals
Estrogens	Female offspring: clitoral enlargement, labial fusion, congenital anomalies
Progestins	Cardiovascular anomalies
DES	Male offspring: semen and testicular abnormalities, reduced fertility; female offspring: abnormal vaginal or cervical growth, masculinization, reproductive organ cancers
Oral contraceptives	Suspected but unconfirmed reports of physiological difficulties, among them anal, cardiac, kidney, and limb abnormalities

Sources: Moore (1989); Mattson and Smith (1993).

human chorionic go-nadotropin (HCG) (CORE-ee-ON-ik goh-NAH-doe-TROE-pin) A hormone produced by the placenta.

placenta The organ formed by the joining of the uterine wall tissue with that of the developing fetus; a major source of hormones during pregnancy.

including amenorrhea (absence of expected menstrual bleeding), abdominal swelling, or nausea, even though she is not pregnant (see "Health: The Inability to Conceive"). Possible causes include tumors and cysts, which may be benign or malignant. Early examination can help detect the sources of such nonpregnancy-related bodily changes, and the problems are more readily treated and cured with early detection.

Most pregnancy tests are based on detection of **human chorionic gonadotropin (HCG)** in a woman's blood or urine. After conception the **placenta,** which connects the uterus to the developing fetus, begins to produce HCG at rapidly increasing levels. HCG secretion reaches its maximum level about nine weeks after conception and then declines (Hatcher et al., 1994). The presence of HCG in a woman's bloodstream may

Health

The Inability to Conceive

Approximately 15 percent of people of childbearing age in the United States experience involuntary childlessness or infertility (Leiblum, 1993). Sterility can result from genetic factors, damage to the reproductive organs, drugs and environmental pollutants, and a variety of other sources.

There are a number of procedures available for the treatment of male and female infertility. Artificial insemination from a donor, surrogate motherhood, and in vitro fertilization/embryo transfer are just a few of the techniques.

Infertility is related to a wide range of negative emotional experiences. An increase in marital conflict and decreases in sexual self-esteem, satisfaction with one's sexual performance, and frequency of sexual intercourse have been reported (Andrews, Abbey, & Halman, 1991; Leiblum, 1993). Research has supported the idea that infertility leads to these psychological problems rather than the psychological problems causing infertility.

---

be detected in a blood sample within a week after conception. Analysis of urine for the presence of HCG is highly accurate as early as the first day of the expected (but missed) menstrual period.

Contemporary at-home pregnancy test kits also work by detecting HCG in urine and are highly reliable if a woman adheres precisely to the directions for their administration. They are useful for early screening if a woman suspects that she is pregnant and cannot obtain an immediate appointment with a health care provider. However, such test kits should always be followed by a visit to a health care provider if the result is positive (indicating that the woman is pregnant). If the result is negative but the conditions that led a woman to believe that she was pregnant persist for the next week, she should also see a health care provider. One dangerous medical condition that can be checked is **ectopic pregnancy.** In an ectopic pregnancy, the fertilized egg implants outside the uterus, usually in a fallopian tube. Such pregnancies are often aborted spontaneously, but if they are not, the growing embryo can rupture the fallopian tube within about six weeks. If a woman with a ruptured tube does not receive treatment for the internal bleeding within about 30 minutes, she may die.

REALITY or MYTH ? **1**

ectopic pregnancy A pregnancy that occurs when a fertilized egg implants itself outside the uterus, usually in a fallopian tube.

Threats to Fetal Development

As noted earlier, one of the reasons that it is essential for a woman to obtain a pregnancy test if she suspects that she has conceived is that certain drugs and diseases threaten fetal development. Furthermore, the damage done by exposure to drugs and diseases is greatest during the first three months of pregnancy. A pregnant woman must consider dosage levels when deciding whether to ingest drugs; a proper dose for a woman of, say, 125 pounds may be a large overdose for a one- or two-pound fetus. The livers of infants do not begin functioning until a week after they are born, and full functioning of the liver does not occur for several more months. When a fetus is exposed to drugs taken by the mother, its liver is incapable of breaking them down as efficiently as an adult's liver would.

Heavy alcohol use during pregnancy is the leading environmental cause of mental retardation in infants, with 40 percent of chronically alcoholic women producing an infant with symptoms of **fetal alcohol syndrome (FAS).** Symptoms of FAS in humans include a short upturned nose, small and underdeveloped midface, short eyeslits, and

fetal alcohol syndrome (FAS) A disorder found in the offspring of problem drinkers that causes a group of specific symptoms, including mental retardation.

ISSUES TO CONSIDER

Do you think society should regulate the behavior of alcoholic women who become pregnant?

missing or minimal ridges between the nose and the mouth. Mental retardation, poor motor development, and retarded physical growth also occur. There are no reports of pregnant women who drank less than two ounces of alcohol a day giving birth to babies with FAS characteristics (Andolsek, 1990). No absolutely safe levels have been established, however, and most health care providers now advise their patients to abstain from alcohol during pregnancy.

Fetal health is also seriously jeopardized when the mother is infected with a sexually transmitted disease. Chlamydia is a sexually transmitted bacterial infection (see Chapter 13) that can be passed from mother to fetus during pregnancy or to the baby during vaginal delivery. Although it is readily treated, many women are asymptomatic (without symptoms) and thus do not seek treatment. Women who have chlamydia during the first trimester of pregnancy have a greater incidence of premature births. All pregnant women should be tested and treated for chlamydia rather than waiting for their babies to get sick with conjunctivitis (which occurs in up to 50 percent of exposed babies) and pneumonia (which is seen in up to 15 percent of exposed babies) (Hatcher et al., 1994).

A major sexually transmitted infection that cannot be cured is genital herpes (see Chapter 13). A woman infected with genital herpes is more likely to have a spontaneous abortion, a stillbirth, or an infant born with congenital abnormalities. If a woman has an active outbreak of herpes at the time of delivery, a Cesarean section should be performed to protect the baby from potential contact with the virus during a vaginal delivery. Finally, there is an increase in the number of babies being born with HIV, the virus that causes AIDS. As noted in Chapter 13, there are interventions that can reduce the risk of an HIV+ woman transmitting HIV to her fetus, but only if she knows she is pregnant.

Stages of Pregnancy

Pregnancy has an enormous impact on a woman's body and emotions. In many cases the emotions of an expectant father are also strongly affected. Impending parenthood alters both women's and men's definitions of themselves and of their relationships. It changes their status among their relatives and in society as a whole, as the quote at the beginning of this chapter conveys.

Paralleling the stages in fetal development and growth described in Chapter 2 is a series of remarkable physiological and psychological changes that women undergo during the nine months of pregnancy. Pregnancy is conventionally divided into three trimesters. Each stage of pregnancy brings characteristic alterations in the woman's body and in her feelings about herself and her role as a mother. For the first-time mother, each sensation is a new experience.

The gestation period lasts approximately 266 days from conception to birth, but the expected delivery date is normally calculated by subtracting three months from the first day of the last menstrual period and then adding 53 weeks to that figure. This method is not foolproof because some women continue to menstruate for a month or more after becoming pregnant. A friend of ours was undergoing a final check before going into surgery for a tumor when it was discovered that the "tumor" was a 4 month-old fetus. She had not suspected that she was pregnant because she had continued to have normal menstrual periods. Five months later she gave birth to a healthy baby girl. Most women stop menstruating when they are pregnant, however, and most babies are born within a week of the date calculated by the method just described.

It is important that couples be aware of the physical, emotional, social, and financial challenges imposed by pregnancy, impending birth, and the responsibilities of parenthood. If a couple has been experiencing serious marital problems, it is a good idea to consider marital counseling to try resolving the conflicts before the child is born. As Reamy and White (1987, p. 178) pointed out, "The idea that a child will bring harmony and intimacy into a dysfunctional marriage is erroneous, if not ludicrous." Difficulties in a couple's relationship that existed prior to pregnancy usually remain or intensify, and new problems may emerge. Among couples who have a stable and mutually satisfying relationship, the decision to have a baby and the sharing of feelings about the pregnancy may add to their sense of commitment and intimacy—two factors that are important for the experience of love (see Chapter 16).

ISSUES TO CONSIDER

What do you think are the effects on two people of having a child when they are experiencing problems in their relationship?

FIRST TRIMESTER.   Most women do not realize that they are pregnant for several weeks or even a month or more following conception. Although women should record the dates of their periods on a calendar, not all do. Those who do not are sometimes unaware that they have skipped a period.

In addition to ceasing menstruation, many women experience swelling in their breasts. Their nipples may become temporarily sensitive, so that manual stimulation or contact with clothing is uncomfortable. In a first pregnancy, the **areolas** of some women darken early in the first trimester. During pregnancy estrogens aid in the development of the milk ducts, and progesterone stimulates the completion of the development of these ducts and **alveoli.**

areola (AIR-ee-OH-lah) The darkened skin surrounding the nipples containing oil-secreting glands.
alveoli (AL-vee-OH-lee) Milk-secreting cells in the breast.

About six weeks after conception, noticeable changes occur in a woman's cervix. Normally, the cervix has a hardness and resiliency similar to those of the end of the nose or the top of the ear. About a month after the first missed menstrual period, however, the cervix feels relatively soft and malleable, a difference that can be detected by a woman who is familiar with the feeling of her cervix as well as by a health care provider during manual inspection.

During the first trimester, about half of all pregnant women have periodic bouts of nausea as a result of elevated levels of HCG and changed carbohydrate metabolism. This condition is called "morning sickness" because it is usually most severe in the morning. For some women, the nausea is relatively mild and can be controlled by eating dry crackers before getting up in the morning; eating small, frequent meals; and avoiding spicy foods. For other women, the nausea is considerably more severe and is accompanied by vomiting. A few women must be hospitalized to control the potential dehydration from constant vomiting. Many women, however, do not experience any of these unpleasant side effects of pregnancy.

Increased fatigue and sleepiness are common during the first trimester. Many women also report feeling more irritable, vulnerable, and dependent than they did prior to conception. The changes in the shapes of their bodies depress some women. At this stage they are not yet "showing" the pregnancy enough to justify wearing maternity clothes, but they may have trouble buttoning slacks or skirts toward the end of the first trimester.

Pregnancy is commonly depicted as a time of calm and radiance, but women often feel ambivalent in the first trimester. Even in a planned pregnancy, a woman is frequently surprised that conception has actually occurred. Women who need to make changes in career plans and commitments or who feel financially stressed are most likely to feel ambivalence. Some women also express fears about pregnancy, labor, and delivery. Such worries are likely to be the most intense when the pregnancy is unwanted or unplanned.

Figure 7.1
Physical Changes During the First Trimester of Pregnancy
The first trimester of pregnancy does not produce major physical changes in most women. Compare this figure with the changes illustrated in Figures 7.3 and 7.6.

ISSUES TO CONSIDER

Why do you think some men develop symptoms that mimic those of their pregnant partners (couvade)?

couvade Phenomenon in which some men develop symptoms similar to those of their pregnant partner.

colostrum (cuh-LAWS-trum) A thin, yellowish fluid secreted from the nipples before and around the time of birth.

quickening The first fetal movements felt by the mother.

Some women, especially those who had difficulty conceiving, worry about possible miscarriage (spontaneous abortion). This concern is realistic—the majority of miscarriages occur during the first trimester.

A pregnant woman tends to look for physical signs to prove to herself that she is truly pregnant. She becomes conscious of small changes in her body. She watches for thickening of her waist, weight gain, and breast development (see Figure 7.1). Even morning sickness, however unpleasant, is confirmation that she is in fact pregnant. Usually by the end of the first trimester she has resolved any ambivalence and has accepted the developing fetus as a temporary part of herself.

Like the expectant mother, the father also needs to adjust to the pregnancy and to the coming changes in his life. Most men feel pride that conception has occurred; at the same time, however, many express ambivalence. The extent of the father's ambivalence is related to a variety of factors, such as his relationship with the mother, his age, their financial status, and whether the pregnancy was planned.

After the initial excitement and announcement of the pregnancy, many fathers feel left out. Attention becomes focused on the mother, who may act differently than she did prior to her pregnancy. Her mood changes and fatigue may confuse the expectant father. He may also experience her obsession with herself as a kind of rejection. Many men worry about their ability to be a good father and spend much time thinking about their own fathers.

Some men develop symptoms, such as fatigue, sleeping difficulties, backaches, and nausea, similar to those of pregnant women. The term **couvade** refers to men developing symptoms similar to those of their pregnant partners. Perhaps these symptoms provide a way for a man to identify with his partner and to participate in the pregnancy.

SECOND TRIMESTER.   For most women, the second trimester is characterized by a sense of well-being and pleasure. The symptoms of the first trimester diminish or disappear entirely, and the threat of miscarriage has diminished. Because they may take better care of themselves during pregnancy, some women report having more energy and feeling healthier in their second trimester than they did before they became pregnant. Some acknowledge the pregnancy by wearing maternity clothes, even if such clothes are not yet necessary. Small amounts of **colostrum,** a thin, yellowish fluid high in proteins and antibodies, may be expelled from the nipples during the second trimester. Colostrum production continues throughout pregnancy. The abdomen increases in fullness, particularly in women who have been pregnant before. The pressure of the enlarging uterus on the bladder interferes with women's activities, as well as their sleep, by increasing the frequency of their need to urinate.

Most health care providers schedule monthly prenatal checkups for women who have reached the beginning of the second trimester. These checkups are extremely important to detect any problems that might threaten the life or well-being of the mother or fetus. During these visits the woman's weight, blood pressure, and urine are checked. Some appointments also include a pelvic examination to determine the position and development of the fetus. Genetic testing or ultrasonography may be ordered for pregnant women over age 35 with family histories of genetic disorders or for those susceptible to any other potential difficulties (see "Health: Tests for Identifying Fetal Abnormalities" and Figure 7.2).

Expectant parents generally are very excited by two events that occur around the middle of the second trimester. One is **quickening,** the woman's first awareness of fetal movement. The other is detection of the fetal heartbeat, amplified with a device known as a Doppler. Some health care providers invite women to bring their partners with them to their next checkup after the heartbeat is detected, so that both expectant parents can hear the fetal heartbeat.

Health

Tests for Identifying Fetal Abnormalities

Three procedures are used to check the fetus for the presence of genetic and other disorders: amniocentesis, chorionic villi sampling (CVS), and ultrasonography. *Amniocentesis*—a diagnostic procedure in which amniotic fluid is extracted from the uterus and fetal cells are analyzed for chromosome defects—is the traditional method for identifying fetal chromosomal defects. In this procedure sound waves are directed at the uterus, and through computer translation the echoes are bounced back in a visual picture (a sonogram or ultrasound scan) of the fetus and its location. With the location of the fetus known, a needle is then inserted into the woman's abdomen until it penetrates the uterus (but avoids the fetus). A small amount of amniotic fluid surrounding the fetus is removed through the needle (refer to Figure 7.2). Cells from the fluid are cultured (grown) for several weeks, and photos of the chromosomes are examined for abnormalities. Amniocentesis is useful for diagnoses only after the first trimester.

Analysis of the fetal chromosomes can detect chromosomal defects such as Down syndrome, as well as the gender of the fetus. In addition, biochemical tests of the cultured cells can detect many problems from genetic abnormalities that cause no visible changes in chromosomes, such as spina bifida (opening in the spine) and cleft palate.

Another genetic test, *chorionic villi sampling (CVS)*, involves insertion of a thin tube through the cervix into the placenta to obtain a sample of chorionic villi. The villi are fingerlike projections of tissue that transfer oxygen, nutrients, and waste between mother and embryo. The villi are composed of the same cells as the fetus.

The advantages of CVS over amniocentesis are that it can be performed at about the eighth week of pregnancy, it is a less invasive procedure, and results are available within 24 hours. The risk of fetal loss following CVS is only slightly higher than with amniocentesis (Andolsek, 1990). Some of this increased risk, however, may be due to the greater risk of miscarriage during the first trimester that exists regardless of whether prenatal diagnostic tests are performed. Furthermore, if a woman elects to terminate the pregnancy

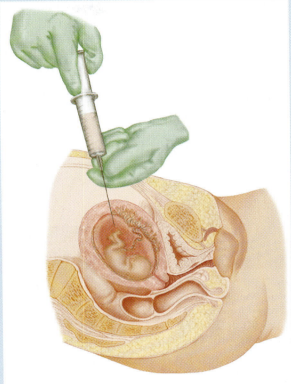

Figure 7.2
Amniocentesis In this procedure, fluid and loose fetal cells are withdrawn from the amniotic sac. The cells are then cultured and examined for abnormalities.

based on the results of CVS analysis, she faces relatively low risk because she is still in her first trimester. Like amniocentesis, CVS can help detect Down syndrome, Tay-Sachs disease, sickle-cell anemia, hemophilia, and about 90 other genetic diseases.

In addition to helping locate the fetus during amniocentesis or CVS, *ultrasonography* (the use of sound waves and a computer to create a visual image of a fetus) is a useful diagnostic tool in its own right. It helps resolve questions about the due date by determining fetal size and development. It can also be used to detect fetal abnormalities, twins, ectopic pregnancies, or tumors.

By the middle of the second trimester, women usually have to replace most of their regular clothing with loose slacks and dresses to allow for the expansion of the uterus. Having adjusted to these changes in appearance, the woman usually takes pleasure in the sensations of pregnancy and begins to picture the fetus as a real person.

Quickening gives a woman a sense of "knowing" the baby. Many women are eager to learn about childbirth and child care during this time (see Figure 7.3).

The changes of early pregnancy also prompt a woman to think about her relationship with her partner and her status as a new mother. Many women feel anxiety about their partners, especially if their mates respond to the pregnancy by withdrawing. Like the mother, an expectant father needs to resolve any mixed feelings he has about the pregnancy. His involvement in preparing for the baby, hearing the baby's heartbeat, and feeling fetal movements usually help him adjust to his new situation (see Figure 7.4).

THIRD TRIMESTER.   During the last three months of pregnancy, most women have an awkward gait and feel rather blimplike. The average weight for a full-term baby is 7½ pounds, but the average woman gains 20 to 30 pounds during pregnancy (see Figure 7.5). Increased fluid retention and fat are responsible for much of the gain.

Figure 7.3
Physical Changes During the Second Trimester of Pregnancy Compare this figure with Figures 7.1 and 7.6.

Figure 7.4
Expectant Father's Connection This expectant father is obviously enjoying listening to and feeling his baby in his partner's uterus.

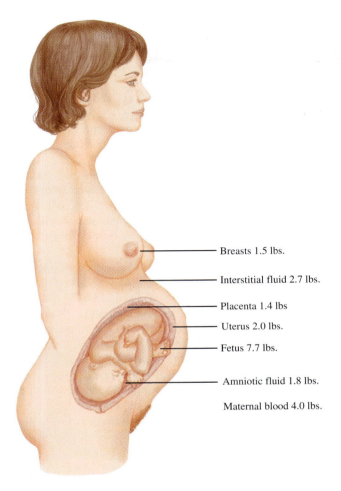

Breasts 1.5 lbs.

Interstitial fluid 2.7 lbs.

Placenta 1.4 lbs

Uterus 2.0 lbs.

Fetus 7.7 lbs.

Amniotic fluid 1.8 lbs.

Maternal blood 4.0 lbs.

Figure 7.5
Weight Gain in Pregnancy The weight of the full-term baby contributes only about one-third of the 20 to 30 pounds gained by the average woman during pregnancy.

The baby's kicking and movement—initially a source of great pleasure and interest—may become downright irritating in the third trimester, particularly during the mother's attempts to sleep. Occasionally the fetus gets hiccups, and the regular spasms can be as distracting as a slowly dripping faucet. An expectant father may feel the kicking and movement readily with his hands or occasionally in the small of his back when the woman snuggles against him in bed. Many women have difficulty finding a comfortable position in which to sleep. The need for frequent urination returns, requiring several trips to the bathroom at night to release the small amount of urine under pressure in the bladder, which is being crowded by the growing fetus.

During the third trimester a pregnant woman generally feels a sense of pride combined with anxiety about the future. Many women simultaneously experience an intense desire for the pregnancy to be over and anxiety about labor and birth. Fears about the baby's health and possible birth defects tend to surface in the last trimester. With increased girth, the woman may need help with some tasks (see Figure 7.6, page 168). For example, if she is somewhat short, she may find that she has

Figure 7.6
Physical Changes During the Last Trimester of Pregnancy
Compare this figure with Figures 7.1 and 7.3.

to move the driver's seat of her car so far back to accommodate her swollen abdomen that she can no longer reach the pedals to drive. Toward the end of this period, the woman usually experiences a burst of energy and a need to prepare a "nest" for the baby. She makes final arrangements for the baby's needs, and she plans for the first few months after the birth.

If the couple has communicated effectively and resolved any problems, the third trimester is likely to be the most peaceful one. The father usually has adjusted to the pregnancy and is ready to become involved in preparing for the baby. He may participate in prepared-childbirth classes and become increasingly supportive of the mother.

If the father has remained detached, however, his early anxieties about the pregnancy may recur. For example, he may worry about family finances, or he may be concerned about his ability to be a good father. Even a detached father-to-be may feel an increased sense of responsibility as the birth approaches.

Sex During Pregnancy

Sexual expression during pregnancy varies widely across cultures and among couples. Depending on the culture, pregnancy provides a rationale either for or against sexual intercourse. In some cultures sexual intercourse ceases for most couples as soon as a woman knows that she is pregnant. When asked about intercourse during pregnancy, the So of northeastern Uganda asked, "Why would you want to do that? There is already someone in there." Among the Mehinaku of Brazil, however, repeated intercourse is perceived as necessary for the growth of the developing fetus (Gregor, 1985).

Coital positions and sites of sexual stimulation generally shift during pregnancy. After the first part of pregnancy, use of the man-above coital position tends to be replaced with a preference for positions that place less pressure on the woman's abdomen (see Figure 7.7).

In addition to changing positions, many couples find that the frequency of coitus declines during the last three months of pregnancy. The reasons for this decline vary from woman to woman, but physical discomfort is probably the most frequent. Other reasons cited by expectant mothers include fear of injuring the baby, lack of interest, feelings of awkwardness or unattractiveness, and health care providers' recommendations (Mattson & Smith, 1993).

Couples' fears notwithstanding, in a healthy pregnancy there is no reason to limit sexual activity. In fact, in a study of fourteen thousand pregnant women, Read and Klebanoff (1993) found that women who reported having engaged in coitus one to four times a week during weeks 23 to 26 (end of second and beginning of third trimesters) were about one-third less likely to have a premature birth than were women who had coitus less frequently. This finding certainly does not indicate that frequent coitus causes full-term delivery, but it does suggest that coitus is unlikely to produce premature delivery. If a woman in her third trimester is uncomfortable with coitus for whatever reason, she and her partner can engage in such noncoital forms of sexual intimacy as manual and oral stimulation of the genitals. Cuddling, kissing, and holding each other can often meet the needs of a pregnant woman and her partner.

Two sexual practices should be avoided during pregnancy. One of these is blowing air into the vagina during cunnilingus as this may cause air embolisms (Fyke, Kazmier, & Harms, 1985). An embolism is any foreign matter such as a blood clot or an air bubble that blocks a blood vessel. In addition, pregnant women should avoid sexual contact with a partner who has a sexually transmitted disease. As described earlier, if a

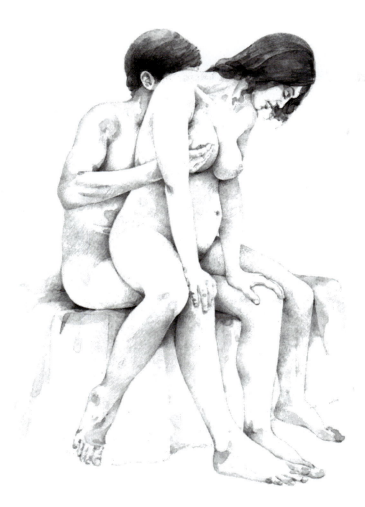

Figure 7.7
Sex During Late Pregnancy During the third trimester, a couple often shifts to coital positions that place less pressure on the woman's abdomen.

woman becomes infected, the disease may be transmitted to her baby during the pregnancy or during vaginal delivery.

LABOR AND BIRTH

As the end of pregnancy draws near, a woman may be reluctant to make appointments or to start new projects because the birth process may begin at any moment. This waiting game, with its persistent phone calls from relatives and friends, can get tedious, and expectant parents become increasingly eager to see their baby. In addition to preparing the household for the baby, many parents spend the last weeks of pregnancy actively preparing for childbirth. In giving birth, the average woman puts in

labor The process of child-birth, consisting of contractions, thinning out and expansion of the cervix, delivery of the baby, and expulsion of the placenta.

about 15 hours of increasingly strenuous work—hence the term **labor** for the stages directly leading to and including birth.

Preparation for Childbirth

During much of the twentieth century in Western countries, preparing for childbirth meant packing a suitcase with clothes for the hospital stay of the mother and newborn baby. Few expectant parents actually prepared for childbirth, and most women received little education about labor and giving birth (see "Highlight: A Personal Account of Childbirth").

Most health care providers and hospitals now encourage expectant parents to enroll in prepared-childbirth classes and to work as a team during labor and childbirth. Expectant parents usually enroll in these classes at the beginning of the third trimester. Instructors typically provide information about pregnancy and the stages of childbirth, dispelling fears and myths about birth. The course also generally includes a tour of the hospital's birthing center or maternity ward unless the couple plans to give birth at home with the help of a midwife. Finally, expectant parents learn exercises and procedures designed to facilitate childbirth. Expectant fathers master massage techniques to help relieve the lower back pain that sometimes accompanies labor contractions. Expectant mothers learn procedures to help them relax and work with contractions instead of bracing against them. They are also taught breathing techniques that are useful during different stages of labor. Participants in these courses have reported that this preparation reduced their anxieties.

Although enrollment in a prepared-childbirth course is now a routine part of the process of pregnancy and birth, the idea of active participation by both the mother and the father became popular only in the late 1960s, partly stemming from changing attitudes toward the use of anesthesia. Anesthesia was not used for childbirth until 1847, at least in part because the Bible held that "children should be brought forth in pain and sorrow." After anesthesia was introduced, however, it quickly became routine in hospital deliveries.

In the book *Childbirth Without Fear* (1932), English physician Grantley Dick-Read questioned the use of anesthetics during labor. His objections were based on the potential danger to the baby and mother. He maintained that the pain stemming from labor contractions could be eliminated or reduced through the kind of education and training for relaxation that are now a routine part of prepared-childbirth classes.

French obstetrician Bernard Lamaze also contributed to our contemporary approach to birth. After observing women in Russia undergoing labor with little pain, he began to train pregnant women and their husbands (or other "coaches") in muscle relaxation and breathing techniques. Lamaze students today also are strongly encouraged to be in top physical condition for labor. Exercises to strengthen the leg muscles are taught because the legs undergo considerable strain during childbirth.

The assistance of a familiar, supportive person is of great benefit to a woman giving birth. During labor and delivery, a woman's coach not only times her contractions (see Figure 7.9, page 176), but also supports and encourages her in relaxation and proper breathing. The use of these techniques is associated with fewer birth complications, less use of anesthesia, and shorter labor than are typical with more traditional approaches to childbirth. Mothers using prepared childbirth also have more positive attitudes following birth, higher self-esteem, and a greater sense of self-control (Olds, London, & Ladewig, 1992).

The techniques used in prepared childbirth are similar to those employed in hypnosis. For example, a woman is told to concentrate on an object—a bead in a necklace,

ISSUES TO CONSIDER

Why would anyone write that "children should be brought forth in pain and sorrow"? Do you think the author was a man or a woman?

A Personal Account of Childbirth

Pregnant women generally receive a great deal of advice and information from other women who have experienced childbirth. Here is mine. —E.R.A.

I have given birth in a hospital and at home, with and without anesthesia, with and without the help of my husband, with and without the benefit of prepared-childbirth instruction. In my experience, the ideal birth takes place at home, without anesthesia, and with the assistance of the expectant father, who has also participated in prepared-childbirth classes. The most important of these four conditions are the help of a mate and the classes. I would avoid anesthesia unless it is really needed, both for the baby's well-being and for the quality of the birth process. Because an unusually prolonged or complicated labor will mar the experience for the mother, however, anesthesia should be used when necessary.

Second-stage labor has been compared to a particularly prolonged bowel movement and to orgasm, but neither approaches the intensity of childbirth. Given my druthers on a Sunday afternoon, I'd prefer orgasm to childbirth. However, the exhaustion produced by the labor of childbirth is followed by exhilaration at birth and a period of euphoria following birth that is unique in my experience.

My advice to expectant parents is to get as much information about pregnancy and birth as possible. The more they know about it, the more fascinating the process. Prepared-childbirth classes and diligent practice of childbirth exercises are invaluable.

Amidst the rhetoric regarding women's and men's liberation, childbirth provides an extraordinarily liberating opportunity for a woman. It presents her with the opportunity to experience the union of her voluntary and involuntary processes in an event that wholly claims her—the expression of life force through her with her utter cooperation.

for example, or a picture on a wall—to aid her in relaxing during labor. She learns to control her breathing and is reassured that she can manage the stress of childbirth.

Labor for Childbirth

Although childbirth may be the most concentrated physical effort that a woman experiences in her life, women who have carried a growing baby for nine months are generally eager for labor to begin. Sometimes they experience **Braxton-Hicks contractions** for weeks prior to the onset of labor. Some women also undergo false labor—periodic contractions that seem to signal the beginning of labor but stop, rather than increase, in frequency and intensity.

Braxton-Hicks contractions
Irregular contractions of the uterus that are often mistaken for the onset of labor.

THE ONSET OF LABOR.   As the due date approaches, pregnant women begin watching for signs of the onset of labor. It is thought that labor begins when the fetus's adrenal glands produce hormones that are secreted into the placenta and uterus. These secretions stimulate the release of prostaglandins that induce contractions in the uterus. The gradual awareness of these contractions is the first symptom of labor for many women. Initially, the contractions may be so mild and infrequent (30 minutes or more apart) that women are unsure that they are actually experiencing them. The contractions gradually increase in frequency, duration, and intensity. Most women are instructed to call their doctors or midwives when the contractions occur at five-minute intervals.

Other symptoms of impending labor that can occur either before or after the onset of contractions include a pinkish discharge from the vagina and/or varying amounts of a watery discharge ("breaking waters") from the vagina. The discharge comes from the rupture of the amniotic sac. During pregnancy the fetus is protected by a cushion of almost two pounds of amniotic fluid. With the onset of labor, the fluid is generally released in varying amounts from a trickle to a gush. After the release of the amniotic fluid, contractions usually increase in frequency and intensity, although some women go through most of labor or even childbirth without the amniotic sac breaking.

LOCATION OF LABOR AND BIRTH.

In 1900 more than 95 percent of American women delivered their babies at home rather than in hospitals. At this point the figures are reversed, with only a small percentage of women giving birth at home. Some of these home deliveries are unplanned, but many families choose to deliver at home with the aid of a physician or midwife. Today's midwives can be nurses who can be certified as nurse-midwives in most states or laypersons who are trained by experienced midwives.

The advantages of home birth are the greater familiarity and comfort of the environment to the mother, the greater accessibility of family and friends who wish to be present at the birth, and the reduced expense. The most obvious disadvantage of home birth is the reduced access to equipment and trained personnel in the event that an emergency develops during labor or delivery.

Although home birth is gaining in popularity, most couples in North America go to a hospital or birthing center for childbirth. Birthing centers—health care facilities usually affiliated with hospitals but physically separated from them—generally allow a woman and her family more control over the experience of childbirth than they are likely to have in a hospital. Birthing centers are typically less expensive than are hospitals and are designed for early discharge from the center, generally within a day of the birth. Birthing centers are supplied with emergency equipment for medical problems and have advance arrangements for transferring a woman to a hospital if an emergency occurs. Research indicates that delivery at birthing centers is associated with a low Cesarean section rate and low or no neonatal mortality (Eakins, 1989). Nurses and nurse-midwives usually staff the facilities. Physicians often attend the deliveries, but some centers are staffed entirely by nurses affiliated with a particular hospital.

Labor is divided into three stages. During first-stage labor, the cervix gradually opens enough to permit passage of the baby. Birth occurs during second-stage labor. The placenta, or afterbirth, is expelled during third-stage labor.

FIRST-STAGE LABOR.

At the beginning of first-stage labor, a woman is given a checkup and a pelvic exam. During the checkup her blood pressure is measured and blood and urine samples are collected. These samples are analyzed for any signs of abnormality that might affect the process or outcome of birth.

The position of the fetus is checked to see whether **engagement** has occurred. With engagement the fetus drops several inches lower in the abdominal cavity, and when the head has gone past the mother's pelvic bone structure, it is said to be engaged. Engagement may happen at any time from a week before birth to several hours after the onset of labor.

During the pelvic exam, some labor contractions are monitored. The uterus becomes very firm, almost rigid, during each uterine contraction. This firmness can be felt by placement of a hand on the abdomen; the characteristic hardness is absent during a false labor contraction. The extent of **effacement** and **dilation**—thinning out and opening up of the cervix—is also checked. If one or more of these signs indicates that the woman is in labor or if the amniotic sac has ruptured and released some amniotic fluid, the woman is prepared ("prepped") for childbirth.

engagement Movement of the fetus into a lower position in the mother's abdominal cavity, with its head past her pelvic bone structure.

effacement Flattening and thinning of the cervix that occur before and during childbirth.

dilation Expansion or opening up of the cervix prior to birth.

At this point many women, particularly those with a first pregnancy, experience one of the two most frustrating events associated with normal childbirth.[1] They are sent home! They may have been having regular contractions five or fewer minutes apart, only to have the contractions come to an abrupt halt after they reach the hospital or birthing center. In recognition of this phenomenon, many hospitals do not admit maternity patients until after the initial checkup and pelvic exam. If the amniotic sac has not ruptured and if the cervix is completely undilated, hours or even a few days may elapse before effective labor begins. In this event it makes no sense to keep a woman in the hospital or birthing center. Nonetheless, after notifying relatives that the baby's birth is imminent, a woman who must return home still pregnant can be disappointed to tears.

When effective labor is in progress, however, women are prepared for childbirth. The abdomen, vulva, and thighs are washed with an antiseptic solution to reduce the chances of infection being transmitted to the baby during birth. Traditionally, women were given enemas and had all their pubic hair shaved, but some researchers have questioned the necessity of both practices.

Shaving of the pubic hair was done to facilitate sterilization of the area. In contemporary obstetric practice, however, shaving is recommended only if an **episiotomy** is planned. Otherwise, shaving of the pubic hair is unnecessary, and the irritation of the vulva that women feel as the hair grows back adds to their postpartum discomfort.

The rationale for the enema was twofold: The bowels should be empty so that feces are not pushed out during birth, and the enema might speed labor. Because women are given no solid foods after labor begins, however, any food that they have eaten previously has already been digested and expelled unless labor is very rapid, in which case the enema does not eliminate the food further up in the intestines. Enemas are currently recommended only if the woman has a large amount of stool in the rectum.

After the preliminary pelvic exam and checkup, the woman is taken to a labor room or birthing room—accompanied by the expectant father or another birth coach—where her contractions prepare her body to expel the baby. The contractions of early first-stage labor feel like a tightening of the abdomen and are generally not uncomfortable. As labor progresses, the tight feeling is accompanied by a sense of pressure, sometimes in the lower back and sometimes inside the abdomen just above the line of the pubic hair. The feelings grow in intensity, particularly after the release of amniotic fluid, but there are "resting" periods of a minute or two between each contraction. The breathing exercises taught in prepared-childbirth classes help a woman to avoid tensing her muscles in opposition to the work of the contractions. Fear and tension may create or heighten the intensity of a contraction.

After the cervix has dilated five or six centimeter (about two inches, or three "fingers"), the hormone oxytocin is secreted by the pituitary, and the frequency and intensity of the contractions increase considerably. The end of first-stage labor is signaled by a relatively short period of intense and seemingly incessant contractions known as **transition.** The transitional contractions complete the dilation of the cervix to 10 centimeters (four inches), so that the baby's head can pass through it.

After the baby's head appears in the vagina, doctors often perform the minor surgical procedure known as an episiotomy—a surgical cut from the bottom of the entrance to the vagina down toward the anus. The supposed purpose of the episiotomy

REALITY or **MYTH** ? **3**

episiotomy (eh-PEE-zee-AW-tuh-mee) An incision made from the bottom of the entrance to the vagina toward the buttocks angled to avoid tearing of anal tissues during childbirth.

transition A short period of intense and very frequent contractions that complete dilation of the cervix to 10 centimeters.

---

1. The other source of frustration for a woman is learning that her cervix has dilated only a few centimeters after she has been in labor for several hours and is sure that delivery is near.

is to decrease the likelihood of vaginal tearing when the baby's head and shoulders pass out of the woman's body. The surgery is performed in more than 60 percent of U.S. deliveries (Olds et al., 1992). However, except in cases in which a woman is delivering an exceptionally large baby or has an exceptionally small vaginal opening, the episiotomy is unnecessary. Furthermore, there is no reduction in rates of tearing among women given episiotomies compared to those who deliver without the surgery (Thacker & Banta, 1983). Even if some slight tearing does occur, the wound tends to mend quite readily without any postpartum stitching, whereas a surgical cut requires stitches, although they usually dissolve within a few days.

SECOND-STAGE LABOR.   In the second stage of labor, the intense and constant contractions of transition are replaced by an extremely strong urge to "bear down"—that is, to push the baby out—with each contraction. Contractions at this stage are strong, but compared to the contractions of transition, they are not particularly uncomfortable, and they are less frequent. Any discomfort is relieved when the woman does push, but depending on the position of the baby, the woman may need to control the urge to bear down, so that the baby's position may be altered by the health provider to decrease the likelihood of tearing of the cervical or vaginal opening. The rapid panting learned in prepared-childbirth classes can be helpful at this time. When the baby is positioned correctly (see Figure 7.8), a woman is told that she may bear down at the next contraction.

Within a period of time that varies from a few minutes to more than an hour, the woman succeeds in pushing the baby out (see Figure 7.9, page 176). After the baby's head has emerged, a woman may feel a wonderful combination of relief, exhaustion, and exhilaration. Controlling the urge to bear down at this point is considerably easier. When the baby's shoulders have emerged, the rest of the baby's body usually pops out readily. Thus ends second-stage labor for normal birth (see "Health: Possible Birth Complications," page 178).

After a normal birth and a quick inspection of the baby's genitals, the midwife or doctor proclaims, "It's a girl!" or "It's a boy!" Depending on the policies of the doctor and hospital and the wishes of the mother, the baby may be given to her immediately to hold and nurse.

When it is clear that the baby is able to rely on its own lungs to obtain oxygen and the umbilical cord has ceased pulsating, the cord is clamped in two places and cut. This procedure is painless for both mother and baby. If the woman has had an episiotomy, the health care provider stitches up the incision.

THIRD-STAGE LABOR AND RECOVERY.   After the baby is born, a woman continues to have a few contractions, usually quite mild, that aid her in expelling the placenta, or so-called afterbirth. Third-stage labor ends with the expulsion of the placenta. It is this process that poses the greatest risk for the mother. As the placenta is expelled, the blood vessels formerly attaching the placenta to the uterus generally close off. If they do not, hemorrhage and shock are possible. To avoid this danger, a nurse monitors the woman's vital signs for an hour or so to ensure that blood vessels close properly.

The baby is bathed, and an antibiotic solution is placed in its eyes to minimize the chances of infection. Having abstained from solid food for 10 hours or more, many women are ravenous and are given a meal. New mothers are generally encouraged to get up and walk around, use the bathroom, or go to the windows of the nursery to peer at their babies as soon as they feel comfortable doing so. Some hospitals and birthing

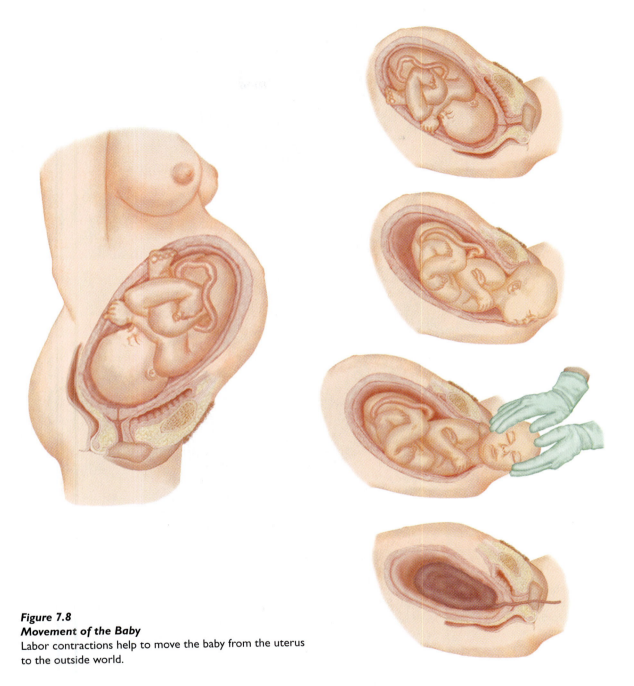

Figure 7.8
Movement of the Baby
Labor contractions help to move the baby from the uterus
to the outside world.

centers provide the option of "rooming in" for the mother. Rooming in means that the baby is housed in a bassinet right next to the mother's bed. This option is particularly convenient for the mother who wishes to breast-feed her baby because she can respond much more quickly to the baby's cry or restlessness than can nursery room staff.

In a day or two, if all is well with the mother and baby, they are released from the hospital or birthing center to go home. The lives of couples or single mothers who are parents for the first time enter a different stage, with a host of new joys and responsibilities.

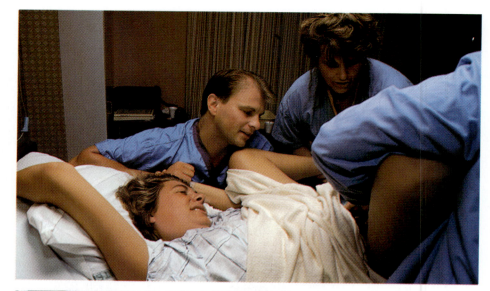

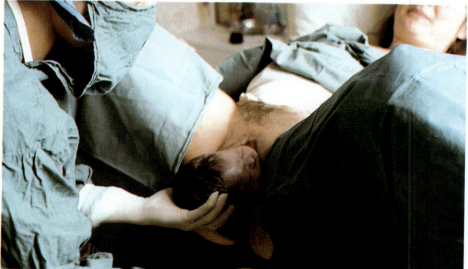

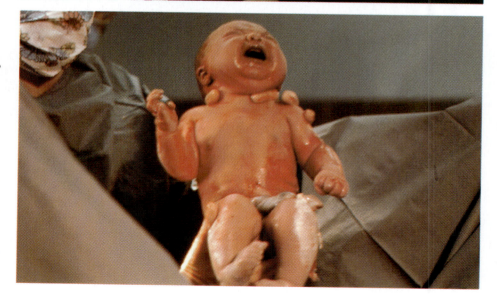

Figure 7.9 Birth

In the top photo, this woman holds onto a rail behind her to help her respond to the urge to bear down to expel the baby. Her partner coaches her during delivery. In the middle photo, the baby's head has emerged from the woman's vagina. After the shoulders have come out, the rest of the baby readily emerges. In the bottom photo, the newly born baby utters its first cry. When it is clear that the baby can breathe on its own, the umbilical cord attaching it to its mother (her placenta) is cut.

POSTPARTUM EVENTS AND DECISIONS

Within hours of their child's birth, the mother and her partner turn their attention to the innumerable decisions they have considered over the course of the pregnancy. Two of these are the method of feeding and, if the infant is a male, the question of circumcision.

Feeding

All mammals, including humans, have the capacity to suckle their offspring. Throughout most of our history, human mothers have breast-fed their babies. During the earlier part of the twentieth century, the popularity of breast-feeding declined throughout the world in favor of the use of bottled milk, or formula. Breast-feeding was perceived as "lower class," and bottled formula was thought to be antiseptic and scientific.

Just prior to birth, the woman's estrogen and progesterone levels fall. This hormonal decline stimulates the pituitary to secrete prolactin, a hormone that aids in milk production and stimulates the alveoli to secrete milk. The release of oxytocin, another pituitary hormone, is activated by the baby's sucking (Huff & Bucci, 1990). Just as oxytocin stimulates contractions of the smooth muscles of the uterus during birth, it stimulates contractions of the cells that surround the alveoli, and these contractions eject the milk into the ducts, so that the baby can easily obtain the milk by sucking. Colostrum provides the newborn with its first liquid food. The colostrum is replaced by milk about 48 hours after birth.

Numerous studies have compared the benefits of bottle and breast-feeding. Breast-fed babies acquire **passive immunity** from their mothers. Because breast milk contains antibodies from the mother's immune system, breast-fed babies are temporarily immune to a variety of diseases, including viruses and respiratory and gastrointestinal infections.

Breast milk is usually better than cow's milk or commercial formulas for the infant's physical well-being for several other reasons. First, babies can digest human milk more easily than they can other animals' milk or vegetable-based formulas such as those made from soybeans. Second, although human milk contains less protein and iron than cow's milk, human infants can use most of the protein and absorb more iron from their mother's milk than from cow's milk (Campbell, Waller, Andolsek, Huff, & Bucci, 1990). Third, breast-fed babies are less likely to suffer from diarrhea or constipation than are bottle-fed babies. Fourth, breast-fed babies tend to have healthier teeth and are less likely to be obese or to get premature atherosclerosis (formation of fatty deposits on the walls of arteries). Because of these benefits, the American Pediatric Society has concluded that breast milk is superior to bottled formula for infants and recommends breast milk as the optimal food for the first four to six months of life. For women who cannot or do not wish to breast-feed their babies but who want them to have the nutritional advantages of human milk, milk banks are now operating in many large metropolitan areas.

Breast-feeding is particularly pleasant when the baby gets older and becomes active and playful (see Figure 7.10). The average baby takes in approximately one thousand calories per day from its mother's breast milk, a circumstance that benefits a woman who gained more weight than she wished during pregnancy. A woman can generally shed pounds steadily without denying herself food if she nurses for six months or so. The oxytocin secretion stimulated by the baby's sucking also stimulates the smooth muscles of the uterus, providing another major benefit to a nursing mother. The resulting involuntary "exercise" of the uterus helps it to return to its normal size more quickly than it would if the woman did not breast-feed. The introduction of solid foods

passive immunity A kind of immunity to some diseases or conditions acquired by a baby when it receives its mother's antibodies through her breast milk.

Health

Possible Birth Complications

Reading about potential difficulties that can occur during pregnancy and childbirth can be alarming, particularly for the couple expecting its first child. With effective prenatal care and a nutritionally balanced maternal diet, however, most couples have little need to worry about their expected baby. About 99 percent of U.S. babies are born healthy and normal (Kochanek & Hudson, 1994).

Several factors can complicate the birth process, however, including atypical fetal positioning, the need for a Cesarean section, multiple births, and variations in the length of gestation. Birth position is one source of childbirth complications that can endanger the baby's or the mother's life. Most babies spend the first two trimesters of pregnancy upright in the mother's uterus. During the third trimester, the fetus generally reverses its position, so that its head is near the cervix and its buttocks and feet are at the top of the uterus. About 90 percent of babies are born head first. This position is the safest and easiest one for birth.

A small number (4 percent) of babies, however, do not reverse their direction before the onset of labor. Instead, they may present the buttocks first (breech presentation) or a shoulder or side first (transverse presentation). In many cases the doctor or midwife can alter the position, so that the baby emerges head first. If attempts at such repositioning are unsuccessful and if the mother is very small or the baby is very large, a Cesarean section (C-section) may be necessary.

About 23 percent of U.S. babies are delivered by C-section rather than vaginally (Rates of Cesarean Delivery—United States, 1993 [1995]). The woman is given general or local anesthesia, an incision is made through the abdomen and uterus, and the baby is removed. Because a C-section is a surgical procedure requiring anesthesia, women tend to be more uncomfortable following this kind of delivery than they are after a vaginal delivery. Typically, women who have a C-section remain hospitalized for four days (MMWR, 1995). They may resume coitus within the usual length of time. Women undergoing a C-section because of problems with the baby's presentation or size, lengthy labor, or other medical emergencies can usually deliver subsequent babies vaginally. But if small pelvic size is the reason for the C-section, then future births may also require this method unless the subsequent babies are small.

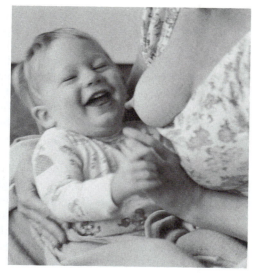

Figure 7.10
Breast-Feeding:
Food and Fun This year-old baby nurses to obtain nutrition, but breast-feeding also provides the baby and mother with an opportunity to cuddle and play. Notice the hand-holding in both photos.

The chances of a baby surviving birth and infancy are reduced by premature birth, low birth weight, and delayed birth. Babies are considered premature when they are born before they are due—that is, sooner than 266 days after conception—and when they weigh less than five and a half pounds. In a study of fourteen thousand pregnant women, Read and Klebanoff (1993) found that more than 11 percent of the mothers delivered their babies prematurely. A baby has a little more than a 50 percent chance of survival if it is born at 24 weeks' gestation. Only 15–18 percent of infants delivered at or before 23 weeks of gestation survive (Hack et al., 1995).

Factors associated with premature birth include complications during pregnancy, ingestion of drugs, maternal malnutrition, inadequate prenatal care, multiple pregnancies, and some infectious and noninfectious illnesses. Women having a first baby after age 40 and those having a series of babies during adolescence are more likely to have premature babies than are women giving birth during their 20s and 30s. Premature babies tend to develop somewhat slowly at first, but if they are given adequate treatment, they generally show normal physical development by the time they are 3 years old.

About 12 percent of babies are born two weeks after they were expected, and 4 percent are born at least three weeks late. Late babies have a mortality rate three times that of babies born when expected. Causes of death include cerebral hemorrhage and suffocation. Although some late babies are heavier than average, others may be underweight because the placenta stopped functioning after the due date. When the symptoms of labor have not appeared several weeks after the due date or when medical problems indicate that birth should be accomplished as quickly as possible, a woman may be given synthetic oxytocin to speed the labor. Oxytocin is the hormone associated with the intense contractions of transition. Labor-inducing drugs should be used only when the risks of prolonged labor outweigh the risks of administering the drug.

Early knowledge of pregnancy and regular prenatal checkups reduce the likelihood of parents experiencing these complications of pregnancy and childbirth. Awareness of, and avoidance of, potential risks can increase the chances that expectant parents will experience a happy and satisfying pregnancy and childbirth.

to supplement breast milk should be implemented by the fourth to the sixth month (Campbell et al., 1990).

Some mothers find the sucking of their nipples sexually arousing, and a few experience orgasm during breast-feeding (Reamy & White, 1987). Depending on a woman's sexual attitudes, such arousal can be either extremely disconcerting or an additional pleasure associated with breast-feeding. Some women begin to breast-feed but terminate the process within a few days because of tender nipples and the engorgement of their breasts with milk, characteristics of the early weeks of breast-feeding. For those women who experience nipple tenderness from breast-feeding, the discomfort is slight to moderate, and it usually peaks at the third day and then decreases rapidly thereafter (de Carvalho, Robertson, & Klaus, 1984). The woman can reduce or eliminate nipple tenderness by allowing the breast milk to dry on the nipples. She can reduce breast engorgement by nursing the baby and by taking a warm shower to release some of the milk.

Just as some drugs and medications taken by a pregnant woman can transfer through the placenta to the fetus, so can they also be received by a baby through breast milk. A nursing mother should check with her health care provider before taking any medications.

REALITY or MYTH ? 4

ISSUES TO CONSIDER

What are the advantages and disadvantages of breast-feeding an infant?

Circumcision

Throughout history diverse operations have been performed on the sex organs of infants, as well as children and young adults. Boys have had their foreskins removed (circumcision) and slits made in the entire length of their penises (subincision). Girls have had their clitorises, their clitoral hoods, and their labia removed. Some women have had their labia sewn together. These operations have been performed in compliance with religious, ritual, hygienic, or sexual beliefs in various cultures. At present these practices remain common only in some parts of the Middle East, Africa, and Australia, as well as in the United States. More than 1 million baby boys are circumcised each year in the United States, and circumcision is the most common surgery performed on children (Niku et al., 1995).

Many contemporary American parents support circumcision, either because their religion prescribes it, because they mistakenly think that it is legally required, or because they believe that the presence of the foreskin causes cancer later in life. Recent research indicates that circumcision is associated with a slightly reduced risk of penile cancer (Niku et al., 1995). Since 1930 about sixty thousand men have been diagnosed with this rare form of cancer. Almost all were uncircumcised. The incidence of penile cancer is believed to be related to personal hygiene. Evidence linking cervical cancer to sexual intercourse with uncircumcised men is inconclusive (Niku et al., 1995). A task force of the American Academy of Pediatrics reviewed the available data and concluded that the evidence on the risks and benefits of circumcision is contradictory. The task force concluded its report with the following recommendation: "Newborn circumcision has potential medical benefits and advantages as well as disadvantages and risks. When circumcision is being considered, the benefits and risks should be explained to the parents and informed consent obtained" (Schoen, Anderson, & Bohen, 1989, p. 390).

Another common belief is that circumcision affects sexual arousal. Some have argued that the removal of the foreskin reduces sensitivity because constant contact with clothing toughens the glans. In earlier times this assumed reduction in sensitivity was considered an advantage in curbing masturbation. More recently, the assumed decrease in sensitivity was believed to delay orgasm in men, thereby enhancing their desirability as sexual partners because women tend to become aroused more slowly than do men. These long-held ideas notwithstanding, the presence or absence of the foreskin is not related to sexual sensitivity, the tendency to masturbate, or the speed of orgasm. As Karen Paige (1978, p. 45) put it, "Sexual sensitivity appears to be in the mind of a man, not in his foreskin."

Circumcision is usually done with an analgesic and/or anesthesia. Various techniques are used, and the complication rate is about 4 percent, which translates into more than fifty thousand complicated circumcisions each year. Hemorrhage, mutilation, infection, and surgical trauma are the most serious complications. Furthermore, evidence suggests that for a short time after the operation, circumcised babies not only have increased heart rates and hormone-release patterns but also manifest greater levels of irritability than do uncircumcised babies (Niku et al., 1995).

A growing number of insurance companies and state Medicare agencies in the United States refuse to cover the cost of circumcision unless it is medically indicated. For example, in rare cases of phimosis (a condition in which the foreskin is so tight that it cannot be retracted from the glans), circumcision is considered medically appropriate. The proportion of newborn U.S. boys who are circumcised has been drop-

ISSUES TO CONSIDER

If you had (or have) a boy, would you (did you) have him circumcised? Why or why not?

ping. In Canada, after an examination of research on the effects of circumcision to determine if the government should continue to pay for the procedure, Cadman, Gafini, and McNamee (1984) concluded that the operation constitutes cosmetic surgery and thus should be paid for by those parents desiring it for their sons.

Postpartum Adjustment

Because giving birth involves both physiological and psychological adjustment, the six weeks following childbirth are inherently stressful. First, the new mother experiences a rapid decline in estrogen and progesterone levels. High levels of estrogen during the menstrual cycle are associated with a general sense of well-being, whereas the low levels that precede the onset of menstruation are often accompanied by unwanted premenstrual symptoms. The decrease in estrogen associated with birth might also be expected to be related to such symptoms as fatigue, depressed mood, and edginess.

Second, both parents may get little sleep because most infants awaken frequently at night. The resulting fatigue can be particularly taxing for the mother, who may still be tired from lack of sleep in the final weeks of pregnancy and from the strenuous activity of giving birth. In addition, the deep sleep phase is reduced in women prior to delivery and typically does not return to normal until the second week following birth (Hostetter & Andolsek, 1990).

Third, for first-time parents, the loss of freedom and the number of tasks involved in caring for a helpless infant can be overwhelming. For couples who were accustomed to accepting last-minute invitations to parties or requests to work overtime, the realization that they cannot act as spontaneously as before can lead to a sense of being trapped, even when the pregnancy was planned. The opportunity for uninterrupted conversation or lovemaking may be sharply curtailed for months after the birth, leaving the mother and/or father feeling neglected, jealous, or resentful of the baby. Some new parents suspect that their seemingly helpless infants are considerably more aware of the surrounding environment than is commonly thought. As one young father we know put it, "That damn kid has ESP. . . . Every time I get his mother alone for a few minutes, he wakes up and starts wailing!"

Although women are generally expected to be elated, even if exhausted, by the arrival of the "blessed event," 87 percent of new mothers experience health problems in the first two months postpartum, such as tiredness, backaches, anemia, breast problems associated with breast-feeding, and depression (Glazener et al., 1995). In light of these factors—changes in hormone levels, loss of sleep, and reduced freedom—it is surprising that "postpartum blues" are not universal.

When these symptoms continue beyond a few weeks, a woman may be diagnosed as experiencing **postpartum depression,** including prolonged dysphoria (absence of enjoyment of life) and loss of concentration and self-esteem. Severe and lengthy symptoms of depression affect only about one or two women per one thousand births (Olds et al., 1992).

postpartum depression Intense sadness or general letdown experienced by some women following childbirth.

Postpartum Sexual Expression

Many physicians have routinely banned coitus for six weeks following birth. This ban may be linked more to societal or religious taboos based on beliefs about women's "uncleanliness" during menstruation and the immediate postpartum period than to empirical data indicating medical risks (Reamy & White, 1987). Yet for the first few weeks after birth, coitus may be the furthest thing from a new mother's mind. Tenderness in the vaginal area (particularly after an episiotomy), general fatigue, diminished levels of estrogen, and the vaginal discharge that occurs in the days following birth all may contribute to temporarily diminished sexual desire. Gradually, these symptoms decline. The original discharge is replaced by **lochia,** a discharge consisting of a smaller amount of red or brown blood that may continue for two to four weeks or more following birth. This discharge need not interfere with intercourse, however, if the woman begins to feel the familiar stirrings of desire.

If a woman has not had an episiotomy, or if the episiotomy has healed quickly, the couple may resume coitus within three or four weeks after birth. In a study of more than one thousand women and their spouses/partners during pregnancy and the year postpartum, Hyde, DeLamater, Plant, and Byrd (1996) found that about 90 percent of couples reported resuming intercourse during the fourth to twelfth month postpartum, but only about 19 percent reported coitus in the month immediately following birth. Nevertheless, the majority of couples did report petting during the first month postpartum. At all times, women and men in the Hyde et al. study were above the midpoint in their ratings of their satisfaction with their sexual relationship—including the first month postpartum. For most women, first postpartum coitus occurs between the first

lochia (LOH-kee-ah) Dark-colored vaginal discharge that follows childbirth for several weeks.

Figure 7.11
Parents as Lovers Even as couples carry out their roles as parents, it is important that they maintain their relationship as a couple.

and second month following birth, with the fifth week being the most common time for resumption of coitus (Reamy & White, 1987).

It is normal for women to feel apprehensive when resuming coital relations; many fear a renewal of the vaginal discomfort that they experienced during childbirth and recovery. But new mothers have other concerns as well. Worries that may inhibit resumption of intercourse include concerns about birth control, vaginal tenderness, harm to internal organs, infections, waking the baby, and decreased vaginal lubrication.

The issues of effective contraception and waking of the baby can be handled readily, with some preplanning. However, if a woman is experiencing perineal tenderness from the birth or from an episiotomy, the couple should postpone coitus until she is more comfortable. A temporary reduction in vaginal lubrication for a short time following childbirth is normal, but water-soluble lubricants can be used until the woman begins to secrete adequate amounts of vaginal lubrication.

Some new mothers also worry about their sexual attractiveness. Stretch marks left over from the pregnancy, extra weight, and loose skin in their abdomens may contribute to their self-doubt. But the stretch marks lose their reddish color and become less noticeable with time, and weight reduction and the firming of abdominal skin and muscles can be accomplished with appropriate diet and exercise. Of additional concern to some women are the shape, size, and tone of the vagina after birth. One of the remarkable features of the vagina, however, is its elasticity. Although it stretches to permit the birth of a baby, the vaginal muscles tighten again fairly soon after birth. The new mother can speed the process by which these muscles regain their tone and strength by doing Kegel exercises. Henderson (1983) instructed a group of new mothers to perform these exercises and found that they had greater muscle tone at their first postpartum checkup than did a control group of women.

Although the physical changes following childbirth temporarily require substantial adjustment, psychological and social changes may pose greater challenges for both parents. First-time parents may find that it takes time to integrate their new roles as parents with their former roles as companions and lovers (see Figure 7.11). A candlelit dinner away from home, a walk in the woods—any activity that gives a couple time away from the baby——may help to speed that integration.

Summary of major points

1. Symptoms of pregnancy.

A missed menstrual period is generally, but not always, the first indication that a woman is pregnant. Most lab tests for pregnancy are based on the detection of the hormone HCG in a blood or urine sample. Reliable test results can be obtained as early as a week after conception. Home pregnancy test kits administered as early as the first day of the expected menstrual period are also highly reliable when done correctly. Although these home tests may be a convenient preliminary indicator of pregnancy, they should not be used as a substitute for a lab test because conditions other than pregnancy can affect test results.

2. The experience of pregnancy.

Although each pregnancy is unique, women commonly experience some fatigue and occasional nausea during the first trimester and lose some interest in sexual interaction. In contrast, during the second trimester most women feel very healthy and energetic, and many describe this period as a time of enhanced sexual interest and pleasure. During the third trimester, pregnant women tend to feel increasingly bulky as the fetus gains in weight and size, and fatigue and discomfort are common. For healthy women so inclined, sexual interaction appears to have no negative effects on the fetus during the third trimester. Fathers also experience pregnancy in stages, with responses ranging from ambivalence to a heightened sense of responsibility.

3. The onset of labor.

Various events signal the onset of labor, including uterine contractions and release of the cervical mucus plug and amniotic fluid. The extent of "prepping" a woman undergoes depends on the policies of the physician or midwife and the hospital or birthing center.

4. The process of labor.

During first-stage labor, increasingly frequent and intense contractions efface and dilate the cervix to widen it for the baby's passage. The most frequent and intense contractions occur during transition at the end of first-stage labor. During second-stage labor, a woman bears down at the height of the birth contractions to help push the baby out of the uterus and vagina. During third-stage labor, the placenta and the umbilical cord are delivered.

5. Postpartum parental decisions.

One issue that must be decided shortly after the birth of a baby is whether to breast-feed. Breast milk is nutritionally superior to bottled milk or formula. Another decision that new parents must make is whether to circumcise a baby boy. The practice of removing the foreskins of infant boys (circumcision) is currently the source of considerable controversy.

6. Postpartum adjustment.

New parents, and particularly new mothers, normally experience fatigue and bouts of depression from a combination of abrupt hormonal changes, loss of sleep, and loss of freedom brought on by the responsibility of caring for a helpless new human. Those who experience these problems can reduce their severity considerably by reserving some time for their own needs as individuals and as a couple. Although emotional intimacy can be maintained throughout childbirth and the postpartum period, sexual intercourse is generally not resumed for three to six weeks following birth. For new parents, the weeks following the birth of a first baby are devoted to adding the new role of co-parents to their former roles as lovers and spouses, and this process has both its stresses and its joys.

CHECK YOUR KNOWLEDGE

1. When a fertilized egg implants outside the uterus, it is called (a) couvade, (b) a zygote transfer, (c) an ectopic pregnancy, (d) a sterile pregnancy. (p. 161)

2. The majority of miscarriages (a) occur in the first trimester, (b) are caused by physical abuse of the mother, (c) are caused by the mother engaging in sexual intercourse during the second trimester, (d) occur in the third trimester. (p. 164)

3. Which of these is not a method for checking a fetus for genetic disorders? (a) amniocentesis, (b) chorionic villi sampling, (c) alveoli tissue sampling, (d) ultrasonography. (p. 165)

4. In North America sexual intercourse during the last trimester of pregnancy is (a) often less frequent than in the earlier trimesters, (b) often more frequent than in the earlier trimesters, (c) forbidden by medical authorities, (d) generally recommended to increase the couple's sense of intimacy. (p. 168)

5. The first, second, and third stages of labor correspond to (a) the gradual opening of the cervix, birth, and the expulsion of the placenta; (b) initial sensation of contractions, the gradual intensification and increasing frequency of contractions, and the culmination of contractions just before birth; (c) the opening of the cervix, the onset of contractions, and birth; (d) the onset of contractions, the opening of the cervix, and birth. (pp. 172–174)

6. Following birth most (a) mothers sleep for 16 to 18 hours a day, (b) mothers experience a rapid decline in estrogen and progesterone, (c) fathers experience a rapid decline in HY antigens, (d) parents are intensely attracted to other people. (p. 181)

7. After an uncomplicated delivery, intercourse is (a) possible within three or four weeks, (b) possible within three or four days, (c) unwise for at least eight weeks, (d) unwise for at least three months. (p. 182)

8. Male circumcision is (a) usually performed on an outpatient basis; (b) almost universal in North America, northern Europe, and Japan; (c) the most common surgery performed on male children in the United States; (d) against the law in most African nations. (p. 180)

8

PREVENTING AND RESOLVING UNWANTED PREGNANCY

THE DEVELOPMENT AND USE OF MODERN CONTRACEPTIVES
Selecting a Contraceptive
Correlates of Contraceptive Use
Highlight: Spontaneous Sex—The Big Lie

METHODS OF CONTRACEPTION
Rhythm
Diaphragm and Spermicide
Cervical Cap
Condom
Female Condoms
Foams and Suppositories
Oral Contraceptives
Hormone Implants and Injections
Intrauterine Devices
Relatively Ineffective Methods

STERILIZATION
Vasectomy
Tubal Ligation

CONTRACEPTIVE TECHNIQUES OF THE FUTURE
Research on Future Methods of Birth Control for Men
Research on Future Methods of Birth Control for Women

UNWANTED PREGNANCY

ABORTION: A HUMAN DILEMMA
The Moral and Legal Debate over Abortion
Highlight: The Legal Status of Abortion in the United States
Reasons for Abortion

ABORTION: THE PROCESS
Abortion Methods Early in Pregnancy
First-Trimester Abortion Methods
Second-Trimester Abortion Methods
Psychological Responses to Abortion
The Male Role in Abortion

UNINTENDED PARENTHOOD
Adolescent Parents
Keeping an Unwanted Child

SUMMARY OF MAJOR POINTS

CHECK YOUR KNOWLEDGE

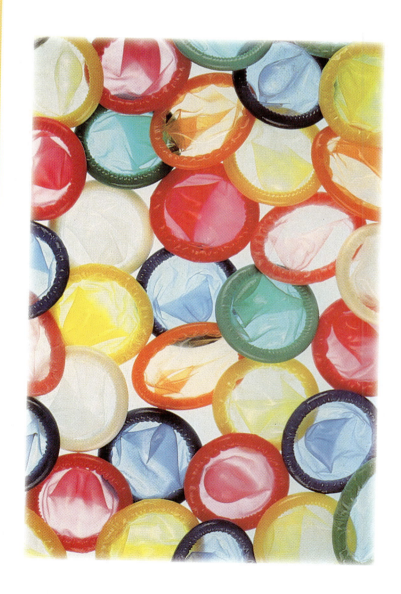

REALITY or MYTH ?

1. The rhythm method is just as effective as the birth control pill in preventing pregnancy.

2. The condom is the only reliable temporary method of male contraception.

3. Female condoms have a lower breakage rate than male condoms.

4. Low-dose oral contraceptives reduce a woman's risk of contracting uterine and ovarian cancers.

5. The majority of Americans support the banning of abortion under any circumstances.

6. Most women experience intense sadness, guilt, and regret for a number of years following an abortion.

HOW many humans can the earth support? Control of the growth of the earth's population is one of the most fundamental problems facing our species. The world's population now surpasses 5 billion, and it is expected to reach 6 billion by the time we reach the year 2000 and possibly climb to 70 billion by the year 2150 if current sexual practices do not change (Haub, 1992). In the *minute* that it takes you to read this paragraph, more than 175 babies will have been added to our population! Many are unplanned or unwanted, and our planet's air, land, and water resources are being overwhelmed by population growth.

In this chapter we describe **contraceptives** and the major political and social factors that influenced their development and legal acceptance. We also examine some of the reasons that people engage in unprotected intercourse. We consider the advantages and disadvantages of each of the temporary and permanent methods of **birth control** currently available, along with some that are now being developed.

After discovering an unwanted pregnancy, a woman has three options: obtaining an abortion; continuing the pregnancy, keeping the baby, and rearing it with or without the help of its father; or placing the baby for adoption. We examine the currently available abortion methods and the legal status of this option. We also consider the short-term and long-term effects of choosing this alternative. If an unmarried woman decides against abortion, she is far more likely now than in the past to bring up the baby rather than to place it for adoption. Recent research suggests, however, that without considerable social and economic support, such a mother and her offspring face numerous difficulties.

contraceptives Any techniques, drugs, or devices that prevent conception.

birth control The regulation of conception, pregnancy, or birth with preventive devices or methods.

THE DEVELOPMENT AND USE OF MODERN CONTRACEPTIVES

Despite the age-old belief that *the* purpose of sexual interaction is to reproduce, people have attempted to practice birth control for thousands of years. In Europe large segments of the population began to use birth control in the latter part of the eighteenth century. They employed such methods as withdrawal, absorbents placed in the vagina, postcoital douching, abortion, and even infanticide (the killing of newborns). With the obvious exception of the last two, these methods were not highly reliable, but they did lower the birthrate. During the nineteenth century, the widespread desire for more effective methods of birth control resulted in the development of the forerunners of modern diaphragms, spermicidal agents, cervical caps, condoms, and methods of female sterilization. The early twentieth century witnessed the development of the intrauterine device (IUD), modern methods of male sterilization, and new techniques for abortion. The latest of the widely available methods of birth control—oral contraception, or "the pill"—was first marketed in 1960.

In 1965 the U.S. Supreme Court overturned state laws prohibiting the dissemination of contraceptive information and devices. Such laws were judged to be unconstitutional because they interfered with a couple's right to privacy. With the marketing of the pill and the IUD in the 1960s and the Supreme Court's removal in 1973 of any legal barriers to a woman's decision to obtain an abortion during the first three months of pregnancy, the goal of greater control over reproduction was realized.

Selecting a Contraceptive

One of the most important considerations in the selection of a birth control method is its effectiveness. We often think of a word such as *effective* in an absolute sense: Either something works, or it does not. But in the realm of birth control, such certainty is impossible. On rare occasions babies have even been born following attempted abortions or sterilizations. Birth control methods are therefore evaluated in terms of their probability of failure. This probability is calculated by determining the number of sexually active women out of one hundred who become pregnant in the course of a year while relying on a particular method (see Table 8.1).

theoretical failure rate The failure rate of a contraceptive method when it is used correctly.

actual failure rate The failure rate of a contraceptive method that takes into account both failure of the method and human failure to use it correctly.

Contraceptive effectiveness is measured in terms of both the theoretical and the actual failure rate. The **theoretical failure rate** is the number of failures that occur when the method is used correctly. In those cases conception results from the failure of the method itself. The **actual failure rate** is the total number of pregnancies that occur as a result of either failure of the method or failure to use a method correctly and consistently.

In choosing a birth control method, you are wise to consider both the advantages and the disadvantages. The advantages include relative effectiveness and convenience. Possible disadvantages include health risks, other undesirable side effects, or the potential need to interrupt lovemaking (for example, to use the condom or diaphragm).

Because of the relatively large proportion of adolescents and young adults who engage in sex without contraception, many subsequently experience an unwanted pregnancy (most research has been conducted with this age group). There are four necessary conditions for the use of contraceptives: existence of legal and reliable contraceptives, contraceptive education, easy access to contraceptives, and motivation to employ contraception. In the case of most U.S. teenagers, only one condition—the existence of legal and reliable contraceptives—has been met. In 1977 the Supreme Court struck down a New York State statute that had prohibited the sale or distribution of nonprescription contraceptives to minors under age 16. This decision, combined with several other rulings, eliminated all legal barriers to the acquisition of contraception by adolescents.

Table 8.1   Yearly Failure Rates of Birth Control Methods

Method	Lowest Expected or Observed Failure Rate[a]	Failure Rate Among Typical Users[b]
Tubal ligation	0.4	0.4
Vasectomy	0.10	0.15
Injectable progestin (Depo-Provera)	0.3	0.3
Combined birth control pills	0.1	
Progestin-only pill	0.5	
Norplant (6 capsules)	0.09	0.09
IUD	1.5	2.0
Condom	3.0	12.0
Diaphragm	6.0	18.0
Contraceptive sponge	9.0	36.0
Cervical cap	9.0	36.0
Foam, creams, jellies, and vaginal suppositories	6.0	21.0
Withdrawal	4.0	19.0
Sympto-thermal	2.0	
Chance (no method of birth control)	85.0	85.0

[a]Designed to complete the sentence "Of 100 women who start out the year using a given method, and who use it correctly and consistently, the lowest observed failure rate has been . . ."

[b]Designed to complete the sentence "Of 100 typical users who start out the year employing a given method, the number who will be pregnant by the end of the year will be . . ."

Sources: Hatcher et al. (1994); Trussell, Strickler, and Vaughn (1993).

Correlates of Contraceptive Use

The lack of contraceptive education remains a major hindrance to contraceptive use. Exposure to formal contraceptive programs increases the likelihood by about one-third that a teenage woman will use a contraceptive method at first intercourse. If contraceptive education occurs in the same year that a teenager becomes sexually active, the odds of use of any method and use of a condom are increased by 70 to 80 percent. Mauldon and Luker (1996) suggested that with greater educational efforts, the proportion of teens using no method might decrease from 41 to 33 percent.

What about the belief that easy access to contraception leads to promiscuity? Evidence shows that use of reliable contraceptives is associated with strong commitment to one partner rather than with promiscuous sexual activity involving a number of different partners (Harvey & Scrimshaw, 1988; Miller, 1986). Even for first intercourse, there is greater use of reliable contraception among partners who are in love or planning to marry than among partners who are less involved with each other. The greater the degree of involvement between two partners the first time they have sex, the more likely they are to use a reliable contraceptive.

Adolescent females who consistently use reliable contraceptives differ from those who do not in background, knowledge, attitudes, and personality. On the basis

ISSUES TO CONSIDER

Assume that you have a child who is about to reach puberty. What education would you have already provided about contraception? What information would you want to give as he or she enters puberty?

HIGHLIGHT

Spontaneous Sex—The Big Lie

People sometimes object to the notion of using contraception on the grounds that birth control methods interfere with the spontaneity of sexual intimacy. This reasoning is based on the false assumption that sexual contact occurs without premeditation or forewarning. In truth, although partners may behave spontaneously during a sexual interaction, the decision to become sexually intimate in the first place is not made without at least one partner preparing for intimacy.

Consider the last time that you had a sexual interaction with another person. It may have involved penis-in-vagina, mutual masturbation, or oral-genital contact, or it may have been as simple as a first kiss. The point is that someone, either you or your partner, had to make decisions with the intention of becoming closer sexually. For those sexual contacts involving the risk of conception, a number of acts necessarily precede vaginal penetration: You need to find a private place, there should be agreement between you and your partner that you want to have coitus, and, of course, there is the little matter of removing your clothing, so that sexual intercourse can proceed!

Except in the case of date rape, both people in the early stages of a relationship have probably thought of the possibility of progressing to sexual intimacy—in delightful fantasies, or perhaps with fear. Their fantasies and communication could include erotic contraceptive and prophylactic messages:

"Oh, honey, I really want to insert your diaphragm, so that I can then insert my penis into your vagina. . . . Would you like me to do that?"

"I just woke up from a really horny dream about you; I want us to have oral sex, but after that, I would like you to put your penis inside my vagina. If that is all right with you, I'll go get the condoms from my purse."

"You are gorgeous to me. I just had a general screening test for STDs, including AIDS, and I'm negative. But it's important for us to be safe, so I would like for us to play with a condom. Can we roll them on, very, very slowly? Your penis is so beautiful and firm, would it be ok if I play with your penis while I put the condom on? Would you play with mine while I roll a condom onto me? Oh, you've gotten even harder—would you like to put your penis into me?"

Incorporation of methods to reduce the negative consequences of sexuality (unwanted conception, STDs) into our sexual interactions can enhance the pleasure of our sexual lives.

---

of research, it is possible to draw a general picture of teenagers from each of these two groups. The socioeconomic status of teenage women who consistently use contraception tends to be higher than that of women who are less conscientious. Moreover, the older, and presumably the more mature, a woman is when she first has intercourse, the greater is the likelihood that she will use birth control (Mauldon & Luker, 1996).

Although religious affiliation was related to contraceptive use in the past, research suggests that this is no longer the case (Tanfer, Grady, Klepinger, & Billy, 1993). Catholics, for example, are now as likely as Protestants to use contraception.

Attitudes toward sex are also strongly associated with contraceptive behavior. Consistent use of contraception is more likely among men and women with positive (erotophilic) attitudes and openness toward sex in general and toward their own sexual activity in particular (Fisher et al., 1988). Some students who discover that they are pregnant come to us seeking information about various community resources. They cannot deny, of course, that they have been sexually intimate, but many of them describe the occurrence of intercourse as somehow accidental or unintentional, using versions of the claim that "the devil made me do it." They blame arousal ("We got carried away"), intoxication ("I got drunk"), or their partner ("He made me do it"; "She should have stopped me"). People who cannot acknowledge that they might be sexually active in some situations are unlikely to employ contraception (see "Highlight: Spontaneous Sex—The Big Lie").

Given the obvious association between sexuality and contraception, it is not surprising that guilt about sex affects attitudes and behavior regarding contraception. In fact, sex guilt may even interfere with a person's ability to learn about contraception. Schwartz (1973) found that when college students heard a lecture containing birth control information that is not commonly known, those who felt guilty about sex received lower scores on a test of their retention of the information than did those who felt less guilty.

If the rearing of children to feel guilty about their sexual feelings were effective in preventing premarital intercourse, then the negative association with sex guilt and teenagers' use of contraceptives would not be of great concern. But research involving sexually active college students indicates that sex guilt may be more effective in blocking contraceptive use than in preventing premarital intercourse (Strassberg & Mahoney, 1988).

Our culture's assumptions about men's and women's differing motivations for intercourse and the possible outcome—pregnancy—is related to the development of contraceptives. The bulk of the blame and responsibility for unwanted pregnancy falls on women. Despite men's apparent willingness to use contraceptives, their use is less likely when a man initiates intercourse than when a woman is the initiator (Harvey & Scrimshaw, 1988). Thus most efforts to increase contraceptive use have targeted women.

Various lines of evidence suggest, however, that men are willing to take contraceptive responsibility, although there is currently only one effective temporary method that men can use: the condom. For example, several cross-cultural studies sponsored by the World Health Organization (1980, 1982) found that a considerable proportion of men reported willingness to use hormonal contraceptives. In the past few decades, researchers and family planning agencies have shown increased interest in male contraceptive behavior.

Although the health risks associated with the use of various contraceptives receive much media publicity, the greatest mortality risk for sexually active women comes from dangers associated with pregnancy and childbirth, which kill one in eleven thousand women each year. In contrast, the lowest mortality rates are associated with the use of a barrier method of contraception, such as a diaphragm or a condom, in combination with legal abortion during the first nine weeks if the barrier method fails and a pregnancy occurs: one in four hundred thousand sexually active women dies from this combination of methods (see Table 8.2).

Table 8.2	**Risks Associated with Life and Fertility**
Risk	**Chance of Death in a Year (U.S.)**
Smoking	1 in 200
Motorcycling	1 in 1,000
Automobile driving	1 in 6,000
Power boating	1 in 6,000
Rock climbing	1 in 7,500
Playing football	1 in 25,000
Canoeing	1 in 100,000
Preventing pregnancy:	
Oral contraceptive, nonsmoker	1 in 63,000
Oral contraceptive, smoker	1 in 16,000
IUD	1 in 100,000
Barrier methods	None
Natural methods	None
Undergoing sterilization:	
Laparoscopic tubal ligation	1 in 67,000
Hysterectomy	1 in 1,600
Vasectomy	1 in 300,000
Deciding about pregnancy:	
Continuing pregnancy	1 in 11,000
Terminating pregnancy	
Illegal abortion	1 in 3,000
Legal abortion	
Before 9 weeks	1 in 260,000
9–12 weeks	1 in 100,000
13–15 weeks	1 in 34,000
After 15 weeks	1 in 10,200

Source: Adapted from Hatcher et al. (1994)

METHODS OF CONTRACEPTION

We now discuss current methods of birth control and their potential advantages and disadvantages, benefits, and impact on sexual response.[1] Because new information about birth control becomes available each year, you should consult a health care provider before making contraceptive choices. In choosing the right method for you, you and your health care provider should take into account your age, lifestyle, personality, and medical history.

Rhythm

rhythm method A birth control technique based on avoidance of sexual intercourse during a woman's fertile period each month.

We begin with the so-called **rhythm method,** mainly because the knowledge a couple needs to make this technique effective can be useful in increasing the effectiveness of almost all other birth control methods. About 4 percent of women report using this method as a contraceptive technique (Forrest & Fordyce, 1993). Essentially, it means abstaining from coitus for at least a week around the time of ovulation. The date of ovulation must therefore be determined.

Knowledge of the time of ovulation is useful to women for several reasons. First, pinpointing the date of ovulation and engaging in intercourse at that time can improve the woman's chances of beginning a wanted pregnancy. Second, the more women know about the cycles and functioning of their own bodies, the more likely they are to recognize potential medical difficulties. The presently available methods of detecting ovulation involve the use of a calendar, the recording of one's daily temperature, the monitoring of cervical mucus, and the use of ovulation detection kits.

THE CALENDAR METHOD.

The calendar method of determining ovulation is based on the law of averages. The average menstrual cycle is about 28 days long, with ovulation occurring, on average, 14 days *prior* to the onset of the menstrual period. To determine when ovulation occurs, a woman must be able to predict accurately the day she will begin her next period. Such forecasting can pose a problem because emotional and biological factors such as illness, fatigue, rigorous exercise, and stress can alter the cycle interval. Menstrual regularity is also rare in the first few and last few years of a woman's reproductive span. Furthermore, women occasionally release more than one egg in a particular cycle, which can throw off the timing.

THE SYMPTO-THERMAL METHOD.

sympto-thermal method A way of determining the date of ovulation based on changes in a woman's basal body temperature and the stretchability of her cervical mucus.

To determine the time of ovulation by the **sympto-thermal method,** a woman takes her temperature each morning before she gets out of bed with a basal body temperature (BBT) thermometer (an ordinary thermometer is not sensitive enough) and examines her cervical mucus. Generally low during the first part of the menstrual cycle, the BBT tends to drop slightly more on the day of ovulation.

The BBT then rises on the day after ovulation and remains relatively high throughout the rest of the cycle (see Figure 8.1). Because the most definite indication of ovulation, the rise in BBT, occurs the day *after* ovulation, successful use of this method depends on a woman keeping track of her cycle for up to six months *and* having a regular cycle. A woman can predict the day she will ovulate only if both conditions are met.

A woman confirms the information she obtains from the BBT by examining the cervical mucus because the amount and characteristics of the mucus vary at different points

---

1. Unless otherwise noted, statistics on effectiveness are based on Hatcher et al. (1994).

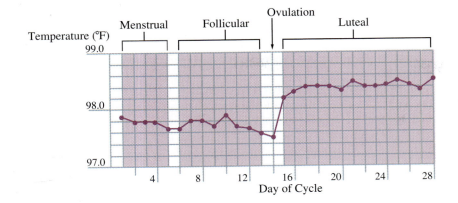

Figure 8.1
Basal Body Temperature (BBT) Chart Note that the temperature pattern for this average woman includes a sharp rise in BBT on day 15, indicating the point of ovulation as day 14.

in the menstrual cycle. During ovulation the mucus stretches and resembles unbeaten raw egg whites in consistency. To check the extent of stretchiness, a woman first inserts her finger into her vagina to obtain a sample of cervical mucus. After withdrawing her finger, she touches it to her thumb and then slowly pulls her thumb and index finger apart. If ovulation is occurring, she will observe a thin, connecting thread of mucus up to an inch long (see Figure 8.2). During the rest of the menstrual cycle, the mucus does not stretch at all.

Ovulation detection kits are now available in drugstores. This test, which monitors the presence of an enzyme associated with ovulation, can only confirm, not predict, ovulation (Hatcher et al., 1994).

Effective use of the sympto-thermal method depends on the woman accurately pinpointing the time of ovulation and avoiding unprotected coitus during the fertile period from five days preceding ovulation until three days following ovulation. For a graphic representation of the sympto-thermal rhythm method, see Figure 8.3. The sympto-

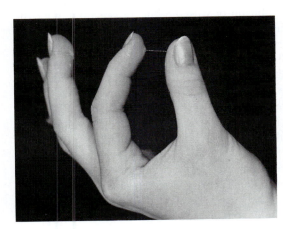

Figure 8.2 (above)
Stretchability of Cervical Mucus at Ovulation At ovulation a woman's cervical mucus stretches to form a connecting thread up to an inch long, as this photo shows.

Figure 8.3 (right)
Hypothetical Menstrual Cycle Illustrating the Use of the Rhythm Method of Contraception

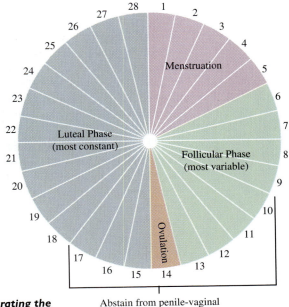

Abstain from penile-vaginal intercourse

thermal method is not as effective as other methods to be described, but it involves far less risk than no method at all. The effectiveness of the method is greatest when a couple engages in coitus only after ovulation. This practice yields a theoretical failure rate of about two pregnancies per one hundred women who engage in coitus on a fairly regular basis for a year.

Drawbacks of the sympto-thermal method include the fact that accurately determining the date of ovulation takes a minimum of six months. Second, although the sympto-thermal method has no direct physical effect on sexuality, it may have psychological effects for some couples. The required periods of abstinence from coitus for one to three weeks out of each cycle depending on the regularity (and thus the predictability) of a woman's menstrual cycle may result in considerable frustration. The temporary ban on coitus need not be a great disadvantage, however, because couples can engage in oral or manual stimulation without fear of conception during those times when a woman is fertile. The major benefit of the sympto-thermal method is that it does not interfere with the woman's reproductive system in any way; therefore, she need not be concerned about potential side effects.

Diaphragm and Spermicide

diaphragm (DYE-uh-fram) A dome-shaped rubber contraceptive device inserted into the vagina to block the cervical opening. The diaphragm should always be used with a spermicide.
spermicide A chemical that kills or immobilizes sperm.

The **diaphragm** is a dome-shaped cap made out of soft rubber that is designed to fit inside the vagina and cover the cervix (see Figure 8.4). It was the first widely available contraceptive for women. Many women abandoned it in favor of the pill during the 1960s, and only about 4 percent of women currently use it as a contraceptive (Forrest & Fordyce, 1993). All diaphragms should be used with a **spermicide.** Spermicides designed to be used with a diaphragm come in tubes of cream or jelly and are available at drugstores without a prescription. Diaphragms may be obtained only by prescription from a physician because they must be fitted to the size of the user.

To use a diaphragm (see Figure 8.5), the user places spermicidal jelly or cream in the center and around the rim of the device. Either the woman or her partner inserts the diaphragm into the vagina with an applicator or with the fingers, positioning the diaphragm so that the side containing the spermicide is next to the cervix. The diaphragm should be inspected regularly for holes or tears.

The diaphragm-spermicide method works in two ways. First, the diaphragm provides a physical barrier across the entrance to the uterus, reducing the likelihood that sperm will reach the egg. Second, the thick spermicide kills or immobilizes the sperm, in addition to providing a physical barrier over the cervix. The diaphragm should be inserted no more than two hours prior to intercourse. It should be left undisturbed for six to eight hours following ejaculation because it takes spermicide that long to be effective.

The failure rate for the diaphragm-spermicide method ranges from the theoretical yearly rate of six per one hundred women to the actual failure rate of eighteen (Trussell, Strickler, & Vaughan, 1993). Failure of the spermicide is generally caused by leakage. The spermicide is most potent if the diaphragm and spermicide are inserted just prior to penile penetration. A couple can thus increase the effectiveness of the method by making insertion of the spermicide-coated diaphragm part of lovemaking.

Diaphragm failure is usually associated with the shifting of the device as a result of particularly vigorous intercourse, changes in the size of the vagina during sexual arousal, or use of the woman-above coital position (Hatcher et al., 1994). Therefore, if conception must be avoided, it is wise to use an additional method of contraception, such as a condom, during ovulation.

The diaphragm is used only when needed and has no influence on subsequent fertility. In rare cases an individual may be allergic to the latex in the diaphragm or to the

Figure 8.4 (left)
Diaphragm and Spermicide

Figure 8.5 (below)
Effective Use of the Diaphragm-Spermicide Method To use this method effectively, a woman should place about a tablespoon of spermicide in the center of the diaphragm and a little spermicide around the rim. The diaphragm is then (a) pinched between the thumb and fingers and (b) inserted lengthwise into the vagina, so that it covers the cervix. The woman should then check to make sure that (c) the diaphragm is covering her cervix and (d) the edge of the diaphragm closest to the vaginal entrance is lodged behind the pubic bone. To remove the device, she inserts a finger under the rim and pulls the diaphragm forward.

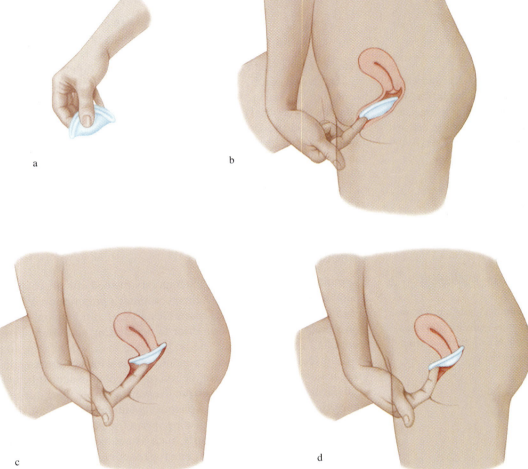

spermicide, but this problem can usually be solved by the woman switching to different brands. The contraceptive effect of the diaphragm is immediately reversible: The partners can simply abandon diaphragm use when they wish to conceive.

A potential drawback of the diaphragm-spermicide method is that it may limit the range of sexual behavior for some couples. For example, the spermicide may inhibit the desire for cunnilingus. Most spermicides are safe and nontoxic, but the odor and

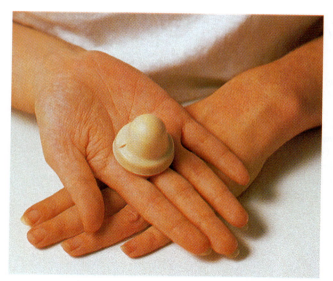

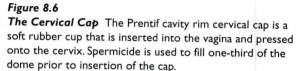

Figure 8.6
The Cervical Cap The Prentif cavity rim cervical cap is a soft rubber cup that is inserted into the vagina and pressed onto the cervix. Spermicide is used to fill one-third of the dome prior to insertion of the cap.

the taste of the standard spermicides are not particularly appealing. Tasteless and odorless spermicides are now available, and fruit-flavored spermicides can be purchased in specialty shops or through mail order catalogues (see Appendix).

Cervical Cap

The **cervical cap** is inserted by the woman or her partner and is removed six or more hours after coitus. The cap is a rubber dome that is available in four sizes to fit a woman's cervix (see Figure 8.6). The cervical cap differs from the diaphragm in that it is smaller and can be inserted earlier. After placing spermicide inside the cap, the woman or her partner may insert it up to six hours before coitus, and like the diaphragm, the cervical cap should not be removed for at least six hours after ejaculation.

The Food and Drug Administration (FDA) concluded that the cervical cap may remain in place without additional applications of spermicide for 48 hours. At a failure rate ranging from 9 to 36 per 100 women, the cap is not quite as effective as the diaphragm (Hatcher et al., 1994). The most frequently cited reason for failure is incorrect or inconsistent use. Reported side effects included unpleasant odor, partner discomfort, and a slightly increased risk of toxic shock syndrome. It is used by less than 1 percent of contracepting women (Forrest & Fordyce, 1993).

cervical cap A contraceptive rubber dome that is fitted to a woman's cervix; spermicide is placed inside the cap before it is pressed onto the cervix.

Condom

REALITY or **MYTH** ? **2**

The **condom** is the only reliable, temporary method of male contraception now widely available. Condoms can be purchased without a prescription. When unrolled, the rubber or cecum (skin) condom resembles a long, thin balloon. Designed to envelop a man's erect penis, it is put on prior to penetration and intercourse (see Figure 8.7). About half an inch of space should be left at the condom's tip, so that there is room for the ejaculated semen; some condoms come with a protruding tip designed to catch the ejaculate. After intercourse the rim of the condom should be held against the base of the penis as it is withdrawn from the woman's vagina so that the condom does not come off. After withdrawal the condom should be taken off and discarded.

condom A sheath placed over the erect penis for prevention of pregnancy and protection against disease.

The condom works by preventing sperm from entering the vagina. Many condoms come with spermicidal lubricants, such as nonoxynol-9, that further boost the condom's effectiveness. The failure rate for condom users ranges between 3 percent and 12 percent per year. Because condom manufacture in the United States is supervised by the FDA, breakage is rare. However, improper treatment of the condom by the purchaser can reduce its effectiveness. Condoms should be kept away from heat; for example, a condom should not be kept in a wallet in one's back pocket.

To increase a condom's effectiveness, a man should wear it during any vaginal penetration, and he should hold on to it firmly while withdrawing. Some men engage in penetration for some time prior to ejaculation and put the condom on only when they intend to ejaculate. This practice raises the failure rate, however, so a couple re-

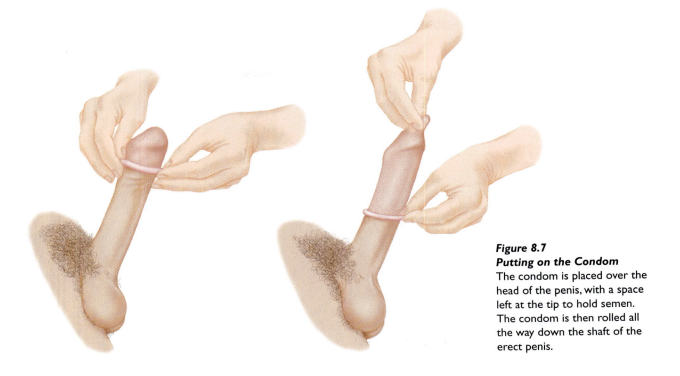

Figure 8.7
Putting on the Condom
The condom is placed over the head of the penis, with a space left at the tip to hold semen. The condom is then rolled all the way down the shaft of the erect penis.

lying on the condom should make sure that it is always worn prior to *any* vaginal penetration.

For additional lubrication, a couple can choose lubricated condoms or employ a water-soluble product such as surgical jelly (K-Y jelly, for example) or saliva. Petroleum jelly (such as Vaseline) should be avoided for two reasons: It may damage the condom, and it is not easily discharged from the vagina.

No negative side effects are associated with condom use, and condoms can prevent the spread of many sexually transmitted diseases (STDs) (see Chapter 13). They also allow a man to take contraceptive responsibility. Almost 75 percent of men in a national survey agreed with the statement that use of a condom shows that the man is a concerned and caring person (Grady, Klepinger, Billy, & Tanfer, 1993).

Most men (75 percent) using condoms report a reduction in sensation to the penis (Grady et al., 1993). According to an old joke, wearing a condom is like taking a shower with a raincoat on. However, a man who ejaculates very quickly may appreciate a slight decrease in sensation, as may his partner, if it prolongs intercourse. About 32 percent of the men in one study (Grady et al., 1993) reported that condom use made sex last longer. Latex condoms inhibit the transfer of heat to some degree, whereas the more expensive cecum condom, made from the intestinal tissue of lambs, allows transmission of changes in temperature and results in a more natural sensation for the couple. However, cecum condoms are at least three times more costly, and they provide less protection from sexually transmitted diseases (Cates & Stone, 1992a).

Some couples may see the act of putting on the condom as an interruption of their sexual expression. Others, however, may incorporate the activity into their pattern of erotic stimulation. Attitudes toward condom use are important. If a couple uses condoms in an erotic fashion (she helps put it on in a sensual way), there tends to be more sexual pleasure (Tanner & Pollack, 1988).

ISSUES TO CONSIDER

Regardless of whether you are male or female, how would you respond to a potential male partner who wants to have sex with you but does not want to use a condom because it reduces the physical sensation in his penis?

Figure 8.8
The Female Condom
The FDA's approval of the female condom in 1992 gave women an opportunity to use a method that provides a woman with protection from both conception and sexually transmitted diseases.

Female Condoms

female condom A pouch placed inside the vagina to line the vaginal walls for prevention of pregnancy and protection against disease.

Several intravaginal pouches, or "female" condoms, have been developed (see Figure 8.8). The **female condom** is generally made of polyurethane or latex and lines the vagina. The female condom can be a highly effective contraceptive method if used correctly (Farr, Gabelnick, Sturgen, & Dorflinger, 1994). In a clinical study of one hundred couples, Robert Hatcher (1991) found that only one female condom in two hundred broke compared to one per one hundred for male condoms. The lower breakage rate may stem from the fact that the female condom is almost twice as thick as most male condoms. Female condoms are more expensive and less acceptable to users than are male condoms (Cates & Stone, 1992a). For example, only about half of a group of British women who used the female condom for at least three months had a positive attitude toward the method (Ford & Mathie, 1993).

Foams and Suppositories

contraceptive foams Spermicidal foams that are injected into the vagina prior to coitus.
contraceptive suppositories Solid contraceptive substances containing a spermicide, inserted in the vagina prior to coitus.

Contraceptive foams and **suppositories** may be purchased without a prescription. These products should be kept cool because heat can decompose them, reducing their effectiveness. Contraceptive foam must be shaken before it is placed in an applicator and inserted in the vagina before intercourse. It should remain in the vagina for six to eight hours after ejaculation. More foam must be injected before each subsequent ejaculation.

A contraceptive suppository should be placed in the vagina at least 10 minutes and no more than two hours before ejaculation. After insertion the suppository melts, filling the vagina with a spermicidal foam. Another suppository must be inserted for each subsequent act of intercourse, and a woman should avoid douching or bathing for at least two hours following intercourse.

The chemical components of spermicides kill or immobilize sperm, and their thick consistency provides a physical barrier to the entrance to the cervix. Used alone, spermicides have a relatively high failure rate of up to 21 per 100 women. Errors in the timing of insertion, as well as coital positions (such as the woman-above position) that allow the foam to move away from the cervix, contribute to the failure rate. Couples can increase the contraceptive effectiveness of spermicides to 95 percent, however, by using them in combination with a condom (Hatcher et al., 1994). Only 1 to 3 percent of women use foams or suppositories for contraception (Forrest & Fordyce, 1993).

The relatively high failure rates of foams and suppositories when used alone are one of their disadvantages. In addition, they are irritating to the genital tissues of some people, which is their only physical side effect. They do not interfere with the reproductive system, and their effects are completely and immediately reversible. In combination with barrier methods, they are also effective in reducing the likelihood of people contracting STDs (Cates & Stone, 1992a).

Although spermicides have no direct physical effects on sexual response, they may have some psychological disadvantages. Some couples object to the noise produced by the extra liquid during thrusting of the penis into the vagina. Furthermore, some women dislike having to wait several hours after coitus before bathing.

Oral Contraceptives

When "the pill" was first marketed in the early 1960s, it was the first widely available, coitus-independent method of birth control; that is, for the first time, a couple could reduce the chances of conception without having to remember in the midst of love-making to insert a diaphragm and spermicide, put on a condom, and so forth. About 40 percent of sexually active U.S. women aged 15 to 44 use the pill for contraception (Forrest & Fordyce, 1993). "The pill" actually refers to about 30 different oral contraceptive products available in the United States, all of which contain estrogen and/or progestin (Klitsch, 1995).[2] When **oral contraceptives** first received FDA approval in 1960, they contained relatively high doses of progestin (10 milligrams) and estrogen (2 milligrams). Today the average combination pill contains much lower levels of both progestin (1 milligram) and estrogen (.5 milligram).

Oral contraceptives require a prescription from a physician. To use the pill, a woman takes one each day for 21 days, stops for 7 days to permit menstrual bleeding, and then begins a new cycle. Oral contraceptives are highly effective, with a maximum failure rate of 3 percent.

Aside from remembering to take the pill at the same time each day, a woman does not have to do anything more to increase the effectiveness of the oral contraceptives, provided that she has the correct dosage. Physicians normally attempt to prescribe the lowest possible effective levels of estrogen and progestin for each woman; sometimes it takes a bit of trial and error to determine the proper dosage.

Unlike the methods previously described, which block the sperm's access to the uterus, the pill derives its effectiveness from altering the reproductive system (see Figure 8.9, page 200). The estrogen and progestin prevent ovulation. In addition, the progestin appears to interfere with the development of the normal lining of the uterus, so that should ovulation and fertilization occur, implantation is inhibited. The progestin also acts to thicken the cervical mucus, with the result that sperm have a difficult time getting through it.

oral contraceptives Pills containing hormones that inhibit ovulation.

---

2. There are various terms for the class of synthetic and naturally secreted progestational (pregnancy-supporting) hormones. For simplicity, we use the generic term *progestin* for synthetic progesterone.

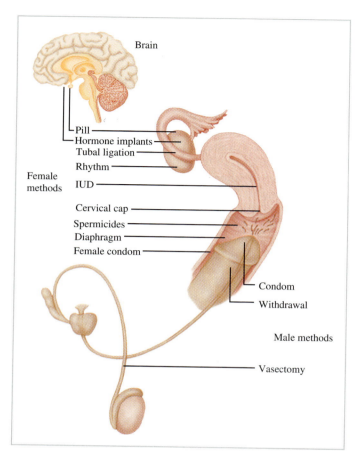

Brain

Female methods

Pill
Hormone implants
Tubal ligation
Rhythm
IUD

Cervical cap
Spermicides
Diaphragm
Female condom

Condom
Withdrawal

Male methods

Vasectomy

Figure 8.9
Location of Contraceptive Effects This drawing indicates the sites of effectiveness for male and female contraceptives.

Because hormones in the pill interact with a woman's system, the side effects of pill use are highly individual, depending on a woman's medical history, age, and personal habits. In general, the side effects are minor and tend to stabilize after a few cycles. They mimic some of the symptoms of early pregnancy, including weight gain, slight breast enlargement and tenderness, reduction in the amount of menstrual discharge during a woman's period, breakthrough bleeding (that is, bleeding not associated with menstruation), emotional depression, and nausea. Headaches, nausea, and dizziness may be a sign that the dosage is too high. Although occasional "spotting" of blood is not unusual, persistent breakthrough bleeding may indicate that the dosage is too low. If any of these conditions arises, a woman should notify her health care provider.

Major side effects from the pill are less common. Involving mainly the cardiovascular (heart and blood vessel) system, they include hemorrhaging and blood clotting, which can be fatal. These cardiovascular problems, although rare, have prompted the FDA to urge the lowest dose pill possible.

The FDA has estimated that from 30 to 40 percent of the 8 to 10 million women who take the pill smoke. The health risks of pill use rise with age and with heavy smoking (15 or more cigarettes a day). Thus, in short, pill users should not smoke cigarettes.

A possible association also exists between pill use and cancer. This link, however, is complicated and has been difficult to evaluate. It is unfortunate that, although some women have avoided the pill because of fear of cancer, actuarial data suggest that low dose contraceptives may actually *reduce* the likelihood of women contracting some forms of cancer and may slow the growth of others (Hatcher et al., 1994). For example, the risk of a woman contracting the most common form of uterine cancer, endometrial cancer, is lower for women who take the pill than for women who do not (Schlesselman, 1990). A similar relationship has been found between pill use and ovarian cancer. In addition, research indicates that pill users have no increased risk of cervical cancer (Hatcher et al., 1994). The pill's risks and benefits with regard to breast cancer are less clear. Because the body of evidence on the association between pill use and breast cancer is contradictory, potential users should obtain the latest information about potential risks from their health care providers.

The pill appears to be a safe, highly effective contraceptive for most women. Oral contraceptives are not messy and are taken independently of coitus. For couples who place a high premium on unplanned coitus, the pill is a highly desirable method. For women with very heavy or lengthy menstrual periods, the pill has the added advantage of decreasing the menstrual flow. Furthermore, for some women, pill use eliminates, or reduces the severity of, menstrual cramps, and consistent pill use almost eliminates unwanted pregnancy.

REALITY or MYTH ? **4**

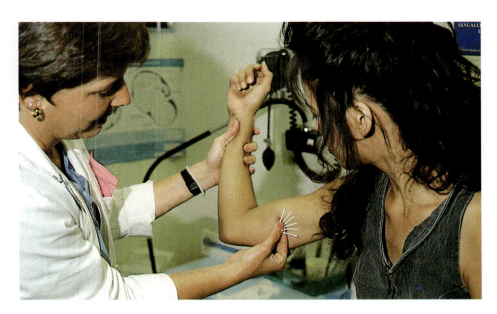

Figure 8.10
Contraceptive Implants
Norplant capsules inserted into a woman's arm provide contraceptive protection by releasing progestin over a five-year period.

Hormone Implants and Injections

In 1990 the FDA approved an implantable slow-release contraceptive for use by U.S. women. Known as **Norplant,** it consists of six thin, flexible capsules, less than one and a half inches long, that are inserted just under the skin of a woman's upper arm (see Figure 8.10). Over a period of five years these capsules slowly and continuously release a synthetic progestin into the user's bloodstream. The method may be relied on for contraception within 24 hours following insertion and is highly effective, with a failure rate of less than 1 percent.

Similar to oral contraceptives, the implants work by suppressing ovulation and thickening cervical mucus, which inhibits the capacity of sperm to enter the uterus. The most common side effects of the method are changes in menstrual symptoms such as irregular bleeding, spotting, and increases and decreases in menstrual flow, especially during the first year (Forrest & Kaeser, 1993). Other possible side effects include headaches, nervousness, nausea, and dizziness. For women who wish to have Norplant removed, either because of side effects or because of a desire to become pregnant, removal—accompanied by a local anesthetic—is readily done by a physician.

About 30 percent of women studied by Darney et al. (1990) reported an improvement in their sex lives after having Norplant inserted, primarily because they were less concerned about pregnancy and thought that sex could be more spontaneous. About 25 percent of the women reported a decrease in frequency of intercourse either because of menstrual changes or, for a very small number of women, decreased libido.

Medroxyprogesterone acetate (Depo-Provera) is a long-acting progestin that has been approved for contraceptive use in the United States. A single injection is given every three months for contraceptive purposes. The first-year probability of failure is less than 1 percent (Hatcher et al., 1994).

Intrauterine Devices

The **intrauterine device** is a small plastic and/or metal device that is placed inside the woman's uterus. The IUD must be inserted by a trained health service provider. An inserter is pushed gently through the cervical opening, and the IUD is released from the

Norplant A contraceptive implant, inserted into a woman's upper arm, that slowly releases hormones to inhibit ovulation.

intrauterine device A small plastic device that is inserted into the uterus for contraception.

inserter into the uterus, where the IUD regains its original shape. The string attached to the IUD hangs from the cervix into the vagina, so that a woman can check it periodically to see that the IUD is still in place. The string also facilitates the removal of the IUD by a physician.

It is not clear precisely how the IUD works, but the low failure rates, ranging from .6 to 2 per 100 women annually, underscore its effectiveness. The mildly irritating effect of the IUD on the uterine wall may stimulate the release of extra amounts of prostaglandins that may in turn trigger spotting or a menstrual period. Thus the IUD may prevent normal development of the uterine lining, so that when a fertilized egg makes its way down the fallopian tube, it cannot implant in the uterus.

IUD insertion involves varying amounts of discomfort, depending on a woman's history and the diameter of the particular IUD inserter. A rare but potentially fatal risk associated with IUD insertion is perforation or puncturing of the uterus. This risk is lessened when experienced professionals perform the insertion. Other adverse side effects of the IUD include cramping, an increase in the amount and duration of menstrual flow, pelvic inflammatory disease (PID; see Chapter 13), expulsion of the IUD, and ectopic pregnancy (see Chapter 7). These side effects are most pronounced during the initial months of use.

The history of the use of the IUD for birth control provides a classic example of why risks and benefits should be weighed carefully by those making contraceptive choices. In 1977, 15 percent of all married women using reversible methods of contraception were wearing IUDs. But by 1986 all but one IUD (Progestasert) had been withdrawn from the market by their manufacturers. Because the string hanging out of the cervix into the vagina makes it easier for bacteria to travel into the uterus, IUD users were as much as six times more likely to develop PID (and subsequent infertility because of scar tissue in the fallopian tubes) than were women who used other contraceptive methods (Cramer et al., 1985; Daling, Weiss, Voight, McKnight, & Moore, 1992). The longer these early IUDs were used, the greater was the risk of PID and infertility.

The two contemporary IUDs—the Copper T and Progestasert—are highly effective. If users carefully follow instructions regarding safer-sex practices, check to make sure that the IUD is in place, and have regular annual pelvic exams, these two IUDs are relatively free of health risks but are still used by only 1 percent of sexually active women (Forrest & Fordyce, 1993).

Relatively Ineffective Methods

The contraceptive methods just described are more effective than is reliance on withdrawal, postcoital douching, or breast-feeding to prevent ovulation. But because millions of people regularly use these three methods, we discuss them briefly.

WITHDRAWAL.   Referred to as *coitus interruptus* in early sex manuals, withdrawal involves removing the penis from the vagina prior to ejaculation. Although the failure rate of this method is as high as 19 percent, it is still lower than the 85 percent pregnancy rate of sexually active women who use no method.

There are two problems with withdrawal. One arises from the vast difference between intentions and actions. Although two people engaged in lovemaking may intend to part before the man ejaculates, they may not always achieve this goal for a variety of psychological and physical reasons. The other problem centers on the secretions of the Cowper's glands. When a man becomes aroused, these glands release clear, slippery droplets at the opening of the penis, and sometimes this fluid contains sperm.

POSTCOITAL DOUCHING.   More than one-third of U.S. women douche regularly, with 18 percent doing so at least once a week (Aral, Mosher, & Cates, 1992). About 3 percent of sexually active women may engage in the practice because of the popular—but inaccurate—belief that postcoital douching has contraceptive benefits (Forrest & Fordyce, 1993).

Some women use carbonated beverages following coitus in a vain attempt to prevent conception. Such acidic solutions do kill sperm, but they must be in contact with the sperm to do so. Therein lies the problem. Sperm start swimming through the cervix and into the uterus in a matter of seconds after ejaculation. Therefore, even if a woman has an acidic douche ready to insert into her vagina right after ejaculation, many sperm may have already escaped to the safety of her uterus. Furthermore, the carbonation in these drinks may even help push the sperm toward the cervical entrance.

BREAST-FEEDING.   Many physicians and laypeople have claimed for years that breast-feeding acts as a natural contraceptive. This claim is based on several observations. First, breast-feeding does appear to delay the return of menstruation following childbirth in some women, although women who rely on the return of menstruation to begin contraceptive use should know that ovulation can occur prior to the resumption of menstruation. Second, cross-cultural comparisons indicate that breast-feeding women take longer to conceive another child than do women who do not breast-feed (Ellison, 1991). In the absence of a sufficient level of calories (a circumstance more likely in nomadic hunter-gatherer groups than among contemporary North American women), ovulation and menstruation are disrupted. The reasons for differences in the return of ovulation and menstruation in various populations are still being investigated. At present, the available data suggest that breast-feeding in and of itself is not a reliable form of contraception.

STERILIZATION

Sterilization—the use of surgical procedures to block an egg's passage through the fallopian tube or the sperm's passage through the vas deferens—has been rapidly gaining in worldwide popularity. More than 14 million Americans and 100 million couples throughout the world rely on sterilization for birth control (Hatcher et al., 1994).

sterilization A surgical procedure performed to make a person incapable of reproduction.

Vasectomy

For males, sterilization means a **vasectomy,** a surgical procedure in which the vas deferens is cut. First performed more than three hundred years ago, the operation has been carried out routinely since 1925. About half a million vasectomies are performed annually in the United States (Klitsch, 1993). Because the effects of a vasectomy can be permanent, it is important for a man or a couple to consider the decision carefully.

The operation, usually performed on an outpatient basis, requires only a local anesthetic. An incision less than one inch long is made either in the middle or on each side of the scrotum. The vas deferens is cut and blocked, and then the incision is sewn up (see Figure 8.11, page 204). Because a vasectomy prevents sperm from traveling beyond the point of incision into the upper part of the vas deferens to join the semen, it is an extremely effective birth control technique, with a failure rate of less than 1 percent. In rare cases, however, the cut ends of the vas deferens manage to reconnect themselves, and additional surgery is required. Vasectomy appears unlikely to raise men's chances of developing either prostate or testicular cancer (Rosenberg et al., 1994).

vasectomy Male sterilization involving cutting or tying of the vas deferens.

ISSUES TO CONSIDER

At what point in your life, if ever, would you consider sterilization to avoid having children?

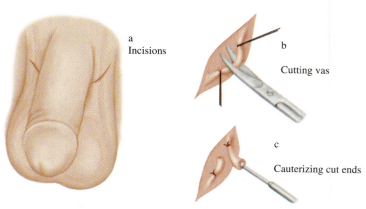

a
Incisions

b
Cutting vas

c
Cauterizing cut ends

Figure 8.11

Vasectomy A vasectomy prevents sperm from traveling out of the scrotum. Drawing *a* shows the site of the incisions in the scrotum. Drawing *b* illustrates the cutting of the vas deferens with surgical scissors, and *c* shows the blocking of the cut ends of the vas deferens to reduce the chances of their growing back together.

After surgery another contraceptive should be used until two successive semen analyses have confirmed the absence of sperm. It takes about four to six weeks and 6 to 36 ejaculations to clear remaining sperm from the vas deferens (Olds, London, & Ladewig, 1992).

Vasectomized men who change their minds after having a vasectomy may have the procedure reversed through a microsurgery procedure called **vasovasectomy.** Across studies, rates of conception following vasovasectomy have ranged from 16 percent to 79 percent (Hatcher et al., 1994). Because vasovasectomy is not 100 percent success-ful, men should not have vasectomies unless they are quite sure that they do not want to father more children. If a man does change his mind after being sterilized, however, he should undergo vasovasectomy as soon as possible.

The major benefit of a vasectomy is that after all sperm have been eliminated from the ejaculate, impregnation is impossible. Vasectomy does not alter hormone produc-tion or the ability to ejaculate because 95 percent of the volume of semen is made up of fluids produced by glands located above the point of incision. Moreover, because va-sectomy does not influence the production of testosterone or other hormones, no physi-ologically based effects on sexual desire or responsiveness would be expected. A wide range of psychological responses may occur, however. Most vasectomized men report either no effect on their sexuality or an improvement in their desire and responsiveness.

vasovasectomy Surgical reversal of vasectomy.

Tubal Ligation

Women are sterilized by having their fallopian tubes cut or tied (ligated), which effec-tively blocks the route normally taken by a mature egg to its potential meeting with sperm. Tubal ligation is considerably more complicated and expensive than vasectomy, generally requiring hospitalization, more extensive anesthesia, and a longer recovery period (see Figure 8.12). Nevertheless, more than half a million U.S. women undergo the procedure annually (Hatcher et al., 1994).

There are a number of variations in female sterilization procedures. One that has been gaining in popularity during the last decade is known as the band-aid operation. This method is performed with a **laparoscope,** which is inserted into the abdomen

laparoscope (LAP-ar-oh-SCOPE) A long, hollow in-strument inserted into the abdominal cavity through an incision directly below the navel.

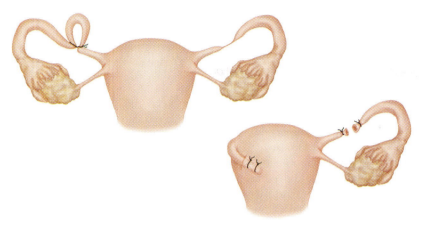

Figure 8.12
Tubal Ligation In the Pomeroy technique (top drawing), the fallopian tube is grasped by its midsection and tied to make a loop, which is then cut. The severed ends scar over, leaving a gap of half an inch or more between the ends of the tube. The lower drawing shows the Irving technique, in which the fallopian tubes are cut rather than tied.

through an incision below the navel after the woman receives an anesthetic. Gas is then pumped into the abdominal cavity, which inflates her abdomen, allowing access to the fallopian tubes. A portion of the tube is grasped and is usually clipped or banded. After the procedure is repeated on the other tube, the gas is released from the abdomen. Finally, the incision is closed with an absorbable suture and covered with a Band-aid. Complications from female sterilization procedures include bowel perforation, infection, hemorrhage, and adverse effects from anesthesia.

Unlike a vasectomized man, a sterilized woman may engage in coitus without any additional contraception as soon as she wants to, although she may have a day or two of slight discomfort following the procedure. Hormone production and the menstrual cycle are unaffected by tubal ligation, and the operation appears to have no physiological effect on sexual desire or response. Psychological effects range from none to positive, with the latter presumably resulting from the elimination of fears of pregnancy. This confidence is well founded, as the failure rate of tubal ligation is less than 1 percent (Hatcher et al., 1994).

Just a few years ago fewer than 25 percent of women who obtained reversals of tubal ligation were subsequently able to conceive. Recent advances in sophisticated microsurgery techniques have led to much higher rates of success in restoring fertility. The overall rate of live births following reversals now ranges from 40 percent to 75 percent (Olds et al., 1992). Like men, however, women should not seek sterilization unless they are quite sure that they do not want (more) children. Women face higher risks than do men when they undergo sterilization and subsequent reversal surgery.

CONTRACEPTIVE TECHNIQUES OF THE FUTURE

It should be abundantly clear by now that most of the currently available, effective methods of contraception are designed to be used by women. Moreover, each poses various problems, although any one of them is preferable to unprotected intercourse followed by an unintended pregnancy. We turn now to current research on methods to control male fertility.

Research on Future Methods of Birth Control for Men

It is unlikely that an effective male method of contraception aside from the condom and sterilization will be available before the year 2000 (Klitsch, 1995). Even after effective methods are found, a number of years will be needed to study the possible long-term side effects before FDA approval can be obtained.

There are a number of hormones currently under study. One testosterone derivative suppresses sperm production enough to provide reliable protection (Klitsch, 1995). However, because weekly injections of testosterone are required, many men would find this an impractical solution. In addition, there is a relatively lengthy period from the beginning of testosterone injections and effective sperm suppression (roughly, four months), so couples would need to use another method of contraception until sperm suppression is achieved (World Health Organization Task Force, 1996; Wu, Farley, Peregoudov, & Waites, 1996). Hormone delivery systems that can deliver testosterone for two to three months and testosterone-derivative implants that are effective for up to a year are being studied.

The most promising vaccines for men use either follicle stimulating hormone (FSH) or luteinizing hormone releasing factor (LHRH). The FSH vaccine eliminates sperm while maintaining normal testosterone levels in monkeys (Hatcher et al., 1994). Alternatively, a vaccine using LHRH shuts down both testosterone and sperm production; to maintain sex drive, men would have to supplement this vaccine with testosterone.

Research on Future Methods of Birth Control for Women

The vaginal ring, developed by the World Health Organization, is a plastic ring that releases progestin or both progestin and estrogen (Klitsch, 1995). It is worn around the cervix for three weeks each month and then is removed during menstruation. The vaginal ring has only a 3 percent failure rate (Hatcher et al., 1994).

Focus on an antipregnancy vaccine for women has involved the hormone human chorionic gonadotropin (HCG). However, because the vaccine also induces abortion, it is unlikely that American companies will pursue this form of birth control within the near future.

Although these birth control methods appear promising, the speed with which they become generally available will be influenced by the amount of money that is devoted to research. An increase in annual expenditures for research and development of new, safe, and effective methods of birth control would accelerate progress.

UNWANTED PREGNANCY

Defining the phrase *unwanted and unintended pregnancy* is tricky. The individual words do not necessarily fit together. A conception may be unintended, but confirmation of the pregnancy may lead a couple to celebrate. Or a pregnancy may be carefully planned but later not wanted for a variety of reasons: the end of a marriage or a relationship, a pregnant woman's exposure to drugs or diseases that could cause birth defects early in pregnancy, or financial setbacks such as loss of a job. Finally, of course, conception may be both unplanned and unwanted.

The number of **abortions** performed annually in the United States—about 1.5 million—provides a minimum estimate of the number of unwanted pregnancies (Henshaw, 1995). In addition, well over 500,000 babies are born annually to unmarried women,

abortion Spontaneous or medical termination of a pregnancy before a fetus can survive outside the uterus.

only a small percentage of whom wanted to conceive. Thus we might conclude that there are in excess of 2 million unwanted conceptions per year. We discuss the fate of these couples and their offspring later in the chapter. First, we consider the most frequently used method of resolving unwanted pregnancy: abortion.

ABORTION: A HUMAN DILEMMA

Deliberate abortion is one of the oldest medical procedures known to humans, practiced throughout history since well before the time of Christ and across Western and non-Western cultures (Bullough, 1994). Attitudes toward the practice have varied greatly. Even the Catholic Church, which currently condemns abortion, has taken an antiabortion stance for only the past century.

During the past decade, slightly under one-third of all pregnant American women obtained abortions each year (Henshaw & Kost, 1996). The majority were performed on relatively young, White, unmarried women in the first eight weeks of pregnancy.

An estimated 36 million to 53 million abortions are performed every year throughout the world. Between 26 million and 31 million of these are legal (Henshaw & Van Vort, 1992). Three-quarters of the world's people live in countries where abortion is legal at least for health reasons, and more than one-half of these reside in areas where abortion can be obtained on request for *any* reason.

The movement toward liberalized abortion laws in many nations has been rooted in three humanitarian principles: (1) the recognition that illegal abortion poses a threat to public health, (2) the belief that social justice requires equal access to abortion for rich and poor alike, and (3) support for a woman's right to control her own body.

The Moral and Legal Debate over Abortion

One dictionary defines murder as "the unlawful killing of one human being by another, esp. with premeditated malice." Lobbyists for a congressional or constitutional ban on abortion make their case on the grounds that abortion is murder. In contrast, supporters of legalized abortion argue that the practice is not murder because the fetus is not a human being with the legal rights of a person. Actually, both arguments seem faulty to us. If abortion is legal, then pregnancy termination is not unlawful, and there is no evidence to suggest that women seeking abortion feel "premeditated malice" toward the fetus. Biologically, the fetus is clearly alive in the uterus (as were the sperm and egg that contributed to conception), so there is human life. However, the fetus is not viable—capable of survival outside the uterus—until late in the second trimester, and more than 90 percent of abortions are performed during the first trimester.

In evaluating the issue of legalized abortion, we must take the alternatives into account. If legal abortion is unavailable, many women will die from self-administered abortions, from abortions performed by others who lack formal training in abortion procedures, or from the complications of unwanted pregnancy and childbirth. In 1965, eight years before *Roe* v. *Wade* (see "Highlight: The Legal Status of Abortion in the United States," page 208), an estimated 20 percent of all deaths related to pregnancy and childbirth were attributable to illegal abortions (Adler et al., 1992). The legalization of abortion has brought about a decrease in the mortality rate of women from pregnancy and childbirth, partly because some women who may be at risk of death from full-term pregnancies are having first-trimester abortions. Maternal mortality is down to an average level of .6 deaths per 100,000 legal abortions worldwide and .4 deaths per 100,000 procedures in the United States (Henshaw & Van Vort, 1992; Koonin, Smith, Ramick, & Lawson, 1992).

The Legal Status of Abortion in the United States

In the past three decades, laws have proliferated liberalizing and then restricting the conditions under which pregnancy could be terminated. In 1970 the New York State legislature ruled that physicians could provide an abortion for any woman requesting it who was less than 24 weeks pregnant. In January 1973 the U.S. Supreme Court ruling in *Roe* v. *Wade* prohibited states from interfering in decisions reached by a woman and her doctor during the first three months of pregnancy. During the second trimester, states could regulate abortion in ways that are reasonably related to maternal health, by requiring, for example, that an abortion be performed in a hospital. The states' right to regulate abortion to protect the fetus during the last trimester remained intact, except if abortion was necessary to protect a woman's life or health.

Although the Supreme Court reaffirmed support for *Roe* v. *Wade* in 1983 and again in 1992, the general trend in the U.S. courts and legislatures has been to try to restrict access to abortion. For example, the access of a minor to abortion has been increasingly regulated. This has been done through the requirement that a parent be notified and/or give consent for a minor to have an abortion. Public funds such as Medicaid have been drastically restricted for women seeking abortion. Federal and state laws remain confusing and, at times, contradictory.

Attitudes toward abortion vary widely among North Americans (see Figure 8.13). For the past few decades, efforts to make abortion readily available figured prominently in the movement to protect women's rights. However, there has been a fervent movement in this country to ban abortion and protect the fetus. In support of this latter position, activists have backed various federal antiabortion bills, including the Human Life Amendment, which would outlaw almost all abortions by declaring that life begins at conception. Antiabortion activists have never been more vocal and visible than in the 1990s. Indeed, militant pro-life activists, apparently motivated by their belief that abortion is murder, have used arson, fire bombings, and blockades as weapons of intimidation and obstruction. It should be noted that the major pro-life organizations have condemned such violence. However, occasionally individuals associated with these organizations have engaged in violence. For example, in 1993 a physician who performed abortions was shot to death on his arrival at work in Pensacola, Florida, by a participant in a pro-life demonstration.

REALITY or MYTH ? 5

Recent research reveals little support for an absolute ban on abortion. Even among those generally opposed to abortion, there is support for the procedure under some circumstances, such as if the mother's health is endangered or if the pregnancy resulted from rape or incest. A Gallup poll conducted in 1995 revealed that 33 percent of respondents supported no restrictions on abortion, whereas 15 percent wanted abortion banned regardless of the circumstances. Although 51 percent believed abortion to be morally wrong, 50 percent felt it should be legal under some circumstances (*Gallup Poll Monthly,* 1995).

People may consider a woman's sexual behavior in making judgments about the appropriateness of abortion. When asked to evaluate a series of fictitious case histories, college students approved of abortion for women who had become pregnant despite the conscientious use of a reliable contraceptive. These students were also more supportive of abortion for women who had become pregnant with a steady partner rather than during a casual sexual encounter (Allgeier, Allgeier, & Rywick, 1979). Participants in the study made a number of revealing comments when describing their reasoning. For instance, one person who approved of abortion for "Ruth" said that if Ruth and her boyfriend "are really close, I could see granting it. She did take precautionary measures." This same person denied "Sue's" abortion request, saying, "If Sue had sexual in-

Figure 8.13
The Abortion Dilemma

tercourse with other men, I don't think she should be granted an abortion, especially since she doesn't know who the father is." Such reasoning ignores both the argument for fetal rights advanced by the antiabortion faction and the argument for women's rights offered by the pro-choice faction. The reasoning observed in this study has the effect of rewarding conscientious women by granting them abortions and "punishing" less responsible women by conferring motherhood on them, or at least full-term pregnancy and birth. Presumably, however, less responsible women are less desirable candidates for motherhood, at least at this point in their lives, than are more responsible women.

Ten years after our series of studies on abortion policies, we were intrigued to learn that a state legislative coordinator for the National Right to Life Committee said that his organization was considering proposals to ban abortions in those cases in which a couple failed to use contraception. Such a law would presumably be difficult to enforce in the absence of witnesses observing the couple at the time of conception!

Reasons for Abortion

Why do women seek abortions? Women usually cite several concurrent reasons; only 7 percent of women in a study of 1,900 abortion patients reported that one factor alone influenced their decision (Torres & Forrest, 1988). A further analysis of these data (Russo, Horn, & Schwartz, 1992) is presented in Table 8.3, on page 210.

More than 75 percent of unmarried minors reported that they were not mature enough to raise a child. Only 5 percent of this group reported avoiding single parenthood as a reason for abortion. External reasons were also important for minors, with desire to complete education, inability to afford a child, concern about social disapproval, and their partner's reaction to the pregnancy as the most common factors influencing their decision to have an abortion. Most states have parental notification laws for minors seeking abortion as well as judicial bypass laws by which minors who fear their parents' reactions can seek a judge's opinion that they are sufficiently mature to make medical decisions for themselves. However, in responding to a given applicant's request for judicial bypass, juvenile court judges varied greatly in their decisions regarding the maturity of applicants (Sensibaugh & Allgeier, 1996).

Among the four groups of adults in Table 8.3, more than one-third indicated they could not afford to have a baby now. Nonmothers who were unmarried were more

Table 8.3   Reasons for Abortions (in Percents)

Reasons	Unmarried Minors Nonmothers (261)	Unmarried Adults Mothers (480)	Unmarried Adults Nonmothers (852)	Married Adults Mothers (204)	Married Adults Nonmothers (46)
I. Internal reasons	77.8	51.5	60.7	55.9	34.8
A. Not ready for childrearing	75.9	23.8	48.5	21.1	34.8
1. Too young/not mature enough to raise a(nother) child	61.3	—	16.1	—	—
2. Can't take the responsibility	33.3	22.3	35.8	18.6	34.8
B. Childbearing completed	—	17.9	—	39.7	—
C. Desire to avoid single parenthood	5.0	18.1	21.4	—	—
D. Health	—	—	—	10.8	6.5
1. Physical problems	—	—	—	7.8	6.5
II. External reasons	70.0	71.3	77.2	66.7	89.1
A. General situational factors	38.3	14.8	33.6	10.3	21.7
1. Education related	36.8	5.2	22.7	—	13.0
2. Job related/would interfere with job/career	8.8	7.1	15.0	6.9	13.0
B. Fetus related	6.5	8.1	11.2	11.8	23.9
1. Prescription medication	—	—	—	5.4	15.2
2. Diagnosed fetal defect	—	—	—	—	6.5
C. Partner related	11.9	24.0	19.0	17.2	28.3
1. Partner not ready/wants abortion	5.0	—	—	—	15.2
2. Relationship may break up/ has broken up	—	7.7	—	5.9	10.9
D. Social disapproval of others	13.8	—	9.3	—	—
1. Doesn't want others to know pregnant	10.7	—	8.5	—	—
E. Other responsibilities/other children need me	—	18.5	—	17.2	—
F. Cannot afford to have a baby	28.4	40.0	44.2	34.3	41.3

Note: Dashes indicate that subcategory had responses of less than 5 percent. Married minors (0.7 percent) and minors who were mothers (3.6 percent) were not included because there were too few for meaningful comparisons.
Sources: Russo, Horn, and Schwartz (1992); Torres and Forrest (1988).

likely to say that they were not mature enough to have a child than were women in the other three groups. Married mothers were more likely to give health-related reasons for abortion. Married nonmothers were more concerned with effects of prescription medications, worries having to do with the fetus, and diagnosed fetal defects as reasons for abortion. These results indicate that a woman's reasons for seeking an abortion are multiple and vary according to life circumstances (Russo et al., 1992).

ABORTION: THE PROCESS

The debate about abortion is complicated by the fact that some methods of contraception can also function as abortives. The IUD, emergency contraceptive pills, and RU-486 can be used as methods of early abortion. Most books listing methods of birth control classify these with contraceptives rather than with abortion methods, presumably because any abortions they cause may occur before a woman knows that she is pregnant.

Abortion Methods Early in Pregnancy

Several early methods exist for women who have engaged in unprotected intercourse and who wish to terminate a potential pregnancy: administration of extra doses of birth control pills, DES (diethylstilbestrol), or RU-486 and menstrual extraction. These methods can be used before the woman knows if she has conceived.

Various hormone preparations are capable of terminating a pregnancy. Extra doses of emergency contraceptive pills (ECPs) involving common oral contraceptives have been shown to reduce the likelihood of conception or implantation of a fertilized egg. In 1996 the FDA concluded that ECPs could be used safely and effectively to avoid pregnancy as late as 72 hours after exposure to sperm. The pills are most effective if begun within 12 to 24 hours of unprotected intercourse. Analyses of results from eight published studies involving a total of 2,839 women indicate that such emergency use of oral contraceptives reduces the risk of pregnancy by about 75 percent (Hatcher et al., 1994). Students interested in ECPs that can be used in emergencies should consult Hatcher et al.'s *Contraceptive Technology* (1994, pp. 415–432). Women with health problems that make the use of oral contraceptives inadvisable should not use ECPs. As soon as possible, the woman should obtain a reliable method of contraception that she can use on a regular basis. ECPs should be used only in emergencies, and they are not as effective as other methods.

The best known of the hormones for abortion—and the only one approved by the FDA—is DES. Taken in what is popularly called the morning-after pill, DES is a highly potent synthetic estrogen. In general, DES is recommended only in an emergency such as rape. Although it is highly effective in interrupting pregnancy, the side effects are quite uncomfortable for many women who use it. DES should not be taken by women for whom estrogen poses a medical hazard.

Another hormonal abortion procedure is RU-486 (mifepristone). Taken orally, this drug blocks the action of progesterone, the hormone that prepares the uterine lining for the implantation of a fertilized egg. RU-486 is most effective if taken within 49 days of the last menstrual period. About 3 percent of women abort within 48 hours of taking the drug. The rest return within 48 hours after taking RU-486 to take **prostaglandins,** which make the uterus contract and bleed and are accompanied by mild to severe cramping. This procedure is reportedly 95 percent to 99 percent effective in inducing abortion (Henshaw & Van Vort, 1992). The major side effect is prolonged uterine

prostaglandins Hormones that stimulate muscle contractions as well as help regulate ovulation and the release of prolactin from the ovaries.

bleeding, but this usually does not require transfusion or curettage (surgical scraping of the uterus). RU-486 was approved for use in France in 1988 and is being used to perform 25 percent of the abortions there (Henshaw & Van Vort, 1992). RU-486 is also available in China and Great Britain but has been banned from use in the United States. Tests of RU-486 began in the United States in 1994; in fall 1996 the FDA announced that it considered RU-486 "approvable," and it is expected to be approved and available in 1998. Because RU-486 holds promise for treating breast cancer, endometriosis, Cushing's disease (forms of leukemia), other cancers, malaria, advanced anemia, and perhaps AIDS, groups concerned with the treatment of these conditions argued for lifting the ban on RU-486 in the United States.

cannula (CAN-u-luh) A tube inserted into the body through which liquid or tissue may be removed.

A third early abortion method, menstrual extraction, involves removal of the menstrual blood and tissue from the uterus with a **cannula** and sometimes a suction machine. This method is generally employed when a woman's period is late by a week or two. A positive pregnancy test is not needed prior to a woman undergoing menstrual extraction; in fact, some women have used the technique simply to shorten the length of their menstrual periods. Casual use of menstrual extraction is not recommended, however, because of the risk of hemorrhage and of introduction of bacteria into the uterus.

The advantages of menstrual extraction are that it is less expensive than a suction abortion (described later) and requires less dilation of the cervix than methods used later in pregnancy. Another advantage of the procedure for some women is that it can be performed before a woman knows whether she is pregnant.

First-Trimester Abortion Methods

More than 90 percent of the abortions performed in the United States occur during the first trimester (Henshaw & Kost, 1996). Methods include suction abortion and dilation and curettage (D&C).

suction abortion Removal of the contents of the uterus through use of a suction machine.

Suction abortion, also called vacuum aspiration, is usually done on an outpatient basis under local anesthesia. It accounts for more than 95 percent of the first-trimester abortions in most Western countries (Henshaw & Kost, 1996). A local anesthetic is injected into the woman's cervix, which is then dilated. A cannula is introduced into the uterus through the cervix. The suction machine draws the blood, fetal tissue, and mucus from the uterus and out through the cannula. This part of the procedure generally takes less than five minutes. A doctor may scrape the uterus with a **curette** to ensure that all fetal material has been removed (see Figure 8.14).

curette (cure-RET) A scoop-like instrument used for scraping bodily tissue.

The woman remains in the recovery room for 30 minutes or so and is then released. She may return to her normal activities the next day, except for intercourse and douching, which she should avoid for several weeks. Bleeding similar to that experienced during menstruation may continue for several days following a suction abortion. The majority of women ovulate within three or four weeks following the abortion, and so a couple should resume intercourse only with a reliable contraceptive. Normal menstrual periods typically return within four to eight weeks of the abortion. Complications of suction abortion may include hemorrhage, uterine perforation, and infection. The most common complication, hemorrhage, afflicts fewer than one of every one hundred women.

Suction abortion has a number of advantages over the dilation and curettage (D&C) and second-trimester methods described later. The time required for the procedure is shorter, recovery is quicker, and complications are fewer because a woman does not have to recover from the effects of general anesthesia. Suction abortion is also considerably less expensive than a D&C because for the latter, hospital costs are involved. Furthermore, the risks associated with a suction abortion are fewer than those associ-

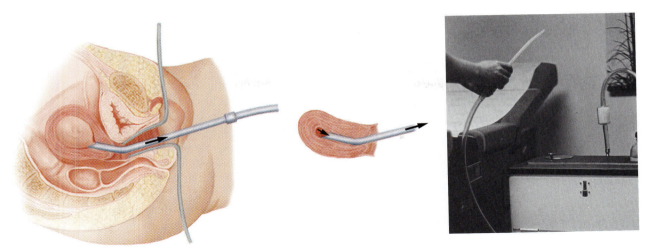

Figure 8.14
Vacuum Curette In abortion by vacuum aspiration, a vacuum curette that is connected by rubber tubing to a suction machine is inserted through the cervix into the uterus. The vacuum-aspiration machine (right) is used to suction the uterine contents into a jar on top of the machine.

ated with pregnancy or childbirth. Most women report little or no pain with suction abortion.

The other first-trimester abortion method is **dilation and curettage**. D&Cs are also performed for various medical reasons on nonpregnant women. This procedure is similar to the suction abortion except that a doctor often administers general, rather than local, anesthesia and uses a curette to scrape out the contents of the uterus instead of suctioning them out. This procedure is still common in developing countries where abortion is legally restricted (Henshaw & Van Vort, 1992).

The D&C is preferable to suction abortion when the pregnancy has progressed to the end of the first trimester. Possible complications from a D&C include those listed for suction abortion (hemorrhage, perforation, and infection) as well as those complications that can be associated with general anesthesia.

Second-Trimester Abortion Methods

Almost 9 percent of American women seeking abortions do so after the first trimester of pregnancy (Henshaw & Kost, 1996). The maternal mortality rate for abortions performed during the second trimester is much greater than that for abortions performed during the first trimester, increasing by about 50 percent for each week beyond the first trimester.

The **dilation and evacuation (D&E)** method, which combines elements of the D&C and vacuum-aspiration methods, is generally used early in the second trimester in a hospital or clinic setting. Until the sixteenth week of pregnancy, the D&E is the safest of the second-trimester methods and takes the shortest time to perform. Starting at the sixteenth week, it has complication and mortality rates equivalent to those of the other methods. Possible complications include infection, perforation of the uterus, and reactions to the anesthesia.

Abortion by means of an **intra-amniotic injection** is another alternative and accounts for about 1 percent of all abortions in the United States (Hatcher et al., 1994).

dilation and curettage (die-LAY-shun and CURE-eh-taj) Dilation of the cervix followed by scraping of the interior of the uterus with a curette.

dilation and evacuation (D&E) An abortion method, generally used in the second trimester, in which the fetus is crushed within the uterus and then extracted through a vacuum curette.

intra-amniotic injection Replacement of amniotic fluid either with prostaglandins or with a salt solution, causing fetal circulatory arrest; used in second-trimester abortions.

With this method, saline (salt) solution, which causes fetal circulatory arrest, is injected into the amniotic sac. The drug pitocin is also administered to induce labor contractions and expulsion of the fetus and placenta. In some cases prostaglandins are used instead of the saline solution.

Major complications occur more frequently from intra-amniotic injections than from D&Es. Complications from saline abortions primarily stem from three factors: (1) accidental injection into the uterine muscle, blood vessels, or abdominal cavity; (2) infection; and (3) absorption of some of the saline solution into the bloodstream. When prostaglandins are used instead of a saline solution, complications may include vomiting, nausea, diarrhea, cervical tearing, and asthmalike symptoms, and this method should not be used with asthmatic women. Abortion via intra-amniotic injection can also be quite painful for some women.

The only major advantage of intra-amniotic abortion is that it is preferable to the alternative of giving birth to a fetus that is likely to be deformed or dead. Fewer than 10 percent of the women who have abortions do so after the first trimester, and many of these women seek abortion only after learning through amniocentesis of major fetal defects.

Another abortion method, **hysterotomy,** is used only when medical conditions rule out a D&E or intra-amniotic injection and when the pregnancy threatens the woman's life. An incision is made in the abdomen through the uterine muscle, and the fetus is removed. Only about .1 percent of abortions require uterine surgery (Tietze, Forrest, & Henshaw, 1988).

hysterotomy (HIS-ter-AW-tuh-mee) Surgical incision into the uterus; when used for abortion, the fetus is removed through the incision.

Psychological Responses to Abortion

Numerous studies conducted since the 1970s have examined the reactions of women to their discovery of an unintentional pregnancy and subsequent decision to obtain an abortion. An overview of this research indicates that the greatest distress occurs before the abortion and that severe negative reactions after an abortion are rare (Adler et al., 1990; Adler et al., 1992). For most women, a legal abortion is followed by a mixture of emotions, with positive feelings predominating over negative feelings. This pattern has been found immediately after and up to eight years after abortion.

As in other stressful situations, the more support and encouragement that women with unwanted pregnancies receive, the more positive they are about their ability to cope with an abortion. Thus events that impair women's expectations for coping with an abortion, such as receiving counseling that emphasizes the negative effects of abortion or being confronted by individuals picketing abortion clinics, may make it more difficult for such women to adjust to an abortion experience.

The Male Role in Abortion

It is not known whether men whose partners seek abortions experience guilt over their part in conception, anger, relief that the woman has chosen to abort, or some combination of emotions. Shusterman (1979) studied the reactions of male partners via reports that were given by abortion clients. The overwhelming majority of women reported that their partners supported the abortion decision, regardless of the length of the relationship. Since 1976 the U.S. Supreme Court has held that a woman has the final say in making an abortion decision.

Some men believe that their legal exclusion from the decision is unfair and denies them a voice in the decision about whether to become a parent. They are right in feeling that the process is unfair. Biologically, they cannot become pregnant, and no amount of legislation can change that fact. However, if a woman is to have control over her body, she must make the final decision about whether to carry a pregnancy to term. Nevertheless, men may not be as powerless as their legal status suggests, for a man's emotional response generally has a substantial impact on his partner. The more involved and supportive the male partner is, the greater are the self-esteem and self-worth of the woman who has had an abortion (Major & Cozzarelli, 1992; Robbins & DeLamater, 1985).

UNINTENDED PARENTHOOD

About half of all pregnancies in the United States are unintended (Mosher & Bachrach, 1996). The rate of unintended pregnancies is higher for teenagers (73 percent) than for women aged 20 to 24 (46 percent) and for women aged 25 to 29 (32 percent). Our informal contacts with unmarried student couples who are dealing with unplanned pregnancy suggest that young men's reactions to the pregnancy of their lovers vary from strong advocacy of abortion to passionate pleas that the woman maintain the pregnancy.

Recourse to marriage as a solution to unintended pregnancy is less prevalent than it used to be. In the 1950s about two-thirds of unmarried pregnant women married their partners, whereas only one-third did so following the legalization of abortion (Baldwin, 1976). Although the birthrate among unmarried teenagers has remained high, at present only about 3 percent of unmarried mothers elect to place their children for adoption (Mosher & Bachrach (1996). The decrease in the popularity of forced marriage and adoption as alternatives for women who maintain pregnancy has resulted in a rise in the number of unmarried mothers. Single parenthood has been increasing for all ages of women who bear children but is particularly high among adolescents.

ISSUES TO CONSIDER

To what extent and under what conditions do you believe that a man who impregnated his partner should have a legal right to require that she maintain a pregnancy that she doesn't want? What if she does want to give birth and raise the child, but the man wants her to abort?

Figure 8.15
Adolescent Parenthood

Adolescent Parents

ISSUES TO CONSIDER

What would your advice be to a 16 year-old pregnant female who does not know who impregnated her?

More than 1 million teenage pregnancies have occurred every year in the United States since 1973 (Henshaw, 1993) (see Figure 8.15). As Table 8.4 shows, a greater proportion of women aged 15 to 19 choose to maintain the pregnancy rather than to have an abortion. In 1988 more than 50 percent of teenage women who gave birth were unmarried, and 85 percent of these pregnancies were unintended (Mosher & Bachrach, 1996). Of those who were married, many of the babies were conceived premaritally. Furthermore, in one study of women who decided to abort, more than half (52 percent) of married women aged 15 to 17 and most of those aged 18 to 19 (60 percent) already had children (Powell-Griner, 1987)!

Pregnancy among adolescents carries more risk than it does among older women. Teenage mothers are more likely than adult mothers to get inadequate prenatal care, to gain insufficient weight during pregnancy, to have labor and delivery problems, to drop out of high school, to have decreased earning potential, and to live in poverty (Alan Guttmacher Institute, 1994; Mosher & Bachrach, 1996).

In the most extensive longitudinal study of the effects of early motherhood, Frank Furstenberg and his colleagues (Furstenberg, 1976; Furstenberg, Brooks-Gunn, & Morgan, 1987) found that early parenthood creates many disadvantages for young women and their children. Young women consistently experienced greater difficulty in realizing their life plans than did a control group of their nonpregnant classmates. As Furstenberg (1976, p. 219) observed: "Their prospects of achieving a stable marriage were damaged by the early pregnancy, and they were having great difficulty supporting a family on their own. Poorly educated, unskilled, often burdened by several small children, many of these women at age 20 or 21 had become resigned to a life of economic deprivation." Although a 17-year follow-up study showed that a number of the women rebounded from their adversity and established adequate lives for themselves, adolescent pregnancy presents formidable obstacles, and many women in the study remained mired in poverty.

Table 8.4   Number of Pregnancies, Legal Abortions, and Births for Adolescent Women[a]

	1975	1980	1985	1988
Under Age 15				
Pregnancies	31,950	29,080	30,930	27,720
Legal abortions	15,260	15,340	16,970	11,461
Births	12,642	10,642	10,220	13,934
Aged 15 to 19				
Pregnancies	1,056,120	1,151,850	1,000,110	1,006,010
Legal abortions	324,930	444,780	339,200	341,218
Births	582,252	552,161	467,485	473,281

[a]Note: The total number of abortions and births does not add up to the number of pregnancies because some of the pregnancies ended in miscarriages.

Sources: Henshaw and Van Vort (1992); Henshaw (1993).

Adolescent mothers who marry are twice as likely to separate or divorce as are married women who have a first child in their 20s. In one study one-third of the 15- to 19-year-old mothers who had married before giving birth were found to have separated or divorced by the time their children were 6 years old (Presser, 1980).

What happens to the children of adolescent mothers? When tested at various ages up to their seventh year, the offspring of adolescents were found to be somewhat lower in IQ and cognitive development than the children of older women. Children whose mothers were employed or in school scored higher than those whose mothers were at home full time. Some studies have shown deficits in the social and emotional development of the children of adolescent mothers, but others have not (Baldwin & Cain, 1980). Many children in the Furstenberg et al. (1987) study appeared destined to experience their own struggles. The children were characterized generally as having high rates of school failure, and adolescent pregnancy by the daughters and juvenile delinquency by the sons were common. Other longitudinal research indicates that the children of adolescent mothers are more likely than the children of older mothers to become adolescent mothers themselves. In fact, the best predictor of whether a teenage girl becomes a mother is the age at which her mother first gave birth.

The fate of most adolescent fathers is similar to that of teenage mothers. Generally having come from poor, relatively uneducated backgrounds, they experience serious social and economic disadvantages when compared with young men who postpone fatherhood until a later age (Hardy, Duggan, Masnyk, & Pearson, 1989; Marsiglio, 1987). Gradually, many of these fathers decrease their contact with their child. Most of the fathers lacked the necessary skills to provide a stable home environment for their families even if they wanted to do so. In short, poverty is the tie that binds most adolescent fathers and mothers, and although some manage to cope with their situation and succeed, the odds are stacked against them.

Two variables are strongly associated with the development and life experiences of adolescent parents and their offspring in the various samples. One of these is the single parent's economic level. The other is the extent of social support received by the single-parent family. The disadvantages experienced by adolescent mothers and their offspring are either reduced or nonexistent when adolescent mothers receive strong social support from older people or have above-average economic resources.

Keeping an Unwanted Child

What about the offspring of women who are unable to obtain wanted abortions? Because of restrictive abortion legislation in effect in several European countries, researchers have had a chance to compare unwanted and wanted children (David, Dytrych, Matejcek, & Schuller, 1988; David, 1992). The children have been studied up through ages 26 to 28.

Comparisons of the unwanted children with the wanted offspring showed that as a group those who had been unwanted were less well adjusted at age 9 and at ages 14 to 16 and had greater psychosocial instability at ages 21 to 23. David et al. (1988, p. 124) reported that their adult relationships "with their families of origin, friends, coworkers, supervisors, and especially with their sexual or marital partners are dogged by serious difficulties." Research on the marital partners of unwanted children (now aged 26 to 28) found that they were similar to their spouses. These families had more difficulties or were more problem-prone than families founded by individuals wanted or accepted in early pregnancy (David, 1992). These results strongly suggest that in the interests of children's well-being, prospective parents should delay parenthood until they want to have children.

Summary of major points

1. The development and acceptance of contraceptives.

Although contraceptive techniques have been used throughout history, their use was illegal in the United States well into the twentieth century. Legal barriers were slowly eliminated, and in the 1960s the pill and the IUD joined the less reliable barrier methods as popular contraceptives. For various reasons, the focus has been on the development of female, rather than male, contraceptives.

2. The evaluation of contraceptive methods.

The prospective contraceptive user should consider the effectiveness and potential side effects of each method, as well as his or her own habits and preferences. Contraceptive effectiveness and risks depend on the lifestyle and medical history of the user, as well as on the likelihood that a method is employed during every act of coitus. For most women, the greatest risk of illness and death is associated with engaging in unprotected intercourse. In the absence of birth control, 85 of every 100 sexually active women become pregnant within a year.

3. Barriers to contraceptive use.

Reluctance to obtain and use contraception is associated with certain psychological and social factors. Those who feel guilty about sexuality and those who are less emotionally committed to their partners are less likely than others to use contraception. Contraceptive knowledge is related to the likelihood of people's use of birth control, but ready access to contraceptives and emotional factors appear to be more important than information in determining contraceptive use.

4. Temporary methods of contraception.

The safest methods of contraception are the barrier methods: the diaphragm and spermicide, the cervical cap and spermicide, the condom, and spermicidal foams and suppositories. These methods are less effective, however, in preventing conception than are the pill, the IUD, and hormonal implants. The effectiveness of the rhythm method may be increased by use of several means of determining the date of ovulation. Although withdrawal, postcoital douching, and breast-feeding may reduce the risk of conception slightly, these three attempts at birth control are not notably effective.

5. Permanent methods of contraception.

Sterilization is the most popular method of contraception. Vasectomy, the severing of the two vasa deferentia, is highly effective and entails little risk of side effects for most men. Female sterilization methods are somewhat more complicated than is the vasectomy because an abdominal incision must be made to expose the fallopian tubes. These methods are highly effective and do not interfere with sexual response. Although physicians report increasing success with sterilization reversals, individuals should not undergo sterilization unless they are certain that they do not wish to conceive.

6. Unintended and/or unwanted pregnancy.

The number of unintended and unwanted conceptions in the United States has been on the rise, particularly among adolescents. Faced with unwanted conception, more than 1.5 million women a year end their pregnancies through abortion, terminating roughly 30 percent of all confirmed conceptions. The number of single women who choose to maintain their pregnancies and take on the responsibilities of parenthood, however, has been increasing dramatically. About 250,000 women do so annually.

7. Access to abortion.

In the historic *Roe* v. *Wade* decision of 1973, the Supreme Court eliminated legal barriers to women's right to abortion during the first two trimesters of pregnancy. Citizens have continued to debate the morality of the procedure, however, and those who oppose abortion have succeeded in getting Congress to pass legislation preventing the use of federal funds for abortions. Those who favor legal abortion maintain that women should have the sole decision regarding the use of their bodies.

8. Abortion procedures.

Most abortions are performed during the first trimester through either the suction or the D&C method, or through a combination of the two. Legal, first-trimester abortions are among the safest of all medical procedures. Second-trimester abortions are considerably more complicated and time-consuming. They are performed through injection of saline solution into the amniotic fluid, injection of prostaglandins, or a D&E. Clearly, first-trimester abortion is preferable, but sometimes situations that occur after the first trimester—such as exposure to teratogenic diseases or conditions—prompt women to seek abortion.

9. Emotional responses to abortion.

Relatively little is known about the psychological reactions of women and men in reaching decisions about unwanted pregnancy. However, the vast majority of women who choose abortion report that positive feelings predominate over negative feelings: Few experience guilt, sorrow, or severe distress.

10. Unintended parenthood.

Compared with women who first give birth in their 20s, teenage mothers (and their offspring) generally suffer a number of long-term disadvantages. Whether particular women and their children experience problems is strongly associated with two factors: financial status and social support. Relatively little is known about the men who are faced with an unwanted pregnancy.

CHECK YOUR KNOWLEDGE

1. The number of conceptions that occur when a contraceptive method is used correctly is known as the (a) actual failure rate, (b) theoretical failure rate, (c) methodological failure rate, (d) effective failure rate. **(p. 188)**

2. The greatest mortality risk for sexually active women is (a) unprotected sexual intercourse, (b) use of a barrier method of contraception, (c) a first-trimester abortion, (d) use of birth control pills. **(p. 191)**

3. Checking the stretchability of cervical mucus is associated with which of the following methods of contraception? (a) vaginal suppositories, (b) sympto-thermal method, (c) spermicide, (d) diaphragm. **(p. 193)**

4. The diaphragm should be left in the vagina following ejaculation for (a) approximately 1 hour, (b) 6 to 8 hours, (c) 12 hours, (d) 24 hours. **(p. 194)**

5. Sterilization (a) is used only when a man has testicular cancer, (b) inhibits sexual arousal in men and women, (c) is an increasingly popular contraceptive technique, (d) is illegal in North America. **(p. 203)**

6. The majority of abortions in the United States are performed on young (a) unmarried white women, (b) unmarried black women, (c) married white women, (d) married black women. **(p. 207)**

7. Which of the following is the safest abortion procedure? (a) D&C, (b) D&E, (c) suction abortion, (d) intra-amniotic injection. **(pp. 212–213)**

8. Most women who have had abortions report that they have which of the following feelings about their decision? (a) resentment, (b) guilt, (c) relief, (d) giddiness. **(p. 214)**

9

GENDER AND SEXUALITY IN CHILDHOOD AND ADOLESCENCE

UNDERSTANDING CHILDHOOD SEXUALITY

Research Controversy: Children's Sexual Knowledge—An Immoral Research Topic?

INFANCY: TRUST VERSUS MISTRUST

Biosexual Development

Sensual Development

Parental Reactions to Early Sensuality

EARLY CHILDHOOD: AUTONOMY VERSUS SHAME AND DOUBT

Language, Gender, and Sexuality

Toilet Training and Gender: Differences in Sexual Associations

Awareness of Gender Differences

PRESCHOOL YEARS: INITIATIVE VERSUS GUILT

Gender-Role Socialization

Gender Similarities and Differences Versus Gender Stereotypes

Sexual Learning

Physical Attractiveness

LATE CHILDHOOD: INDUSTRY VERSUS INFERIORITY

Sexual Rehearsal

Homosociality

Sex Education

Across Cultures: The Relationship Between the Provision of Sex and Contraceptive Education and Unwanted Pregnancies in Western Nations

ADOLESCENCE: IDENTITY VERSUS ROLE CONFUSION

Gender-Role Identification in Adolescence

Sexual Exploration in Adolescence

The Sexual Double Standard

SUMMARY OF MAJOR POINTS

CHECK YOUR KNOWLEDGE

1 At birth, males are capable of having erections and females can lubricate vaginally.

2 All gender stereotypes are inaccurate.

3 Males are not able to have an orgasm until they reach puberty (adolescence).

4 In this culture, some homosexual behavior is often a normal part of growing up.

5 Sex education programs emphasizing postponement and protection appear to be more effective in delaying sexual initiation and decreasing pregnancy rates than are abstinence-only programs.

6 Men report more anxiety and less guilt about their first coital experience than do women.

MOST people in our culture assume that humans are nonsexual for many years after birth. Infants are the epitome of innocence, and in North America sexuality represents the opposite of innocence (see Figure 9.1). In fact, first coitus is sometimes referred to as the "end of innocence."

In this chapter we explore childhood and adolescent sexuality and gender. We begin by considering researchers' persistent difficulties in obtaining information about sexual behavior in childhood and early adolescence—difficulties that are associated with our culture's attitudes toward sexuality. We then examine various theories about

Figure 9.1
The Innocent Infant Most people make assumptions about infants that influence treatment of and expectations about them.

221

the influence of early relationships with family members on personality development. The biological, psychological, and social aspects of gender identity and sexual development are considered, as well as the role of sexual play as a rehearsal for adult interactions and a source of information about sexuality. Next, we evaluate the quality of sex education both at home and in school and its association with sexual attitudes and knowledge from infancy through adulthood. Then, we outline the process of sexual maturation that marks the end of childhood, and the exploration of sexual behaviors and personal identities through which most adolescents pass. Finally, we consider some of the behaviors involved in initial experiences of sexual intimacy with a partner.

UNDERSTANDING CHILDHOOD SEXUALITY

Our cultural assumption that the innocence of infancy is the opposite of sexuality has a number of effects. One is that few investigators have dared to delve into sexual feelings and experiences early in the life span because of the taboos that surround childhood eroticism. Even after children reach school age, researchers have difficulty obtaining permission to ask questions about what youngsters know about sex, and it is extremely unlikely that researchers would be allowed to ask children what they do sexually (see "Research Controversy: Children's Sexual Knowledge—An Immoral Research Topic?").

Just as conducting research on childhood sexuality tends to be forbidden in North American culture, the exploration and expression of childhood sexuality tend to be prohibited or discouraged by parents and other caretakers. In many respects, scientists encounter the same set of problems that children face in their search for sexual information. Children with an active curiosity about sexuality elicit concern, anxiety, and reprimands from parents and other adults. Similarly, investigators of childhood sexuality and advocates of sex education programs are confronted with suspicion and, at times, public outcry.

Why do some people find sexual feeling and expression a source of deep pleasure, whereas others feel relatively little interest in this area of life, and still others experience shame, embarrassment, or fear that inhibits their ability to interact sexually with a person whom they love dearly? Such questions have stimulated theorists to devise models of how we acquire variations in our personalities (see Table 9.1, page 224).

As we pointed out in Chapter 1, Sigmund Freud believed that personality variations result from differences in individuals' experiences as they attempt to cope with sexual energy during successive stages of early childhood. Freud theorized that if development went awry during these early years, psychotherapy could help an adult to understand, but not necessarily eliminate, the effects of negative early experiences.

Erik Erikson (1968a, 1968b) also proposed that humans go through stages of personality development. He saw development as a process in which each person must resolve successive dilemmas. He described eight stages of life occurring throughout the life span, each of which involves a crisis or opportunity for the individual. Successful resolution of life crises enables us to become healthier, more well-developed, integrated, and mature human beings. Like Freud and other theorists, Erikson perceived the first years of life as extremely important in personality development. Unlike Freud, though, he thought that positive experiences later in life can offset less-than-desirable early experiences. Similarly, the effect of positive experiences and development during infancy can be overwhelmed by the negative effects of crises arising later in life.

We examine the process of development primarily through Erickson's theoretical framework but discuss other theoretical approaches when there is information that is relevant to them.

Research Controversy

Children's Sexual Knowledge—An Immoral Research Topic?

Ronald and Juliette Goldman (1982) have described some of the difficulties faced by those who attempt to investigate children's sexuality. The Goldmans interviewed 838 children in Australia, Britain, the United States, Canada, and Sweden, at the ages of 5, 7, 9, 11, 13, and 15. To understand children's thinking about sexuality, they asked each of these children 63 questions.

After examining previous research in the area in the course of designing the study, the Goldmans wrote, "The paucity of published articles reinforced our conviction for the need to undertake what was to prove a difficult and demanding project for the next two years" (1982, pp. xvi–xvii). In selecting the specific topics to be investigated, the Goldmans noted that gathering information on a number of sexual behaviors, including childhood masturbation, would have been

extremely valuable, but we judged from trial responses that to have included such items would have gone beyond the limits set by social taboos in home, school, and community. . . . Operating within the constraints evident within the public school systems the content had to be adjusted to what was realistically possible and acceptable. The influence of these and other sexual taboos, preventing discussion, exploration or research in certain areas, is in itself an indication of the need for research into sexual thinking. (pp. 62–63)

The Goldmans carefully designed their interviews to avoid offending school boards and parents, who had to read a description of the research and sign consent forms before children could participate. The researchers experienced no difficulties in obtaining their samples from three of the five countries. The exceptions were the United States and Canada—specifically, the cities of Buffalo and Niagara Falls, New York, and the province of Ontario, Canada:

On both sides of the Canadian-USA border, despite the continuous efforts of university colleagues to help us make contacts and gain access to schools, we encountered widespread negative attitudes, and considerable opposition. This was so pronounced that after more than a month of fruitless effort, we almost gave up and returned to Britain.

The overall reason for these difficulties would appear to be the direct political control exercised by elected Boards of Education in the USA, to whom area superintendents of schools are responsible. These Boards are usually composed of lay persons who act as watchdogs, if not leaders, of the community. . . . By a misfortune of timing, we were trying to gain entry to schools in New York State only a few weeks before the local Boards of Education elections. Administrators were plainly anxious that our project might provide political ammunition during those elections and leave them exposed to public criticism. . . . One superintendent said to us that he didn't want his home bombed, and another, due to retire shortly, reported that he would not put his pension at risk. (pp. 73–74)

INFANCY: TRUST VERSUS MISTRUST

After nine months in the protective uterine environment, an infant emerges into the outside world and is immediately assigned a gender: "It's a girl (boy)!" Research shows that the behavior of the adults varies according to whether they believe an infant is male or female regardless of its actual gender (see Figure 9.2, page 225). In one study, an infant was introduced as a little girl to one group of mothers and as a little boy to another group of mothers. The mothers were more likely to offer dolls to and smile at the "female" infant and more likely to offer trains to the "male" infant (Will, Self, & Datan, 1976). Gender stereotyping of infants is more prevalent among children, adolescents, and young adults than it is among older adults (Stern & Karraker, 1989; Vogel, Lake, Evans, & Karraker, 1991).

In the womb, the fetus's basic needs are satisfied automatically and continuously through the umbilical cord. After birth, an infant must depend on the responsiveness of adults for its nourishment. Cuddling within the womb is replaced by cuddling with caretakers. An infant whose needs are satisfied in a loving and consistent way develops a trusting stance toward others. If caretakers are unloving or react inconsistently to the infant's needs, the child may form an attitude of generalized mistrust. An infant who lacks a trusting stance toward life is unlikely to have an optimistic approach toward the future—that is, hope. Instead, according to Erikson, the infant will worry constantly about the satisfaction of current needs and will therefore be tied to the present. Thus, the quality of the attachment between an infant and caretakers is a critical aspect of the infant's development (Belsky, 1991; Shaver & Hazan, 1994).

Table 9.1   Models of Development and Sexual Capacities

Stages	Ages	Freud's Stages	Erikson's Crises	Capacities
Infancy	Birth to 18 months	Oral stage	Basic trust vs. mistrust	Sensuality via sucking, touching, holding, bodily contact
				Genital exploration, erection of penis, lubrication of vagina, and capacity for orgasm
Early childhood	18 months to 3 years	Anal stage	Autonomy vs. doubt, shame	Development of sphincter control; ability in males to produce erections
				Awareness of nongenital gender differences and gender identity
				Development of language and potential to begin to acquire sexual vocabulary (names of body parts, processes)
Preschool years	3 to 5 years	Phallic stage (Oedipus/Electra complexes)	Initiative vs. guilt	Deliberate pleasurable self-stimulation
				Curiosity about sexual and reproductive processes
				Well-developed gender identity
Late childhood	5 to 11 years	Latency	Industry vs. inferiority	Active sexual exploration with both same- and other-gender friends
				Active desire for sex information
				Prepubescent surge in hormones, growth of internal and external sexual organs
Adolescence	12 to 20 years	Genital stage	Identity vs. role confusion	Development of capacities to ejaculate and to menstruate; sexual maturation
				Increasingly intense romantic attachments
				Absorption in questions regarding self and identity

Figure 9.2
Describe This Child's Personality Adults respond differently to an infant, depending on whether they are told that the baby is a boy or a girl.

In discussing early development, we must be careful not to define children's activities by adult standards. By the time we reach adulthood, most of us have learned to differentiate—in fact, to segregate—our sexual feelings and experiences from our other sensations and activities. Young children do not appear to make these distinctions, however. With this in mind, let us consider eroticism during infancy.

Biosexual Development

Before birth the fetus absorbs hormones secreted by the mother, and these effects do not disappear immediately. Thus, for a brief time after birth, infants show several signs associated with reproductive maturity. The genitals and breasts of baby boys and girls are typically large and prominent. A milky substance is secreted from the nipples of breast-fed infants, who continue to receive some hormones through their mother's milk. Prolactin, responsible for the production of the mother's milk, is found in these infants' urine. Female infants also may have slight vaginal bleeding suggestive of menstruation. All of these characteristics suggestive of reproductive maturity gradually disappear well before the end of a baby's fourth month.

The ovaries of baby girls have a ribbonlike appearance at birth. They increase quite slowly in size and weight until puberty, when they develop dramatically. Until that time, estrogen secretion is slight and constant; the adrenal glands are thought to be the source of the estrogen. The uterus of a baby girl is tiny, and the fallopian tubes have a coiled appearance.

The structure of the testes and epididymis of baby boys is established by the middle of the gestation period. Some interstitial cells, which produce testosterone, are present at birth. After some fluctuation in testosterone levels in the first seven months of a male infant's development, testosterone levels remain fairly similar to those in female infants from the third month until the onset of puberty. Adrenal androgen levels, however, rise a few years before puberty begins, which may influence skeletal maturation (Vermeulen, 1986). Like girls, boys experience little development in their sexual and reproductive structures until the onset of puberty.

Sensual Development

Before a baby begins to acquire language, communication between the infant and the outer world takes place largely through physical sensations. The ways in which adults hold and caress the infant, as well as their responses to the child's discomfort, affect a child's emerging concept of his or her own body and developing sensuality (Hatfield, 1994).

It is apparent that human infants are able to decipher body language before they can understand the content of words. Well-intentioned caretakers who are extremely tense and nervous in their attempts to calm a distressed infant tend to do just the opposite. Conversely, the pleasure and contentment of a nursing mother are mirrored in the pleasure of her infant. A nursing infant sometimes even shows body tension and release similar to that observed during erotic interaction between adults. The important factors in the infant's sensual development are probably the body contact, cuddling, and caressing that accompany feeding rather than the actual source of nourishment (breast or bottle).

 From birth on, male babies are capable of erections, and female babies are capable of vaginal lubrication. If erections are not observed during waking hours, they may be seen during the stage of sleep accompanied by rapid eye movement (REM). REM sleep is associated with dream states in children and adults, and erections in males frequently appear during these periods of dreaming.

The signs of infant eroticism—erections and lubrication—are primarily reflexive during the first year of life; that is, touching or brushing the genital area may bring about a "sexual" reflex. The infant does not, as far as we know, fantasize or purposely try to bring about erection or lubrication. Yet there are exceptions. According to one report (Kinsey et al., 1953), six infants under 1 year of age were observed masturbating. In general, however, genital fondling by infants is not goal directed, as is adult masturbation. For infants and young children, touching or rubbing the penis or vulva is a generally pleasurable activity like many other sensuous pursuits, such as sucking their fingers and playing with their toes. Only as they mature do children start to masturbate with the intent to have orgasm. Some preliminary reports of children in their first year suggested little or no difference between boys and girls in the frequency of autoerotic play (Roiphe & Galenson, 1981).

Parental Reactions to Early Sensuality

Our cultural norm of segregating the sexual from the rest of our experience begins during infancy. Most parents make a happy fuss over their infant's discovery of his or her own toes, ears, and fingers. But if they make a fuss over the discovery of the penis or the vulva, it is not likely to be a happy or positive fuss. Parents either ignore the discovery, or they actively discourage genital exploration by moving the little fingers or covering the genitals with a diaper. What significance do infants attach to the fact that when they suck on their toes, their parents imitate their behavior and also suck on their infants' toes, but when they pull on the labia or penis, parents do not laughingly join in?

Assumptions that humans naturally differentiate between the genital and nongenital explorations of their infants and naturally avoid any genital contact with infants are not supported by evidence from other cultures (Frayser, 1994). Not only are self-exploration and stimulation accepted in many societies, but in some cultures adults use genital fondling as a method of soothing cranky babies. Mothers in Trinidad, for example, masturbate their babies to calm them and to induce sleep.

Certain learning experiences during infancy may be important for developing the capacity to give and receive erotic pleasure in adulthood. Many expressions of tenderness between parents and their offspring—snuggling, hugging, stroking, and caressing—are similar to intimate behaviors between adults. People who receive little sensual contact during infancy and childhood often have difficulty in accepting and giving tenderness when they grow up. Many of the techniques that sex therapists employ can be viewed as attempts to teach inhibited adults how to recapture the pleasure of sensual interaction.

EARLY CHILDHOOD: AUTONOMY VERSUS SHAME AND DOUBT

During the first year of life, children are highly dependent. At some point before the end of their first year or shortly into the beginning of their second, however, babies demonstrate rapidly rising levels of physical and verbal competency.

Erikson (1968a) described the challenge of this second stage as the conflict of autonomy versus shame and doubt. The child's task at this developmental stage is to form a sense of autonomy and a balance between it and feelings of shame and doubt. Children who are encouraged to develop their competencies in a protective environment begin to acquire a sense of autonomy, or the ability to direct and control themselves. Too much protectiveness and interference thwart the toddler's developing sense of competency; too little protection may cause a toddler to experience the world as a painful and unsafe place. In the first case, Erikson says, the child experiences shame, and in the other, doubt.

Language, Gender, and Sexuality

A baby quickly acquires a sense of being either male or female through their interactions with adults and older children. By the time children begin to talk (generally between the first and second year), they can apply the appropriate gender label to themselves. By recognizing basic differences between genders, children begin to grasp the concept of **gender identity.**

A baby girl assigned a female gender at birth will perceive and describe herself as a girl, thereby developing a female gender identity by the time she is 2. She learns the behaviors that are expected of females in her culture and incorporates these behaviors into her personality. As she learns about becoming a female, she is learning about **gender roles.** As she gradually assumes the characteristics of this role, she is acquiring a **gender-role identification.**

By this time, children may have already learned to differentiate between their sexual anatomy and other parts of the body. When such differentiation begins to occur, parents are likely to bolster a child's impression that there is something mysteriously taboo about the genital regions. Children may note that whereas parents are willing to provide such labels as "nose" and "eyes," they consistently appear reluctant to say "penis" and "vagina." Some parents give minimal information, labeling the entire genital area "your bottom," "your privates," or "down there." Others refuse to provide any label, saying instead, "Never mind."

gender identity The feeling or conviction that one is a male or a female.

gender roles The traits and behaviors expected of males and females in a particular culture.

gender-role identification The process by which individuals incorporate behaviors and characteristics of a culturally defined gender role into their own personalities.

Toilet Training and Gender: Differences in Sexual Associations

Within a few months of their second birthday, toddlers begin to demonstrate some rudimentary control of their sphincter muscles, so they are able to deposit their urine and feces in whatever place the culture deems appropriate. Parents employ a variety of toilet-training techniques, but a common theme in parental instruction in our culture is an emphasis on the dirtiness of feces and urine. Long after children have learned appropriate places to eliminate bodily wastes, they may retain the accompanying lesson that the genital area is bad, dirty, and not to be touched for fear of contact with smelly and filthy bodily discharges. This association can be seen in our culture's labeling of sexual stories, allusions, or jokes as "dirty."

Both genders are taught the association between dirt and the genitals, but two differences may account for different sexual attitudes and behaviors of boys and girls. Typically, boys are taught to wipe themselves with toilet paper after they defecate but not after they urinate. Conversely, little girls are taught to wipe themselves always after using the toilet. Because differentiating the urethra from the clitoris and the vagina from the anus is considerably harder than differentiating the penis from the anus, girls may assume that the urethra, clitoris, and vagina are all dirty. When they reach puberty, many girls are taught that menstrual bleeding is unclean, an idea further stamping in the connection between the genitals and dirt for females. The association of dirtiness with the reproductive organs can lead to significant problems with sexual expression later in life.

ISSUES TO CONSIDER

How does the association of "dirty" and genitals arise in childhood? Are there ways of minimizing this association?

Awareness of Gender Differences

Toddlers can label accurately the gender of others, apparently based on external appearances stemming from gender-role norms, such as hair styles and clothing (Fagot, 1995). In their interview study with children, Ronald and Juliette Goldman (1982) found that most children under the age of 9 were unable to give an accurate description of how to tell whether a newborn baby was a boy or a girl.

There is, however, considerable difference from one culture to another and from one child to another in awareness of genital differences. This variation suggests that such awareness is at least partially due to differences in the opportunities children have to observe males and females (see Figure 9.3). One little boy we know had apparently been oblivious to any anatomical difference among his sisters, his parents, and himself, despite the fact that he had been taking baths with one or another family member since birth. One day shortly before his second birthday, when he and his mother were taking a bath, he began to stare at her vulva. A look of great consternation came over his face, and he asked, "Where *penis?*"

Figure 9.3

Natural Sex Education Some parents insist that their young children be clothed at all times, whereas others consider nudity acceptable under certain conditions. These children have the opportunity to observe other children nude and therefore may have healthier and more positive attitudes about the human body.

PRESCHOOL YEARS: INITIATIVE VERSUS GUILT

According to Erikson, the crisis/opportunity of ages 3 to 5 involves the conflict of initiative versus guilt. Whether children emerge from this stage with their sense of initiative favorably outbalancing their sense of guilt depends largely on how adults respond to the children's self-initiated activities.

Both Erikson and Freud believed that during this stage, the child begins to internalize reprimands and prohibitions from authorities. Thus authority figures are no longer necessary to evoke shame over the youngster's wrongdoing. The child's own internal sense of right and wrong becomes important in guiding behavior.

It is noteworthy that Freud believed that boys' internalization of parental moral values was more complete than was girls'. He thought that this supposedly greater morality in boys resulted from their higher anxiety, arising from fear of castration by their fathers as punishment for boys' intense attraction to their mothers—the **Oedipus complex.** To resolve the conflict between their attraction to their mother and fear of their father, boys internalize their father's beliefs and values by the time they are about five years old. Although Freud wrote that girls also feel attraction to their fathers—the **Electra complex**—they have less to fear, because they had supposedly already been punished by castration. Thus, they internalize their mother's values with less intensity and develop less of a conscience.

Oedipus complex (EH-dih-pus) In Freudian theory, a son's sexual desire for his mother.

Electra complex In Freudian theory, a daughter's sexual desire for her father.

In contrast with Freud's theory about the development of values and morality, however, females appear to be more controlled by societal dictates than do males, a gender difference that social learning theorists attribute to differential socialization rather than to the possession of a penis or a clitoris. Social learning theorists believe that children continue throughout their development to build up associations of positive and negative consequences of their behavior; thus, they learn to engage in some acts and avoid others.

Gender-Role Socialization

The process of **gender-role socialization** occurs throughout childhood and adolescence as the child is influenced by the family, peer group, and school system. The behavior and traits seen as characteristic of masculinity or femininity are culturally defined.

gender-role socialization The training of children by parents and other caretakers to behave in ways considered appropriate for their gender.

The specific traits and behaviors that are expected of males and females vary from one culture to the next. In our culture, males have been expected to be active, aggressive, athletic, and unemotional. Females have been expected to be passive, nurturant, yielding, emotional, and gentle. In New Guinea, though, among the Mundugamor, aggressiveness is expected and observed in both men and women. In contrast, the mountain-dwelling Arapesh women and men of New Guinea both behave in ways that are traditionally associated with women in our culture. Among the lake-dwelling Tchambuli of that island, the traditional roles of our culture are reversed, with females being aggressive and males being gentle and nurturant (Mead, 1935).

Both parents usually engage in differentiation based on the gender of their offspring, but distinctions that fathers make are more pronounced than those that mothers make. Fathers rate their sons as being better coordinated, hardier, and stronger than their daughters. In their observations of groups of 3-year-old boys and girls and their parents, Jacklin, DiPietro, and Maccoby (1984) found that father-son pairs displayed higher levels of rough-and-tumble play than any other parent-child combination. They concluded that fathers assume more of a role than do mothers in socializing their children to play according to traditional gender roles.

If you have observed parents interacting with their children, you may wonder about the effectiveness of such gender-role training. To the casual observer, some 4-year-old girls appear to be quite resistant to parental attempts to encourage them to remain neat and clean, a stereotypically feminine behavior. Similarly, it may seem to you that the crying howl of the frustrated or hurt little boy is so loud that he could not possibly hear his parents' admonition that "big boys don't cry." Nonetheless, such parental efforts to push little boys and girls into gender-stereotypic attitudes and behaviors are not only effective but also begin to show their effects early in life.

Gender Similarities and Differences Versus Gender Stereotypes

gender difference A difference in physique, ability, attitude, or behavior found between groups of males and females.

overlapping distributions A statistical term describing situations in which the levels of a variable for some members of two groups are the same, although a difference exists between the overall levels of the particular variable for the two groups.

gender stereotype A belief about the characteristics of a person based on gender.

Some additional concepts are important to understanding gender similarities and differences. A **gender difference** is a reliable difference between the average male and the average female that has been scientifically observed when large groups of males and females have been studied. For example, the average male is taller than the average female. It is important to realize, however, that even where gender differences exist, the groups generally overlap. For example, the distribution of height in males overlaps the distribution of height in females: Some females are taller than the average male, and some males are shorter than the average female. So knowledge of someone's gender does not allow us to predict his or her height.

Such **overlapping distributions** (see Figure 9.4) characterize almost all aspects of gender, and of sexual behaviors as well, including sexual appetite, speed of arousal and orgasm, frequency of masturbation, and desire for sexual variety. Nonetheless, it is commonly believed that males have larger sexual appetites than do females. Such a belief about the characteristics of a person based on his or her gender is a **gender stereotype.** A gender stereotype may be accurate or inaccurate. For example, the stereotype that females are less likely to masturbate than males, or at least to report masturbating, has been supported by research (Laumann et al., 1994; Leitenberg et al., 1993). In contrast, the gender stereotype that females are less aroused by explicit sexual material has not been supported by contemporary research (Laan & Everaerd, 1995). Regardless of the accuracy or inaccuracy of a given gender stereotype, we cannot use it as a basis for predicting the behavior of a particular male or female because of the overlapping distribution of gender characteristics and sexual behavior in males and females.

 ?

Sexual Learning

Just as they display a keen interest in learning about how to be a boy or girl in their culture, most children also reveal a marked curiosity about sexuality during their preschool years. Discouraging and punishing their sexual exploration will lead children to feel guilty about sex. Acknowledging children's curiosity without ridiculing or inhibiting fantasy activity, on the other hand, fosters a sense of competence and encourages assertiveness.

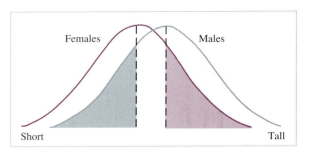

Figure 9.4
Overlapping Distributions
If we plot the heights of males and females, we find that the average male is taller than the average female. Note, however, that there are many females who are taller than the average male (see color-shaded area) and many males who are shorter than the average female (see gray-shaded area). The distributions of numerous social and physical characteristics of males and females overlap in this way.

Figure 9.5
Childhood Expressions of Affection

The capacity for self-stimulation and orgasm seems to be potentially available to most children by the age of 5. Kinsey and his colleagues (1953) estimated that almost all boys could have orgasm without ejaculation three to five years before reaching puberty, and more than half could reach orgasm by 3 to 4 years of age. Equivalent systematic research is lacking for females.

During the preschool years, children's sexuality becomes more social. Children kiss, hug, or hold hands in obvious imitation of adults (see Figure 9.5). Much of their curiosity about sexuality is woven into their play. This play facilitates their intellectual and social development, permitting them to explore their environment, learn about objects, and solve problems. Through acting out roles in fantasy play, children learn to understand others and practice roles they will assume as they grow older. They can test without fear the outer limits of what is acceptable. In our culture, much of children's curiosity about their own and others' bodies is expressed through such well-known games as "playing house" and "playing doctor." Interest in these games may be fueled to some extent by parents' failure to provide children with explicit information about sexual anatomy and by the absence of opportunities in traditional families for casual observations of parents and siblings when they are nude.

THE PRIMAL SCENE: PSYCHOSEXUAL TRAUMA OR SEX EDUCATION? A child's witnessing of parental lovemaking is referred to as the **primal scene.** Many psychoanalytic therapists believe that this experience can have traumatic effects on a child's psychosexual development. This belief stems, in part, from reports of therapy patients who said that they were shocked and horrified during childhood when they stumbled on their parents having sexual intercourse. Inferences were then made about an association between such exposure and the problems that brought these patients into therapy. However, there is no empirical evidence linking accidental observation of parental lovemaking with subsequent psychological harm (Okami, 1995).

Although they were not directly investigating the impact of the observation of parental lovemaking on offspring, Lewis and Janda (1988) found that the current sexual

primal scene A child's observations of parental coitus.

adjustment of college students was unrelated to the extent of their childhood memories of parental nudity, exposure to nudity in general, and sleeping in the parents' bed.

Given these results, we speculate that the effects of observing parental sexual activity depend on the general family environment. If parents tend to be extremely private about their affection, avoiding any touching, hugging, or kissing except when they are alone; if they avoid any nudity; and if they punish their child's interest in and exploration of his or her own body, the child who observes his or her parents making love witnesses a host of new experiences: nudity and parental contact plus the specific behaviors associated with active intercourse. A child raised in such a household could have even more difficulty interpreting the primal scene if the parents scold the child and angrily send him or her out of the room, or if they avoid giving any sort of explanation. It would seem reasonable for this child to have a fearful reaction, perhaps interpreting the event as a violent one in which the parents were hurting each other.

In contrast, a child reared in a generally less restrictive atmosphere would have fewer new experiences to interpret. Upon discovering his or her parents having intercourse, the child might be likely to ask a question already posed in numerous other circumstances: "What're you doing?" If the parents respond with something like, "We're cuddling; do you want to come cuddle for a few minutes before you go back to bed?" the child's reaction will probably not be much different from his or her response if the parents were snuggling fully clothed on the couch while watching television when the child wandered in. Parents who opt for this alternative need not worry about the child seeing the father's erection, because loss of erection is notoriously rapid when a man is startled or interrupted. Thus the father's penis would probably be quite flaccid long before the child could climb into bed.

CHILDREN'S SEXUAL KNOWLEDGE.   A major study by Ronald and Juliette Goldman (1982) yielded some fascinating information about children's developing understanding of sexuality. The Goldmans interviewed 838 children in Australia, Britain, Canada, Sweden, and the United States whose ages ranged from 5 to 15 years. Among the 63 questions the Goldmans asked children was, "How can anyone know a newborn baby is a boy or a girl?" They also asked how boys and girls grow differently as they get older. The Goldmans (1982) suggested that if Freud's hypotheses are correct regarding the Oedipal conflict, its resolution at about age 5, and **latency** (the subsequent period of so-called sexual disinterest and inactivity),

> *one would expect many 5-year-olds to be aware of sexual differences and to show relatively little embarrassment when asked the question about newborn babies, and for inhibitions to occur strongly at 7 years with recognition of differences being repressed until about 10 or 11 years of age. A similar observation might be made about castration fears, but there is little evidence for these in the responses of the sample.* (p. 194)

Presumably children who were afraid of being castrated or who believed themselves to be already castrated would be aware of the physical differences between males and females. However, at the age of 5, a large majority of the children in the four English-speaking countries gave responses that demonstrated no awareness of genital differences, whereas less than half (43 percent) of the Swedish children did so. Thus, there is little evidence for the occurrence of the Oedipal or Electra complexes among children in this study.

This variation between the English-speaking children and the Swedish children may be due to differences in the educational policies of these cultures. In 1956 Sweden instituted mandatory sex education in school from kindergarten on and also empha-

latency In psychoanalytic theory, a stage lasting from about 6 years of age until puberty, in which there is little observable interest in sexual activity.

ISSUES TO CONSIDER

How does the Goldmans' study on children's sexual knowledge cast doubt on Freud's theory of the Oedipal and Electra complexes?

sized gender-role egalitarianism in its educational system. In contrast, almost four decades later, the English-speaking countries are still debating the content of sex-education programs beginning in elementary or middle school. Thus, it should not be surprising that not until the age of 9 have the majority of children advanced to some awareness of genital differences between males and females. These findings do not support Freud's idea that genital anxieties or envies motivate children to accept as their own the values and attitudes of their same-gender parents.

Physical Attractiveness

Although preschool children may be unaware of genital differences between males and females, they do appear to notice physical attractiveness. The strong connection in most cultures between physical attractiveness and sexual desirability may have its roots in early childhood.

Children as young as 2 months old differentiate between slides of attractive and unattractive female faces (Langlois et al., 1987). These infants spent more time looking at the attractive faces than they did the unattractive faces. Because these slides were rated as to their attractiveness by college students, it appears that infants and adults use similar standards in evaluating others' attractiveness. Children as young as 3 to 5 years old attribute positive qualities and abilities to attractive individuals and negative qualities and abilities to unattractive individuals, just as adults do (Ecker & Weinstein, 1983; Langlois & Roggman, 1990). Because preferences for physically attractive faces emerge so early in development, evolutionary theorists have suggested that recognition of signs of good health such as facial and body symmetry—how closely each side of the face and body matches the other—may be part of our genetic heritage. In general, body symmetry is associated with biological health and hardiness in most organisms.

Furthermore, the ways in which others treat and respond to children are influenced by the attractiveness of the children. Some research has suggested that children with unattractive body builds or faces may indeed develop the undesirable characteristics attributed to them because of their looks (Langlois & Casey, 1984). In other words, these children may learn to behave in a manner that is consistent with others' expectations. As they become older, they may generalize these negative feelings about themselves to include their sexuality. Misled by the cultural myth that only the physically attractive are sexually appealing, they may doubt their desirability as sexual beings.

LATE CHILDHOOD: INDUSTRY VERSUS INFERIORITY

In modern industrialized societies, the child's world expands dramatically with entrance into school. By the sixth year of life, children spend a large portion of their day in the company of peers rather than with family members.

The developmental task of late childhood, according to Erikson, is to strike a balance within the personality by resolving the conflict of industry versus inferiority. For children who are essentially trusting, autonomous, and able to take initiative, there is now the opportunity to be responsible for schoolwork and other school-related activities. If parents and other caretakers respond positively to the child's work, his or her self-confidence continues to develop. Conversely, sarcastic and derogatory responses undermine the child's sense of industry, leading to a feeling of inferiority instead. If children doubt their skill or status among their peers, they may become discouraged from pursuing further learning.

Freud described the ages of 6 to 11 as a period of latency, a time of disinterest and inactivity regarding sexuality. Let us examine children's behavior during this stage.

Sexual Rehearsal

Childhood sexual play has been observed among the young of many cultures in situations where it was not inhibited by adults (Frayser, 1994). The aborigines of Australia's northern coast, for example, had no taboo against infantile sexuality until they came into contact with Western ideas. Aborigine children aged 5 or 6 engaged in coital-positioning play. Adults responded to these childhood rehearsals with amusement: "Isn't it cute? They will know how to do it right when they grow up" (Money, 1976, p. 13).

We do not know why some children engage in such rehearsal of adult sexual interaction. Perhaps it is a natural developmental stage that all children would act out if not inhibited. Of the Kinsey group's (1948, 1953) sample, 57 percent of the adult males and 48 percent of the adult females reported memories of some sex play, mostly between ages 8 and 13.

Most sexual activity in childhood tends to center around discovering and playing with one's own body or those of peers. For example, 61 percent of college students in one study reported that they had had some sexual experience with another child before the age of 13 (Leitenberg, Greenwald, & Tarran, 1989). When these students were compared to students who reported no sexual experience with another child before age 13, there were no differences between the two groups in sexual adjustment during young adulthood. In general, the occurrence or nonoccurrence of sexual activity with another child has little impact on later sexual behavior. Even when the sexual activity involved a sibling, as happened in 17 percent of the cases, there was no apparent connection to sexual adjustment in young adulthood (Greenwald & Leitenberg, 1989).

Perhaps because the threat or use of force was almost nonexistent in the reports of students in this study, negative outcomes were minimal. Other studies have shown negative reactions to preadolescent sexual activity with siblings when there were larger age differences between the siblings and if force was used to obtain sexual contact (Finkelhor, 1980). Despite our cultural beliefs about the detrimental effects of such preadolescent contacts, current research indicates little relationship between these experiences and the sexual adjustment of young adults, provided that force was not involved.

Homosociality

Young people begin to broaden their social contacts as they move into seventh grade and beyond. Cliques—small groups of intimate friends—become important. These tend to be same-gender groups in late childhood and early adolescence, becoming heterosexual in the later stages of adolescence, although many teenagers belong to both kinds of groups. Sharp differentiation of masculine and feminine gender roles, and the development of competence in interpersonal relationships, are facilitated by close association with same-gender peers. This gender segregation is called **homosociality**. It usually begins around age 8 and peaks in late childhood at about ages 10 to 13. During this time, children may express considerable distaste for children of the other gender.

Because children play almost exclusively with members of their own gender, it is not surprising to find that homosexual behavior is more common during this period than later in adolescence (Leitenberg et al., 1989). Homosexual activities are a common element in sexual development in our culture, and such experiences seldom determine one's orientation toward sexual partners of the same or other gender in adulthood (Bell, Weinberg, & Hammersmith, 1981; Van Wyk & Geist, 1984). Fearing this possi-

REALITY or MYTH ? **4**

bility, however, parents who find their children in sexual exploration with other children of the same gender may attach adult meanings to the activity. Inappropriate overreactions by parents may be one of the sources of the widespread antipathy toward same-gender contacts and homosexuality, an attitude known as antigay prejudice.

Some of this same-gender (and other-gender) sex play stems from an intrinsic curiosity about sexuality. Ironically, the relative neglect of sex education in North America may contribute to such exploration.

Sex Education

The arguments advanced by those who oppose sex education reflect an unstated assumption: that we can choose whether children and adolescents receive sex education. It should be amply clear from the evidence that we have discussed so far that children learn about sex from birth on, although the accuracy of their knowledge varies considerably as a function of the source and goals of that education.

It is difficult for many children to make sense of this thing called sexuality, and they may wonder why it is so important and yet so shrouded in secrecy. Most children hear about sexual intercourse and its connection to pregnancy by the age of 8 or 9. However, many of them associate the processes of coitus and birth with the anus. Children's reaction to coitus as they perceive it may be one of shock, disbelief, and disgust. A friend of ours overheard his son discussing sex and reproduction with another boy, who explained that babies were caused by daddies' sticking their things into mommies' bottoms to plant a seed so that a year later "the mommy poops out a baby." Our friend's son's reaction was, "Yuck!"

Another idea that children sometimes form about pregnancy is the "digestive fallacy." The Goldmans (1982, p. 49) described it: "Mother eats food and she becomes fat. The food is the baby and it comes out where food normally comes out, through the anus." Such inaccurate explanations were given by the majority of North American children in the Goldmans' study until around the age of 11. At that age, 50 percent gave realistic descriptions, and at age 13, 79 percent did so. It is clear from this research that in the absence of information about sex and reproduction, children devise their own explanations.

Figure 9.6
Sources of Sex Information

Where would you have preferred to receive information about sex? Various studies have shown that the majority of respondents would choose to get their sex education from their parents. However, in samples of people ranging in age from 9 to over 50 years of age, only 10 percent of males and 16 percent of females listed "parent" as their primary source of information about sexuality (Ansuini, Fiddler-Woite, & Woite, 1996). Because parents do not provide sufficient details about sex, most young people seek information elsewhere (see Figure 9.6, page 235).

When parents and children communicate about sexuality, it appears that attitudes and values are generally conveyed, rather than facts. The sexual knowledge of children who learned about sex at home has not been found to be superior to that of children who learned about sex from other sources (Fisher, 1986).

When sex education courses are offered in the public schools, fewer than 3 percent of parents refuse to let their children participate, and Gallup polls indicate widespread support among both teachers and the general public for such courses (Marsiglio & Mott, 1986). Although most school districts in large U.S. cities provide information about sex-related topics, either as a separate course or as part of another subject, the quality and comprehensiveness of sex education programs vary widely (Kenney, Guardado, & Brown, 1989). Several studies of the effects of these courses indicate that they improve the accuracy of students' knowledge about sex but do not necessarily produce major changes in sexual attitudes and values (Kirby, Barth, Leland, & Fetro, 1991). The importance of sex education, whether at home or school, has been underlined by statistics that have been gathered on adolescent sexual activity and contraceptive use.

The majority of Americans become sexually active before age 17 (see Figure 9.7). The proportion of teenage American women who had engaged in premarital intercourse was 29 percent in 1970 and had increased to 52 percent by 1988 (Mosher & Bachrach, 1996). Higher proportions of boys than of girls initiate early intercourse (see Table 9.2). Predictors of having first sex by age 14 are having a mother who began having sex at an early age and who has worked extensively outside the house (Mott, Fondell, Hu, Kowaleski-Jones, & Menaghan, 1996). By the end of the 1980s, more than half of teenage women used a contraceptive at first intercourse—primarily the condom. In the early 1980s, 28 percent were protected by a condom; that percentage increased to 55 percent by the end of the 1980s. Despite the increase in the use of contraceptives, the proportion of births to unmarried mothers has also been rising rather dramatically over the past half-century. In 1940, 4 percent of American births were to unwed mothers, compared with 11 percent in 1970 and 32 percent in 1995 (Mosher & Bachrach, 1996; Rosenberg et al., 1996).

In response to these sobering trends, hundreds of sexuality education curricula have been implemented in middle and high schools in the United States in the past two decades (Kirby et al., 1991). They can be broadly

Figure 9.7
Sexual Intimacy Among Adolescents

Table 9.2 Cumulative Percentages of Adolescents Who Have Become Sexually Active by a Given Age			
Age	Boys	Girls	Total
13	14.7	2.7	8.6
14	24.6	10.8	17.7
15	35.0	27.3	31.2
16	63.1	47.1	54.9
17	72.1	65.8	68.6

Source: Mott et al. (1996)

characterized as employing one of two approaches. One teaches sexual abstinence until marriage and avoids discussing methods for responsible nonmarital (or even marital) sexual activity, including contraception for couples who do not wish to conceive and use of condoms to reduce the risk of disease. The other approach emphasizes postponement of early sexual involvement but provides education for responsible sexual contacts when couples decide they are ready to have sex.

ABSTINENCE-ONLY PROGRAMS.

The abstinence-only approach in the United States has received political backing and major funding from the federal government. This approach does not differentiate between those circumstances that promote pleasuring, bonding, and wanted procreation from those circumstances that expose persons to disease, coercion, and unwanted pregnancy.

Sex education foe Phyllis Schlafly, backed by her Eagle Forum organization, has appeared frequently on television to argue against sex education programs, claiming that the high levels of unintended adolescent pregnancy in the United States have been *caused* by school-based sex education. This stance is clearly contradicted by the cross-national study done by Elise Jones and her colleagues (1986; see "Across Cultures: The Relationship Between the Provision of Sex and Contraceptive Education and Unwanted Pregnancies in Western Nations," page 238) and by U.S. studies comparing the sexual behaviors and pregnancy rates of adolescents who have and have not received education about sex and contraception (Howard & McCabe, 1990; Kirby et al., 1991).

Unfortunately, the U.S. government has promoted abstinence to the exclusion of sex and contraceptive education. The Adolescent Family Life Act, passed in 1981, permitted the Office of Adolescent Pregnancy Programs to provide millions of dollars annually to fund projects to promote abstinence from sexual interaction until marriage (Goodheart, 1992).

There has not been much systematic evaluation of the effectiveness of abstinence-only programs. What research does exist suggests that these programs are not only ineffective in delaying sexual initiation, but actually may be associated with earlier sexual initiation—the reverse effect from that intended (Christopher & Roosa, 1990; Roosa & Christopher, 1990).

POSTPONEMENT AND PROTECTION PROGRAMS.

Fortunately, there are other programs that include more thorough sex and contraceptive education. Outcome evaluations of these programs show considerably more promise (Frost & Forrest, 1995).

 REALITY or MYTH? 5

The longitudinal Reducing the Risk (RTR) program of Douglas Kirby and his colleagues (1991) is among the most well developed of the existing U.S. programs. This program directs instructors to describe social pressures to have sex, describing common "lines" that are used in the attempt to obtain sexual access, and to teach students to develop strategies and skills in response to social pressures to have sex. Students have opportunities to practice talking to one another about abstinence and contraception. The situations they are given to role-play increase in difficulty over the course of the program. The RTR program also gives students practice in obtaining contraceptive information from stores and clinics.

Kirby et al. (1991) studied high school students, primarily tenth graders, enrolled in 13 California high schools. Among students who were sexually inexperienced at the start of the program, exposure to the RTR program was significantly related to lower likelihood of having experienced coitus 18 months following the program. Students who completed the program also had a 40 percent reduction in unprotected intercourse!

ISSUES TO CONSIDER

If you were on your local school board, what type of sex education, if any, would you support for your schools?

Across Cultures

The Relationship Between the Provision of Sex and Contraceptive Education and Unwanted Pregnancies in Western Nations

The quality of sex and contraceptive education and the timing of its provision vary dramatically among Western nations. Elise Jones and her colleagues (1986, 1988) examined teenage pregnancy rates in 37 developed countries to isolate variables that might explain why teenage pregnancy rates are so much higher in the United States than in other Western nations (see the accompanying figure).

A culture's openness about sex is related to low rates of teenage pregnancy. Despite the soaring U.S. teen pregnancy statistics, the authors not only found the United States far less open about sex than most of the other countries, but also described the United States as having "an ambivalent, sometimes puritanical attitude about sex" (Jones et al., 1986, p. 230).

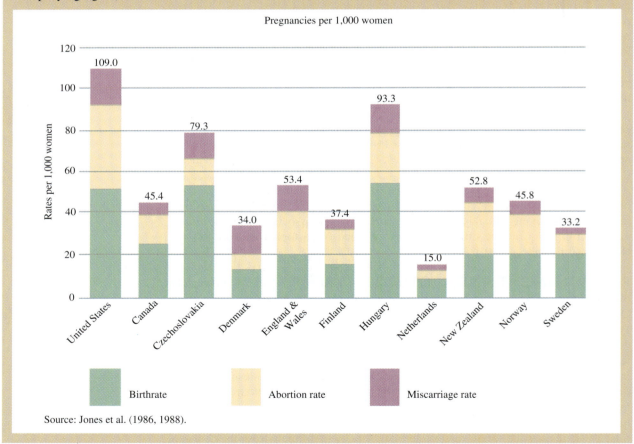

Pregnancies per 1,000 women

Source: Jones et al. (1986, 1988).

Other postponement and protection programs have also shown the ability to delay sexual initiation, increase contraceptive use, and decrease pregnancy rates among adolescents (Frost & Forrest, 1995). These programs were most successful when aimed at younger people, before they had begun to engage in sexual activity with a partner.

We might usefully compare our culture's approach to sex education with the ways in which we deal with young people's wishes to learn to drive. Adults might have various responses to adolescents' desire to drive. They might (1) prohibit adolescents from driving, (2) hand them the car keys with little instruction in safe and responsible driving, (3) wring their hands and mutter, "Tsk, tsk," at the incidence of car accidents among untrained and unlicensed drivers, or (4) provide extensive classroom instruction and practical tutoring in driving and encourage enrollment in these courses by giving course credit, reduced insurance premiums, and the like. In general, our society has taken the fourth of these alternatives regarding driving.

In contrast, we have used all *but* the fourth alternative to deal with children's and adolescents' capacity for sexual interaction. First, we discourage sexual expression. Second, although children and adolescents already have the keys, so to speak, we try to keep them from realizing that they possess those keys rather than showing them how to use them. Thus, when they discover the keys anyway, they use them, with minimal instruction on safe and responsible sexual expression. Third, we complain about the incidence of "accidents," such as unintended conceptions or sexually transmitted diseases (STDs) among adolescents untrained in responsible sexual interactions.

Taking the fourth approach—providing extensive instruction to prospective drivers—does not totally eliminate car accidents, and we cannot expect that offering thorough sex education would completely eliminate unplanned pregnancies or STDs either. However, following the model used for driver education would be a step in the right direction when dealing with adolescent sexuality; that is, children and adolescents could be given extensive classroom instruction on responsible sexual expression. This instruction could include practical tutoring in techniques for inserting diaphragms or putting on condoms (using plastic models of the body), as well as information about obtaining contraception, discussing sexual feelings and responsibilities with another person, and recognizing the difference between sexual feelings and sexual actions. Emphasis on the enormous responsibility of child care and the emotional and financial investment involved in rearing a child for at least two decades could be provided as well. Explicit discussion of these issues in the classroom might furnish a much-needed model for explicit discussion of issues between young people when they decide to become sexually involved.

Regardless of their education for handling their emerging sexual feelings as they enter puberty, pubescent development occurs—and along with it, the capacity for procreation. We turn now to this stage in the life cycle.

ADOLESCENCE: IDENTITY VERSUS ROLE CONFUSION

In the light of the fact that adolescence (roughly, the years from ages 12 to 20) has been characterized as a time of turbulence, rebelliousness, and stress, the responses of young teenagers to two questions asked by the Goldmans (1982) are somewhat surprising. The Goldmans inquired, "What is the best time to be alive?" and then asked for reasons for the choices. Prior to age 13, children's responses were quite variable, but the majority of 13-year-old respondents chose the teenage years. Some of their reasons: "As a teenager, you're at your physical peak. It's a crucial time which decides what happens [to you] later. You've got your head together more. You know more about life than when you were younger. Your brain works better. You know what to expect" (p. 119).

The responses suggest that these teenagers were well on their way to achieving the solid self-concept that Erikson (1968b) proposed is the developmental goal of this period: identity versus role confusion. Erikson noted that the biological events of puberty bring on a physiological revolution (see Chapters 2 and 3), and he pointed out that the adolescent must contend with playing a variety of different roles. One of the most profound is the acquisition of gender-role identification and its interaction with sexual roles.

If you have children or younger brothers and sisters at around puberty, you may remember with amusement one conspicuous aspect of their transition from childhood into adolescence. After years of relative unconcern about appearance, teenagers monopolize bathrooms and mirrors with astounding obsessiveness. Other family members may have difficulty obtaining even a few moments of privacy in the bathroom, let alone the opportunity for a bath, because the adolescent's third shower of the day has used up all the hot water.

The adolescent experiments with different roles and fantasies, just as he or she tries out clothing and hairstyles. At this stage, the adolescent runs the risk of developing a fragmented identity: too much freedom may result in confusion about personal identity, but too little does not permit an exploration of role possibilities and may leave the adolescent ill equipped to deal with adult life. Erikson suggested that moderate levels of freedom, accompanied by structure and advice from parents and other caretakers, can help the adolescent to integrate his or her exploration of various roles into a coherent identity.

In contrast to Erikson, Freud emphasized the biological and genital changes of puberty. Freud called this period—in his framework, the last step in psychosexual development—the genital stage. He hypothesized a resurgence of sexual energy and activity with the onset of puberty. Freud also believed that adolescents experience renewed sexual interest in the parent of the other gender, which generally expresses itself in adolescent crushes on older people.

An emphasis on learned sexual behavior characterizes the approaches taken by such sociological theorists as Gagnon and Simon (1973; Gagnon, 1990). In their view, basic sexual roles and scripts gradually emerge during adolescence. Sexual fantasies develop, serving as rehearsals for eventual interactions and as ways of exploring different sexual scripts. Out of a relatively chaotic approach to sociosexual transactions, complicated sexual scripts emerge. The body parts that can be touched and the circumstances under which they can be caressed, as well as all the subtleties of dating, are incorporated into the adolescent's behavioral repertoire.

Gender-Role Identification in Adolescence

Attitudes and beliefs about appropriate behavior for males and females as a function of gender have changed remarkably in the past few decades, and as we will see, these changes are associated with attitudes about acceptable sexual behavior for men and women. Just three decades ago, behavioral scientists and mental health professionals alike assumed that mentally healthy women were quite different in their personality traits from mentally healthy men. Take a minute to rank yourself on the scale shown in Table 9.3 to see how gender-role identification was measured.

The developers of measures of gender-role identification made two major assumptions. First, they assumed that the checkmarks of a healthy woman should fall fairly close to the items on the left-hand side of the scales, and those of a healthy adult man close to the right-hand side. Second, they presupposed that identification with masculine characteristics was the opposite of identification with feminine characteristics; that is, a person was either passive or active, yielding or stubborn. In reality, of course, most of us are yielding under some conditions and stubborn under others.

Armed with these measures, many therapists labeled men "psychologically disturbed" if some of their checkmarks fell to the left-hand side. Similarly, a woman ranking herself as "aggressive," "taking leadership roles," and so forth was considered to be in need of therapy. These people then might have undergone psychotherapy for "gender-role confusion" or "inappropriate gender-role identity." Although use of these la-

Table 9.3   Feminine or Masculine?

To use this scale, place a checkmark on each line at the point along the scale that most closely represents your personality.*

Passive ————————	Active
Dependent ————————	Independent
Like to take care of others ————————	Don't like to take care of others
Yielding ————————	Stubborn
Nonaggressive ————————	Aggressive
Soft-spoken ————————	Use harsh language

*We have placed the so-called masculine traits on one side and feminine traits on the other to make it easy to see the configuration of traits supposedly attributable to the "healthy" man or woman. In practice, the masculine and feminine traits are usually reversed on about half the scales so that they are counterbalanced.

ISSUES TO CONSIDER

What are the advantages and disadvantages of being androgynous?

bels represented an improvement over such phrases as "penis envy" to describe women who felt constrained by traditional gender roles, the concept that men and women are— or should be—distinctly different psychologically was still accepted without question.

Sandra Bem developed a gender-identity measure, the Bem Sex Role Inventory (1974), that treats identification with masculine traits as independent of identification with feminine traits. In Bem's scoring system, people who describe themselves as having masculine and feminine traits and behaviors in equal measure are called **androgynous.** Those persons who endorse characteristics traditionally associated with their biological sex are called **sex-typed** or **gender-typed.** Bem's both/and concept of psychological identification quickly replaced the either/or notion that had dominated earlier personality measures.

Bem and others using the scale found that androgynous people, regardless of their gender, responded more flexibly to a variety of situations. They could be nurturant when dealing with people in need but assertive when their rights were in danger of being violated. Sex-typed persons were more limited. Although they could respond readily with behaviors stereotypic of their gender, when a behavior or trait traditionally displayed by the other gender was more appropriate (for instance, nurturance in women, assertiveness in men), they were constrained and uncomfortable (Bem, 1975; Bem & Lenney, 1976; Bem, Martyna, & Watson, 1976).

We will have more to say about gender roles and their relationship to sexual attitudes and behavior as we continue our examination of the development of sexuality across the life span.

androgyny (ann-DRAW-jih-nee) The ability of a person to express both stereotypically masculine and stereotypically feminine traits and behaviors; from the Greek *andro*, meaning "male," and *gyn*, meaning "female."

sex-typed identification (also called *gender-typed identification*) Incorporation into the personality of the behaviors and characteristics expected for one's gender in a particular culture, with avoidance of those characteristics expected of the other gender.

Sexual Exploration in Adolescence

Much has been written, particularly in the popular press, about high levels of sexual permissiveness among adolescents today. The attention is understandable, for research consistently shows that by age 18 the majority of males and females in North America have engaged in coitus and a variety of other sexual activities (Day, 1992; King et al., 1988; Laumann et al., 1994; Miller & Heaton, 1991).

Scientific and societal interpretations of increased adolescent sexual activity vary considerably. Some people consider increases in adolescent sexual expression, including masturbation, to be symptomatic of a decadent society; they voice concern that such early "self-indulgence" leads to promiscuity, an inability to form permanent relationships, and soaring divorce rates. Taking a different view, others maintain that because the onset of sexual maturity (from a biological perspective) occurs in early adolescence, cultural restrictiveness regarding masturbation and nonmarital sexual interaction is unrealistic.

Adolescents are usually anxious and awkward during their initial experiences with sexual and quasi-sexual contact. Many of their early dates may be seen as practice for the more serious pairing that occurs later in adolescence. Through self-stimulation, experimentation with same-gender friends, behavioral scripts provided by the culture (for example, through peers and the media), and increasingly intimate sexual interactions, adolescents gradually learn to express their sexual feelings. By the time they approach the end of adolescence, the majority of Americans have engaged in premarital sex.

The Sexual Double Standard

sexual double standard The belief that a particular behavior is acceptable for one gender but not for the other.

Although an enormous shift has occurred in attitudes toward premarital sexual expression in the past two decades, North Americans must still contend with a **sexual double standard.** Early studies indicated that both men and women accepted the idea of premarital sexual experience for men but not for women. Some more recent studies have found equal levels of approval for premarital sex for men and women (DeLamater & MacCorquodale, 1979), but other evidence suggests that it may be too soon to dismiss the double standard totally. Although it has become socially acceptable for both men and women to engage in premarital intercourse, men and women are stereotypically expected to play different roles in those encounters. Specifically, men are the initiators of sexual interaction, whereas women set limits on the extent of the sexual contact.

Naomi McCormick (1979) studied the strategies that men and women use both to initiate and avoid sexual intimacy. She asked students to imagine that they were alone with an attractive person with whom they had "necked" but not yet had sexual intercourse. The respondents indicated how they might influence that person to have sexual intercourse, as well as what strategies they would use to avoid having sex. When McCormick presented these same strategies to another group of volunteers,

Figure 9.8
Changing Sexual Patterns
In the past, men were more likely to have first intercourse with a prostitute or casual partner, whereas contemporary adolescents, both males and females, generally have first coitus with a steady partner with whom they feel an emotional bond.

these participants rated the strategies for seeking intercourse as primarily employed by men, and the strategies for avoiding sex as predominantly used by women. These differences appear to be due to different motivational systems. Men's motives for sexual intercourse more often include pleasure, fun, and physical reasons, whereas women's motives are more often based on love, commitment, and emotions (Buss, 1994; Carroll, Volk, & Hyde, 1985).

Do these beliefs accurately reflect gender-role behavior in sexual interactions today? Research results on this question are mixed, suggesting that we are in a state of transition regarding the influence of traditional gender-role stereotypes in sexual interactions. Men tend to hold more positive attitudes toward the idea of women's taking the initiative in dating and sexual intimacy than do women. Ilsa Lottes (1993) found that initiating sexual activity was becoming more common among college females.

Before they come to the end of adolescence, most people have begun having sexual intercourse (see Figure 9.8). The majority of adolescents today describe their first sexual partner as someone toward whom they felt emotional attachment or love (Miller, Christopherson, & King, 1993). In contrast, four decades ago men were more likely than they are currently to have first intercourse with a casual acquaintance or a prostitute. In reviewing research regarding the degree of commitment that people report toward their first sexual partner, John DeLamater and Patricia MacCorquodale (1979) concluded that women have become more permissive: They engage in intercourse with men toward whom they feel affection rather than waiting until a love relationship develops or until they become engaged to marry. Conversely, men are becoming less permissive: They are more likely than they were formerly to have first intercourse with a person toward whom they feel emotional attachment or love. The net effect of these shifts is a reduction in gender differences regarding the kind of relationship with the first coital partner.

The emotional responses of men and women to their first coital experience vary considerably (Sprecher, Barbee, & Schwartz, 1995; Weis, 1983). Men report experiencing more anxiety and pleasure and less guilt than do women. The greater pleasure that men experience may stem, in part, from their greater likelihood of having orgasm during first coitus. Both men and women reported less anxiety, more pleasure, and less guilt when sex occurred in a close relationship rather than a casual one.

The motives for and experience of first intercourse are related to subsequent sexual behavior and current and future relationships (Cate, Long, Angera, & Draper, 1993). In the next chapter, we consider sexual intimacy during the adult life span, beginning with a discussion of the relationship between sexual and emotional intimacy.

ISSUES TO CONSIDER

Do you think a sexual double standard still exists in North America? Why or why not?

SUMMARY OF MAJOR POINTS

1. **Barriers to knowledge and theoretical perspectives.**

Information about sexuality early in the life span has been difficult to obtain, partly because of the belief that children are not sexual and partly because of taboos against asking children about their sexual feelings and behaviors.

2. **Infantile sexuality.**

Infants are capable of responses that adults label as sexual, including erection and vaginal lubrication. But these responses are primarily reflexive, not intentional. Experiencing cuddling and sensual contact as an infant seems to be important in developing healthy adult sexuality.

3. Early childhood (18 months to 3 years).

Parents convey attitudes about sexuality as they help their offspring develop language skills and bodily control of elimination. Casual genital stimulation occurs among children, but apparently without the goal of reaching orgasm. During early childhood, children learn their own gender and begin to demonstrate some awareness of gender differences using such cues as hair and clothing styles.

4. Preschool years (3 years to 5 years).

At this stage, children show increasing independence and self-direction. Although they continue to need protection, their movement toward initiative must also be supported. During this period, children begin to internalize parental and societal expectations about "right" and "wrong" behavior.

5. Gender stereotypes versus gender differences.

Research has demonstrated that males and females are more similar than they are different. Most attributes exist on overlapping distributions. Before accepting a cultural belief about a supposed gender difference, it is important to determine whether (a) the difference exists and (b) the difference characterizes all males and females or typifies the average male versus the average female.

6. Sexual exploration in childhood.

During early childhood, children actively explore their environment, and their curiosity about sexuality is evident. They play quasi-sexual games and act out adult roles, but the majority do not connect differences in genital anatomy with maleness or femaleness. Variations in physical attractiveness, important in determining adult evaluations of others, begin to influence children in early childhood.

7. School-age children.

During the elementary school years, sexual exploration with others may be stimulated more by curiosity than by arousal. Friendships at this age are primarily homosocial, and sexual play with children of the same gender is common. Freud's theory of latency—that children between ages 6 and 11 are uninterested in sex and are sexually inactive—is not supported by research. Instead, children appear to become increasingly interested in and curious about sexuality as they get older.

8. Sex education.

Although children want to obtain information about human sexuality and reproduction, relatively few North American children enter puberty with accurate information about sexuality in general or about the changes occurring in their own bodies. Comparisons of abstinence-only programs with postponement and contraceptive protection programs suggest that the latter are more effective in encouraging young people to postpone sexual activity and to use contraceptives when they do become sexually intimate.

9. Adolescence.

A primary task of adolescence is to begin the development of a coherent identity as a person. One aspect of this developmental stage involves a person's recognition of himself or herself as a male or a female—gender-role identification. Research in the past few decades has suggested that androgyny—the incorporation of characteristics stereotypic of both masculinity and femininity into one's identity—may be beneficial for personality development.

10. The sexual double standard.

The sexual double standard—the idea that premarital sex is acceptable for males but not for females—has been diminishing over the past several decades. Nonetheless, men are still expected to initiate initial sexual contact, and women are expected to set limits on the extent of sexual intimacy.

CHECK YOUR KNOWLEDGE

1. Which group of people is *least* likely to stereotype boy versus girl infants? (a) children, (b) adolescents, (c)younger adults, (d) older adults. **(p. 223)**

2. The capacities for _____ *first* emerge in _____. (a) erection; males at birth; (b) vaginal lubrication; girls shortly after first menstruation; (c) orgasm; males and females during puberty; (d) masturbation; boys after puberty. **(p. 226)**

3. The primal scene refers to (a) a child's witnessing parental coitus, (b) early childhood sex play, (c) a child's observing animal coitus, (d) Adam and Eve's first attempt at coitus. **(p. 231)**

4. The Goldmans' research on children's sexual knowledge found that _____ were most knowledgeable. (a) Americans, (b) Canadians, (c) Swedes, (d) Australians. **(p. 232)**

5. The tendency to segregate into same-gender social groups in late childhood and early adolescence is called (a) gender reciprocity, (b) homosociality, (c) latent homosexuality, (d) heterosociality. **(p. 234)**

6. Comparisons of the effectiveness of abstinence-only with postponement-and-protection sex education programs have found that _____ the onset of sexual activity. (a) the former produces delays in, (b) neither approach affects, (c) the latter produces delays in, (d) no such comparisons have been made about. **(p. 237)**

7. Erikson's theory of identity versus role confusion refers to (a) sibling rivalry, (b) an adolescent's supposed renewed sexual interest in a parent, (c) the incorporation of sexual fantasies into a unified adult pattern of sexual behavior, (d) the variety of roles that an adolescent can adopt as a lifestyle. **(p. 239)**

8. Males' first coital experience is usually (a) with a casual acquaintance, (b) with a prostitute, (c) with someone toward whom they feel emotional attachment or love, (d) described as physically uncomfortable. **(p. 243)**

10

GENDER AND SEXUALITY IN ADULTHOOD

YOUNG ADULTHOOD
Highlight: Back-Burner Relationships
The Relationship Between Sexual Intimacy and Emotional Intimacy
Lifestyle Choices and Shifting Norms

MARRIAGE AND LONG-TERM COMMITMENTS
Sex, Time, and Parenthood
Family Formation and Division of Labor

LONG-TERM RELATIONSHIPS
Sexual Pleasure and Marital Longevity
Attraction Versus Attachment in Long-Term Relationships
Extramarital Sexual Relations
Across Cultures: The Relationship of Equity to Likelihood of Having Extramarital Sex
Separation and Divorce
Adjustment to Separation: Who Suffers Most?

AGING AND SEXUALITY
Midlife Changes and Assessments
Menopause
The Double Standard of Aging
Midlife Challenges and Gender Roles

OLD AGE
Physiological Changes
Health: Aging of the Male Sexual System
Social Stereotypes and Self-Image
Health: Aging of the Female Sexual System
Decreasing Sexual Activity: Aging or Other Factors?

SUMMARY OF MAJOR POINTS
CHECK YOUR KNOWLEDGE

REALITY or MYTH ?

1 Cohabiting couples have sex more frequently than do married couples.

2 Married partners who are both employed have sex less frequently than do married couples in which one partner works outside the home.

3 Financial problems are the most common reason for couples to divorce in those countries that have been studied.

4 Women experience more severe emotional problems following the breakup of a relationship than do men.

5 Hormone-replacement therapy alleviates the symptoms of male menopause.

6 Young married couples who have an active sex life are more likely to maintain regular sexual activity in their old age than are less sexually active young couples.

THE passage from adolescence to adulthood is often subtle and poorly marked, leaving the person concerned and sometimes confused about his or her identity and proper behavior. In this chapter we examine the phases of exploring sexual behaviors and developing personal identities through which most adults pass. We also look at how sexuality in young adulthood relates to the eventual development of emotional intimacy and the commitment to a long-term relationship in adulthood. A variety of lifestyle options is available to young heterosexual adults, including marrying early, postponing marriage, cohabiting, and remaining single. With the exception of marriage, gays and bisexuals also face the task of selecting among these lifestyle options. We discuss what is known about the costs and benefits of each of these alternatives. As is true in all other societies, the vast majority of North Americans marry, and some of those who do not marry form long-lasting intimate bonds in the absence of a marriage license (Laumann et al., 1994). Thus, the relationship of marriage to the level of sexual activity and satisfaction are also considered. We review research on extramarital affairs and examine how the quality of sexual expression bears on a couple's decision to separate and divorce. Factors related to postseparation adjustment are also discussed. Finally, we explore the relationship of sexual pleasure to biological, social, and psychological changes among middle-aged and elderly people.

YOUNG ADULTHOOD

The age at which adolescence ends and adulthood begins is not always clear. Is a 24-year-old graduate student who still depends on his parents for financial support an adult? Is an 18-year-old factory worker who supports herself and has her own apartment an adolescent? Becoming independent of one's parents usually signals the transition from adolescence to adulthood. People achieve such independence at different ages, depending in part on their educational and vocational aspirations.

Regardless of the exact age at which it begins, young adulthood brings new challenges. Erik Erikson described three stages of adulthood (see Table 10.1, page 248).

Table 10.1   Erikson's Stages of Development During Adulthood

Age	Crisis or Stage	Sexual Expression and Capacities
Young adulthood (20–39)	Intimacy versus isolation	Sexual intimacy, capacity for reproduction[a]
Middle age (40–64)	Generativity versus stagnation	Parenting, adapting to the aging of the body
Old age (65→)	Ego integrity versus despair	Loss of many attributes considered attractive and sexual

[a] A person acquires the capacity for reproduction during puberty, but does not generally attain the emotional maturity and economic resources important for the process until young adulthood.

Erikson (1968b) proposed that the major task young adults face is developing their capacity to be intimate. Having shaped a firm sense of identity during adolescence, the individual is now able to risk forming close bonds with other people. Although long-term relationships, whether between married or unmarried partners, can enrich life and increase the individual's sense of purpose and value, such associations can also be experienced as threatening. A close attachment to another person provides someone with whom to celebrate successes and recover from disappointments. But for some people, the vulnerability that accompanies a close bond is too great a risk; another person can smother you, reject you, or let you down. Some individuals deal with the uncertainty by maintaining shallow levels of intimacy, either because they perceive close relationships as a source of entrapment or because they fear loss and rejection. Erikson described these persons as resolving the developmental crisis by maintaining isolation. However, those who resolve the crisis through marriage are not necessarily any happier, as we discuss later.

The process of getting to know a potential partner for a long-term relationship is variously known as dating, going out, going together, or seeing someone. The phenomenon of dating as a means of selecting a marriage partner is a relatively recent (circa 1920) social invention in North America. Current trends in premarital sexual behavior and their related expectations seem to depend on the stage of development in the dating relationship as well as on gender-role stereotypes. Roche (1986) conceptualized the progress of a dating relationship as a progression through five stages:

Stage 1: Couple dates without affection.

Stage 2: Couple dates with affection.

Stage 3: Dating individuals consider themselves to be "in love."

Stage 4: Each individual dates the loved person exclusively.

Stage 5: Couple becomes engaged to marry.

Roche asked heterosexual college students and young adults to indicate what they considered to be proper sexual behavior, ranging from no physical contact to sexual intercourse, during these five stages. During the first three stages, men condoned greater permissiveness and reported that they engaged in significantly more petting than did women. In the last two stages, these gender differences essentially disappeared. Men and women agreed about the appropriateness of light and heavy petting and intercourse during stages 4 and 5, and large numbers of both genders reported engaging in sexual intercourse during those stages. The only gender difference to emerge for later stages involved oral-genital sex, with more men (86 percent) than women (71 percent) indicating that oral sex was appropriate at stage 4. It is important to note that both men and

HIGHLIGHT

Back-Burner Relationships

Christine Cregan Sensibaugh and her colleagues (Sensibaugh, Yarab, & Allgeier, 1996) discovered a phenomenon that they termed back-burner relationships. This is a practice in which one is in an ongoing committed relationship but engages in activities to attain or maintain the romantic interest of another person. These activities may or may not include genital contact. Other phrases used for the retention of a person on the back burner are "stringing someone along" and "keeping someone on the line." In their survey of 350 heterosexual college students, Sensibaugh et al. found that more than 75 percent of the respondents reported having been involved in a back-burner relationship as either the person keeping a back burner (the control position), the primary partner, or the back burner. About half the sample indicated being in the control position and in the back-burner position, but only a quarter reported having been the primary partner of someone who kept a back burner. The most commonly reported motive for having a back burner by both men and women was to obtain additional attention. Men and women differed in other motives, however. Men were more likely than women to indicate the desire for additional access to sex, whereas women were more likely than men to indicate that they wanted the additional attention that they got from the back burner.

women reported greater permissiveness in their actual behavior than in their definitions of proper behavior.

A large majority of the students in Roche's study thought that sexual intercourse was acceptable for a couple who were "in love" and dating each other exclusively (see "Highlight: Back-Burner Relationships"). However, attitudes about premarital sex do not appear to be reflected in the actual behavior of young people (Laumann et al., 1994). DeBuono, Zinner, Daamen, and McCormack (1990) compared the prevalence of sexual intercourse in college women during 1975, 1986, and 1989. Depending on the year, 87 percent to 88 percent of the women had had coitus. Although acquired immunodeficiency syndrome (AIDS) has apparently not reduced the likelihood of premarital coitus, condom use, sometimes combined with other contraceptive methods, increased at each time period: 12 percent in 1975, 21 percent in 1986, and 41 percent in 1989. No differences were found, however, in the number of sexual partners or the likelihood of engaging in fellatio, cunnilingus, or anal sex.

The Relationship Between Sexual Intimacy and Emotional Intimacy

Although nonmarital sexual intimacy has become almost universal in North American culture, contemporary attitudes about this practice vary widely. Some individuals believe that early sexual intercourse is an effective and acceptable means by which couples can develop intimacy. Others assert that engaging in intercourse early in a relationship can preclude greater closeness and commitment.

Generally, we lack the **longitudinal research** needed to answer questions about the role of early emotional and sexual intimacy in relationships. However, Letitia Anne Peplau, Zick Rubin, and Charles Hill (1977) examined 231 dating couples over a two-year period during their sophomore and junior years of college. At the beginning of the study, the couples had been dating for an average of about eight months. Few had made definite plans to marry, although about a fifth of them were living together. On the basis of the couples' responses, the researchers identified three patterns of sexual behavior and emotional intimacy: sexually liberal (had coitus within a month of their first date), sexually moderate (waited to engage in coitus until later in their relationship), and sexually traditional (planned to avoid coitus until marriage).

longitudinal research Research carried out with the same sample of people over a period of months or years.

ISSUES TO CONSIDER

Based on what you know about these couples so far, which group do you expect to have the highest proportion of couples who ultimately marry one another?

The Peplau group (1977) was interested in the association between the timing of first coitus and the outcome of the relationship. At the end of two years, Peplau et al. were able to obtain information about 221 of the original 231 couples: 20 percent had married, 34 percent were still dating, and the remaining 46 percent had broken up. It may surprise you to learn that there was no association between the pattern of their sexual behavior when first contacted (coitus within a month, later coitus, or abstention) and the outcome of their relationship (marriage, dating, or separation) two years later. Peplau et al. found no evidence that sexual intimacy early in a relationship either short-circuits or encourages a long-term commitment. Similarly, abstinence was unrelated to the likelihood of developing a lasting relationship.

To what extent are norms shifting in other areas relevant to sexuality, relationship and family formation, and other lifestyle issues? We now turn to the available research on these and other questions.

Lifestyle Choices and Shifting Norms

Young adults face major decisions regarding lifestyles, jobs or careers, and relationships. Their choices can have far-reaching consequences for structuring their lives throughout adulthood, including old age.

Until recently, most individuals reaching adulthood perceived their main tasks to be finding gainful employment and selecting a mate with whom to have children. If marriage was postponed, the delay was due more to economic conditions than to personal choice. Anyone who did not take religious vows was expected to take marital vows, and those who did not were frequently the objects of pity. It was assumed that permanently single people were atypical with respect to physical attractiveness, sexual feeling, or emotional adjustment. Such judgments fell particularly hard on unmarried women, who were commonly referred to as old maids or spinsters.

Choices for men and women today have become considerably more diverse. Instead of the issue of whom to marry, the question centers on whether to marry, and if so, when. Instead of discussing how many children to have, it has become acceptable, at least among some segments of society, to talk about whether to have any children at all. In addition, most people begin engaging in sexual intercourse before they reach the end of adolescence and before they marry.

Women have made significant progress toward achieving economic and social equality, but is there any evidence of corresponding changes in women's roles in romantic and marital relationships? If attitudes are changing, what is the influence of new attitudes on contemporary choices regarding lifestyles?

SINGLE LIFESTYLES.   When we think of a household, we usually assume that it consists of at least two people. The proportion of households that contain only one person, however, is rising rapidly. Almost 25 percent of households are composed of a single occupant, as compared to 7 percent in 1949, a spurt of 40 percent. The growing incidence of one-person households has stemmed primarily from an increase in the number of never-married persons who either do not intend to marry or are postponing marriage.

ISSUES TO CONSIDER

In what ways do you think the trend toward later marriages affects men and women who wish to marry at younger ages?

With the median age at first marriage gradually rising to the mid-20s in the 1990s (27 years for men, 25 years for women in 1994), more people are single during part or all of their young adulthood (U.S. Bureau of the Census, 1996). Even among those who marry, more than half return to single status through separation or divorce, and many others return to single status as the result of a spouse's death. The rise in the number of one-person households consisting of divorced or separated men under age 35 has been particularly marked. Among women, the number of widows continues to grow, but not so much as the numbers of never-married, divorced, and separated women (U.S. Bureau of the Census, 1996).

Although there is no particular type of person who remains single, women with graduate-school training and women with little education (fewer than five years) contribute disproportionately to the ranks of the never married (Saluter, 1992). Women with graduate training may perceive marriage as interfering with their career plans. Those with little education may be seen as undesirable partners, especially if their lack of education stems from problems such as low income and mental or physical disabilities.

Singles, particularly those over 25 years old, are the victims of a number of misconceptions. One of the most common is that they are "swingers." The stereotype of the promiscuous and carefree bed hopper who pursues endless amorous adventures is an enduring fantasy. It is interesting that the alleged swinging lifestyle of an unattached man is often viewed with envy or fascination, whereas single women are often seen as threatening, particularly by their married counterparts. Another misconception about singles is that they are not married because they have been unable to find anyone willing to marry them. Emotional instability, physical unattractiveness, and low intelligence may be attributed to individuals to explain why they are unmarried. The underlying assumption appears to be that all normal people marry. In addition, singles must often endure insinuations that they are homosexual. Fear of homosexuality is so pervasive in our culture that any deviation from marriage leaves one vulnerable to the charge. The conclusion that an unmarried person must be promiscuous, unattractive, or gay, however, reflects ignorance about single lifestyles.

In departing from the conventional choice of marriage, at least for a period of time, single men and women must develop an alternative network of relationships that provide support and intimacy. Many singles form friendships in the workplace, in school, at parties, and through hobbies and sports. Remaining single has become a workable and satisfying alternative to marriage for many men and women, one that can last for a few years or a lifetime. A form of legal, if not emotional, singleness that has become popular is cohabitation.

COHABITATION.   The practice of sharing a residence with a sexual partner before marriage or instead of marriage—**cohabitation**—has rapidly increased in popularity in the past three decades. About 25 percent of college students report having cohabited for some period of time (Newcomb, 1986; Thornton, 1988). In the United States as a whole, the proportion of persons who lived with a partner before marrying for the first time increased from 11 percent in 1970 to nearly half for recent first marriages (Bumpass, Sweet, & Cherlin, 1991). The actual number of people cohabiting is higher because about 20 percent of cohabitors do not ever expect to marry or marry again.

cohabitation An arrangement in which an unmarried couple live together.

Although most cohabitors plan to marry at some point, they do not necessarily intend to marry the person with whom they are living. The majority of cohabiting relationships break up or end in marriage within 18 months (Bumpass et al., 1991; Laumann et al., 1994). However, about 20 percent of cohabiting couples have lived together for more than five years. Roughly half of cohabiting couples end their relationships before marriage, and marriages that are preceded by cohabitation have higher dissolution rates than marriages without previous cohabitation (DeMaris & Rao, 1992; Laumann et al., 1994).

The mention of cohabiting usually elicits a stereotyped image of two young people adjusting to living together, but 40 percent of cohabiting households include children. Most cohabitors report that their lives would be pretty much the same if they were married (Bumpass et al., 1991).

Cohabitors and noncohabitors have been compared on a variety of demographic and personality measures (Byers & Heinlein, 1989; DeMaris & Rao, 1992; Laumann et al., 1994). In general, cohabitation is more prevalent in large urban centers. Cohabitors tend to have higher expectations for marriage than do their noncohabiting counterparts. Moreover, cohabitors are more experienced sexually and become intimately involved at younger ages than noncohabitors. Both groups reported similar levels of sexual satisfaction, although cohabiting couples report having sex more frequently than do married couples (Laumann et al., 1994; Sprecher & McKinney, 1994).

Couples who cohabit in part to avoid legal hassles in case they separate may find some recent court cases sobering. In contrast to laws governing marital relationships, laws concerning cohabitation and the ending of cohabiting relationships have not been particularly well defined. As a result, there is the potential for complicated, lengthy, and expensive legal battles if long-term cohabitants decide to separate. Many attorneys advise a couple intending to cohabit to sign a contract regarding the division of property and income acquired during the relationship to clarify the situation that will arise if or when the individuals decide to separate.

Whether they want to make a contract, all gay or straight couples who decide to live together, regardless of their marital status, can benefit from considering various material and emotional issues. Therapists working with couples having relationship difficulties often hear such statements as, "Well, I thought I could change him [her]," and "I didn't think it was important" in response to questions about whether the client was aware of a particular preference, behavior, or personality characteristics of his or her partner before making a commitment to live with the individual. If they are able to resolve important differences between them, about 40 percent of cohabiting couples go on to marry one another (Laumann et al., 1994).

REALITY or **MYTH** ? **I**

ISSUES TO CONSIDER

Is cohabiting just part of a developmental sequence that begins with romantic attraction and proceeds to sexual intimacy, then cohabitation, and finally marriage? Or does the increase in the practice of cohabitation indicate vast changes in our society, from which a new family form is emerging?

MARRIAGE AND LONG-TERM COMMITMENTS

In the traditional view of marriage portrayed in countless movie and TV scripts, marriage is a climactic event, after which a couple live "happily ever after." Many people retain an image of a young couple who, after finishing their educations, getting satisfying jobs, and spending a period of time engaged to each other, exchange wedding vows. Within a few years, they greet the first of several babies, who are brought up to expect the same idealized future.

How accurate is this depiction of families today? Recent census data provide extensive information about the characteristics of contemporary U.S. families. Table 10.2 reveals the contrast between the dream and the reality of U.S. marriages. Some elements of the cultural dream are based on the assumption that there are certain prerequisites for rearing emotionally healthy children. Biases against single-parent or gay-parent families, for example, may rest on the assumption that without both a mother and a father present throughout childhood, a child will become maladjusted. There is no evidence, however, to suggest that the offspring of single or gay parents are more poorly adjusted than are their counterparts from intact heterosexual families.

Sex, Time, and Parenthood

High levels of passion are characteristic of the initial stages of a sexual relationship. Research conducted over the past 50 years has consistently shown that married couples engage in sexual intercourse two or three times a week during the early years of marriage, with the frequency of intercourse declining over time. The drop in sexual activity

Table 10.2   Contemporary American Families: Dreams and Reality

Cultural Dream	Cultural Reality
1. Couples get married and then live with one another.	1. More than 10 million unmarried couples share a household.
2. Pair-bonding takes place between one man and one woman.	2. Approximately 3% of the population live in two-person, same-gender households.
3. "Normal" people marry in their early 20s.	3. About 40 million people aged 25 or older are unmarried.
4. A couple's first baby is conceived after the wedding.	4. About 30% of all first births are to unmarried women.
5. First marriage endures until the death of one spouse.	5. More than half of all first marriages end in divorce or separation.
6. Children live with both their biological parents until age 18.	6. Only 42% of children live with both biological parents.
7. Children are raised by both a mother and a father.	7. More than 10% of all family groups with children under age 18 are headed by a single parent.
8. After a child is born, the mother ceases employment until the child has left home.	8. More than half of women with children under 3 years old are in the labor force.

Sources: Ahlberg & DeVita, 1992; Martin & Bumpass, 1989; Saluter, 1992; U.S. Bureau of the Census, 1996.

over the duration of a relationship also holds true for couples who cohabit and for gay and lesbian couples (Laumann et al., 1994; Sprecher & McKinney, 1994).

Parenthood is one factor in the reduced frequency of heterosexual couples' sexual contact (Call, Sprecher, & Schwartz, 1995). When they are parents, a couple who formerly made love when they got home from work regularly find themselves faced with fussing babies and demanding children. By the time the children go to sleep for the night, the ardor that the couple may have felt while making dinner may have faded to a wistful, "Well, honey, maybe tomorrow."

Further, the assumption that there is a tomorrow may decrease a couple's sense of urgency about expressing their sexual feelings immediately. For many couples, the reduced level of sexual activity may be merely a practical response: the presence of children decreases the opportunity for sexual expression.

Despite the challenges presented by the employment of both partners in a relationship, sometimes referred to as the DINS (double income, no sex) dilemma, employment of both spouses does not appear to affect the frequency of marital sexual intercourse (Call et al., 1995; Olson & DeFrain, 1994). It appears that couples who want to have sex make the time for it, rendering the DINS dilemma inaccurate.

REALITY or MYTH ? 2

Family Formation and Division of Labor

First-time parenthood can radically alter the relationship between partners. No longer just lovers or spouses, they now share the responsibilities of child rearing.

Even if both spouses were employed prior to the pregnancy, women tend to cease or limit their outside employment for varying lengths of time after giving birth. The length of time women remain at home after giving birth has decreased in recent years. By 1994, about two out of three mothers with children under 1 year old were employed outside the home (U.S. Bureau of the Census, 1996).

If one spouse is gone all day (typically the husband) and the other one remains in the house with the baby (typically the wife, at least for a while), the homebound spouse may begin to take most of the responsibility for such family tasks as house cleaning, grocery shopping, child care, and meal preparation. The spouse at home may begin to feel dependent on the employed spouse for stimulation and for contact with the outside world. But the employed spouse, preoccupied with tasks, relationships, and issues taking place outside the house, may view home as a place to relax and withdraw from work and relationship pressures. This difference in expectations can strain a formerly egalitarian relationship.

Further, when the wife does return to work, she typically continues to take responsibility for the bulk of household and parenting tasks. The division in household labor between men and women was investigated by analyses of diaries kept by married couples in a national sample of more than five hundred American couples (Pleck, 1983). These couples recorded all their daily activities for one year. Employed husbands spent fewer than 14 hours a week on all family work, compared to 28 hours for employed wives and almost 49 hours for wives not employed outside the house. Husbands performed about 32 percent of the couple's total family work if the wife was employed and 21 percent of the family work if the wife was not employed. Such overloads on women have also been found in Canadian samples (Douthitt, 1989). Although men's contribution to housework has increased, working women still do two to three times as much family work as do husbands (Major, 1993; Silverstein, 1996).

The demands placed on women by having multiple and time-consuming roles can leave little time for leisure or intimacy. Working couples who desire more time for sexual intimacy could discuss the possibility of the husband's expanding his contribution to household chores and the wife's reducing the time spent on housework. If each partner assumes responsibility for about half the housework, the couple has additional time to spend on their relationship. For example, in Joseph Pleck's (1983) study, there were about 42 hours a week of housework, of which the wife was responsible for 28 hours and the husband for 14 hours. A husband who increases his share to 21 hours could give the couple 7 hours a week to devote to pleasurable pursuits.

Regardless of the frequency of sexual behavior, couples grow older. In the next section we examine the association of long-term relationships with the quality and frequency of sexual expression.

LONG-TERM RELATIONSHIPS

The phrase "until death do us part," included in most marriage vows, had a far more literal meaning for most of human history than it does today. In nineteenth-century America, marriage lasted an average of only 12 years before one of the partners died. Today, extended human longevity allows for much longer relationships, which may be complicated by the intrusion of some of the problems common to middle and old age. Most of our examination of long-term relationships focuses on marriage because there is little information about extended relationships among unmarried people.

Sexual Pleasure and Marital Longevity

Kinsey et al. (1953) noted that a decrease in women's orgasm rates frequently preceded divorce and separation, but the meaning of this change was unclear. Did the marital problems leading to divorce affect wives' sexual responsiveness? Or was it the other way around: did the decline in responsiveness lead to increased marital distance and ultimately divorce? Several studies of married couples have indicated that happy marriages can exist between couples whose sexual encounters are not particularly frequent or earthshaking (Blumstein & Schwartz, 1983; Laumann et al., 1994). Sexual incompatibility, however, has been found to be associated with breakups of relationships among dating, married, and homosexual couples (Call et al., 1995; Hatfield & Rapson, 1996; Laumann et al., 1994; Sprecher & McKinney, 1994).

Marital satisfaction is positively related to how often a couple has sex (Blumstein & Schwartz, 1983; Call et al., 1995). Specifically, the more often that sexual intimacy occurs, the more satisfied couples are with their marriage. However as the length of a relationship continues, frequent sex becomes less crucial for marital satisfaction (Call et al., 1995). Over the course of a long-term relationship, many people begin to value personal attachment more highly than sexual attraction.

Attraction Versus Attachment in Long-Term Relationships

The decreasing importance of sexuality in a marriage over time, at least in the successful long-term relationships that have been studied, has been examined in terms of sexual attraction and **attachment.** Troll and Smith (1976) suggested that there is an inverse relationship between these two factors: Sexual attraction is high in the beginning of a new relationship, and attachment is low; over the years, sexual attraction diminishes as novelty wanes, and attachment increases. If marital satisfaction or happiness is measured in terms of sexual attraction, a steady decrease over time is inevitable, with perhaps a temporary rise when the children's departure creates a new domestic situation for husband and wife. If marital satisfaction is measured in terms of attachment, security, and loyalty, however, couples' marital happiness tends to increase over time.

As we have seen, the initial phases of most romantic relationships are characterized by passion and sexual intimacy. The experience of being swept away (see Figure 10.1) does not last long, however, as many parents have advised their unheeding offspring over the years. After couples begin to see each other regularly, passion typically lasts approximately 18 months to 3 years (Fisher, 1992). In short, passion and sexual intimacy appear to be more important to loving relationships in early adulthood, whereas tender feelings of affection and loyalty are more important to loving relationships in the second half of adult life (Byrne & Murnen, 1988; Fisher, 1992).

attachment The feeling of strong connection to another person.

Figure 10.1
Attraction in New Relationships Passion and the desire to be close to one another characterize the beginning of most romantic relationships.

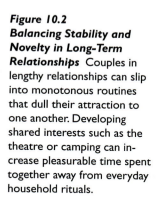

Figure 10.2
Balancing Stability and Novelty in Long-Term Relationships Couples in lengthy relationships can slip into monotonous routines that dull their attraction to one another. Developing shared interests such as the theatre or camping can increase pleasurable time spent together away from everyday household rituals.

Partially because of the inherent tension between the desires for new sexual experiences versus those for continuity and comfort, monogamous relationships are perhaps the most difficult of all human contracts. Additional strain may be added by the fact that such relationships are expected to satisfy so many varied needs for the individuals involved. The needs for passion, security, and play, to name a few, are channeled into monogamous marriages that are typically strained by concerns about children, vocations, and economics. Slowly and often imperceptibly, these relationships can drift toward dispassionate companionship. As a relationship becomes habitual over time, the partners become limited to a constricted range of experiences because it is difficult to preserve the excitement of a relationship that is enmeshed in the rituals of security (see Figure 10.2). Some people have attempted to resolve this dilemma by continuing their primary relationship while simultaneously having sexual relations with others outside their marriage.

Extramarital Sexual Relations

Extramarital sex can involve either covert or overt activity. Covert activities encompass all extramarital sexual relations that occur without the spouse's knowledge. Overt extramarital sex may take several different forms: open marriage, swinging, mate swapping, and group marriage. In these agreed-upon arrangements, both marital partners engage in extramarital sexual activity.

Regardless of the form that extramarital sex assumes, a majority of respondents in Western societies disapprove of extramarital relationships (Bringle & Buunk, 1991; Laumann et al., 1994). Nonetheless, in Laumann et al.'s national sample, about 25 percent of men and 16 percent of women reported having had an extramarital affair. In Tom Smith's (1991) national sample, about 21 percent of men and 13 percent of women indicated that they had had an extramarital affair. These findings are in contrast to previous estimates that at least half of married people have had extramarital sex (Blumstein & Schwartz, 1983; Buss & Schmitt, 1993). This apparent decline in extramarital sex may stem from fear of contracting AIDS (Billy et al., 1993; Smith, 1991).

Why do people have extramarital sex? There is a strong relationship between an individual's sexual attitudes and his or her behavior with respect to premarital sex (Reiss, Anderson, & Sponaugle, 1980). The more tolerant or permissive one's attitudes are toward premarital sex, the more likely it is that one will engage in that activity. For extramarital sex, the relationship between attitudes and behavior may be considerably weaker (Glass & Wright, 1992), in part because of "stronger cultural norms [against extramarital sex] which may not stop the behavior but will produce guilt" (Reiss et al., 1980, p. 398).

The old line, "My wife [husband] doesn't understand me," reflects a pervasive cultural belief that a person strays from the marital bed because of marital discontent or dissatisfaction with the quality of the couple's sex life. Research indicates associations between the likelihood of having affairs and unhappy marriages, but the studies also indicate that happily married people sometimes have extramarital affairs (Bringle & Buunk, 1991). Factors other than marital happiness may be responsible for the associations found. For example, the belief that one's marriage should fulfill all interpersonal needs may be unrealistic.

Some people may choose to have extramarital relationships not just because of the sexual variety but because of other shared interests. Friendships between men and women may also provide a strong inducement for extramarital affairs. Anxiety over waning attractiveness, particularly among men, has been implicated as another motivation for extramarital sex, which provides a way for the man to prove to himself that he is still sexually attractive and virile. Although husbands are more likely to be involved in extramarital affairs than are wives (Buss, 1994; Laumann et al., 1994), they are also more likely to perceive affairs as destructive—if their wives are "unfaithful"! Like men, women often start affairs in their late 30s or early 40s seeking passion, a reaffirmation of their sexual attractiveness, and the excitement of courtship and love (Bringle & Buunk, 1991; Lawson, 1988). Sexual relationships outside marriage are not limited to middle age, of course. They can and do occur at any time during a marriage. Teenagers and grandparents have affairs and give a variety of reasons for doing so.

Under what conditions do people perceive extramarital sex as justified? Glass and Wright (1992) distributed questionnaires to adults at an airport and during the lunch hour in downtown Baltimore. Based on the responses of married people in their sample, four factors or reasons emerged: (1) sexual factors (excitement, enjoyment, curiosity, and novelty), (2) emotional intimacy, (3) extrinsic motivation (career advancement, revenge on spouse), and (4) love. Men were more likely to endorse sex as a justification, and women were more likely to see love as a justification for extramarital involvement.

Sometimes a marital imbalance leads a husband or wife to feel justified in seeking an extramarital relationship. Walster, Walster, and Berscheid (1978) have distinguished two kinds of imbalance. First, we may feel overbenefited when our marital rewards are greater than our costs. Second, we may experience deprivation when we perceive our investment as greater than our rewards. Finally, **equity** exists when we perceive our rewards as being equal to our investment in the marriage.

It is important to note that rewards and investments can be defined in various ways. People bring diverse contributions to a relationship—financial assets, practical know-how, or physical appeal, for example. Walster et al. found some support for their hypothesis that spouses who perceive themselves to be either overbenefited or in an equitable relationship would be less likely to involve themselves in extramarital affairs

ISSUES TO CONSIDER

What prompts married people to have sexual relations outside their marriages? Conversely, why do some married people avoid sexual intimacy with anyone but their spouses?

equity In a personal relationship, a perceived balance between the benefits the relationship provides and the personal investment it requires.

Across Cultures

The Relationship of Equity to Likelihood of Having Extramarital Sex

In a study of married Dutch persons, 30 percent of whom had been involved in extramarital affairs, Prins, Buunk, and VanYperen (1993) also examined the relationship of equity to the likelihood of such extramarital liaisons. Women who felt deprived *or* advantaged in their marital relationships were more likely to have extramarital relations than were those women who reported equity in their marital relations. In contrast, men's likelihood of engaging in extramarital sex was less related to their relative sense of equity in their marital relationships. Prins et al. also found that although men reported stronger desires to engage in extramarital sex, there were no differences in the percentage of men and women reporting involvement in such affairs.

than would spouses who saw themselves as deprived (see "Across Cultures: The Relationship of Equity to Likelihood of Having Extramarital Sex").

Separation and Divorce

The U.S. divorce rate has been on the rise since the beginning of the Industrial Revolution (Fisher, 1992). This increase started to level off in the early 1980s, although more than half of recent first marriages still end in separation or divorce (Sprecher & Fehr, 1998). Most industrialized nations have experienced similar patterns, although divorce is more common in the United States than elsewhere (Ahlburg & DeVita, 1992).

Pessimists point to these statistics as reflections of widespread instability, the decline of the family, and moral decay in contemporary society. This concern about the demise of the family is not new. The following comment appeared in the Boston *Quarterly Review* in 1859: "The family in its old sense is disappearing from our land, and not only our free institutions are threatened but the very existence of our society is endangered" (Cherlin, 1981, pp. 2–3).

Optimists take a different view, suggesting that the numbers simply underscore high expectations for the quality of marital relationships. We are, they say, unwilling to settle for the "lives of quiet desperation" that have characterized the many marriages held together for the sake of children or religious or financial considerations. Optimists cite another statistic to support their point: 60 percent to 80 percent of divorced people marry a second partner depending on the group studied (Ahlburg & DeVita, 1992; Sprecher & Fehr, 1998). It seems that these people are rejecting a particular spouse but not the institution of marriage.

How is it that two people can enter marriage full of love, hope, and commitment, only to have the relationship dissolve? Although the causes of divorce are complex and there is not enough evidence to answer this question definitively, certain conditions are associated with the longevity of relationships. Age at marriage and educational level are two of the most consistent (White, 1991). Teenage marriages are more than twice as likely to end than are unions of people in their 20s, with the most stable first marriages occurring among women who wed after the age of 30 (Martin & Bumpass, 1989; Norton & Moorman, 1987). Divorce peaks between the ages of 20 and 24 for both genders in the United States, which is slightly younger than for other societies for which data are available (Fisher, 1992). The proportion of divorces is highest at around the fourth year of marriage in most of the 24 societies that anthropologist Helen Fisher studied. In the United States, the peak is found somewhat earlier, occurring around the third year of marriage (Fisher, 1992; Kurdek, 1993). Divorce then becomes less and less frequent.

REALITY or MYTH ? 3

An analysis of 160 societies indicated that infidelity, particularly by the wife, was the most common reason given for divorce (Betzig, 1989). Infertility was the next most commonly mentioned reason. Cruelty, especially by the husband, ranked third world-wide among reasons for divorce. Although these reasons are closely related to sex and reproduction, divorce in the United States today seems to be less tied to sex and repro-ductive reasons. Individuals' accounts of their own divorces implicate such factors as substance abuse, infidelity, personal or sexual incompatibility, physical and emotional abuse, financial problems, and gender-role disagreements (White, 1991).

Adjustment to Separation: Who Suffers Most?

Women are stereotypically portrayed as far more dependent on love and marital rela-tionships than are men, and thus more devastated by separation and divorce. The evi-dence suggests, however, that the responses of men and women to separation and divorce are somewhat more complicated than usually portrayed.

REALITY or MYTH ? 4

Men are more likely to experience depression and illnesses requiring hospitaliza-tion following divorce than are women. Women's reactions are less severe but more fre-quent and long-lasting; they include mild depression and anxiety about living alone (Hatfield & Rapson, 1996; Kitson & Morgan, 1991). In addition, some divorced women feel helpless, unattractive, isolated, and concerned about loss of status (Hether-ington, Cox, & Cox, 1982).

These gender differences may have roots in many factors, including the fact that after divorce, a woman's financial resources are reduced by about 30 percent (Kitson & Morgan, 1991). Related to their standard of living is the greater difficulty women may experience in finding employment that provides sufficient income following the loss of the husband's paycheck. In divorce settlements, the custody of children is still gener-ally awarded to women, and the responsibility for rearing children single-handedly may restrict the ability of women to pursue new social relationships.

After divorce, men and women usually do not become celibate. Even when con-cerns about contracting AIDS became widespread, only 20 percent of the separated and 26 percent of the divorced people in Smith's (1991) nationally representative sample reported abstinence during the previous 12 months.

Regardless of marital status, at some point during their 40s or 50s, people begin to assess what they have done with their lives so far, as they come to grips with the fact that they no longer have as much time remaining in their lives as they had during young adulthood.

AGING AND SEXUALITY

Most sex research has focused on individuals in late adolescence or early adult-hood. The fact that people beyond early adulthood have received only limited research attention is probably due to several factors, including our species' relative in-experience with aging, traditional beliefs about the purposes of sex, and the greater ease of obtaining samples of college students than of older adults to participate in research.

For most of human existence, relatively few individuals lived to advanced ages. Even in the United States, which, in terms of human history has existed for an extremely brief period, it is only in the twentieth century that living beyond age 40 has become commonplace. Because life was short and seldom sweet, it was crucial for our ancestors to reproduce as early and as frequently as possible. The historical equation of reproduction with sexuality, strengthened by thousands of years of struggling to survive as a species, may still affect our vision of sexuality. The identification of sexuality with fertility perpetuates the idea that people beyond their reproductive years are sexless. Decreases in reproductive capacity, however, need not eliminate sexual feelings and responsiveness.

Nonetheless, in North America, sexuality is generally treated as a quality and activity limited to the young. Many older members of society accept this stereotype, and some of them welcome the release from what they perceive to be a burdensome obligation. Other people, however, find that age brings a different kind of release. As one woman put it,

> *The older I get, the more I enjoy sex. When I was in my teens and 20s, I spent a lot of time thinking about how I should act, and I felt shy about my body. I know that objectively, I was a lot more attractive then than I am now in my late 40s. But I feel so much freer and prettier now that I don't worry about what I'm supposed to do or how I'm supposed to look. Instead of thinking about what my partner thinks of my body, I'm appreciating my body for the pleasure it gives me. (Authors' files)*

Midlife Changes and Assessments

Erikson (1968b) described the developmental challenge of this period as the conflict of generativity versus stagnation. Generativity is a concern for the future of our species, expressed not only in involvement with our own children, if we have them, but with children in general. Successful resolution of this stage requires looking beyond our own goals of personal gratification and yields a sense of intense connection to the well-being of others in our family, community, and nation and to humanity in general (see Figure 10.3). People who do not resolve the crisis of this stage feel little connection

Figure 10.3 Generativity Versus Stagnation This middle-aged man enjoys sharing his love of art with these children. Talking about art with young people provides him with an ongoing sense of involvement in life and the transmission of knowledge to future generations (generativity).

with anything beyond their own personal gratification. For such persons, the aging process involves stagnation. Failing to form a deep connection with others, these people experience aging simply as an inevitable movement toward loss of physical and personal power and death. Embedded in this period are the biological changes associated with aging.

Menopause

The average woman experiences **menopause,** the gradual ending of ovulation, menstruation, and reproductive capacity, at around age 51. However, it can occur any time between the ages of 35 and 60. There is usually a seven-year transitional period, known as the perimenopausal stage, characterized by increasing irregularity of menstrual-cycle length and bleeding pattern (Cutler, Garcia, & McCoy, 1987).

One of the most common changes associated with menopause is the decline in sex hormones. This decline is the source of the "hot flashes" and sudden sweating that many menopausal women report. Fatigue, depression, and headaches are also common, and some women experience reductions in vaginal lubrication. These symptoms, linked to decreases in estrogen secretion, can persist for several years. The administration of hormone-replacement therapy, usually low doses of estrogen and progesterone, reduces unwanted symptoms associated with menopause. Estrogen suppositories or creams placed in the vagina several times a week may also reduce problems associated with estrogen deficiency.

Although medical experts once widely agreed that menopausal women experience a declining level of sexual response in correspondence with declining levels of estrogen, more recent studies have found a great deal of variation in sexual response during this period (Cutler et al., 1987; Luria & Meade, 1984). Although very low estrogen levels are associated with infrequent sexual activity, no one knows whether low levels of estrogen cause, or are the result of, low levels of sexual activity. However, research does indicate that menopause need not bring women's sexual responsiveness to an end.

The continuance or decline of sexual responsiveness at menopause may be partially a function of a woman's social class. In Hallstrom's (1977) study of 800 women, upper-social-class menopausal women showed less decline in sexual interest, capacity for orgasm, and coital frequency than did menopausal women of lower social classes, who revealed age-related deficits in their sexual responses.

What about "male menopause"? A review of the male menopause literature indicates that a significant number of men experience psychological and social difficulties in middle age, but these appear to stem from cultural and lifestyle changes, such as retirement and loss of status associated with employment, rather than from hormonal changes (Fetherstone & Hepworth, 1985).

menopause The end of menstruation, ovulation, and a woman's reproductive capacity.

 REALITY or MYTH ? 5

The Double Standard of Aging

In our culture, aging is more of a challenge for women than for men, for two reasons. First, because female reproductive capacity terminates at menopause, whereas male reproductive capacity wanes gradually, women beyond the age of menopause are more likely to be stereotyped as sexless. (If this stereotype were accurate, there would be little reason to study the sexuality of older women.) Second, the physical characteristics regarded as attractive in females—smooth skin, slim physique, firm breasts—tend to decline earlier than the physical qualities considered sexy in men. A woman's youthful physical appearance has traditionally defined her attractiveness. In contrast, a man with gray or white hair is often described as distinguished, and the lines on his

Figure 10.4 *(left)*
Sexy Sean Actor Sean Connery continues to be a box-office draw despite being in his 60s. In contrast, aging actresses often find it difficult to obtain leading roles.
Figure 10.5 *(right)*
Fabulous Tina Tina Turner demonstrates that aging women can be sensuous and vibrant.

ISSUES TO CONSIDER

Do you think there is still a double standard of aging and sexuality for men and women?

face, increasing and becoming more deeply etched with age, are considered to bestow character (see Figure 10.4). His sexual value is defined more by power and status than by physical characteristics.

The visual media perpetuate such stereotypes and help to create unrealistic fantasies. Hollywood generally rejects women of 40 and over as vital sexual beings but hands many romantic leads to men of that age or older. Actress Joanne Woodward, in a television interview, compared herself to her husband, actor Paul Newman, as follows: "He gets prettier; I get older." But there are signs that this double standard is gradually changing with the aging of the general population. Television shows such as *Murphy Brown,* starring Candice Bergen, and *Cybill,* starring Cybill Shepherd, feature women in their 40s and 50s who are depicted as quite interested in sex. These portrayals are contributing to the portrayal of older women as intelligent, attractive, and sexy (see Figure 10.5).

Midlife Challenges and Gender Roles

There is evidence that gender roles become less important from middle age onward and that people take on personality attributes traditionally defined as characteristic of the other gender; that is, as men become older, they tend to express their affiliative and nurturant feelings, whereas women become more responsive to and less guilty about their egocentric and assertive impulses (Neugarten & Gutmann, 1968). In traditional societies, women become more assertive as they become older, often becoming more influential in their social groups. Fisher (1992) suggested that biology may play a role. Levels of estrogen decline with menopause, allowing testosterone, which has been linked with assertiveness, to exert greater influence. Psychologically, there is a counterbalancing of personality traits between men and women, and more complex conceptions of what it means to be male and female develop (Hatfield & Rapson, 1996). Although many adults experience a time during which they question the value of what they have done and are doing, such soul searching is by no means automatic.

For both men and women, the average frequency of intercourse declines as they advance into old age (Cash, Sprecher, & Schwartz, 1995; Laumann et al., 1994). However, there is considerable variation in the sexual practices of older people.

OLD AGE

Erikson maintained that the challenge of the last stage of life is to resolve the conflict of integrity versus despair. During self-assessment at this stage, the emphasis is on evaluating the kind of person one has been and the meaning that one's life has had. This evaluative process can produce a sense of satisfaction and integrity. People who have been relatively successful in resolving earlier crises can view their lives as having been purposeful, and the resultant sense of integrity can soften the fear of death. Conversely, the realization that there is not enough time left to try to improve or alter what has been done with one's life may engender a sense of pointlessness and despair. In addition to various psychological changes, aging brings some inevitable physiological changes. (See Figure 10.6.)

Physiological Changes

Changes occur in the phases of the sexual response cycle (Rowland, Greenleaf, Dorfman, & Davidson, 1993), particularly after age 60. Masters and Johnson (1966) studied changes in the sexual responses of people from late adolescence to the age of 89. (For a summary of Masters and Johnson's major findings regarding males, see "Health: Aging of the Male Sexual System" on page 264.) For example, an aging male whose penis has been erect for a relatively lengthy period during lovemaking may experience ejaculation as a seeping out of semen rather than a forceful expulsion of seminal fluid.

Figure 10.6
Gender and Sexuality over the Life Cycle Gender differences peak in the reproductive years and gradually diminish as males and females advance into their later years.

Health

Aging of the Male Sexual System

1. Males' sexual responsiveness, as measured by ejaculation, masturbation, nocturnal emission, coitus, orgasm, and level of sexual excitement, wanes or declines.

2. Erection of the penis takes longer to occur. The erection can be maintained, however, for extended periods of time without ejaculation.

3. Full erection often does not occur until just before ejaculation.

4. The penis is likely to return to a flaccid state following ejaculation rather than remain erect for a number of minutes.

5. The refractory period between orgasm and subsequent erection and ejaculation increases. After age 60, 12 to 24 hours may be required before an erection can be attained again.

6. The pleasure associated with ejaculation may decrease because ejaculation may be experienced as seepage rather than forceful expulsion.

7. A single-stage rather than a two-stage ejaculatory response may be experienced.

8. The amount of seminal fluid is markedly reduced.

9. Nipple erection and the sex flush of the skin do not occur as frequently.

10. Secondary erectile dysfunction increases significantly after 50 years of age.

Source: Adapted from Masters & Johnson, 1966.

As mentioned earlier, estrogen production in women usually begins to decline after age 40, and the decrease continues until about age 60. With the reduction in estrogen secretion, the vaginal walls of postmenopausal women thin out. The rate and amount of vaginal lubrication also diminish, although Masters and Johnson reported exceptions to this rule. Women who were consistently sexually active, having coitus once or twice a week, showed no decline in vaginal lubrication.

Breast tissue atrophies somewhat as the glandular material is slowly replaced by fibrous tissue. Further, the reduced secretion of estrogen after menopause can lead to osteoporosis, or bone deterioration, and many physicians now recommend hormone-replacement therapy to reduce the risk of osteoporosis (bone loss). (For a summary of other results obtained in Masters and Johnson's observation of the aging process in women, see "Health: Aging of the Female Sexual System.")

Social Stereotypes and Self-Image

Social and psychological factors can either diminish the effects of aging or make them more severe. As the elderly population increases and we learn more about sexuality among the aged, social recognition and acceptance of the sensual appeal of older people may become more common.

In the early 1990s, several groups of older women were featured in talk shows and in live performances around the United States; among them were the Sensuous Seniors and the Dancing Grannies, who dressed in body suits and performed aerobic dancing to popular music. Ranging in age from their 50s to their 70s, these women appeared to be more agile than many adolescents and young adults. In addition to altering stereotypes about aging women, the vigorous exercise regimen the Dancing Grannies followed probably has beneficial effects on their self-esteem and physical health. They

Health

Aging of the Female Sexual System

1. The vagina decreases in length and width.
2. The vagina loses some of its elasticity and ability to expand.
3. The vaginal walls become thin and light pinkish in color, in contrast to their earlier thick and reddish appearance.
4. The rate and amount of vaginal lubrication diminish, sometimes making sexual intercourse painful or difficult.
5. The uterus and cervix shrink in size.
6. Uterine cramping or contractions may make intercourse painful.
7. An urgent need to urinate is frequently experienced after intercourse.
8. Vaginal burning or irritation and pain centered around the pelvis may be experienced in association with sexual activities.
9. Nipple erection during sexual intercourse loses some of its intensity.
10. The sex flush of the skin does not occur as frequently.
11. Vaginal contractions during orgasm last for a shorter period of time.

Source: Adapted from Masters & Johnson, 1966.

were not seeking to portray themselves as young women. Instead, their goal was to demonstrate that elderly women can be sensuous, healthy, and vibrant.

In sum, our culture has traditionally propagated stereotypes suggesting that individuals become sexually inactive in their middle and senior years. The persistence of such ideas may make people feel guilt or worry if they continue to have sexual feelings as they advance into and beyond middle age. But just how widespread is termination of sexual expression during old age?

Decreasing Sexual Activity: Aging or Other Factors?

Older people's sexual activity generally follows the patterns established in younger years. If sex has been a source of caring and comfort, it can provide warmth and security in advanced years. But if sex has caused conflict or pain or if a person has seldom been interested in or rewarded by sexual activity, old age can represent a welcome opportunity to end sexual relations. Of course, for some elderly people, sexual interactions end because they lack a partner. In the general population, there is a steady decline in frequency of sexual activity with age, although this pattern varies considerably from one person to the next.

The average man's sexual responsiveness diminishes as he ages. Laumann et al. (1994) found no other factor than age for men that affected the frequency of total sexual outlet as much. It is more difficult to assess women's sexual expression over the life cycle than men's, for several reasons. First, for unmarried women, societal restrictions tend to inhibit coital activity. Second, for married women, coital activity is likely to be influenced by a husband's sexual inclinations, which show a decline over time. A third complication in measuring female sexuality through the years is that women tend to have orgasm less consistently than do men.

The largest survey to date on sexuality and the elderly relied on responses to a questionnaire appearing in *Consumer Reports* (Brecher, 1984). Among the many

Table 10.3   Sexual Activity in Those 50 Years of Age and Older

	In Their 50s	60s	70 and Over
Men who masturbate	66%	50%	43%
Frequency of masturbation per week for these men	1.2	0.8	0.7
Husbands who have sex with their wives	87%	78%	59%
Frequency of sex per week for these men	1.3	1.0	0.6
Women who masturbate	47%	37%	33%
Frequency of masturbation per week for these women	0.7	0.6	0.7
Wives who have sex with their husbands	88%	76%	65%
Frequency of sex per week for these women	1.3	1.0	0.6

Source: Brecher, 1984.

Figure 10.7
Lack of Opportunity
Because, on average, women live longer than men, heterosexual women who have lost their life partners often have difficulty in finding a new partner with whom to be emotionally and sexually intimate.

findings was the fact that 59 percent of the men and 65 percent of the women 70 years or older still engage in sexual intercourse, and half of them make love at least once a week. Some of the other findings are presented in Table 10.3. It is apparent that many people in this age range remain sexually active. Sexual activity was not limited to the marital relationship. Almost 25 percent of the husbands and 8 percent of the wives reported that they had engaged in extramarital sex at least once after age 50.

People tend to assume that aging persons lose their capacity for sexual arousal and response as a result of the physiological changes described earlier. However, because the quality and frequency of sexual expression vary greatly over the later years, re-

searchers have suggested that several other factors may also determine whether sexual expression continues.

A group of Duke University scientists reported that the decline in sexual interest and activity over the second half of life is at least partially a reflection of variations in the patterns of different generations rather than just an age-related decline. A longitudinal study of married couples ranging in age from 60 to 94 indicated that patterns of sexual activity remained more stable in middle and later life than was previously thought (George & Weiler, 1981; Newman & Nichols, 1960; Pfeiffer et al., 1968; Verwoerdt et al., 1969). Only about 8 percent of the men and 15 percent of the women reported a cessation of sexual activities.

Although the Duke scientists found a progressive decline in the frequency of sexual expression with advancing age, they also discovered great variations in sexual capacity among their older volunteers. The ability to engage in sexual activity has been reported among 70-, 80-, and 90-year-old people (Brecher, 1984; Karlen, 1994; Weizman & Hart, 1987). After age 80, the most common sexual activity for both men and women was touching and caressing without sexual intercourse, followed in popularity by masturbation, and then sexual intercourse (Bretschneider & McCoy, 1988). Sexual activity appears to be associated with two other factors in addition to physiological capability: past sexual activity and the availability of a partner (see Figure 10.7).

The advice that one should maintain a regular program of physical exercise to be physically fit in later years ("use it or lose it") appears to apply to sexual capacities as well. Volunteers who engaged in sexual activity relatively frequently during early adulthood and middle age were more sexually active during old age than were volunteers who were less sexually active during their youth and middle age.

More than the sum of biological drives, the erotic impulse is an expression of basic desires for human contact, love, and life itself. The erotic impulse may be a fundamental expression of an appetite for life; starvation of this appetite through premature denial of our continuing erotic impulses may contribute to feelings of isolation and despair. Correlational data support this speculation: Older persons who have intimate relationships are more likely than those who do not to enjoy high levels of both objective and self-perceived well-being (see Figure 10.8). These findings suggest that sexual feelings and expression should be nurtured rather than suppressed. Healthful activities during their younger years may help individuals who wish to be sexy, sensuous seniors to increase their likelihood of achieving that goal.

Figure 10.8
Tactile Comfort and Aging
Touching can provide a sense of connection and pleasure with other people across the lifespan.

ISSUES TO CONSIDER

Would you feel comfortable talking about sexuality with an older person such as a grandparent or an elderly neighbor? Why or why not?

SUMMARY OF MAJOR POINTS

1. Young adulthood and sexual-lifestyle choices.

The decision to remain single for varying lengths of time, or permanently, has become more acceptable. Choosing singleness does not necessarily mean choosing celibacy. In general, cohabiting individuals do not differ greatly from people who opt to marry before living together. The primary differences appear to be a greater likelihood of flexibility in gender roles and more sexual experience beginning at an earlier age among those who cohabit.

2. Parenthood and sexuality.

Although children can provide immense satisfaction to a couple, they also appear to have a rather dampening effect on the flexibility of a husband and wife's timing of sexual expression. The presence of children also reduces the frequency of a couple's sexual interaction.

3. Long-term relationships.

Contrary to cultural myths regarding the timing of and the roles involved in marriage and parenthood, the majority of women today, regardless of whether they have children, are employed outside the home. The decades since the 1960s have been a period of transition in social attitudes about the tasks and roles of spouses. Sexual satisfaction appears to be less important to perceptions of marital satisfaction as people get older. Sexual boredom can be problematic in long-term relationships if couples develop rigid and highly predictable patterns of relating to each other.

4. Extramarital relations.

Disapproval of extramarital sex remains high in the United States. There is evidence, however, that substantial numbers of men and women have been sexually intimate with people other than their spouses. Most married people who have extramarital encounters do so without the agreement, approval, or knowledge of their spouses. Research conducted at the end of the 1980s indicates that Americans have begun to reduce their involvement in extramarital affairs.

5. Separation and divorce.

More than half of contemporary first marriages end in separation or divorce. A small proportion of divorced men tend to have serious reactions that are more severe than those experienced by women. However, a larger proportion of women than men suffer minor adjustment problems, many linked to access to economic resources and control over their lives. Most men and women are sexually active after divorce, and the majority eventually remarry.

6. Cultural attitudes toward aging.

Our society is youth oriented in its views of what constitutes eroticism, and we tend to equate sexual functioning with reproductive ability, particularly in women. A double standard of aging has led postmenopausal women to be viewed as having lost their erotic appeal, whereas men are considered sexy as they gain status and power with age.

7. Sexual expression among the elderly.

There is considerable variation in the frequency of sexual expression among elderly people. Longitudinal research indicates that people who enjoy frequent sexual stimulation and interaction during middle age show relatively little decline in sexual expression as they age. There is some reduction in the speed of arousal and orgasmic response, but the frequency of sexual contact among elderly people who remain sexually active is quite stable. Correlational data indicate greater health, life satisfaction, and general well-being among elderly people who are sexually active and have intimate relationships than among those who do not engage in sexual or sensual activity.

CHECK YOUR KNOWLEDGE

1. Which of the following stereotypes is *not* often associated with single lifestyles? (a) promiscuous, (b) gay, (c) attractive, (d) emotionally unstable. **(p. 251)**

2. Compared to cohabitors, noncohabitors generally report that they have (a) lower expectations for marriage, (b) less satisfactory sexual lives, (c) less sexual experience, (d) more legal problems. **(p. 252)**

3. Employed husbands spend (a) as much time at family work as their wives do if the latter are employed, (b) spend less time at family work if their wives are employed, (c) spend more time at family work if their wives are unemployed, (d) have begun to increase their contribution to family work. **(p. 254)**

4. Passionate feelings in a relationship typically last (a) 6 months to a year, (b) 18 months to 3 years, (c) 5 to 7 years, (d) for the duration of a relationship. **(p. 255)**

5. Which of these is *not* related to divorce rates? (a) marital age, (b) educational level, (c) political affiliation, (d) infidelity. **(pp. 258–259)**

6. Erikson's developmental crisis of the midlife years involves (a) integrity versus despair, (b) sexuality versus money, (c) identity versus role confusion, (d) generativity versus stagnation. **(p. 260)**

7. Menopause is (a) the end of a woman's reproductive capacity, (b) the end of a woman's sexual interest, (c) the end of a man's reproductive capacity, (d) marked by extreme fluctuations in the production of estrogen. **(p. 261)**

8. Recent longitudinal studies of older married couples suggest that sexual activity (a) increases among couples who were sexually active in their earlier years; (b) mirrors levels of sexual activity earlier in their relationship; (c) is unrelated to their earlier levels of sexual activity; (d) none of the above, as the sexual activity of older married couples has not been studied. **(p. 267)**

11

SEXUAL ORIENTATION

WHAT IS SEXUAL ORIENTATION?
Cross-Species Perspectives
Highlight: Variations in Sexual Orientation and Gender Identity
Cross-Cultural Perspectives
Across Cultures: Rigid Versus Fluid Definitions of Orientation

HOMOSEXUAL BEHAVIOR AND GAY IDENTITY
Self-Definition
Sexual Expression

EXPLANATIONS OF SEXUAL ORIENTATION
Biological Correlates
Family Experiences
Gender-Role Nonconformity During Childhood

SEXUAL ORIENTATION AND ADJUSTMENT
Antigay Prejudice
Changing Views of Mental Health
Therapy

DISCRIMINATION AND LIBERATION
Discrimination
The Gay Liberation Movement

BISEXUALITY
Incidence
Characteristics
Identity Versus Experience
Bisexual Identity: Stable or Transitional?

SUMMARY OF MAJOR POINTS

CHECK YOUR KNOWLEDGE

REALITY or MYTH ?

1 Homosexual behavior occurs among other species in addition to humans.

2 Research has found that lesbians slightly outnumber gay men in the United States.

3 Almost all homosexuals can be identified by their personal characteristics.

4 An imbalance of sex hormones is the most frequent cause of homosexuality.

5 Homosexuals are allowed in the military as long as they are not public about their sexual orientation.

6 Many people who have had sexual experience with both genders do not consider themselves bisexual.

W E each have a sexual orientation. Some of us feel sexual arousal toward individuals of the same gender; others are attracted to people of the other gender. Some of us find people of both genders sexually appealing.

In this chapter we survey research on human sexual orientation. Most of this research has focused on attraction to people of the same gender—that is, homosexuality—and our coverage will reflect that bias. Studies of heterosexual orientation have been neglected, perhaps because funding agencies and researchers have perceived heterosexuality as being "natural" or "normal" and thus needing no explanation. We look at homosexuality in other species and cultures, and we also examine the relationship of gender-role identity to sexual orientation. We discuss what is known about the incidence of homosexual behavior and about the characteristics of gay lifestyles. Current explanations of the development of sexual orientation are reviewed. The phenomenon of antigay prejudice, sometimes called **homophobia,** has captured the attention of researchers, and we discuss what their studies have shown about this bias and its consequences. We examine the assumption that people who have an erotic orientation toward others of the same gender are in need of psychotherapy, and we describe attempts to alter sexual orientation. The legal and social treatment of gay people within our culture and the emergence of the gay liberation movement are considered. Finally, we consider bisexuals—people for whom gender is not an influence in erotic attraction to others—and we consider whether this identity is transitional or stable.

ISSUES TO CONSIDER

Why would anyone study sexual orientation?

homophobia Fear of and hostility toward homosexuality.

WHAT IS SEXUAL ORIENTATION?

M ost North Americans reserve the label *heterosexual* for people who have had sexual interactions only with members of the other gender. All others, regardless of how many homosexual or heterosexual interactions they have had, are lumped into the *homosexual* category. How accurate is the common assumption that a heterosexual has sex exclusively with members of the other gender and that a homosexual is

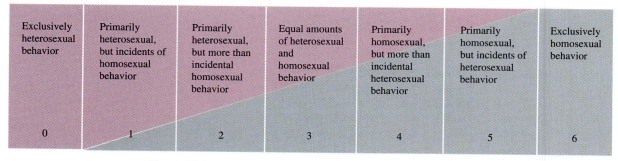

Exclusively heterosexual behavior	Primarily heterosexual, but incidents of homosexual behavior	Primarily heterosexual, but more than incidental homosexual behavior	Equal amounts of heterosexual and homosexual behavior	Primarily homosexual, but more than incidental heterosexual behavior	Primarily homosexual, but incidents of heterosexual behavior	Exclusively homosexual behavior
0	1	2	3	4	5	6

Figure 11.1

Heterosexual–Homosexual Rating Scale Rather than treating people as either heterosexual or homosexual, the Kinsey group placed individuals along a continuum divided into seven categories, as this figure shows.

anyone who has ever had sex with a person of the same gender? Although we noted in Chapter 1 that the Kinsey group's sample was not representative of the U.S. population, Kinsey et al. (1948) found that 37 percent of men and 13 percent of women in their sample had had at least one homosexual encounter. Kinsey and his colleagues introduced an orientation rating scale that subsequent researchers have used extensively (see Figure 11.1). Based on their sexual behaviors and erotic feelings, individuals are assigned a place or number on Kinsey's seven-point continuum from exclusive heterosexuality to exclusive homosexuality. Who goes into which group, and why?

Although the Kinsey group did take psychological reactions to people of the same and other gender into account in classifying sexual orientation—that is, fantasies and feelings about same-gender people by individuals who did not have homosexual contacts—they emphasized behavioral criteria. In contrast, social scientists such as Michael Storms (1980, 1981) and Matthew Hogben and Donn Byrne (1998) have presented evidence that an individual's erotic fantasies and feelings are central to the development of sexual orientation. These erotic fantasies motivate and give direction to sexual behavior and to the selection of partners. In using the terms *gay, homosexual,* and **lesbian** in this chapter, we are referring to people who are motivated by a definite erotic desire for members of the same gender and who usually (but not necessarily) engage in overt sexual relations with them.

Many people confuse gender identity with sexual orientation; that is, they assume that homosexual orientation occurs because of inappropriate gender identification. Consequently, men who prefer male sexual partners are frequently portrayed in the media as highly effeminate, or in slang terms "swishy." But in fact, the gender-role identities of gay men and lesbians are often consistent with their biological gender. Later in the chapter, we will examine several possible explanations for variations in orientation, but for now we can say that the stereotypes of gay men as effeminate and lesbians as masculine are, more often than not, inaccurate. For example, Mary and Susan may both be quite stereotypically feminine in their gender identities, yet they may be involved in a lesbian love affair with each other. There is also a tendency to confuse transvestism and transsexuality with sexual orientation. (See "Highlight: Variations in Sexual Orientation and Gender Identity" for definitions of some key terms.)

lesbian A woman who is attracted to or has sex with other women.

Cross-Species Perspectives

REALITY or **MYTH ?** **1**

Homosexual behavior is fairly common among nonhuman mammals. Mounting of one male by another has been observed among rodents and primates. Male-male mountings

HIGHLIGHT

Variations in Sexual Orientation and Gender Identity

Heterosexuals. People who have sexual relationships primarily or exclusively with members of the other gender.

Homosexuals. People who have sexual relationships primarily or exclusively with members of their own gender.

Bisexuals. People who have sexual relationships with members of either gender, although not necessarily at the same time.

Transsexuals. People who appear biologically to be members of one gender but who feel psychologically as if they were members of the other gender.

Transvestites. People who become sexually aroused when wearing clothing stereotypical of the other gender. (Most contemporary transvestites are heterosexual males.)

---

are much more likely to occur when one of the males displays feminine behavior, although this behavior is not necessarily a sexual act. For example, among some types of monkeys, a male adopts a "receptive" posture as a gesture of appeasement after an argument with a more dominant male (de Waal, 1995). Female-female mounting is also common among mammals. This appears to be true of chimpanzees, several types of monkeys, cows, lions, and domestic cats.

In summary, we can conclude that homosexual interaction is not limited to human beings. It has been observed in many species that researchers have studied (Pavelka, 1995). Animal studies have given us little insight, however, into human homosexual behavior, so it is advisable to keep in mind Frank Beach's (1976, p. 298) warning:

> The fact that some animals engage in homosexual behavior has often been mentioned in discussions of human sexuality, with the implication that the mere existence of the similarity proves something or other about homosexuality in man; e.g., that homosexuality is "biologically normal." The conclusion may or may not be correct but the empirical evidence is irrelevant and neither supports nor denies the deduction.

Cross-Cultural Perspectives

Our information about homosexual expression in other cultures is primarily based on anthropologists' observations. In *Patterns of Sexual Behavior* (1951), Cleland Ford and Frank Beach reviewed reports of about 190 cultures for which information about sexuality was available. They reported that homosexual behavior was not found to be a predominant sexual activity among adults in any of those societies. In the majority of the groups for which information on homosexuality was available, same-gender sexual relations were considered to be normal and socially acceptable, at least for certain members of the community. In about a third of the societies, homosexual behavior was reported to be rare, absent, or carried on only in secrecy.

The Sambia of New Guinea is an example of a culture that prescribes a period of ritualized homosexuality for boys. In fact, in New Guinea, up to 20 percent of the total number of distinct cultures in that region practice some form of ritualized homosexuality (Herdt, 1984). In these cultures, semen is believed to be a precious resource that must be transferred to a young male to enable him to reach maturity. Techniques for achieving this transfer include oral intercourse, anal intercourse, and masturbation, followed by a smearing of semen over the body. Most of these young males become heterosexual, marry, and father children.

Across Cultures

Rigid Versus Fluid Definitions of Orientation

Psychologist Michael Stevenson (1998) received a Fulbright scholarship to study in Indonesia. He described an experience on the flight to Jakarta in which he was sitting next to a middle-aged married Indonesian man. The man asked Stevenson a variety of increasingly personal questions (including inquiring about whether Stevenson had been circumcised!), and made it quite clear that he was interested in a sexual liaison with Stevenson. Stevenson indicated a number of times that he was not interested, but the man insisted in giving Stevenson his telephone number. After arriving in Jakarta, Stevenson asked if the behavior of his fellow passenger was commonplace. He was told that it was not typical, but it also was not unusual.

Stevenson wrote that because of the diversity in cultures in Indonesia, it was inappropriate to make many generalizations about sexual orientation. However, one generalization that can be made is that the whole definition of sexual orientation appears to be more fluid in Indonesia than characterizes how North Americans perceive orientation. Specifically, it appears that the use of the rigid labels *heterosexual* or *homosexual* that is common in North America to refer to both behavior and identity is not applied in most Indonesian cultures. Although Indonesians recognize that a heterosexually married man may have recreational sex with another man, he is not then labeled as homosexual or, for that matter, bisexual.

Davenport (1965) provided an excellent account of a group of Melanesian people living on a Pacific island, where adult male homosexual relations with adolescents and homosexual relations between two adolescents were completely acceptable and openly discussed. Mutual masturbation and anal intercourse were considered normal within these relationships, although oral-genital activity was unknown. When a man was about 20 years old, he married a woman, but he could still engage in extramarital homosexual relations. Thus men in this society demonstrated either heterosexual or bisexual behavior. Davenport found no adult males who were exclusively homosexual.

Popular Western stereotypes suggest that homosexuals adopt either male (the butch) or female (the femme) roles. A homosexual man who inserts his penis during fellatio or anal intercourse is considered to be active and masculine, whereas a man who receives the penis is seen as passive or feminine. Based on his preference in sexual activities, each "type" supposedly also exhibits stereotypically masculine or feminine attributes in nonsexual areas. Much of North American and British research, however, does not support this rigid stereotyping. A substantial proportion of male homosexuals show a wide variety of traits associated with both masculine and feminine roles and engage in all forms of, and positions in, homosexual activity. Further, most homosexual men are attracted to masculine rather than to effeminate male partners. Similarly, lesbians are attracted to each other on the basis of their femininity (Bailey, Kim, & Hills, 1997; Blumstein & Schwartz, 1983; Schreurs, 1993).

Most of this research has focused on middle- and upper-class Western males in developed countries (Carrier, 1980). In contrast to these men, substantial numbers of males in Mexico, Brazil, Greece, and Turkey express a clear preference for playing either the active or the passive role when engaging in homosexual relations. These cultures have rigidly defined gender roles that shape heterosexual as well as homosexual interaction. Apparently there is little stigma attached to the active, inserter role in homosexual contacts in these groups because this role is considered to be masculine. A man's penetration of another man is viewed as an accomplishment of sorts, like sexual penetration of a woman. But a person who takes the submissive, receptive role is ridiculed and stigmatized as effeminate. In Brazil, for example, the average person does not perceive the man who takes the active sexual role as homosexual (Parker, 1991). When two men engage in sex, only the receptive or feminine man is labeled as homosexual.

It seems, then, that in those cultures or subcultures where rigid gender-role stereotypes prevail, cultural expectations will lead to narrowly prescribed sexual relationships. In predominantly middle- and upper-class North America, where gender roles are more flexible, we find greater variation in sexual expression among both heterosexuals and homosexuals, and less pressure to engage exclusively in sexual activities associated with stereotypically masculine or feminine roles. For example, fellatio appears to be more common among Americans than among, say, Mexicans (Carrier, 1980). Homosexual Mexican males, reflecting their societal values, are expected to achieve sexual satisfaction through anal intercourse rather than fellatio, just as heterosexual Mexicans are expected to prefer sexual intercourse to fellatio (see "Across Cultures: Rigid Versus Fluid Definitions of Orientation"). To date, there has been little cross-cultural research on lesbianism (Hatfield & Rapson, 1996).

HOMOSEXUAL BEHAVIOR AND GAY IDENTITY

What is the extent of homosexual behavior in our society? The answer depends on how we ask the question. Since the Kinsey group's research, in which they found that more than a third of men and about 13 percent of women had same-gender sexual encounters, there have been a number of attempts to assess sexual orientation in the United States and other countries. Some of these studies have used national probability sampling, tapping a more representative group than did the Kinsey group (Billy et al., 1993; Laumann et al., 1994). These researchers have come up with markedly lower estimates of the prevalence of homosexuality among Americans. For example, Sell, Wells, and Wypij (1995) compared the prevalence of homosexuality in the United States, Britain, and France (see Table 11.1).

It is difficult to determine whether the lower numbers reflect more representative sampling techniques or a failure to elicit honest answers from the respondents. Given the differing results, the best estimate seems to be that about 4 percent to 6 percent of

Table 11.1	Homosexual Attraction and Behavior Across Cultures		
	United States	**Britain**	**France**
Percentage reporting homosexual attraction but no homosexual behavior since age 15			
Males	8.7	7.9	8.5
Females	11.1	8.6	11.7
Percentage reporting some sexual contact with someone of the same gender in the previous five years			
Males	6.2	4.5	10.7
Females	3.6	2.1	3.3
Percentage reporting homosexual attraction and homosexual behavior since age 15			
Males	20.8	16.3	18.5
Females	17.7	18.6	18.5

Source: Adapted from Sell, Wells, and Wypij (1995).

men and 2 percent to 4 percent of women are predominantly homosexual for a large part of their lives (Diamond, 1993; LeVay, 1996).

A substantial number of people who engage in homosexual behavior do not become exclusively homosexual. The typical male pattern involves homosexual contact during preadolescence and the teens, followed by little or no further homosexual activity. This finding raises an interesting question about sexual orientation: Why do a large number of males who engage in youthful homosexual activity eventually indulge primarily in heterosexual relations and presumably maintain a heterosexual identity, whereas others adopt a homosexual identity? On a more concrete level, how do people who have had one or more homosexual contacts know whether they are homosexual or heterosexual? Or, if they have developed a strong emotional attachment to a member of the same gender, how do they decide whether this attachment should be classified as a homosexual orientation or a deep friendship that includes sexual expression? These questions all involve our identities and self-definitions as sexual beings.

Self-Definition

The search for meaning and self-definition is at no other time more pressing than during adolescence. During childhood and adolescence, most people experience a great deal of confusion and ambiguity about sexual thoughts, feelings, and behavior. What is normal, and what is deviant or abnormal? What is the appropriate role to choose in relationships with others? In moving awkwardly through this complicated process, a person begins to construct a sexual identity. For most people, one aspect of that identity is heterosexual, but for some it is homosexual or, more rarely, bisexual. The many paths that lead to a homosexual identity are far more difficult to travel because of the sanctions against homosexual behavior.

Those adults who define themselves as homosexual often experience a sense of being "different" in childhood and adolescence (Telljohann & Price, 1993). One study of 1,000 gay people indicated that "homosexual feelings" occurred typically at age 14 among males and about age 16 among females. For both males and females, the feelings had arisen at least two years before they ever made genital contact with a person of the same gender (Bell et al., 1981).

Acquiring a gay identity is a gradual process, however. The emergence of homosexual feelings is usually followed by an individual's adoption of the label *gay,* association with other gay individuals, and a first homosexual love relationship (Harry, 1993; Rust, 1993a). There is evidence that young men identify themselves as gay at an earlier age if they are able to meet openly with gay men in a supportive environment where homosexuality is considered normal (Boxer & Cohler, 1989). This sort of environment is most likely to be found in large cities where there are well-developed support systems for gays.

After individuals define themselves as gay, the stage is set for a number of other important decisions. Should they remain "in the closet," keeping their sexual orientation as private as possible? If they decide to "come out"—that is, to acknowledge their gay identity to others—how publicly should they express their orientation? Should they tell their family and friends? What about employers? The coming-out phase is a complex one in the individual's life, during which he or she adopts a gay identity and explores the homosexual community. Most men come out at about age 19 or 20; women tend to come out somewhat later, in their early 20s (Harry, 1993; Rust, 1993a). This coming-out process may have unintended positive consequences for gay men and lesbians. The best predictor of heterosexuals' attitudes toward gay men is personal contact with a gay man or lesbian. Of the respondents in a national survey, 35 percent

Figure 11.2
Public Display of Affection
Gay men who openly express their affection toward their partners are often criticized for "flaunting" their homosexuality. It is rare, however, to hear a heterosexual couple who hugs in public be condemned for flaunting their sexuality.

of those who had a friend, acquaintance, or relative who was homosexual had more positive attitudes toward gay men than did those who had no such contact (Herek & Glunt, 1993). Thus acknowledging one's homosexual orientation to close associates may lead to more positive attitudes toward homosexuals.

Although sexual orientation is just one aspect of identity, our society tends to view the sexual orientation of homosexuals as an extremely important, if not the most important, aspect of a person's identity. Regardless of their occupations, accomplishments, temperaments, and the myriad other factors that make up the complexities of being human, people who choose to express their sexuality with others of the same gender are culturally defined, first and foremost, as homosexuals; this definition affects the ways in which others interpret all their actions.

This link between homosexual orientation and other personal characteristics and behaviors is even more problematic when we consider that most homosexuals and heterosexuals cannot easily identify the sexual orientation of other individuals. In one study, students observed videotapes of interviews of heterosexual and homosexual males and females (Berger, Hank, Rauzi, & Simkins, 1987). Almost 80 percent of the students were unable to identify accurately the sexual orientation of those shown in the videotapes beyond chance expectations. The difference so emphasized in our society is not readily apparent to most of us.

Some homosexuals openly express their affection (see Figure 11.2). Faced with the intolerance of conventional heterosexual society, other homosexuals carefully shroud their sexual orientation in secrecy. Most choose a position somewhere between these two extremes (Cox & Gallois, 1996; Harry, 1993). Homosexuals who tend to be overt

REALITY or MYTH ? **3**

Figure 11.3
Same–Sex Marriage
Hawaii is the only state that recognizes homosexual marriage. The state has appealed Circuit Court Judge Kevin S. C. Chang's decision to the Hawaiian Supreme Court. Chang has ruled that the state had failed to prove that same-sex marriages would harm children or anyone else.

about their orientation are most likely to volunteer for research on the topic. Therefore, we know more about the lifestyles of those people than we do about less openly gay persons.

Almost all gay men and lesbian women have been involved at some point in a relatively steady relationship with a same-gender partner (McWhirter & Mattison, 1984; Schreurs, 1993). In Alan Bell and Martin Weinberg's (1978) study, more than 50 percent of the men and approximately 70 percent of the women were currently involved in a steady relationship (see Figure 11.3).

Sexual Expression

Homosexuals use the same methods of sexual expression as heterosexuals, with the obvious exception of coitus. For lesbians, the most common sexual activities are hugging, snuggling, kissing (see Figure 11.4), cunnilingus, mutual masturbation, and *tribadism* (Fassinger & Morrow, 1995; Schreurs, 1993). To perform the last, one woman lies on top of the other, making rhythmic thrusting movements to stimulate their clitorises (see Chapter 5). The use of dildos and the practice of analingus (stimulation of the anal area with the tongue) appear to be relatively rare among lesbians (Schreurs, 1993), despite their popularity in erotic films and books. Gay men most frequently engage in fellatio, mutual masturbation, anal intercourse, and interfemoral intercourse—rubbing the penis between the partner's legs until orgasm (Bell & Weinberg, 1978; Weinrich, 1994).

Comparisons of the values of gay and heterosexual men and women have yielded many similarities in the groups' rankings of the values (described later) that they con-

Figure 11.4
Gay Lovemaking
Masters and Johnson (1979) claimed that gay couples may have a more relaxed and less goal-oriented approach to sexual intimacy than do heterosexual couples. However, the degree of relaxation is probably a function of the length of a relationship and level of commitment, regardless of people's sexual orientation.

sidered important in a relationship. Their romantic view of love, degree of commitment, and satisfaction with their relationships were also similar (Fowlkes, 1994). But gay men differed from heterosexuals in that they attached less importance to sexual exclusivity in a relationship. In terms of psychological adjustment and measures of satisfaction and commitment, there appear to be no differences between monogamous and nonmonogamous gay male couples (Blasband & Peplau, 1985; Kurdek & Schmitt, 1985/1986). Apparently, both types of relationships can be satisfying for gay males.

Researchers have also found differences between dependent or traditional women involved in lesbian relationships and independent, feminist lesbians (Peplau & Gordon, 1983). Mirroring the tendency of traditional heterosexual women, traditional lesbian women were especially dependent on their partners for fulfilling their needs. In contrast, the independent, feminist lesbians sought satisfaction from professional and community involvement, not just from their love relationships.

GENDER DIFFERENCES.   Most of the differences that have been found between gay men and lesbian women are those that might be expected from the different socialization experiences of Western males and females (Leigh, 1989; Schreurs & Buunk, 1995). For example, women, regardless of sexual orientation, rank emotional expressiveness and equality in their love relationships as more important than do gay and straight men. And in contrast to many gay male relationships, lesbian love affairs are relatively long-lasting ones in which the couples show a considerable degree of fidelity to each other (Kurdek & Schmitt, 1987; Schreurs & Buunk, 1995). Perhaps for this reason, public **cruising** is much less frequent among lesbians than among gay men. Only 17 percent of lesbians, Black and White, had actively sought sexual encounters during the year previous to the research. When the women did cruise, the activity was

cruising Socializing in a variety of locations in the attempt to find a partner.

almost entirely limited to bars and private parties. In contrast, about 85 percent of Black and White men reported cruising about once a month (Bell & Weinberg, 1978). We might expect the frequency of cruising to have diminished with the advent of HIV/AIDS, but no current data are available.

One of the most striking differences between homosexual men and women lies in their number of sexual partners. Almost half the White homosexual men in the Bell and Weinberg (1978) study said that they had had at least 50 different sexual partners during their lives, and 28 percent claimed 1,000 or more partners. In contrast, none of the lesbians in the total sample reported having had this many partners, and more than half had been involved with fewer than 10 sexual partners. One of the unfortunate consequences of the male pattern is that about two out of three reported having had a sexually transmitted disease at one time or another, whereas only 1 of the 293 women in this study had ever contracted an STD from homosexual activity.

Both gay men and heterosexual men report similar levels of sexual interest. Lesbian and heterosexual women also have similar levels of sexual interest, but it is lower than that of gay and heterosexual men. However, gay men come closer to fulfilling their desires by having sex more frequently and with more partners than do heterosexual men, perhaps because they are not constrained by the unwillingness of women to have sex with them (Bailey, Gauling, Agyei, & Gladue, 1994).

ISSUES TO CONSIDER

In what ways are gay males more like heterosexual males than they are like lesbians?

AGING.   There is no particular reason to believe that the biological effects of aging on sexual response are any different for homosexuals than for heterosexuals (Kye, 1995). Masters and Johnson (1979) have demonstrated that sexual response does not differ according to sexual orientation, and it is difficult to imagine factors that would alter this fact in the second half of life.

Most studies (Bell & Weinberg, 1978; Kinsey et al., 1948, 1953; McWhirter & Mattison, 1984) indicate that homosexuals experience the same general age-related changes in their sexual behavior as do their heterosexual counterparts. Linda Wolf (1979) nevertheless found that although the aging gay people whom she interviewed experienced many of the life changes that are characteristic of our culture at large, their sexual orientation did produce unique challenges as they dealt with the effects of menopause, the changes of midlife, and plans for retirement activities. For gay men, psychological adjustment in later life is associated with a strong commitment to homosexuality, integration into the gay community, low concern with concealment of sexual orientation, and a satisfactory sex life, usually within an exclusive relationship (Berger, 1996).

There is a stereotype in Western societies of the aging homosexual as fearful and lonely. This stereotype has not been supported by research (Berger, 1996; Kye, 1995). In fact, Martin Weinberg and Colin Williams (1975) found that older respondents tended to have better self-concepts and to be more stable than younger gays. Among older respondents, more women than men tended to be sexually active, but those men who were still sexually active did not differ from the women in frequency of sexual expression. Women showed more interest than men did in long-term relationships. One difference that emerged from this research was that lesbians were less anxious about growing old than were gay men. The reverse has been found to be true among heterosexuals. Perhaps this is a reflection of the gender of the person one wishes to attract. Because men are attracted to youth and beauty, those people who wish to be sexually attractive to men—heterosexual women and gay men—may become overly concerned about their own youth and beauty, a fact that might make them more vulnerable to eating disorders, for example, in their efforts to remain thin and attractive (Gettelman & Thompson, 1993).

Homosexuals who are open about their lifestyles may not experience the midlife crisis that many heterosexuals encounter (Kyes, 1995). Relatively early in life, most homosexuals go through a crisis that heterosexuals do not: They must face and manage a conventionally nonaccepted sexual lifestyle. It may be that if this challenge is successfully resolved, the individual's ability to cope with the changes of aging are strengthened. In addition, the majority of homosexuals are not faced with the family responsibilities and changes in family involvement that often confront heterosexuals as they age.

SITUATIONAL SAME-GENDER CONTACTS: PRISONS. In gender-segregated institutions such as prisons, homosexual relations are fairly common. Homosexual behavior under these conditions is frequently spurred by the lack of opportunity for heterosexual contact and is known as transient or situational homosexuality. In one early study of prison life, about 40 percent of the convict population was found to have engaged in homosexual activity (Clemmer, 1958). Of these, only about 10 percent had engaged in such behavior before they went to jail.

Same-gender sexual interactions in men's prisons are often based on the wish to dominate those perceived as weaker or possessing "feminine" characteristics (Long & Sultan, 1987; Struckman-Johnson, Struckman-Johnson, Rucker, Bumby, & Donaldson, 1996). In a situation similar to those reported in the earlier discussion of cross-cultural research on homosexuality, the dominant man does not view himself as homosexual, and seldom is there reciprocal sex. That is, the dominant man uses the "weaker" man for sexual release but does not in turn provide sexual pleasure for the subordinate man (see "Highlight: Male Rape," Chapter 14).

There has been little research on sexuality in female prisons. In one study of several midwestern state prisons, only 7 percent of women prisoners reported experiencing sexual coercion, compared to 22 percent of men prisoners (Struckman-Johnson et al., 1996). As might be expected from our earlier discussion of lesbian relationships, women prisoners usually integrate sexuality into an ongoing relationship. Most of the women who engage in same-gender relations in prison do not think of themselves as homosexuals, and they usually return to heterosexual behavior when they are released.

EXPLANATIONS OF SEXUAL ORIENTATION

Historically, most hypotheses that have been advanced to explain sexual orientation have included the notion that people are gay because of defects: inherited disorders, deviant hormonal exposure, harmful family patterns, early onset of sexual maturity, or gender-role nonconformity. If not for negative influences, it was thought, the individual would be heterosexual. We consider this assumption after reviewing the data relevant to each hypothesis.

Biological Correlates

Interest in a hereditary basis for homosexuality dates back to the eighteenth century, when all sexual variations were assumed to be a sign of a degenerate family tree. Not surprisingly, most theorizing regarding homosexuality and heredity has portrayed homosexuality as maladaptive. For example, an early investigator of homosexuality wrote:

> *The urgency of [research] with respect to the genetic aspects of homosexual behavior is underscored by the ominous fact that* adult homosexuality continues to be an inexhaustible source of unhappiness, discontent, and a distorted sense of human values. *(Kallmann, 1952, p. 296, emphasis added)*

concordance rate The likelihood that if one person manifests a certain trait, a relative
(twin, sibling, uncle, etc.) will
manifest that same trait.

As this statement demonstrates, Kallmann was not the most objective observer of homosexuality. In 1952, he conducted an extensive study of sexual orientation in twins, in which he examined **concordance rates.** Kallmann reported that the concordance rate was nearly 100 percent for monozygotic (genetically identical) twins and about 10 percent for dizygotic (not genetically identical) twins. This work was criticized because many of the men in his study came from prisons and psychiatric institutions, and because there was no information about how Kallmann judged whether the twins were monozygotic (MZ) or dizygotic (DZ).

More recent twin studies have shown concordance rates for homosexual orientation in males to be as high as 66 percent for MZ twins and 30 percent for DZ twins (Bailey & Pillard, 1991; Whitam, Diamond, & Martin, 1993). For women, 48 percent of the MZ twins were lesbian or bisexual compared to 16 percent of DZ twins and 6 percent of adoptive sisters (Bailey, Pillard, Neale, & Agyei, 1993). These findings suggest a genetic contribution to homosexual orientation.

The idea of a genetic or biological basis for some male homosexuals is reinforced by the report by Dean Hamer and his colleagues (Hamer, Hu, Magnusen, Hu, & Pattatucci, 1993). They found a region on the X chromosome that appears to contain a gene or genes for homosexual orientation. Thirty-three of the 40 pairs of homosexual brothers had similar genetic markers and appear to have inherited the chromosome responsible for the trait from their mothers. See Figure 11.5 for data from their study showing the relationship of the maternal connection to homosexual orientation in men. For example, in Family A, Generation I, the woman's brother is gay. The woman (let's call her Sally) has one daughter and four sons, one of whom is gay. Sally's daughter then produces a daughter who is straight and a son who is gay. It should be noted that Hamer and his colleagues think that homosexuality arises from a variety of causes, both genetic and environmental.

In keeping with this emphasis on biology, there have been reports of differences between the brains of homosexual and heterosexual men (LeVay, 1991, 1996; Swaab, Gooren, & Hofman, 1995). One of the four regions in the hypothalamus of the brain, the INAH-3, is generally larger in men than in women. Based on research with animals, the region appears to be involved in male-typical sexual behavior. In an intriguing study, Simon LeVay hypothesized that the volume of INAH-3 would show a size difference not just with biological sex, but with sexual orientation.

LeVay (1991) obtained statistically significant differences in the volume of the INAH-3 region between the three groups in his sample. As predicted, heterosexual men had a higher volume in that region of the hypothalamus than did homosexual men. Homosexual men were intermediate between heterosexual men and heterosexual women in the INAH-3 volume, with the women having the lowest volume. We must emphasize that these results are preliminary and have been questioned as to their relevance to sexual orientation (De Cecco & Parker, 1995). Further, LeVay wanted relatively young deceased participants to control for the effects of aging, but he could not find enough deceased young lesbian women, as lesbians tend to be quite healthy.

In the 1930s and 1940s, several attempts were made to treat homosexual men with androgens. This approach was based on the idea that gay men were not masculine enough, so they needed a booster of masculinizing hormones. Although the androgen administration usually succeeded in increasing sexual interest and activity, partner orientation remained unchanged.

REALITY or MYTH ? 4

The vast majority of homosexual males appear to have testosterone levels within the normal range (Banks & Gartrell, 1995). Research on sex hormones is even more difficult in females than in males because of the fluctuation in women's hormone lev-

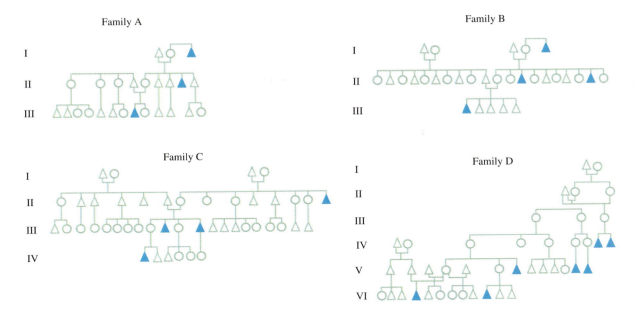

Figure 11.5
Family Trees of Homosexual Males Samples of homosexual males and their families were asked by Hamer et al. (1993) to identify, if possible, other family members who were/are gay. Families A and B both have a single gay man in each of three maternally related generations. In Family C two gay brothers have a maternally related gay uncle and nephew. Family D, for whom information was obtained about six generations, contains seven (known) gay males. These gay men are all related through the sequential marriage of two sisters to the same husband in generation II. As Hamer et al. (1993) put it, in addition to evidence of transmission of gay male orientation through the maternal line, the striking aspect of these genealogies "is the absence of transmission through the paternal line and the paucity of female homosexuals" (p. 323).

els. Past studies indicate that the majority of lesbians appear to have testosterone and estrogen levels within the normal range (Banks & Gartrell, 1995; LeVay, 1996).

Anthony Bogaert and Ray Blanchard (1996) hypothesized that differences in sexual differentiation in the brain during prenatal development might result in differences in the height, weight, and age of puberty in homosexual versus heterosexual men. With a sample of more than six hundred men, half of whom described themselves as homosexual and the other half as heterosexual, the authors found that on average, the gay men were shorter, weighed less, and reported earlier onset of puberty than did the heterosexual men. Their findings confirmed those of earlier researchers. To our knowledge, no one has made similar comparisons of samples of lesbian versus heterosexual women, but if differences in prenatal brain differentiation contribute to one's orientation, then lesbian women, compared to heterosexual women, should be heavier, taller, and have later onset of puberty.

There is growing interest in the possible prenatal hormonal contribution to sexual orientation, but we are probably decades away from adequately testing this theoretical link. Even if such a prenatal contribution exists, whether it is overtly expressed would probably depend on many other lifetime experiences.

Family Experiences

triangular family system In psychoanalytic theory, the notion that a male homosexual's parents consist of an intimate, controlling mother and a detached, rejecting father.

Several researchers influenced by psychoanalytic theory have explored the role of early family influences in the development of sexual orientation. In one such study, Bieber, Dane, and Prince (1962) described a **triangular family system** to account for the development of male homosexuality. According to this hypothesis, a homosexual is typically the child of an overly intimate, controlling mother and a detached, hostile, rejecting father. Bieber and coworkers based their system on the differences they found between a group of homosexual men and a group of heterosexual men in psychoanalysis. Even so, 38 percent of the homosexuals did not come from a triangular family system, and 32 percent of the heterosexuals reported such a family background. At best, the Bieber research suggests that many people in therapy, regardless of their sexual orientation, may be the products of a triangular system. More objective research has not supported the hypothesis that orientation toward same-gender partners stems from being raised in a triangular family system (Milic & Crowne, 1986; Newcomb, 1985; Siegelman, 1987).

Some of the conflicting results emerging from studies of homosexuals' family backgrounds can be attributed to variations in the populations from which the homosexual samples were drawn; in certain studies these populations consisted of patients or prisoners. Marvin Siegelman (1972a, 1972b) attempted to reduce the potential bias introduced with such samples by administering questionnaires, including one that measured neuroticism, to groups of "normal" (not in therapy) homosexuals and heterosexuals. When he compared homosexual and heterosexual men who were low in neuroticism, there were *no* differences in the parental backgrounds of the two groups. The same was true of women who scored low in neuroticism.

Overall, his research supports the idea that parental characteristics may correlate with tendencies toward neuroticism in both homosexuals and heterosexuals but are not related to sexual orientation per se. Therefore, the evidence on family background and sexual orientation supports the position taken by Evelyn Hooker (1969) about three decades ago that disturbed parental relations are neither necessary nor sufficient conditions for the development of homosexuality.

Gender-Role Nonconformity During Childhood

A growing body of evidence indicates that one pathway to becoming a homosexual in adulthood is nonconformity to societal expectations for one's gender in early childhood. Researchers have reported that "feminine" boys have a much higher probability of becoming adults with a homosexual orientation than do more "masculine" boys (Bailey, Miller, & Willerman, 1993; Green, 1987; Phillips & Over, 1992). Similarly, lesbians recalled more male-stereotypic behaviors in childhood than did heterosexual women in the United States, Brazil, Peru, and the Philippines (Phillips & Over, 1995; Whitam & Mathy, 1986). Homosexual men were more likely to characterize their childhoods as having involved interest in toys stereotypic for girls, cross-dressing, preference for girls' games and activities, preference for the company of women, being regarded as a sissy, and preference for boys in childhood sex play (Whitam, 1977).

Not all homosexuals display traits or interests atypical of their gender in childhood. About half the homosexual men in the Bell et al. (1981) research appeared to have masculine identities, interests, and activities in childhood, compared to about three-fourths of heterosexual men. About one-fifth of lesbian women, compared to one-third of heterosexual women, reported being highly "feminine" while growing up.

The link between homosexuality and gender nonconformity in childhood has been questioned because of the way in which it was established. In the Bell group's study, individuals were asked to describe their childhoods. Beyond the usual difficulties associated with remembering events long past, this population may have introduced an additional bias. Having already accepted a gay identity and a set of beliefs about homosexuality, they may have unintentionally edited their memories to make those memories consistent with their current belief systems. Such bias may be particularly problematic when the sample is recruited from members of the gay-liberation movement.

Richard Green (1987) avoided the problem of inaccurate memories by conducting a longitudinal study in which boys who were effeminate during childhood were compared to a control group of conventional boys. Following these boys into adolescence, he found that the gender nonconformists were more likely to become homosexual than were members of the control group.

Michael Ross (1980) suggested that researchers would find less rigid gender stereotyping in less traditional countries. Studies in Sweden and Australia support his hypothesis. Swedish homosexuals, reared in a society in which adopting nontraditional gender roles is acceptable, recalled less feminine childhood play than did Australian homosexuals, who typically were reared to adopt traditional gender roles. Thus early atypical gender-conforming interests and activities may be related to homosexuality in cultures that emphasize rigid distinctions between masculinity and femininity.

Of the factors that we have considered thus far, only this last one—gender-role nonconformity in childhood—appears to have a fairly solid link to homosexual orientation. Sexual orientation appears to be fairly well established in males by age 18 and in females by age 21. Masturbatory fantasies may reinforce these sexual orientations through sexual arousal and orgasm (Storms, 1980, 1981; Van Wyk & Geist, 1984).

In his Exotic Becomes Erotic model, which subsumes a number of the proposed explanations for orientation that we have already described, Daryl Bem (1996) hypothesized that biological variables (genes, prenatal hormones, brain neuroanatomy) do not directly cause a particular orientation. Instead, these factors result in childhood temperaments that may influence a child's preferences for gender-typical or -atypical activities and peers. According to Bem, such preferences then lead children to feel different from their peers of the same or the other gender and to see the peers from whom they feel different as dissimilar, unfamiliar, and exotic. This perception stimulates heightened physiological arousal that is erotically responsive to (some) members of the gender they perceive as different from themselves in terms of interests and activities. Thus, the exotic (different) becomes erotic (see Figure 11.6).

Bem's model can also incorporate the findings we previously discussed regarding the correlation between gender-role nonconformity during childhood and subsequent development of homosexual orientation. It also has the advantage of explaining the correlation between gender-role conformity and subsequent development of heterosexual orientation. Bem's hypotheses need to be investigated empirically, and we hope that his model will stimulate research on the sources of sexual orientation. In summary, there appear to be many different paths to the development of erotic orientation that vary from one culture and historical period to another.

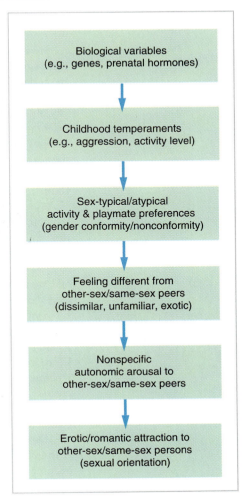

Figure 11.6
Bem's Model of the Development of Sexual Orientation Daryl Bem has hypothesized a temporal sequence of events leading to sexual orientation for most men and women.

SEXUAL ORIENTATION AND ADJUSTMENT

Over the years, homosexuals in North America have been accused of being men-tally ill or maladjusted. Mental health professionals have tried to "cure" homo-sexuals, and researchers have attempted to measure emotional health and adjustment as a function of a person's sexual orientation. However, many gay people experience adjustment problems because of the prejudice against homosexuality that they face in their daily lives. We now examine this antigay prejudice.

Antigay Prejudice

At the outset, it is important to understand the difference between prejudice and dis-crimination. Most of us have prejudices—negative (or positive) attitudes and stereo-types about particular groups—but we do not necessarily act on these prejudices in ways that interfere with the rights of people who belong to those groups. When our prejudices are expressed in behaviors that harm others, our actions constitute discrimi-nation, a topic we will discuss later in this chapter. Although evidence is lacking to sup-port most contemporary North American stereotypes about homosexuals, such as the idea that all gays are maladjusted, negative attitudes against homosexuals remain wide-spread (Schwanberg, 1993; Weinrich, 1994).

For many people, aversion to homosexuals approaches a true phobia—that is, a persistent and irrational fear. National surveys measuring attitudes toward homosexual relations between adults found that a majority of those questioned believed that such relations were wrong (Davis & Smith, 1984; Herek & Glunt, 1993; Pratte, 1993). In their worst forms, homophobia and antigay discrimination are responsible for the ver-bal and physical abuse of gays. In recent surveys, as many as 92 percent of lesbians and gay men reported that they had been verbally abused or threatened because they were gay. As many as 24 percent report experiencing physical attacks because of their sexual orientation (Herek, 1992; Otis & Skinner, 1996). Some commentators speculate that antigay hate crimes are rising as part of the public reaction to the AIDS epidemic. And the response of governments and public health officials to the AIDS crisis may have lagged because most of the early victims of AIDS in North America were gay men (Shilts, 1987).

Negative attitudes toward homosexuals are more prevalent among men than among women. In addition, compared with people who are tolerant of others' sexual orienta-tion, antihomosexuals attend church more frequently and are more likely to be affili-ated with fundamentalist religions and to come from rural areas. Moreover, they tend to be more authoritarian, feel guiltier about sex, display greater gender-role rigidity, and are more likely to view sex as primarily for procreative purposes than do those who are tolerant of gays (Herek & Capitanio, 1995; Herek & Glunt, 1993; Kurdek, 1988).

Implicit in many negative attitudes toward gays is the fear that homosexuality is contagious. Perhaps the most damaging myth about homosexuals is that they are abusers of impressionable young children whom they will seduce and lure into a gay lifestyle. Despite the fact that research has not supported it, this belief has caused over-whelming hardships for teachers who are homosexual and for gay parents seeking child custody. Most teenagers have their first homosexual experiences with other adolescents rather than with adults. Furthermore, most child sexual abuse is committed by hetero-sexual men, not gays.

On a related note, because the vast majority of homosexuals are reared in homes with heterosexual role models, it is unlikely that the offspring of gay parents would become homosexual as a result of the early childhood models they encountered (see

ISSUES TO CONSIDER

What are the potential ben-efits and risks to children raised by gay parents?

Figure 11.7
Gay Parenting These lesbian parents are helping their son with an art project. There is no evidence that the offspring of lesbian parents are more likely to become homosexual or maladjusted than are children raised by heterosexual parents.

Figure 11.7). In fact, research involving lesbian mothers has shown that the mothers' sexual orientation does not produce homosexuality in their children or have damaging consequences for their offspring's development (Coleman, 1990; Golombok & Tasker, 1996; Tasker & Golombok, 1997).

One of the possible explanations of homophobia dates back to Sigmund Freud, who speculated that a fear of homosexuality was a defensive reaction against one's own erotic feelings toward someone of the same gender. In an interesting probe of this idea, Adams, Wright, and Lohr (1996) divided a group of male college students into homophobic and nonhomophobic groups on the basis of their scores on a measure of homophobia. Both groups were exposed to sexually explicit videotapes of heterosexual, gay male, and lesbian sexual interactions. More homophobic men (54 percent) displayed an increase in penile erection to the gay male tapes than did nonhomophobic men (24 percent). When questioned later, however, the homophobic men significantly underreported their arousal, suggesting that they were unaware of it or denying it. Thus, it may be that some of their dislike of homosexuals stemmed from a fear of being vulnerable to their own erotic feelings toward men, and they demeaned these feelings because they found them incongruent with their image of themselves as heterosexual.

Despite research to the contrary, many people find it difficult to accept the idea that homosexual lifestyles offer legitimate and productive alternatives for some individuals. By treating homosexuals as perverted or diseased, others can affirm their own normalcy. Thus a sense of "rightness" is maintained by dwelling on the "wrongness" of homosexual lifestyles. Faced with such discriminatory attitudes and behavior on the part of some public officials, it is not surprising that homosexuals have grown more militant.

Changing Views of Mental Health

Homosexuals have had to deal with the predominant view that they are "sick." Unlike most people with illnesses, however, homosexuals also have had to cope with the knowledge that the behaviors associated with their "illness" were illegal.

It was not until 1974 that members of the American Psychiatric Association ratified a resolution that "homosexuality per se implies no impairment in judgment, stability, reliability or general social or vocational capabilities," thus removing homosexuality from the list of official mental disorders. This removal was due partly to research conducted over the past four decades that failed to establish any direct connection between homosexual orientation and mental or emotional disorders. To some extent, it was also a response to the growing social and political influence of gay people who fought against psychiatric labeling and criminal prosecution.

Early research on the psychological adjustment of homosexuals relied on clinical reports of homosexuals in therapy. The investigators, who were usually therapists, tended to assume that homosexuals were maladjusted; why else would they be in therapy? In another research approach, homosexuals in therapy were compared with control groups of heterosexuals who were usually not in therapy. This design, too, provided evidence that homosexuals were maladjusted. The results of these studies then tended to be generalized to all homosexuals. Assumptions that homosexuals are maladjusted started changing when researchers began to draw samples from populations of homosexuals who were not in therapy. In general, there is no evidence of major differences in adjustment between homosexuals and heterosexuals (Gonsiorek, 1991; Weinrich, 1994).

A small proportion of homosexuals have been found to have significant problems with adjustment. For example, Bell and Weinberg (1978) reported that about 12 percent of the gay men and 5 percent of the lesbian women in their total sample could be classified as dysfunctional. These individuals experienced numerous problems in their day-to-day lives and appeared to fit society's stereotype of the maladjusted homosexual. What is remarkable, however, is that most gays function as well as their heterosexual counterparts despite society's negative sanctions. Their adjustment in the face of overwhelming societal burdens is testimony to the adaptiveness and resourcefulness of the human being.

ISSUES TO CONSIDER

Why do you think homosexuality was once considered a mental illness?

Therapy

In the past, clinicians treating homosexuals widely assumed that their clients' sexual orientation, rather than the social oppression they experienced because of their orientation, was the crux of their problems. In fact, the psychoanalyst Kenneth Lewes (1988) has outlined how conservative psychoanalytic thought attributed difficulties of both homosexual men and heterosexual women to individual defects rather than to societal expectations. For example, until recently, a woman at home with young children who went to a psychoanalyst and complained of depression was thought to be maladjusted. Similarly, a homosexual who sought therapy because of feelings of alienation from his family was assumed to be neurotic, with "conversion" to heterosexual orientation the recommended treatment. In contrast, many therapists today explore whether the woman's depression stems from feeling trapped all day without adult companionship, and whether the gay man's alienation is rooted in fear of familial rejection if he acknowledges his orientation.

In addition to being ethically questionable, the use of psychoanalysis and behavior therapy to change sexual orientation has been ineffective (Davison, 1991). Most therapists report a "cure" rate ranging from 10 percent to 30 percent, depending on the length of client follow-up. In all likelihood, the impetus among clinicians to change or "cure" homosexuals stems from the difficulties of recognizing a difference without labeling it as psychologically abnormal.

Despite bias among some clinicians, many therapists now concentrate on helping their clients to accept their sexual orientation and to develop their potential to survive in an antigay society, rather than on attempting to change sexual orientation—unless such a change is the client's own goal (Gonsiorek, 1995; Lewes, 1995).

DISCRIMINATION AND GAY LIBERATION

Earlier, we noted the difference between prejudice (attitudes) and discrimination (behaviors). Now we consider how discrimination has contributed to the formation of the gay liberation movement.

Discrimination

The discrimination against people who are, or are thought to be, homosexuals has a long and far-reaching history. Gays' civil rights have been limited by discrimination in such areas as housing, employment, immigration, naturalization, child custody, and military service. It can range from being snubbed or derided while shopping (Walters & Curran, 1996) to being incarcerated for breaking "sexual" laws that are almost never used to prosecute heterosexuals. For example, in 1996, the U.S. Congress passed, and President Clinton signed, the Defense of Marriage Act (DOMA), which prohibited federal recognition of marriage between gays. Passage of this legislation was ironic given the belief of some DOMA supporters that all gays are promiscuous. Such people would presumably wish to support the legalization of marital vows for gays.

U.S. criminal law has contributed more than its fair share of discrimination against individuals who engage in homosexual acts. In general, homosexuals have been prosecuted under state sodomy laws. These laws generally outlaw "unnatural acts"—nonprocreative activity such as oral sex and anal intercourse. Although many heterosexuals could be prosecuted for breaking these laws, homosexuals traditionally have been singled out for prosecution for these "criminal" activities. Slowly but surely, states have been decriminalizing sodomy. As of 1997, more than half the states no longer considered sodomy a crime. In Canada sodomy is known as buggery and includes having sexual relations with animals. An individual can be charged with the offense only if a participant is under age 21, or if the act takes place publicly or involves an animal (*Pocket Criminal Code,* 1987).

In the military, a person who engages in homosexual behavior because of orientation or the lack of heterosexual opportunity faces grave penalties. He or she is in conflict with a Pentagon rule, which states, "Persons who engage in homosexual conduct" or "demonstrate a propensity" to do so "adversely affect the ability of the armed forces to maintain discipline, good order, and morale." According to Pentagon figures, more than a thousand men and women are discharged annually for violating this rule. The discharges are usually honorable, provided that the offender leaves the service and does not contest the expulsion.

The ban on gays in the military provoked sharp debate in the 1990s (Shilts, 1993). President Clinton initially pledged to end the military's ban on homosexuals, but in the ensuing furor he accepted a compromise proposal: "Don't ask, don't tell, don't pursue." Theoretically, this would permit gays in the military as long as they make no

REALITY or MYTH ? 5

Figure 11.8
Gay Political Demonstrations
Political demonstrations by homosexuals have brought attention to the pervasive discrimination they experience at the hands of the heterosexual majority.

public declarations of their orientation. However, in 1993, when the policy was zero tolerance for homosexuals, 682 gays were discharged; in 1996 when the military was smaller and the new policy was in effect, more than 850 gays were discharged. And in 1996, in contrast to the "don't ask . . . don't pursue" policy, a man was discharged after a colleague, charged with homosexual rape, was offered a plea bargain if he would name other gays (Komarow, 1997). Until gays are fully accepted in the military and elsewhere, they continue to face stigma and potential extortion.

The Gay Liberation Movement

Spiraling concerns about homosexual rights in the 1980s and 1990s resulted from gays' efforts to organize and influence the political process in the time-honored American tradition of participatory democracy. The beginning of the gay liberation movement in the United States is usually traced back to an incident on June 27, 1969, when police raided the Stonewall Inn, a gay bar in New York City. The patrons became angry and pelted the officers with bottles and stones until police reinforcements arrived and the crowd dispersed. For the next five nights, crowds of homosexuals, joined by heterosexual sympathizers, gathered in the vicinity of the inn to protest the vice-squad raid and to confront the police. Within a month after the Stonewall riots, the Gay Liberation Front had been organized in New York City. Although groups concerned with gay rights had existed since the 1950s, it was the Stonewall riots that marked the emergence of homosexuals' political activism.

Much recent gay activism has been channeled into obtaining increased funding for AIDS research and education (see Figure 11.8). With the growth of gay liberation, a wide variety of support systems for gay individuals has evolved in urban areas. Friends or partners can be found in gay social clubs, churches, political organizations, and discussion groups. Large cities have easily identifiable gay neighborhoods with bookstores, physicians, realtors, clothing stores, lawyers, and many other resources that cater to a gay clientele.

We hope that homosexuals will someday be treated as ordinary people and that sexual orientation will become strictly a private issue. This can happen only when society accepts and protects all its noncoercive variations.

BISEXUALITY

Sandra Bem, famous for her studies of gender role identification, denied being **bisexual**, but, like many bisexuals, she considers gender to be irrelevant in what attracts her to other people:

bisexual The capacity to feel erotic attraction toward or to engage in sexual interaction with both men and women.

> *I am not now and never have been a "heterosexual." But neither have I ever been a "lesbian" or a "bisexual.". . . The sex-of-partner dimension implicit in the three categories . . . seems irrelevant to my own particular pattern of erotic attractions and sexual experiences. Although some of the (very few) individuals to whom I have been attracted . . . have been men and some have been women, what those individuals have in common has nothing to do with either their biological sex or mine—from which I conclude, not that I am attracted to both sexes, but that my sexuality is organized around dimensions other than sex. (1993, p. vii)*

Bisexuality, the sexual attraction to both men and women, has received little scientific or social attention in a world polarized into homosexual and heterosexual camps. The homosexual subculture often views the bisexual as someone who is going through a phase of heterosexual encounters because he or she is unwilling to come to grips with being homosexual (Rust, 1993b; Weinberg, Williams, & Pryor, 1994). The heterosexual community, meanwhile, tends to lump bisexuals into the general category of homosexuals or view them as confused heterosexuals who need guidance.

Researchers have reported, however, that a substantial number of men report bisexual attraction and engage in sex with both men and women during adulthood (Doll et al., 1992; Lever, Kanouse, Rogers, Carson, & Hertz, 1992; Stokes, McKirnan, & Burzette, 1993).

Incidence

How many people can be classified as bisexuals? As with other classifications, the number depends on the definition of the term. If the criterion is at least one overt sexual experience with a member of each gender, then a third of the Kinsey group's (1948) males fell into the bisexual category. If the additional 13 percent who reported having had erotic feelings toward both genders but overt experience with only one of them are added, the total was 46 percent of the sample. Although comparable figures for the Kinsey group's (1953) females are difficult to report, about a third as many females as males reported overt experience with both genders, and about half as many females as males reported erotic responses to both genders. Looking at this question from another standpoint, 52 percent of the exclusively homosexual and 93 percent of the predominantly homosexual males in Bell and Weinberg's (1978) study reported that they had engaged in heterosexual coitus at least once. The comparable figures for females were 77 percent and 93 percent, respectively.

Characteristics

Although we all have the potential to respond erotically to both genders, only some of us do so. What factors lead some people to interact sexually with both men and women?

Answers to that question and many others about bisexuality must be tentative because few studies have investigated people describing themselves as bisexual. In one such study, Philip Blumstein and Pepper Schwartz (1976) interviewed 156 bisexuals and found three themes to be particularly prevalent among the respondents. The first of these was sexual experimentation in the context of friendship. Some of the individuals had progressed from intense emotional attachment to sexual involvement with a friend, although they had never previously had an erotic attraction to a person of that gender. The second theme was interaction in group sex. This pathway to bisexuality is quite common for women who are involved in swinging, and who are often encouraged by their husbands or friends to engage in same-gender sexual activity (Weinberg et al., 1994). In this situation, Blumstein and Schwartz's respondents focused on the pleasurable feelings of these encounters rather than on the gender of the person providing the pleasure. The third theme was the presence of a belief system in which bisexuality was seen as a normal state. Some respondents in the study had embraced bisexual identification because they felt that a truly free person should be able to love both genders. Although some respondents had not actually engaged in bisexual relations, many agreed intellectually with the idea of inborn bisexuality.

Bisexuals tend to display higher levels of eroticism in their fantasy and behavior than do their heterosexual counterparts. They report more heterosexual fantasies, begin heterosexual activity sooner and engage in it more frequently, masturbate more, report stronger orgasms, and are more sexually adventurous than are heterosexuals (Van Wyk & Geist, 1984).

Bisexually experienced men, compared to heterosexual men, report engaging in more high-risk behaviors (multiple partners, anal sex) and are more likely to report having had an STD in the past five years. However, the frequency of these risk characteristics among bisexual men is less than that found among homosexual men (Lever et al., 1992).

Particularly disturbing is that many bisexually active men do not tell their female partners about their homosexual contacts. In a study of 350 behaviorally bisexual men, 71 percent did not reveal this behavior to their female sexual partners, and 59 percent did not disclose to their steady female partner in the previous six months (Stokes, McKirnan, Doll, & Burzette, 1996). Thus, these women are unknowingly at risk for contracting sexually transmitted diseases, including HIV.

Comparisons of bisexual men and women who have been heterosexually married show several gender differences. Bisexual women tend to marry at an early age, and they are more likely than bisexual men to become aware of their homosexual feelings after they wed. Bisexual women are also more likely than bisexual men to terminate their marriages early because of conflicts arising from their bisexuality and sexual dissatisfaction (Bell & Weinberg, 1978; Coleman, 1987). The fact that the marriages of bisexual women are shorter than the marriages of bisexual men may stem from the differing sexual socialization of males and females. Like lesbians, bisexual women seem less inclined to engage in multiple sexual relationships than bisexual or homosexual men. The conflict generated by their feelings for a woman in the face of their desire for monogamy may prompt some bisexual women to end their marriages. Bisexuals have begun to develop broad social networks. The first international conference was held in Amsterdam in 1991 (Rust, 1993b).

Identity Versus Experience

Many people who have experienced a sexual relationship with both genders do not think of themselves as bisexual. Janet Lever and her colleagues (1992) found that more than two-thirds of bisexually experienced men labeled themselves as heterosexual. One of the most prominent characteristics of whether a bisexually active man identified himself as bisexual was adolescent homosexual experience. The greater the amount of adolescent homosexual experience, the more likely the men were to label themselves as bisexual (Lever et al., 1992). However, many men engage in sexual activities with both genders and continue to consider themselves heterosexuals (Weinberg et al., 1994).

Thus, substantial numbers of people who consider themselves to be either heterosexual or homosexual have the capacity to be sexually aroused by and/or to engage in sexual activity with members of both genders. Many of these individuals engage in same-gender sexual activity only once or a few times, usually in adolescence, and therefore do not really qualify as bisexuals.

Bisexual Identity: Stable or Transitional?

One question faced by people who engage in sexual activity with both genders concerns whether their dual attraction is a stable identity, simply a "phase" out of which they will grow, or a transition to homosexuality. Paula Rust (1993b) interviewed lesbian women about their beliefs concerning bisexual women. Most lesbian women believed that bisexuality was more likely than lesbian identity to be a phase or a way of denying one's true sexuality. They also believed that bisexual women are less personally and politically loyal and more able and willing to "pass" as heterosexuals than are lesbians. However, Rust found that most lesbians were not particularly hostile toward bisexual women. More than half of a small sample of men and women who currently considered themselves as bisexual or gay reported having identified with the other orientation (gay or bisexual, respectively) in the past (Rosario et al., 1996).

In their interviews with more than 500 Black and White bisexually active men, McKirnan, Stokes, Doll, and Burzette (1995) found that bisexual behavior appeared to be relatively stable, and 60 percent of the respondents had bisexual sexual contacts in the past six months. More than half the men had begun bisexual activity at least five years prior to the study. However, Stokes et al. (1993) found that men who initially identified themselves as bisexual were more likely to change toward a more homosexual than heterosexual identity, although more than half remained stable in their identification as bisexual—at least over the period of a year.

Other researchers have found that over a five-year period, 33 percent of men and 40 percent of women retained a bisexual identity, whereas others moved toward either a more homosexual or heterosexual identity (Weinberg et al., 1994). Despite these variations in the permanence of bisexual orientation, bisexuals as a group appear to be as well adjusted psychologically as the heterosexuals and homosexuals who have been studied (Coleman, 1987).

Perhaps as wider recognition is accorded bisexual orientation, more people will claim this label. Bisexuality may soften the hard edges of the homosexual and heterosexual categories, which ignore so many people who do not fit neatly into either. If Freud, Kinsey, and the behaviorists are right regarding the human potential for bisexual responses, then recognition of this possibility, whether a person acts on it or not, may be the way out of an illusory heterosexual-homosexual dichotomy.

REALITY or MYTH ? 6

ISSUES TO CONSIDER

Having read the chapter, what do you believe is the cause of your own sexual orientation?

Summary of major points

1. **Sexual orientation.**

Most individuals confine their sexual interactions to the other gender, although many people who define themselves as heterosexuals have also experienced erotic attraction to members of their own gender. Homosexuals feel attraction toward and interact sexually with people of the same gender. Aside from sexual orientation toward individuals of the same gender, research has uncovered few reliable differences between heterosexuals and homosexuals.

2. **Gender differences and sexual orientation.**

Gay males tend to seek variety and relatively impersonal sex in a pattern more similar to that of heterosexual males than to that of heterosexual females. Lesbian relationships and values resemble those of heterosexual females. These gender differences are consistent with variations in the ways in which males and females are socialized. It is not known, however, whether socialization is entirely responsible for these differences.

3. **Explanations of sexual orientation.**

The assumption that homosexual orientation stems from either genetic or hormonal conditions or a social situation such as a disturbed family relationship dominated early research into the causes of homosexuality. Although there is little evidence to support most of these assumptions, preliminary data suggest a biological contribution to at least some types of homosexuality. Gender-role nonconformity in young boys has also been associated with adult homosexuality.

4. **Sexual orientation and adjustment.**

Many early studies of the psychological adjustment of homosexuals compared gays in therapy with heterosexuals not in therapy. This research led to the conclusion that gays were maladjusted. More appropriate comparisons have failed to identify reliable differences in people as a function of their sexual orientation.

5. **Discrimination and liberation.**

Fear, hatred, and discrimination toward homosexuals characterize the attitudes of many people in our culture. In the United States, the civil rights of homosexuals have been limited in such areas as housing, military service, and the enforcement of certain laws regulating sexual behavior. In response to this history, gays have organized politically to pursue equal protection under the law.

6. **Bisexuality.**

Bisexuals are capable of feeling erotic attraction toward and engaging in sexual intimacy with individuals of both genders. They present an interesting question for future research: Why do some people restrict their range of potential partners to one gender (either the same or the other gender), and other people (bisexuals) consider gender unimportant in selecting partners? From this standpoint, exclusive heterosexuals are similar to exclusive homosexuals. Bisexuality appears to be a stable identity and behavior for some people, whereas for others, it represents a transitory phase, usually to homosexual identity and behavior.

CHECK YOUR KNOWLEDGE

1. Which of the following is true? (a) Homosexual orientation results from cross-gender identification in adulthood. (b) Humans are the only species that engage in homosexual behavior. (c) In many traditional cultures, such as Mexico, Brazil, and Turkey, a man who inserts his penis into another man is not considered homosexual. (d) Engaging in homosexual behavior to orgasm almost always leads to a gay identity. **(pp. 274–275)**

2. In their survey of about 190 cultures, Ford and Beach found that homosexual behavior (a) between adults was predominant in a few cultures, (b) was rare or secret in the majority of the cultures studied, (c) between male adolescents was socially required in the majority of the cultures, (d) was normal and socially acceptable for certain members of the community in the majority of cultures studied. **(p. 273)**

3. Probably the best estimate of the percentage of people who are predominantly homosexual for a large part of their lives is (a) 2 to 6 percent, (b) 12 to 16 percent, (c) 23 to 27 percent, (d) 35 to 39 percent. **(pp. 275–276)**

4. "Coming out" refers to a homosexual person's (a) first experience of homosexual feelings, (b) first homosexual encounter that leads to orgasm, (c) acknowledgment to others of his or her gay identity, (d) feelings of love toward someone of the same gender. **(p. 276)**

5. The most accepted explanation for homosexuality is (a) mutations; (b) an excess of testosterone in both male and female homosexuals; (c) a family background consisting of an intimate, controlling mother and a detached, rejecting father; (d) there is no one accepted explanation for homosexual orientation. **(pp. 281–285)**

6. Negative attitudes toward homosexuals are associated with (a) affiliation with fundamentalist religions, (b) erotophilia, (c) residence in urban areas, (d) gender-role flexibility. **(p. 286)**

7. In the United States, the gay liberation movement is usually dated back to (a) the 1920s, (b) the World War II era, (c) the late 1960s and early 1970s, (d) the onset of the AIDS epidemic in the early 1980s. **(p. 290)**

8. Which of the following is *not* a reason that bisexuals give for their sexual orientation? (a) sexual experimentation in the context of friendship, (b) bisexual pornography, (c) group sex, (d) a belief that bisexuality is normal. **(p. 292)**

12

SEX FOR PROFIT

VARIETIES OF SEXUAL PRODUCTS AND SERVICES
Magazines and Newspapers
Advertisements
Television Programs
Erotic Movies and Videos
Highlight: Romance Novels— Erotica for Women?
Adult Bookstores
Telephone Sex
Cyberspace
Erotic Dancing
Other Forms of Erotica

EROTICA AND THE LAW

THE EFFECTS OF EROTICA
Nonviolent Erotica
Highlight: Public Policy and Erotica
Violent Erotica
Prolonged Exposure
Cultural Variations
Children and Erotica

PROSTITUTION (COMMERCIAL SEX WORK)
The Oldest Profession
Commercial Sex Work in Contemporary Society
Across Cultures: Japanese Telephone Clubs That Offer Sex with Girls
Across Cultures: Sex Tourism

SUMMARY OF MAJOR POINTS

CHECK YOUR KNOWLEDGE

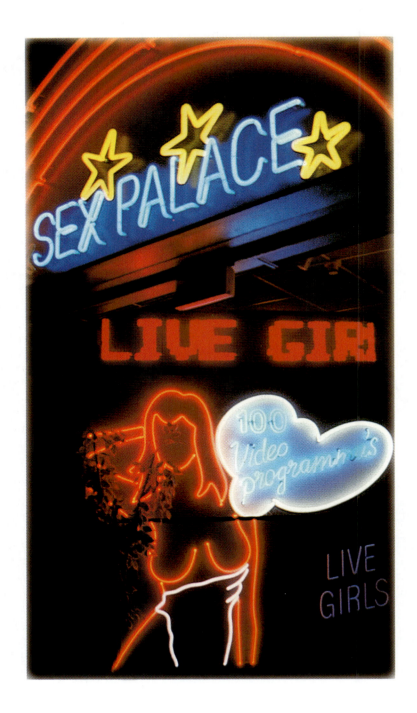

REALITY or MYTH ?

1 The use of sex to sell magazines and other products is ineffective.

2 X-rated erotic movies contain more violence than PG-13 or R-rated films.

3 Most North Americans agree on what material they consider obscene.

4 Viewing sexually explicit material increases a person's likelihood of committing a sex crime.

5 The depiction of child sexual activity is illegal in North America.

6 Some prostitutes enjoy their work as well as the income that it produces.

T H E next time you watch television or look at a magazine, notice how frequently the commercials or advertisements emphasize sex appeal. Attractive and seductive young models promote everything from mouthwash to cars. With the growing use of sexual messages in advertising and the prevalence of graphic depictions of sexuality in films and in print, it is assumed that using sex to sell a product makes money.

In this chapter we describe the intersection of sexuality and the profit motive. Much of the controversy about sexual products centers on their possible effect on consumers, particularly those who are young and impressionable. We review what is known about the effects of exposure to various types of erotic media and discuss laws concerning sexually explicit material. In addition to viewing and listening to erotic material, consumers can buy sexual services from prostitutes. Both women and men sell sexual access to their bodies, but prostitution is primarily a female profession, and most buyers are males. We consider different kinds of prostitutes, legal constraints on prostitution, and the characteristics associated with prostitutes and with those who purchase their services.

VARIETIES OF SEXUAL PRODUCTS AND SERVICES

Erotic material may be viewed in magazines, in theaters, or at home on television programs, videocassettes, and the Internet; it is found in nightclubs featuring adult entertainment, adult bookstores, and even advertisements for products that have no readily apparent connection with sexuality. Before discussing the profits generated by these materials, we need to define a few key terms.

The word **erotica** generally refers to sexually oriented material that is acceptable to the viewer. **Pornography** is sexually oriented material that is not acceptable to the viewer. What one person may find appealing, pleasant, and arousing, another may judge disgusting, unpleasant, and nonarousing.

erotica Sexually oriented material that is acceptable to the viewer.

pornography Sexually oriented material that is not acceptable to the viewer.

297

hard-core erotica Erotica that explicitly depicts the genitals and sexual acts.

soft-core erotica Erotica that is suggestive, but not explicit, in portraying sexual acts.

Hard-core erotica or pornography is sexual material that explicitly depicts sexual acts. X-rated movies and materials displayed in adult bookstores are usually hard core. **Soft-core erotica** or pornography is sexual material that is suggestive, but not explicit, in portraying sex acts. Magazines that can be purchased from most newsstands, such as *Playboy* and *Penthouse,* are examples of soft-core erotica.

Magazines and Newspapers

Soft-core erotica made major inroads in the magazine business in 1953, the same year that Kinsey and his group published their research on women's sexuality, when *Playboy,* the first national magazine to display bare breasts and buttocks, was launched. Other similar magazines soon followed, and depiction of the genitals became increasingly common. These magazines reached their peak circulation in the 1970s and then began to lose readership, perhaps because they were less explicit than the more hard-core magazines (Kimmel & Linders, 1996).

Nonetheless, the continuing power of sex in selling magazines is reflected in the sales figures for the annual swimsuit issue of *Sports Illustrated*. In 1995 *Sports Illustrated* sold almost twice as many copies of its swimsuit issue than of its other monthly issues. Revenues for the issue and tie-ins (videos, calendars) reached about one-third of the magazine's net income for that entire year.

 REALITY or MYTH ? ❶

Advertisements

The electronic and print media and advertisers have shown people in various states of undress and intimate poses. Examine the advertisement in Figure 12.1. The use of sexual images has become overt, and analyses of the content of advertisements during the past two decades support the conclusion that nude or seminude models (females much more so than males) are a common element in advertising in the United States and other countries (Wiles, Wiles, & Tjernlund, 1996).

This trend may reflect a belief by the advertising industry that sex sells, but does it? Does sexual content in an advertisement increase the likelihood that consumers will purchase a particular item? The answer appears to be no, unless the product is related to sexuality (Gould, 1994). For products that are unrelated to sexuality, research indicates that overt sexual content in ads is less effective than nonsexual content. Although

**Figure 12.1
The Use of Partial Nudity to Sell Products**

provocative stimuli may grab attention initially, memory of a brand name and comprehension of an ad's message are reduced when there is irrelevant sexual content in the advertisement (Severn, Belch, & Belch, 1990). Despite the absence of evidence for the effectiveness of using sex appeal to sell products, the advertising industry nevertheless continues to turn out sexually explicit ads.

This explicitness brings up the question of what limits, if any, should apply to the advertising industry's attempts to sell products by linking them with sexuality. Not surprisingly, data indicate that erotophobic persons report less enjoyment of and less exposure to erotic material compared to erotophilic persons. In addition, erotophobic people generally report higher approval of censoring erotic materials than do erotophilic people (Fisher et al., 1988; Lopez & George, 1995). (See Chapter 4 for definitions of erotophilic [positive] and erotophobic [negative] emotional responses to sexual feelings and experiences.)

Television Programs

The use of sex in the electronic and print media is hardly limited to advertisements. One study of sexual behavior during prime time on the major networks found an average of 10 incidents of sexual behavior per hour (Lowry & Shidler, 1993). Almost all depictions in this medium are of heterosexual activity that is recreational and mostly between unmarried partners (Brown & Steele, 1996).

As you know from your own viewing experience, one difficulty with television's presentation of sex is that programs depicting sexual encounters rarely deal with the possible consequences of sexual activity. For example, characters shown engaging in sex with each other seldom discuss potential negative outcomes, such as unwanted pregnancy and STDs and what they can do to reduce these risks. The absence of modeling responsible sexual decision making may lead viewers into an unrealistic view of the range of consequences for sexual behavior.

Hamburg (1992) and Hechinger (1992) have more globally described television viewing patterns and sexual content. Overall, the average 18-year-old has spent only half as much time in school as watching television. U.S. viewers are exposed each year to almost ten thousand scenes of suggested sex or innuendo, and more than 90 percent of sex portrayals on TV involve people who either are unmarried or are married to someone else!

The tendency to exaggerate the glamour of sexuality has led fundamentalist religious groups to advocate the censorship of erotic activity on television. Other organizations, including Planned Parenthood, suggest that when sexual activity is portrayed, the possible unwanted consequences should also be presented. "They did it 20,000 times on television last year. How come nobody got pregnant?" was a slogan used by the Planned Parenthood Federation of America in an adolescent pregnancy prevention program a number of years ago (Meischke, 1995). Similar advice could be given to the producers of the numerous explicit sexual scenes featured in many music videos. The controversy about the effects of the commercial portrayal of sex intensifies when we turn to films and books that directly aim to evoke sexual arousal.

Erotic Movies and Videos

In the 1970s the market for sexually explicit films flourished. The market for cinematic erotica took another turn in the 1980s when the video recorder began to chip into the profits of adult theaters and magazines. The steadily climbing sales and rentals of hard-core videocassettes suggest that consumers prefer watching these films in the privacy of the home rather than in a theater (Kimmel & Linders, 1996).

Hard-core or X-rated movies probably contain the most explicit depictions of sexuality that North America has produced, but their plots are typically dull and predictable. Sociologist Ira Reiss characterized most X-rated films as having a thin plot and unimpressive acting:

> *The scenes focus upon oral, anal, and coital acts with extensive closeups of that action. The acts are mostly heterosexual, and when they are homosexual, unless the film is made specifically for male homosexuals, the focus is upon lesbian sexual acts. The absence of male homosexuality is due to the strong*

ISSUES TO CONSIDER

Should erotophobic persons have to tolerate exposure to the sexually suggestive material that permeates contemporary advertising and other media?

ISSUES TO CONSIDER

The next time you watch a sex scene in a network show or on MTV, think about how you would inject information about responsible sexual behavior into the script.

HIGHLIGHT

Romance Novels—Erotica for Women?

Romance novels have been phenomenally successful, selling millions of copies and appearing regularly on best-seller lists. They are female fantasies, written mainly by women. The erotic romance generally features a young woman whose innocence is violated by an older man; his repeated assaults result in pregnancy and marriage. The struggle between the two for dominance, the man's eventual triumph, and his ultimate domestication are consistent plot elements. In one study, readers of these novels reported having sexual relations twice as often as nonreaders of romance; in addition, they often used fantasy as a complement to intercourse, whereas nonreaders did so rarely, if at all (Coles & Shamp, 1984). Romance novels are a kind of soft-core erotica that women find socially acceptable.

Reiss (1986) suggested that in one sense female erotic fantasy may be based on the same principle as male erotic fantasy; that is, it is enhanced by removing the negotiating power of one's sexual partner. In romance novels, the male is depicted as obsessed with romance. His intense love for the heroine renders him helpless to resist; he must pursue her and give her what she desires. Feminine gender-role expectations are compatible with this scenario, and a woman can relax her sexual guard and feel safe (Thompson, 1994).

Women are pressured to be both selective and sexually responsive in North American culture. Men are socialized to become sexual initiators, ready to perform at the drop of an eyelash. Is it any wonder that women and men often prefer different types of erotica?

attempt to appeal to Western heterosexual males' lustful feelings in these films. Little or no physical violence against women occurs in the vast majority of these films. (1986, pp. 174–175)

The typical X-rated film is a fantasy about sexually insatiable women who are incapable of resisting any type of male sexual advance. In a matter of seconds, regardless of the male's approach, the woman is overcome by her sexual passion and willingly participates in all sorts of sexual activities. In a culture in which males are socialized to be sexual initiators—a role in which they are vulnerable to rejection by females who are not sexually interested in them—it is not difficult to see why the insatiable female fantasy is so popular. The female counterpart to this male fantasy can be seen in women's romance novels (see "Highlight: Romance Novels—Erotica for Women?") and, more recently, explicit novels, and sexual films made from a feminist perspective (cf. Candida Royale's Femme Productions).

Historically, most erotica has been aimed at arousing males. Men's seemingly greater interest in obtaining erotic material probably explains this marketing strategy. In one college sample, men reported viewing erotic material an average of about six hours a month, whereas women reported viewing such material only about two and a half hours a month (Padgett, Brislin-Slutz, & Neal, 1989).

Hard-core and X-rated movies are often the targets of groups that advocate censorship. However, these films generally contain less violence than R-rated films or other movies that children are permitted to see. The highest incidence of violence occurs in PG-13 videos, followed by R-rated videos, with X-rated videos trailing far behind (Scott & Cuvelier, 1993).

In Laumann et al.'s (1994) representative sample of American adults, 23 percent of men and 11 percent of women indicated they had watched X-rated movies or videos. Consumers of X-rated videos do not fit into any easily identifiable category. Reiss (1986) examined six annual surveys of representative groups of Americans 18 and older, conducted between 1973 and 1983 by the National Opinion Research Center. The higher the educational attainment, the more likely the person was to have attended an X-rated movie. Of particular relevance to feminists' concerns that X-rated movies

 **REALITY** or **MYTH** ? **2**

may promote gender inequality was Reiss's finding that for each year between 1973 and 1983, people who attended X-rated movies were more, not less, egalitarian in their gender-role attitudes than those who did not. Similarly, patrons of an adult movie theater who responded to questionnaires placed on a counter in the theater had more positive attitudes toward women than did college men and women (Padgett et al., 1989). Thus research does not support the idea that erotica fosters positive attitudes toward the subordination of women.

Adult Bookstores

Paralleling the expanding market for sexually explicit films, adult bookstores have also shown growing profits. These bookstores sell hard-core erotica of a sort not readily available at other retail stores. In addition to printed media and videos, a range of other products is often available, including such sex toys as vibrators, massage oils, dildos, and other sexual aids. Some stores also offer live sex shows featuring everything from nude dancing to simulated live sexual acts (see Figure 12.2).

A study of 26 adult bookstores in the Philadelphia area found a strong overlap between the stores and such forms of vice as drug distribution, gambling, and prostitution (Potter, 1989). All of these establishments had peep-show areas where a customer could enter a booth and insert coins or tokens to watch a film. Twelve had booths where a viewer could pay for a curtain or blind to be raised. In the booth, a male or female employee behind a glass partition converses with the customer through a telephone or intercom system. The employee gradually undresses and engages in sexual talk with the customer. Eventually, the employee carefully solicits the customer and, for additional payment, goes to the customer's side of the booth (or the two retire to another part of the store) for sex.

Glory holes were also provided in 24 of the 26 stores in their peep-show areas (Potter, 1989). A glory hole is a circular opening two to six inches in diameter in the

Figure 12.2
Adult Bookstore This 17-year-old boy checks out the display in the window of an adult bookstore in Copenhagen, Denmark. The Scandinavian countries are generally more tolerant of erotica than are their North American counterparts.

side wall of the booth, through which genitals may be inserted. The booths usually feature homosexual themes, and their purpose is to allow two men in adjacent cubicles to engage in manual or oral stimulation.

In Philadelphia, the retail pornography outlets are intertwined with prostitution and are part of organized criminal networks. Investigations by the Federal Bureau of Investigation have revealed complicated patterns of common ownership of pornography outlets, massage parlors, and after-hours clubs in that city. These patterns are not unique to Philadelphia. Similar arrangements flourish in many other cities, contributing to an estimated annual gross income of up to $9 billion (Potter, 1989).

Telephone Sex

Those who seek sexual stimulation at a distance can dial a 900 telephone number and listen to explicit sexual talk for a price. The so-called dial-a-porn industry allows a caller to have a conversation with a paid performer at the other end of the line or to listen to a prerecorded message (Glasock & LaRose, 1993). Roughly 1 percent of all men and no women report using this service (Laumann et al., 1994). For fees that range from $3 to $12 a minute, a caller can indulge in sexual fantasies with a phone worker who will talk "dirty" to the caller and charge the episode to that person's monthly telephone bill or credit card. Advertisements for such services can be found in the personal ad sections of many newspapers and in sexually oriented magazines.

For this illusion of sexual fulfillment, the caller is often treated to a worker's feigned interest in his fantasy. Many calls are forwarded to the worker's home, where he or she may try to titillate the customer while going about such ordinary pursuits as cleaning the kitchen or reading the paper (Borna, Chapman, & Menezes, 1993).

Cyberspace

The computer has combined with modern telephone technology to create a highly efficient means for the transmission of information. It should come as no surprise that one of the oldest human desires has hooked up with the latest technology. Computer

Figure 12.3
Example of Explicit Sex on the World Wide Web The World Wide Web, like other communication modes, has its share of sexual displays and services. Just as they have supported censoring other media, some politicans have advocated censorship for sexually oriented material that finds its way onto computer screens.

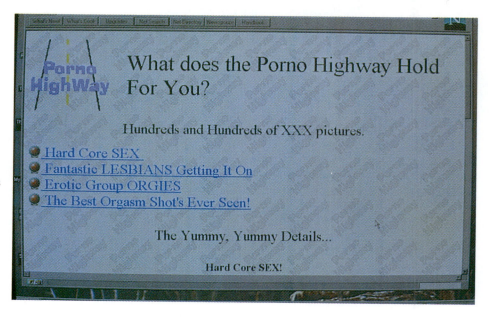

bulletin-board systems, known as BBSs, are roughly equivalent to high-tech electronic telephone party lines. By connecting to a particular BBS, one can use a computer to contact individuals or companies with similar interests in the United States or other places in the world. Users can meet through the computer, exchange messages and engage in erotic banter, exchange telephone numbers, arrange dates, and upload and download files.

Adult-oriented BBS, with names like ThrobNet and KinkNet, feature libraries of X-rated films and interactive adult games such as "The Interactive Adventures of Seymore Butts." In this game, the wrong answer gets Seymore a refusal or a slap in the face; the right answer lands him in bed, where the viewer gets to see hard-core sex.

Some on-line BBS services make direct approaches to people with atypical interests (Durkin & Bryant, 1995). Sadomasochism, bestiality, or almost anything else imaginable is available (see Figure 12.3). Of particular concern have been highly publicized incidents of individuals obtaining child erotica and attempting to contact youngsters (usually through deception) to arrange meetings for sexual purposes. This has led some legislators in the United States and other countries to propose various types of censorship in computer communication. We will undoubtedly see more attention to the censorship issue in the coming years.

Erotic Dancing

Erotic dancing—the gradual shedding of clothes to music in bars, restaurants, theaters, clubs, and private shows—has a long history. Depending on the locale, strippers may shed all their clothes or strip down to scanty G-strings (the rule in most U.S. cities). In table topping, the disrobing dancers perform on the tables where the customers are seated.

Erotic dancing, also known as stripteasing, has been primarily a form of entertainment provided by women. Three factors appear to be associated with women's entrance into this profession. These include residing in an area where such opportunities for employment are available, being aware of the potential for earning a reasonable living through the profession, and perceiving—based on assessments from others—that one is sufficiently attractive and qualified to succeed in the job (Forsyth & Deshotels, 1997; Thompson & Harred, 1992).

The majority of strip clubs pay the dancers the minimum wage or nothing at all. For their income, the dancers depend on tips and, in some cases, subsequent paid sex with the customers. Similar to restaurants, the strip clubs vary in their atmosphere and cost to customers. Although only a small proportion of the 1,500 clubs in the United States can be described as "upscale," their numbers are growing in metropolitan areas. Such establishments, known as "gentlemen's clubs," provide additional services such as exercise rooms, tanning salons, hair salons, and fax machines (Forsyth & Deshotels, 1997).

Craig Forsyth and Tina Deshotels (1997) interviewed erotic dancers about their profession and goals. Many of the women reported taking drugs to reduce their inhibitions about nude or semi-nude dancing, with marijuana being the most commonly used intoxicant. Although their interactions with men at the clubs were typically impersonal, many of the dancers said that the clubs provided good places to meet men and indicated that they would quit dancing to marry the right man. If fact, most dancers saw marriage as a future goal.

More recently, men have increasingly entered this occupation (see Figure 12.4, page 304). In contrast to most female strippers, male strippers apparently are motivated frequently by the opportunity to meet women (or men) with whom they may subsequently engage in sex—and not necessarily for money (Dressel & Peterson, 1982).

ISSUES TO CONSIDER

Do you think the government should censor erotic material on the Internet? If not, why not? If you favor censorship, what guidelines would you propose?

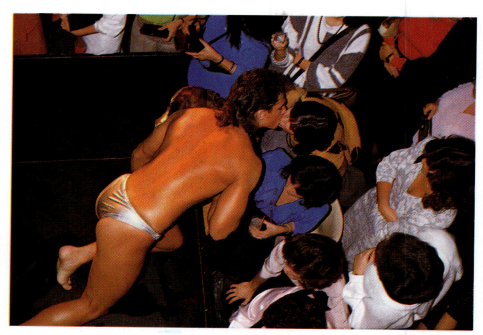

Figure 12.4
Male Stripping: A Relatively Recent Social Phenomenon
Contact between a male dancer and women in the audience is not unusual in the stripping business.

Male strip shows often involve costumed individuals or group performances in various scenarios; members of the audience may approach a dancer offering a tip, after which physical contact such as kissing or fondling may occur.

Male and female strippers alike believe that society views them in a negative light. Thus they often describe themselves to others as entertainers or dancers in an effort to avoid negative stereotypes (Thompson & Harred, 1992).

Other Forms of Erotica

Individuals can employ erotica to arouse themselves or a sexual companion. Used with a partner, erotic materials can enhance lovemaking, but some forms can serve as a substitute for those who lack a partner.

A wide array of products are billed as enhancing sexual proficiency. Vibrators, dildos, creams, pastes, and lubricants are just a few of the more tame items competing for the consumer's business. See the Appendix for these and more exotic paraphernalia. About 2 percent of men and women report using vibrators or dildos (Laumann et al., 1994). Individuals or couples may use such sexual aids to heighten their sensations during masturbation or coitus. For example, a number of companies manufacture scented lubricants, with some variations aimed at women and others at men. There is no evidence that these kinds of stimulants are harmful, and some do, in fact, produce the sensations—warmth, numbing—claimed. For those who prefer human-like playthings, there are various inflatable dolls that can be used as a sexual partner.

Other advertised products are of more dubious quality. Several years ago, we received a promotional piece on a so-called sex pill for men, called NSP-270, that purportedly would compensate for certain male "nutritional deficiencies" and promote penis growth. Although the literature contains some remarkable graphs in which penis-shaped bars indicate the length of a man's penis before and after he has taken

NSP-270, readers never learn which famous California medical school has developed this "nutrient."

Although people widely condemn erotica and sexual aids, the trade would not be flourishing if consumers did not support it with their money.

ISSUES TO CONSIDER

What other forms of erotica have you encountered that we have not mentioned?

EROTICA AND THE LAW

The word **obscenity** is often used interchangeably with the word *pornography,* but obscenity also has a legal meaning. In U.S. law, obscenity refers to illegal erotica. In the United States, laws regulating erotic material date back to the nineteenth century. The most important one is the Comstock Act, named after its major advocate, Anthony Comstock, the most prominent member of the New York Society for the Suppression of Vice. The Comstock Act, passed in 1873, made mailing obscene, **lascivious,** or **lewd** material a felony. Still in effect, the law is enforced by the Inspection Service of the U.S. Postal Service.

Enforcement of the obscenity laws has been uneven because of the difficulty in defining what is obscene. In 1957 the Supreme Court, in *Roth* v. *United States,* attempted to provide a more precise definition of obscenity, and this definition remains the current legal one. In its decision, the Court stated that for material to be considered obscene, it must meet three essential criteria: (1) it must be offensive to contemporary community standards, (2) the dominant theme of the work must appeal to **prurient** interest in sex, and (3) the work must be devoid of serious literary, artistic, political, or scientific value. This ruling did not lead to a clarification of the legal issues. The meaning of "community standards" is vague. A community can encompass both fundamentalist churches and a university with a liberal faculty; Republicans and Democrats; conservatives and liberals; and elderly, middle-aged, and young persons. How does one arrive at the community standard?

In an attempt to determine whether a single "community standard" response to erotic materials could be found, college students participated in a study of "judgments about photographs" (Allgeier, Yachanin, Smith, & Myers, 1984). Students at the university where this research was done are quite conservative, and most regularly attend religious services. They were asked to rate photographs portraying nudity, heterosexual and homosexual activity, group sex, and so on. There was considerable variation in the ratings of how arousing, pornographic, and offensive each photo was. The absence of similarity of responses in this homogeneous group suggests that establishing a community standard would be even more difficult in a population as diverse as that found in U.S. cities.

The Supreme Court attempted to clarify the definition of obscenity again in a 1987 decision. The Court ruled six to three that some sexually explicit works may not be obscene even if most people in a city or state think that the works have no serious literary, artistic, political, or scientific value. According to Justice Byron White, "The proper inquiry is not whether an ordinary member of any given community would find literary, artistic, political, or scientific value but whether a reasonable person would find such value in the material taken as a whole." The question remains, of course, about how we define a reasonable person.

Contemporary social pressure to censor erotic depictions comes from two groups, one of which includes mainly political conservatives and religious fundamentalists. This group generally supports strict regulation of sexual behavior and considers use of erotica a pathway to sexual degeneracy. The second group consists of feminists who object to erotica that they consider degrading to women. They see certain forms of

obscenity The legal term for material that is foul, disgusting, lewd, and offensive to accepted standards of decency.

lascivious Tending to stimulate sexual desire.
lewd Sexually unchaste; inciting lust or debauchery.

prurient Provoking lasciviousness.

REALITY or MYTH ? 3

erotica as leading to aggression against women. Many feminists also assert that erotica reinforces traditional gender roles by emphasizing the subordination of women and the power of men in sexual relationships.

In 1992 Canada redefined obscenity as sexually explicit material that involves violence or degradation. Adult erotica, no matter how explicit, is not considered obscene. Erotic material that contains violence, degradation, bondage, or children is considered illicit obscenity. In effect, the Canadian court decided that a threat to women's equality is an acceptable ground for some limitation of free speech. As of this writing, Canada is the only nation that has defined obscenity in terms of harm to women rather than as material that offends moral values. It should be noted, however, that many feminists do not support censorship of sexually explicit materials (McCormick, 1994).

We know of no research exploring judgments of whether certain themes are perceived as degrading to men. In fact, we are not sure how anyone would construct heterosexual erotica that contained elements that would be judged by women—or men—as degrading to men, short of the rape of men by women, as described in Chapter 14.

Judgments of the themes of sexually explicit material are a separate issue from judgments about whether such material should be censored. National surveys conducted almost every year from 1973 to 1986 in the United States by the National Opinion Research Center indicated that the majority of respondents in every survey agreed that the distribution of pornography to adults should not be illegal (Smith, 1987).

More important than whether people approve of the availability of erotica is whether particular kinds of erotica can be harmful. A choice confronting any society is the degree to which it wants to suppress material that may trigger antisocial behavior in some of its citizens. To protect the First Amendment rights of free expression, the courts have ruled that only those forms of expression that have a "virtual certainty" of producing potential harm can be banned. The conclusions of several national commissions concerning whether certain types of erotica cause harm are presented in "Highlight: Public Policy and Erotica."

THE EFFECTS OF EROTICA

There is intense controversy over the effects of exposure to erotica, particularly violent erotica. We now examine what is known about erotica and its effects.

Nonviolent Erotica

We deal with the issue of violent erotica shortly, but in this section our focus is on erotica that portrays consensual sexual activities. Does erotic material containing no aggression against women stimulate people to engage in sexual acts that they would normally avoid? Or does this material provide a sexual outlet for individuals who might use other means to satisfy their sexual desires if erotica were not available? Is exposure to erotica related to sex crimes and violence?

Since 1970 there have been many studies done exposing research volunteers to nonaggressive sexual material. A review of these studies reveals no support for the belief that exposure to nonviolent erotica affects the rate of sex crimes, attitudes toward rape, or evaluations of rape victims (Davis & Bauserman, 1993; Kimmel & Linders, 1996; Winick & Evans, 1996). This is true for both short-term (less than an hour) and long-term (anything beyond an hour) exposure to nonviolent erotica.

HIGHLIGHT

Public Policy and Erotica

President Lyndon Johnson appointed the U.S. Commission on Obscenity and Pornography in the late 1960s. After funding much research and holding many hearings, the commission released its report in 1970. The commission's efforts were reported in nine technical volumes, two of which were specifically concerned with the effects of erotica.

Essentially, the commission arrived at a "no harm" conclusion, maintaining that, according to the available evidence, exposure to or use of explicit sexual material does not play a significant role in causing crime, delinquency, sexual deviancy, or severe emotional disturbances (Amoroso, Brown, Pruesse, Ware, & Pithey, 1971). Overall, the commission recommended that federal, state, and local legislation should not interfere with the right of adults who wish to read, obtain, or view explicitly sexual materials. In the 1970s and 1980s, similar committees in Britain and Canada reached similar conclusions.

In 1985 the United States Attorney General's Commission on Pornography was formed. Also known as the Meese Commission (named after Attorney General Edwin Meese III), it delivered its final report in 1986 after hearing testimony from witnesses around the country and reviewing more than five thousand magazines, books, and films (see Figure 12.5, page 308). The commission claimed to have found a "causal relationship between sexual violence and exposure to erotica that featured children and/or violence." Its assertion of this causal link has provoked serious criticisms of its conclusions. A number of studies have examined the correlation between exposure to explicit materials containing sexual violence, and attitudes toward women and assault. However, the correlational design of the studies reviewed by the commission did not allow any conclusions about the causes of sexually assaultive behavior on adults or children.

Despite the fact that the Meese Commission's conclusions were not warranted by the data its members reviewed, the commission made 92 specific recommendations aimed at halting the spread of erotica. Many of these recommendations related to a more rigorous enforcement of the law with respect to erotic materials.

Violent Erotica

To examine the effect of exposure to violent pornography, Neil Malamuth and Edward Donnerstein (1984) presented to men a series of slides and tapes of women reading stories that included either coercive (use of force) or consensual (mutually consenting) sexual interaction. These researchers used self-reported arousal as well as genital measures of erection to assess men's responses to these forms of erotica. Before participating in the studies, volunteers were asked to indicate the likelihood that they would commit rape if they could be sure of not getting caught. Those who revealed that they thought they might engage in coercive sexual acts were classified as force-oriented.

Although the designs of these studies varied, the stimuli usually consisted of a story of an attractive woman wandering along a deserted road. A man finds her there, but when he approaches her, she faints. He carries her to his car, and when she awakens they engage in sex. In one version of this basic story, the woman is tied up and forced to have sex in the car. In other variations, she clearly consents to the act. Regardless of which rendition they saw, male volunteers found this story arousing, as indicated by both self-reports and the extent of their erections. This finding is consistent with others showing that certain rape portrayals elicit relatively high sexual arousal in nonrapists (Malamuth, 1984; Malamuth & Check, 1983).

Even a rape portrayal emphasizing the victim's pain and distress may, under certain conditions, stimulate high levels of sexual arousal in viewers. But this effect appears to vary as a function of whether the viewer describes himself as force-oriented (Malamuth, 1981). Force–oriented volunteers reported having more arousal fantasies after exposure to the rape version than after exposure to the consensual version.

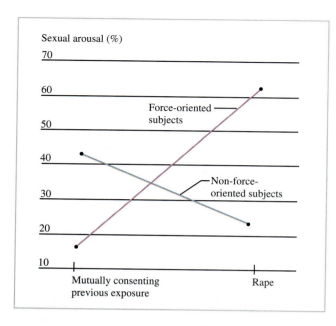

Sexual arousal (%)

Force-oriented subjects

Non-force-oriented subjects

Mutually consenting previous exposure

Rape

Figure 12.5
Violent Pornography and Sexual Arousal As this graph illustrates, men who indicate some likelihood that they would commit rape (force-oriented men) are more aroused by violent pornography than are men who indicate they would not (non–force-oriented).

Non–force-oriented men, however, reported having more arousing fantasies in response to the variations of the story involving mutual consent than in response to the rape variation (see Figure 12.5).

What about the kind of violent pornography that depicts a positive reaction on the part of the victim? As Donnerstein (1984) pointed out, pornographic media quite often portray victims of assault as responding favorably to a rape. Further, in real life, convicted rapists often fail to perceive their assaults as coercive, believing that their victims desired intercourse and enjoyed their sexual attentions (McCormick, 1994). Exposure to violent pornography has been shown to heighten sexual arousal in some men, promote acceptance of rape-supportive attitudes, and foster negative attitudes toward women (Donnerstein & Linz, 1986; Malamuth, 1984).

Donnerstein reasoned that exposure to stories in which a woman is depicted as having a positive reaction to sexual assault would increase aggressive behavior against women. To test this hypothesis, each male volunteer was paired with a female confederate, who either angered the man or treated him in a neutral manner. Each man then watched one of four films: a neutral version, a variation that involved consensual interaction, a version in which the victim had a negative reaction to forced sex, or a variation in which the victim's reaction to forced sex was positive. After viewing one of these films, the volunteer was given an opportunity to administer simulated electric shocks to the female confederate. Of the volunteers who had been angered prior to watching the movie, those who had viewed either of the forced-sex films chose to give higher levels of electric shock to the female confederate than did those who viewed either of the other films. Even the nonangered men became more aggressive (as measured by electric shock level) following exposure to the version of the film showing a positive reaction to forced sex. When a male confederate angered a male volunteer prior to his exposure to the film, the versions of the film did not affect aggression toward the male confederate (Donnerstein, 1984).

To determine if the limited range of responses provided by previous experimenters had affected findings, William Fisher and Guy Grenier (1994) provided a broader range of alternatives for volunteers. That is, after being angered by the female confederate and shown sexual material containing violent content, men in Fisher and Grenier's research could select shock, verbal feedback, or the alternative of simply being debriefed (told the true purpose of a study), receiving their experimental credit, and terminating their participation in the study. Almost all participants selected the last alternative. This research is preliminary and needs to be replicated by others to see if the finding holds up.

What is the effect of violent pornography on women's arousal? To investigate this question, Wendy Stock (1982) presented college women with variations in rape depictions while measuring their genital responses and their subjective reports of arousal. Based on the women's responses, Stock concluded that women are not aroused by rape when described realistically. But she did find heightened arousal as a result of viewing distorted portrayals of rape in which victims do not suffer. This is, of course, not the experience of most victims of rape. The belief of some rapists and members of the general public that women secretly enjoy rape is not supported by Stock's findings. Her work suggests that society should be concerned about rape representations that lead viewers to perceive sexual assault as an erotic experience for the victim.

Our present knowledge does not permit us to determine whether men who report strong arousal to rape depictions and who are aroused by their own rape fantasies will actually commit rape.

The likelihood of a link between arousal in response to violent pornography and the commission of sexual assault was strengthened by the research of Gene Abel and his colleagues (1977) more than two decades ago. They found that convicted rapists were as aroused by rape depictions as they were by portrayals of sexual interactions involving mutual consent. Nonrapists, in contrast, were more aroused by portrayals of consensual sex than by portrayals of forced sex.

Violent pornography degrades both women and men because it depicts women as wanting to be attacked, harmed, and assaulted and portrays men as wanting to inflict pain on other human beings. Because of the demeaning nature of violent erotica and its possible negative effects, some people favor banning it. Before censorship could be instituted, however, someone would have to determine what kinds of violent material should be prohibited. Who should make that determination? Another problem is that the effect of censorship in the past has been to increase the profits of the producers of banned material. If violent pornography is found to pose a danger to women, we believe that the withdrawal of consumer support would be far more effective in stopping the production of aggressive pornography than would attempts at censorship.

Prolonged Exposure

The 1970 Commission on Obscenity and Pornography found that continued or repeated exposure to erotic stimuli resulted in a decrease in sexual arousal and interest in such material. But this conclusion has been challenged by the work of Zillmann and Bryant (1984, 1988). They concluded that following long-term exposure (4 hours and 48 minutes over a six-week period) to erotica that did not contain overt violence, men and women became more tolerant of bizarre and violent forms of erotica, less supportive of statements about gender equality, and more lenient in assigning punishment to a rapist whose crime was described in a newspaper account.

Prolonged exposure also produced other effects, such as discontent with the physical appearance and sexual performance of an intimate partner and the questioning of the values of marriage. It deepened men's callousness toward women, as reflected in increased acceptance of such statements as these: "A woman doesn't mean no until she slaps you" and "If they are old enough to bleed, they are old enough to butcher." The material Zillmann and Bryant used commonly depicted women as sexually insatiable. Perhaps short-term exposure is not sufficient to produce changes in attitudes that reflect this unrealistic view of women. Long-term exposure to erotica, however, did not increase aggressive behaviors. On the other hand, prolonged exposure to pornography that portrays violence against women has consistently been linked to negative effects, such as lessened sensitivity toward rape victims and greater acceptance of force in sexual encounters (Davis & Bauserman, 1993; Linz, 1989).

These findings make it difficult to reach any firm conclusions on the effects of prolonged exposure to nonviolent erotica. Moreover, even in those cases in which negative effects have been found, we do not know how long these effects last. For example, it appears that any changes that occur after short-term exposure to violent erotica are not deeply ingrained and may fade when the participants receive an educational debriefing

ISSUES TO CONSIDER

In making a video that portrays sexual assault, how would you convey the message that rape is a frightening, traumatizing experience for its victims?

reminding them that the material is fictional, women do not enjoy sexual coercion, and so forth (Allen, D'Alessio, Emmers, & Gebhardt, 1996; Malamuth & Check, 1984). Such debriefings are required by university ethics committees and the federal government of agencies that receive federal research funds. Research on debriefing after prolonged exposure to erotica should be conducted to determine whether those effects are short-lived.

As we have emphasized in this chapter, there is no scientific consensus on whether serious harm is likely to result from exposure to erotica. We believe that the basic issue is violent images, not erotic images. It is interesting that our culture exposes the young to graphic details of violence on television and movie screens and in magazines without the same intense public concern that attends exposure to erotica or pornography (Brown & Steele, 1996).

Cultural Variations

Cultural practices and value systems may temper the influence of viewing erotica. For example, bondage and rape themes are prominent in both novels and films in Japan. In Japanese films, the plot often involves the rape of a high school girl, a theme that is also evident in cheap erotic novels and sexual cartoons. Abramson and Hayashi (1984) pointed out that one of the best ways to ensure the commercial success of a Japanese adult film is to include the bondage and rape of a young woman.

The popularity of this theme might lead one to suspect that Japan would have a high rate of sexual assault. Yet Japan has one of the lowest reported rates (i.e., number of rapes per 100,000 people) among the industrialized countries in the world; the reported rape rate in the United States is more than 14 times higher. The assault laws in the two countries are essentially the same, and Japanese women are as reluctant to report assault as are U.S. women. A possible explanation for Japan's low assault rate is that the message expressed in erotica is mediated by cultural values. In Japan, people are socialized to have a strong sense of personal responsibility, respect, and commitment to society and to experience shame if they behave improperly (Dion & Dion, 1993).

Children and Erotica

The use of children as models for sexually explicit magazine photos and as stars of erotic movies has become a major concern of many social agencies and citizens' groups. Both houses of Congress held hearings on child erotica in 1977. Witnesses at the hearings estimated that as many as half a million children were involved in the production of erotica. After these hearings, the federal government and nearly all state governments enacted laws against the production, distribution, and possession of child erotica.

Involvement in the production of erotica is a form of sexual exploitation that is associated with various adverse emotional, behavioral, and physical reactions in children, as well as in adults who were exploited as children (Finkelhor & Browne, 1985). Evidence of these reactions comes from clinical studies of children who were seeing therapists or other professionals, however, so we need to be careful in generalizing these findings to all children involved in such activity. Furthermore, most children and adolescents lured into making erotica also participated in prostitution or other sexual activities with adults (Burgess, Hartman, MacCausland, & Powers, 1984), and many came from homes where they experienced neglect and abuse (Silbert & Pines, 1984). It is hard to isolate the effects of their experiences in making erotica from the effects of these other experiences.

Some people oppose prosecuting those who ensnare children in the manufacture of erotica. Their claim is that these products provide viewers with sexual release and that having such an outlet for their sexual tension prevents the consumers from actually seeking young people for sexual activities. Current law, however, bars children from participating in the production of erotica because they are incapable of giving informed consent.

Those adults who pay, entice, or coerce children to engage in this activity can be prosecuted under child-abuse laws rather than under obscenity laws. We favor this course of action for three reasons. First, obscenity laws may at times violate First Amendment guarantees of freedom of expression. Second, it is generally accepted that the First Amendment permits the outlawing only of material that is considered offensive to public taste and morality, and, as we have seen, this judgment is often difficult to make. Third, children, whether clothed or nude, are not obscene; it is the exploitation of children that is obscene. Adults who abuse their responsibilities toward children by exploiting them are therefore guilty of child abuse.

In 1982 the Supreme Court ruled unanimously that states may prosecute publishers and sellers of child erotica without having to prove that the materials showing children engaging in sexual acts are legally obscene or appeal to prurient interests. According to the Court, the simple inclusion of children engaging in sexual acts is enough to justify prosecution.

PROSTITUTION (COMMERCIAL SEX WORK)

We have considered how advertisers use sex to sell products and how materials such as erotic magazines and films, as well as sexual aids, are designed to elicit sexual arousal. In this section, we examine the direct sale of sexual services.

The Oldest Profession

Prostitution appears to have been practiced at least as far back as we have historical records, and hence it is often called the world's oldest profession. The word *prostitute* comes from the Latin *prostituere,* which means "to expose." Under Roman law, prostitution was defined as the sale of one's body indiscriminately and without pleasure.

Prostitution flourished in ancient Rome; street prostitutes offered their services to patrons of the theater, races, and gladiator contests. As a prelude to the contests between gladiators, patrons would view shows featuring a variety of sexual acts. After the contest was over, those patrons interested in having sex were taken by the prostitutes to the arches beneath the public buildings, known as the *cellae fornicae*. This practice was so common that the word **fornication** came to mean engaging in nonmarital sexual intercourse (Bullough & Bullough, 1987). Through recessions and boom times, prostitution remained a means of employment for poverty-stricken females before and after the Roman Empire.

In the Victorian era in England, a period noted for its supposed purity and prudery, prostitution flourished. Officially, the prostitute was a social outcast, but implicitly she was tolerated. She provided an outlet through which the proper nineteenth-century man could satisfy his passion. Victorian prostitutes were most often women who had been caught in the squalor and degradation of the slums that developed around the mining and milling industries. Selling sexual favors was their main hope for survival.

prostitution The practice of selling sexual stimulation or interaction.

fornication Sexual intercourse between people who are not married to each other.

Commercial Sex Work in Contemporary Society

Although there is still a strong relationship between poverty and prostitution, in some ways the nature of prostitution has changed markedly in the twentieth century. In the first part of the century, most transactions with prostitutes were conducted in houses where prostitution was the sole business. The employees worked, ate, and slept there. Because small red lights were used to indicate that the houses were open for business, the areas in which they were clustered became known as red-light districts. In some nations in northern Europe, as well as in some counties in the state of Nevada, houses of prostitution continue to operate legally. For the most part, however, prostitutes in contemporary America operate out of a variety of other settings that reflect the economic status of the prostitute.

streetwalkers A prostitute who solicits on the street.

pimp A prostitute's business manager.

Streetwalkers (see Figure 12.6) are on the lowest rung of the ladder in the hierarchy of prostitution and at greatest risk of being victimized on the job (Boles, 1998; Vanwesenbeeck, de Graaf, van Zessen, Straver, & Visser, 1995). They solicit on the street and often work for, or are attached to, a **pimp,** who usually has more than one woman working for him. He protects them from outside assaults and generally takes care of them, although by the nature of his business, he is also highly manipulative of the women. The pimp usually takes a considerable share of the prostitute's earnings in exchange for his "protection." Some streetwalkers are recruited from among drug abusers and young runaways. However, most pimps are not interested in substance abusers because of economic reasons. Substance abuse is expensive, and addicted prostitutes are not reliable employees (McCormick, 1994). A growing exception to the foregoing, however, occurs in crack houses in which prostitutes exchange sex for drugs, particularly crack cocaine, which puts crack users and their sex partners at special risk for HIV transmission (Boles, 1998; Inciardi, 1995). This greater risk occurs because the crack cocaine tends to lengthen the time spent in sexual stimulation and the experience of orgasm, thus increasing the risk of likelihood of vaginal, anal, or penile tearing of the skin. In addition, crack-using prostitutes tend not to use condoms with their multiple partners.

Streetwalkers have traditionally worked during the night, but daytime solicitation has become common in large cities. Some streetwalkers, for example, solicit by day in X-rated movie houses. After an arrangement has been struck, the streetwalker usually takes her "trick" (customer) to her apartment or to a cheap hotel, where the manager or room clerk typically is fully aware of the situation. A relatively new variation in streetwalking occurs in truck stops and highway rest areas. At truck stops, women known as "commercial beavers" provide sexual services in the drivers' cabs (McCormick, 1994).

Bar and hotel prostitutes are somewhat higher in the hierarchy of prostitutes than are streetwalkers. The bar girl usually enters into an arrangement with the owner or manager of the bar where she works, and she may receive a percentage of the drinks that she entices the customer to buy for both of them. More frequently, the bar girl is tolerated by the ownership because of the business she attracts. Unlike the streetwalker, the bar girl sometimes finds herself in competition with women who go to bars seeking romance, and she may have to solicit aggressively. The customer may become quite disgruntled if he at first thinks the bar girl is taking an interest in him because of his lovable personality and then discovers that there is a price attached to any sexual activity. The bar girl's fee for sex is generally higher than that charged by the streetwalker.

Because hotel managers generally frown on open solicitation, hotel prostitutes must be subtle and skilled in sending nonverbal messages to potential clients. After a deal has been made, sexual activity usually takes place in the customer's hotel room

Figure 12.6
Film Depiction of a
Streetwalker In the popular
movie *Pretty Woman,* Julia
Roberts plays a streetwalker.
She provides Richard Gere
with sexual favors and he
subsequently falls in love with
her. The experience of most
streetwalkers includes much
less glamour, wealth, and
playfulness.

or apartment. Many hotel prostitutes work a bar one day and a hotel the next. They generally operate without pimps.

One of the more visible forms of prostitution is the storefront variety. In this version, women are employed by massage parlors or thinly disguised business fronts such as escort services to provide sexual services to the customers. Although there are legitimate massage parlors and escort services, many run an operation involving both massage and masturbation (M&M) of customers. For an additional fee, the "hand whores" may also provide oral sex or, less frequently, coitus. Many women employed by massage parlors and escort services are amateurs: college students, homemakers, sales clerks, nurses, secretaries, and women in other occupations who are supplementing their incomes (McCormick, 1994). Women hired to entertain at conventions through escort services are sometimes prostitutes. They may be asked to service delegates, visitors, and convention personnel, as well as to perform before a limited audience. The performances involve dancing, stripping, and lesbian and heterosexual activities. The convention prostitute may have a pimp who acts as a booking agent.

At the top of the prostitution hierarchy is the **call girl.** She usually works out of a comfortable apartment, and if she has a pimp, he acts as her business manager. Typically, her prices are high and her clientele is screened, with solicitation generally occurring by telephone. New customers are located through referrals and word of mouth. The call girl is likely to provide services other than purely sexual ones, such as serving as an attractive date for dinner or a party. It is widely believed that many corporations and government agencies employ call girls to entertain important customers, agents, and dignitaries. Although the use of call girls by government agencies, particularly intelligence agencies, is probably not as great as espionage novels suggest, prostitutes' involvement in espionage has a long history.

call girl A high-priced prostitute whose customers are solicited by telephone or by word-of-mouth references.

MALE PROSTITUTES.   It should not be surprising that the possibility of earning money for sexual favors has attracted males as well as females. Like their female counterparts, most male prostitutes often sell their bodies for financial gain as well as sexual pleasure (Calhoun & Weaver, 1996).

Many heterosexual male prostitutes function in a manner similar to that of call girls. These men may be kept by an older woman, or they may work for an escort service for single, wealthy women. The **gigolo's** relationship to the client is generally well defined, requiring little or no emotional involvement.

Much more common are males who sell their sexual favors to other men; in fact, most male prostitutes describe themselves as homosexual or bisexual (Earls & David, 1989). The homosexual prostitute is called a "hustler" or sometimes a "boy." Such men usually ply their trade on the street or in gay bars and baths. Unlike female streetwalkers, male prostitutes usually do not have pimps (Calhoun & Weaver, 1996). In the homosexual culture, prostitutes drift in and out of the occupation; homosexual prostitutes are more likely to be part-timers than are heterosexual prostitutes (Luckenbill, 1985).

Male prostitutes tend to be more suspicious, mistrustful, hopeless, lonely, and isolated than are nonprostitute males (Simon, Morse, Osofsky, Balson, & Gaumer, 1992). These characteristics may be a response to the chaotic and often dangerous environment in which they exist. This environment may intensify the psychological characteristics that led them to "the life" in the first place. More than 80 percent of the 211 men in Simon et al.'s study used multiple drugs, with alcohol, marijuana, and cocaine being the most common; 28 percent reported injecting drugs and sharing needles with their customers. This intravenous drug use is alarming from a public health standpoint because of the possibility of transmitting HIV and other STDs. Condom use was infrequent or never occurred, according to the men and their customers (Morse, Simon, Balson, & Osofsky, 1992).

Streetwalking men in Atlanta, Georgia, were interviewed by Jacqueline Boles and Kirk Elifson (1994). Although you might assume that these men were gay, only 18 percent of their sample self-identified as homosexual, about a third were bisexual, and the rest described themselves as heterosexual. The bisexuals tended to make statements such as, "I have [paid] sex with men and I have a girlfriend; I guess that makes me a bi" (p. 44). HIV infection rates for men in each sexual identity group were higher for those who frequently engaged in receptive anal sex, had many sexual partners, used drugs frequently, and had a history of other STDs.

THE TRADE.   Prostitution is a topic that proper society prefers to avoid contemplating. Perhaps because of societal disdain, not only do stereotypes abound but knowledge about prostitution is lacking. It is not uncommon to hear laypersons describe female prostitutes as man-hating lesbians or nymphomaniacs.

The research on female prostitutes indicates that their attitudes toward their clients and toward men in general are varied rather than uniformly negative (Diana, 1985; McCormick, 1994). Contrary to the popular belief that prostitutes are sexually unresponsive during their work, a study of streetwalkers in Philadelphia found that 70 percent of the women reported enjoying intercourse all, most, or some of the time; 83 percent reported the same degree of pleasure from receiving oral sex; and 63 percent enjoyed giving oral sex (Savitz & Rosen, 1988).

Another stereotype about female prostitutes—that is, that most are lesbians—is also not supported by research. Most female prostitutes consider themselves heterosexual or bisexual, not homosexual (Diana, 1985; Savitz & Rosen, 1988). Prostitutes sometimes engage in sex with another woman in response to a customer's desires; for example, a male-female couple may hire a prostitute to have sex with one or both of them.

gigolo A man who is paid to be a woman's escort and to provide her with sexual services; a kept man.

 **REALITY** or **MYTH** ? **6**

The financial fortune of prostitutes depends on how many tricks they can turn in a working day. (Call girls are typically an exception to this assembly-line approach because they are often hired for an entire evening by a customer.) The more customers a prostitute can bring to orgasm, the more money he or she makes. Thus after a client pays for a particular service, the prostitute generally attempts to bring the customer to orgasm as quickly as possible, usually after two to three minutes of sexual contact. The most frequently reported practice to accomplish this goal is oral sex, as cited by both prostitutes (Freund, Leonard, & Lee, 1989) and their customers (Wallace, Mann, & Beatrice, 1988). Most prostitutes prefer oral sex because it takes less effort than coitus, the next most common sexual practice. In third place is a "half and half": oral stimulation followed by coitus. These kinds of sexual contacts, along with the manual stimulation of customers' genitals, account for almost all sexual transactions between prostitutes and their clients. Vaginal intercourse is more likely to occur if the customer is a regular client, that is, has frequent sexual contacts with the same prostitute over a long period of time—specifically, one to three times a week over 1 to 14 years (Freund et al., 1989).

The number of customers whom a prostitute services in a working day or night varies greatly, depending on such factors as client availability, the prostitute's mood, and negative characteristics of a potential customer. Published accounts indicate an average of 4 to 12 sexual encounters per workday (Diana, 1985; Freund et al., 1989). The large number of sexual contacts, of course, puts the prostitute (and customer) at an elevated risk of contracting STDs if they do not use condoms. The specter of fatal illness has altered the sexual practices of prostitutes, with many now regularly employing condoms and abstaining from high-risk sexual behaviors (Earls & David, 1989; Freund et al., 1989). Condom use in sexual encounters has been reported by 38 percent to 74 percent of prostitutes (Cohen, Hauer, Poole, & Wofsy, 1987; Freund et al., 1989; Wallace et al., 1988). Condom use varies depending on the sexual activity. Of male clients of female streetwalkers, 72 percent of the clients reported using condoms during vaginal intercourse, and 33 percent reported doing so during oral sex (Freund, Lee, & Leonard, 1991).

PROSTITUTION AND THE LAW.

Legal definitions of prostitution vary from one time and place to another, but they generally include some notion of indiscriminate sexual activity or promiscuity as well as barter. State legal codes typically forbid making money from the provision of sexual fulfillment. For example, a 1968 ruling of the supreme court of Oregon stated: "The feature which distinguishes a prostitute from other women who engage in illicit intercourse is the indiscrimination with which she offers herself to men for hire" (Rosenbleet & Pariente, 1973, p. 381). Prostitution and commercialized vice include sex offenses such as (1) prostitution; (2) keeping a **brothel**—a house where prostitutes and customers meet for sexual activity; (3) **pandering** or **procuring**—serving as a go-between in commercial sexual transactions (also called pimping), transporting, or detaining women for immoral purposes; and (4) all attempts to commit any of the preceding (Maguire & Pastore, 1995).

Every state in the United States has laws regulating prostitution, soliciting for prostitution, or loitering for the purpose of prostitution. Nevada is the only state in which counties are given the option to allow prostitution, and several do. These counties, however, confine prostitution to brothels and have laws against soliciting customers in other vicinities.

The frequency of this "criminal" violation, and the numbers of men and women involved in it, are difficult to estimate. Prostitution is not an offense reported by a victim or complaint, and hence the statistics based on arrests are not a clear reflection of

ISSUES TO CONSIDER

If a man or a woman engages in sex with another person in exchange for a favor, a promotion, influence, or dinner, is this prostitution?

brothel A house where prostitutes and customers meet for sexual activity.

pandering Serving as a go-between in commercial sexual transactions; generally pimping or procuring.

procuring Obtaining customers for a prostitute.

the incidence of this activity. Arrests tend to be sporadic, and differences in the number of arrests from one locality to another may reflect the attitude of local law enforcement officials rather than the incidence of prostitution.

[Prostitution represents the only sexual offense for which women are prosecuted more often than are men.] In 1994 there were more than 95,000 arrests for prostitution and commercialized vice in the United States (Maguire & Pastore, 1995). The fact that a disproportionate number of Blacks were arrested (46 percent) probably reflects prostitution's link to economic factors. Those individuals who are arrested for prostitution are usually streetwalkers, who tend to come from the lower socioeconomic strata of our society.

Enforcement agents often deploy a vice-squad undercover officer to pose as a **john**—a slang term for a prostitute's customer. The prostitute is arrested when she offers a sexual service for a price. To avoid arrest, the experienced prostitute is careful about how she words her proposition to a potential customer. She may ask him whether he wants a good time or some fun. She also approaches the matter of her fees in a roundabout way. If a prostitute is arrested and convicted, she is usually fined but typically does not spend much time in jail. Either her pimp or a friend usually secures bail money. Fines tend to be minimal and jail sentences short.

Patronizing a prostitute is illegal in some states, but there has been little concerted effort to prosecute customers. In some states, however, the patron of prostitution does

john A slang term for the customer of a prostitute.

Figure 12.7
"Tiny Annie" and Her Friends These streetwalker children are seeking customers in Seattle, Washington. Tiny Annie was reported to say, "For a blow-job, it would be $30 on up and for a lay it would be $40 on up. Most of these [veteran] ho's charge more than us little kids do."

Across Cultures

Japanese Telephone Clubs That Offer Sex with Girls

Japanese school girls have found an occupation to increase their ability to buy high-status objects such as Chanel perfume and designer clothes. As one 16-year-old girl put it, "Girls in my school tend to be split up into the girls who have such things and those who don't. If you have the brand-name things, you're important" (Stroh, 1996). To acquire these things, some girls participate in "telephone clubs" where they can call men and decide after talking with them whether to meet them for sex. The girls can earn up to $1,000 from each liaison with an older man.

These telephone clubs started appearing in the mid-1980s. In the past few years, the number of these clubs across Japan has increased to more than 2,200. A recent survey indicated that as many as 25 percent of high school girls had called a telephone club at least once (Stroh, 1996). The system works like this: Men pay about $20 to rent small rooms in the clubs where they can watch TV and wait for girls to call them. The girls call toll-free numbers advertised in public phone booths and on packets of tissues that are distributed on street corners.

In 1995, about 1,500 men were arrested for having sex with teenage girls they met through telephone clubs, and more than 5,000 girls aged 18 and younger were questioned for involvement in sex-related offenses and prostitution (which is illegal in Japan)—a 16 percent increase from the previous year (Stroh, 1996). In 1996, a school principal near Tokyo was arrested for running a prostitution ring involving 280 14- to 17-year-old girls.

face a fine of $500 or more and a year or more in jail. A customer is most likely to be arrested when a female police officer poses as a prostitute and entices him into asking for a sexual service and offering money for it. The punishment for pimping is much more severe than that for prostitution, although few pimps are arrested.

It is the working man or woman in the prostitution network who bears the brunt of legal penalties. To protect themselves, many prostitutes have joined the local and national unions that have emerged in North America and Western Europe. The decriminalization of prostitution would have a number of advantages for the prostitute and for society. City and state governments spend a great deal of money trying to control prostitution, with little success (Boles, 1998). If prostitution were legalized, pimps would likely lose much of their influence on the trade. Prostitutes could be licensed, taxed, and regularly examined for STDs. The civil rights of prostitutes and of their consenting adult clients could be protected. Children would also be barred from entering prostitution.

The lure of money for unskilled labor is often difficult to resist (see "Across Cultures: Japanese Telephone Clubs That Offer Sex with Girls"). One disturbing statistic is the increase in U.S. arrests for prostitution of those under 18 years of age. Between the 1960s and 1980s, the annual arrests for this age group shot up almost 400 percent (Maguire et al., 1992). In 1982 the U.S. General Accounting Office compiled a report on teenage prostitutes and estimated there were as many as 2.4 million adolescent prostitutes. Many of these children were runaways, some as young as 12 or 13, who were tempted or coerced into prostitution as a means of supporting themselves (see Figure 12.7).

BECOMING A PROSTITUTE.   A number of studies have been done to examine the factors or circumstances associated with a female's becoming a prostitute (Boles, 1998; Bullough & Bullough, 1996). Poverty, disenchantment with life prospects, a tedious job, failure in school, a turbulent home life, and physical and sexual abuse are some of the factors associated with entry into prostitution. Although these background conditions may predispose an individual toward prostitution, they are not sufficient to guarantee entry into the trade. If they were, there would be a lot more prostitutes, given the number of women who come from an impoverished background or who have experienced physical or sexual abuse.

What is necessary is contact with someone involved in the world of prostitution: a prostitute or pimp, or a bartender or hotel clerk. Through these associations, a female learns about the world of prostitution. If she decides to become part of this world, she typically develops a relationship with a pimp. She is taught the tricks of the trade: how to protect herself from disease, dangerous customers, and police officers, and how to do the least amount of work for the most money. In one study of two hundred street prostitutes, almost 80 percent reported having started prostitution as juveniles. About one-third of these women also reported having been involved as juveniles in sexually explicit activity that was photographed. Contrary to the popular notion, "once a prostitute, always a prostitute," the average span of a prostitute's career is about five years (Potterat, Woodhouse, Muth, & Muth, 1990).

Like their female counterparts, male prostitutes often come from a background of poverty, strained parental relations, poor education, and little or no work experience (Boles, 1998). If they seek or are exposed to experienced hustlers or customers, they may choose to enter the trade. Unlike female prostitutes, they usually do not have a pimp, and they are not trained or supervised in the trade. They learn how to hustle by observation and through interaction with other hustlers and customers (Calhoun & Weaver, 1996).

THE PROSTITUTE'S CLIENTELE.

The clients of prostitutes have not been studied thoroughly. Kinsey and his colleagues (1948) found that about 69 percent of the White men in their sample had had some sexual experience with prostitutes. Many of these men reported only one or two experiences. Laumann et al.'s (1994) data indicated that the use of prostitutes' services appears to be on the decline. Only 3 percent of men in the study reported that their first coitus was with a paid partner.

Using peepholes, one-way mirrors, and other observation posts more than two decades ago, Stein (1974) witnessed hundreds of sessions between cooperating prostitutes and their clients. She described the men whom she observed:

> At first I looked for signs of "abnormality" in the clients. I felt that any man who paid for sex must be some kind of "loser." I was disappointed. I saw a few "losers," of course, but most of the clients were agreeable, reasonably attractive, upper-middle-class men, businessmen or professionals. (p. 10)

Studies of massage-parlor patrons on the West Coast (Armstrong, 1978) and in Illinois (Simpson & Schill, 1977) indicated that the typical customer appeared to be indistinguishable from the average U.S. male. Interviews with 30 johns who had paid for sex an average of 50 times revealed that almost all were involved in personal relationships that included sexual activity. They purchased sex by choice rather than out of necessity (Holzman & Pines, 1982). In their association with prostitutes, many of these men experienced feelings and displayed behaviors that were typical of regular courtships. For example, before meeting a prostitute, they attempted to make themselves physically appealing by bathing, dressing fashionably, and using cologne. Many were aroused by the potential adventure and danger of associating with a prostitute.

Across Cultures

Sex Tourism

Sexual tourism has received increasing recognition in the news media. Many Japanese, North American, Australian, and European men travel to places such as Thailand to view sex shows, purchase erotic materials, and engage in sex. The promotion of Thailand as a tourist sexual resort has been looked on tolerantly by government officials, who view it as an economic asset (Manderson, 1995). Although there are other countries in which sex tourism is promoted, Thailand has remained a major destination for men seeking sexual adventure. Manderson (1995) described the atmosphere in the Patpong area of Bangkok, the capital of Thailand. This is an area of nightclubs, drinking lounges, and go-go bars. Most of the sex performances are oriented toward heterosexual males, although transvestite, transsexual, and same-gender sex workers are also part of the panorama.

Most sex performances take place in the bars. Customers are expected to buy the "bar girls" a drink. If they negotiate sex, they pay the bar a "fine," and then the sex workers receive a set fee (half of which goes to the brothel keeper) and possibly a tip.

On stage, women engage in a variety of sexually exotic acts. Single acts include using the vagina to smoke cigarettes, open bottles of soft drinks, pick up sushi with chopsticks partially inserted in the vagina, and many other similar demonstrations. Duo acts may be faked but also include heterosexual and lesbian sexual interaction. "Heterosexual acts work through a menu of poses that display penile length, stroke-style, female agility, usually without ejaculation because there are often several performances in an evening. Lesbian sex involves caressing, tribadism, and cunnilingus" (Manderson, 1995, p. 313).

There are many harmful aspects to this sex industry such as young children from poor families being sold to sexual entrepreneurs who immerse them in the world of prostitution. In addition, it is estimated that a majority of these commercial sex workers are infected with HIV. Such an environment presents a true health hazard. What has been promoted as a sexual paradise for tourists can become a sexual hell for those who contract incurable STDs.

Freund et al.'s (1991) interviewers approached men in their cars, sometimes with introductions by prostitutes, and obtained responses from 101 male clients of prostitutes. These men averaged about 40 years of age (ranging from 21 to 72). Their ethnic background was similar to that of the general population in the area (Camden, New Jersey), and they reported an average of about five years of paying for sex. Most were regular clients, with 93 percent reporting visits monthly or more frequently and 63 percent seeing a prostitute weekly or more frequently. About half had had sex with the same prostitute or the same small group of prostitutes. (See "Across Cultures: Sex Tourism.")

A FINAL NOTE.   Prostitution exists because of the market for it. The same statement applies to erotica and other uses of sex for profit by advertisers and movie and video producers. People are often attracted to participation in erotic or pornographic ventures or to prostitution because these enterprises provide more income than they imagine they might be able to obtain through other employment. Their motivation is, of course, the same one that prompts people to offer any service for which there is a societal demand. Viewing or using erotica or sexual aids by oneself or with a steady partner may continue to flourish because these activities do not expose people to AIDS. In contrast, the novelty or adventure associated with buying sexual intimacy from prostitutes will likely be tempered by the possibility of contracting a fatal disease. In the next chapter, appropriately, we turn to a discussion of STDs, with a large proportion of the analysis devoted to the impact of AIDS.

Summary of Major Points

1. Soft-core and hard-core erotica.

Materials designed to elicit sexual arousal can be divided into soft-core and hard-core erotica. Soft-core magazines endured substantial losses in readership in the 1980s. Part of this decline is probably attributable to the greater availability of hard-core or X-rated materials and increased sales of sexually explicit videocassette films that consumers can view in the privacy of the home.

2. Sex and the consumer.

Sexuality is a major theme in the U.S. marketplace. It is a staple of television programming and permeates advertising. The images used by advertisers and filmmakers glamorize sex without mentioning the possible consequences of sexual activity. Erotic products, advertisements, and services can be found in magazines, newspapers, theaters, and adult bookstores. Consumers can purchase sexual services through telephone sex, strip shows, theaters, or bars.

3. Obscenity.

For material to be considered obscene, it must meet three essential criteria: (1) it must be offensive to contemporary community standards, (2) its dominant theme must appeal to prurient interest in sex, and (3) the work must be devoid of serious literary, artistic, political, or scientific value. In 1987 the Supreme Court ruled that the proper application of community standards is not whether most people in a locality would find literary, artistic, political, or scientific value in allegedly obscene material but whether a reasonable person would find such value in the material taken as a whole.

4. Effects of erotica.

The evidence indicates that most forms of erotica do not trigger sexual aggression in or cause harm to observers. Two exceptions may be violent erotica and child pornography.

5. Violent erotica.

Researchers have concluded that the majority of college men do not find violent pornography as arousing as depictions of consensual relationships. A sizable minority of men, however, are more aroused by aggressive sexual depictions than by consensual erotica; such responses are also characteristic of convicted rapists.

6. Children and erotica.

The Supreme Court ruled in 1982 that states may prosecute the publishers and sellers of child erotica without having to prove that their materials are legally obscene. Because children are not legally capable of informed consent, those adults who pay, entice, or coerce them to engage in sexual activity can be prosecuted under child abuse laws.

7. Prostitution.

Prostitution has flourished since the beginning of recorded history. Most of its practitioners have come from impoverished backgrounds. Every state in the nation has laws regulating prostitution. Usually the prostitute rather than the customer is prosecuted. Some prostitutes have organized unions that provide services to improve the working conditions of prostitutes.

CHECK YOUR KNOWLEDGE

1. Pornography refers to sexual material that (a) depicts violence, (b) the Supreme Court considers illegal, (c) is not acceptable to the viewer, (d) explicitly depicts the genitals or sexual acts. **(p. 297)**

2. Sex on prime-time television usually depicts couples who are (a) married, (b) using birth control effectively, (c) unmarried, (d) using birth control ineffectively. **(p. 299)**

3. Most X-rated movies are (a) more violent than other types of commercial films (e.g., R-rated films), (b) representative in their depiction of sexually liberated women, (c) watched primarily by men, (d) illegal in most states. **(p. 300)**

4. In *Roth* v. *United States,* the U.S. Supreme Court defined as essential criteria for obscenity all of the following *except* (a) it must be offensive to community standards, (b) the dominant theme of the work must appeal to prurient interest in sex, (c) it must not depict sexually stimulated genitals, (d) it must be devoid of serious literary, artistic, political, or scientific value. **(p. 305)**

5. Research on the relationship between viewing erotica and rape suggests that (a) most men would commit rape if they were certain of not getting caught; (b) when female victims are shown as enjoying forced sex, male aggression (as measured by electric shock) decreases; (c) most men report having more sexual fantasies after exposure to a depiction of rape than before; (d) some rape depictions produce sexual arousal in noncoercive men. **(pp. 307–308)**

6. These are usually the most financially successful prostitutes: (a) commercial beavers, (b) call girls, (c) massage parlor employees, (d) streetwalkers. **(p. 313)**

7. The male equivalent of a call girl is a (a) gigolo, (b) bisexual prostitute, (c) homosexual hustler, (d) dominatrix. **(p. 314)**

8. Legal penalties for prostitution are most likely to be given to (a) prostitutes, (b) pimps, (c) customers, (d) brothel owners. **(pp. 316–317)**

13

SEXUALLY TRANSMITTED DISEASES

ATTITUDES TOWARD SEXUALLY TRANSMITTED DISEASES

Attitudes Toward People with STDs

Health: How Accurate Is Your Knowledge of AIDS?

The Relationship of AIDS Knowledge and Attitudes

Attempts to Reduce STD Transmission

BACTERIAL INFECTIONS

Gonorrhea

Syphilis

Chlamydia and Nongonococcal Urethritis (NGU)

Research Controversy: Ethical Principles and the Tuskegee Study

Cystitis

Prostatitis

Other Bacterial Infections

Pelvic Inflammatory Disease (PID)

ACQUIRED IMMUNODEFICIENCY SYNDROME (AIDS)

Highlight: An Epidemic of Stigma

Prevalence

Causes

Risk Factors

Symptoms

Diagnosis

Opportunistic Infections

Treatment

Health: Being Tested for HIV Antibodies

Protection Against AIDS

OTHER VIRAL STDS

Herpes Simplex Type II

Genital Warts/Human Papilloma Virus

Hepatitis B

PARASITIC INFECTIONS

Candidiasis

Trichomoniasis

Pediculosis Pubis

SAFER-SEX PRACTICES: REDUCING THE RISK OF CONTRACTING STDS

Relationship Negotiation

Other Practices That Reduce Risk

SUMMARY OF MAJOR POINTS

CHECK YOUR KNOWLEDGE

REALITY or MYTH ?

1 People are more knowledgeable about HIV/AIDS than they are about other sexually transmitted diseases (STDs).

2 Most cases of gonorrhea take several years to be cured even with proper medical treatment.

3 Brain damage can be one of the results of untreated syphilis.

4 All babies born from mothers infected with HIV/AIDS contract HIV/AIDS themselves.

5 Blood transfusions are responsible for causing about half of all AIDS cases in the United States.

6 There is a vaccine for hepatitis B virus.

SEXUAL intimacy can be a source of ecstatic pleasure, but it also carries the risk of exposure to infection from sexually transmitted diseases (STDs). *STD* is the term used to describe more than 25 infectious organisms that are transmitted through sexual activity and the many disorders that they cause. More than 12 million Americans contract an STD each year; many result in severe consequences if left untreated, including infertility, ectopic pregnancy, cancer, and even death. Two-thirds of STD cases afflict persons under 25 years old, and 3 million teenagers become infected each year with STDs (Tanfer, Cubbins, & Billy, 1995).

We begin this chapter by examining how attitudes about sexuality and morality may increase the likelihood of contracting and transmitting STDs. Then we review the common STDs and genital infections and discuss measures that reduce the risk of contracting or transmitting an STD.

ATTITUDES TOWARD SEXUALLY TRANSMITTED DISEASES

Some years ago, an anthropologist (Miner, 1956) wrote a description of a people called the Nacirema. These people were notable for their obsessive rituals and their worship at altars made of large white bowls on pedestals of varying heights. Each Nacirema family owned at least three of these bowls, sometimes as many as ten, and they engaged in rituals in front of them half a dozen or more times a day. The cleanliness rituals they performed were thought to bring moral goodness.

Nacirema is *American* spelled backward. Indeed, our culture places a high premium on cleanliness, health, and physical beauty. From childhood on, hygiene and health are linked to moral goodness, and dirtiness is linked to disease. Although the emphasis on hygienic practices is valuable in reducing sickness and increasing longevity, some negative side effects are associated with our national obsession with cleanliness and health. Among these are the counterproductive personal and societal responses to STDs, which originate in our linking of dirt and disease with sin and sexuality and usually begin in childhood (see Chapter 9).

When a person contracts an STD (formerly called a venereal disease, or VD), the rational response is to have it diagnosed and treated immediately and to notify partners so that they may do the same. The shame and embarrassment associated with STDs, however, often inhibit reasonable and healthy responses to dealing with these infections and infestations.

It is important for sexually active people to obtain diagnosis and treatment of any suspicious symptoms because most STDs are readily cured in their early stages. Further, the partners of a person with an STD must be informed that they have been exposed because as many as 80 percent of women and many men may be **asymptomatic** with some of the STDs (Fact Sheet, 1997). Failure to obtain early diagnosis and treatment can lead to various medical problems, including sterility and even death. Because of the high proportion of asymptomatic infections, sexually active people should be tested for STDs during annual pelvic (female) or urologic (male) examinations.

asymptomatic (A-symp-toe-MAH-tik) Without recognizable symptoms.

Many people who are diagnosed as having an STD are reluctant to name their partners to physicians or clinic personnel. On one level, it is quite understandable that they would rather deliver the bad news themselves. Instead of doing so, however, these individuals may indirectly attempt to discover whether the partner has any symptoms of the particular disease. If the partner appears to be healthy, they may decide to avoid disclosing their own infection, on the assumption that the partner did not catch it. In the case of a marital partner who contracts an STD during extramarital relations, fear of seriously disrupting or even destroying the marriage may dissuade him or her from informing an apparently healthy spouse.

The absence of recognizable symptoms does not provide insurance that the partner does not have the genital infection. Gonorrhea, for example, is notoriously "silent" in women, with an estimated 80 percent having no recognizable symptoms during the early, and readily treatable, stages of the infection. Many men are also asymptomatic.

Attitudes Toward People with STDs

In addition to dealing with the medical consequences of STDs, infected persons experience difficult psychological reactions. They have lowered self-esteem, feelings of isolation and loss of control, and a negative body image (Catotti, Clarke, & Catoe, 1993; Perlow & Perlow, 1983). Some of the negative psychological reactions and feelings of psychological isolation that infected persons experience may stem from expectations that others will reject them—a fear that may be realistic.

All sexually active people are at risk of contracting STDs, however, and extensive education of the general public and complete reporting by STD patients are important for controlling the spread of these diseases. Sexually active people can also take responsibility for controlling STDs by getting themselves screened annually or whenever changing sexual partners. A person who contracts an STD should tell his or her sexual partners so that they can be tested and, if necessary, treated. After treatment for a curable STD, patients should be retested to be sure that they no longer have the STD.

Some STDs are not curable; the most notable contemporary example, of course, is AIDS. The deaths of such public figures as actor Rock Hudson and pianist Liberace and the spread of AIDS among highly visible heterosexuals such as basketball star Magic Johnson have done what the deaths of thousands of anonymous AIDS victims were not able to do: spurred governmental and public response to the epidemic (Moskowitz, Binson, & Catania, 1997; Shilts, 1987). A film, *And the Band Played On*, based on Randy Shilts's gripping and well-documented book, was released on video in 1993, and we highly recommend it, especially for students interested in the worldwide competition among public health researchers attempting to deal with the spread of AIDS. Shilts died of complications from AIDS in 1994 (see Figure 13.1).

Figure 13.1
Randy Shilts Randy Shilts was an investigative reporter whose book, *And the Band Played On*, documented the search for the cause of AIDS.

Health

How Accurate Is Your Knowledge of HIV/AIDS?

In responding to these questions, put a T (true) or F (false) in front of each statement.

1. AIDS is caused by bacteria.

2. AIDS can be inherited.

3. A healthy person who is HIV-positive can transmit HIV to another person.

4. HIV can be transmitted through semen.

5. Unlike the common cold, HIV cannot be transmitted through the open air.

6. AIDS can be treated in its earliest stage with penicillin.

7. A pregnant woman who has HIV can give it to her baby.

8. Most people can tell by someone's physical appearance if that person is HIV-infected.

9. Using latex condoms properly reduces the risk of getting HIV/AIDS.

10. A vaccine for AIDS will be available for the general population within a year.

The Relationship of AIDS Knowledge and Attitudes

STD research recently has primarily focused on students' attitudes and knowledge about AIDS, undoubtedly due to the devastating impact of this infection compared to infection with other STDs. However, much of what we have learned about the social dimensions of AIDS is also applicable to other STDs. Before reading further, you may wish to take the test on AIDS knowledge above ("Health: How Accurate Is Your Knowledge of HIV/AIDS?") to see how well informed you are. After you have finished reading the chapter, go back to the test to see how accurate your knowledge was.

Studies of Americans, from teenagers through the elderly, show that people are more knowledgeable about HIV and AIDS than they are about other STDS (Benton, Mintzes, Kendrick, & Solomon, 1993; Brown, DiClemente, & Beausoleil, 1992; Sweat & Lein, 1995). Younger people are generally more knowledgeable about AIDS than older people. There are few ethnic or racial differences in HIV/AIDS knowledge when socioeconomic status (SES) is controlled. That is, people of lower SES have less knowledge about HIV/AIDS than do people of higher SES regardless of their ethnic or racial background (Sweat & Lein, 1995).

What is the effect of being knowledgeable about HIV/AIDS? Researchers have shown that HIV/AIDS knowledge is consistently related to behavior change and lower rates of unsafe sexual activity (Caron, Davis, Wynn, & Roberts, 1992; Fisher & Fisher, 1992; Mickler, 1993). The relationship between knowledge and altered risk behavior, however, is not a very strong one.

College students are generally knowledgeable about AIDS and HIV, but most report that they take no special precautions against HIV infection. Although this does not mean that knowledge is unimportant, it highlights the need for HIV/AIDS education to do more than simply promote information and dispel myths about AIDS. To address this issue, education programs have been developed to increase student involvement and motivation and to teach them the necessary behavioral skills to reduce unsafe sexual behaviors. Peer counseling, group discussions, role playing, sexual assertiveness training, and skill training have been used successfully to reduce risky sexual behaviors (Sikkema, Winnett, & Lombard, 1995; Smith & Katner, 1995; Weisse, Turbiasz & Witney, 1995). Effective AIDS education appears to be best served by programs that combine these strategies with providing accurate information.

ISSUES TO CONSIDER

What would you include in the design of an educational program to prevent unsafe sexual activities?

Attempts to Reduce STD Transmission

In addition to education programs, public health authorities have employed numerous approaches to try to alter sexual practices and thereby reduce the spread of AIDS and other STDs. However, behavior change among sexually active heterosexual adolescents and young adults has been difficult to achieve (Fisher & Fisher, 1992; Melnick et al., 1993). For example, a national survey of college students revealed that nearly 50 percent of the heterosexual respondents reported multiple sexual partners and that approximately 60 percent used condoms less than half the time when they engaged in sexual intercourse (DiClemente, Forrest, & Mickler, 1990).

More recent surveys of adolescents, however, show that they have made moderate changes in their sexual practices or contraceptives in response to the AIDS epidemic. For example, condom use has increased among high school and college students (Ashcraft & Schlueter, 1996; CDC, 1995; Tanfer, Cubbins, & Billy, 1995).

ISSUES TO CONSIDER

Given the percentages of people who report having lied to obtain sex, what steps would you take to determine the truthfulness of a potential sexual partner about the person's STD status?

When behavior changes are made, the most commonly reported are reducing the number of sex partners and being more careful in partner selection (Melnick et al., 1993). Taking care in partner selection is no guarantee of freedom from risk, however (Misovich, Fisher, & Fisher, 1996). Not all people tell the truth. In their study of college students, Cochran and Mays (1990) found that 34 percent of men and 10 percent of women reported having lied to have sex. Further, about 20 percent of the men said that to get sex, they would lie about having tested negative for HIV antibodies.

In a survey of adolescents, Ralph DiClemente (1989) found that a perception of susceptibility to HIV infection was strongly associated with a reduction in high-risk behaviors. Compared to their White counterparts, minority adolescents regarded themselves as less susceptible to AIDS (Mays & Cochran, 1988). In Jeff Fisher's (1988) study of potential factors affecting condom use among adolescents, perceived peer-group behavior was the only factor that differentiated adolescents who used condoms from those who did not. Those who viewed their peers as supporting condom use were almost twice as likely to report using condoms.

In a longitudinal study of gay men, Joseph and coworkers (1987) reported that, even among adults, the belief that one's friends were adopting recommended behavior changes was positively and consistently related to adopting safer-sex practices, becoming monogamous, and reducing the number of partners and the frequency of sexual activity. The authors suggested that "the norms shared within a network . . . may be the most important in influencing the adoption of behaviors consistent with risk reduction" (Joseph et al., 1987, p. 86).

Despite all efforts to reduce their spread, people still contract STDs. We turn now to the symptoms, consequences, and treatment of specific STDs (see Table 13.1), including diseases and infections caused by bacteria, viruses, and parasites. Of these, viral infections are the most problematic because they cannot be killed by antibiotics.

BACTERIAL INFECTIONS

Bacteria are one-celled organisms that can be seen only through a microscope. STDs caused by bacteria are relatively easy to cure. They include gonorrhea, syphilis, chlamydia, nongonococcal urethritis, cystitis, prostatitis, gardnerella vaginalis, shigellosis, and chancroid.

Table 13.1   Symptoms of Sexually Transmitted Diseases and Genital Infections

Bacterial Infections	Annual Estimated Incidence	Symptoms
Gonorrhea	800,000	*In males:* painful urination; smelly, thick, yellow urethral discharge, appearing 2 to 10 days after sex with infected person. *In females:* vaginal discharge; some pain during urination; mild pelvic discomfort and/or abnormal menstruation (but most women are asymptomatic).
Syphilis	101,000	Hard, round, painless sore or chancre with raised edges that appears 2 weeks to a month after contact.
Chlamydia and nongonococcal urethritis (NGU)	4,000,000	*In females:* mild irritation in the genitals; itching and burning during urination; some cervical swelling (but most women are asymptomatic). *In males:* thin, relatively clear, whitish discharge; mild discomfort during urination 1 to 3 weeks after contact.
Cystitis		Painful urination; lower back pain; constant urge to urinate.
Prostatitis		Groin and lower back pain; fever; burning sensation during and following ejaculation; thin mucous discharge from urethra before first morning urination. Prostatitis can be either congestive (from infrequent ejaculation) or infectious (from *E. coli* bacteria).
Gardnerella vaginalis		Leukorrhea and unpleasant odor.
Shigellosis	24,000	Pain; fever; diarrhea; inflammation of the mucous membranes of the large intestines; sometimes vomiting and a burning sensation in the anus.
Pelvic inflammatory disease (PID)	1,000,000	Intense lower abdominal and/or back pain; tenderness and fever; pain when cervix is moved from side to side. Symptoms usually develop within weeks after the STD that causes PID is contracted.

Viral Infections	Annual Estimated Incidence	Symptoms
Acquired immunodeficiency syndrome (AIDS)	80,000	Swollen lymph nodes; unexplained weight loss; loss of appetite; persistent fevers or night sweats; chronic fatigue; unexplained diarrhea; bloody stools; unexplained bleeding from any body opening; skin rashes; easy bruising; persistent, severe headaches; chronic, dry cough not caused by smoking or a cold; chronic, whitish coating on the tongue or throat.
Herpes simplex type II (genital herpes)	200,000–500,000	Small blisters on the genitals or vulva, developing 3 to 7 days after contact. After tingling, itching, and creating a burning sensation, they break open and spread.
Genital warts (HPV)	500,000–1,000,000	Soft, pink, painless single or multiple growths resembling cauliflowers on the genitals or vulva.
Hepatitis B		Nausea; vomiting; fatigue; mental depression; jaundice; dark urine.

Gonorrhea

gonorrhea An STD caused by the bacterium *Neisseria gonorrhoeae.*

Gonorrhea ("clap," "drip") infection is caused by gonococcus bacteria (*Neisseria gonorrhoeae*), which thrive on mucous membranes in the mouth, vagina, cervix, urethra, and anus. The bacteria can be acquired by kissing or engaging in oral, anal, or vaginal sex with an infected person. Although the bacteria from urethral discharge can survive for up to 24 hours on towels and toilet seats (Neinstein, Goldering, & Carpenter, 1984), transmission from these sources has not been demonstrated. The probability of contracting gonorrhea from having intercourse once with an infected partner is about 50 percent for women and 20 percent for men, and the risk increases with each additional sexual contact. In their national sample, Laumann et al. (1994) found that the self-reported lifetime incidence (the number of people who said that they had the disease at least once) of gonorrhea among participants was 6.6 percent.

REALITY or **MYTH** ? **2**

There is little need to worry about the effects of gonorrhea if it is diagnosed and treated quickly. Gonorrhea symptoms usually appear within 2 to 10 days after intimate contact with an infected person. Symptoms in men include painful urination and a smelly urethral discharge that is thick and yellow (see Figure 13.2). Some men experience no symptoms or discomfort, however. Of women who contract gonorrhea, 80 percent have mild symptoms or no symptoms at all. Symptoms in the remaining 20 percent of women include altered vaginal discharge, some pain during urination, mild pelvic discomfort, and/or abnormal menstruation.

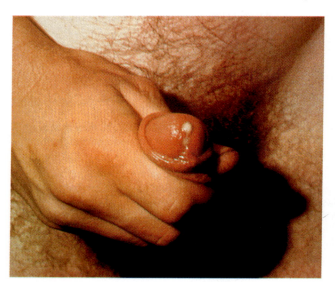

Figure 13.2
Gonorrhea Symptoms Symptoms of gonorrhea include a yellowish discharge from the urethra and painful urination.

Gonorrhea is treated with antibiotics, which usually efficiently kill the bacteria. A follow-up test should be performed to ensure a successful cure. Gonorrhea strains that are resistant to antibiotics appear to be increasing and account for more than 5 percent of all gonorrhea cases in the United States (Aral & Holmes, 1991). Men engaging in high-risk sexual behaviors are more likely to contract antibiotic-resistant forms of gonorrhea. People who have been cured are not immune to future infection. Thus, another reason that a sexual partner with gonorrhea should be examined and treated is to avoid reinfecting a partner who has been cured.

If not diagnosed and treated within a few weeks, gonorrhea can have serious complications. In males, these may include infection of the prostate, testes, and epididymis, potentially causing sterility. The bladder, kidneys, and rectum of males and females may also be infected with gonorrhea. In females, untreated gonorrhea and other infections may produce pelvic inflammatory disease (see p. 332). Furthermore, women may pass untreated gonorrhea to a baby during childbirth, possibly causing blindness in the infant.

Syphilis

syphilis An STD caused by the bacterium *Treponema pallidum.*
chancre (SHANG-ker) A dull-red, painless, hard, round ulcer with raised edges that forms where the spirochete causing syphilis enters a person's body.

Syphilis is caused by a spirochete, a tiny, corkscrew-shaped bacterium named *Treponema pallidum.* Transmitted through intimate sexual contact with an infected person, syphilis first produces a usually painless **chancre,** a hard, round, dull-red sore or ulcer with raised edges. A chancre can form in the mouth, vagina, urethra, or rectum, or on the anus, external genitals, or nipples, so almost any act of sexual intimacy with a person who has infectious syphilis can allow the microorganism to invade the uninfected person. The probability of infection from one contact with a syphilis carrier is about 30 percent. Less than 1 percent of Laumann et al.'s (1994) national sample reported having been diagnosed with syphilis during their lifetime.

The chancre typically appears two weeks to a month after exposure to an infectious case of syphilis (see Figure 13.3). Because it is usually painless, a female may not realize that she has the chancre if it breaks out in the vagina, on the cervix, or in the rectum. Similarly, if the chancre erupts within a male's urethra or rectum, he may be unaware of it. After several weeks, the chancre spontaneously disappears, often leaving syphilis patients with the false impression that they have no infection.

Syphilis is usually diagnosed through examination of a blood sample for antibodies. If syphilis is present, it is readily treated with a long-acting antibiotic different from the one used to treat gonorrhea. Just as with gonorrhea, exposure to syphilis does not ensure future immunity, so a treated person can be reinfected during subsequent sexual contact with a syphilis carrier.

If not treated, syphilis goes into a second stage, called secondary syphilis, about two weeks to two months after the chancre has healed. Secondary syphilis is characterized by a generalized body rash, sometimes accompanied by headache, fever, indigestion, sore throat, and pains in the joints or muscles. Syphilis is highly contagious during both its primary and secondary stages.

Following the secondary stage, a latent stage begins that can last for 1 to 40 years. It is called *latent* because no external symptoms are observable, but the spirochetes are nonetheless burrowing their way into internal organs such as the brain, spinal cord, bones, and bodily tissues. After syphilis has been latent for about a year, an untreated person is no longer infectious.

Finally, third-stage, or late, syphilis is reached by about a third to half of all untreated victims. Treatment even at this advanced stage can cure syphilis, but heart failure, loss of muscle control, blindness, deafness, brain damage, and other complications may have already occurred (see "Research Controversy: Ethical Principles and the Tuskegee Study," page 330).

Untreated syphilis can infect a fetus as well as the infected person and his or her sexual partner, because the spirochetes can cross the placental barrier after the sixteenth to eighteenth week of pregnancy. Thus all pregnant women should be tested for syphilis at the time of the first prenatal visit. Infected pregnant women are administered the same regimen of antibiotics as are infected nonpregnant women. After birth, their infants are also treated. In 90 percent of the cases in which a pregnant woman's syphilis is not treated during early pregnancy, the fetus is miscarried, stillborn, or born with congenital syphilis. The newborn can be treated to prevent further damage, but treatment will not undo the damage that has already been done, which may include partial blindness, deafness, and deformities of the bones and teeth.

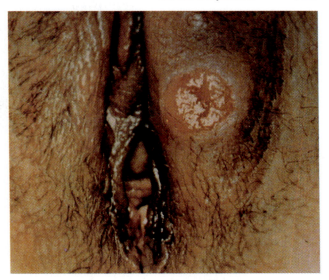

Figure 13.3
Syphilis Chancre The chancre is a painless sore that appears where the spirochete entered the body.

Chlamydia and Nongonococcal Urethritis (NGU)

The STD **chlamydia,** the source of many vaginal and urethral infections in women and men, is caused by *Chlamydia trachomatis* or T-strain *Mycoplasma,* which are both bacterial microorganisms. These bacteria were not identified until the 1970s. Before that time, infections that did not result from the gonococcus bacterium or other known organisms were diagnosed as **nongonococcal urethritis (NGU)** in men and as vaginitis

chlamydia (clah-MID-ee-uh) An STD, frequently asymptomatic in women, caused by the bacterium *Chlamydia trachomatis.*

Research Controversy

Ethical Principles and the Tuskegee Study

In 1932 the U.S. Public Health Service sponsored a research program in Tuskegee, Alabama, to study the long-term effects of untreated syphilis—a research project that exemplifies the violation of all four ethical principles of research (Jones, 1993). Syphilis is now easily cured in its early stages, but it can lead to mental and physical disability and death if left untreated.

In the 1930s mercury and two arsenic compounds were known to be effective in killing the bacteria that cause syphilis. Unfortunately, these drugs are also highly toxic, and patients experienced serious, and occasionally fatal, reactions to the drugs. When the study began, therefore, the treatments may have been worse than the disease, at least in the short term. The Tuskegee study, however, involved no treatment; its goal was to examine the long-term effects of untreated syphilis in Blacks (Jones, 1993).

To obtain research participants, the Public Health Service held meetings at Black schools and churches in Macon County, Alabama, at which it was announced that "government doctors" were giving free blood tests. As residents of one of the poorest counties in the South, most of the citizens had never even seen a doctor, much less been treated by one. The response to the announcement was overwhelmingly positive, and thus began one of the most tragic human studies of the twentieth century. Between 1932 and 1972, approximately 625 Black males in the county who were identified as having syphilis received blood tests and underwent physical examinations to determine the progression of the disease. This study may have had some ethical justification during the 1930s, when the treatment for syphilis was dangerous. But the withholding of treatment after 1943, the year in which it was discovered that penicillin could kill the bacteria without killing the victim, represented a serious violation of the risk-benefit principle.

The lack of ethical principles of the researchers became clear when the men visited local clinics for checkups for other disorders. The Public Health Service informed the attending physicians that the men were not to be treated for syphilis because they were part of an experiment; World War II military authorities dealing with draftees got similar instructions. The denial of effective treatment not only endangered the lives of the men being studied without their informed consent, but also resulted in the transmission of syphilis to their wives and of congenital syphilis to their children. The principle of informed consent was also seriously violated because the men did not even realize that effective treatment for syphilis was being withheld from them. They were told that they had "bad blood" and that they were being studied by the government.

Only 120 in the group were known to be still alive in 1974. Most of the remaining 500 or so syphilis victims could not be located and were presumed dead. In 1997, President Clinton formally apologized for the government's abuse to the eight people who were still alive. An award-winning HBO film, *Miss Evers' Boys,* depicts the events surrounding the Tuskegee study and is available on video.

---

nongonococcal urethritis (NGU) (non-GON-oh-KOK-al yur-ree-THRY-tis) A term for urethral infections in men that are usually caused by the chlamydia bacterium.

in women. Chlamydia in men is still frequently referred to as NGU, and about 40 percent of NGU cases are due to chlamydia infection (CDC, 1993). The self-reported lifetime incidence of both chlamydia and NGU is 3.2 percent (Laumann et al., 1994). With more than 4 million chlamydia infections reported annually, it is the most prevalent bacterial STD in the United States (DeLisle, 1997). As with gonorrhea, the risk for acquiring chlamydia from having intercourse once with an infected partner is greater for women (40 percent) than it is for men (20 percent).

Chlamydia is transmitted primarily through sexual contact, but it can be spread from one body site to another (e.g., by touching urethral discharge and then the eyes). It can also be transmitted nonsexually, through contact with the fingers or feces of an infected person. Symptoms generally appear one to three weeks after contact with the infection.

In males, chlamydia symptoms include a thin, relatively clear, whitish discharge. NGU may also trigger inflammation of the urethra and mild discomfort during urination, but approximately 50 percent of men have no symptoms or such mild ones that they do not seek treatment (DeLisle, 1997). Symptoms among the 25 percent of women who have them include mild irritation in the genitals, as well as itching and burning during urination.

Chlamydia and NGU can be treated effectively with antibiotics. If left undiagnosed and untreated, both can profoundly affect health and fertility. Infection of the epididymis in men and the fallopian tubes in women can create scar tissue that blocks the passage of sperm or egg, causing permanent sterility. Of infants born to women with untreated chlamydia, up to 20 percent become infected with chlamydia pneumonia, and up to 50 percent develop conjunctivitis, a serious eye infection. In fact, chlamydia is recognized as the greatest cause of preventable blindness in the world (DeLisle, 1986).

Cystitis

Cystitis is sometimes called honeymoon cystitis because it is often brought on by frequent or vigorous intercourse. This condition can occur in both men and women but is more common among women. It is caused by various bacteria, including *Escherichia (E.) coli,* which can be transmitted either nonsexually or sexually. Wiping from the anus toward the urethra (rather than the reverse) after a bowel movement may bring *E. coli* from the rectum to the urethral opening. Strenuous intercourse may have the same effect. Within a day or two after bacteria are introduced into the urethra, the person may experience a more or less constant urge to urinate, burning during urination, and pain in the lower back or abdomen. Sulfa drugs are usually effective in curing the condition, and drinking large quantities of fluids, including cranberry juice, helps to eliminate the infection.

> **cystitis** (sis-TYE-tis) A general term for any inflammation of the urinary bladder marked by pain and frequent urination.

For some unfortunate people, nine out of ten of whom are women, cystitis becomes chronic and is called interstitial cystitis (IC) (Webster, 1996). Almost half a million Americans suffer from IC. In addition to low back pain and the burning sensation associated with very frequent urination, many people with IC also must contend with painful intercourse. A variety of treatment approaches have been used to attempt to relieve the symptoms of IC, but no effective cure has been developed.

Prostatitis

Prostatitis refers to any infection or inflammation of the prostate gland. Prostatitis affects up to 40 percent of U.S. men. There are two major types: infectious prostatitis, caused by *E. coli* bacteria, and congestive prostatitis.

> **prostatitis** (praw-stay-TYE-tis) Inflammation of the prostate gland.

Infectious prostatitis can result from the transmission of bacteria during sexual contact. Celibate men can be afflicted with congestive prostatitis (technically not an STD), which may stem from infrequent ejaculation or abstention from sexual activity. Some men are asymptomatic, but when symptoms are present, they include pain in the groin and lower back, fever, and a burning sensation during and following ejaculation. Another symptom is a thin, watery discharge from the urethra in the morning before urinating. Infectious prostatitis is commonly treated with antibiotics, and the inflammation of the prostate can be reduced by palpating, or manipulating, that organ.

Other Bacterial Infections

gardnerella vaginalis Infection producing a thin, smelly discharge; afflicts both men and women.

shigellosis (SHIH-geh-LOW-sis) A form of dysentery (diarrhea) that can be transmitted by sexual contact.

chancroid (CANE-kroid) An STD characterized by soft, painful genital sores.

vaginitis (VAH-jih-NYE-tis) A general term for any inflammation of the vagina.

leukorrhea (LOO-kor-EE-ah) A whitish discharge from the vagina, often caused by a fungus infection.

Three other STDs caused by various bacteria are **gardnerella vaginalis, shigellosis,** and **chancroid.** Gardnerella vaginalis is sometimes referred to as **vaginitis;** however, this term is misleading. As with some other bacterial infections that are diagnosed as vaginitis, both males and females may contract and transmit these infections although it is more prevalent among women during their reproductive years.

Gardnerella vaginalis results in thin **leukorrhea,** which ranges in color from gray to greenish-yellow and has an unpleasant odor. It is treated by oral administration of the prescription drug Flagyl (metronidazole) to the infected woman and her partner. Men infected with gardnerella vaginalis are typically asymptomatic, but some men do develop symptoms, which include urethritis and inflammation of the foreskin or glans.

Shigellosis is an acute diarrheal disease that can be contracted through sexual contact or contact with feces carrying the bacteria. In the 1990s approximately 17,000 to 24,000 cases of shigellosis were reported annually in the United States (CDC, 1996). Oral stimulation of the anus of an individual with shigellosis exposes the stimulator to the disease. Pain, fever, diarrhea, and inflammation of the mucous membranes of the large intestine are among the symptoms of shigellosis. Shigellosis is diagnosed by culturing a stool specimen. It can be treated with ampicillin or tetracycline, although *Shigella* bacteria rapidly develop resistance to antibiotics.

The number of reported chancroid cases in the United States has been rising since the 1980s (CDC, 1993). About three to five days after contact, a small pimple surrounded by a reddened area appears at the site of infection, usually on the genitals. Within a day or two, it becomes filled with pus and breaks open to form irregular, soft ulcerations. The softness of the chancroid sores and their painfulness distinguish them from the hard and painless chancres of syphilis. In more than half of chancroid cases, the lymph nodes on the infected side of the groin become inflamed and swollen. These enlarged lymph nodes, called buboes, can rupture and ooze a thick, creamy pus. Diagnosis is made through physical examination. Treatment by antibiotics is highly effective.

Pelvic Inflammatory Disease (PID)

pelvic inflammatory disease (PID) Swelling and inflammation of the uterine tissues, fallopian tubes, and sometimes the ovaries.

The most common serious complication of untreated gonorrhea, chlamydia, and other genital infections in females is **pelvic inflammatory disease (PID).** About 2 percent of U.S. women aged 18 to 59 report having been diagnosed with PID. This translates into more than 2 million cases of PID annually in the United States (Laumann et al., 1994). In addition to the expense of diagnostic tests, doctor's office visits, medicine, hospitalization, surgical fees, and time lost from work, there are costs to PID sufferers that cannot be measured in dollar amounts. These include pain, anxiety, and the elevated risk of ectopic pregnancy and sterility.

PID develops when chlamydia, gonorrhea, or other infections move through the cervix to infect the uterine lining or fallopian tubes. PID can develop within weeks after a woman contracts the STD. Sexually active women who use oral contraceptives are half as likely to be hospitalized for PID as women who do not use contraception (Cates & Stone, 1992b). Smoking cigarettes and douching are also associated with an increased risk of contracting PID (Scholes et al., 1993).

Some women with acute PID experience intense lower abdominal pain, tenderness, and fever. These women are fortunate because their symptoms at least make it likely that the PID will be discovered and treated before permanent damage is done. Many women with acute PID have less well-defined symptoms and thus may not seek treatment. The vast majority of patients with acute PID respond quickly to treatment with antibiotics (DeLisle, 1997).

ACQUIRED IMMUNODEFICIENCY SYNDROME (AIDS)

The STDs discussed so far are caused by bacteria and are treated relatively easily. Scientists have not been as successful in finding cures for infections caused by viruses. In the past two decades, we have witnessed the rapid spread throughout the world of HIV, the virus that can lead to **acquired immunodeficiency syndrome (AIDS)** (see Figure 13.4). AIDS has been devastating not only in terms of its impact on patients and the family members and friends who love them, but also in terms of the increase in antigay discrimination that it has spawned (see "Highlight: An Epidemic

acquired immunodeficiency syndrome (AIDS) A virally caused condition in which severe suppression of the immune system reduces the body's ability to fight diseases.

Figure 13.4

HIV Infection Now and in the Future Throughout the world, more than 1.8 million people have been infected with HIV since the mid-1970s. The majority live in Africa, but Asia is estimated to become the next site of widespread infection. Experts expect the number of infections worldwide will exceed 40 million by the year 2000.

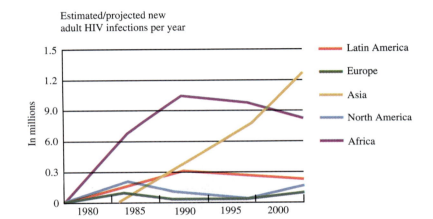

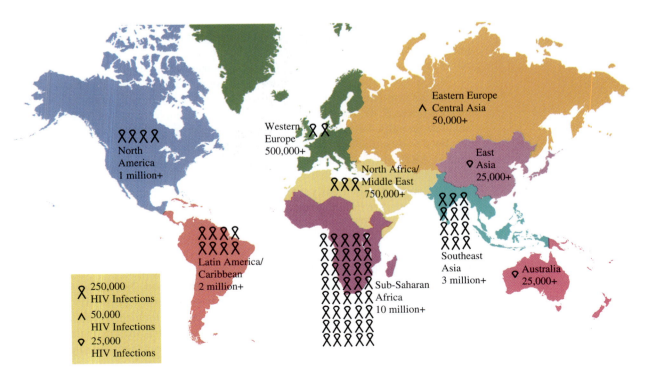

HIGHLIGHT

An Epidemic of Stigma

As we will see in the next chapter, Sexual Coercion, some of us have a tendency to blame the victim. This victim-blaming phenomenon has been seen in the responses of some people to other members of our society who have contracted HIV. Proposition 64, a referendum to quarantine people found to be HIV+ (positive), was placed on the ballot in the 1986 California election. Voters defeated the proposal, but the fact that many people favored such a quarantine—despite no evidence indicating that AIDS could be spread through casual contact—provides a vivid example of the way in which society sometimes blames the victim.

In an article from which we have taken the title for this box, researchers Gregory Herek and Eric Glunt (1988) quoted several instances in which discriminatory behavior appeared to be stimulated by the stigma associated with AIDS.

In White Plains, New York, a mail carrier refused to deliver mail to an AIDS Task Force office for two weeks because he feared catching the disease ("Mail Service Ordered to AIDS Center," 1987).

In Arcadia, Florida, three brothers tested positive for HIV. After word spread of their infection, their barber refused to cut the boys' hair, and the family's minister suggested that they stay away from Sunday church services. Eventually, the family's house was burned down (Robinson, 1987).

In a 1986 [article] in the New York Times, *William F. Buckley, Jr., proposed that "everyone detected with AIDS should be tattooed on the upper forearm, to protect common-needle users, and on the buttocks, to prevent the victimization of other homosexuals" (p. A27).*

In the American Spectator, *Christopher Monckton (1987) wrote: "Every member of the population should be blood tested every month to detect the presence of antibodies against [AIDS], and all those found to be infected with the virus, even if only as carriers, should be isolated compulsorily, immediately, and permanently" (p. 30).*

After you read the section on AIDS, you may want to return to this box to consider whether the available data on the disease support the attitudes and policies described here.

---

of Stigma"). The fact that it first gained publicity in North America primarily among homosexual men in the United States led some to call AIDS the "gay plague;" however, AIDS is caused by a virus, not by a person's sexual orientation.

AIDS first captured the attention of physicians in 1981, but the syndrome had existed for some time prior to the 1980s. In February, 1952, a 28-year-old Tennessee man known as R. G. was admitted to a hospital in Memphis, gasping for air. Over the next few months, he suffered one debilitating infection after another until his overwhelmed body could not cope any longer and he died. Although not recognized at the time as AIDS, it ran a course typical of this illness, and was later identified, earning R. G. a place in medical history (Ewald, 1994).

The origin of AIDS has yet to be determined, although most scientists agree that the HIV viruses are basically ape or monkey viruses because of their genetic similarities. Antibodies to HIV have been found in human blood samples that were collected in the 1960s and 1970s in central and east Africa, lending some support to the hypothesis that AIDS originated there (Ewald, 1994). If the origin of HIV is ultimately determined, that knowledge may contribute to finding a vaccine and a cure.

immunosuppression The suppression of natural immunologic responses, which produces lowered resistance to disease.

AIDS patients suffer from severe **immunosuppression.** Normally, our immune systems protect us from various diseases to which we are exposed, but HIV, perhaps in combination with other physiological factors, cripples the immune system. Patients are then vulnerable to numerous opportunistic infections—that is, infections that take hold because the impairment of the body's immune system gives them the opportunity to flourish.

Prevalence

Before 1981, only 92 people in the United States were diagnosed as having the symptoms later to be called AIDS. From 1981 through December 1996, state and territorial health departments reported more than 581,000 cases of AIDS among men, women, and children. Another 75,000 adults and children have tested positive for HIV, but do not yet show symptoms of AIDS. A study of almost 17,000 students at 19 universities found 1 in 500 to be HIV-positive (Gayle, Keeling, Garcia-Tunon, et al., 1991). More than 357,000 AIDS-related deaths have occurred (CDC, 1996). Because of reporting delays and other factors (e.g., some patients move and then die without the knowledge of their former physicians), these numbers are minimal estimates, as reporting by states of AIDS cases to the Centers for Disease Control (CDC) is about 85 percent complete and reports of deaths are about 90 percent complete (CDC, 1996). By 1993 AIDS ranked as the leading cause of death among adults 25 to 44 years of age.

Minority group members have been disproportionately represented among U.S. citizens infected with HIV (CDC, 1996). However, members of ethnic minorities in the United States are also overrepresented among the least educated and poorest segments of American society, and it may be that their poverty and lack of education are more predictive of their greater risk of HIV infection than their ethnic minority status. Intravenous (IV) drug use rather than homosexual activity appears to be the source of most HIV infection among minorities.

AIDS is most prevalent in large, urban centers, but an increasing proportion of all cases is being reported from smaller cities and rural areas (CDC, 1996). The rates of AIDS cases among men who have sex with men have been dropping and now account for fewer than half of all cases. In descending order of risk, following receptive anal sex, are injecting drug use (and needle sharing), hemophilia/coagulation disorder, heterosexual contact, receiving a blood transfusion, and receipt of transplanted tissues, organs, or artificial insemination from an HIV-positive donor (CDC, 1996).

Data from Haiti and Africa underscore the fact that it is intimate contact with an infected person rather than an individual's sexual orientation that places one at risk of contracting HIV. In central Africa, AIDS is far more prevalent among heterosexuals than among homosexual men, and antibodies to HIV are as common in women as in men.

CHILDREN WITH AIDS.   HIV can pass from an infected mother to her fetus during pregnancy and to a baby through breast milk. About 22 percent of all babies born to mothers with HIV become infected with the virus. However, if their HIV-infected mothers are treated with **AZT (zidovudine)** during their pregnancies, the rate of HIV infection among the children is reduced by two-thirds (about 7 percent of babies) (Davis et al., 1995). Among children diagnosed as having AIDS, 88 percent had at least one parent with AIDS or with increased risk of developing AIDS. Another 7 percent had contracted AIDS during blood transfusions.

Causes

The **retrovirus** that causes AIDS was identified in 1983 in France and in 1984 in the United States and given the name **human immunodeficiency virus (HIV)** (Shilts, 1987). There are at least five strains of HIV (Science, 1992). The two most prominent are HIV-I, found primarily in the West and responsible for the vast majority of the world's AIDS cases, and HIV-II, most commonly found in Africa.

HIV must make DNA copies of its own RNA structure before it can reproduce inside a host cell. Within days after the virus has entered the body, many people

---

ISSUES TO CONSIDER

Why do you think that HIV/AIDS is more prevalent among the poor and less educated?

AZT (zidovudine) Drug used in the treatment of AIDS.

retrovirus A form of virus that cannot reproduce inside a host cell until it has made DNA copies of its own RNA structure.

human immunodeficiency virus (HIV) The retrovirus that causes AIDS.

experience flu-like symptoms. At this time, HIV particles are reproducing in their favorite target, specialized white blood cells called helper T-cells (also called CD4 cells), which are vital to the functioning of the immune system. When the helper T-cells are attacked, the body uses all its resources to protect these cells.

After the body has swept the virus from the blood and trapped it in the lymph nodes, HIV continues to churn out copies of itself. The immune system reacts with two strategies that initially limit damage. First, it activates antibodies to neutralize HIV particles. Then specialized white blood cells, called killer T-cells, attack and digest infected tissue. If they have themselves tested for HIV antibodies, this is the stage during which most people discover they are HIV positive.

This asymptomatic stage can last from 5 to 12 years. Each year, however, more HIV escapes from the lymph nodes into the blood. The immune system becomes progressively weaker as more and more helper T-cells die. Eventually HIV destroys the ability of the body's immune system to fight diseases.

HIV has been found in blood, semen, vaginal secretions, and breast milk and less frequently in the saliva, tears, and urine of infected individuals. Researchers believe that the risk of contracting AIDS from the saliva, tears, or urine of an infected person is extremely low.

Risk Factors

The risk of acquiring HIV and developing AIDS appears to be highest among individuals with large numbers of sexual partners and frequent sexual contacts: the more partners a person has, the more likely he or she is to encounter someone carrying the virus (Tanfer et al., 1995). Engaging in sexual practices with an HIV-infected partner that expose you to blood or semen increases the likelihood of contracting HIV. Those sexual practices that cause fissures or tears in a body opening generate higher risk—by providing HIV with access to the bloodstream—than do practices that are unlikely to damage sensitive bodily tissues. Thus, HIV is most prevalent in people who engage in unprotected receptive fisting (insertion of the fist into the anus, which produces fissures that leave receivers vulnerable to contraction of HIV if they engage in anal sex), receptive anal coitus, receptive fellatio, and analingus.

People with a history of other STDs such as gonorrhea, chlamydia, and syphilis are also at higher risk of contracting AIDS than are individuals who have never been infected with these agents (Fisher & Fisher, 1992; The Institute for Medicine, 1997). Scientists do not know the precise reasons for this correlation, but it is possible that a person who has had other STDs has a weakened skin area where the infection occurred, making the area more vulnerable to HIV infection. Another possible reason for this relationship is that both treatable STDs and HIV infection are more likely to occur among persons with multiple partners.

Sharing needles during intravenous drug use, too, places people at risk of exposure to HIV-infected blood. In rare cases, individuals have contracted AIDS from contaminated blood products received during medical treatment, but this risk has been greatly reduced with improvements in the screening procedures for HIV infection. About 1 percent of the U.S. cases of AIDS have resulted from receiving transfusions of contaminated blood (CDC, 1996). There is no risk in giving blood, for which sterile, disposable needles are used. AIDS rarely results from casual contact, and then only if contact with the body fluids of infected persons occurs (Hochhauser & Rothenberger, 1992). Casual contacts with AIDS patients that do not involve the exchange of body products, such as shaking hands, hugging, or providing health care, are not risk factors.

Symptoms

Acquired immunodeficiency syndrome is called a syndrome because a variety of life-threatening conditions are associated with it. Some of the same symptoms are also associated with other diseases and infections, such as the flu and colds, or with physical and psychological stress. The presence of one of these symptoms, such as swollen lymph nodes, does not necessarily indicate that a person has contracted HIV, particularly if he or she is not engaging in risky behaviors and is not the partner of someone who is infected with HIV.

Common early signs of AIDS are **lymphadenopathy,** unexplained weight loss, loss of appetite, persistent fevers or night sweats, chronic fatigue, unexplained diarrhea or bloody stools, unexplained bleeding from any body opening, skin rashes, easy bruising, persistent severe headaches, chronic dry cough not caused by smoking or a cold, and a chronic whitish coating on the tongue or throat. All of these symptoms result from the opportunistic infections that accompany AIDS.

lymphadenopathy Condition involving swollen lymph nodes in the neck, armpits, and/or groin.

Diagnosis

People are diagnosed as having AIDS when they develop one of the opportunistic infections or diseases associated with AIDS and when they receive a positive result from tests for HIV. There may be as long as a six-month period between contracting the infection and testing positive for HIV. The opportunistic infections most commonly suffered by AIDS patients are pneumocystis carinii pneumonia (PCP), Kaposi's sarcoma, and cytomegalovirus infection. In 1993, three other infections were added: pulmonary tuberculosis, recurrent pneumonia, and invasive cervical cancer. In that same year, the definition of AIDS infection was expanded to include a laboratory measure of severe immunosuppression (CD4+ T-lymphocyte count of fewer than 200 cells or less than 14 percent of total lymphocytes) (CDC, 1996).

Although the CDC concluded that the available blood tests for HIV antibodies, such as the ELISA test, are highly accurate, they are not perfect. That is, occasionally a person receives a false-positive result (erroneously indicating HIV antibodies when there are none) or a false-negative result (incorrectly indicating no HIV antibodies when they are in fact present). (See "Health: Being Tested for HIV Antibodies," page 339). For further accuracy, follow-up testing can be done using the Western Blot test.

In 1996, the Food and Drug Administration (FDA) approved an HIV test that can be taken at home. By calling a toll-free number and punching in a code number, the user gets a recorded message if the result is negative. With a positive result, a trained counselor answers the call and refers the consumer to a local clinic for further testing. HIV home tests have been shown to be as accurate as tests provided through clinics or doctors' offices (Frank et al., 1997).

ISSUES TO CONSIDER

Would you be more willing to take a home test than a test at a health care clinic to determine your HIV status? Why or why not?

Opportunistic Infections

Pneumocystis carinii pneumonia (PCP) used to be a rare parasitic infection of the lungs usually observed only in cancer patients who were undergoing chemotherapy or in organ-transplant patients who were given drugs to suppress their immune systems. PCP is now the most common opportunistic disease associated with AIDS. The drugs used to treat PCP can prevent it if they are given early enough in the course of the HIV infection (Redfield & Burke, 1988). Approximately 60 percent of AIDS patients experience serious side effects from these drugs, however, and researchers are therefore

pneumocystis carinii pneumonia (PCP) (NEW-moh-SIS-tis kah-RYE-nee-EYE) A form of pneumonia that commonly appears in persons whose immune systems are highly suppressed.

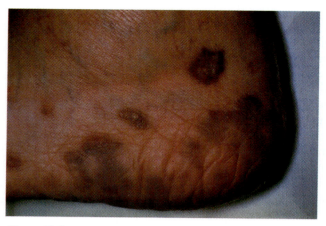

Figure 13.5
Kaposi's Sarcoma (KS)
Kaposi's sarcoma was once a rare form of cancer. A virulent variety of the disease afflicts some AIDS patients, often appearing first as a lesion on the palate. This patient has lesions on his heel.

Kaposi's sarcoma (KS)
(KAP-up-seez sar-KOH-mah) Formerly, a rare type of cancer of the skin and connective tissue. It is now more common as one of the opportunistic infections that attacks AIDS patients.

cytomegalovirus (CMV)
(sye-toe-MEG-uh-low-VYE-rus) One of a group of viruses causing cell enlargement in various internal organs.

AIDS dementia complex
Infection of the brain by HIV, resulting in the deterioration and loss of nerve cells.

testing other medications in the ongoing search for more effective and less dangerous treatments.

Kaposi's sarcoma (KS) is a rare form of cancer of the skin and connective tissues (bones, fats, and muscles), which in the past mainly affected elderly men in Western societies. In some parts of Africa, KS now accounts for 9 percent of all cancers detected in men. Some KS patients develop lesions on their palate (roof of the mouth), face, arms, and other skin areas (see Figure 13.5). Men who develop KS have a shorter interval from the time they are diagnosed with HIV to the development of AIDS than do men without KS (Lifson et al., 1990).

Cytomegalovirus (CMV) infections, which are caused by a group of herpes viruses, result in enlargement of the cells in various parts of the body, including the lungs, intestines, and central nervous system. CMV symptoms include fever, blindness, pneumonia, colitis, and low blood-cell counts. Other opportunistic infections attacking AIDS patients without KS or PCP account for only a small proportion of cases.

AIDS patients are understandably depressed when their disease is diagnosed. In some cases, the depression may be a response to the impact of HIV on the spinal cord and brain, which can produce neurological deficits called **AIDS dementia complex.** Brains of infected persons decrease in size through the atrophy (wasting away) of some nerve cells. In the early stages of AIDS dementia, patients may experience forgetfulness, social withdrawal, and difficulty concentrating. Then problems with walking and talking develop, and response time in visual and motor tasks becomes impaired. Later, AIDS dementia patients experience seizures and spasms.

Treatment

A cure for AIDS will probably not be found in the foreseeable future, but there are treatments for some of the opportunistic infections that attack people with impaired immune systems, and some drugs slow the effects of the AIDS virus. Zidovudine (AZT) is more effective than placebos in extending the lives of AIDS patients and was licensed by the FDA in 1987. Despite AZT's effectiveness in reducing the severity of illness and extending the lives of AIDS patients, the drug has potentially severe side effects. Another problem with AZT is that HIV can become resistant to the drug with long-term treatment. However, the combination of several other drugs with AZT appears to increase its effectiveness. Newer drugs called protease inhibitors have been shown to extend the lives of people infected with AIDS (Katz & Gerberding, 1997). These drug "cocktails" block production of a key enzyme, protease, that the virus needs to replicate itself. Ritohvair, Indinavir, and Saquinavir are examples of protease inhibitors.

Noting that HIV/AIDS infections are associated with depression, reduced sexual desire, and sexual dysfunctions, Wagner, Rabkin, and Rabkin (1997) conducted a study with a group of AIDS patients in which they provided testosterone injection therapy. Compared to a control group of AIDS patients (who subsequently received the testosterone treatment), those receiving the therapy showed increased pleasure with life, sexual desire, and sexual functioning. Some of the men engaged in masturbation, some had sex with partners and used condoms, but a few of the men engaged in unprotected insertive sex with a partner who was unaware of the patients' AIDS status. Testosterone treatment could improve the quality of life for AIDS patients (Tiefer,

Health

Being Tested for HIV Antibodies

As I sit here dispassionately describing the testing process for HIV antibodies, I vividly remember my own experience of being tested. I realized that the hepatitis that my husband and I had contracted while in Africa is one of the infections associated with AIDS. A local hospital had a free and anonymous AIDS testing program, and one of my students asked whether I thought it really was confidential. He is gay, and he was afraid that if he were tested, his parents, potential employers, and others might find out. I was willing to be tested with him because I thought that it might be beneficial to find out firsthand about the procedures and the extent of anonymity. We made appointments, and on a snowy Monday evening we drove to the hospital to have the ELISA test done.

When we arrived at the hospital's testing site, the receptionist gave us each a slip with a four-digit number on it and told us to have a seat. Soon a volunteer counselor came out and called my number. He gave me a short questionnaire to fill out anonymously, on which I was to indicate such details as my age, gender, sexual orientation, marital status, number of sexual partners in the recent past, and drug-use patterns. When I returned the questionnaire, he read it over and asked why I wanted to be tested because I did not seem to fit any of the high-risk groups. I explained about Africa and related my other reasons. He then competently obtained my informed consent (see Chapter 1) regarding the blood test and the hospital's procedures to guarantee anonymity.

I was shown a videotape reviewing much of the same material that the counselor had presented. A nurse took a blood sample, wrote my number on the vial, and directed me back to the receptionist, who scheduled my appointment for the following week. I found my friend, and we drove home, comparing notes on the way. He was worried, and we talked about his potential risk. After I dropped him at his dorm, I began to feel anxious about my own test results. I talked with Rick about it, and during the next week I thought a great deal about what I might do if the test result were positive.

I was relieved when told that my test was negative, and I was delighted to see the huge grin on my friend's face when he returned to the waiting room. On the drive home, we talked about our anxiety during the past week, which was nothing compared to the fear, anguish, and eventual physical pain of those who get positive test results and go on to develop AIDS.　—E.R.A.

1997), but this study raised ethical concerns about continuing to provide testosterone injection therapy to the few men who reported having engaged in unsafe sexual behavior (Fisher, 1997).

Scientists have been working on developing vaccines against HIV since the mid-1980s. So far, the results have not been very encouraging. Research on HIV vaccines must be conducted with humans, and that raises controversial ethical problems (see Chapter 1). Furthermore, there are many strains of HIV, and the virus is constantly changing. In 1996, Liu et al. reported that approximately 1 percent of people have a "defective" gene that renders them immune to the effects of HIV. Further research with that gene may lead to the development of a treatment or vaccine for HIV/AIDS.

Protection Against AIDS

Unless a person is celibate or involved with an uninfected partner in a monogamous relationship, he or she should take direct steps to reduce the risk of HIV infection. Methods of lowering one's risk of contracting STDs, including HIV/AIDS, are described at the end of this chapter.

The relationship between having a history of other STDs and contracting AIDS may simply be evidence of the fact that people with AIDS and those with other STDs

ISSUES TO CONSIDER

If you were a member of the research team providing testosterone injection therapy, what would you do about the few men who subsequently reported engaging in unsafe sexual behavior? Remember that research participants are generally guaranteed confidentiality, and refusing to provide further therapy to those few men who reported engaging in risky sexual behavior would reduce the likelihood that they or other men in the study would report honestly their sexual behaviors.

share certain risk factors. For example, they may have unprotected sex with a large number of partners, not use a barrier contraceptive method (the condom, the diaphragm, and the female condom), or engage in sexual practices that increase the likelihood of infection if they have sex with an infected partner (Wagstaff et al., 1995).

One of the reasons that AIDS initially may have been more prevalent among homosexuals than among U.S. heterosexuals is that homosexuals do not use contraceptives. Barrier methods of contraception reduce the risk of HIV transmission when used properly. The protective effect of barrier methods is supported by the fact that AIDS is as prevalent among females as males in some African populations, most of whom do not use these contraceptives. Asking about the health and sexual risk-taking behaviors of potential partners is crucial in slowing the spread of AIDS, but it is also important in reducing the incidence of other viral STDs, a topic to which we turn now.

OTHER VIRAL STDS

Like AIDS, the other sexually transmitted viruses are incurable at present. They can be treated, but no methods are yet available to purge the virus from the body and thus prevent recurrent episodes of these diseases. These virally produced STDs include genital herpes, genital warts, and hepatitis B.

Herpes Simplex Type II

Many people have experienced the episodic, mildly painful, and unsightly fever blisters or cold sores of herpes simplex type I. Although most people do not welcome the irritating sores, herpes I is not worrisome after the lesions have healed.

herpes simplex type II A viral infection contracted through physical contact with an infected person during an active outbreak of the sores.

A related virus, **herpes simplex type II** (called herpes II or genital herpes), causes most genital herpes infections, although herpes I may also appear on the genitals if they are orally stimulated by a partner with an active outbreak of herpes I around the mouth. Conversely, herpes II may develop in the mouth if an individual orally stimulates the genitals of a partner who has an active infection of herpes II.

The CDC estimates that there are about half a million new cases of herpes II each year, with several million people experiencing recurrent episodes annually. About 30 million Americans are believed to have herpes II (Fact Sheet, 1997).

Genital herpes is most often contracted through physical contact with the open herpes II sores of an infected person. In its dormant phase, the disease is less contagious. The symptoms, which include small blisters similar to those created by herpes I, generally appear at the site of the infection three to seven days after infection (see Figure 13.6). They may tingle and itch, or they may produce a burning sensation. When the blisters break open, the infection can spread to other parts of the body. The open wounds are also susceptible to secondary infections from skin bacteria. Other symptoms of genital herpes include fever and swollen lymph glands. In women, herpes II blisters commonly break out on the outer and inner lips of the vagina, the clitoral hood, and the cervix. In men, the blisters tend to erupt on the glans or foreskin of the penis.

With the first outbreak of genital herpes, only about 20 percent of patients recognize symptoms (Corey, 1994). Patients with mild symptoms may be more likely to transmit herpes to others because they do not realize that they have the virus. Primary herpes infections pro-

Figure 13.6
Herpes II Sores Herpes II patients experience periodic outbreaks of these sores.

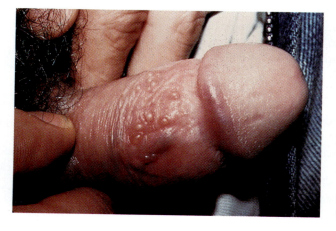

duce open sores that last for an average of 16 to 21 days in men and 10 to 16 days in women. In general, symptoms and complications of recurrent outbreaks are milder than those associated with the primary outbreak of herpes.

Laboratory studies reveal that some contraceptives are effective in reducing the risk of transmitting or contracting herpes II. Spermicides containing nonoxynol-9 have been shown to deactivate the herpes virus on contact (Catotti et al., 1993). Condoms also block the passage of the virus in laboratory tests. Although sexual contact should be avoided during active herpes II outbreaks, laboratory studies suggest that sexual intercourse is probably safe during remission of herpes II. Remission can occur for years after the initial episode, and during this time there are no outbreaks of the symptoms. Nonetheless, couples engaging in sex during this stage should use condoms with liberal amounts of spermicide.

Pregnant women with genital herpes can transmit the disease to a fetus. And a woman who has an active case of primary genital herpes has about a 50 percent risk of transmitting it to the baby during vaginal delivery. Women who have visible lesions during labor or have recently tested positive for herpes II should deliver via cesarean section (Catotti et al., 1993; Kroon & Whitley, 1994).

Accurate diagnosis of genital herpes is enhanced by obtaining samples of the infected tissue early in the infection and subjecting them to laboratory analysis. Although researchers are working on a cure, current treatments only reduce the discomfort of the symptoms; they do not eliminate the virus. In some patients, however, the disease appears to go into remission, with no further outbreaks of the symptoms for years after the initial episodes. The drug acyclovir relieves pain, shortens the time required for the healing of herpes lesions, and can suppress recurrent outbreaks in some patients (Sacks, 1995). Other methods for treating the symptoms of genital herpes are available or under development, so genital herpes patients should check with their health care providers for the latest information.

Many people experience intense emotional reactions when they are initially diagnosed as having genital herpes. Herpes patients can receive counseling about ways of reducing or avoiding stressful factors in their lives and of coping with recurrent outbreaks. Herpes II patients have banded together to form the Herpes Resource Center, which disseminates information about recent research and sources of emotional support for those with herpes II. (Consult the Appendix for further information.)

genital warts An STD that can also be contracted nonsexually; caused by the human papilloma virus.

Genital Warts / Human Papilloma Virus

Genital warts are caused by the human papilloma virus (HPV). They are soft, pink, painless, single or multiple growths resembling a small cauliflower (see Figure 13.7). The virus is transmitted through direct contact with the warts during vaginal, oral, or anal intercourse, but it may also be contracted through nonsexual contact. The warts, which are highly contagious, begin to appear one to three months after contact and are diagnosed visually. They may be removed by freezing (cryotherapy), burning, dehydration with an electrical needle, or surgery. If the warts are unusual or persistent, they should be biopsied to determine whether they are precancerous. Approximately 60 HPV types have been identified so far, and a number of these are now believed to cause nearly all cancer of the penis, anus, cervix, vagina, and vulva (Institute of Medicine, 1996; Koutsky et al., 1992). If they are on the penis or in the vagina, abstinence from intercourse or the use of a condom until the warts have been removed can lessen the likelihood of transmitting the virus.

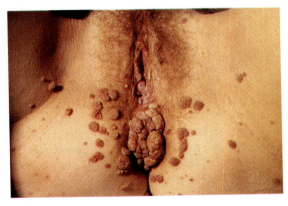

Figure 13.7
Genital Warts The common genital wart is a soft, pink lesion that can be sexually transmitted.

More than a million cases of genital warts requiring treatment have been reported each year in the United States (Fact Sheet, 1997). Most male partners of women with genital warts or HPV have no visible genital warts, and there is no screening test for the presence of the HPV in men without visible warts.

Although genital warts sometimes regress without treatment, they may spread and grow to the point where they block the vaginal or rectal opening. Further, the virus can be transmitted to a baby during vaginal delivery if the warts are located on the cervix or in the vagina.

Hepatitis B

hepatitis B A virus that attacks the liver; often sexually transmitted.

There are different types of hepatitis, each of which is thought to be caused by a different virus (Stevens et al., 1990). In all forms of hepatitis, the virus attacks the liver. Our main concern here is with **hepatitis B,** because it can be transmitted through exposure to the blood, saliva, or semen of infectious carriers, although saliva and semen tend to have lower concentrations of the virus than does blood. The causative agent is called the hepatitis B virus (HBV). Approximately three hundred thousand people, most of them young adults, are infected each year. About ten thousand require hospitalization, and about two hundred and fifty of the patients die annually, usually of liver cancer (The Institute for Medicine, 1996). Up to 10 percent of young adults with HBV infections become carriers, and the United States has an estimated pool of half a million to one million carriers.

HBV infection usually begins within 30 to 120 days after exposure to an infectious carrier. The most common symptoms are mild fever, fatigue, sore muscles, headache, upset stomach, skin rash, joint pains, and dark urine. The characteristic external sign is a yellowing of the whites of the eyes. The skin may also become yellow, or jaundiced. The disease is diagnosed by a specific blood test, the hepatitis B surface-antigen test.

 ? **6**

We are happy to end this sobering section on the effects of sexually transmitted viral infections by reporting that an effective vaccine against HBV was licensed in 1981, making hepatitis B the one viral STD that can be prevented by a vaccine. The CDC reported that people who develop adequate antibody levels after vaccination have almost complete protection against HBV.

PARASITIC INFECTIONS

We now turn to some of the sexually transmitted infections caused by parasites, fungi, and yeasts.

Candidiasis

The yeastlike fungus *Candida albicans* (also known as moniliasis, and commonly called a yeast infection) normally lives in the mouth, the digestive tract, and the vagina. Growth of the fungus is usually restricted by the presence of other bacteria. When these controlling bacteria are reduced in number by antibiotics, frequent douching, pregnancy, diabetes, or other conditions, such as oral contraceptive use, that reduce the acidity of the vaginal environment, the unrestricted growth of the fungus in the vagina can result in infection.

candidiasis (KAN-dih-DYE-ah-sis) An infection of the vulva and vagina caused by the excess growth of a fungus that occurs normally in the body.

Candidiasis produces a thick, white vaginal discharge resembling the curd of cottage cheese, an unpleasant yeasty odor, and severe itching. The vaginal walls may be inflamed, the labia sometimes swell, and intercourse may be painful. Candidiasis is diagnosed by visually examining a fresh specimen of discharge or by growing the fungus in a culture. It is treated with antibiotic-antifungal compounds in suppositories or ointments, many of which are available without a prescription. During treatment, couples should abstain from coitus or use a condom to avoid infection or reinfection of the partners.

Trichomoniasis

Trichomoniasis is a parasitic infection with an estimated annual incidence of 3 million cases (Fact Sheet, 1997; The Institute for Medicine, 1996). It is caused by a parasite called *Trichomonas vaginalis*. It can be transmitted through sexual interaction, but infection can also result from contact with infected wet towels and wet bathing suits.

The incubation period ranges from four days to a month. A minority of women with this infection produce a frothy yellow-green or white vaginal discharge with a strong odor, and some men have an inflamed urethra (urethritis). The majority of people with trichomoniasis, however, are asymptomatic (Grodstein, Goldman, & Cramer, 1993).

A diagnosis is made by examining a sample of the discharge for trichomonads under a microscope. Both the person who has been diagnosed as having trichomoniasis and his or her partner(s) are given medication to eliminate the infection.

trichomoniasis (TRIK-uh-muh-NYE-ah-sis) An inflammation of the vagina characterized by a whitish discharge, caused by a parasite.

Pediculosis Pubis

Pediculosis pubis, or crabs, is an infestation of six-legged lice about the size of a pinhead. They inhabit hairy areas of the pubic region, anus, underarms, and eyelashes. Eggs, or nits, are laid by the female. These nits mature in two or three weeks and begin feeding on blood, producing inflammation of the skin and itching. They may be transmitted sexually or nonsexually through contact with infected bedding, towels, or clothing. Like scabies, crabs can be eliminated by shampooing the infected areas with the nonprescription medicine Kwell (called Kwellada in Canada).

pediculosis pubis (peh-DIK-you-Low-sis PYOU-bis) A lice infestation of the pubic hair; commonly referred to as crabs.

SAFER-SEX PRACTICES: REDUCING THE RISK OF CONTRACTING STDs

There has been a lot of discussion about "safe sex" in the media, but you may have noticed that we have consistently used the phrase "safer sex" in this book. The reason is that, from the standpoint of wanting to avoid an STD (or, for that matter, an unwanted pregnancy), there is no such thing as safe sex if genital contact is involved. There are, however, practices that reduce risk: abstinence, avoiding anonymous "one-night stands," communicating clearly about your sexual policies with a person prior to deciding whether to become sexually intimate with him or her, limiting sexual activities to contacts that do not involve bodily penetration, and using condoms during any sexual intimacy.

For many couples, one of the most difficult steps in deciding whether to become more sexually intimate and engage in safer-sex practices is discussing the matter with each other. But frank and open dialogue is absolutely essential if you are to make wise decisions about developing a relationship that may affect your physical and psychological well-being for the rest of your life. To make sexual decisions in the dark, so to speak, is like driving with your eyes closed. In addition, one benefit of the discussions you have prior to making that decision is that they may ultimately enhance your emotional and physical intimacy as a couple.

Relationship Negotiation

Most of us are sexually attracted to many different people in our lives, but we generally go through a screening process (although we may not think of it that way) as we try to decide whether to act on our feelings. We are selective about our choice of sexual partners and practices. Being selective, however, requires that you devote some time to deciding your sexual policies. "Sexual policies" and "selective" may sound abstract and vague, but determining sexual policies so that you can be selective involves a series of concrete steps:

1. *Clarify your sexual policies.* Make decisions about your sexual policies when you are calm and able to think clearly, not when you are sexually aroused and have to make a decision about a particular person. In forming your policies, ask yourself questions about the conditions under which you wish to become physically and emotionally intimate with another person:

   a. Do I want to select partners who are capable of valuing others as much as they value themselves?
   b. What kind of relationship am I seeking, with what level of mutual commitment?

   We know two students—one a heterosexual woman and the other a gay man—who, for different reasons, plan to avoid serious commitments for a couple of years. Neither of them is against casual relationships, but both make it clear to potential partners that they are not emotionally available for any intense or long-term relationship.

2. *Communicate your policies to a potential partner.* After you become aware that you and another person are interested in each other, it is important to spend some time getting to know one another before deciding to become sexually intimate. Your prospective partner may appear to meet the criteria that you established in your sexual policies, but first impressions are not always accurate.

3. *Identify the extent to which your own past sexual behaviors pose a potential risk to the person in whom you are interested.* If you have been sexually active with others, have you been tested for STDs to make sure that you will not transmit an STD to this new person? You should be able to give this new person that information, although you need not deliver a litany of names and specific episodes

4. *Ask about your potential partner's risk of having contracted an STD.* If that person cares about you, she or he should willingly provide you with the same information that you provide. If the individual refuses to tell you about the frequency of past sexual experiences with different partners, perhaps your criteria for an intimate sexual relationship have not been met.

5. *Postpone physical intimacy involving the exchange of body fluids until laboratory tests have verified that you are both free of STDs.* You may perceive our emphasis on getting yourself tested before entering a new relationship as an expensive practice that kills sexual spontaneity. But keep in mind that it is not nearly so expensive as contracting an STD, particularly one of the incurable viral diseases. In addition, a clinic in your area may provide testing services free or on a sliding scale based on income.

   If, after considering your own values and establishing open communication, you and the other person decide that you feel sufficiently committed to each other to make love, both of you can reduce the risk of infection by incorporating safer-sex practices into your lovemaking. If a couple approaches the situation with some imagination and humor, these practices can be both erotic and romantic as well as safer. They need not resemble a medical examination or a police body search. If you care enough about your partner to want to be sexually intimate with him or her, you should also want to protect that person—as well as yourself—against possible disease.

6. *Shower or bathe together before becoming sexually intimate.* Washing yourselves and each other can be highly erotic (see Figure 13.8). It also gives you both the opportunity to observe each other's bodies.

7. *Learn about each other's bodies.* You may want to invest in some pink light bulbs for your bedroom (or wherever you choose to have sex). If you notice any unusual characteristics (for example, bumps or discharge), you should ask about them. If you suspect that one of you has symptoms of an STD, you should delay further physical intimacy.

8. *Use latex condoms together with spermicides.* The combination can be highly effective in reducing the likelihood of transmitting most STDs. If you find the usual spermicides less than aesthetically pleasing, you may want to obtain one of the flavored spermicides. In the event that you and your partner decide to make a long-term, monogamous commitment to one another and neither of you is infected, latex condom and spermicide use can be abandoned (and will have to be if your long-term commitment includes plans for children!).

Figure 13.8
Bathing Together By bathing or showering together, you can enjoy erotic play and have an opportunity to see each other's bodies.

Other Practices That Reduce Risk

Our intention in providing the following list of practices is not to be moralistic but to help you avoid contracting AIDS or any of the other STDs:

1. Do not use intravenous drugs, isobutyl, or poppers (amyl nitrate) (see Chapter 4).

2. Do not share needles or any other IV-drug equipment.

3. Do not use the belongings of others that contain any of their body fluids (blood, saliva, urine, semen, and so forth).

4. Avoid unprotected sexual intimacy with IV-drug users. Many of the new AIDS cases result from people who inject drugs and share needles or have had unprotected sexual contact with IV-drug users.

5. Finally, remain abstinent until you are confident that sexual activity between you and a desired partner will not pose health risks for either of you.

If you are sexually active and nonmonogamous, following these safer-sex and general health practices is extremely important. You may also want to change your sexual lifestyle until vaccines against viral STDs become available. Our capacities to provide one another with sexual pleasure can be seriously jeopardized by AIDS or other STDs. If one does not practice abstinence, there is no absolute guarantee that a sexual contact will not result in an STD. Although those who wish to remain sexually active and healthy may not be thrilled about altering their sexual practices to avoid disease, for most people, survival is more important than high-risk sexual encounters with a variety of partners.

> **Note:** AIDS information is available from the following sources. *United States:* For a tape recording of the latest information, call, toll-free, 1-800-342-AIDS. AIDS information is available (although not always toll-free) from the Department of Health in each state and the District of Columbia. To inquire about a toll-free number in your locale, call 1-800-555-1212. *Canada:* National AIDS Centre, Ottawa, 1-613-957-1772. Toronto Area Gay Hotline, 1-416-964-6600.

Summary of major points

1. Attitudes, knowledge, and diagnosis of STDs.

Unfortunately, inadequate knowledge, negative attitudes, and shame about STDs often interfere with responsible health practices. Early diagnosis and treatment of STDs are necessary to avoid the dangerous long-term effects of undetected STDs that can readily be cured. In addition, knowledge of our STD status is important so that we do not spread them, particularly when they involve the currently incurable viral STDs.

2. Categories of STDs.

STDs can be classified into three major categories: bacterial infections, viral diseases, and parasitic infestations. Except for viral STDs, these can be readily cured in their early stages. Contracting an STD in the past may increase one's chances of contracting HIV; thus sexually active people should take preventive measures to avoid any STD.

3. Bacterial STDs.

The bacterial infections include gonorrhea, syphilis, chlamydia, nongonococcal urethritis (NGU), cystitis, prostatitis, gardnerella vaginalis, shigellosis, and chancroid. The most common serious complication of untreated bacterial genital infections in women is PID. A variety of medications are successful in treating these conditions, particularly if they are used in the early stages of the infection.

4. Viral STDs.

The viral STDs include AIDS, herpes II, genital warts, and hepatitis B. Although there are treatments for the symptoms and for some complications of these diseases, none can be cured. There is a vaccine for hepatitis B, however, and people at risk of contracting it should be vaccinated.

5. Parasitic STDs.

Infections caused by parasites, fungi, and yeasts include candidiasis, trichomoniasis, and pediculosis pubis. Antibiotic and antifungal compounds are generally effective in treating these infections.

6. Safer-sex practices.

Except for celibacy, there is no way to eliminate the risk of contracting STDs. But sexually active people can sharply reduce the likelihood of contracting AIDS and other STDs by refraining from IV drug use, avoiding contact with others' body fluids (including blood and semen), and adopting safer-sex practices. Reducing exposure to STDs involves careful selection of partners and the correct and consistent use of latex condoms and ample amounts of spermicide. Condoms reduce the likelihood of transmitting or contracting most STDs, and spermicides are effective in killing many of the organisms that cause STDs, including herpes.

CHECK YOUR KNOWLEDGE

1. Which of the following is true about gonorrhea? (a) Shortly after contracting gonorrhea, women develop highly noticeable symptoms. (b) It is transmissible by kissing as well as by sexual intercourse. (c) It is always curable by antibiotics, so no follow-up test is needed. (d) It cannot be transmitted to infants during childbirth. **(p. 328)**

2. The most prevalent bacterial STD in the United States is (a) syphilis, (b) chlamydia, (c) AIDS, (d) cystitis. **(p. 330)**

3. Which of the following is *not* true of pelvic inflammatory disease (PID)? (a) It is the most common serious complication of untreated gonorrhea, chlamydia, and other genital infections in females. (b) It is a cause of ectopic pregnancy and sterility. (c) It is frequently contracted in the absence of any other STD.(d) It is incurable. **(p. 332)**

4. HIV is (a) the antibody whose presence in a person's blood shows infection with AIDS, (b) the abbreviation for the two groups most at risk for contracting AIDS: homosexuals and intravenous drug users, (c) the retrovirus that causes AIDS, (d) a drug that slows the course of AIDS infection. **(p. 335)**

5. Which of the following statements about the spread of HIV is *not* true? (a) It is more likely to occur among people with a history of other STDs. (b) The risk of contracting HIV rises dramatically with the number of sexual partners one has. (c) The disease is sometimes contracted in the process of donating blood. (d) Pregnant women can transmit the virus to their fetuses. **(p. 336)**

6. The safer-sex practices that reduce the risk of contracting HIV or other STDs include all of the following *except* (a) using male condoms, (b) using female condoms, (c) limiting the number of sexual contacts, (d) douching. **(p. 343–346)**

7. Chlamydia is (a) caused by a virus, (b) an infection affecting only women, (c) an infection affecting only men, (d) transmissible primarily by sexual contact. **(p. 330)**

8. The risk of contracting herpes II from an infected partner during sexual activity is reduced by (a) engaging only in oral sex, (b) using a condom and spermicide, (c) taking antibiotics before having sex, (d) avoiding orgasm during coitus. **(p. 341)**

14

SEXUAL COERCION

SEXUAL ASSAULT
The Magnitude of the Problem
Rape Stereotypes
The Sexual Assault Offender
Victims of Sexual Coercion
Highlight: Male Rape
What Provokes Sexual Assault?
The Aftermath of Sexual
  Assault
What Should Assault
  Victims Do?
Highlight: Was He Asking
  for It?
Sexual Assault and the
  Criminal Justice System
Factors Associated with Being
  Sexually Assaulted

SEXUAL HARASSMENT
Sexual Harassment in
  Occupational Settings
Highlight: Research Findings
  on Sexual Harassment
Sexual Harassment in
  Educational Settings
Sexual Harassment in
  Therapeutic Settings

SEXUAL ABUSE OF
CHILDREN
Prevalence of Sexual Abuse
  of Children
Risk Factors for Sexual Abuse
  During Childhood
Health: Memories of Sexual
  Abuse During Childhood
Characteristics of Child-Adult
  Sexual Contacts
Long-Term Correlates of Child-
  Adult Sexual Contacts

GENDER DIFFERENCES
IN SEXUALLY COERCIVE
BEHAVIOR

SUMMARY OF MAJOR
POINTS

CHECK YOUR
KNOWLEDGE

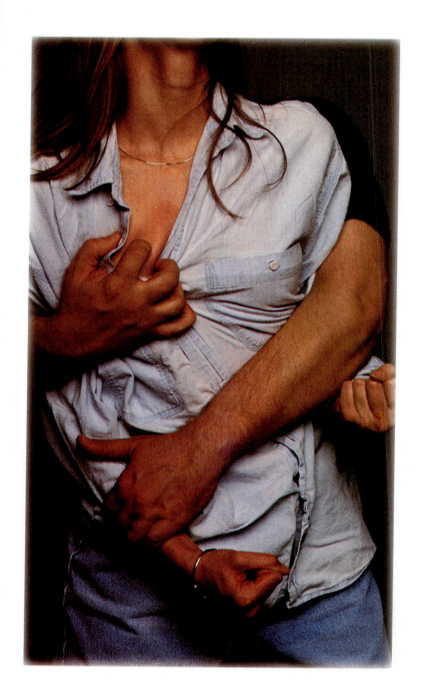

1   About 60 percent of American males report that they have forced a woman to engage in sexual acts against her will.

2   Men can be forced by women to have sex against their will.

3   Women generally enjoy rape, although they are unlikely to admit it.

4   Most cases of sexual harassment in the workplace are reported to the employer.

5   Most therapists report feeling sexual attraction toward some clients.

6   A majority of the sexual crimes against children are committed by adults who are friends or relatives of the victim.

THE ways in which human beings relate to one another sexually reflect the complexity of human emotions and motivations. Sexual activity can be a medium for expressing the deepest and most pleasurable feelings we have, or a vehicle for the degradation and abuse of another. In this chapter we discuss sexual interactions that are marked by various forms of coercion. First, we consider sexual assault, in which one person is forced by physical or psychological means into sexual activity by one or more other people. Second, we examine sexual harassment, in which economic, evaluative, or psychological power is used to pressure another person into sexual relations. Finally, we discuss child sexual abuse.

SEXUAL ASSAULT

Sexual assault is one of the most exploitive forms of sexual encounter. Often including **rape,** it is an expression of aggression through sex. In this section, we look at some of the myths that surround rape and sexual assault. Then we survey the characteristics of sexual aggressors and victims, and the factors associated with sexual assault. Finally, we look at the consequences of sexual assault for the victim and the responses by police and the courts to the offense.

sexual assault Forcing another person to have sexual contact.

rape Sexual intercourse that occurs without consent under actual or threatened force.

The Magnitude of the Problem

In the United States there was one reported rape for every 270 women in 1995 (Federal Bureau of Investigation, 1996). The number of sexual assaults reported annually to criminal justice authorities is a vast underestimate of the actual number of assaults committed each year because most assault victims do not report the crime (McCormick, 1994). Sexual assault is a frightening invasion of personhood. We need, however, to keep this abhorrent act in perspective. The vast majority of men do not rape women. About 3 percent of men and 1.5 percent of women ages 18 to 59 report having forced a person to do something sexual (Laumann et al., 1994). Although this is undoubtedly an underestimate because some men and women may be reluctant to admit such antisocial activity, it still underlines the fact that most people do not rape, despite the claims of some who contend that all men are rapists or potential rapists.

Most early research on sexual assault was conducted with those victims who reported the assault to authorities and with convicted rapists. More recent research involving surveys of nonreporting victims and legally unidentified rapists has challenged a number of common myths about sexual assault.

Rape Stereotypes

There are many stereotypes about sexual assault. Some of these are supported by evidence; others are utterly false. One of the most common myths about rape is that it occurs because women tempt men beyond men's ability to control themselves. At least two beliefs are reflected in this myth. One is that the victim is at least partially responsible for the attack. This idea is called **victim precipitation.** It has its historical roots in the ancient notion that women are dangerous seductresses and that men must be wary of women's power to excite them into a state of uncontrollable lust.

victim precipitation The notion that the victim of an attack is at least partially responsible for the attack.

This belief is closely related to the second idea: that after lust has been triggered, men are powerless to prevent themselves from sexually attacking the person who elicited the lust. To evaluate the accuracy of these beliefs, we review what is known about the perpetrators of the crime, the victims of rape, and the circumstances under which rape occurs.

The Sexual Assault Offender

Until recently, information about the characteristics of sexual-assault offenders was limited to those who had been arrested for an assault. Only about a third of reported sexual assaults in 1992 resulted in the arrest of alleged assailants, however (Federal Bureau of Investigation, 1996). In the remaining cases reported to authorities, the assailants could not be found, there was not enough evidence to proceed legally, or police did not believe that a rape had occurred.

Further, recent research suggests that it is inappropriate to generalize from small samples of convicted rapists to the total population of those who coerce others into sexual contact. Hence we differentiate between *convicted* rapists and *unidentified* rapists, the latter being persons who admit anonymously that they have forced others to have sexual contact but whose victims did not report them to authorities, or who were reported but not caught, arrested, or convicted.

Although the ages of those arrested for sexual assault range from 10 to 65, men aged 18 to 24 account for most arrests (Federal Bureau of Investigation, 1996). Women, gay men, and young boys have also been convicted of rape. The majority of convicted rapists use weapons to coerce their victims, and in three-quarters of the cases, physical force is also employed. The majority of offenders are either drinking or drunk at the time of the sexual assault (Abbey, Ross, McDuffie, & McAuslan, 1996).

In contrast to convicted rapists, unidentified rapists rarely use weapons; instead, they rely on verbal coercion, threats, and physical restraint. The deliberate attempt to intoxicate their victims with alcohol or other drugs appears to be a common coercive strategy that both convicted and unidentified assailants use (Abbey et al., 1996; Barbaree, Hudson, & Seto, 1993).

SOCIALIZATION EXPERIENCES OF SEX OFFENDERS.   Examination of the childhood and adolescence of convicted sex offenders and unidentified assailants has yielded both similarities and differences in the two groups.

Convicted Assailants. First, as noted by William Prendergast (1994), a psychologist who worked with sex offenders in a prison environment for about three decades, many of these men lack self-confidence from an early age. They may compensate for their general sense of inadequacy with exaggerated demonstrations of masculinity, which include assault.

Second, a high proportion of convicted rapists were themselves victims of violent sexual abuse, physical assault, or neglect during their preschool, childhood, and adolescent years (Dhawan & Marshall, 1996; Graham, 1996).

Third, it is perhaps not surprising, given the first two findings, that many adult sex offenders report a pattern of having sexually victimized others during their childhood and adolescence (Barbaree et al., 1993).

Unidentified Assailants. In the case of unidentified offenders, the individuals' backgrounds may be more representative of the general population than are those of convicted rapists. Research comparing unidentified assailants and nonassailants has found no differences in race, social class, or place of residence between the two groups (Ageton, 1983).

The socialization experiences of unidentified assailants, however, do appear to differ from those of nonassailants. Suzanne Ageton's (1983) data from unidentified adolescent offenders showed a pattern of estrangement from the values of families and teachers. These boys engaged in various delinquent activities and identified with delinquent peer groups. Compared with their nonassaultive peers, they expected to receive more negative labeling from both their parents and their teachers. In Ageton's five-year study, these differences in assaultive and nonassaultive males were found before as well as after they had coerced females to have sex.

Similarly, Eugene Kanin's (1985) data indicated that college males who engaged in sexually coercive behavior said that their best friends would "definitely approve" of forcing particular types of women to have sex with them. If the males perceived their potential victims to be "loose," "teasers," "pick-ups," or "economic exploiters," then coercion was justified in their own eyes, and they expected that their peers would approve of their behavior.

ATTITUDES AND PERSONALITY TRAITS OF ASSAILANTS.
Studies in which the personality and attitudes of unidentified rapists were compared with those of nonassaultive men have revealed several factors related to high levels of sexual aggression. With a sample of men ranging in age from 18 to 47, Malamuth (1996) found that hostility toward women, acceptance of interpersonal violence, and dominance as a sexual motive were positively related to self-reported sexual aggression. In Rapaport and Burkhart's (1984) research, the more coercion the unidentified assailants reported, the lower their scores were on measures of responsibility and positive socialization. The assailants in Rapaport and Burkhart's research also saw sexual aggression as more acceptable than did the nonassailants.

In an intriguing study of college students, Mahoney, Shively, and Traw (1986) obtained self-reports of coercive behavior and measures of **hypermasculinity.** A man's rating on the hypermasculinity scale (Mosher & Sirkin, 1984) is determined by asking him to indicate which of two statements from 30 pairs better describes him. For example, most hypermasculine men would choose the statement, "You have to screw some women before they know who is boss," in preference to the statement, "You have to love some women before they know you don't want to be boss." Not surprisingly, hypermasculine men reported having engaged in more sexually coercive behavior than did their counterparts who were more likely to select the less aggressive alternative.

ISSUES TO CONSIDER

How do identified sexual offenders differ from unidentified sexual offenders?

hypermasculinity Exaggeration of male dominance through an emphasis on male virility, strength, and aggression.

hyperfemininity Exaggerated adherence to a stereotypic feminine gender role.

In the light of the Mahoney group's (1986) findings and Kanin's (1985) conclusion that assailants and their peers perceived some types of women as legitimate targets of coercion, it is tempting to speculate that hypermasculine males are most attracted to the **hyperfeminine** women whom they perceive as deserving of assault (Murnen & Byrne, 1991).

SEXUAL CHARACTERISTICS OF ASSAILANTS.   It is common to think of rapists as sexually preoccupied people with high sex drives. A rather different picture emerged from the work of A. Nicholas Groth and Ann Burgess (1977), who studied men convicted of sexual assault, women who were victims of sexual assault, and victims' descriptions of the assault to the police. Only a quarter of the convicted rapists had no problems with erection or ejaculation during the assault. About one-third of the men showed clear evidence of sexual dysfunction of some type.

ISSUES TO CONSIDER

Why do you think that convicted rapists often experience sexual problems during forced sex?

Ironically, practically none of the convicted rapists reported similar dysfunctions in their sexual relations with consenting partners. Rather, their dysfunctions appeared to be specific to the context of rape. These observations are consistent with the notion that rape is not primarily sexually motivated but instead is an attempt to dominate and subjugate another person. There remains the larger question, however, of why the anger, resentment, and need to control are expressed sexually.

Studies of unidentified rapists are more supportive of the notion that rapists have strong sexual appetites. Compared with nonrapists, the unidentified rapists in Kanin's (1985) sample had had a greater number of sexual partners, as well as considerably more sexual outlets: the average number of orgasms per month from coitus, fellatio, and masturbation was 6, compared to 0.8 for the nonassailants. When asked how often they attempted to seduce a new date, 62 percent of the unidentified rapists responded "most of the time," compared to 19 percent of the nonrapists.

Part of the discrepancy between results of studies of convicted rapists and those of studies of unidentified rapists regarding aggressive versus sexual motivations may stem from the level of relationship between the rapist and the victim. Women who are raped by strangers are far more likely to report the assault, resulting in an overrepresentation of stranger assaults among convicted rapists (McCormick, 1994). It may be that convicted males who rape strangers are using sex to express aggressive, hostile motives, whereas males who rape acquaintances are using aggressiveness to achieve sexual goals, a notion to which we will return when we examine hypotheses about the causes of rape. Before turning to that topic, we consider victims of sexual coercion.

Victims of Sexual Coercion

Victims of sexual assault come from all walks of life. In trying to describe the typical victim of sexual coercion, we face some of the same generalization problems that have plagued research on rapists. We will distinguish among those victims who report their assaults to authorities and victims who do not report their assaults but anonymously acknowledge during victimization surveys that they have been assaulted.

Many people think of the typical sexual assault as the rape of a young woman by someone whom she does not know. However, about 75 percent of sexual assaults reported to authorities involve people who know each other, and among legally unidentified victims, the overwhelming majority know their assailants (Federal Bureau of Investigation, 1996; Lonsway, 1996). Sometimes they have just met, sometimes they have been casually dating for a while, and sometimes they are married to each other. Many sexual assaults involve more than one assailant. Further, some of the victims of sexual assault by individuals or gangs are male.

MALE VICTIMS OF ASSAULT.   Popular stereotypes of rape victims do not usually include males. Even when we consider men as rape victims, we think of them as being at risk of sexual assault only when they are in prison and only by male assailants. Indeed, many men are raped in prison. In an ambitious study of prison rape in several prisons in a midwestern state, Cindy Struckman-Johnson et al. (1996; see also Struckman-Johnson, 1998) found that 22 percent of imprisoned men anonymously reported having been raped (compared to 7 percent of imprisoned women). A quarter of the rapes of men were gang assaults. Women (staff) were among the perpetrators in 5 percent of the cases, and they were the sole perpetrators in 2 percent of the cases.

Reports of male victims from rape-crisis centers and the data from several recent studies document that nonimprisoned men can also be sexually assaulted by women (Struckman-Johnson & Struckman-Johnson, 1994). In Laumann et al.'s (1994) national study, 3.6 percent of the men reported having been forced into sexual contact, which would generalize to more than 3 million American males.

Perhaps because of the traditional definition of rape as an act committed by a male against a female, most researchers studying acquaintance assault have constructed their measures on the assumption that males are perpetrators and females are victims. Struckman-Johnson (1988) administered a survey to college students that allowed them—regardless of their gender—to respond as assailants, victims, or both. In her sample, 22 percent of the women and 16 percent of the men reported that they had experienced at least one forced-sex episode.

As might be expected, the strategies used to obtain sex by men and women differed. In Struckman-Johnson's (1988) study, 53 percent of the female victims, compared to 9 percent of the male victims, reported sexual coercion through physical restraint. In contrast, male victims were more likely to report the use of psychological force (48 percent) than were female victims (16 percent). For 12 percent of the incidents, the force used included physical restraint, physical intimidation, threat of harm, or harm (Struckman-Johnson & Struckman-Johnson, 1994). Like victimized women, men who are raped find the event traumatic and the reporting of it difficult (see "Highlight: Male Rape," page 354).

Later in the chapter, we describe the after-effects of rape on women. Following rape by women, many college men experience the same sorts of disruptions in eating, sleeping, sexual relationships, social relationships, and psychological functioning as college women and women in the general community report (Struckman-Johnson, 1991). The self-reported negative emotional impact was less when the coercion was from female than from male perpetrators. In addition to the fear, anger, and self-blame that is commonly felt by women who have experienced coercion, the men coerced by women felt that their masculinity had been threatened; in contrast, heterosexual men coerced by men were concerned about perceptions of their sexual orientation (Struckman-Johnson et al., 1996).

FEMALE VICTIMS OF ASSAULT.   The true incidence of the sexual assault of women is difficult to estimate because the relevant statistics are compiled in different ways by different sources. Further, police reports include only a fraction of incidents because many victims do not report the assault. Even when they do, legal authorities do not always believe the victim. A nationally representative sample of adolescents revealed rates of sexual assaults of females by adolescent males as much as 300 times higher than police reports show (Ageton, 1983).

Studies of adolescents are particularly important because of the consistent finding (among both victims who report to authorities and those who report only anonymously on victimization surveys) that females in their adolescence and early 20s are at greatest

HIGHLIGHT

Male Rape

This account was sent to us by a young convict after he took a human sexuality course in prison:

> It was the policy for inmates to shower—all at once—in a large shower room. While showering, I was aware of a hand brushing against my genitals. As I turned and looked around, I observed a young male on his hands and knees as a much larger youth began raping him anally. The cries were loud and scary as the incident continued. I pretended not to notice as another man stepped in front of the youth and began to force his penis into the youth's mouth. I stood there in sheer disbelief as the youth became a sexual "sandwich" for the two larger youths. After they had both ejaculated, they punched and kicked the smaller man until he lay still on the floor—blood and semen running from his anus. . . . It was not a pretty sight. It is a memory which is deeply imbedded in my mind— as vivid as though it was yesterday. Whatever happened to the young man who was victimized? He committed suicide three days later.

risk of sexual assault (McCormick, 1994). Although research on victims who report the assault to authorities has suggested that they come predominantly from lower socioeconomic classes, such studies may overrepresent the poor because victims who can afford to do so may seek treatment from private sources to avoid having to deal with the police and the media. Findings based on representative samples show that a woman's risk of sexual assault is unrelated to her social class (Ageton, 1983).

The popular perceptions notwithstanding, the overwhelming majority of female victims know their assailants. The level of relationship varies considerably across studies; assailants range from casual acquaintances of the victims to friends, teachers, neighbors, classmates, dates, lovers, fiancés, and spouses. In Laumann et al.'s (1994) national sample, only 4 percent of women who experienced forced sexual activity claimed that the perpetrator was a stranger. Among samples of college students, between 86 percent and 98 percent of the victims knew their attackers (Koss, Dinero, Seibel, & Cox, 1988; Mynatt & Allgeier, 1990).

Acquaintance assault (sometimes called date rape) first received attention when Kirkpatrick and Kanin (1957) found that 62 percent of college women they surveyed reported experiencing at least one episode of offensive force in the year before they entered college. At least one incident of offensive sexual aggression during the previous year in college was also reported by 56 percent of these women.

Perhaps the most startling statistics emerged from a study of the responses of college men to a questionnaire containing inquiries about the use of offensive sexual aggression (Kanin, 1969). Specifically, the men were asked whether they had personally attempted to have sexual intercourse with a woman by using force that was disagreeable and offensive to her. About 22 percent of these men admitted to the use of force.

The form and the extent of force that female victims experience seem to vary as a function of whether the assailant is a stranger or an acquaintance. As we might expect, acquaintance assaults are less likely to involve either a weapon or physical injury to the victim than are assaults by strangers (Allgeier, 1987; Koss et al., 1988). Among college students, the pattern of assaults sometimes involves a man's attempt to engage in a particular sexual activity with little or no prior sexual play.

Perpetrators of sexual assault often deliberately attempt to intoxicate victims with drugs or alcohol. As Katie Roiphe (1993) pointed out, a man may give a woman alcohol or drugs, but she chooses whether to consume them unless drugs are slipped into her drink. Such deceptive behavior has been occurring with the drug *Rohypnol,* known on the street as "roofies." This odorless, colorless, tasteless tranquilizer is dropped into victims' drinks, causing them to pass out and have little memory of what happens next. In response to highly publicized reports of women being raped after being victimized by this ploy, President Clinton signed a bill in 1996 outlawing Rohypnol and other "date-rape drugs." The bill subjects rapists to an additional 20 years in prison if they use a narcotic to incapacitate their victims.

The majority of assaulted women feel extremely hostile following the attack, with about a third reporting anger or disgust, or both. Other emotional reactions include fear, guilt, and emotional pain. Women with relatively assertive personalities, however, make fewer internal attributions of responsibility; that is, they engage in less self-blame for the assault than do women who are relatively nonassertive (Mynatt & Allgeier, 1990). An interesting finding emerged from Mary Koss et al.'s (1988) study in that 73 percent of the women they categorized as rape victims did not define their experience as rape. These women apparently did not recognize that their self-reported experience met the legal criteria for sexual assault. Further clouding our interpretations of rape, 42 percent of women categorized as rape victims in Koss's study later had consensual sex with the man who had allegedly raped them earlier (Gilbert, 1992).

As with acquaintance rape, sex forced on women by their husbands is seldom defined by the women as rape or sexual assault and is almost never reported to authorities (Russell, 1984). Among the college-student sample that Koss et al. (1988) studied, 351 of the women (11 percent) were married. Of these, 13 percent reported having been raped by spouses or family members.

What Provokes Sexual Assault?

Among the current hypotheses used to explain rape are victim precipitation, uncontrollable lust, uncontrollable aggression, exaggerated gender-role identity, and exposure to violent pornography. As noted in Chapter 12, exposure to violent pornography has been shown to increase acceptance of rape myths and negative attitudes toward women. We do not know whether exposure to violent pornography sufficiently lowers inhibitions against aggression in the real world to the point that a man who is irritated by a woman and then sees violent pornography would actually seek out that woman to rape her. We now turn to other ideas, starting with the hypothesis that has received the least support: the notion that victims cause assailants to rape them.

VICTIM PRECIPITATION.   The majority of adults—both men and women—blame the victims of sexual assault for provocative behaviors before, during, and after they have been forced to engage in sex. Almost all research on blaming victims for sexual assault has focused on attitudes toward female victims.

The belief that a victim precipitates assault by her behavior comes in a number of guises. About two-thirds of a sample of U.S. citizens agreed that "women provoke rape by their appearance or behavior" (Feild & Bienen, 1980). Teenagers—males and females alike—are less likely to perceive an open shirt, tight jeans, or a tight bathing suit as a signal of sexual interest or availability when worn by a man rather than by a woman (Zellman & Goodchilds, 1983). In addition to being held responsible for assaults because of the way they dress, women, according to various surveys, are also held accountable if they hitchhike or enter a man's apartment (McCormick, 1994).

At odds with the stereotypes of victims' provoking their own assaults were the results of a study sponsored by the Federal Commission on Crimes of Violence, which concluded that only 4 percent to 6 percent of rape charges involve victim precipitation (Curtis, 1974). That study was conducted more than two decades ago; the assault rate has risen since that time, but there is no reason to believe that low rates of victim precipitation have changed.

ISSUES TO CONSIDER

To what extent do you be-
lieve that rapists are motivated by sexual arousal
versus needs to dominate
and aggress against their
victims? Do you think that
rapists from different populations (e.g., stranger rapists,
acquaintance rapists) may
differ in their motives?

UNCONTROLLED LUST OR UNCONTROLLED AGGRESSION?

Belief in victim precipitation may stem in part from the assumption that a rapist attacks a victim out of an intense, overpowering sexual drive unleashed by a sexually provoca-tive woman. As Feild and Bienen (1980) pointed out, if a relatively unattractive victim charges rape, she may be perceived as lying—"No one would be turned on by her." However, if the victim is attractive, some observers would maintain that the rapist was so overcome with passion that he could not help himself. Clearly, both approaches im-ply that the rapist's motivation is sexual rather than assaultive. Despite this common belief, most experts have concluded that sexual arousal and aggression fuse into a volatile pathway to rape (Malamuth, 1996; Muehlenhard, Danoff-Burg, & Powch, 1996).

Some evidence that unidentified males who rape acquaintances may have both aggressive and sexual motives comes from Kanin (1985), who found that the male as-sailants in his sample perceived themselves to be sexually deprived. Although the aver-age number of monthly sexual outlets they reported far exceeded the number reported by nonassailants (6 versus fewer than 1), the number of sexual outlets they desired was 4.5 orgasms per week, compared to 2.8 for nonassailants. Because nonassailants also reported a desire for greater sexual contact than they were having but did not feel com-pelled to force women to engage in nonconsensual sex, what is it that motivates the rapist to engage in sexual aggression? Assailants reported receiving considerably more pressure from their peers to engage in sexual activity than did nonassailants. This finding provides some support for the idea that exaggerated gender-role norms and identification may underlie the perpetration of sexual assault, a hypothesis to which we now turn.

EXAGGERATED GENDER-ROLE IDENTITY.

The traditional socializa-tion of men and women may set the stage for conflict and sexual assault. Men are trained to believe that a truly masculine man is aggressive and has intense sexual needs (Byers, 1996; Hall & Barongan, 1997). Traditional socialization also encourages the belief that women are not particularly interested in sex but that they can be "awakened" sexually with enough persuasion and seductive power. Accordingly, some rapists be-lieve that even though their victims struggled, the women secretly enjoyed the rapist's sexual prowess. In other words, the assumption is that just because a woman *says* no, it does not necessarily signify that she *means* no. Further, the rapist may believe that even if the woman means no initially, the sexual episode will lead her to change her mind (McCormick, 1994; Muehlenhard, 1988).

The belief that men ought to—or at least inevitably do—push for sexual intimacy and that women must therefore set limits is deeply ingrained in both Eastern and West-ern cultural traditions (Hall & Barongan, 1997). Thus, as noted in Chapter 4, it is im-portant that parents and others who help to shape young people's outlook and behavior take responsibility for teaching youths (1) to communicate what they do and do not want in their interpersonal interactions and (2) to listen to and respect what the other person is saying, so that they may reduce the potential conflict arising from traditional male and female roles. Children and adolescents need to understand that violence is not a solution to anything and that it is possible to clarify their interest or lack of in-terest in sexual intimacy by discussing sexual feelings honestly and directly with po-tential partners.

We hope that research over the next few years will yield more information relevant to these hypotheses about the causes of sexual assault. In the meantime, both research and the efforts of various advocacy groups have done a great deal to reduce the pain associated with the aftermath of rape.

The Aftermath of Sexual Assault

The anguish wrought by sexual assault often extends far beyond the actual experience (see Figure 14.1). For about a third of victims, the rape episode itself is only the preface to a series of traumatic events that can go on for years (Kilpatrick, Edmunds, & Seymour, 1992). Further, the common belief that rape by a stranger is more traumatic than rape by a boyfriend or husband is not supported by research on assault (Golding, 1996; Kilpatrick, Best, Saunders, & Veronen, 1988). The Kilpatrick group's study found that women assaulted by spouses or dates were as likely as those attacked by strangers to be "depressed, fearful, obsessive-compulsive, and sexually dysfunctional years after the assault" (p. 343).

On the basis of their research with victims of rape seen at Boston City Hospital, Burgess and Holmstrom (1974) described a **rape-trauma syndrome.** The syndrome consists of two phases. The *acute* phase, which can last for several weeks after the rape, generally includes one of two basic reactions. With an *expressive* reaction, the victim cries frequently and expresses feelings of fear, anxiety, tension, and anger. With a *controlled* reaction, the woman is composed, calm, and subdued.

Following the acute phase, women go through a long-term *reorganization* phase. During this period, which can last more than a year, women experience a variety of reactions. Some move repeatedly and switch jobs or even stop going to work. Fears of any situation resembling that in which the rape occurred are common. A rape survivor may experience disruptions in consensual sexual relationships; avoidance of sexual activities that he or she formerly enjoyed; or disturbances related to specific activities that took place during the event, such as swallowing if the assault involved forced oral penetration. Sexual assault can also cause excessive menstrual bleeding, genital burning, missed menstrual periods, and painful intercourse (Golding, 1996).

Finally, some victims have a *silent* rape reaction. They experience the kinds of reactions described above but do not tell anyone about the assault. They are thereby deprived of the opportunity to obtain the support and counseling that may help them to resolve their fears and their undeserved feelings of guilt.

In addition to their personal reactions, many assault victims have to contend with a series of painful and humiliating episodes in police stations and in the courts (see "Highlight: Was He Asking for It?" on page 358). The aftermath of the described mugging seems ridiculously farfetched. It is not so unusual, however, when the crime is sexual assault. In fact, by substituting the idea of sex for the idea of money in the questions in the Highlight, you can obtain a fairly realistic picture of the kind of interrogation that many victims of sexual assault have endured.

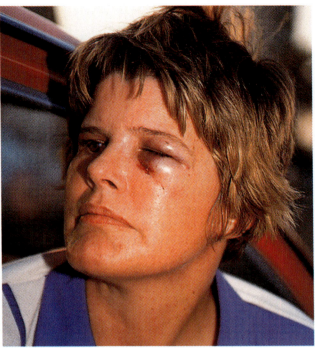

Figure 14.1
The Assault Victim This woman's face reflects the trauma of a sexual assault.

rape-trauma syndrome
Emotional and behavioral consequences that victims experience after being raped.

What Should Assault Victims Do?

A victim of sexual assault should call the nearest rape-crisis center for help immediately, before changing clothes, bathing, or doing anything else. Many crisis centers provide a volunteer to accompany the victim during everything from initial medical

HIGHLIGHT

Was He Asking for It?

John Jones walks six blocks from his office to the subway every day after work. Occasionally, he gives some coins to some of the beggars who solicit money along his route.

One evening, he stayed at work later than usual because he had been invited to a dinner party and needed to change his clothes. He brought a nice shirt and a sport coat with him to work and changed in the restroom. It was dark and rainy when he left the office. The other office workers had left for home earlier, and the street was deserted. About halfway to the subway, John noticed one of the beggars to whom he had occasionally given spare change approaching him. The man held out his hand, but John smiled and said, "Sorry, but I'm afraid I don't have any extra today," and continued on his way. He thought that the beggar was following him, so with some apprehension, he began walking more quickly. The next thing he knew, he had been tackled to the ground, and the beggar told him to give him his wallet or "I'll cut you up good!" It had gotten quite dark, so John could not see if the man had a knife or some other weapon; he decided that maybe it would be best if he just gave up the wallet. The beggar grabbed it and ran off.

John staggered home to call the police. When he got home, he still felt upset, so he fixed a drink, took a shower, and changed into dry clothes to try to calm down before making the call. He was told to come to the station to file a report.

Throughout his dealings with the police, and later, in court, John was exposed continuously to statements and questioning that suggested that he had not really been robbed or that he had provoked the beggar into the assault:

1. It is six blocks between your office and the subway, so why didn't you take a cab? Aren't you asking for it when you parade the street every night?

2. Have you ever given away money to anyone before?

3. Did you ever give money to the person you *claim* mugged you?

4. You don't look like you've been hurt; how do we know that a mugging occurred?

5. Can you prove your wallet was taken?

6. Why were you so dressed up? Wasn't that just inviting the assault?

7. You've given him a dollar or two before and now you claim he took your wallet containing $50, but in giving him some money, weren't you in effect consenting to give him all your money?

8. You didn't resist the mugger; therefore, you must have really wanted to give him your wallet.

9. You said that he threatened you, but you didn't see the knife, and in fact, you handed over your wallet to him, so it doesn't sound like a mugging at all.

10. If you really were mugged, why did you wait two hours before calling? Maybe you really wanted to give the man your money at the time but then changed your mind later.

treatment to final court appearances. Some centers also offer group-counseling sessions to help victims cope with the immediate and long-term effects of the attack. There are many of these centers throughout North America.

In the course of the medical examination and treatment administered after an assault, a victim usually receives a physical examination and an inspection of the genitals or other areas violated during the assault. A sperm sample is collected if possible, and other evidence of assault is documented. Many states have recently passed laws requiring the county or state to pay the cost of such medical examinations.

After undergoing a medical examination and treatment, the victim should report the assault to the police. The majority of victims, however, do not do so. Many are reluctant because they feel guilty and responsible for the assault. Further, some victims fear rejection by their mates, family members, and friends in the event that the assault becomes public knowledge. The small proportion of victims who overcome their fears and inhibitions enough to report the assault have no guarantee that the police will record the charge or that the rapist will be convicted.

Sexual Assault and the Criminal Justice System

Legal authorities may determine that an assault charge is unfounded for many reasons. If there are obvious discrepancies in the victim's story or if the police conclude from their investigation that no offense occurred or was attempted, they will declare the charge unfounded.

Kanin (1994) studied the forcible-rape cases in a small city in a midwestern state over a nine-year period. Of the 109 reported rapes, 41 percent were discovered to be false. Revenge, attention seeking, and the need for an alibi (e.g., an unmarried adolescent becomes pregnant and tries to avoid responsibility) were the most common motives for the false allegations. Unfortunately, these cases complicate and detract from the efforts to reduce our high rates of sexual assault.

When a case is determined to be unfounded, it is not included in the crime statistics, and the authorities do not deal with it in any way. Under these conditions, victims may find themselves in the unexpected and bewildering predicament of having come to the police for aid (depicted by the media as the courageous and correct course to take), only to have the door slammed in their faces.

The assistance of a female crisis center volunteer is potentially useful in reducing the likelihood that the police will judge an assault charge unfounded. Moreover, McCahill, Meyer, and Fischman's study (1979) of rape reports in Philadelphia showed that the presence of another woman during the report—whether she was the police officer taking the report or the secretary taking notes during the interview—was associated with a reduced proportion of rape charges that were declared unfounded.

About half of all complaints that are declared founded do not result in an arrest. Moreover, of those arrested, only 58 percent are prosecuted, and of those prosecuted, 46 percent are acquitted or have their cases dismissed. Based on these figures, a rapist's chances of being convicted for assault are only 4 in 100 (Feild & Bienen, 1980). Most of us would be willing to bet quite a bit of money if the probability of losing were only 4 percent.

STATE LAWS ON SEXUAL ASSAULT.   In an effort to improve these rather grim statistics, dramatic changes are being made in the legal definition of assault and the treatment of the victim whose case does reach the courtroom. When victims, aided by crisis center volunteers, report assaults to the police and tell their stories in court, they not only diminish their own feelings of helplessness but also have the satisfaction of reducing the likelihood that the rapist will be able to attack others in the future.

Many states no longer employ the term *rape* because of its connotation of forced penile-vaginal penetration. The broader phrase sexual assault, which implies coercive sexual contact that does not necessarily involve penile-vaginal intercourse, has become more common.

Also, many states have rewritten their laws in gender-neutral terms so that the victim and the offender can be either male or female. Previously, sexual assaults on males were prosecuted under sodomy laws. The problem with using sodomy laws is that both participants, the perpetrator and the victim, are usually charged.

The issue of consent remains a crucial one in the definition of sexual assault. For example, in **statutory rape,** an older person is charged with having sex with another person who is not considered old enough to give consent to sexual activity, even if the

statutory rape Sexual intercourse with a person who is under the legal age of consent in a given state.

younger person willingly engaged in or even initiated sexual contact. Our statutory rape laws can be traced to England more than seven hundred years ago, when ravishing a maiden "under the age of 12" became illegal (Donovan, 1997). These laws became part of the American legal system through English common law. Today, the age of consent in the United States varies by state and ranges from 14 to 18 years of age.

Returning to the issue of force, in the hypothetical story in "Highlight: Was He Asking for It?" on page 358, it was implied that the mugged man consented to the assault because he had earlier given away money to many people, including the mugger. That is, of course, patently absurd. However, the same logic has prevailed in both societal attitudes toward rape victims and the arguments of attorneys who are defending alleged rapists. That is, if a victim had ever consented to sex with anyone, or if she and the offender had ever engaged in a sexual interaction—even kissing—then the traditional view was that she must have consented to whatever sexual acts her assailant desired. In response to objections that such assumptions essentially put the victim rather than the assailant on trial, the U.S. Congress passed a law in 1979 known as the Rape Victim's Privacy Act. This law limits the extent to which evidence of the victim's previous sexual experience with people other than the defendant can be introduced.

Another major change in some states' sexual assault laws is the elimination of the requirement that, to prove a sexual assault, the victim must have resisted. Under some circumstances, passive submission may be the victim's best strategy. Some victims who adopt passivity, however, are later described by defense attorneys as having consented to the sexual contact. To prove nonconsent, victims had to have done everything in their power to resist the assault, even if their actions might have exposed them to further brutality and injury. In part because of the work of rape-crisis centers throughout the country, lawmakers and judges are beginning to realize that a woman need not have the kind of injuries shown in Figure 14.1 to be a nonconsenting victim of sexual assault.

Clearly, the victims of sexual coercion face ongoing difficulties long after they experience an episode of sexual assault. It would be desirable to find a means of preventing all sexual coercion. Because that goal is unlikely to be met, however, people should take steps themselves to reduce their risk of being sexually assaulted.

Factors Associated with Being Sexually Assaulted

Because none of us is free of the risk of sexual coercion, assault victims should not be blamed for attacks they suffer. Accumulating evidence, however, indicates that there are strategies that can be used to reduce the likelihood of an assault or to fend off an assault attempt.

Marital status is correlated with risk of assault, with single women being at greatest risk, followed by divorced or separated women; married women are at least risk (Russell, 1984). Of course, it is difficult or impossible to alter factors such as age—as noted earlier, women in their adolescence or early 20s are at greater risk than are older women—or marital status to try to reduce the risk of assault.

Other risk factors have been identified that are somewhat more controllable. The chances of victimization increase as women lead "riskier" (less protected or less "traditional") lives—for example, by being sexually active, living apart from parents and (if in college) outside a dorm, lacking a visible male partner, experimenting with drugs, or consuming alcohol (Abbey et al., 1996; Mynatt & Allgeier, 1990). Among adolescent women, those who are alienated from their parents and teachers, identify with a delinquent peer group, and engage in delinquent acts themselves are more likely to become victims of sexual assault than are their nonalienated counterparts (Ageton, 1983).

The general sexual climate within the peer groups of victims differs from that within the peer groups of nonvictims. Hall and Flannery (1985) found that girls aged 14 to 17 whose best friends were not sexually active were less likely to have been raped than those whose best friends were sexually active. The authors suggested that if a young woman is part of a peer group known to be sexually active and is sexually active herself, the man who rapes her may perceive her as being interested in sex and as having led him on.

In addition, the consensual sexual experience of sexual-assault victims is greater than that of nonvictims (Abbey et al., 1996; Koss & Dinero, 1988). In Koss's research, victims reported an average of 12 sexual partners, whereas nonvictims reported an average of 4 partners. Compared with nonvictims, those women experiencing rape were more likely to have had as their first sexual partners strangers, casual dates, or married men, and they were less likely to have had steady boyfriends or a fiancé as their first sexual partners. Victims in the Koss study were also less likely than nonvictims to report that they believed that their first intercourse experience would lead to marriage.

REDUCING YOUR RISK OF SEXUAL ASSAULT.
Many of these steps are more applicable to acquaintance assault than to assault by strangers, but, as we have seen, most assaults involve acquaintances. Much of this discussion also applies to potential male victims.

1. *Determine your sexual policies.* If you have not thought about what you need in a relationship before you would feel comfortable with or desirous of sexual contact, you may communicate considerable ambivalence about your wishes to a partner, who may interpret your ambiguity as a desire to "be persuaded." Thus it may be helpful to make a list of your general sexual policies. What kind of person would you find acceptable as a potential sexual partner? How well would you want to know this person prior to physical intimacy? How much commitment would you need before you found sexual relations acceptable? Where and when would sexual contact be comfortable for you? Add any other factors that you consider important in making a decision about having a sexual relationship. People sometimes alter their policies, but it is advantageous for you to clarify in your own mind the general conditions under which sexual intimacy is acceptable to you.

2. *Discuss your policies regarding sexual activities.* We commonly negotiate such nonsexual activities as where to eat dinner and what movie to see. Why not explicitly negotiate the acceptability and timing of sexual activities as well? Although evidence directly demonstrates that such negotiations do not eliminate the risk of assault attempts, the directness and firmness with which a person communicates nonconsent to sexual activity are positively related to resisting successfully an attempt at forced sexual contact (Byers & Lewis, 1988; Quinsey & Upfold, 1985).

3. *Negotiate in public, and avoid being alone with a person until you believe that you can trust him or her.* Quinsey and Upfold's (1985) analysis of attempted versus completed rapes indicated that rapists were least likely to be deterred when the attempt was made inside a building or car and against someone whom they knew.

4. *Avoid becoming intoxicated if you are with a person with whom you do not wish to become intimate.* Use of alcohol or drugs by assailants and victims is common at the time of a sexual assault (Abbey et al., 1996; Barbaree et al., 1993).

Figure 14.2
Self-Defense Against Sexual Assault Women can develop a sense of confidence by learning methods of self-protection to prevent sexual victimization.

Intoxication lowers the inhibitions of a potential assailant; it may also impede the ability of a potential victim to escape an assault attempt.

5. *Make your feelings known both verbally and nonverbally.* In the event that someone does try to force you to have sex, communicate in every way possible that you do not want sexual contact (see Figure 14.2). Men have cited victim resistance as the primary reason for the failure of an assault attempt. Some self-identified rapists in Kanin's (1985) sample reported surprise that their victims had been so easily intimidated; the assailants described other occasions of assault attempts that clearly had been rebuffed. Victim resistance of any kind tends to deter assault, and screaming is a particularly strong deterrent (Muehlenhard, Andrews, & Beal, 1996). Most males interpret screaming as strong evidence of nonconsent (Byers & Lewis, 1988). The fact that a scream is more likely to be effective if someone other than the assailant can hear it is another reason to avoid being alone with a person until you believe that you can trust him or her.

One important qualification should be added here. Although the vast majority of assaults are carried out by acquaintances and do not involve the threat of lethal weapons, if someone attempts to assault you using a weapon as the means of coercion, resistance may be ill advised.

In summary, take as much active control of your environment as you can. Remember, however, that following all of these steps will not eliminate the possibility of being sexually assaulted or seriously injured during an assault. There are no absolute rules for dealing with all assaults; ultimately, you must decide which strategy seems most likely to get you out of the particular assault situation with the least amount of harm. We live in a society in which violence is commonplace, and hostility and aggression are often expressed against inappropriate targets. We hope that the information provided in this chapter will help you reduce your risk of being sexually assaulted. In the next section we consider another form of coercion that some of the preceding steps may be useful in combating: the abuse of power to harass sexually.

SEXUAL HARASSMENT

Sexual harassment appears in diverse guises and in many different environments. For example, an employer may use the power to hire, promote, and fire to force an employee into having sexual relations (see Figure 14.3). An instructor may use the power to grade to coerce sexual intimacy. Harassment can also take place between health care providers and clients, between clergy and parishioners, and between those of different ranks in the military. All of these situations involve interactions between two people who are not equal in power, and the individual with greater economic, evaluative, or psychological power may employ that advantage to obtain sexual gratification from an individual who is in a subordinate position.

Sexual harassment is quite common. An overview of studies on sexual harassment in a variety of settings suggests that employees or students have at least a 40 percent chance of encountering sexual harassment in their place of work or study (Barak, Fisher, & Houston, 1992).

sexual harassment The use of status and/or power to coerce or attempt to coerce a person into having sex; also, suggestive or lewd comments directed at a person in occupational, educational, or therapeutic settings.

Sexual Harassment in Occupational Settings

Sexual harassment was not clearly perceived as a legal or social problem before the mid-1970s. Initially, the law defined sexual harassment rather narrowly as constituting the requirement that sexual relations be part of getting or keeping a job. Equal Employment Opportunity Commission (EEOC) rulings on sexual harassment in 1980 expanded the definition to encompass *any* unwanted verbal or nonverbal sexual behavior in the workplace. The EEOC ruled that unwelcome sexual advances, requests for sexual favors, and other verbal or physical contact of a sexual nature constitute sexual harassment when (1) submission to such conduct is made either explicitly or implicitly a term or condition of an individual's employment; (2) submission to or rejection of such conduct by an individual is used as the basis for employment decisions affecting the individual; or (3) such conduct has the purpose or effect of unreasonably interfering

Figure 14.3
Sexual Harassment at Work
Sexual harassment may involve physical force, or it may occur in more subtle ways, as in this photo. This man's intrusion into an employee's physical space may go unreported because she fears losing her job.

HIGHLIGHT

Research Findings on Sexual Harassment

1. About a third to half of working women have suffered some negative consequences from sexual harassment, whereas few men report problems in this area.

2. When asked whether they had ever quit a job because of sexual harassment, up to 15 percent of respondents said yes.

3. Married women are less likely to report having been harassed than are single, divorced, or cohabiting women.

4. Men are more flattered by sexual overtures from women at work than are women by such approaches from men.

5. About half of men who initiate are supervisors. The more severe the harassment is, the more likely the initiator is to be a supervisor rather than a coworker.

6. Men who rate high on a measure of likelihood to harass sexually hold adversarial sexual beliefs, have difficulty assuming others' perspectives, endorse traditional male gender-role stereotypes, are high in authoritarianism, and report a higher likelihood of raping if they believe they will not be caught.

Sources: Barak, Fisher, & Houston, 1992; Bingham & Scherer, 1993; Fitzgerald, Swan, & Fischer, 1995; Gutek, 1995; Pryor, 1994.

with an individual's work performance or creating an intimidating, hostile, or offensive working environment.

Early research on harassment relied on self-selected respondents, such as women attending a meeting on the topic of harassment, the vast majority of whom had experienced on-the-job harassment (Silverman, 1976). Later studies employing random samples of workers probably provide a more accurate estimate of the extent of harassment in the United States; some of the findings from these studies are presented in "Highlight: Research Findings on Sexual Harassment."

Grieco (1987) mailed questionnaires to all nurses in Boone County, Missouri, inquiring about their experiences with harassment during their careers. More than half indicated that they had experienced grossly inappropriate comments and brief minor touching or breast fondling and mauling. A greater proportion of female nurses (82 percent) than male nurses (67 percent) reported having been harassed. The fact that the majority of both men and women reported harassment suggests that the phenomenon is common, although harassment of women is the predominant mode of sexual harassment in the workplace (Berdahl, Magley, & Waldo, 1996).

Harassment victims report various reactions to the unwanted approaches, including nervousness, loss of motivation, sleeplessness, uncontrolled anger or crying, and weight loss. Nonetheless, they are unlikely to report the episode(s) to authorities (Fitzgerald, Swan, & Fischer, 1995; Gutek, 1985). Awareness of the problem has increased recently, however, with the rise in demonstrations by women's groups to call attention to the issue and because of some well-publicized lawsuits.

Like perpetrators of sexual assault, those who sexually harass their employees or coworkers appear to have a strong need for dominance and power (Fiske & Glick, 1995). Men tend to perceive behaviors that challenge male dominance in the workplace as harassing, whereas women experience behaviors that reinforce female subordinance as harassing (Berdahl et al., 1996).

Not all sexual intimacy between coworkers constitutes harassment. As Barbara Gutek (1992) pointed out, mutual attraction and flirtation commonly occur in the workplace, and men and women alike sometimes seek, and find, marriage partners at work. Mutually consenting adult sexual relations are difficult to attain, however, when there is an imbalance of power between partners in work or educational settings, the topic to which we turn now.

Sexual Harassment in Educational Settings

Harassment in educational settings is quite prevalent at both the undergraduate and the graduate-school levels. In their review of studies conducted at 11 universities, Allen and Okawa (1987) found that, in response to anonymous questionnaires, between 13 percent and 33 percent of students reported experiencing harassment, which ranged from instructors' leering and patting in an offensive manner to threats or bribery to gain sexual intimacy. Although you may think that these students are imagining that their instructors' interest in them is not just academic, Fitzgerald, Weitzman, Gold, and Ormerod (1988) administered an anonymous survey to male faculty, and 25 percent of them reported having had sexual encounters with students. Only one faculty member described the relationship as harassment. Somers (1982) found that 8 percent of the women in her sample reported that either they themselves or others whom they knew had dropped a class or avoided a particular instructor or teaching assistant because of his embarrassing sexual language or advances.

As with sexual assault, the reporting of harassment to academic authorities is uncommon. For example, in Allen and Okawa's (1987) study, although 81 percent of harassed students at the University of Illinois knew that campus policy prohibited sexual harassment, only 5 percent of those who had experienced harassment reported it to any university office or official. This low rate of reporting may stem from students' reporting experiences that objectively constitute sexual harassment on anonymous surveys, but rarely perceiving themselves as having been sexually harassed (Barak et al., 1992).

If you are sexually harassed by an instructor, you should contact authorities on your campus about the incident. Seek out another professor whom you trust or the chairperson of the department. If these people are not supportive, talk with someone at the campus affirmative-action or civil-rights office. Sometimes students are reluctant to report such incidents for fear that the instructor in question will give them failing grades or will be fired. Affirmative-action regulations protect people who file harassment complaints from grade discrimination. If you believe that the instructor who has made advances toward you is not approaching other students and if there have been no other reports of harassment, the instructor generally is put on probation and watched closely. Assuming that there are no further reports of harassment, no career damage occurs. It is common, however, for instructors who engage in such behavior to do so with many students; thus those who are reluctant to report an incident should consider the welfare of their fellow students, who could also become targets, rather than that of the harassing instructor.

Sexual Harassment in Therapeutic Settings

The issue of power differences is particularly stark in the case of the sexual harassment of a patient or client by a physician or psychotherapist. Physicians and psychologists are highly trained, powerful members of society. They usually have more status than the patients or clients who, because of illness or psychological difficulties, seek their help. For the patient or client, compounding the problem of dealing with sexual harassment is the fact that a client's charge of abuse may be ascribed by the therapist or physician to the client's mental instability.

Occasionally, one-sided or mutual attraction may develop between the professional and the patient: 87 percent of the 575 psychotherapists surveyed by Pope,

ISSUES TO CONSIDER

How would you deal with an instructor who made sexual advances toward you?

REALITY or MYTH ? 5

Keith-Spiegel, and Tabachnick (1986) reported feeling sexual attraction toward certain clients. As noted in Chapter 6, such feelings are normal, but professionals who act on their erotic feelings with people who come to them for help are not serving their clients' best interests.

To examine whether clinical and counseling psychology graduate students are obtaining training on how to deal with their sexual feelings toward clients, Sherral Austin and Elizabeth Allgeier (1997) sampled those who were in at least their fourth year of training in American graduate programs and were applying for clinical internships. Most (78 percent) reported that they had experienced sexual feelings toward at least one client, but fewer than half believed that their training had provided more than adequate preparation for handling such feelings. Almost half (43 percent) described their training for dealing with sexual attraction toward clients as less than adequate.

Studies with different samples indicate that 5 percent to 10 percent of therapists act on their feelings and become sexually intimate with their clients (Pope et al., 1986). Further, about three-quarters of therapists who have sex with their clients do so with numerous clients. Pope and Bouhoutsos (1987) reported that one therapist had been involved in sexual relations with more than one hundred clients. Cases involving physicians and their patients have also been reported (Dale, 1986; Plaut & Foster, 1986).

The long-term correlates of such contact for the clients or patients are almost always negative, ranging from hesitation about seeking further professional help to depression, hospitalization, and suicide (Bouhoutsos, Holroyd, Lerman, Forer, & Greenberg, 1983; Grunebaum, 1986; Sonne, Meyer, Borys, & Marshall, 1985; Zelen, 1985).

In addition to the problems attending sexual relationships between people unequal in status, problems arise from the fact that professionals' and clients' motives for sexual intimacy are likely to be quite different. Professionals—including members of the clergy—may perceive themselves as offering therapeutic contact for a brief period of time, but clients, generally dependent while seeking therapeutic or medical help, may believe that they are in love and that their sexual contact is part of a long-term primary relationship, perhaps leading to marriage. Another type of abuse in which the person who initiates sex has more power than the person invited to engage in sexual activity is that of the adult who tries to engage in sexual activity with children.

SEXUAL ABUSE OF CHILDREN

Adult-child sexual interactions by definition involve coercion because children are not legally capable of giving informed consent to sexual activity. An individual who provides informed consent understands both the meaning and the possible consequences of an action, but most children and young adolescents do not have a clear understanding of sexuality. One of the main reasons adults are severely punished for sexual activities with children is that they take advantage of a child's naiveté.

When a sexual relationship involves two people who are related to each other, it is called **incest.** In general, incest refers to any sexual interaction between individuals who are so closely related that marriage between them would be illegal. The word *incest* comes from Latin and means "impure" or "soiled." Although incest can occur between two people of any age, it most frequently involves a child and an adult family member or sibling.

Sexual activity between a child and an adult is a crime in every state. Doctors, psychologists, teachers, and health professionals who work with children are legally required to report to legal authorities all suspected cases of the sexual abuse of chil-

incest Sexual activities between family members who are too closely related to be able to marry legally.

dren. By law, authorities must investigate these reports, and district attorneys must prosecute the cases.

Prevalence of Sexual Abuse of Children

In attempting to determine the prevalence of any phenomenon in a nation, it is useful to have a nationally representative sample, but until the 1990s, when Finkelhor, Hotaling, Lewis, and Smith (1990) and Laumann et al. (1994) reported their results, no such data were available on the prevalence of the sexual abuse of children. Finkelhor et al. (1990) asked respondents questions by telephone about past experiences (occurring at age 18 or under) with what they might now consider to be sexual abuse: attempts by others to touch them sexually, initiate sexual acts including intercourse, photograph them in the nude, exhibit themselves, or perform sex acts in their presence. Of the respondents, 27 percent of the women and 16 percent of the men answered yes to one of the questions. Detailed follow-up questions were then posed to probe their experience. Using an interview procedure, the Laumann (1994) group found that 17 percent of women and 12 percent of men reported being touched sexually during childhood.

In the United States, the number of allegations of the sexual abuse[1] of children reported annually to child protective services leaped from an estimated 34,000 in 1976 to 400,000 in 1995 (U.S. Department of Health and Human Services, 1997). This huge jump in reported child sexual abuse probably resulted from increased media attention and the enforcement of state laws requiring health professionals to report suspected cases of sexual abuse, rather than from a sudden epidemic in the incidence of the sexual abuse of children. The actual incidence of child abuse is not showing systematic marked increases. In surveys, the experience is reported equally frequently by people of different age **cohorts** (Finkelhor et al., 1990; Laumann et al., 1994). If sexual abuse were increasing, we would expect to see higher rates among younger people, but that is not the case.

However, particular conditions—more or less prominent at various points in the past few generations—may increase the likelihood of child sexual abuse (and other forms of abuse and violence, such as sexual assault). We look at these next.

cohort A group from a particular generation; for example, those born from 1970 to 1979 are members of a different cohort from those from 1980 to 1989.

Risk Factors for Sexual Abuse During Childhood

Based on their nationally representative study of adults, Finkelhor et al. (1990) identified two risk factors for males and three primary risk factors for females for sexual abuse during childhood. For males, the risk factors were living with their mothers alone or living with two nonbiological parents. For females, the risk factors included having an unhappy family life, living without a biological parent, and having an inadequate sex education.

Based on his earlier sample of college students, Finkelhor (1984) identified some of these factors plus some additional risk variables. Notably, being reared by a sex-punitive mother was correlated with experiencing sexual abuse. By "sex-punitive mother," Finkelhor meant a mother who warned, scolded, and punished her children for asking questions about sexuality, for masturbating, and for looking at sexually suggestive or

---

1. We occasionally use the phrase "child abuse" synonymously with the phrase "sexual abuse of children." The kind of child abuse that involves the neglect of children or the nonsexual physical beatings and other abuse of children has not disappeared, but as Okami (1990) pointed out, such destructive behavior has taken a back seat to the sexual abuse of children in the concerns of our society. It is also beyond the scope of this book.

Memories of Sexual Abuse During Childhood

Much publicity has accompanied cases in which men and women recall being sexually abused many years after the event(s) occurred. In some cases, people report the abuse as long as three decades later. Most of these recovered memories occur when the individuals see therapists who help them discover past abuse.

One of the more publicized cases involved Cardinal Joseph Bernardin (who died in 1996) in which a man reported recalling, while hypnotized, repeated sexual abuse by the cardinal decades earlier. The "therapist" had no training in hypnosis and had a master's degree from an unaccredited institution (Pendergrast, 1995). The man later retracted his allegation. In 1994, when the man was dying of complications from AIDS, Cardinal Bernardin said mass for him and anointed him in an emotional reconciliation.

Three different patterns are apparent in current cases involving memories of childhood sexual abuse. In one, an adult tells a therapist or other health care professional about having experienced sexual contact with an adult when he or she was a child. The therapist and client explore the current meanings of the event and attempt to resolve the client's feelings so that the event does not intrude on the client's current functioning or relationships.

In a second pattern, a client clearly remembers an episode of having had sexual contact with an adult while he or she was a child, but has sought therapy for current problems and does not perceive the childhood experience as contributing much to these now-pressing issues. The therapist can either accept the client's perception and work with him or her to resolve current problems or treat the childhood event as if it is the reason for the client's present difficulties.

In a third pattern—one described by Pendergrast (1995) and that we have also seen among our students—some therapists operate on the assumption that any current difficulties (e.g., depression, relationship difficulties, sexual dysfunctions) stem from having been sexually abused as a child. For example, one of

explicit pictures. Finkelhor found that girls with sex-punitive mothers were 75 percent more vulnerable to sexual victimization than was the typical girl in the sample. In general, it appears that children in disrupted, isolated, and economically poor families are at higher risk of sexual abuse than youngsters in more stable and middle-class families, although child abuse occurs at all social levels (Finkelhor et al., 1990; Kinsey et al., 1953).

Characteristics of Adult-Child Sexual Contacts

A review of the research that has focused on children who have been sexually abused, or on adults who remember having been sexually abused as children, indicates that heterosexual men are the perpetrators in 95 percent of the cases of sexual abuse of girls and 80 percent of the cases of sexual abuse of boys (Finkelhor & Russell, 1984). Second, sexual abusers are not generally violent (Okami & Goldberg, 1992). In a national sample, physical force was used in only 19 percent of incidents involving girls and 15 percent of episodes involving boys (Finkelhor et al., 1990). Third, children, like  women, are far more likely to be sexually abused by acquaintances—relatives, siblings, family friends, and neighbors—than by strangers (Finkelhor et al., 1990; Laumann et al., 1994).

Long-Term Correlates of Child-Adult Sexual Contacts

Although most people vehemently condemn child-adult sexual contacts and claim that such experiences have profound effects on the child that last into adulthood, a few defend such relationships. For example, in 1984 the Dutch psychologist Theodorus Sandfort published a report of his research with 25 boys, aged 10 to 16, who were involved in sexual relationships with adult males. Most of the boys described their sexual relationships our students told us about her sister who was having some adjustment problems during late adolescence. Her family decided to have her treated in a private psychiatric hospital. The therapist she saw was convinced that her current difficulties stemmed from childhood sexual abuse. He asked a series of questions about her relationship with her father. While she was growing up and her father hugged her, where did he put his hands? Did he ever kiss her on the lips? Did he ever enter the bathroom or her bedroom while she was changing her clothes? The therapist's leading questions continued despite the girl's contention that she had never been abused. The therapist had her locked in her room for several days, but she was finally able to contact her family, who obtained her release. In this pattern, the therapist was clearly convinced that adult difficulties must have resulted from sexual contact during childhood.

Most people think of memory as a recording of all the events they have ever experienced, much like a camcorder records whatever is filmed. However, memory is much more variable than that. It is com-

mon for people not to remember many events in their lives. In addition, we constantly add, delete, and reconstruct our past experiences to bring them in line with our current beliefs.

A few years ago, the television program *20/20* showed a segment on research done with children, "Out of the Mouth of Babes." Over a series of many weeks, the children were repeatedly asked questions about events that did not happen. For example, they were asked about getting their finger caught in a mouse trap, or having their genitals examined by a pediatrician. Initially, the children denied that the event had happened. But over the weeks of questioning, gradually the children reported the event and developed elaborate details about the (nonoccurring) event.

Recovered-memory syndrome is not just an academic issue. Families have been broken up and people sentenced to prison because of "recovered memories." A report of a long-"repressed" memory of abuse from a client should certainly be treated as a possibility but one that needs further investigation and evidence before it is accepted as "truth."

as predominantly positive and did not perceive them as representing abuse of authority by adults.

In contrast, many therapists claim that sex during childhood almost always leads to maladjustment. Although a great deal has been written about these "effects" that sexual relations with adults may have on children, most of the literature is either speculative or based on biased samples from which little can be concluded (Rind, 1995; Rind & Tromovitch, 1997). For example, because psychotherapists often uncover child-adult sexual incidents in the backgrounds of their clients, they have sometimes concluded that these experiences underlie the problems that led the person to seek therapy (see "Health: Memories of Sexual Abuse During Childhood"). Similarly, because substantial numbers of prostitutes have backgrounds that include sexual contact with adults during their childhoods, some observers have assumed that early sexual experience leads to prostitution.

Why are studies of nonclinical populations (people who are not in therapy) important? Because they give us a better picture of the association of child-adult sexual contact than do clinical reports. If someone who has experienced abuse believes that everyone with such experiences will have problems later in life, they probably will attribute all life difficulties to the childhood abuse rather than looking at factors in their current life circumstances. In contrast, knowing that many people are not permanently harmed by many types of childhood sexual experiences allows a wider range of options in explaining their current life situations.

One review indicated that compared to women with no history of childhood sexual abuse, those women who did report such a history were more likely to experience depression, sexual dysfunction, anxiety or fear, homosexual experience, and revictimization experiences (Beitchman et al., 1992). Revictimization—also known as victim

ISSUES TO CONSIDER

What do you think about the possibility of repressing the memory of traumatic events and then remembering them many years later? If a friend or relative reported such an experience, how would you respond?

recidivism—refers to findings that adults who report unwanted childhood sexual experiences are also more likely than adults who do not report such experiences to report unwanted sexual experiences in adulthood (Possage & Allgeier, 1992; Stevenson & Gajarsky, 1991).

Systematic surveys of normal populations, however, suggest that child-adult sexual contacts *per se* do not inevitably lead to long-term problems in adult functioning (Kilpatrick, 1992; Laumann et al., 1994; Rind & Tromovitch, 1997). In a survey of 501 predominantly middle-class women, the majority (55 percent) reported having had some sexual experience with peers or adults during childhood (Kilpatrick, 1986). The presence or absence of sexual contact during childhood, however, was unrelated to stressful family relations, depression, marital satisfaction, sexual satisfaction, or self-esteem in adulthood.

We might expect that children's sexual experience with a relative—particularly a parent—would have more damaging consequences than sexual abuse by a nonrelative because incest would presumably disrupt the child's sense of stability within the family. In support of this hypothesis, Kilpatrick (1986) found that adults whose childhood sexual experiences involved a parent or other relative who used pressure, force, or guilt to obtain the sexual contact did show somewhat more impairment in their adult functioning in all of the areas measured except sexual satisfaction. In terms of its impact on adult functioning, however, the crucial issue appears to be the use of invasive force and coercion by a relative during childhood rather than the sexual contact. Another study of a random sample of more than 1,000 college student women also indicated that the

Figure 14.4
Most Adult-Child Interactions Do Not Involve Sexual Contact Most adults who spend time coaching, teaching, or advising children are invested in the children's well-being.

majority of respondents had unwanted sexual contacts during childhood (Hrabowy & Allgeier, 1987). The more invasive the act was, the more currently troubled the women were by it. Even so, the level of invasiveness was not related to the general measures of psychological adjustment.

Many mental health professionals believe that the reactions of parents, relatives, and adult authorities to sexual incidents are the key factors in determining the effect of these events on children. Young children have little understanding of what is sexual. Therefore, they have difficulty in labeling the incident, if they seek to label it at all. Older children are more aware of sex and thus, depending on what they have learned about sexuality, are more likely to react to abusive incidents with vague feelings of wrongdoing or guilt over their participation, even if they were coerced. Their feelings of guilt can be either reduced or increased by adults' reactions.

Fear is a child's most common reaction to a forced sexual interaction with an adult (Finkelhor, 1979). Fear may also be the primary reason that children avoid telling anyone about an incident of abuse by an adult. In one study of adults, only 26 percent of women and 15 percent of men reported that they told someone about sexual abuse at the time of the experience (Laumann et al., 1994).

When a child does report a sexual contact with an adult to a parent or other authority figure, the adult may, for various reasons, cover it up rather than report it. First, he or she may not believe the child. Such nonrecognition of the sexual contact may be the response that is most damaging to the child's self-concept. Even when an adult believes a child, the adult may avoid reporting the incident for fear of entanglement with legal or social-welfare authorities. If the offender is a family member or close friend, a parent or adult who learns of the incident is less likely to report, perhaps because of fears that the child or the adult offender will be removed from the home (Gaines & Allgeier, 1993). This concern is a relatively realistic one: many of our legal and social policies regarding the sexual abuse of children have had the unintended side effect of further disrupting the family rather than aiding the adjustment of children, particularly when the adult-child contact involves relatives.

If adults overreact to incidents of child sexual abuse, the young victims may feel that they are guilty of some unspeakable act and may blame themselves for what occurred. If adults act reasonably, attributing responsibility to the offending adult where it belongs, children can come away from the experience with minimal distress. It is also important that parents not focus on the sexual nature of the incident. Sexual activity per se, whether it involves exhibitionism, fondling of the genitals, or sexual intercourse, has no relationship to the degree of trauma experienced by children (Bagley, 1996; Finkelhor, 1979; Higgins & McCabe, 1994).

If a child is able to talk with a supportive person, whether a family member or a counselor, about an abusive sexual interaction, residual feelings of shame or fear may subside. It is important for the child or adolescent to vent the emotions and concerns that may stem from such contacts. An anxious overreaction on the part of family members, friends, or therapists may communicate to a child or adolescent that there is something wrong with him or her. Instead, a supportive person should discuss the situation with the adolescent or child in a matter-of-fact way and use the following guidelines in the conversation:

1. Sexual feelings and the desire for sexual attention are perfectly normal.

2. It is inappropriate for adults to interact sexually with children.

3. Sex is not evil, nor are all adults bad. In fact, the adult with whom the child had sexual contact is not necessarily a "bad" person. The behavior of the adult under these conditions, however, was inappropriate.

It is crucial to stress that the child is not responsible and should not feel guilty. Clearly, the use of children by adults to meet their own needs is exploitive.

Before ending this section, it may be helpful to put the phenomenon of child sexual abuse into perspective. First, we should note that most people who concern themselves with children do so out of goodwill and caring, with no intent to exploit (see Figure 14.4, page 370). Second, we should examine rates of other forms of victimization of children. David Finkelhor, one of the foremost authorities on the topic of sexual abuse, has provided rates of childhood victimization ranging from the least common to the most common per 1,000 U.S. children (Finkelhor & Dziuba-Leatherman, 1994). As may be seen by inspection of Figure 14.5, of the 14 forms of victimization, assault by siblings ranks first, childhood sexual abuse ranks tenth, and homicide ranks fourteenth. It is curious that the more prevalent forms of childhood victimization have received far less publicity than childhood sexual abuse.

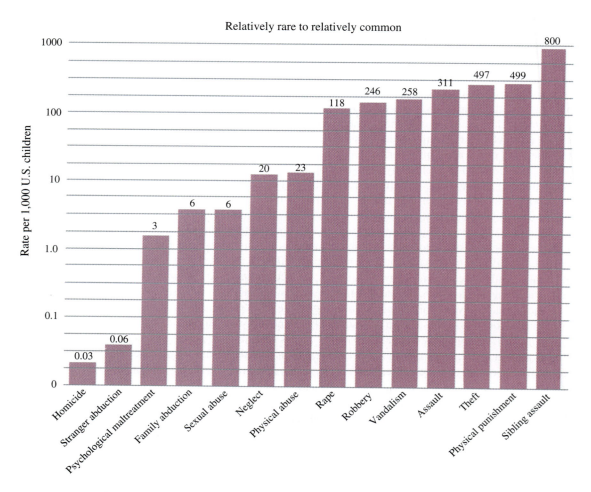

Figure 14.5
Forms of Child Victimization These rates of various forms of victimization of children demonstrate that many potentially harmful behaviors are far more common than the highly publicized crime of child sexual abuse.

GENDER DIFFERENCES IN SEXUALLY COERCIVE BEHAVIOR

We conclude by examining a finding that has cropped up throughout this chapter: most victims of rape, harassment, child sexual abuse, and incest are females, and most perpetrators are males. Some people might use this finding to buttress an argument that males are innately dominating and aggressive and that females are destined to be victims, submissive and masochistic. But for various reasons, this simplistic explanation is unconvincing. First, in all coercive episodes, there are instances in which males are the victims and females the perpetrators. Second, most males do not coerce sexually, and many females experience a lifetime free of sexual victimization. Third, research on cross-cultural differences in the incidence of rape, discussed in Chapter 12, suggests that rape and other forms of sexual coercion may result from social factors (Hall & Barongan, 1997).

One key to reducing the occurrence of sexual coercion of children might be to determine why the overwhelming majority of assailants are males and victims are females. Our informal language is replete with phrases that suggest the sexual stimulus value of young females. Rarely does one hear references to a romantic or erotic relationship between a woman and her "boy," but it is difficult to listen to a popular music station for long without hearing an adult male singing about his "girl" or "baby." The common pairing of "man" with "girl," strictly speaking, refers to a pedophilic relationship, although we may not think of it in that way unless sensitized to the issue.

Women in most cultures involve themselves with men who are older and larger than they are, whereas men generally select partners who are younger and smaller (Buss, 1994). Thus erotic arousal in response to children would presumably require less of an alteration of culturally sanctioned sexual preferences for men than for women.

Women are traditionally socialized to expect men to initiate sexual contact, whereas men learn to take the initiative in sexual relations and to overcome any (anticipated) female resistance. This cultural pattern may make men more likely than women to initiate sexual contacts with children.

In the absence of sexual partners, men seem to suffer more of a loss of self-esteem than do women (Buss, 1994). Under these conditions, men may be more likely to use children sexually to regain their self-esteem.

Females are more frequently the recipients of sexual coercion than are males. As a result, they may be more likely to empathize with feelings of exploitation and thus be less likely to express their sexual feelings toward children.

Finally, throughout most of history, women and children have been viewed as the property of men. Father-initiated sexual activity within the family often has been seen as a right and thus, although not approved of, has usually not been punished. Wives, who have been seen as the property of their husbands, have had few rights, sexual or otherwise.

If differential socialization and differential expectations of men and women contribute to the phenomenon of sexual coercion, then certain trends in North American society may help to reduce the incidence of all forms of coercion. As more egalitarian and less possessive sexual relationships become the norm, the equation of sexuality with dominance and aggression may be lessened (Hall & Barongan, 1997).

Summary of major points

1. Varieties of sexual assault.

A large majority of sexual assaults are carried out by people who are acquainted casually or intimately with the victim. Date rape is prevalent in our culture, and about one-quarter of the college men in one sample reported that they had attempted to force sexual relations. Many college women anonymously report that men have forced or attempted to force them to have sex. Males and spouses also experience sexual coercion. Although the majority of rapists and victims are in their adolescence or early 20s, sexual assault may occur from prepubescence to old age.

2. Characteristics of sexual assailants.

Convicted sex offenders tend to be aggressive and lacking in self-esteem. Many report having been sexually and/or physically abused during childhood and adolescence. Moreover, the stereotype of the assailant as a sexually driven male without access to willing partners is not supported by research. Unidentified assailants tend to be alienated from their families and supported by peers, who encourage and approve of both sexual exploits and the victimization of particular categories of women.

3. Sexual assault stereotypes.

Three major hypotheses have been advanced as possible explanations of sexual assault: victim precipitation, uncontrolled lust or uncontrolled aggression, and exaggerated gender-role identity. The notion that victims precipitate sexual assault is completely unsubstantiated in about 95 percent of the cases. There is some support for the theory that offenders are motivated by aggression and general feelings of inadequacy, but little evidence exists in favor of the uncontrolled-lust hypothesis.

4. Reducing vulnerability to sexual assault.

Ways to reduce chances of being sexually assaulted include knowing one's own sexual policies, avoiding being alone or intoxicated with a person one does not know well, and communicating one's disinterest in having sex in a clear, firm, and straightforward manner. In the event that a potential assailant persists, multiple strategies (talking, screaming, running away, and so forth) are more effective in dissuading the attack than are single strategies.

5. Sexual harassment.

Harassment of subordinates by employers and of students by teachers appears to be relatively common. In addition, sexual harassment occasionally occurs between therapists and clients, with a number of reported negative side effects for the clients. Legislation protects employees from unwanted sexual approaches.

6. The sexual coercion of children.

Because children do not understand the nature and potential consequences of sexual activity, they are unable to give informed consent to such interaction. The long-term correlates of sexual contacts vary considerably as a function of the age difference between the child and the perpetrator, the degree of force, and the level of invasiveness. Despite some psychologists' claims, based on their clinical cases, that such experiences cause adult maladjustment, studies of normal samples indicate few differences in measures of psychological adjustment as a function of having had unwanted sexual experiences during childhood. The responses of other adults in the child's environment to the sexual episode may be related to the extent to which the child can cope with the experience. A child who reports having been sexually victimized by an adult should receive support and counseling to reduce his or her feelings of guilt and responsibility.

7. **Gender differences in sexual coercion.**   Males are far more likely to use sexual coercion than are females, and females are far more likely to be sexually coerced than are males. Several theories attempt to explain the reasons for these gender differences. To the extent that differences in the sexual socialization of men and women contribute to the problem, the growing support for gender equality in personal, educational, and occupational environments may gradually reduce the prevalence of all forms of sexual coercion.

CHECK YOUR KNOWLEDGE

1. All of the following statements are rape myths *except*: (a) The majority of rape victims are attractive women who are attacked while walking alone at night. (b) The majority of rapists have other sexual outlets. (c) The majority of women who charge rape actually consent to the act and then change their minds later. (d) Most rapes occur between people who do not know each other. **(pp. 352–355)**

2. Sexual assaults are more likely to be reported to authorities when the assailant is a (a) stranger, (b) casual acquaintance, (c) steady date, (d) spouse. **(p. 352)**

3. A woman's chances of experiencing sexual assault decrease if she is (a) single, (b) sexually active, (c) identified with a delinquent group, (d) married. **(p. 360)**

4. Male victims of sexual assault (a) unlike females, often report enjoying the experience, (b) are almost always homosexual, (c) are less likely than female victims to report that physical force was used against them, (d) are more likely to report the assault than are female victims. **(p. 353)**

5. Sexual harassment is (a) most common in jobs that require manual labor, (b) more commonly reported by men than by women, (c) a third-degree felony in most states, (d) often motivated by a need for dominance and power. **(p. 364)**

6. Which of the following is *not* a risk factor for childhood sexual abuse? (a) having an inadequate sex education, (b) having more sisters than brothers, (c) having a sexually punitive mother, (d) living without a biological parent **(pp. 367–368)**

7. During the past four decades, reports of sexual abuse of children have (a) increased dramatically, (b) dropped dramatically, (c) shown few systematic fluctuations, (d) been related to the decade in which the child was born. **(p. 367)**

8. Research shows that children who experience sexual contact with an adult during childhood will (a) almost always have emotional problems during adulthood, (b) usually become gay or lesbian, (c) generally not enjoy sex in adulthood, (d) usually show adult adjustment that does not differ from that of adults who did not experience sexual contact during childhood. **(pp. 368–371)**

15

ATYPICAL SEXUAL ACTIVITY

THE PARAPHILIAS

THE NONINVASIVE CONSENSUAL PARAPHILIAS

Fetishes

Transvestism

Transsexuality

Sexual Sadism and Sexual Masochism

Highlight: Pain and Sexual Arousal

THE INVASIVE PARAPHILIAS

Voyeurism

Exhibitionism

Frotteurism

Pedophilia

Zoophilia

Necrophilia and Miscellaneous "Philias"

Compulsive Sexual Behavior

Highlight: Uncommon Paraphilias

TREATMENT OF THE INVASIVE PARAPHILIAS

Psychotherapy

Surgical Castration

Chemical Treatment

Cognitive-Behavior Therapies

Other Approaches

SUMMARY OF MAJOR POINTS

CHECK YOUR KNOWLEDGE

REALITY or MYTH ?

1 Transvestites are individuals who experience sexual pleasure from dressing in the clothes of the other gender.

2 Female-to-male sex-reassignment surgery (SRS) is usually less successful than male-to-female SRS.

3 Most transsexuals describe first experiencing gender cross-identification when they are in their early 30s.

4 Women show little sexual interest in watching partners undress.

5 Men who expose themselves in public (exhibitionists) or "peep" (voyeurs) are seldom dangerous.

6 Pedophiles tend to be younger and use greater levels of violence with children than do men who rape adult women.

OU pervert!
High school students commonly use this epithet, usually jokingly, to label someone who engages in a quasi-sexual behavior deviating slightly from the norm. What does the word **perversion** mean? One dictionary defines *perversion* as a maladjustment involving aberrant or deviant ways of seeking sexual satisfaction. A problem with this label and other similar terms, such as *deviation,* is that what is considered aberrant or deviant at one time and place might be considered normal at other times and places.

Some of the atypical behaviors we will cover do not involve or victimize others and so are considered to be more curious or annoying than dangerous. Other paraphilias are invasive of others' rights and thus can be seen as part of the continuum of coercive sexual behavior. In considering societal responses to paraphilias, it is important to differentiate between those that are simply variations from normal or typical behavior and those that infringe on the lives of other people.

In this chapter we examine noninvasive fetishes, transvestism, and transsexuality. We also review the characteristics and possible motivations of those who engage in uncommon and invasive practices, including people who are sexually attracted to children. The various treatments given to those who have strayed from what North American culture considers normal sexual behavior are examined.

THE PARAPHILIAS

ecause beliefs change with respect to what sexual activities are normal, many professionals prefer to avoid the terms *perversion* or *sexual deviance*. Someone who practices an atypical sexual activity is not necessarily dangerous or in need of therapy. **Paraphilia** (the love of the unusual, or atypical, sexual activity) is the term now used for a restricted group of sexual behaviors that are considered unusual by the society of the person performing them.

paraphilia (par-rah-FIL-ee-ah) Love of the unusual; the term now used to describe sexual activities that were formerly labeled deviance (*para:* "beside or amiss"; *philia:* "love").

ISSUES TO CONSIDER

How would you define "abnormal" sexual behavior?

Because of social and legal restrictions, reliable data on the frequency of paraphilic behaviors are limited. Most of our information about the paraphilias comes from people who have been arrested or are in therapy. But it is likely that most people who engage in paraphilias do not fall into either of these two categories, so our ability to generalize most research findings is restricted.

One solidly supported generalization about paraphilias, however, does appear to be appropriate: males are far more likely to engage in paraphilias than are females. More than 90 percent of people who are arrested for sexual offenses other than prostitution in the United States are males (Uniform Crime Reports, 1996).

Atypical sexual patterns can coexist with emotional disorders. People who confine their sexual outlets to strange and occasionally bizarre activities sometimes have trouble relating to other adults in a meaningful way. Yet many individuals who engage in paraphilic acts are also able to take part in "normal" sexual behavior with adult partners without relying on paraphilic fantasies or behaviors to generate sexual excitement.

THE NONINVASIVE CONSENSUAL PARAPHILIAS

Many types of atypical sexual behavior involve consensual adults: people who mutually agree to observe, participate in, or just put up with the behavior in question. No one's rights are violated, and the vast majority of society's members are unaware that the behaviors even exist, except for those who watch daytime talk shows.

Fetishes

fetishism Obtaining sexual excitement primarily or exclusively from an inanimate object or a particular part of the body.

Fetishism refers to the use of nonliving objects as a preferred or exclusive means of inducing sexual arousal. Thus some object comes to symbolize or embody the sexual arousal value usually reserved for human beings. To some extent, we are all fetishists, in that various objects can sexually arouse us. We may associate items of clothing with particular body parts or with a particular person. Bras, underpants, and jock straps have definite associations with specific body parts and may acquire the capacity to arouse us sexually by themselves. Similarly, cars, perfumes, or hairstyles that we associate with a loved one can arouse us.

Fetishism is thought to be primarily a male characteristic. There have been very few documented cases of female fetishism (Arndt, 1991). Most frequently, fetish objects are used in connection with fantasy and masturbation. Sometimes they are employed to build arousal during sexual intercourse or in combination with other forms of sexual expression.

Although the list of possible fetish objects is inexhaustible, certain items are more likely than others to be associated with sexual arousal, perhaps because they are more similar in texture or appearance to the genitals. Shoes, boots, and undergarments are frequent objects of fetishistic interest. In addition, items made of leather, rubber, fur, or silk seem to be particularly popular fetishes in North American culture.

Feet and their coverings have been used as symbols for sex in many cultures throughout history, and the foot has been one of the most common phallic symbols. Shoes are generally made of leather, which is animal skin. Perhaps it is this juxtaposition of skin against skin that gives objects like shoes their erotic appeal. Aromas are an important source of arousal for many people, and leather certainly has a distinctive odor. An evolutionary theorist might suggest that the shoe or leather fetishist may only be carrying to an extreme a general human attraction toward these objects.

Learning approaches stress the association between the fetishistic object and sexual arousal. Sexual arousal and orgasm, which are both reflexive responses, may be accidentally elicited by a strong emotional experience that happens to involve some particular object or body part. This initial conditioning experience may be strengthened through the reinforcement of masturbation and orgasm. Fetishism usually develops around puberty (Weinberg, Williams, & Calhan, 1995).

Transvestism

A man who has strong urges to dress in women's clothing and who becomes sexually aroused while wearing feminine apparel is called a **transvestite,** or TV. For most transvestites, cross-dressing is not an attempt to reject their biological gender. Although transvestism can be seen as a mild expression of discontent with one's biological sex and gender roles, it seldom entails the extreme rejection of one's biological sex seen in transsexualism (the belief that one is really a member of the other gender). Both gay and straight men can be transvestites (Bullough & Bullough, 1997). In addition, some gay men cross-dress to attract a partner, but wearing clothes of the other gender does not in and of itself sexually arouse most homosexuals. (See Figure 15.1.)

Cross-dressing was reported in Greek legend and among Roman emperors. It existed during the Middle Ages, and it is recognized and accepted today in many cultures (Bullough & Bullough, 1997; Stevenson, 1998). Although in both industrialized and nonindustrialized cultures it is usually men who practice transvestism, Vern Bullough and Bonnie Bullough (1997) noted that prior to the twentieth century, there were more reports of female than of male cross-dressers. One of the major charges against Joan of Arc in her trial for heresy was her preference for male hairstyles and attire.

REALITY or **MYTH** ? **1**

transvestite A person sexually stimulated or gratified by wearing the clothes stereotypic of the other gender.

Figure 15.1 Men in Women's Clothes Cross-dressing can take many forms, from the elaborate attire of glamorous drag performer RuPaul, on the left, to the more practical attire of the man on the right.

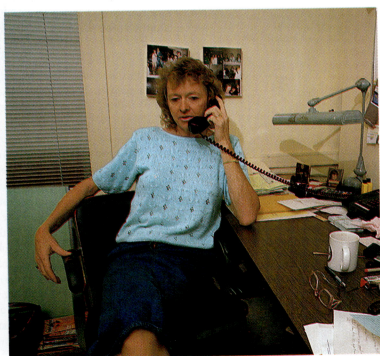

Until the late 1960s, most of our information about transvestites came from the reports of clinicians working with men who wished to be rid of their desire to cross-dress. Since that time, several research teams have sampled groups of transvestites from the general population to survey a nonclinical group.

Several aspects of research on nonclinical samples tend to contradict commonly held stereotypes about transvestites. For example, respondents generally described themselves as heterosexual; only a small percentage considered themselves exclusively homosexual. Most reported having been treated as boys—not as girls—during childhood, and very few reported being cross-dressed by their parents. Most began cross-dressing before puberty (Bullough & Bullough, 1997; Schott, 1995). Most studies have yielded no evidence that transvestism is associated with any major psychiatric symptoms (Beatrice, 1985; Bentler, Sherman, & Prince, 1970).

Cross-dressing is usually done at periodic intervals a little more than once a month. Masturbation may take place during the cross-dressing episode, but often the cross-dressing itself produces orgasm. Although most transvestites report that they feel like women when cross-dressed, they said that they feel like men when nude, as well as when dressed in their usual attire. When transvestites were exposed to films of nudes, their erotic responses, as measured by penile volume, fell within the normal range for heterosexual males (Buhrich & McConaghy, 1977).

As might be expected, given the strength of attitudes in our own culture regarding gender roles, the desire to cross-dress introduces some novel problems into transvestites' relationships. Most either had been or still were married. The majority of the transvestites in Neil Buhrich's (1976) sample thought that their desire to cross-dress would disappear with marriage, so they did not tell their partners about it before marriage. Some wives were unaware of their husbands' cross-dressing, even after they had been married for years. When wives did find out that their husbands were transvestites, their responses ran the gamut from complete disapproval and antagonism to acceptance and cooperation, the latter to the point of the wives lending their husbands their own clothing. Wives sometimes accompany their husbands when they appear in public in feminine attire (Brown & Collier, 1989). And many wives report having sex with their husbands when their husband is cross-dressed (Bullough & Weinberg, 1988).

EXPLANATIONS OF TRANSVESTISM.   We have no conclusive explanation of the urge to cross-dress. Male hormone deficiency has been suggested as one cause, but comparisons of transvestites with nontransvestites have found no differences between the groups in testosterone levels (Buhrich et al., 1979).

One particularly puzzling aspect of transvestism is its apparent absence among contemporary Western females. Some scholars have argued that female transvestism is rare because norms with respect to what one may wear are far less restrictive for females than they are for males. For example, if you caught your aunt foraging in the kitchen for a midnight snack dressed in your uncle's pajama top, you might think she looked cute. Your reaction would probably be quite different, however, if you were to find your uncle rummaging through the refrigerator with your aunt's negligée on.

Several factors argue against this difference in restrictiveness as the cause of gender differences in the incidence of transvestism. First, most women who wear men's garb do not appear to derive the sexual satisfaction that males experience when they cross-dress. Second, Buhrich's (1976) research suggested that transvestites' urge to cross-dress is not satisfied by wearing ambiguous or unisex attire. Instead, they tend to desire apparel that is exclusively for females—for example, lacy bras, slips, and garter belts. (Similar behavior on the part of a female might be to don a pair of jockey shorts.) Third, transvestism most frequently appears in cultures with relaxed rather than restrictive gender-role norms. In all probability, then, the restrictiveness of norms for male clothing styles is not responsible for the incidence of male transvestism and the absence of female transvestism in the twentieth century.

The anthropologist Robert Munroe and his colleagues (Munroe & Munroe, 1977; Munroe, Whiting, & Hally, 1969) reviewed cross-cultural research on transvestism to explore whether any social or economic factors were associated with the practice. They found transvestism was most likely to be prevalent in cultures having two characteristics: relaxed gender-role norms and greater pressure on the male than on the female to ensure the family's economic survival. In contrast to cultures with rigid gender-role norms and a lower status for women, cultures with relaxed norms grant women many of the privileges accorded to men. At the same time, women in most cultures do not have as much pressure and responsibility for economic survival placed on them as men do. Men's economic burdens may perhaps lead some males to take a "vacation" by temporarily abandoning their role as provider and symbolically adopting women's roles, behaviors, and attire. Even if this speculation is eventually supported by further evidence, it still leaves many questions unanswered, including why the urge to cross-dress begins so early in life and why it is associated with arousal.

Whatever the explanation of the desire to cross-dress, it is clear that transvestites are not rejecting their biological sex. Instead, they find pleasure in occasionally donning the intimate attire typically worn by members of the other gender in their society. In contrast, transsexuals dislike the anatomical attributes of their biological sex, and many of them seek the anatomical characteristics of the other gender. We turn now to that phenomenon.

Transsexuality

As members of a culture that is fascinated by sexual symbols of manhood (for example, penis size and functioning) and womanhood (such as breast size), many of us cannot comprehend the feelings of a person consumed with an ardent desire to be rid of the physical attributes of his or her gender. Indeed, most people in our culture who are dissatisfied with their sexual organs seek to enhance rather than to eliminate them.

But for some men, their male sexual organs are in conflict with their feminine psychological identity. These men are male-to-female (M-F) transsexuals. Similarly, for the female-to-male (F-M) transsexual, the physical symbols of the female biological sex are at odds with their masculine identification.

DEFINITION AND INCIDENCE.   A **transsexual** is a biologically normal male or female who feels that he or she is a member of the other gender. Although transsexualism has only recently been defined, historical records describe a number of individuals who managed to live as members of the other gender (Bullough & Bullough, 1993).

It is easy to become confused if you try to categorize a transsexual's sexual orientation. From a genetic standpoint, we could conclude that many transsexuals have homosexual orientations because they are genetic males who are attracted to men or genetic females who are attracted to women. On the other hand, from a psychological standpoint, most M-F transsexuals feel as if they are really women and perceive their attraction to men as demonstrating heterosexual orientation. In various studies of transsexuals, up to a third of transsexuals reported little or no sexual activity before surgery and were classified as asexual (Blanchard, 1989; Freund, Steiner, & Chan, 1982).

transsexual A person whose gender identity is different from his or her anatomical sex.

ISSUES TO CONSIDER

Do you think transsexualism stems more from psychological or biological variations?

M-F TRANSSEXUALISM.   Although not the first to seek and obtain surgery, George Jorgensen, in the early 1950s, was the first American whose sex reassignment was widely publicized. His childhood and adolescence were similar in many ways to those of other transsexuals. He remembered wishing for a pretty doll with long golden hair for Christmas when he was five years old; he was disappointed to get a red model train instead (Jorgensen, 1967). He avoided rough-and-tumble games and fistfights and described himself as having been frail and introverted as a child. At the age of 19, he was drafted into military service. At that point he weighed 98 pounds and had under-developed genitals and almost no beard.

He experienced emotional feelings for several men but did not view these attachments as homosexual. He felt himself to be a woman. He wanted to relate to men and to the world at large as a woman, and he read everything that he could find about sex hormones. He moved to Copenhagen, Denmark, in 1950 after hearing that surgery for his condition might be available. In 1952, after taking estrogen on a regular basis, he underwent a series of three operations. Two months later, at the age of 26, she returned to the United States as Christine Jorgensen.

Jorgensen never regretted her decision, and she felt that if she had not been able to get the surgery, she might not have survived. Christine Jorgensen never married but was engaged twice and reported having been in love with several men. She died in 1989.

Subsequent research involving transsexuals who have undergone gender reassignment in the United States over the past few decades suggests that Jorgensen's feelings are quite representative. Some transsexuals, lacking access to sex-reassignment surgery, have been so desperate that they have attempted self-castration.

For most M-F transsexuals, identification with females and a preference for girl's clothing, or cross-dressing, begin at an early age. On psychological inventories, the scores of feminine boys are very similar to those of girls of the same age (Bullough & Bullough, 1993). In adolescence and adulthood, some transsexuals engage in hyper-feminine behavior, characterized by "an overwhelming aroma of perfume, seductive behavior, and attire which is inappropriate to the occasion" (Pauly, 1974, p. 510). Researchers have also noted tendencies among transsexuals to give responses on psychological inventories that are more stereotypically feminine than those given by control groups of women (McCauley & Ehrhardt, 1977).

The sexual practices of those who believe that their biological gender is the wrong one reflect their convictions about their true identities. M-F transsexuals who marry women tend to visualize themselves as women during coitus with their wives (Blanchard, 1993). Transsexuals who have anal intercourse with men do not view the act as homosexual because they believe themselves to be female, regardless of whether they have undergone surgery.

For people who experience no conflict between their anatomy and their gender identity, the desire for sex-reassignment surgery may be the most difficult aspect of transsexualism to comprehend. For many transsexuals, however, the elimination of the penis as well as other reminders of their genetic gender provides a welcome relief.

More than 40 hospitals and clinics in North America have provided transsexuals with therapy and surgery since the first sex-reassignment operation was performed at the Johns Hopkins University Hospital in Baltimore in 1966 (Pauly & Edgerton, 1986). Applicants for surgery are first evaluated psychologically; individuals who appear to be suffering from disturbances other than a conflict of gender identity are not accepted for surgery.

M-F Sex Reassignment.   Those transsexuals who are accepted for surgery are instructed to live as women by adopting women's clothing and a feminine lifestyle for a

year or two if they had not already been doing so (Diamond, 1996b). If they successfully accommodate to this lifestyle, they are given an estrogenic compound to increase the softness of their skin, the size of their breasts, and the fat deposits on their hips. The growth of facial and body hair is reduced by this hormone, and pubic hair begins to grow in a typically female pattern. Muscle strength and libido diminish, and a gradual reduction takes place in the frequency of erection and ejaculation and the amount of semen. The estrogen treatment does not alter voice pitch, so M-F trans-

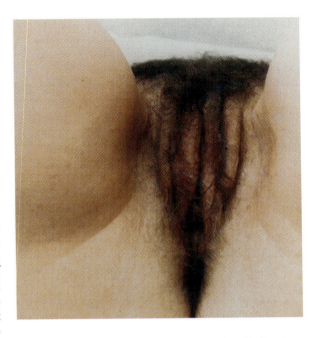

Figure 15.2 Male-to-Female Sex Reassignment Surgery

sexuals often take lessons to change their voice. The hormonal therapy has little effect on penis length but does reduce the size of the testicles. These effects can be accentuated by administration of drugs that lower testosterone levels (Asscheman & Gooren, 1992).

If, after a year or more, a transsexual still wishes sex-reassignment surgery, a series of operations is performed. The testes and penis are removed, and silicone may be implanted in the breasts. Labia and a facsimile of a vagina are constructed (see Figure 15.2). The skin of the penis, with its sensitive nerve endings, is laid inside the vagina, and a form is placed within the vagina for several hours each day to keep the grafted skin from growing together. Body and facial hair may be removed by electrolysis, and plastic surgery may be performed to feminize the person's appearance. With the removal of the testes, the source of sperm and most of the masculinizing hormones is eliminated, and sterility results. M-F transsexuals may engage in sexual intercourse, however, and many report erotic feelings and orgasm after their operations (Lief & Hubschman, 1993).

F-M TRANSSEXUALISM.   Although there are some similarities between male and female transsexuals, several studies also suggest intriguing differences in both overt behavior and certain aspects of sex-reassignment surgery.

Most F-M transsexuals report having thought of themselves as boys for as long as they can remember, with cross-identification first occurring at about three or four years of age (Pauly, 1985). The sense of being male despite having anatomical and assigned roles as females is a source of pain and confusion for F-M transsexuals (Bullough & Bullough, 1993). Puberty is an especially difficult time for female transsexuals. F-M transsexuals feel intense revulsion toward menarche and other aspects of female development (Steiner, 1985).

Many F-M transsexuals report an awareness of having been attracted to females during early adolescence, but they generally do not begin having sexual relations with women until about five years later, at about the age of 18. Their sexual partners are often markedly feminine, heterosexual women, although some report relationships with gay men (Devor, 1993). During sexual relations, many F-M transsexuals do not allow their partners to see them nude, penetrate their vaginas, or touch their breasts and genitals (McCauley & Ehrhardt, 1980). Of those who do permit touching, most limit the contact to clitoral stimulation. Transsexuals whose clitorises have been enlarged through androgenic compounds often imagine their clitorises to be penises. Pauly's (1985) research suggested that F-M transsexuals take on the masculine role more believably than their M-F counterparts take on the feminine role. The responses of most F-M transsexuals on diagnostic inventories indicate no severe psychological disturbance other than gender-identity conflict (Coleman, Bockting, & Gooren, 1993).

F-M Gender Reassignment.   After psychological screening, applicants for F-M sex-reassignment surgery are asked to live as males for a year or more. If they are successful in this adaptation, they are given androgenic compounds. These masculinizing compounds stimulate the growth of facial and body hair, slightly decrease breast size, increase the size of the clitoris, suppress menstruation, and deepen the voice (Asscheman & Gooren, 1992).

If the person still desires surgery after having lived as a male for a year or so, a series of operations is performed. Because it is easier to remove than to add body parts, F-M sex-reassignment surgery is more complex (Lief & Hubschman, 1993). It is also frequently less successful for F-M transsexuals than for their M-F counterparts.

For some F-M transsexuals, the lack of success with constructing an artificial penis leads them to avoid this surgery, as shown in this excerpt (Brame, Brame, & Jacobs, 1993):

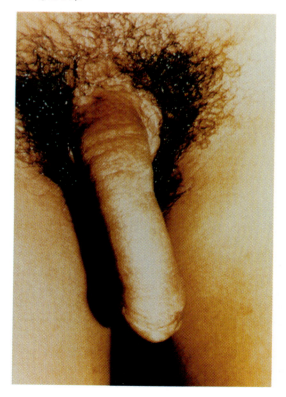

Figure 15.3 Female-to-Male Sex Reassignment Surgery

There's a lot of reconstruction. The male-to-female stuff is peanuts by comparison. Female-to-male is also more expensive than the male-to- female. I was quoted a cost [of] around $60,000. There are other things I can think of to buy with $60,000 than a dick that doesn't work. (p. 424)

For those who choose to have this surgery, skin from the labia and abdomen is used to fashion a penis and scrotum. An artificial testis may be placed in each side of the scrotum. The penis looks quite realistic (see Figure 15.3), but no surgical procedure at present can create a penis that becomes erect in response to sexual stimulation. Although the artificial penis does not respond to physical stimulation, erotic feelings and orgasm remain if the clitoris has been left embedded at the base of the penis. Additional surgery can involve removing the breasts, uterus, and ovaries and sealing off the vagina. Removing the ovaries eliminates eggs and the primary source of estrogen so, like the M-F transsexual, the F-M transsexual can no longer reproduce.

Ideally, a postsurgical transsexual continues to receive medical follow-up and counseling. Such therapy can also be beneficial to a transsexual's family and lover. Unfortunately, these postoperative practices are not always followed, partially because transsexuals tend to relocate to a different city following recovery from surgery.

CONTROVERSIES ABOUT TRANSSEXUALISM.

Some individuals function in a psychologically healthy fashion except for a deeply felt conflict between anatomical features and psychological gender identity, and for them, the use of the term *transsexual* may be appropriate. Others may blame their inability to deal effectively with various life challenges on a gender-identity conflict. Further, researchers' estimates (Pauly & Edgerton, 1986) indicate that about a third of applicants for sex-reassignment surgery are homosexuals who cannot accept their sexual orientation and apply for reassignment surgery mainly in the hope of bringing their practices into compliance with a heterosexually oriented society. Still other people may view the painful surgery as a method of punishing themselves for real or imagined "sins." None of these individuals fits the definition of a transsexual.

EXPLANATIONS OF TRANSSEXUALISM.

There is no agreement as to why some people feel an intense conflict over gender identity. Some studies have reported abnormal brain wave patterns in about one-third of transsexuals, but the significance of these findings is still not known (Hoenig, 1985; Pauly, 1974). Postmortem study of the brains of transsexuals has not shown differences between them and "normal" brains (Emory, Williams, Cole, Amparo, & Meyer, 1991).

Hormonal explanations of transsexualism have fared no better. Most adult transsexuals have hormone levels that fall within the normal range for their genetic gender (Jones, 1974; Goodman et al., 1985).

Because gender identity is learned very early in life, and most transsexuals report cross-identification well before puberty, the dynamics within the family might be linked to the development of transsexuality. However, no systematic patterns have emerged with respect to parents.

In summary, until further research has been done focusing on large samples of transsexuals, the most honest answer we can give to the question of what causes transsexualism is that we do not know.

TREATMENT: SURGERY OR PSYCHOTHERAPY?

Until the 1960s, the U.S. medical profession was generally opposed to sex-reassignment surgery, defining the problem of transsexualism as psychological rather than medical in nature.

To some extent, people's attitudes regarding the appropriateness of surgery depend on what they view as the source of the problem. Virginia Prince (1977) suggested that surgical solutions to conflicts of gender identity represent a confusion between biology and psychology. In her succinctly stated opinion, surgery "is only a painful, expensive, dangerous and misguided attempt to achieve between the legs what must eventually and inevitably be achieved between the ears." Physicians who are faced with a desperate plea for surgery on the part of a transsexual whose conflict is a source of great pain and who may have contemplated or even attempted suicide obviously have a difficult choice.

Most transsexuals claim to be happier following surgery than prior to it and report that they would go through the procedure again (Lief & Hubschman, 1993; van Kesteren, Gooren, & Megens, 1996). There appear to be gender differences in postsurgical adjustment, however. F-M transsexuals more often have stable relationships with a partner and appear more socially adjusted than M-F transsexuals do (Kockott & Fahrner, 1988; Verschoor & Poortinga, 1988). Psychological adjustment has also been found to be greater in postsurgical transsexuals than in presurgical transsexuals. The quality of the surgery too may affect postsurgical adjustment (Pfäfflin, 1992; Ross & Need, 1989).

One study, however, indicates that surgery is not necessarily essential to a transsexual's psychosocial adjustment. A comparison of the social and psychological adjustment of 34 postsurgical transsexuals with that of 66 transsexuals who did not receive surgery revealed improvements in both groups (Meyer & Reter, 1979). For example, both experienced a 70 percent decrease in the number of visits to psychiatrists over a six-year period.

There is a need for further research to determine whether the operation makes enough of a difference to justify the pain, expense, and drastic anatomical and hormonal alterations. The evidence does clearly suggest, however, that sex-reassignment surgery can alleviate the emotional distress associated with feeling that one is of a different gender than one's anatomy indicates (Green & Fleming, 1990; Pfäfflin, 1992).

Earlier, we alluded to hypotheses that some individuals seeking reassignment surgery may be motivated by the desire to punish themselves for real or imagined "sins." Such a connection between sexuality and the infliction of real or symbolic pain is a theme for those engaging in sadomasochistic activities, a topic to which we turn now.

ISSUES TO CONSIDER

Assume that you have a sibling or close friend who is convinced that he or she is really a member of the other gender and is living in the wrong body. Based on what you have read, what advice would you give?

Sexual Sadism and Sexual Masochism

sexual sadism The intentional infliction of pain or humiliation on another person for sexual excitement.

Sexual sadism refers to the infliction of physical or psychological pain on another living creature to produce sexual excitement. In this section, our consideration is limited to consenting partners, for sadism performed on an unwilling victim is sexual assault.

Only those pain-inflicting acts that sexually excite the inflictor can be classified as sadistic. In mild forms of sadism, the administering of pain can be primarily symbolic, such as beating someone with a soft object that is designed to resemble a hard club. In these cases, the partner just pretends to be in pain. At the other end of the continuum is the sadist who can become aroused only if the partner is savagely attacked or even murdered. In this case, it is not the dead body that excites the sadist but the victim's suffering and dying.

sexual masochism Sexual gratification through experiencing pain and humiliation.

Sexual masochism refers to experiencing sexual arousal by suffering physical or psychological pain that is produced in specific ways. The individual may be aroused by being whipped, cut, pricked, bound, spanked, or verbally humiliated. A masochist responds sexually only to particular sorts of pain. A masochist who becomes sexually aroused while being whipped, for example, does not respond with erection or vaginal lubrication if a car door is slammed on his or her finger. The masochist usually has specific requirements with respect to the manner in which pain is inflicted, the area of the body assaulted, and the person who inflicts the pain (see "Highlight: Pain and Sexual Arousal"). If the pattern is not followed, then the pain will lose its arousal power.

Most information about sadism and masochism comes from clinical case reports, but another source is several questionnaire studies that have been conducted with individuals located through sadomasochistic magazines and clubs (Breslow, Evans, & Langley, 1985; Spengler, 1977). More than half the respondents indicated that they

HIGHLIGHT

Pain and Sexual Arousal

One of the unusual relationships that can exist between the perception of pain and sexual arousal is illustrated in the following excerpt from Brame, Brame, and Jacob's (1993) book, *Different Loving: An Exploration of the World of Sexual Dominance and Submission:*

> The real nature of S&M was driven home to me about 15 years ago. I was doing a movie called House of Sin. There was an S&M scene [with] a mistress and her slave, who were, in real life, living together. She had him on the floor, with his hands tied behind him. She had a dog chain wrapped around his cock and balls and was lifting him off the floor by his cock and balls and smacking him across the nuts, hard enough so that every

> guy in the room had his legs crossed. Two things stuck in my mind: First, that while this was happening, this guy had an incredible erection, and two, as soon as I yelled, "Cut!" he immediately started to bitch and moan about the fact that he was lying on a hardwood floor and didn't have a pillow behind his head. At that moment I realized that what she was doing to his genitals was not painful; the little bit of pressure on the back of his head, that's what his brain was interpreting as pain. But the hard pressure of her hand coming in contact with his nuts was erotically stimulating. I realized that in S&M, if it's painful, you're doing it wrong. (pp. 42–43)

played both dominant and submissive roles within the sadomasochistic context. This finding suggests that many people who participate in sexual activities involving the intentional infliction of pain are more accurately described by the compound term *sadomasochist* than by the single word *sadist* or *masochist.*

Male respondents indicated that they first became aware of their sadomasochistic interests at around age 15 years, whereas females reported that they became interested in sadomasochism at about age 22. Both men and women viewed sadomasochism as primarily sexual foreplay. Perhaps because there appear to be more men than women involved in the sadomasochistic subculture, female respondents had sadomasochistic sex more often and with more partners than did males. Table 15.1 on page 389 shows the respondents' behavioral preferences. The more extreme forms of sexual activity associated with sadomasochism, such as torture and use of excrement, were relatively rare.

The most popular sadomasochistic sexual activities, which include spanking and master-slave relationships, are featured in sadomasochistic magazines and movies. Sadomasochists may belong to special clubs, contact like-minded others on the Internet, or visit prostitutes who indulge their fantasies (Ernulf & Innala, 1995; Chivers & Blanchard, 1996).

Sadomasochistic sexual practices may also include bondage and discipline, a pattern in which a sexual partner is tied up and then sexually stimulated. The exchange may involve dog collars, leashes, and chains but usually follows predetermined patterns and stops short of physical harm (see Figure 15.4, page 388).

What seems to be central to sadomasochistic activities is a master-slave relationship. The partner playing the master can exercise complete control over the other person for a time, and the partner playing the slave can give up all personal responsibility. Sexual expression is controlled and predictable in these carefully structured situations (Brame et al., 1993; Weinberg, 1994), and it is common for couples to engage in elaborate negotiations about their specific roles before beginning sadomasochistic play.

SADOMASOCHISM AND BELIEFS ABOUT GENDER DIFFERENCES.

Men and women both engage in sadism, and their masochistic partners are both men and women. Research on normal populations suggests that there is a slight difference in the proportion of males and females who enjoy sadomasochism in some form. For

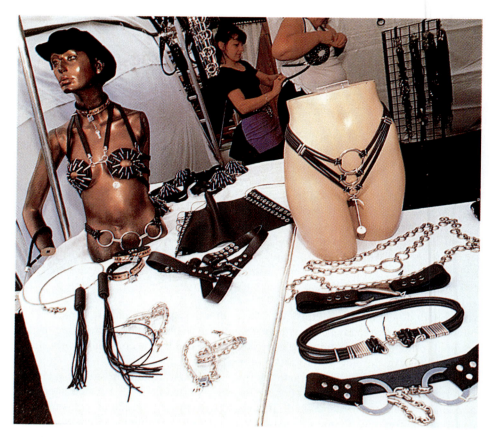

Figure 15.4 Tools of Bondage and Discipline The bondage apparel displayed in this sex-specialty shop is designed for sadomasochistic activities.

example, Kinsey et al. (1953) found that 22 percent of men and 12 percent of women reported some sexual arousal from sadistic stories.

There appear to be gender differences, however, in how males and females approach masochism. Male masochism appears to be an escape strategy from the traditional male role (Baumeister, 1988a). Being humiliated and degraded, and sacrificing or postponing one's own sexual pleasure, contradict the masculine archetype. This escape from self may reduce high levels of self-awareness and intensify a focus on the immediate present and bodily sensations. Female masochism follows a different route in escaping from one's everyday self by exaggerating the female stereotype. The woman devotes herself to her partner's pleasure, and her role is transformed to "remove responsibility, insecurity, and sexual inhibition" (Baumeister, 1988b, p. 497). Again, we emphasize the difference between consensual sadomasochistic activities versus invasive sadism in which one person attempts to, or does, exert complete control over another person against that person's will.

THE INVASIVE PARAPHILIAS

Invasive paraphilias involve behaviors that violate other people's personal space. For clinical professionals to consider a diagnosis of paraphilia, a person must display recurring, intense sexual urges and fantasies—carried out behaviorally—that can disrupt other people's lives. Many people who are arrested for invasive paraphilic be-

ISSUES TO CONSIDER

Do you think that men's masochism might be associated with *withdrawal* (escape) from the traditional male role and women's masochism might be associated with an *exaggeration* of the female stereotype? If so, why?

Table 15.1   A Comparison of the Sadomasochistic Preferences of Females and Males

Interest	Male (%)	Female (%)
Spanking	79	80
Master-slave relationships	79	76
Oral sex	77	90
Masturbation	70	73
Bondage	67	88
Humiliation	65	61
Erotic lingerie	63	88
Restraint	60	83
Anal sex	58	51
Pain	51	34
Whipping	47	39
Rubber/leather	42	42
Boots/shoes	40	49
Verbal abuse	40	51
Stringent bondage	39	54
Enemas	33	22
Torture	32	32
Golden showers	30	37
Transvestism	28	20
Petticoat punishment (forced cross-dressing)	25	20
Other toilet activities	19	12

Note: Some of these activities are part of the usual sex play of couples; these same activities (e.g., oral sex, golden showers, erotic lingerie) are considered part of a sadomasochistic pattern when the dominant "demands" it or the submissive "pleads" for it. "Golden showers" refers to urophilia—obtaining erotic pleasure from incorporation of urination in erotic play.

Source: Based on responses to questionnaires completed by people located through sadomasochistic magazines and clubs, by Breslow, Evans, and Langley (1985). *Archives of Sexual Behavior, 14,* p. 315. Copyright 1985 by Plenum Publishing Company. Reprinted by permission.

haviors do not qualify for a clinical label because they do not meet these criteria. They may resort to the paraphilia for lack of a socially appropriate sex partner, because of an unusual opportunity, or out of a desire to experiment. As we consider the major paraphilias, it is important to remember that personal or subjective biases often play a greater role in labeling a person as sexually atypical than do objective, scientific facts (Levine & Troiden, 1988).

Voyeurism

Voyeurism refers to obtaining sexual gratification by observing others without their consent who are undressing, naked, or participating in sexual activity. Many people enjoy observing nudity and sexual activity, as the popularity of erotic literature and X-rated movies and videotapes demonstrates. You may therefore wonder where the

voyeurism (VOY-yer-ism) Obtaining sexual arousal by observing people without their consent when they are undressed or engaging in sexual activity.

Figure 15.5 Culturally Approved Watching Observing scantily attired or nude performers in clubs or bars is not considered voyeurism, because the participants being observed have consented to the activity.

dividing line is between "normal" looking and voyeurism (see Figure 15.5). After all, in our culture, watching women has been as accepted a male pastime as watching the Super Bowl, and it is certainly a component of courtship behavior. In their national sample, Laumann et al. (1994) found that, for men, watching their partners undress was a more popular sexual activity than receiving oral sex.

Although women traditionally have been assumed to possess little interest in the uncovered bodies of men, the popularity of male strip shows and photos of men in women's magazines such as *Cosmopolitan* is evidence to the contrary. Like girl-watching, women's interest in these phenomena is considered normal rather than voyeuristic. Further in Laumann et al.'s (1994) sample, women rated watching their partners undress as just slightly less appealing than receiving oral sex.

Looking becomes voyeurism, a criminal offense, when the voyeur observes people who are unaware that they are being watched or are unwilling to be observed. Because only a few states prohibit voyeurism, voyeurs are often prosecuted under anti-loitering and disorderly conduct laws. For the voyeur, the viewing of strangers without consent is the primary or preferred sexual activity.

Convicted voyeurs are almost always male. Many women enjoy observing nude males, but women seldom invest the energy required to seek out unsuspecting men for observation. This gender difference may stem from cultural constraints against women's actively seeking out sexual stimuli. Alternatively, the difference may be due to men's greater receptivity or sensitivity to visual sexual stimuli. One hypothesis holds that men's keener interest in visual sexual stimuli is rooted in our evolutionary past. That is, women's physical attractiveness may have symbolized general health and therefore reproductive fitness (Buss, 1994; Fisher, 1992). Male sexual arousal at the sight of nude or partially nude females was therefore a critical part of the process leading to reproduction.

It is also possible, however, that there are more female voyeurs than arrest and conviction records indicate. A man out for a walk who stops to view a nude woman in a window may be arrested for voyeurism. But if a man undresses in front of a window and a woman stops to look, the man may be as likely to be arrested for exhibitionism as the woman for voyeurism. Police and court records may reflect this bias.

CHARACTERISTICS OF VOYEURS.   Voyeurs tend to be young and male, with the average age at first conviction being 24 (Gebhard, Gagnon, Pomeroy, & Christenson, 1965). Paul Gebhard and his associates found that few voyeurs had serious mental disorders, and alcohol or drugs were seldom involved in their "peeping." Some voyeurs resemble other sex offenders in that they display deficient sexual relationships, but others are able to interact sexually with consenting partners with no evidence of dysfunction.

The voyeur derives sexual arousal from the notion that he is violating the privacy of his victims. Like practitioners of other criminal sexual variations, the "peeping Tom" may be stimulated by the danger of apprehension. The willingness to run risks is what distinguishes the voyeur from the average woman watcher. The voyeur may scale high fences, bore holes in bedroom walls, risk injury from watchdogs, and endure terrible weather conditions to observe what excites him. The act of looking is usually accompanied by sexual excitement, and frequently by orgasm. Sometimes the voyeur masturbates while he is gazing at unsuspecting targets, or he may do so later when remembering the scene.

As with other paraphilias, the cause of voyeurism is not clear. Behaviorists emphasize that the initial association of sexual arousal with peeping may be accidental. If a male masturbates while peeping or later while recalling the act in fantasy, the association is strengthened. Repeated incidents can lead to reliance on peeping as the main source of sexual arousal.

Some psychoanalysts trace the disorder back to childhood episodes in which the individual witnessed his parents having intercourse. For persons who have poorly developed social and sexual skills, voyeurism provides a means of sexual gratification that avoids the potential threat of sexual interaction. Taking the risk of being caught may bolster the voyeur's often deficient sense of masculinity, just as it does for the exhibitionist.

Exhibitionism

Exhibitionism refers to obtaining erotic gratification from displaying one's genitals. The public display of the genitals, or indecent exposure, is illegal in every state. Exposing one's genitals to another person in private is, of course, a normal part of sexual interaction. It is only when this activity becomes the primary or preferred source of sexual gratification and involves unwilling or unsuspecting victims that it becomes problematic (see Figure 15.6, page 392).

As with most other paraphilias, exhibitionism is almost exclusively a male activity. There are only three published cases of exhibitionism in women who were not developmentally disabled, epileptic, or schizophrenic (Arndt, 1991).

Exhibitionism is the most common sexual offense, accounting for about a third of all sex-crime arrests (Arndt, 1991). Generally indecent exposure is a misdemeanor unless it is committed under "aggravating" circumstances, which include having minors as victims or having a number of previous convictions for indecent exposure. Exhibitionism occurs primarily during warm weather (May to September), in the middle of

exhibitionism Obtaining sexual gratification by exposing one's genitals to an unwilling observer.

ISSUES TO CONSIDER

Why do you think that the exposure of men's genitals is a crime and women's exposure of their genitals is usually commercial entertainment?

Figure 15.6 Public Nudity
What is shown in this photo—voyeurism, exhibitionism, or self-expression?

the week, between 3:00 P.M. and 6:00 P.M., and in public settings (Arndt, 1991; MacDonald, 1973). Contrary to the American Psychiatric Association's definition of exhibitionism as involving the baring of the genitals to strangers, a study of college women found that 36 percent of the reported exposure episodes involved men whom the victims knew (Cox, 1988). This suggests that a change in the psychiatric definition of exhibitionism may be appropriate.

It is common for the exhibitionist to have an erection when he exposes himself. About half of one sample of 130 exhibitionists reported always or almost always having erections when exhibiting (Langevin et al., 1979). Almost half this group reported masturbating when exposing themselves.

Many exhibitionists use the episode as a source of fantasy for later masturbation. There is evidence to suggest that indulging in such fantasies during masturbation may be critical in the development and maintenance of exhibitionist behavior (Blair & Lanyon, 1981).

CHARACTERISTICS OF EXHIBITIONISTS.

Exhibitionistic men are typically in their 20s the first time they expose themselves (Arndt, 1991). The most frequent targets of these displays are 16- to 30-year-old women (Langevin et al., 1979). A substantial number of men in the Langevin et al. (1979) study wanted the women to whom they exposed themselves to be impressed by the size of their penises. They described the desire for sexual relationships with their victims as a secondary motivation.

Exhibitionists generally score in the normal range on measures of intelligence, personality, and psychological adjustment (Arndt, 1991; Levin & Stava, 1987). Although no difference in testosterone levels has been found between exhibitionists and other men, certain biological conditions may contribute to exhibitionism. Some developmentally disabled individuals may not be fully aware of the social disapproval associated with the exposure of their genitals at inappropriate times and places. Likewise, older men may suffer from senile brain deterioration that can lead to decreased self-control.

All definitions of exhibitionism include the association of exposure with sexual excitement. The sexual arousal may be generated by the response of the woman to whom men expose themselves. However, nearly half the 130 exhibitionists studied by Langevin et al. (1979) reported that they exposed themselves without physical gratification. These men may be as motivated by the thrill-seeking aspect of risking arrest for their exhibitionism as they are by its overt sexual aspects. For many exhibitionists, self-exposure may be a way of compensating for timidity and lack of assertiveness. The exhibitionistic act may make them feel like powerful men, and the danger of being apprehended and prosecuted as criminals may contribute to this feeling. The psychoanalytic view of exhibitionism fits with this general picture: it is thought that by displaying the penis, exhibitionists seek to prove to the world and, most important, to adult women that they are indeed men.

The association of masculinity with exposing must be extremely powerful, because being convicted of a sex offense can result in social and professional ruin. Once ruined, many exhibitionists have little to deter them from subsequent "flashing." One-third of the convicted offenders in one study had four to six previous convictions, and another 10 percent had been convicted seven times or more (Gebhard et al., 1965). This recidivism rate may reflect the fact that many exhibitionists display themselves repeatedly in the same place and at the same time of day with seeming disregard of the danger of being caught again.

Many exhibitionists expose themselves even when they have opportunities for consensual sexual contact. A wife or lover can admire an exhibitionist's penis for only so long. Perhaps "the exhibitionist may be like an actor on the stage who wants an audience but does not want it to participate in his act" (Langevin et al., 1979, p. 328).

Although most experts consider exhibitionism and voyeurism to be distinct syndromes, many individuals indulge in both activities and a number of other invasive sexual behaviors as well, including rape. Using interviews and guaranteeing confidentiality, Gene Abel and Jeanne Rouleau (1990) found that a group of 142 men incarcerated for exhibitionism had committed a total of 71,696 invasive paraphilic acts, only a quarter of which were exhibitionism. These men reported 10 different kinds of invasive paraphilias including rape. Of a group of more than 600 men referred to a clinic for sexual offenses, all those who had engaged in voyeurism also had committed other sexual offenses (Langevin, Paitich, & Russon, 1985). Exhibitionism and voyeurism are almost always related to other paraphilias. Thus, targets of these paraphilias should not treat them as harmless. Instead, they should get away from the perpetrator as quickly as they can and report the behavior to police.

REALITY or **MYTH** ? **5**

OBSCENE TELEPHONE CALLS.   People who describe sexual activities to a listener over the telephone can be thought of as exhibitionists. They are "exhibiting" verbally. Like the man who exposes his genitals, the obscene caller enjoys the frightened or startled response of the victim. Masturbation during or shortly after making the call is common, and almost all obscene calls are made by men rather than women. In one study, 61 percent of the women had received obscene phone calls (Herold, Mantle, & Zemitis, 1979).

The recipient of such telephone calls can be unnerved if the calls are made repeatedly by someone who breathes heavily or describes sexual acts. Nevertheless, a person who receives an obscene telephone call should try to react in a calm manner and get off the phone as quickly as possible. A man recently called our house purportedly wanting to do a survey on female lingerie, and he has called many of our women students with the same ploy. When I (E.R.A.) answered the phone and heard his pitch, I said, "Certainly. Just let me turn on the speaker phone so that my husband can hear." The caller immediately hung up. If you are the recipient of such repeated calls, you should report the calls to the telephone company and to the police. Persistent obscene calls can sometimes be traced. Even if you have caller ID, it is probably best to let the police or telephone company handle the situation.

Frotteurism

Frotteurism is characterized by touching or rubbing one's body against a nonconsenting person, usually a woman. The frotteur typically rubs his penis, usually covered, against a woman to achieve sexual arousal and/or orgasm. Subways, buses, and other crowded situations provide opportunities for such gratification, which typically elicits either little notice or only minor annoyance from the target.

frotteurism   Obtaining sexual arousal by touching or rubbing one's body against the body of an unsuspecting or nonconsenting person.

Frotteurism often occurs in conjunction with other paraphilias. In one study, almost 70 percent of males referred for frotteurism were found to have been involved in voyeurism, exhibitionism, or rape (Freund & Blanchard, 1986).

The paraphilias that we have just described—voyeurism, exhibitionism, and frotteurism—are also behaviors that may be practiced by people who are sexually attracted to children: pedophiles.

Pedophilia

pedophilia (PEH-doe-FIL-ee-ah) Sexual contact between an adult and a child.

The term **pedophilia** has its origin in Greek and literally means "love of children." The pedophile, or sexual abuser of children, is usually envisioned as a "dirty old man" who lures an innocent young girl into a dark alley or the woods, where he rapes her. As such, child molesters are regarded with even more disgust and rage than are rapists who prey on adults. In prisons, the sexual abuser of a child tends to be the prisoner most despised by guards and other inmates alike. How accurate is this stereotype of pedophiles? At the outset, we should note that people who approach children sexually (primarily men) are usually either related to, or acquaintances of, the youngsters.

Those convicted of sexual offenses against minors tend to be older than other convicted sex offenders. Their average age at conviction is 35, and about a quarter are over 45 (Arndt, 1991; Gebhard et al., 1965). Past clinical and survey literature has described the pedophile as conservative, socially inadequate, psychosexually immature, and psychologically disturbed, but Paul Okami and Amy Goldberg (1992) found no evidence to support these assumptions in their review of the literature. Even if we consider solely convicted child sex offenders, clear-cut psychiatric disturbance is not generally apparent, although many child offenders tend toward shyness, loneliness, low self-esteem, isolation, and sensitivity to the evaluations of others (Okami & Goldberg, 1992). In general, the younger the victim is, the more likely it is that the sexual offender exhibits psychopathology (Kalichman, 1991). Similar to sexually coercive college males, convicted offenders of sexual crimes against children do not appear to lack appropriate social skills (Koralewski & Conger, 1992; Okami & Goldberg, 1992).

There is some evidence that "child sex offenders" adjust their sexual behaviors to the age level of their partner or victim (Okami & Goldberg, 1992). That is, they will engage in the early stages of a normal courtship sequence, looking and touching, but they generally avoid more intimate forms of sexual contact. In only 4 percent of cases studied by David Finkelhor (1979) did the prepubescent girls report that coitus had occurred between them and the offender. The contact was confined to exhibitionism in 20 percent of the episodes and to touching and fondling of the genitals in another 38 percent of child-adult sexual interactions.

A primary and relatively permanent sexual interest in children (true pedophilia) actually characterizes only a quarter to a third of imprisoned child molesters. The rest of those convicted of the offense appear to have made advances to a child for situational reasons. That is, the contact occurred during periods of stress, frustration, or lack of other sexual outlets, or during an unusual opportunity (Arndt, 1991; Gebhard et al., 1965).

If a person develops a sexual interest in children, how is this interest translated into behavior? From time to time, all of us experience arousal under inappropriate conditions or toward inappropriate people, and we choose not to act on our arousal. You may feel attracted to your best friend's partner, or you may get inexplicably "turned on" while sitting in class one day, but you inhibit your feelings to avoid hurting your friends or embarrassing yourself. The sexual abuser, however, may be uninhibited as a result of various factors, a major one being alcohol (Arndt, 1991).

Cognitive distortions or unusual thought processes are also thought to allow the offender to bypass his normal inhibitions. In a study of 101 child sex offenders undergoing treatment, the following cognitive distortions were the most frequently mentioned when the men were asked to report what they were thinking at the time of the offense (Neidigh & Krop, 1992, p. 212):

> *"She enjoyed it."*
>
> *"This won't hurt her or affect her in any way."*
>
> *"This is not so bad, it's not really wrong."*

It has also been suggested that the exposure of pedophiles to child pornography may incite them to act on their sexual fantasies about children (Russell, 1984). Experimental research relevant to this hypothesis is not available because no one has yet been able to design ethically acceptable research to test it. It is apparent that we know very little about pedophilia beyond clinical observations. We hope that knowledge about this disorder will change in the near future.

Zoophilia

A human's sexual interaction with a member of another species—a dog, horse, or sheep, for example—is known as **zoophilia,** or bestiality. The use of animals as the preferred or exclusive means of obtaining erotic pleasure is relatively rare; most often an animal is employed sexually because the person lacks a human partner.

References to sexual contact between animals and humans appear throughout recorded history. Such contact is depicted often in ancient mythology and classical art (see Figure 15.7). Some modern pornography also contains depictions of sexual relations between humans (usually women) and animals. It has been suggested that a devotee of this kind of pornography is excited by the degradation of the woman rather than by the sexual activity itself.

zoophilia (ZOO-oh-FIL-ee-ah) Sexual activity with animals.

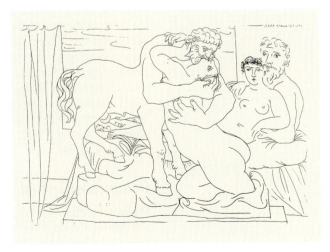

Figure 15.7 Picasso's Etching of the Centaur and a Woman Artistic depictions of sexual contact between humans and animals stretch back to the beginnings of recorded history.

INCIDENCE AND CHARACTERISTICS.
About 8 percent of the males and 4 percent of the females in the Kinsey group's (1948, 1953) samples reported having had sexual experience with animals, but rates among boys raised on farms were considerably higher. About 17 percent of farm boys experienced sexual arousal to the point of orgasm as a result of contact with animals. The same percentage of boys had animal contacts that did not result in orgasm. Coitus with animals such as calves and sheep was the most common form of sexual interaction reported by the Kinsey group's adolescent male volunteers. In another common pattern, reported especially among residents of urban areas, household pets—most often dogs and sometimes cats—stimulated their owners' genitals.

The great majority of animal contacts reported by the Kinsey group's male volunteers occurred during adolescence, prior to the beginning of sexual relations with other people. By adulthood, most of the men had abandoned their sexual contacts with animals.

Table 15.2 Erotic Responses to Observing Animals in Coitus		
Erotic Response	**By Females (%)**	**By Males (%)**
Definite and/or frequent	5	11
Some	11	21
Never	84	68
Number of people interviewed	5,250	4,082

Source: Adapted from Kinsey, A.C., Pomeroy, W., Martin, C., Gebhard, P. *Sexual Behavior in the Human Female*, p. 663. Philadelphia: Saunders, 1953. By permission of the Kinsey Institute for Research in Sex, Gender, and Reproduction, Inc.

It appears that substantial numbers of people find observation of animals in coitus to be sexually arousing (see Table 15.2). Almost a third of the men and 16 percent of the women in the Kinsey (1953) group reported that they had experienced an erotic response when observing copulating animals.

In addition to arguing that sexual contact with animals per se was not aberrant, Kinsey expressed concern over the fact that the laws in most states treat bestiality as a crime and punish it with stiff prison terms. Kinsey suggested that the incidence of sex with animals closely paralleled that of prostitution and homosexuality, and thus he questioned whether zoophilia should even be classified as a paraphilia.

Necrophilia and Miscellaneous "Philias"

necrophilia Sexual arousal and/or activity with a corpse.

Having sexual relations with a corpse is called **necrophilia.** Clinically, necrophilia differs from extreme sadism in that the source of sexual excitement appears to have nothing to do with the pain or death of the sex object. Instead, the excitement is associated with the dead body.

Despite jokes about morticians who enjoy sex with corpses, necrophilia appears to be extremely rare. Those few persons who have reported necrophilic behavior typically have had severe emotional problems. After a man was discovered fondling a woman's corpse in an Iowa funeral home, legislators were unable to find any law banning such behavior, so they passed a bill to outlaw sexual abuse of a corpse in 1996.

One of the more bizarre "philias" involves using a rope, belt, or the like to apply pressure to one's neck, thus decreasing the oxygen supply to the brain and elevating the carbon-dioxide level in the blood. This produces a state of euphoria that enhances the pleasure derived from masturbation to orgasm. Tragically, this practice, called *asphyxiophilia*, often leads to death by hanging even though the victim may have tried to use safety mechanisms to avoid death (Innala & Ernulf, 1989). It has been estimated that between 500 and 1,000 deaths occur yearly in the United States as a result of asphyxiophilia (McAnulty, 1995). See "Highlight: Uncommon Paraphilias" for a listing of other unusual practices.

Compulsive Sexual Behavior

Many individuals who engage in paraphilic behaviors would be described by psychologist Patrick Carnes (1983, 1991) as "sexual addicts." Just as alcoholism or drug dependency involves a pathological relationship with a mood-altering chemical, so "sexual addiction" involves a pathological relationship with mood-altering sexual experiences.

Uncommon Paraphilias

In addition to the paraphilias that we have already described in some detail, some people are aroused by other objects that most people do not find sexually stimulating. *Partialism* refers to an exclusive focus on a particular part of the body for arousal. *Coprophilia* is arousal associated with feces, either depositing them on the partner or having them deposited on oneself. *Urophilia* is similar, except that the arousal stems from urine instead of feces. *Klismaphilia* refers to arousal from receiving enemas.

A person occasionally experiencing arousal from one of these sources might not be diagnosed as having a paraphilia needing treatment unless the person is very distressed by it. The *DSM-IV* differentiates between persons with mild (has fantasies or urges but has never acted on them), moderate (has occasionally acted on them), and severe (has repeatedly acted on them) paraphilic urges.

According to Carnes, who has developed a treatment program for sexual addiction, addiction progresses through a four-step cycle that intensifies with each repetition:

1. *Preoccupation*—a trancelike engrossment in thoughts of sex, which creates a compulsive search for sexual stimulation.

2. *Ritualization*—special routines that precede sexual behavior and intensify sexual arousal and excitement.

3. *Compulsive sexual behavior*—the sexual act itself, which addicts are unable to control or stop.

4. *Despair*—the feeling of utter hopelessness that addicts of every kind have about their behavior.

Trancelike states are often a part of intense sexual encounters in normal relationships. In the addict's case, however, the individual is preoccupied with sex and intensifies his or her preoccupation through rituals. For example, the exhibitionist may develop a number of regular routes that he habitually follows at certain times when he wants to expose himself. Eventually, the compulsive sexual behavior begins to be noticed because the person can no longer control it. The despair that the person experiences after the sexual act can be numbed or alleviated by sexual preoccupation, which begins the cycle anew. Carnes advocates treatment based on family therapy and the 12-step treatment model used in the Alcoholics Anonymous program. At present, adequate information is lacking about the effectiveness of this approach for reducing compulsive sexual behavior.

The concept of sexual addiction or compulsion is highly controversial (Coleman, 1991; Levine & Troiden, 1988). As John Money (1988) has suggested, the notion of addiction to sex is not logical. In the context of sexual arousal, there can only be addiction to some*thing* or some*one*. Pointing out that an alcoholic is not addicted to thirst but to alcohol, Money fears that the logical treatment outcome for sexual addiction would be sexual abstinence. Martin Levine and Richard Troiden (1988) expressed concern about the invention of a new "disease" that would threaten the liberties of sexually variant people. These criticisms of the notion of sexual addiction are especially revealing when we consider that the medical establishment defined masturbation, oral sex, homosexuality, and high numbers of sexual partners ("promiscuity") as forms of mental illness in 1952. The fact that these behaviors are no longer considered pathological reflects altered social values rather than advances in clinical research.

TREATMENT OF THE INVASIVE PARAPHILIAS

The public's widespread sense of moral outrage toward paraphiliacs is reflected in many of the painful and dubious treatments administered to individuals who engage in paraphilias. Electroconvulsive therapy or shock treatment, castration, and mood-altering drugs have all been used at one time or another to treat sexual offenders.

Psychotherapy

Conventional counseling or psychotherapy has not been very effective in modifying paraphiliacs' behavior. Success rates in this area compare with those of standard psychotherapy treating drug addiction or alcoholism. The reasons for the poor track record of traditional treatments are unclear. Some researchers have speculated that the unusual behavior is crucial for paraphiliacs' mental stability (Stoller, 1977). According to this view, without their paraphilia, patients would undergo severe mental deterioration.

Another view is that although people are punished for sexual deviance, they also experience rewards. For example, paraphiliacs whose activities make them liable to arrest, such as exhibitionists, voyeurs, and pedophiliacs, seem to have a strong need to run great risks. The constant danger of arrest becomes as arousing as the sexual activity itself.

The difficulties encountered in treating paraphiliacs may be related to the restrictive and often emotionally impoverished environments that many of them experienced as children and adolescents. It is difficult to undo the effects of years of conditioning in one or two hours a week of therapy. Like rapists, convicted sex offenders report more physical and sexual abuse in their childhood than do those convicted of nonsexual crimes (Barbaree et al., 1993; Dwyer & Amberson, 1989). The odds of being convicted of a sex crime were eight times greater for those who reported physical abuse as a child than for those who did not.

All explanations of the paraphilias are still speculative. Attempts to treat these problems, however, have not been deterred by the scarcity of information about them.

Surgical Castration

"It is evident that castration turns the clock back to medieval times, when amputation of the hands was practiced as a means of curing thievery" (Heim & Hursch, 1979, p. 303). In the past, castration was used for many reasons: to prevent procreation by those who were judged undesirable, to punish certain crimes, and, more recently, to treat violent sexual offenders. Castration was recommended as a treatment for "sexual overexcitement" in the late eighteenth century and was first used as a therapy in 1889 (Karpman, 1954). Castration can involve excision of the testes or removal of the entire external genital system, including the penis. Castration for "therapeutic" purposes involves removal of the testes only.

Although the surgical castration of incarcerated sexual offenders is not unknown in North America, it has been practiced on a much wider scale in some northern European countries. The appeal of castration as a treatment for sexual offenders lies in the belief that testosterone, produced by the testes, is necessary for sexual behavior.

This reasoning has a straightforward appeal, but we hope by now you are convinced that the causes of sexual behavior are far more complicated than this surgical treatment suggests. Reducing the amount of testosterone in the blood system does not always change sexual behavior. Contrary to the prevalent myth that the sex offender has an abnormally strong sex drive, many sex offenders have little sexual desire or are sexually dysfunctional (Gebhard et al., 1965; Groth & Burgess, 1977). Presumably castration would not have a marked effect on the behavior of an offender who already had a weak sex drive.

There is substantial evidence that the effect of castration on male sex drive is strongly influenced by an individual's psychological attitude toward castration. As Clellan Ford and Frank Beach (1951, p. 232) stated:

> *We consider it more probable that some men, being convinced in advance that the operation will deprive them of potency, actually experience a lessening of sexual ability. Other individuals unprejudiced by such anticipatory effects are able to copulate frequently despite loss of hormonal support.*

This reasoning is supported by follow-up research with castrated sex offenders in West Germany (Heim, 1981). Questionnaires were mailed to a group of sex criminals who had been castrated before release from prison. These individuals had been out of jail for periods ranging from 4 months to 13 years. They reported sharp reductions in the frequency of coitus, masturbation, sexual thoughts, sex drive, and sexual arousability. However, almost a third of the men could still have sexual intercourse.

Chemical Treatment

Certain treatments involve the administration of chemicals to inhibit desire in sex offenders. Chemical treatment has the same goal as surgical castration, but with a major advantage for the offender: he keeps his testes.

Estrogens have been found to reduce sex drive in paraphilic men, but they are no longer used because they can have feminizing effects on the male physique, including enlargement of the breasts (Bradford, 1993). In contrast, there are antiandrogenic drugs that interfere with the action of testosterone but do not feminize the body. Medroxyprogesterone (MPA; trade name, Depo-Provera) and cyproterone acetate (CPA) are the most commonly used antiandrogens in North America. They block the effects of testosterone on the target organs. This treatment does not affect the direction of sexual behavior (toward gender, sexual acts, and so on), but it does reduce or inhibit sexual response. In 1996, California passed a law requiring repeat child sex offenders to undergo weekly injections of Depo-Provera. Clinical studies indicate that these antiandrogens are fairly effective in suppressing sexual fantasy, desire, and arousal in men (Bradford & Pawlak, 1993; Money, 1988). When used in conjunction with counseling, they benefit some sex offenders. The best candidates for this treatment are self-referred, highly motivated men with good social support (Cooper, 1986).

Adequate empirical studies of the effects of these chemicals on sexual behavior are still needed, and side effects and short- and long-term behavior changes need to be assessed. At present, they offer considerable promise in the treatment of sex offenders. Chemical treatments are often combined with cognitive-behavior therapies.

Cognitive-Behavior Therapies

Cognitive-behavior therapists teach techniques to decrease or control paraphiliac sexual motivation and behavior. The cognitive component involves modifying distorted ideas or cognitions that paraphiliacs use to justify their behavior. Most comprehensive cognitive-behavior therapy programs generally include the following components (Abel, Osborn, Anthony, & Gardos, 1992, p. 256):

1. Behavior therapy to reduce inappropriate sexual arousal and to enhance or maintain appropriate sexual arousal.

2. Training to develop or to enhance prosocial skills.

ISSUES TO CONSIDER

Do you believe that the state has the right to require surgical or chemical treatment for sex offenders?

3. Modification of distorted cognitions and development of victim empathy.

4. Relapse prevention.

An example of a comprehensive cognitive-behavior approach to the treatment of exhibitionism was reported by Marshall, Eccles, and Barbaree (1991). They instructed exhibitionists to carry smelling salts (which have an unpleasant odor) to inhale whenever they felt the urge to expose themselves. This helped the offender to develop control over his thoughts by associating aversive smell with deviant fantasies. Additional aspects of this program include training in assertion and stress management, changing cognitive distortions through role playing, and training in relationship skills. Recent cognitive-behavioral therapies have been shown to be effective in treating paraphilias and reducing repeat offenses (Abel et al., 1992; Pithers, 1993).

Other Approaches

In addition to the medical and cognitive-behavior therapies, a wide range of other therapeutic techniques can help clients to develop more socially approved sexual-arousal patterns and skills. For example, in directed masturbation therapy, the client is instructed to masturbate to socially acceptable sexual fantasies and to cease masturbating to paraphilic themes (Laws & Marshall, 1991). As the client learns that he can successfully masturbate to nondeviant themes, he gradually changes his self-definition from sexually deviant to normal. Other approaches include family or systems psychotherapy, group therapy, psychoanalysis, and systematic desensitization.

A factor complicating the effective treatment of convicted sex offenders is the reality that therapy typically is conducted while the offenders are incarcerated, in either psychiatric hospitals or prison environments. Prisons tend to have small numbers of therapists, and, given their caseloads, they often can offer only minimal treatment.

Despite these problems, cognitive-behavior therapies and chemical approaches appear to be effective in treating sex offenders. The question facing society is whether to opt for treatment or to incarcerate offenders without therapy. The latter option is the one most commonly adopted, and it is associated with recidivism and, eventually, more victims.

Summary of major points

1. Fetishism.

A fetishist requires the presence of an inanimate object to become sexually aroused. To the extent to which we learn to associate inanimate objects such as clothing with arousal, we all have minor fetishes.

2. Transvestism.

Often confused with homosexuality or transsexuality, transvestism, or cross-dressing, usually is practiced by individuals who are biologically and psychologically masculine but who derive erotic pleasure from wearing stereotypically feminine attire.

3. Transsexualism.

Some people whose genetic, gonadal, hormonal, and genital gender development all coincide nevertheless believe themselves to be members of the other gender. Although the causes of transsexuality are unclear, many transsexuals who undergo surgical sex reassignment report greater happiness and adjustment in their new status. But surgery does not improve adjustment for all transsexuals. Given the drastic nature of sex-reassignment surgery, some scientists have called for a halt to transsexual surgery until we have a better understanding of transsexual identity.

4. Sadomasochism. Sadists are aroused by inflicting pain on others and masochists are erotically stimulated by receiving pain. Sadomasochism is distinguished from sexual assault in that both participants consent to the activity. A variant of this fetish, bondage and discipline, involves symbolic dominance and submission more than it involves physical pain.

5. Voyeurism and exhibitionism. Voyeurism involves observing others without their consent who are nude and/or sexually involved, and exhibitionism is showing others one's genitals without being invited to do so. As far as is known, voyeurs and exhibitionists are almost exclusively male. Victims of voyeurs and exhibitionists may be startled or frightened by the intrusion, but a calm response is generally most effective in discouraging the behavior and is least likely to reward the perpetrator.

6. Pedophilia. Adults convicted of sexual contacts with children resemble convicted rapists with respect to feelings of inadequacy, although they do not appear to be as aggressive as rapists. Factors that impair judgment, such as alcohol and emotional disturbance, are quite common among those convicted of sexual relations with children.

7. Zoophilia. Most individuals who report engaging in sex with animals do not describe it as a preferred or exclusive mode of sexual interaction. When zoophilia occurs, it usually takes place during adolescence and is abandoned in adulthood.

8. Compulsive sexual behavior. Many paraphilias seem similar to addictions to alcohol or drugs. The individual engages in a behavior to alter his or her mood and seems unable to control the behavior.

9. Treatment of the invasive paraphilias. Numerous approaches are used to treat paraphiliacs. Many early treatments resembled punishments more than effective therapies. Cognitive-behavior therapies and pharmacological treatments appear to be effective in treating paraphilias. Whether these treatments are employed depends on whether society emphasizes rehabilitation and treatment or incarceration and punishment.

Check your knowledge

1. Transvestism is a (a) symptom of homosexual tendencies, (b) symptom of schizophrenia, (c) behavior that some heterosexuals enjoy, (d) consequence of being raised in a household where there was no strong father figure. **(p. 380)**

2. Transvestism (a) is caused by prenatal exposure to high levels of inappropriate hormones, (b) results from unusual bonding patterns between parents and children, (c) probably results from abnormal genetic inheritance, (d) is caused by unknown factors. **(pp. 380–381)**

3. A transsexual is (a) an androgynous person, (b) a person of either gender who enjoys dressing as a member of the other gender but is not homosexual, (c) a person who is sexually attracted to either gender, (d) a biologically normal male or female who believes that he or she is a member of the other gender. **(p. 381)**

4. Exhibitionism is (a) a genetic disorder, (b) the most frequently committed sexual offense, (c) most frequently committed by bisexuals, (d) most often performed in the presence of elderly women. **(pp. 391–392)**

5. Compared to other sex offenders, pedophiles are typically (a) younger, (b) older, (c) more violent, (d) more assertive. **(p. 394)**

6. Zoophilia involves (a) enjoying viewing monkeys and other captive animals engaging in sexual activity, (b) taking a young child to a zoo with the idea of later persuading the child to have sex, (c) human-animal sexual contact, (d) forcing animals of two different species to have sexual contact. **(p. 395)**

7. Most sadomasochists are (a) dangerous psychopaths, (b) people who are sexually aroused by ritualized pain and/or degradation, (c) persons who enjoy receiving and/or inflicting any kind of actual pain, (d) all of the above. **(pp. 386–387)**

8. In the treatment of paraphilias, the most effective procedure appears to be (a) psychotherapy or family therapy, (b) surgical castration, (c) chemical treatment or cognitive-behavior therapy, (d) psychoanalysis. **(pp. 398–400)**

16

LOVING SEXUAL INTERACTIONS

BEING LOVED
Early Experience
**Highlight: Attachment Styles
and Adult Relationships**

SELF-LOVE
Self-Love Versus Selfishness

LOVING OTHERS
Constructions of Love
Forms of Love
Love Versus Lust
**Across Cultures: What Do You
Look for in a Partner?**

LOVE AS DEPENDENCY,
JEALOUSY, AND OTHER
UNLOVELY FEELINGS
Dependency and Control
Jealousy
Highlight: Dating Infidelity

LOVING SEXUAL
INTERACTIONS
*Vitality in Long-Term
Relationships*
**Highlight: Make Love,
Not War**

SUMMARY OF MAJOR
POINTS

CHECK YOUR
KNOWLEDGE

REALITY or MYTH ?

1 People who love themselves are more able to be loving with other people.

2 Men make a stronger distinction between love and sex than do women.

3 Infatuation is not considered real love by most researchers.

4 Limerence is a form of love experienced only by couples who have been involved in a lengthy relationship.

5 Men's jealousy is a major reason for marital murder in North America.

6 After a person has formed a romantic relationship with someone, he or she will not be sexually attracted to or have fantasies about anyone else.

S EX, as we have seen, can be used for the domination and exploitation of others, but it can also be fun, relaxing, and physically rewarding. And sexual interactions, in the context of strong attachment, mutual respect, and concern for a partner's feelings and well-being, can allow us to realize our potential to take part in one of the most remarkable experiences available to human beings. A loving sexual relationship can provide what Abraham Maslow (1962) called a **peak experience.**

How we develop the capacity to participate in a loving sexual relationship is the topic of this final chapter. First, we look at the relationship between being loved during infancy and childhood and the capacity to love others during adulthood. We then examine models of the development of love relationships. Finally, we turn to some of the problems that couples need to resolve in order to develop enduring relationships characterized by loving sexual expression.

peak experience Maslow's term for a personal experience that generates feelings of ecstasy, peace, and unity with the universe.

BEING LOVED

What is love? It can be a momentary feeling or attitude that results in a loving act, such as helping a hurt person. It can be a more enduring feeling or attitude directed toward a specific person over a long period of time. Love can take a variety of forms, which we consider later in the chapter. For now, we rely on science-fiction writer Robert Heinlein's (1961) definition: love is the feeling that someone else's needs and well-being are as important to you as your own.

Early Experience

What does a child need to grow into a mature, loving person? We cannot systematically vary the environment in which children are raised in order to examine, experimentally, the effects of different kinds of child rearing on personality development. However, observations of abused and neglected children, experimental research with primates, and cross-cultural correlational studies offer clues to the importance of early experience in creating our capacity to grow physically and emotionally, to love ourselves, and to form loving bonds with others.

THE PRIMATE STUDIES.

Erik Erikson's contention that consistent loving care during infancy and childhood is necessary for the development of basic trust is supported by experimental research with primates (Harlow & Mears, 1979). Young monkeys undergo a relatively lengthy period of dependence on adult care that is somewhat similar to that of human children. Rhesus monkey mothers are protective and typically nurse their infants for a year or more. The kind of care that the monkey receives profoundly affects its later behavior, as does its contact with other infant and juvenile monkeys.

In one famous study, monkeys were separated from their mothers shortly after birth and reared in a laboratory. The infants were put into cages with one of two surrogate mothers. One surrogate was a plain wire-mesh cylinder from which the monkeys could receive milk from a bottle. The other was a terrycloth-covered form, but no milk was available from that surrogate. When the monkeys were allowed to choose between the two surrogate mothers, even those who got their milk from the wire mother spent more time clinging to the cloth mother (see Figure 16.1). The cloth "mother" seemed to provide more comfort to the infant monkeys (Harlow & Harlow, 1962).

In another series of studies, young rhesus monkeys were brought up in isolation. Lighting, temperature, cage cleaning, food, and water were provided by remote control, and the totally isolated monkeys saw no living beings. The longer the monkeys were isolated, the more abnormal and maladjusted they became. Monkeys reared in isolation for six months were described as social misfits; monkeys isolated for the first year of life appeared to be little more than "semi-animated vegetables" (Suomi & Harlow, 1971). As they advanced into childhood and adolescence, these monkeys were still social misfits compared with those who were reared with their mothers and peers. The monkeys who had been isolated for six months had biologically normal reproductive systems but were sexually incompetent.

Those monkeys isolated for a year did not even approximate the botched sexual behavior of the six-month isolates; they attempted no sexual contact at all. The lack of successful mating on the part of these isolates may have been fortunate, for isolated females who had been impregnated accidentally or artificially were generally rejecting or incompetent mothers. Early deprivation thus has devastating effects on monkeys' sexual behavior in adolescence and adulthood.

An intriguing series of studies has demonstrated that these maladjustments may not be permanent or irreversible. In a kind of sex-therapy procedure, isolated monkeys were paired with younger normal monkeys for specific periods of time, such as two hours a day for three days a week. The individual therapy sessions were augmented with group therapy involving two isolates and two "therapists" (normal monkeys). After six months of therapy, the isolates showed remarkable improvement in their behavior. By adolescence, the isolates' sexual behavior was normal for their age (Novak & Harlow, 1975; Suomi, Harlow, & McKinney, 1972).

Figure 16.1
Contact Comfort That infant monkeys need contact comfort is revealed by their choosing a cloth-covered surrogate more frequently than a wire surrogate that provides milk.

Harry Harlow postulated that if the infant experiences a severe lack or loss of contact comfort from the parents, normal body contact will be extremely difficult to accept when the time arrives for social play and peer love:

> *It is this knowledge of learning what the body as a whole can do, in air and sea, on land and snow, that reinforces the first pleasure in mastery and also gives the first confidence in self. . . . The basis for self-esteem is a prerequisite for the love of living and loving, no matter what love at what age or stage. (Harlow & Mears, 1979, p. 170)*

DEPRIVATION OR ENHANCEMENT?

Human infants reared in an orphanage or an institution where they receive only rudimentary care come closest to experiencing the deprivation encountered by the monkeys in the Harlow studies. In the past, institutionalized babies were traditionally kept in individual cubicles separated from other infants, and their adult contact was brief and hurried. For example, in one case, eight infants had to share one nurse (Spitz, 1947). These children were thus deprived of the range of sensory stimulation that a child normally receives from being picked up, cuddled, talked to, played with, and rocked. An impoverished environment of this kind was associated with major disturbances in interpersonal relationships and with emotional problems during childhood and adolescence (Casler, 1968).

Because of the remarkable similarities between human infants and other primate infants, John Bowlby (1973) hypothesized that the attachment between infant and caregiver forms the basis for later attachments in adulthood.

A major contribution to understanding how differences in early caregiving are related to personality differences in young children was made by Mary Ainsworth and her colleagues (Ainsworth, Blehar, Waters, & Wall, 1978). They observed mother-infant pairs at home and in a laboratory situation called the Strange Situation. They were interested in seeing how infants would react to novel toys, an unfamiliar adult, and a brief separation from their mother. Ainsworth et al. reported three major kinds of attachment patterns: secure, anxious-ambivalent, and avoidant. Secure parent-child attachment is marked by parents' noticing, understanding, and responding to infant needs. Anxious-ambivalent attachment is characterized by parents who sometimes respond to the needs of the infant and sometimes do not. In avoidant attachment, there is a great deal of parental neglect of the infant.

This classic study has been replicated and extended by many other researchers (Elicker, Englund, & Sroufe, 1992). Attachment behaviors that are assessed at age 1 appear to be good predictors of later childhood social behaviors. Securely attached children are more socially competent, have higher self-esteem, and have more satisfying relationships than do avoidant and anxious-ambivalent children.

Attachment styles have also been found to be related to romantic relationships in adults (Feeney & Noller, 1990; Shaver & Hazen, 1994; Ward, Hudson, & Marshall, 1996). A summary of these findings is presented in "Highlight: Attachment Styles and Adult Relationships" (see page 407). Although there has been no longitudinal research tracing attachment styles from infancy through adulthood, evidence is accumulating to support the hypothesis that early attachment between infants and their caretakers plays an important role in the infants' later relationships.

In Chapter 14 we reviewed numerous studies that examined the childhood experiences of adults who sexually assault others. These studies indicate that a high proportion of sexually violent adults were themselves physically and sexually abused

ISSUES TO CONSIDER

How would you try to help an adult who was deprived of adequate human contact and affection during childhood?

Figure 16.2
A Child Who Is Loved Becomes a Loving Child
Children who receive physical affection during childhood are likely to become trusting and affectionate adults.

during childhood. Just as abuse breeds violence, caring breeds love. At first the child is a passive recipient of the care and affection of its parents, but before long, a loved child becomes a loving child (see Figure 16.2). From a very early age, loved children derive a great deal of pleasure from displaying affection for their parents and others.

Sigmund Freud contended that this love contains a sexual component. Children's love clearly includes the sensual pleasure derived from intimate body contact with members of the family (see Figure 16.3). The idea that the child desires sexual intercourse, however, depends on whether the child can understand this activity. At this point we have no evidence that young children have such a concept, and the Goldmans' (1982) research strongly suggests that they do not. In fact, many preadolescent children, upon hearing about the activity leading to conception, express revulsion. Children's occasional expression of the desire to marry one or both of their parents probably stems not from copulatory urges but from their love of their parents, their observation of the pleasure that their parents take in their marriage, and a desire to maintain an ongoing connection with their parents.

HIGHLIGHT

Attachment Styles and Adult Relationships

Attachment styles are associated with many behaviors exhibited by individuals with their romantic partners.

People with secure attachment

seldom worry about being abandoned by their partner

believe other people are well intentioned

view their relationship as a trusting partnership

place highest value and derive most pleasure from relationships rather than from work

People with anxious-ambivalent attachment

often worry that their partners do not love them or will leave them

would like others to be closer to them

feel it is easy to fall in love

experience high degrees of sexual attraction and jealousy

report frequent emotional ups and downs

more frequently experience obsessive love

worry about love interfering with work

People with avoidant attachment

are uncomfortable being close to others

tend to fear intimacy

are afraid of becoming dependent on another

expect that love relationships are destined to fail

report emotional ups and downs

experience high degrees of jealousy

tend to prefer work over love relationships

Because of the absence of longitudinal research or of studies of attempts of people to change their attachment styles, we do not know the extent to which individuals can alter attachment styles developed during infancy. However, evidence is accumulating in support of the basic tenets of attachment theory, and research is needed on the possibility of altering one's attachment style in adulthood.

Sources: Feeney & Noller, 1990, 1991; Hazan & Shaver, 1990; Shaver & Hazen, 1993; Ward et al., 1996.

CROSS-CULTURAL OBSERVATIONS.   In some cultures, infants and children are given minimal physical affection and body contact in the belief that the withholding of physical intimacy makes them grow up to be independent and self-reliant. In other cultures, adults take great pleasure in holding, caressing, stroking, and playing with babies (Hatfield, 1994; Thayer, 1987). James Prescott (1975) examined

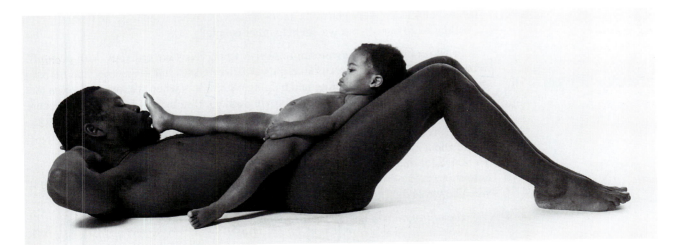

Figure 16.3   Physical Intimacy   Children enjoy the pleasure of physical intimacy without thinking of it as sexual.

the relationship between the treatment of infants and the level of adult violence in 49 cultures. Those cultures in which infants are reared with a great deal of physical affection tend to display little physical violence; conversely, those cultures in which infants are deprived of physical affection display high levels of physical violence among adults.

On the basis of these observations, Prescott (1975) suggested that affection and aggression are, to some extent, mutually exclusive. That is, children reared with physical affection are likely to be affectionate and nonviolent as adults. Prescott believed that in the absence of physical affection during infancy and childhood, brain development is restricted, with the result that adult aggressiveness becomes more likely. Social learning theorists suggest a modeling effect: children learn affectionate or aggressive behavior from affectionate or aggressive parents and peers. Whether the mechanisms producing affectionate or aggressive adults are due to structural alterations in the brain or to social learning experiences, or both, it is clear that children who receive love and physical affection are more likely to give love and to respect themselves.

ISSUES TO CONSIDER

Why do cultures who rear children with physical affection tend to display little physical violence?

SELF-LOVE

Most of us have heard exhortations against selfishness from our parents, religious leaders, and teachers all our lives. In stressing that one of the factors most consistently associated with healthy psychological functioning and adjustment is self-esteem, are we advocating selfishness? Not at all; there is a world of difference between self-esteem, or self-love, and selfishness.

Self-Love Versus Selfishness

Answering the following questions illuminates the enormous gulf between self-love and selfishness.

1. When was the last time you felt unhappy with yourself (insecure, hassled, irritable)?

2. When did you last feel very happy with yourself (proud of yourself, pleased with some of your personal qualities)?

3. How did you behave toward others on those two occasions? On which occasion were you kinder, more generous, more sensitive to others' feelings, and more willing to go out of your way to help other people?

In all probability, you were more selfish when you were unhappy with yourself. When we dislike ourselves, our energies are directed toward protecting and helping ourselves, not toward protecting and helping others. It is when we love ourselves that we are most capable of giving to and loving others. Similarly, when we are insecure and ashamed of our bodies, our energies are concentrated on hiding and protecting ourselves. It is difficult to make love to another person when we are ashamed or embarrassed about our own feelings and our own bodies.

Love for oneself, then, is intricately connected with love for any other being. According to Erich Fromm (who can be forgiven for his sexist language, given the time when he wrote this!),

> *The affirmation of one's own life, happiness, growth, freedom is rooted in one's capacity to love. . . . If an individual is able to love productively, he loves himself too; if he can love only others, he cannot love at all. (1956, p. 60)*

LOVING OTHERS

riters have tried throughout history to describe love's elusive qualities:

Love is patient and kind; love is not jealous or boastful;
It is not arrogant or rude. Love does not insist on its own way;
it is not irritable or resentful;
It does not rejoice at wrong, but rejoices in the right.
Love bears all things, believes all things, hopes all things,
endures all things.
(St. Paul, I Corinthians 13: 4–7)

Death and delight, anguish and joy, anxiety and the wonder of birth—
these are the warp and woof of which the fabric of human love is woven.
(Rollo May)

Love is aim-inhibited sexuality. (Freud, 1955, p. 142)

Although love has fascinated philosophers, theologians, writers, poets, and artists for ages, only recently have scientists attempted to describe and measure it.

Constructions of Love

The scientific investigation of love has increased markedly since the mid-1960s. Many recent studies have focused on romantic love, at least in part owing to researchers' reliance on college students as volunteers. Although romantic love is thought to be in full bloom during late adolescence, it remains to be seen whether the results obtained from this age group are characteristic of other points in the life span. Researchers have explored the relationship between love and friendship (Hendrick & Hendrick, 1992; Sternberg, 1991), passionate and companionate love (Hatfield & Rapson, 1993), and attachment and love (Shaver & Hazan, 1993). The components and forms of love have also been probed (Hendrick & Hendrick, 1993; Sternberg, 1991).

Many scales employed to measure love reflect a stereotypically feminine perspective that emphasizes emotional expression and shared feelings. These measures have resulted in what Cancian (1986) has called the feminization of love and may yield an incomplete conception of it. For example, in one study, some of the behaviors described as love were "communicating without words," "sharing someone's feelings," and "letting someone know all about you" (Foa et al., 1987). Generally, these are the expressive aspects of love, and women tend to have more expressive skill than do men. Instrumental behaviors, more stereotypical of men than of women, are usually neglected in measures of love. Practical help, shared physical activities, and emphasis on physical sex are some of the characteristics associated with men. Because many of our measures of love reflect the stereotypically feminine ideal, it is not surprising that women emerge as more capable of love than do men. For example, a woman would be perceived as showing love if, at the end of a long day, she shares her feelings about a hassle at work or asks about her partner's feelings (expressive behaviors). If, on that same evening, her partner noticed that her tire was flat and decided to change it for her (an instrumental behavior), this would not necessarily be perceived as showing love.

Rather than trying to make men become more "loving" by becoming more stereotypically feminine, Cancian (1986) argued for a more androgynous conception of love that is both expressive and instrumental. As she put it:

> Who is more loving: a couple who confide most of their experiences to each other but rarely cooperate or give each other practical help, or a couple who help each other through many crises and cooperate in running a household but rarely discuss their personal experiences? Both relationships are limited. Most people would probably choose a combination: A relationship that integrates both feminine and masculine styles of loving, an androgynous love. (p. 709)

Given the foregoing analysis and in the light of gender differences in attitudes about sex described throughout this book, it should come as no surprise that there are also gender differences in attitudes about love. Men tend to differentiate love and sex more strongly than do women (Hendrick & Hendrick, 1993). This pattern of results is also found in Sweden, although the differences are not as pronounced, indicating a greater likelihood of fusing sex and love in that culture. There is also evidence that the tendency to differentiate between love and sex decreases as people grow older (Foa et al., 1987; Sprague & Quadagno, 1989).

Men are more likely than women to view love as a game to be played out with a number of partners (Hendrick & Hendrick, 1993). This orientation can lead to the manipulation of others and sexual aggression, and men who perceive love as a game may be wary of emotional investment. Women are more likely to merge love and friendship than are men. Perhaps because women have been socialized to view sex as a precious commodity that must be guarded, they are also more pragmatic about love than are males. That is, they emphasize "love planning" based on the potential of a lover to meet particular criteria.

ISSUES TO CONSIDER

Why do you think women are more likely to merge love and friendship than are men?

Forms of Love

Psychologist Robert J. Sternberg (1986, 1991) devised a theoretical framework to account for the various forms that loving can take. We use this model for the light it sheds on different kinds of love, although there is some question as to how distinct from one another some of these variants are (Hendrick & Hendrick, 1992). Sternberg maintained that love could be understood in terms of three components: (1) intimacy, which includes the feelings of closeness and connectedness that one experiences in loving relationships; (2) passion, which refers to the drives that lead to romance, physical attraction, and sexual interaction in a loving relationship; and (3) decision and commitment, which encompass (in the short run) the decision that one loves another and (in the long run) the commitment to maintain the love.

Intimacy, according to Sternberg, is the *emotional* component of love. It grows steadily in the early phases of a relationship but later tends to level off. It is the major component of most loving relationships that we have with family, friends, and lovers.

Passion is the *motivational* component of love. Passion develops quickly in relationships but then typically levels off. It involves a high degree of physiological arousal and an intense desire to be united with the loved one. In its purest form, it can be seen in the experience of "love at first sight."

Decision and commitment are the *cognitive* components of love. Commitment increases gradually at first and then grows more rapidly as a relationship develops. The love of a parent for a child is often distinguished by a high level of commitment.

Although these three components are all important parts of loving relationships, their strength may differ from one relationship to another and may change over time within the same relationship. Sternberg represents the various possible relationships as triangles (see Figure 16.4, p. 412). The absence of all three components is nonlove (see part a of Figure 16.4), which describes the majority of our relationships—those with casual acquaintances. When all three components of Sternberg's love triangle are present in a relationship, there exists what he calls consummate or complete love (see part h of Figure 16.4). According to Sternberg, that is the kind of love that people strive for but find difficult to sustain. It is possible only in very special relationships.

FRIENDSHIP.   The first type of love that most of us experience outside our families is a close friendship with a person of the same gender. Friendship, or liking, is reserved for close friends; passing acquaintances do not inspire it. According to Sternberg, a friendship occurs when one experiences the intimacy component of love without passion and decision/commitment (see part b of Figure 16.4). Also known as **philia** and **platonic love,** friendship is a form of love in which we are as concerned with the well-being of our friend as we are with our own well-being. Friendships can evolve into relationships characterized by passionate arousal and long-term commitment; when this occurs, the friendship goes beyond liking and becomes another form of love.

Most people view friendship as a relationship between equals that is characterized by sharing and caring (Blieszner & Adams, 1992). It is interesting that throughout most of history, the experience of this kind of love between a man and a woman was seen as unlikely or impossible. Among the early Greeks, the deepest love was believed to exist in the friendship of two males, who might also be involved in an erotic love relationship.

With the movement toward equality for men and women in the twentieth century, intense friendship is no longer confined to partners of the same gender. Nonetheless, 75 percent of the respondents in a magazine survey (*Psychology Today,* 1979) saw same-gender friendships as different from other-gender friendships. Friendships between men and women were seen as more difficult and complicated because of potential sexual tensions, the lack of social support for male-female friendships, and the belief that men and women have less in common than do friends of the same gender. Although there are still challenges to same-gender friendships, they do not seem to be as important today to college students (Monsour, Harris, & Kurzwell, 1994).

INFATUATION.   One dictionary defines infatuate as "to inspire with a foolish or extravagant love or admiration." In Sternberg's framework, **infatuation** involves passionate arousal without the intimacy and decision and commitment components of love (see part c of Figure 16.4). Infatuated love is "love at first sight." It is essentially the same kind of love that Dorothy Tennov (1979) called **limerence**—a love characterized by preoccupation, acute longing, exaggeration of the other's good qualities, seesawing emotion, and aching in the chest. These characteristics can be experienced as either intensely pleasurable or painful, depending on the response of the loved one, or "limerent object."

Unlike other forms of love, limerence is an all-or-nothing state that men and women experience in similar ways. Based on several hundred descriptions of limerence obtained through personal interviews, Tennov (1979) outlined a number of traits that a person in this state may exhibit:

1. *Preoccupation with the limerent object.* You are unable to think about anything else but the object of your affection. Everything you do is calculated in terms of how the limerent object would respond—whether he or she would like or dislike it. You may feel happy or sad depending on the degree of attention you get from your limerent object.

philia Love involving concern with the well-being of a friend.
platonic love Nonsexual love for another person, often referred to as spiritual love.

 **? 3**

infatuation Foolish and irrational love.

limerence (LIH-mer-ence) Love marked by obsession and preoccupation with the loved one.

 **? 4**

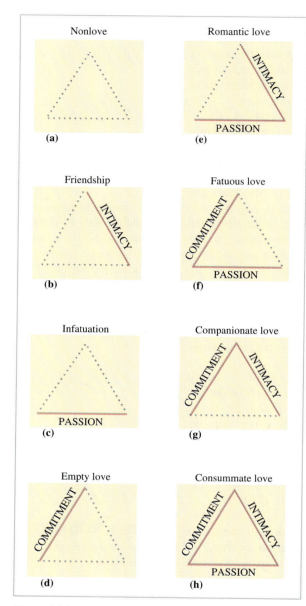

Figure 16.4
The Forms of Love

2. *Intrusive or unintentional thinking about the limerent object.* In addition to spending a great deal of time intentionally fantasizing about the limerent object, you find that thoughts about your beloved intrude and interfere with other mental activity in an apparently involuntary way. You may be working on a paper or performing some task at work when thoughts and fantasies of the love object come to the fore.

3. *Desire for exclusivity with the limerent object.* You crave the limerent object and no one else. You want commitment to ensure exclusivity even when it is premature or inappropriate. This can lead you to smother the object of your affection with attention and pressure rather than allowing the relationship to develop gradually.

Tennov proposed that limerence develops in stages, the first being admiration for another person who possesses valued qualities and for whom one feels a basic liking. This stage is followed by an awareness of sexual attraction. Once admiration and sexual attraction are present, the next step is to undergo an experience that raises the probability that these feelings might be reciprocated. This experience could be something as simple as observing a look or gesture or being asked to go to dinner or a party.

At this point in the development of limerence, the first "crystallization" occurs: one begins to focus on the good qualities of the limerent object and to disregard his or her bad qualities. After the first crystallization, if the two people develop a mutual attraction, the intensity of the romantic involvement is relatively mild. Doubt about the limerent object's commitment, however, can evoke extreme, or "crazy," limerence. The interaction between hopefulness and uncertainty leads to the second crystallization, which results in feeling an intense attraction to the other person.

Limerence is a tantalizing state that promises great things that never can be fully realized. In the beginning it can also be devastating, especially if the limerent object is lost abruptly. Tennov outlines three ways in which limerent attraction can end:

1. The development of a deeper relationship, which evolves if one is able to withstand the major disappointments and emptiness of fading limerence.

2. Abandonment owing to a lack of reciprocity on the part of the limerent object.

3. The transfer of attention to another limerent object—a continuation of the limerent state.

Tennov maintains that full-blown limerence cannot develop without an element of uncertainty.

ROMANTIC LOVE.   The deeper relationship that may blossom out of limerent love, or infatuation, is characterized by romantic love. Romantic love comprises intimacy as well as passion (see part e of Figure 16.4). It is the "Romeo and Juliet" type of love: liking with the added excitement of physical attraction and arousal but without commitment.

Humans' first experience of romantic love can occur during infancy and childhood. Infants normally display a passionate attachment to their parents (Shaver, Hazen, & Bradshaw, 1988). Much like adolescent and young adult lovers, they get intense pleasure in parental attention and approval, and they express distress when separated and affection when reunited. Five-year-olds often display passionate love for others by reporting that there is another child they cannot stop thinking about, whom they want to be near, and whom they would like to touch and be touched by (Carlson & Hatfield, 1992). The Greeks called this form of love **eros.**

eros Erotic love.

Many people wonder whether it is possible to have a romantic love relationship with more than one person in a lifetime. When an intense romantic relationship ends, it is common to feel that you will never again experience romantic love. Yet as people who find another mate after separation, divorce, or the death of a beloved partner discover, it is possible to form a romantic bond with more than one person.

Some researchers, unlike Tennov and Sternberg, maintain that romantic love does not differ from infatuation. For example, Ellen Berscheid and Elaine Walster (1978) contended that defining our feelings as love depends on a two-stage process: we first become physiologically aroused, and then cognitive labeling takes place.

Prior to the development of Berscheid and Walster's model, many researchers assumed that loving is an intense form of liking, governed by the same principles. Voluminous research by Byrne (1971) and others had indicated that we like those who share our values and attitudes and who evaluate us positively. We find associating with someone who shares our beliefs and attitudes rewarding, because he or she affirms our perceptions of the world. And obviously, we find compliments or positive evaluations rewarding.

Berscheid and Walster conceded that we are more disposed to like those who reward us than those who do not, but they point to the fact that people have been known to become highly infatuated with a person whom others perceive as not rewarding or even as punishing. From this phenomenon comes the axiom, "Love is blind."

Berscheid and Walster cited two other reasons for their rejection of the idea that loving is simply a more intense form of liking, explained by the same principles: **unrequited love** and jealousy. In unrequited love you feel and/or express intense feelings for another person, but the object of your desire behaves as if you do not exist or, worse, appears to be repelled by you. Jealousy is not an emotion that most of us find rewarding, and yet many of us have experienced heightened feelings of desire for a person after thinking that he or she was attracted to someone else.

unrequited love Intense romantic/erotic attraction toward another person who does not have the same feelings toward you.

Based on these and other similar observations, Berscheid and Walster proposed that we are more likely to label our feelings toward someone as love when we are physiologically aroused. An obvious source of physiological arousal, of course, is sexual arousal. But Berscheid and Walster argued that *any* source of physiological arousal—for example, fear, euphoria, or anxiety—can increase the likelihood of our defining our feeling as love.

The second step, cognitive labeling, occurs because we seek an explanation for our feelings. Most of us are conditioned over a long period to associate feelings of arousal with romantic attraction. Berscheid and Walster's two-stage theory of love (or infatuation) helps to explain why we may perceive punishing sources of arousal such as jealousy and anxiety as indicators of the strength of our feelings for others.

EMPTY LOVE.   Sternberg describes empty love as commitment without intimacy or passion (see part d of Figure 16.4). It can be the kind of love, for example, that is seen in a 25-year-old marriage that has become stagnant. Intimacy and passion have died out, and all that remains is commitment. Although North Americans may associate this type of love with the final stages of a long-term relationship, in other societies it may be the starting point of a relationship. For example, in cultures in which marriages are arranged, a couple may begin a relationship with little beyond a commitment to try to love each other (Hatfield & Rapson, 1996).

FATUOUS LOVE.   Fatuous love involves passion and commitment but no intimacy (see part f of Figure 16.4, page 412). Sternberg (1991) described it as the form of love that we associate with whirlwind courtships. Girl meets boy; the next week they are engaged; a month later they are married. This type of love is fatuous, or foolish, because a commitment is made based only on the heady chemistry of passion without the stabilizing effect of intimacy. Fatuous love is unlikely to sustain a long-term relationship.

Figure 16.5
Companionate Love Based on their facial expressions and posture, this couple seems to have developed the friendship, mutual trust, and reliance characteristic of companionate love.

COMPANIONATE LOVE.   Companionate love involves intimacy and commitment but no passion (see part g of Figure 16.4, page 412). It is essentially a long-term friendship such as often develops in marriage after a couple's passion has died down (see Figure 16.5).

Strongly connected couples beyond the surging emotions of passion usually develop a system of shared values. The extent of support and interplay is often unspoken and habitual, and only upon death or divorce do they become aware of how much they have lost. Having been concerned with what was not working well, they may have failed to realize fully how many of their joint pursuits did work (Carlson & Hatfield, 1992).

CONSUMMATE LOVE.   Consummate love is the combination of all three components of Sternberg's triangle. Although it is most often associated with romantic relationships, it can occur in other contexts. One can experience a love for one's child, for example, that has the deep emotional involvement of the intimacy component, the satisfaction of motivational needs (such as nurturance and self-esteem) of the passion component, and the dedication of the decision/commitment component. Achieving consummate love, according to Sternberg, is like losing weight: difficult but not impossible. After the goal has been reached, maintaining it—whether keeping the weight off or keeping the consummate love alive—becomes the problem.

Love Versus Lust

lust A strong sexual desire or need.

One dictionary defines **lust** as "an intense longing" and "sexual desire often to an intense or unrestrained degree." In Sternberg's (1986) theory, lust is the passionate component of love. Lust or passion can be so strong as to elicit the feelings and behaviors often associated with emotional disturbance. Infatuated people may be distracted by obsessional thoughts about the object of their affection. Normally poised and well coordinated, they may find themselves speechless and clumsy in the presence of the person to whom they are attracted. Mood shifts from euphoria to depression are common, and a person's priorities may be drastically altered, at least temporarily. For some people, the experience of falling in love bears a striking resemblance to temporary insanity. Perhaps this similarity underlies the expression, "I'm crazy about you."

FEELINGS VERSUS BEHAVIORS.   Like fear, hunger, happiness, and anxiety, lust is a human feeling. You cannot choose to experience or to avoid feelings, but you can control your responses to them. If you are dieting, you may choose to have just one egg at breakfast rather than two, even though you may still be hungry after eating the single egg. If you experience irritation with your partner while at a party, you may choose to scream and yell publicly or you may opt to postpone your reaction until the two of you are alone. Similarly, if you are feeling lust, you may deal with it in various ways, including having sex with the nearest willing person, masturbating, running a mile, or taking a cold shower. We are responsible for the specific acts and behaviors we choose, but because we do not choose the specific feelings we have, guilt (or pride) over our feelings is inappropriate. Feelings are neither good nor bad, moral nor immoral, although some feelings are more pleasant than others.

CONFUSING LUST AND LOVE.   Lust is a normal, healthy human emotion that can be very pleasurable for two people when they both desire sexual expression with one another. It is reasonable for two adults who are sexually attracted to each other to choose to express their lust by becoming sexually intimate. If the two people do not deal honestly with their feelings prior to engaging in sexual activity, however, these feelings can lead to considerable pain and guilt.

Differences in the sexual socialization of males and females in North American culture contribute to the difficulties that adolescents in particular have in communicating their feelings. Specifically, females are traditionally taught to look for a partner for an enduring romantic relationship, whereas males are culturally conditioned to seek sexual experience per se. Feeling lust (but not love), a young man may attempt sexual activity with a young woman. She may interpret his sexual attentions as love, and indeed he may say, "I love you," to persuade her to agree to sexual intimacy. If his acts are based primarily on feelings of lust, he attains his goal when he has an orgasm.

The young woman's objectives and expectations may be quite different. For her, sexual intimacy may be a means to the goal of an enduring relationship rather than an end in itself. There is no reason that a young man and woman (or any other couple, for that matter) should not have sexual relations that are based on lust, but honest communication and agreement about expectations must occur prior to sexual intimacy if people are to avoid using others or feeling used. In the absence of honest disclosure of feelings and goals, prospective sex partners may exploit one another.

As noted earlier, there is an old cliché suggesting that men use love to get sex and women use sex to get love. With North American culture's progress toward gender equality in recent decades, some men complain that women exploit them sexually, and women may protest that "just because I went to bed with him, he thinks he owns me." There is evidence to suggest, however, that young women are still more likely than young men to find sex acceptable only in a love relationship (Buss, 1994; Roche, 1986). (See "Across Cultures: What Do You Look for in a Partner?" on page 416.)

A striking example of this gender difference is reflected in two studies by Russell Clark and Elaine Hatfield (1989). In these experiments, male and female confederates of average attractiveness approached students on a college campus and said, "I have been noticing you around campus. I find you to be very attractive." The confederate then asked the students one of three questions: (1) Would you go out with me tonight? (2) Would you come over to my apartment tonight? or (3) Would you go to bed with me tonight? None of the women who were approached agreed to go to bed with the male confederate, whereas more than two-thirds of the males agreed to such a proposal.

ISSUES TO CONSIDER

The Clark and Hatfield studies were done in 1978 and 1982, before the threat of AIDS was well known. Do you think men have become more reluctant to agree to sexual encounters with women whom they do not know? What reasons do you think women might have for refusing that men do not have?

Across Cultures

What Do You Look for in a Partner?

A great deal of attention has been applied to how we select potential mates. We have presented 10 of the 18 scales employed by Buss et al. (1989). Indicate the importance to you of the following mate characteristics by putting the number that best reflects your feelings in front of each quality. Scale:

Irrelevant   Extremely important

$$0 \text{——} 1 \text{——} 2 \text{——} 3$$

___ 1. Dependable

___ 2. Chaste (no previous sexual intercourse)

___ 3. High in financial prospects

___ 4. Intelligent

___ 5. Good looking (physical attractiveness)

___ 6. Sociable (outgoing, friendly)

___ 7. Ambitious and industrious

___ 8. You are in love with the person

___ 9. Gets along with your family

___ 10. Considerate

Assume that you and your classmates are able to gather responses—after getting your instructor's permission, of course—from other people to this questionnaire. If your hypotheses are guided by evolutionary theory, you would probably assume that, compared to women, men would give higher ratings to physical attractiveness as indications of reproductive fitness. In contrast, you might hypothesize that women, compared to men, would give higher ratings to a potential partner's ability to be a good provider, as shown by high ratings for financial prospects and for ambitiousness and industriousness.

In a study of staggering proportions designed to test these same hypotheses, David Buss and his colleagues (1989) studied 37 cultures in Africa, Asia, Europe, Canada, Australia, New Zealand, South America, and the United States. The measures consisted of 18 characteristics, including the following target items: physical attractiveness, good financial prospects, and ambition and industriousness. In support of Buss's hypotheses, women placed higher value on the financial prospects of potential partners than men did: differences occurred in 36 of the 37 samples. In 29 of the 37 samples, women rated a potential partner's ambition and industriousness more highly than men did, providing moderate support for that expectation. In 34 of the 37 samples, men rated the physical attractiveness of a potential partner as more important in selecting a mate than did women. Thus this hypothesis received strong support.

These studies illustrate the pronounced difference between men and women in willingness to engage in sexual intimacy outside the context of a committed or loving relationship. People may also differ in the meanings that they attach to the word *love*, and we turn now to this issue.

LOVE AS DEPENDENCY, JEALOUSY, AND OTHER UNLOVELY FEELINGS

Even when two people sincerely believe that they love each other, problems may arise because of differences in their interpretations of the word *love*. As we have seen, love can take many different forms. It may connote both passion and a commitment so strong that a temporary absence of sexual pleasure is cheerfully accepted. It may carry the message that "I will sacrifice for you and you should sacrifice for me." It may mean, "I have the right to control you," or it may sometimes be used to express a state of tension. At other times, love can communicate a sense of peacefulness.

Dependency and Control

It has been proposed that humans have a fundamental need for social attachment that is conditioned in particular ways by specific cultures (Baumeister & Leary, 1995; Shaver et al., 1988). One way that North American adolescents and adults satisfy this need is through romantic love. Dependency has been seen as a central component of romantic love by a number of researchers (Dion & Dion, 1988).

North Americans tend to prepare their offspring to seek security through emotional attachment to other people. In its extreme form, the association of security with attachment can lead to exaggerated expectations about what another person in a relationship can provide. Some people seek security and self-gratification through one other person, who provides a buffer against an often tumultuous and threatening world. Just as people can become dependent on drugs, work, or (as we saw in Chapter 15) atypical sexual practices, so can they become desperately attached to another person. Such an attachment may lead to what Peele and Brodsky (1975) call interpersonal addiction, the classic syndrome involving both tolerance and withdrawal.

You are probably familiar with the concepts of tolerance and withdrawal as applied to substance abuse. As people's dependency on a particular drug grows, they acquire a tolerance for it, and their bodies require more and more of the substance to provide a reassuring "high." Over time, most addicted people become increasingly unable to cope with the problems and uncertainties that attracted them to the drug. They cannot envision everyday life without the drug and feel unable to free themselves from its grip. When the drug is not available, their bodies react to withdrawal with fever, sweating, shivering, and alternating patterns of insomnia and drowsiness. Addicts even experience anxiety over the potential unavailability of the drug.

Just as drug addicts seek security in chemicals, some individuals seek comfort and security in an emotional attachment to another person. They can become so addicted to another that they let go of all other interests and activities (see Figure 16.6). According to Peele and Brodsky (1974, p. 25),

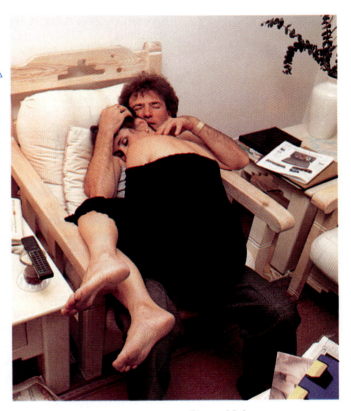

Figure 16.6
Dependency or Love?
Some individuals feel that they cannot live without their lover, regardless of how that lover treats them in return. *Dependency* is a more accurate word for such feelings than *love*.

> As an addictive relationship unfolds, the lovers may seem to be seeing each other for the pleasure and excitement of it, but this doesn't last. After a while, the lovers are just there for each other, not for mutual growth or self-expression, but for comfort and familiarity. They reach a tolerance for each other. As for withdrawal, we have all seen the emotional and physical havoc that follows in the wake of some breakups, and the desperate ploys a jilted lover will try in order to get another "shot" of his or her beloved.

Lovers sometimes talk as if their love were unconditional. This outlook is reinforced in traditional North American marriage vows, by which the couple pledge to love one another in sickness and in health, for richer or for poorer, and so forth. Certainly a marital commitment should not be severed because of changes in a partner's health or wealth. The concept of unconditional love applied to a relationship between adults, however, often masks dependency. Adults who value themselves do not unconditionally accept a relationship with a partner who abuses them. For example, an unhappy woman who puts up with a continued pattern of physical or emotional abuse from her partner may be remaining in the relationship out of dependency, not love. The man who fails to assert his rights as an adult to determine his own activities and time schedules may do so not from love but from the inability or unwillingness to function as an independent adult. We should note that many scholars do not agree with addiction models as an explanation of complex social behaviors.

Just as we may confuse love with dependency, we may define an emotion as love when it is actually jealousy. Of all the feelings we experience, jealousy is among the most unpleasant. In the grip of this painful emotion, the most poised, self-confident, attractive person can disintegrate into a frightened, hostile, suspicious, defensive, complaining being.

Jealousy

One of the potential drawbacks of becoming attached to another person is that the bond can make us vulnerable to jealousy. Feelings of jealousy can be so intense and unpleasant as to provoke us to attempt to control and possess the sexual thoughts, feelings, and expression of the person to whom we are attached. There is evidence that men and women differ in their perceptions of the behaviors that indicate infidelity and elicit jealousy (see "Highlight: Dating Infidelity").

Because jealousy, or at least competition for mates, is apparent among mammals, Alfred Kinsey, as well as many contemporary evolutionary theorists (Buss, 1994; Fisher, 1992; Symons, 1979), considered jealousy and competition to be a part of our evolutionary inheritance. Male jealousy is a major motive in the murder of married women in North America (Buss, 1994; Fisher, 1992). Ira Reiss (1986) also believed jealousy to be a universal emotion, but he did not link it to our genetic heritage. Instead, he maintained that all societies set boundaries for important relationships, particularly marriages. When the boundaries of a relationship are violated, jealousy arises. The observation that not everyone experiences jealousy upon learning of a mate's sexual interaction with another person suggests, however, that the capacity for jealousy can be affected by psychological and social experiences. That is, in cultures that permit polygamous marriages, husbands and wives do not associate outside sexual activity with anger and with fear of rejection and loss to the same degree that North Americans do (Allgeier, 1992).

Some researchers have concluded that the extent to which jealousy dominates and overwhelms an individual's sense of well-being is related to such individual characteristics as insecurity, inadequacy, and dependency (Buss, 1994; Fisher, 1992). Women are more likely to experience jealousy when they are feeling inadequate. On the basis of his longitudinal research, White (1981; White & Helbick, 1988) concluded that the feelings of inadequacy evoke the jealousy. In men, he believed, the relationship is reversed: men become aware of jealousy and then begin to feel inadequate.

There is evidence that some people deliberately provoke jealousy in their partners. Women are more likely than men to report this behavior. The most common method of provoking jealousy reported by White's respondents was talking to the mate about how appealing someone else was, and the most common motive was to get more attention from the mate. Other methods included flirting, dating others, pretending to be attached to someone else, and talking about a former partner.

We know a woman who has had a number of extramarital affairs and characterizes them all as a form of revenge. That is, whenever she learned of another of her husband's affairs, she sought an extramarital relationship to even the score. Women's general response to jealousy, however, is to increase efforts to make themselves attractive to the primary partner. In contrast, men seek outside relationships for solace and retribution. Jealousy is more common among younger than older people and among less

H I G H L I G H T

Dating Infidelity

Before a serious commitment exists between two people, it is common for each of them to go out with other people. Difficulties can arise, of course, if one member of a couple believes that they are at a later stage in the dating relationship than the other partner does, or if they have different values about the extent of dating and sexual exclusivity that should exist between them at a specific dating stage. To examine a phenomenon that they labeled *dating infidelity*, Roscoe, Cavanaugh, and Kennedy (1988) gathered the responses of 247 unmarried college students to the following questions:

1. What behaviors do you think constitute being "unfaithful" to a dating partner provided the couple is in a serious dating relationship (in other words, they have assumed that they are to date only each other)?

2. What are some reasons a person in a serious dating relationship would be "unfaithful" to a dating partner?

3. What would you do if you learned that your dating partner was "unfaithful" to you? (p. 37)

If you are currently in what you consider to be a serious dating relationship, you and your partner might want to discuss these questions with one another. In general, students in the Roscoe et al. study described three major behaviors as constituting infidelity if done with someone else: dating or spending time; having sexual intercourse; and engaging in other sexual interactions, such as flirting, kissing, necking, and petting. Men and women differed in their views of infidelity, however, with more women than men listing dating or spending time with another and keeping secrets from the primary partner. In contrast, men were more likely than women to state that having sexual interactions with another person constituted unfaithfulness.

The top three reasons why students thought infidelity would occur were dissatisfaction with the relationship; boredom; and revenge, anger, or jealousy. More women than men listed relationship dissatisfaction as a reason, and more men than women listed sexual incompatibility and lack of communication or understanding as a potential cause for infidelity. If they learned that their dating partner had been unfaithful, 44 percent of the students said that they would terminate the relationship, with women more likely than men to indicate that they would first discuss the situation with the partner.

A final interesting set of findings from Roscoe et al.'s (1988) research concerned their examination of students' attitudes as a function of whether they reported always having been faithful. A slight majority of both men and women stated that they had not always been faithful in a dating relationship. Those who had engaged in dating infidelity at some time, compared to those who had always been faithful, were more likely to give the following reasons for a person's dating infidelity: dissatisfaction with the relationship, sexual incompatibility, and being insecure or unsure about the relationship.

educated than more educated people, and it is more intense in new relationships than in those of longer duration. Finally, people who report overall dissatisfaction with their lives have more frequent bouts of jealousy than do happier people (Wiederman & Allgeier, 1993).

Jealousy is a fact of life for most Americans. Some researchers maintain that in the context of Western norms that revere pairing, family orientation, ownership, private property, competition, and the ideal of the perfect relationship, jealousy is inevitable (Reiss, 1986; Wiederman & Allgeier, 1993).

Most researchers studying jealousy have examined people's reactions to the idea of their spouse's engaging in extramarital sexual contact, or their committed partners having extradyadic (ED: *extra* means additional, *dyad* means "pair") sexual relationships. However, in a series of studies, Yarab and Allgeier (1997; see also Yarab, Sensibaugh & Allgeier, 1997) asked a large number of undergraduates to describe behaviors by their partners that they would judge as unfaithful and likely make them feel jealous. This procedure yielded a large number of behaviors (e.g., having lunch with a member of the other gender) that did not necessarily involve sexual activity. The researchers

ISSUES TO CONSIDER

Have you ever felt jealousy in a relationship? If so, how did you cope with the feeling, and what advice would you have for others who experience jealousy?

retained the behaviors mentioned most commonly and administered them to a new group of volunteers. One of the most surprising findings from their series of studies was that respondents perceived their partner's having sexual fantasies about someone

REALITY or MYTH ? **6**

else as unfaithful, jealousy-inducing, and threatening to the primary relationship. Even more interesting was that many respondents reported ED behaviors with others and having fantasies toward others. However, they perceived their own ED behaviors and fantasies as not indicative of unfaithfulness and not as a threat to their primary relationship! That is, respondents exhibited a double standard. The phrase *double standard* is usually used in the context of gender differences. In this case, however, double standard refers to the finding that we judge the same behaviors, including fantasy, as more threatening to our primary relationship when our partners engage in them than when we engage in them. We seem to feel that we can handle such experiences without their threatening our primary relationships, but our partners cannot engage in the same behaviors and fantasies without endangering their primary relationships with us.

How can one cope with the painful feelings of jealousy and minimize the destructive behaviors that those feelings sometimes elicit? Persons who feel threatened by jealousy in a relationship commonly withdraw from their partner or go on the attack. Either response can stimulate a similar reaction—withdrawal or counterattack—in the partner. These responses may be perceived by the jealous partner as further evidence that his or her fears are justified. An alternative reaction to feelings of jealousy is to *acknowledge* one's feelings and to describe their source: "Paul, I'm feeling jealous and afraid that you've lost interest in me because of the time you spent talking with Michelle at the party." Because this reaction is not an attack or a withdrawal, Paul may be more disposed to provide reassurance and a hug than he would be if his partner stomped angrily into the bedroom, muttering, "Well, you certainly have the hots for Michelle, don't you?" If one partner continually punishes the other partner by attacking or withdrawing when there has been no real violation of their relationship agreement, the accusations may produce the violation that the jealous partner fears.

There are instances in which, because one partner *has* violated the agreement between the couple, the other partner's jealousy and anger are justified. In that case, too, successful resolution is more likely if the partner presents an honest, direct description of his or her feelings about the other person's behavior.

Finally, some couples have problems in negotiating their differences because of the dominance of their desire for intimate contact. In an intriguing article called "Intimate Terrorism," Michael Miller (1977, p. 79) eloquently described some of the difficulties inherent in intimate relationships after they have progressed beyond initial infatuation:

> *Intimacy is as much about power as it is about love. The power struggle is rarely explicit at first, because infatuation and courtship are so satisfying, but it begins to surface when the relationship becomes a matter of daily living.*

ISSUES TO CONSIDER

Why would intimate relationships be as much about power as about love?

LOVING SEXUAL INTERACTIONS

Earlier we described Peele and Brodsky's (1975) concept of addiction. By way of contrast, they also described some of the characteristics of mature love, and the following five questions are based on their work. If you are part of a loving sexual relationship, you and your partner might want to answer these questions individually and then discuss your responses.

1. Have you continued to maintain individual interests, including meaningful personal relationships with people other than your partner?

2. Are you and your lover friends? If your erotic involvement ended, would you continue to see one another as friends?

3. Have you maintained a secure belief in your own value as an independent person?

4. Is your relationship integrated with the rest of your life rather than set off or isolated from your other activities?

5. Finally, do you feel improved by the relationship? Have you become stronger, more attractive, more accomplished, and more sensitive since becoming involved with your partner?

Few of us can give an unqualified and enthusiastic "yes" in response to all five questions. In any case, relationships—especially good ones—are always changing, and thus your answers may differ from one month or year to the next. If either you or your partner feels, however, that the answer to two or more of these questions is a sad "no," you may want to discuss the possibility of making some changes in your relationship.

The quality of a relationship is not appropriately measured by its complete absence of problems. There is no such thing as a perfect relationship that is always problem-free. Instead, the qualities that are important in a loving sexual (or, for that matter, non-sexual) relationship are honesty, integrity, and concern for resolving problems in such a way as best to meet the needs of *both* partners.

A couple can have a richly satisfying relationship without seeing eye to eye on everything. In fact, if they are both healthy, independent adults, differences of opinion are inevitable. (For an example of how differences and disagreements are handled in another species, see "Highlight: Make Love, Not War," page 422.) Disagreements about fundamental aspects of the relationship, however, may make the couple's long-term investment in the union inadvisable. For example, before making a long-term commitment, a couple should discuss their feelings regarding whether they should be sexually exclusive or free to have other sexual relationships, whether they want children, and whether their relationship will be characterized by highly traditional or egalitarian roles. There are many other areas in which agreement is not at all necessary. For example, whereas a woman who believes that a couple should share all activities may feel deserted as a result of her mate's solo interest in gardening or golf, people with well-developed avocations may welcome the fact that their spouses also have independent interests and hobbies. In fact, the combination of taking part in some activities independently of one another and cultivating common interests is related to the satisfaction of partners in a long-term relationship.

Vitality in Long-Term Relationships

At the beginning of a relationship, there is a great deal of arousal that is not purely sexual. Uncertainty about how the relationship will turn out generates its own excitement or arousal. Not knowing how the other person feels, and wondering about our own attractiveness and sexual performance, lend a dimension of vulnerability and risk to initial involvement with another person.

After a relationship has existed for a while, the sexual arousal may be as strong as it was initially, but if the relationship is characterized by mutual trust and commitment, the other contributions to the feelings of arousal may fade. In any good ongoing relationship—whether with parents, children, siblings, roommates, or coworkers—there are cycles. Different points in the cycle are characterized by periods of intense connection, irritation, indifference, and dislike. In some couples, the individuals fall into rigid ways of relating to each other socially and sexually. Reliance on inflexible and highly

HIGHLIGHT

Make Love, Not War

Imagine a society in which there is minimal violence, no warfare, and disputes are settled by engaging in sexual behavior. Don't look for such a group among humans, but among a close relative with whom we share more than 98 percent of our genetic characteristics: the bonobo (buh-NO-boh). Once known as the pygmy chimpanzee, these elegant primates are believed to have split off from our human ancestors and other chimpanzees about eight million years ago.

The bonobo have woven sexuality into the fabric of their social life. They engage in many forms of sexual stimulation that are not limited to adult male-female interaction. Tongue kissing, oral sex, genital massage, and face-to-fact coitus are just part of their sexual repertoire (de Waal, 1995).

The bonobo often engage in sexual activities when they are in competition for attention, food, or some other object. Their sexual activities appear to ease tension. For example, when I (A.R.A.) was visiting the San Diego Zoo in 1996, I watched a bonobo mother nursing her infant. While attempting to nurse, the mother was being annoyed by a male adolescent. The mother put up with his irritating behavior for several minutes, but when he persisted, she seemed to shrug in resignation. She set down her infant, then chased and caught the adolescent. She lay on top of him and rubbed her genitals against his for about 10 seconds. After dismounting, she resumed feeding her baby. The adolescent wandered off in apparent contentment and did not bother her again while I was observing.

You might think that my observation of the way in which the bonobo use sexual activity to reduce conflict stems from the fact that the group I observed were in captivity in a zoo. However, Frans de Waal (1995) re-ported that bonobo observed in their natural habitats in Africa engage in the same pattern of using sex to defuse disagreements.

Some of the bonobo's interesting use of sexual activity has to do with their social structure, which has been described as female-centered and egalitarian. The strongest social bonds are formed among females, although the females also bond with males. The status of a male depends on the position of his mother, to whom he remains closely bonded for her entire life. If a male gets "of out hand," the smaller females band together to discourage him.

The net result is that bonobo usually substitute sex for aggression. Or, perhaps, the bonobo might see humans as peculiar creatures who substitute aggression for sex! Is there a lesson for us in the way in which the bonobo handle conflict?

predictable schedules, social activities, and patterns of sexual interaction can deaden the sense of passion and excitement in the relationship and lead to automatic rather than spontaneous interaction.

Even among couples who have relatively flexible relationships, expectations based on the dizzying feelings that occur during courtship can cause difficulties. We have some recently married friends who are now going through the normal adjustment process associated with marriage. At times during their premarital affair, they would ignore work or other obligations in favor of romantic time alone together. Now they have integrated their relationship into the rest of their activities, but in their busy lives, time for sex no longer "spontaneously" occurs. Of course, it never did. It is simply the case that earlier, the couple gave sexual intimacy the highest priority in their hierarchy of activities, whereas now it has taken its place as one of numerous other important commitments. For them and for all of us who value the pleasure and intimacy shared during loving sexual interactions, it is essential to set aside periods of leisure time for emotional and sexual bonding.

Another trap that busy people should avoid is viewing sex as one more task in the roster of daily chores. People who typically view participation in sexual interaction with their partner as just another of their many duties are more likely to develop sexual problems in response to stresses from work or other sources. A sexual relationship that is vulnerable to stress often follows a conventional but unrealistic script in which the partners feel compelled to play their respective roles. Heavy breathing, erections, lubrication, and orgasm are the criteria. It is the type of sex you have to be up for, and the kind of sex you avoid if you have a headache rather than the kind that relieves headaches; the kind that risks coronaries rather than the kind that relaxes; the kind that is just another duty rather than the kind that is a break from daily responsibilities.

In contrast, sexual intimacy can be viewed as a relief from life's chores and responsibilities. The partners involve themselves sexually for reassurance and support rather than to try to live out some rare media depiction. They can be genuinely irresponsible. Free to express insecurities, worries, and doubts, they can obtain relief from such feelings, with orgasms being a secondary goal. Individuals who view their sexual relationship in this way are less likely to develop sexual problems when they are under stress, depressed, or suffering from midlife crisis or physical pain.

People who like themselves and take pleasure in life are exciting to be around. Thus, it is important for each of us to do things that enhance both our self-regard and our daily pleasure if we wish to have vital and loving sexual interactions with our partners.

In addition, it is essential that we give ourselves the time and leisure to share feelings about our experiences and about each other. At times, engaging in honest sharing can be painful and exhausting, and leaving ourselves vulnerable can be threatening. If we develop our own capacities to love and choose our partner wisely, however, we can share our vulnerability with another independent adult. Making the commitment to nourish our relationships with mutual giving and receiving can provide us with one of life's greatest rewards: loving sexual interactions.

Summary of major points

1. Early experiences and the capacity to love.	Experimental studies with primates, research in a number of cultures, and observations of the development of neglected and abused children all suggest that the young need physical and emotional affection to become well-adjusted adults.
2. Self-love versus selfishness.	Although sometimes confused, these two characteristics have different sources and consequences. When we feel competent and pleased with ourselves, we are far kinder to others than when the reverse is true. At those times when we do not love and respect ourselves, we withdraw and act selfishly. Self-love and appreciation, then, are related to loving and appreciating others.

3. Three forms of love.

The different forms that love can take may be understood in terms of three components: intimacy, passion, and decision/commitment. Romantic love, for example, includes intimacy and passion but not decision/commitment. Whereas infatuation involves only passionate arousal, romantic love is liking with the added excitement of physical attraction and arousal. Other types of love are friendship, empty love, fatuous love, companionate love, and consummate love.

4. Love versus lust.

Initially, erotic lovers typically feel arousal from a number of sources, including sexual desire and anxiety over rejection. Whether they are experiencing lust, infatuation, or the beginning stages of an enduring romantic love, an obsessional preoccupation with the other person is common. A mutual lustful attraction can be highly, if briefly, pleasurable to some couples, but difficulties can arise if one partner is motivated by lust and the other by a commitment to developing an enduring romantic bond. The sharing of feelings and intentions by both partners can minimize the feelings of guilt and exploitation that can arise when two people have conflicting motivations for a relationship.

5. Dependency and jealousy.

These two arousal-laden emotions are frequently confused with the arousal associated with erotic love. Dependency and jealousy are more commonly and intensely experienced by people who lack self-confidence and self-esteem, and both can result in manipulative, exploitive, and nonloving behavior. Most of us feel these painful emotions at some point. Communicating feelings instead of accusing and attacking one's partner reduces the destructive effects of dependency and jealousy.

6. Loving sexual interactions.

Independent, mature, self-confident adults have the greatest capacity for healthy, mutually enhancing, loving sexual interactions. When two such adults form an erotic bond, they can enjoy their similarities and yet be comfortable with their differences. Making another person the exclusive focus of one's life can reduce the vitality of a relationship. If, instead, each partner develops his or her own potential, each is better able to contribute his or her unique qualities to a mutually satisfying and stimulating relationship. This ideal is not easily attained or constantly maintained, but striving toward it contributes to the hope, pride, and pleasure that characterize enduring and loving sexual interactions.

CHECK YOUR KNOWLEDGE

1. Harlow's experiments with primates established that (a) monkeys raised in isolation for at least six months irreversibly become adult social and sexual misfits, (b) monkeys' and humans' need for nurturing as infants are fundamentally different, (c) controlled interactions with younger "normal" monkeys can restore isolated monkeys' ability to function sexually and socially, (d) monkeys raised in isolation were not able to reproduce as adults. **(p. 404)**

2. In Sternberg's formulation, romantic love means (a) passion alone, (b) passion and intimacy but not commitment, (c) passion, intimacy, and commitment together, (d) commitment and passion but not intimacy. **(p. 412)**

3. Sternberg believes that "consummate" or "complete" love is (a) often sought but rarely attained, (b) attained early in a relationship but often diminished over time, (c) generally attained after long intimacy, (d) impossible for normal human beings. **(p. 414)**

4. Early studies of attachment used a research technique called (a) Isolation Rearing, (b) the Strange Situation, (c) Exaggerated Stimulus Enhancement, (d) Soft Love. **(p. 405)**

5. Which of the following is *not* characteristic of a limerent state? (a) a desire for exclusivity, (b) preoccupation with

partner, (c) intrusive thinking, (d) platonic convergence. **(pp. 411–412)**

6. Jealousy is more common among people who are (a) highly educated, (b) sexual addicts, (c) young, (d) old. **(pp. 418–420)**

7. Feelings of jealousy are (a) similar in all cultures, (b) the same in men as in women, (c) associated with feelings of inadequacy, (d) caused by emotional disorders. **(p. 418)**

8. For couples to maintain vitality in long-term relationships, they should (a) give information about their feelings to each other, (b) restrict themselves from having friendships with other people, (c) be sure to have sex frequently with each other even when they aren't feeling much arousal, (d) avoid discussions of problems and hassles. **(pp. 421–423)**

APPENDIX

Sources of Information About Sexuality

Former students frequently approach us for current information about some of the topics we had covered in class. Some students are also interested in further training in human sexuality or in joining professional organizations devoted to furthering research, therapy, and education about human sexuality. Other students are faced with writing term papers in other courses about issues raised in the human sexuality class, and they request names of relevant journals and organizations. Accordingly, we recommend the following sources of information.

Professional Organizations

American Association of Sex Educators, Counselors, and Therapists (AASECT)
Executive Director, AASECT
Suite 2-A, 103 A Avenue South
Mount Vernon, IA 52314-0238

Association of Gay and Lesbian Psychiatrists
1439 Pineville Rd.
New Hope, PA 18938

Coalition on Sexuality and Disability
132 Holbrook Rd.
Holbrook, NY 11741

Feminist Alliance Against Rape
P.O. Box 21033
Washington, D.C. 20009

Harry Benjamin International Gender Dysphoria Association
18333 Egret Bay Blvd., Suite 560
Houston, TX 77058

National Council on Family Relations
3989 Central Ave. N.E., Suite 550
Minneapolis, MN 55421

National Gay Task Force Fund for Human Dignity
80 Fifth Ave., #1601
New York, NY 10011

Planned Parenthood Federation of America
810 Seventh Ave.
New York, NY 10019

Sex Information and Education Council of Canada (SIECAN)
Executive Director, SIECAN
850 Coxwell
East York, Ontario M4C 5R1

Sex Information and Education Council of the United States (SIECUS)
Executive Director, SIECUS
130 W. 42nd St.
New York, NY 10036

The Society for the Scientific Study of Sexuality (SSSS)
Executive Director, SSSS
P.O. Box 208
Mt. Vernon, IA 52314
E-mail: TheSociety@worldnet.att.net
Website: http://www.ssc.wisc.edu/ssss

Society for Sex Therapy and Research (SSTAR)
Stanley Althoff, Secretary
University Hospital of Cleveland
2074 Abington Rd.
Cleveland, OH 44106

World Association of Sexology (WAS)
c/o Eli Coleman
1300 So. 2nd St., Suite 180
Minneapolis, MN 55454-1015

American Board of Sexology
1929 18th St. NW, Suite 1166
Washington, DC 20009

Journals Publishing Sexuality Research Reports

Research on sexuality is published in numerous journals, so our list is necessarily selective. To track down journals that publish research on your topic, check the text references on the subject, and look at recent issues of the journals listed there. For example, if you are interested in the phenomenon of sexual coercion, read that chapter in the text (Chapter 14), list the authors cited and the journals in which they have published, and go to the library for the most current information. You will find the journals listed below in many university libraries.

AIDS Education and Prevention As implied by its name, contains research reports relevant to evaluations of programs aimed at reducing the risk of contracting HIV.
Archives of Sexual Behavior Publishes articles on all sexuality topics, but tends to emphasize research on variations in sexual orientation and gender-role identification.
Canadian Journal of Human Sexuality Published by the Sex Information and Education Council of Canada, articles in CJHS come from a variety of disciplines related to the study of human sexuality.
Family Planning Perspectives Published by the Alan Guttmacher Institute, the research wing of Planned Parenthood. Focuses on research on reproductive decision making and methods of birth control.
Journal of Divorce As implied by its name, publishes research on correlates of relationship termination.

Journal of the History of Sexuality Publishes historical analyses across topics relevant to sexuality.

Journal of Homosexuality Contains research on the development and correlates of particular sexual orientations.

Journal of Marriage and the Family Features research on variables associated with the quality of marital and family functioning.

Journal of Psychology and Human Sexuality Focuses on psychological variables and their relationship to a wide range of sexual issues.

Journal of Sex and Marital Therapy Reports on the effectiveness of different therapeutic techniques for individuals with sexual or marital difficulties.

Journal of Sex Education and Therapy Publishes research on correlates of sexual knowledge, as well as research that evaluates the effectiveness of various kinds of sex education and therapy.

The Journal of Sex Research The oldest journal dedicated exclusively to research on human sexual experience.

Lifestyles Publishes articles relevant to cohabitation, aging and sexuality, and lifestyle variations.

Personal Relationships Focuses on research on romantic attraction, intimacy, and attachment.

Sex Over Forty Publishes information and research on sexuality and aging.

Sex Roles: A Journal of Research Focuses on all aspects of gender roles and norms, including their interaction with sexual relationships.

Sexual Well-Being Newsletter devoted to sexuality and health.

Sexuality and Disability Contains information relevant to the sexual expression of persons with disabilities.

SIECUS Reports Published by the Sex Education and Information Council of the United States. Emphasizes topics relevant to sex education but also publishes articles on all topics in the human sexuality field, as well as reviews of contemporary books and audiovisual materials.

Self-Help Organizations

In many cases, you can find the service or information you are seeking by consulting either the White Pages or Yellow Pages in your local telephone book. If there is a crisis center in your area, its staff can also provide referrals. In the event that the information or service that you want is not locally available, the following sources can be helpful.

Contraception

The Planned Parenthood Federation of America, (800) 829-7732, can provide referrals to the nearest Planned Parenthood clinic or other contraception clinic for those seeking information, contraceptives, and checkups. These services may also be offered by the student health service at your college or university, or by the local public health department.

Erotic Products

Eve's Garden, 119 West 57th St., New York, NY 10019, (800) 848-3837, offers a variety of products from books about sexuality to sexual toys, vibrators, massage creams, and erotic contraceptives. You may write to Eve's Garden for a catalog of mail-order products.

Gay and Lesbian Issues

Parents and Friends of Lesbians and Gays (PFLAG), P.O. Box 27605, Central Station, Washington, DC 20038, (202) 638-4200, is a volunteer peer group whose goal is to help parents accept and understand their gay offspring.

Association of Gay and Lesbian Psychiatrists, 1439 Pineville Rd., New Hope, PA 12938, can be a useful organization for gay individuals or couples seeking a therapist who will not operate on the assumption that their problems stem from their sexual orientation.

The National Gay Task Force has a hotline for reporting violence against gays. Call (202) 332-6483. The Hate Crimes hotline may also be called: (800) 347-4283.

Intersexuality

The Intersex Society of North America (ISNA) is a peer support, education and advocacy group founded and operated by and for intersexuals. Contact ISNA at P.O. Box 31791, San Francisco, CA 94131. E-mail: info@isna.org.

Sexual Dysfunctions

The American Association for Sex Educators, Counselors, and Therapists, (319) 895-8407, can provide you with the names of people in your area whom the organization has certified as sex therapists. Your county or state mental health board can also give the names of licensed therapists in your area.

For those who would like information on erectile dysfunctions, the following organizations may be contacted: Impotence Information Center, Department USA, P.O. Box 9, Minneapolis, MN 55440, (800) 843-4315; or Impotents Anonymous, 119 S. Ruth St., Maryville, TN 37801, (615) 983-6092.

Sexual Information

The Sex Information and Education Council of the United States (SIECUS), listed earlier under "Professional Organizations," also responds to phone calls from individuals with personal questions or concerns about sexuality at (212) 206-7798.

Sexually Transmitted Diseases

The Public Health Service offers several AIDS hotlines. Call (800) 342-AIDS. This telephone number is staffed 24 hours a day, 7 days a week. Spanish speakers may call (800) 344-7432, from 8 a.m. to 2 a.m. daily, EST. There is a TTY number for the hearing impaired: (800) 243-7889, Monday through Friday from 10 a.m. to 10 p.m, EST.

The Herpes Resource Center, 260 Sheridan Ave., Palo Alto, CA 94306, (919) 361-2120, provides information about herpes.

The STD National Hotline can be consulted for information about sexually transmitted diseases and referrals to STD clinics. Call (800) 227-8922.

GLOSSARY

abortion Spontaneous or medical termination of a pregnancy before a fetus can survive outside the uterus.

acquired immunodeficiency syndrome (AIDS) A virally caused condition in which severe suppression of the immune system reduces the body's ability to fight diseases.

actual failure rate The failure rate of a contraceptive method that takes into account both failure of the method and human failure to use it correctly.

AIDS dementia complex Infection of the brain by HIV, resulting in the deterioration and loss of nerve cells.

alveoli (AL-vee-OH-lee) Milk-secreting cells in the breast.

amniotic sac The pouch containing a watery fluid that envelops a developing fetus in the uterus.

amygdala (UH-MIG-duh-la) Brain center involved in the regulation of sexual motivation.

analingus (A-nil-LING-gus) Oral stimulation of the tissues surrounding the anus.

androgens Generic term for hormones that promote development and functioning of the male reproductive system.

androgyny (ann-DRAH-jih-nee) The ability of a person to express both stereotypically masculine and stereotypically feminine traits and behaviors; from the Greek *andro*, meaning "male," and *gyn*, meaning "female."

areola (AIR-ee-OH-lah) The darkened skin surrounding the nipples, containing oil-secreting glands.

asymptomatic (A-symp-toe-MAH-tik) Without recognizable symptoms.

attachment The feeling of strong connection to another person.

autoeroticism Sexual stimulation of oneself.

autosomes The 22 pairs of chromosomes that are involved in general body development in humans.

AZT (Zidovudine) Drug used in the treatment of AIDS.

behaviorism A theoretical approach that emphasizes the importance of studying observable activity.

bias An attitude for or against a particular theory or hypothesis that influences one's judgment.

birth control The regulation of conception, pregnancy, or birth by preventive devices or methods.

bisexual The capacity to feel erotic attraction toward or to engage in sexual interaction with both men and women.

body cells All the cells in the body except germ cells.

Braxton-Hicks contractions Irregular contractions of the uterus that are often mistaken for the onset of labor.

brothel A house where prostitutes and customers meet for sexual activity.

call girl A high-priced prostitute whose customers are solicited by telephone or by word-of-mouth references.

candidiasis (KAN-dih-DYE-ah-sis) An infection of the vulva and vagina caused by the excess growth of a fungus that occurs normally in the body.

cannula (CAN-u-luh) A tube inserted into the body through which liquid or tissue may be removed.

cerebrum (ser-REE-brum) The surface layer of cell bodies that constitutes the bulk of the human brain.

cervical cap Contraceptive rubber dome that is fitted to a woman's cervix; spermicide is placed inside the cap before it is pressed onto the cervix.

cervix (SIR-vix) The lower end of the uterus that opens into the vagina.

chancre (SHANG-ker) A dull-red, painless, hard, round ulcer with raised edges that forms where the spirochete causing syphilis enters a person's body.

chancroid (CANE-kroid) An STD characterized by soft, painful genital sores.

chlamydia (clah-MID-ee-uh) An STD, frequently asymptomatic in women, caused by the bacterium *Chlamydia trachomatis.*

chromosomes The strands of deoxyribonucleic acid (DNA) and protein in the nucleus of each cell. They contain the genes that provide information vital for the duplication of cells and the transmission of inherited characteristics.

clitoris (CLIH-tor-iss) Small highly sensitive erectile tissue located just above the point where the minor lips converge at the top of the vulva; its only known function is to provide female sexual pleasure.

cognitive Related to the act or process of engaging in mental activity.

cohabitation An arrangement in which an unmarried couple live together.

cohort A group from a particular generation; for example, those born from 1970 to 1979 are members of a different cohort from those born from 1980 to 1989.

colostrum (cuh-LAH-strum) A thin, yellowish fluid secreted from the nipples before and around the time of birth.

concordance rate The likelihood that if one person manifests a certain trait, a relative (twin, sibling, uncle, etc.) will manifest that same trait.

conditioned response (CR) An acquired response to a stimulus that did not originally evoke such a response.

conditioned stimulus (CS) In classical conditioning, a stimulus that is paired with an unconditioned stimulus until it evokes a response that was previously associated with the unconditioned stimulus.

condom   A sheath placed over the erect penis for prevention of pregnancy and protection against disease.

contraceptive foams   Spermicidal foams that are injected into the vagina prior to coitus.

contraceptive suppositories   Solid contraceptive substances containing a spermicide, inserted in the vagina prior to coitus.

contraceptives   Techniques, drugs, or devices that prevent conception.

control variables   Variables that are held constant or controlled to reduce their influence on the dependent variable.

copulation (kop-you-LAY-shun)   Sexual intercourse involving insertion of the penis into the vagina.

corona (cor-OH-nah)   The sensitive rim of the glans.

corpora cavernosa (COR-por-uh kah-vur-NOH-sah)   Two columns within the penis that contain small cavities capable of filling with blood to produce an erection.

corpus luteum (COR-pus LOO-tee-um)   The cell mass that remains after a follicle has released an egg; it secretes progesterone and estrogen.

corpus spongiosum (COR-puhs spun-jee-OH-sum)   A column of spongy tissue within the penis that surrounds the urethra and is capable of blood engorgement during sexual arousal.

correlational method   A research method involving the measurement of two or more variables to determine the extent of their relationship.

couvade   Phenomenon in which some men develop symptoms similar to those of their pregnant partner.

Cowper's glands (COW-perz)   Two small glands that secrete a clear alkaline fluid into the urethra during sexual arousal.

cremaster muscle (CRE-mah-ster)   Muscle that runs from the testes into the spermatic cord and controls the proximity of the testes to the body.

cruising   Socializing in a variety of locations in the attempt to find a partner.

cunnilingus (KUN-nih-LING-gus)   Oral stimulation of the female genitals.

curette (cure-RET)   A scooplike instrument used for scraping bodily tissue.

cystitis (sis-TYE-tis)   A general term for any inflammation of the urinary bladder marked by pain and frequent urination.

cytomegalovirus (CMV) (sye-toe-MEG-uh-low-VYE-rus)   One of a group of viruses causing cell enlargement in various internal organs.

deoxyribonucleic acid (DNA) (dee-OX-see-RYE-boh-new-KLAY-ik)   A chemically complex nucleic acid that is a principal element of genes.

dependent variables   Variables that are measured or observed.

diaphragm (DYE-uh-fram)   A dome-shaped rubber contraceptive device inserted into the vagina to block the cervical opening. The diaphragm should always be used with a spermicide.

dihydrotestosterone (DHT)   A hormone produced from testosterone that is responsible for the development of the external genitals of the male fetus.

dilation and curettage (D&C) (die-LAY-shun and CURE-eh-taj)   Dilation of the cervix followed by scraping of the interior of the uterus with a curette.

dilation and evacuation (D&E)   An abortion method generally used in the second trimester, in which the fetus is crushed within the uterus and then extracted through a vacuum curette.

dilation   Expansion or opening up of the cervix prior to birth.

dyspareunia (DIS-par-OO-nee-ah)   Recurrent and persistent pain associated with intercourse for a woman or man.

ectopic pregnancy   A pregnancy that occurs when a fertilized egg implants itself outside the uterus, usually in a fallopian tube.

effacement   Flattening and thinning of the cervix that occurs before and during childbirth.

ego   In psychoanalytic theory, the rational level of personality.

ejaculation   Expulsion of seminal fluid out of the urethra during orgasm.

ejaculatory ducts (ee-JAK-u-la-TOR-ee)   Tubelike passageways that carry semen from the prostate gland to the urethra.

Electra complex   In Freudian theory, a daughter's sexual desire for her father.

embryo   The unborn organism from the second to about the eighth week of pregnancy. *See fetus*

emission   Propulsion of sperm and fluid to the base of the urethra during orgasm.

endocrine glands (EN-doe-crin)   Ductless glands that discharge their products directly into the bloodstream.

endometrium (en-doe-MEE-tree-um)   The lining of the uterus, part of which is shed during menstruation.

engagement   Movement of the fetus into a lower position in the mother's abdominal cavity, with its head past her pelvic bone structure.

epididymis (ep-ih-DIH-dih-mis)   Tightly coiled tubules, located at the top of the testes, in which sperm are stored.

episiotomy (eh-PEE-zee-AW-tuh-mee)   An incision made from the bottom of the entrance to the vagina down toward the anus to avoid tearing vaginal and anal tissues during childbirth.

equity   In a personal relationship, a perceived balance between the benefits the relationship provides and the personal investment it requires.

erectile dysfunction   Recurrent and persistent inability to attain or maintain a firm erection, despite adequate stimulation.

erogenous zones   Areas of the body that are erotically sensitive to tactile stimulation.

eros   Erotic love.

erotica   Sexually oriented material that is acceptable to the viewer.

erotophilic   Having a positive emotional response to sexual feelings and experiences.

erotophobic   Having a negative emotional response to sexual feelings and experiences.

estradiol   The major natural estrogen, secreted by the ovaries, testes, and placenta.

estrogens   Generic term for hormones that promote development and functioning of the female reproductive system.

exhibitionism   Obtaining sexual gratification by exposing one's genitals to an unwilling observer.

experimental method   A research method involving the manipulation of one or more independent variables to determine their influence on dependent variables.

fallopian tube (fah-LOW-pee-an)   Tube through which eggs (ova) are transported from the ovaries to the uterus.

fantasies   Usually pleasant mental images unrestrained by the realities of the external world.

fellatio (fell-LAY-she-oh)   Oral stimulation of the male genitals.

female condom   A pouch placed inside the vagina to line the vaginal walls for prevention of pregnancy and protection against disease.

fetal alcohol syndrome (FAS)   A disorder found in the offspring of problem drinkers. FAS causes a group of specific symptoms, including mental retardation.

fetishism   Obtaining sexual excitement primarily or exclusively from an inanimate object or a particular part of the body.

fetus   The unborn organism from the ninth week until birth.

fitness   A measure of one's success in transmitting genes to the next generation (reproductive success).

follicle-stimulating hormone (FSH)   A gonadotropin that induces maturation of ovarian follicles in females and sperm production in males.

follicles (FALL-ih-kulz)   In the ovary, sacs of estogen-secreting cells that contain an egg.

follicular phase   Menstrual-cycle phase during which FSH stimulates the growth of the ovarian follicles.

foreplay   Term used by some people to refer to sexual behavior occurring before intercourse.

fornication   Sexual intercourse between people who are not married to each other.

frenulum (FREN-yu-lum)   A small piece of skin on the underside of the male glans where the glans meets the body of the penis.

frotteurism   Obtaining sexual arousal by touching or rubbing one's body against the body of an unsuspecting or nonconsenting person.

gardnerella vaginalis   Infection producing a thin, smelly discharge; afflicts both men and women.

gender (JEN-der)   The social-psychological characteristics associated with being a male or a female in a particular culture.

gender difference   A difference in physique, ability, attitude, or behavior found between groups of males and females.

gender identity   The feeling or conviction that one is a male or a female.

gender roles   The traits and behaviors expected of males and females in a particular culture.

gender stereotype   A belief about the characteristics of a person, based on gender.

gender-role identification   The process by which individuals incorporate behaviors and characteristics of a culturally defined gender role into their own personalities.

gender-role socialization   The training of children by parents and other caretakers to behave in ways considered appropriate for their gender.

generalizability   The extent to which findings from a particular sample can be described as representing wider populations and situations.

genes   Part of DNA molecules, found in chromosomes of cells, that are responsible for the transmission of hereditary material from parents to offspring.

genital tubercle   A small protruding bud of fetal tissue that develops into either a penis or a clitoris.

genital warts   An STD that can also be contracted nonsexually; caused by the human papilloma virus.

germ cells   Sperm or egg cells.

gestation   The entire period of prenatal development from conception to birth.

gigolo   A man who is paid to be a woman's escort and to provide her with sexual services; a kept man.

glans   The sensitive tip of the penis or clitoris.

gonadotropins (goh-NAH-doe-TROE-pinz)   Chemicals produced by the pituitary gland that stimulate the gonads.

gonorrhea   An STD caused by the bacterium *Neisseria gonorrhoea*.

Gräfenberg spot (GRAY-fen-berg)   Also known as the G-spot; an area of sensitivity accessed through the upper wall of the vagina.

habituation   A decrease in sexual arousal in response to repeated and/or long-term exposure to the same stimulus (e.g., a sexual partner of long duration).

hard-core erotica   Erotica that explicitly depicts the genitals and sexual acts.

hepatitis B   A virus that attacks the liver; often sexually transmitted.

hermaphroditism   Condition in which a person is born with both male and female characteristics, such as an ovary on one side and a testis on the other.

herpes simplex type II   A viral infection contracted through physical contact with an infected person during an active outbreak of the sores.

homophobia   Fear of and hostility toward homosexuality.

homosociality   A period in middle and late childhood in which social and personal activities are centered around members of the same gender.

hormone (HOR-mohn)   The internal secretion of an endocrine gland that is distributed via the bloodstream.

human chorionic gonadotropin (HCG) (CORE-ee-ON-ik goh-NAH-doe-TROE-pin)   A hormone produced by the placenta.

human immunodeficiency virus (HIV)   The retrovirus that causes AIDS.

hymen (HYE-men)   Layer of tissue that partially covers the vaginal entrance of most females at birth.

hyperfemininity   Exaggerated adherence to a stereotypic feminine gender role.

hypermasculinity   Exaggeration of male dominance through an emphasis on male virility, strength, and aggression.

hypoactive sexual desire disorder   Deficiency or absence of both sexual fantasies and desire for sexual activity with anyone.

hypothesis (hy-PAW-theh-sis)   Statement of a specific relationship between or among two or more variables.

hysterectomy   Surgical removal of the uterus.

hysterotomy (HIS-ter-oh-AW-tuh-mee)   Surgical incision into the uterus; when used for abortion, the fetus is removed through the incision.

id   In psychoanalytic theory, the source of psychic energy derived from instinctive drives.

immunosuppression   The suppression of natural immunologic responses, which produces lowered resistance to disease.

incest   Sexual activities between family members who are too closely related to be able to marry legally.

inclusive fitness   A measure of the total contribution of genes to the next generation by oneself and those with whom one shares genes, such as siblings and cousins.

independent variables   Variables that are manipulated or varied by an experimenter.

infatuation   Foolish or irrational love.

inner lips   The hairless lips between the outer lips that enclose the clitoris and vaginal opening.

instincts   As Freud used this term, biological excitations that lead to mental activity.

intersexuality   A condition in which a person is born with both male and female characteristics, such as an ovary on one side and a testis on the other, with an ova-testis on each side, or with ambiguous genitals.

interstitial cells   Cells in the spaces between the seminiferous tubules that secrete hormones.

intra-amniotic injection   Replacement of amniotic fluid either with prostaglandins or with a salt solution, causing fetal circulatory arrest; used in second-trimester abortions.

intrauterine device (IUD)   Small plastic device that is inserted into the uterus for contraception.

john   A slang term for the customer of a prostitute.

Kaposi's sarcoma (KS) (KAP-uh-seez sar-KOH-mah)   Formerly, a rare type of cancer of the skin and connective tissue. It is now more common as one of the opportunistic infections that attacks AIDS patients.

labioscrotal swelling   The fetal tissue that develops into either the scrotum in a male or the two outer vaginal lips in a female.

labor   The process of childbirth, consisting of contractions, thinning out and expansion of the cervix, delivery of the baby, and expulsion of the placenta.

laparoscope (LAP-ar-oh-SCOPE)   A long, hollow instrument inserted into the abdominal cavity through an incision directly below the navel.

lascivious   Tending to stimulate sexual desire.

latency   In psychoanalytic theory, a stage lasting from about 6 years of age until puberty, in which there is little observable interest in sexual activity.

lesbian   A woman who is attracted to or has sex with other women.

leukorrhea (LOO-kor-EE-ah)   A whitish discharge from the vagina, often caused by a fungus infection.

lewd   Sexually unchaste; inciting lust or debauchery.

limbic system   The set of structures around the midbrain involved in regulating emotional and motivational behaviors.

limerence (LIH-mer-ence)   Love marked by obsession and preoccupation with the loved one.

lochia (LOH-kee-ah)   Dark-colored vaginal discharge that follows childbirth for several weeks.

longitudinal research   Research carried out with the same sample of people over a period of months or years.

lubricant   A shiny, slippery fluid secreted through the walls of the vagina during sexual arousal.

lust   Intense sexual desire.

luteal phase   Menstrual-cycle stage following ovulation during which growth of the uterine lining is stimulated by secretion of progesterone from the corpus luteum.

luteinizing hormone (LH)   A gonadotropin that stimulates female ovulation and male androgen secretion.

lymphadenopathy   Condition involving swollen lymph nodes in the neck, armpits, and/or groin.

meiosis (my-OH-sis)   Cell division leading to the formation of a zygote in which the number of chromosomes is reduced by half.

menarche (MEN-ark)   The first menstrual period.

menopause   The end of menstruation, ovulation, and a woman's reproductive capacity.

menstruation   The sloughing of the uterus's endometrial lining, which is then discharged through the vaginal opening.

mitosis (my-TOE-sis)   A form of cell division in which the nucleus divides into two daughter cells, each of which receives one nucleus and is an exact duplicate of the parent cell.

modeling   Learning through observation of others.

mons pubis   In adult females, cushion of fatty tissue above the labia that is covered by pubic hair.

motile   Exhibiting or demonstrating the power of motion.

Müllerian-duct system   Fetal tissue that develops into the internal female reproductive structures if the fetus is genetically female.

Müllerian-inhibiting substance (MIS)   A hormone secreted by the fetal testes that inhibits the growth and development of the Müllerian-duct system.

muscle tension   Involuntary contractions of muscles during sexual response.

myometrium (MY-oh-MEE-tree-um)   The smooth muscle layer of the uterine wall.

natural selection   The process whereby species evolve as a result of variations in the reproductive success of their ancestors.

necrophilia   Sexual arousal and/or activity with a corpse.

nocturnal emission   Ejaculation of semen during sleep.

nondemand pleasuring   Partners taking turns in exploring and caressing each other's bodies without attempting to arouse their partner sexually.

nongonococcal urethritis (NGU) (non-GON-oh-KOK-al-yur-ree-THRY-tis)   A term for urethral infections in men that are usually caused by the chlamydia bacterium.

Norplant   A contraceptive implant, inserted into a woman's upper arm, that slowly releases hormones to inhibit ovulation.

nymphomania   Excessive and uncontrollable sexual desire in women.

obscenity   The legal term for material that is foul, disgusting, lewd, and offensive to accepted standards of decency.

obsessive-compulsive reaction   Engaging in compulsive behaviors in reaction to persistent or obsessive thoughts.

Oedipus complex (EH-dih-pus)   In Freudian theory, a son's sexual desire for his mother.

operational definition   Description of a variable in such a way that it can be measured.

oral contraceptives   Pills containing hormones that inhibit ovulation.

outer lips   The hair-covered lips that enfold the inner lips, clitoris, and vaginal entrance.

ovaries   (OH-vah-rees)   Two small organs that produce eggs and hormones, located above and to each side of the uterus.

overlapping distribution   A statistical term describing situations in which the levels of a variable for some members of two groups are the same, although a difference exists between the overall levels of the particular variable for the two groups.

ovulation   The release of a mature egg from an ovary.

pandering   Serving as a go-between in commercial sexual transactions; generally pimping or procuring.

paraphilia (par-rah-FIL-ee-ah)   Love of the unusual; the term now used to describe sexual activities that were formerly labeled deviance (*para*, from "beside or amiss," and *philia*, "love").

passive immunity   A kind of immunity to some diseases or conditions acquired by a baby when it receives its mother's antibodies through her breast milk.

peak experience   Maslow's term for a personal experience that generates feelings of ecstasy, peace, and unity with the universe.

pediculosis pubis (peh-DIK-you-LOW-sis PYOU-bis)   A lice infestation of the pubic hair; commonly referred to as "crabs."

pedophilia (PEH-doe-FIL-ee-ah)   Sexual contact between an adult and a child.

pelvic inflammatory disease (PID)   Swelling and inflammation of the uterine tissues, fallopian tubes, and sometimes the ovaries.

pelvic nerve   The parasympathetic nerve involved in involuntary sexual responses of the genitals.

penis (PEE-nis)   The male sexual organ.

perimetrium (pehr-ih-MEE-tree-um)   The thin connective tissue membrane covering the outside of the uterus.

perversion   Deviance from the normal in sexual activities or desires.

phallus   The penis.

pheromones (FARE-oh-mohnz)   Externally secreted chemical substances to which other members of the same species respond.

philia   Love involving concern with the well-being of a friend.

pimp   A prostitute's business manager.

placebos   Treatments or drugs that supposedly have some effect on people, but that in reality should have no effect.

placenta   The organ formed by the joining of the tissue of the uterine wall with that of the developing fetus; a major source of hormones during pregnancy.

platonic love   Nonsexual love for another person, often referred to as *spiritual love.*

pneumocystis carinii pneumonia (PCP) (NEW-moh-SIS-tis kah-RYE-nee-EYE)   A form of pneumonia that commonly appears in persons whose immune systems are highly suppressed.

pornography   Sexually oriented material that is not acceptable to the viewer.

postpartum (post-PAR-tum)   Relating to the time immediately following birth.

postpartum depression   Intense sadness or general letdown experienced by some women following childbirth.

premature ejaculation   Ejaculation before the man wants it to occur.

premenstrual phase   The six days prior to menstruation, when the corpus luteum begins to disintegrate if the egg has not been fertilized.

priapism (PRE-uh-PIZ-um)   Prolonged and painful erection, without sexual desire.

primal scene   A child's observations of parental coitus.

proceptivity   The initiation and escalation of a sexual interaction with another person.

procuring   Obtaining customers for a prostitute.

progestins   Generic term for hormones that prepare the female reproductive system for pregnancy.

prostaglandins   Hormones that stimulate muscle contractions as well as help to regulate ovulation and the release of prolactin from the ovaries.

prostate gland   Gland located at the base of the male bladder that supplies most of the seminal fluid.

prostatitis (praw-stay-TYE-tis)   Inflammation of the prostate gland.

prosthesis   Artificial replacement for a body part.

prostitution   The practice of selling sexual stimulation or interaction.

prurient   Provoking lasciviousness.

pubococcygeus (PC) muscle (pew-bow-cawk-SEE-gee-us)   The muscle that surrounds the vaginal entrance and walls.

pudendal nerve (poo-DEN-dal)   Nerve that passes from the external genitals through spinal cord segments S2 through S4, and that transmit sensations from the genitals.

quickening   The first fetal movements felt by the mother.

rape trauma syndrome   Emotional and behavioral consequences that victims experience after being raped.

rape   Sexual intercourse that occurs without consent under actual or threatened force.

reductionism   Explaining complex processes in terms of basic physical/chemical activities (for example, explaining human sexual desire in terms of hormonal activity).

refractory period   A period of time following ejaculation during which nerves cannot respond to further stimulation.

reliability   The extent to which a measure elicits the same response at different times.

replication   The practice of repeating a study with a different group of research participants to determine whether the results of previous research are reliable.

repression   Not paying attention to thoughts or feelings because they are threatening.

reproductive success   The extent to which organisms are able to produce offspring who survive long enough to pass on their genes to successive generations.

reticular activating system (RAS)   The system of nerve paths within the brain that is involved in arousal.

retrograde ejaculation   A condition in which the base of the bladder does not contract during ejaculation, resulting in semen discharging into the man's bladder.

retrovirus   A form of virus that cannot reproduce inside a host cell until it has made DNA copies of its own RNA structure.

rhythm method   A birth control technique based on avoidance of sexual intercourse during a woman's fertile period each month.

sampling   The process of selecting a representative part of a population.

satyriasis (SAH-ter-RYE-uh-sis)   Excessive and uncontrollable sexual desire in men.

scripts   Largely unconscious, culturally determined mental plans that individuals use to organize and guide their behavior.

scrotum (SCROH-tum)   Sac that contains the testes.

self-report bias   Bias introduced into the results of a study stemming either from participants' desire to appear "normal" or from memory lapses.

semen (SEE-men)   Milky-white alkaline fluid containing sperm; a product of fluids from the epididymis, seminal vesicles, prostate, and Cowper's glands, combined with sperm from the testes.

seminal vesicles (SEM-ih-nal VES-ih-kelz)   Two saclike organs lying on either side of the prostate that deposit fluid into the ejaculatory ducts to contribute to semen.

seminiferous tubules (sem-ih-NIF-er-us)   Long, thin, tightly coiled tubes, located in the testes, that produce sperm.

sensate focus   Concentration on sensations produced by touching.

sex chromosomes   The pair of chromosomes that determines whether an individual is female or male.

sex guilt   Sense of guilt resulting from the violation of personal standards of proper sexual behavior.

sex linkage   The connection between the sex chromosomes and the genes one inherits. When a person inherits a sex chromosome, he or she also inherits the genes it carries.

sex-typed identification (also called *gender-typed identification*)   Incorporation into the personality of the behaviors and characteristics expected for one's gender in a particular culture, with avoidance of those characteristics expected of the other gender.

sexual arousal disorder   Failure to attain or maintain erection or vaginal lubrication and swelling despite adequate stimulation.

sexual assault   Forcing another person to have sexual contact.

sexual aversion disorder   Extreme dislike and avoidance of genital sexual contact with a partner.

sexual double standard   The belief that a particular behavior is acceptable for one gender but not for the other.

sexual harassment   The use of status and/or power to coerce or attempt to coerce a person into having sex; also, suggestive or lewd comments directed at a person in occupational, educational, or therapeutic settings.

sexual masochism   Sexual gratification through experiencing pain and humiliation.

sexual sadism   The intentional infliction of pain or humiliation on another person for sexual excitement.

sexual surrogate   A member of a sex-therapy team whose role is to have sexual interactions with a client as part of the therapy.

shigellosis (SHIH-geh-LOW-sis)   A form of dysentery (diarrhea) that can be transmitted by sexual contact.

socialization   The process of developing the skills needed to interact with others in one's culture.

soft-core erotica   Erotica that is suggestive, but not explicit, in portraying sexual acts.

spectating   Evaluating one's own sexual performance rather than involving oneself in the sexual experience with one's partner.

spermatic cord (spur-MAH-tik)   Cord that suspends the testes and contains the vas deferens, blood vessels, nerves, and cremaster muscles.

spermicide   A chemical that kills or immobilizes sperm.

squeeze technique   A treatment for premature ejaculation in which a man signals his partner to apply manual pressure to his penis to delay ejaculation.

statutory rape   Sexual intercourse with a person who is under the legal age of consent in a given state.

sterilization   A surgical procedure performed to make a person incapable of reproduction.

streetwalker   A prostitute who solicits on the street.

stress   Physical, emotional, or mental strain or tension.

suction abortion   Removal of the contents of the uterus through use of a suction machine.

superego   In psychoanalytic theory, the level of personality corresponding to the conscience.

sympto-thermal method   A way of determining the date of ovulation based on changes in a woman's basal body temperature and the stretchability of her cervical mucus.

syphilis   An STD caused by the bacterium *Treponema pallidum.*

systematic desensitization   A behavior therapy in which deep relaxation is used to reduce anxiety associated with certain situations.

testes (TES-tees)   Two small oval organs located in the scrotum that produce mature sperm and sex hormones.

testosterone   The major natural androgen.

thalamus (THAL-uh-mus)   The major brain center involved in the transmission of sensory impulses to the cerebral cortex.

theoretical failure rate   The failure rate of a contraceptive method when it is used correctly.

transition   A short period of intense and very frequent contractions that complete dilation of the cervix to 10 cm.

transsexual   A person whose gender identity is different from his or her anatomical sex.

transvestite   A person sexually stimulated or gratified by wearing the clothes stereotypic of the other gender.

triangular family system   In psychoanalytic theory, the notion that a male homosexual's parents consist of an intimate, controlling mother and a detached, rejecting father.

tribadism   Sexual activity in which one woman lies on top of another and moves rhythmically for clitoral stimulation.

trichomoniasis (TRIK-uh-muh-NYE-ah-sis)   An inflammation of the vagina characterized by a whitish discharged, caused by a parasite.

umbilical cord   The connection of the fetus to the placenta, through which the fetus is nourished.

unconditioned response (UCR)   A stimulus-evoked response that is not dependent on experience or learning.

unconditioned stimulus (UCS)   A stimulus that evokes a response that is not dependent on prior learning.

unrequited love   Intense romantic/erotic attraction toward another person who does not have the same feelings toward you.

urethra (ur-REE-thrah)   Duct or tube through which urine and ejaculate leave the body.

urogenital folds   Folds or strips on each side of the genital tubercle of the fetus that fuse to form the urethral tube in a male or the inner vaginal lips in a female.

uterus (YOU-tur-us)   The place where a fertilized egg is implanted and the fetus develops during gestation.

vagina (vah-JYE-nah)   The female's muscular tube that extends from the uterus to the vulva.

vaginismus (VAH-jih-NIS-mus)   Involuntary spasms of the pelvic muscles surrounding the other third of the vagina.

vaginitis (VAH-jih-NYE-tis)   A general term for any inflammation of the vagina.

validity   The extent to which an instrument measures what it is designed to measure.

variable   Any situation or behavior capable of change or variation.

vas deferens (VAS DEH-fur-renz)   Slender duct through which sperm are transported from each testis to the ejaculatory duct at the base of the urethra.

vasectomy   Male sterilization involving cutting or tying of the vas deferens.

vasocongestion   Engorgement with blood.

vasovasectomy   Surgical reversal of vasectomy.

victim precipitation   The notion that the victim of an attack is at least partially responsible for the attack.

volunteer bias   Bias introduced into the results of a study stemming from systematic differences between those who volunteer for research and those who avoid participation.

voyeurism (VOY-yer-ism)   Obtaining sexual arousal by observing people without their consent when they are undressed or engaging in sexual activity.

vulva (VULL-vah)   External female genitals, including the mons pubis, outer and inner lips, clitoris, and vaginal opening.

wet dream   Slang phrase for orgasm and/or ejaculation while asleep.

Wolffian-duct system   Fetal tissue that develops into the internal male reproductive structures if the fetus is genetically male.

zoophilia (ZOO-oh-FIL-ee-ah)   Sexual activity with animals.

zygote (ZYE-goat)   The developing organism, from fertilization to implantation.

REFERENCES

Abbey, A. (1987). Misperceptions of friendly behavior as sexual interest: A survey of naturally occurring incidents. *Psychology of Women Quarterly, 11,* 173–194.

Abbey, A., Ross, L. T., McDuffie, D., & McAuslan, P. (1996). Alcohol and dating risk factors for sexual assault among college women. *Psychology of Women Quarterly, 20,* 147–169.

Abel, G. G., Barlow, D. H., Blanchard, E., & Guild, D. (1977). The components of rapists' sexual arousal. *Archives of General Psychiatry, 34,* 895–903.

Abel, G. G., Osborn, C., Anthony, D., & Gardos, P. (1992). Current treatment of paraphiliacs. *Annual Review of Sex Research, 3,* 255–290.

Abel, G. G., & Rouleau, J.-L. (1990). The nature and extent of sexual assault. In W. L. Marshall, D. R. Laws, & H. E. Barbaree (Eds.), *Handbook of sexual assault* (pp. 9–21). New York: Plenum.

Abortion's long siege. (1992, April 27). *Newsweek, 44–47.*

Abramson, P. R., & Hayashi, H. (1984). Pornography in Japan: Cross-cultural and theoretical considerations. In N. M. Malamuth & E. Donnerstein (Eds.), *Pornography and sexual aggression* (pp. 173–183). Orlando, FL: Academic Press.

Adams, H. E., Wright, L. W., Jr., & Lohr, B. A. (1996). Is homophobia associated with homosexual arousal? *Journal of Abnormal Psychology,*

Adler, N. E., David, H. P., Major, B. N., & Roth, S. H., Russo, N. F., & Wyatt, G. E. (1990). Psychological responses after abortion. *Science, 248,* 41–44.

Adler, N. E., David, H. P., Major, B. N., Roth, S. H., Russo, N. F., & Wyatt, G. E. (1992). Psychological factors in abortion: A review. *American Psychologist, 47,* 1194–1204.

Ageton, S. S. (1983). *Sexual assault among adolescents.* Lexington, MA: Lexington Books.

Ahlburg, D. A., & DeVita, C. J. (1992). New realities of the American family. *Population Bulletin, 47,* 2, 1–42.

Ainsworth, M. D. S., Blehar, M. C., Waters, E., & Wall, S. (1978). *Patterns of attachment: A psychological study of the strange situation.* Hillsdale, NJ: Erlbaum.

Alan Guttmacher Institute. (1994). *Sex and America's teenagers.* New York: Author.

Alfonso, V. C., Allison, D. B., & Dunn, G. M. (1992). Sexual fantasy and satisfaction: A multidimensional analysis of gender differences. *Journal of Psychology and Human Sexuality, 5,* 19–37.

Allen, D., & Okawa, J. B. (1987). A counseling center looks at sexual harassment. *Journal of NAWDAC, 50,* 9–15.

Allen, M., D'Alessio, D., Emmers, T. M., & Gebhardt, L. (1996).The role of educational briefings in mitigating effects of experimental exposure to violent sexually explicit material: A meta-analysis. *The Journal of Sex Research, 33,* 135–141.

Allgeier, A. R. (1983). Informational barriers to contraception. In D. Byrne & W. Fisher (Eds.), *Adolescents, sex, and contraception* (pp. 143–169). Hillsdale, NJ: Erlbaum.

Allgeier, E. R. (1984). The personal perils of sex researchers: Vern Bullough and William Masters. *SIECUS Report, 12* (4), 16–19.

Allgeier, E. R. (1992). So-so sexuality: Field research on gender roles with a preliterate polygynous tribe. In G. G. Brannigan & M. R. Merrens (Eds.), *The undaunted psychologist: Adventures in research* (pp. 218–234). New York: McGraw Hill.

Allgeier, E. R., Allgeier, A. R., & Rywick, T. (1979). Abortion: Reward for conscientious contraceptive use? *The Journal of Sex Research, 15,* 64–75.

Allgeier, E. R., & Wiederman, M. M. (1994). How useful is evolutionary psychology for understanding contemporary human sexual behavior? *Annual Review of Sex Research, 5,* 218–256.

Allgeier, E. R., Yachanin, S. A., Smith, K. H., & Myers, J. G. (1984, May). *Are erotic photographs pornographic, offensive, and/or arousing? Correlations among judgments.* Paper presented at the meeting of the Midwestern Psychological Association, Chicago, IL.

American Cancer Society. (1993). *Cancer facts and figures—1993.* Atlanta: Author.

American Cancer Society. (1996). *Cancer facts and figures—1996.* Atlanta: Author.

American Psychiatric Association (1980). *Diagnostic and statistical manual of mental disorders* (3rd ed.). Washington, DC: American Psychiatric Association.

American Psychiatric Association (1994). *Diagnostic and statistical manual of mental disorders* (4th ed.). Washington, DC: American Psychiatric Association.

Amoroso, D. M., Brown, M., Pruesse, M., Ware, E. E., & Pithey, D. W. (1971). An investigation of behavioral, psychological, and physical reactions to pornographic stimuli. In *Technical Report of the Commission on Obscenity and Pornography* (Vol. 8, pp. 1–40). Washington, DC: GPO.

Andolsek, K. M. (1990). *Obstetric care: Standards of prenatal, intrapartum, and postpartum management.* Philadelphia: Lea & Febiger.

Andrews, F. M., Abbey, A., & Halman, L. J. (1991). Stress from infertility, marriage factors, and subjective well-being of wives and husbands. *Journal of Health and Social Behavior, 32,* 238–253.

Ansuini, C., Fiddler-Woite, J., & Woite, R. (1996). The source, accuracy, and impact of initial sexuality information on lifetime wellness. *Adolescence, 31,* 283–289.

Apfelbaum, B. (1984). The ego-analytic approach to body-work sex therapy. *The Journal of Sex Research, 20,* 44–70.

Apfelbaum, B. (1989). Retarded ejaculation: A much-misunderstood syndrome. In S. R. Leiblum & R. C. Rosen (Eds.), *Principles and practices of sex therapy* (2nd ed., pp. 168–206). New York: Guilford.

Aral, S. O., & Holmes, K. K. (1991). Sexually transmitted diseases in the AIDS era. *Scientific American, 264,* 62–69.

Aral, S. O., Mosher, W. D., & Cates, W., Jr., (1992). Vaginal douching among women of reproductive age in the United States: 1988. *American Journal of Public Health, 82,* 210–214.

Armstrong, E. G. (1978). Massage parlors and their customers. *Archives of Sexual Behavior, 7,* 117–125.

Arndt, W. B. (1991). *Gender disorders and the paraphilias.* Madison, CT: International Universities Press.

Arndt, W. B., Foehl, J. C., & Good, F. E. (1985). Specific sexual fantasy themes: A multidimensional study. *Journal of Personality and Social Psychology, 48,* 472–480.

Aron, A., Aron, E. N., Tudor, M., & Nelson, G. (1991). Close relationships as including other in the self. *Journal of Personality and Social Psychology, 60,* 241–253.

Ashcraft, D. M., & Schlueter, D. (1996, May). *Safer-sex practices of rural area college students from 1976 to 1995.* Paper presented at the Eastern and Midcontinent Region Meeting of the Society for the Scientific Study of Sexuality, Pittsburgh, PA.

Asscheman, H., & Gooren, L. J. G. (1992). Hormone treatment in transsexuals. *Journal of Psychology and Human Sexuality, 5,* 39–54.

Austin, S., & Allgeier, E. R. (1997, November). Education of student clinicians regarding sexual feelings toward clients. Paper presented at the Meeting of the American Association of Behavior Therapists. Miami, FL.

Bagley, C. (1996). A typology of child sexual abuse: The interaction of emotional, physical, and sexual abuse as predictors of adult psychiatric sequelae in women. *Canadian Journal of Human Sexuality, 5,* 101–112.

Bailey, J. M., Gauling, S., Agyei, Y., & Gladue, B. A. (1994). Effects of gender and sexual orientation on evolutionarily relevant aspects of human mating psychology. *Journal of Personality and Social Psychology, 66,* 1081–1093.

Bailey, J. M., Kim, P. Y., Hills, A., & Linsenmeier, J. A. W. (in press). Butch, femme, or straight-acting? Partner preferences of gay men and lesbians. *Journal of Personality and Social Psychology.*

Bailey, J. M., Miller, J. S., & Willerman, L. (1993). Maternally related childhood gender nonconformity in homosexuals and heterosexuals. *Archives of Sexual Behavior, 22,* 461–469.

Bailey, J. M., & Pillard, R. C. (1991). A genetic study of male sexual orientation. *Archives of General Psychiatry, 48,* 1089–1096.

Bailey, J. M., Pillard, R. C., Neale, M. C., & Agyei, Y. (1993). Heritable factors influence female sexual orientation. *Archives of General Psychiatry, 50,* 217–223.

Baldwin, W. (1976). *Adolescent pregnancy and child-bearing: Growing concerns for Americans.* Washington, DC: Population Reference Bureau.

Baldwin, W., & Cain, V. S. (1980). The children of teenage parents. *Family Planning Perspectives, 12,* 34–39, 42–43.

Bandura, A. (1986). *Social foundations of thought and action.* Englewood Cliffs, NJ: Prentice-Hall.

Banks, A., & Gartrell, N. K. (1995). Hormones and sexual orientation: A questionable link. *Journal of Homosexuality, 28,* 247–268.

Barak, A., Fisher, W. A., & Houston, S. (1992). Individual difference correlates of the experience of sexual harassment among female university students. *Journal of Applied Social Psychology, 22,* 17–37.

Barbach, L. G. (1976). *For yourself: The fulfillment of female sexuality.* New York: Anchor/Doubleday.

Barbach, L. G. (1980). Group treatment of anorgasmic women. In S. R. Leiblum & L. A. Pervin (Eds.), *Principles and practice of sex therapy* (pp. 107–146). New York: Guilford.

Barbach, L. G., & Levine, L. (1980). *Shared intimacies: Women's sexual experiences.* New York: Anchor.

Barbaree, H. E., Hudson, S. M., & Seto, M. C. (1993). Sexual assault in society: The role of the juvenile offender. In H. E. Barbaree, W. L. Marshall, & S. M. Hudson (Eds.), *The juvenile sex offender* (pp. 1–24). New York: Guilford.

Bart, P. B. (1981). A study of women who both were raped and avoided rape. *Journal of Social Issues, 37* (4), 123–137.

Batra, A. K., & Lue, T. F. (1990). Physiology and pathology of penile erection. *Annual Review of Sex Research, 1,* 251–263.

Baumeister, R. F. (1988a). Masochism as escape from self. *The Journal of Sex Research, 25,* 28–59.

Baumeister, R. F. (1988b). Gender differences in masochistic scripts. *The Journal of Sex Research, 25,* 478–499.

Baumeister, R. F., & Leary, M. R. (1995). The need to belong: Desire for interpersonal attachments as a fundamental human motivation. *Psychological Bulletin, 117,* 497–529.

Beach, F. A. (Ed.). (1976). *Human sexuality in four perspectives.* Baltimore, MD: Johns Hopkins University Press.

Beatrice, J. (1985). A psychological comparison of heterosexuals, transvestites, preoperative transsexuals, and postoperative transsexuals. *Journal of Nervous and Mental Disease, 173,* 358–365.

Beck, J. G. (1993). Vaginismus. In W. O'Donahue & J. H. Geer (Eds.), *Handbook of sexual dysfunctions: Assessment and treatment* (pp. 381–397). Boston: Allyn & Bacon.

Beere, C. A. (1990). *Sex and gender issues: A handbook of tests and measures.* New York: Greenwood.

Beigel, H. G. (1953). The meaning of coital postures. *International Journal of Sexology, 4,* 136–143.

Beitchman, J. H., Zucker, K. J., Hood, J. E., DaCosta, G. A., Akman, D., & Cassavia, E. (1992). A review of the long-term effects of child sexual abuse. *Child Abuse and Neglect, 16,* 101–118.

Bell, A. R., & Weinberg, M. S. (1978). *Homosexualities.* New York: Simon & Schuster.

Bell, A. R., Weinberg, M. S., & Hammersmith, S. K. (1981). *Sexual preference: Its development in men and women.* Bloomington: Indiana University Press.

Belsky, J. (1991). Parental and nonparental child care and children's socioemotional development. In A. Bouth (Ed.), *Contemporary families: Looking forward, looking back* (pp. 122–140). Minneapolis: National Council on Family Relations.

Belzer, E. G. (1981). Orgasmic expulsions of women: A review and heuristic inquiry. *The Journal of Sex Research, 17,* 1–12.

Bem, D. J. (1996). Exotic becomes erotic: A developmental theory of sexual orientation. *Psychological Review, 103,* 320–335.

Bem, S. L. (1974). The measurement of psychological androgyny. *Journal of Consulting and Clinical Psychology, 42,* 155–162.

Bem, S. L. (1975). Sex-role adaptability: One consequence of psychological androgyny. *Journal of Personality and Social Psychology, 31,* 634–643.

Bem, S. L. (1993). *The lenses of gender: Transforming the debate on sexual inequality.* New Haven: Yale University Press.

Bem, S. L., & Lenney, E. (1976). Sex typing and avoidance of cross-sex behavior. *Journal of Personality and Social Psychology, 3,* 48–54.

Bem, S. L., Martyna, W., & Watson, C. (1976). Sex typing and androgyny: Further exploration of the expressive domain. *Journal of Personality and Social Psychology, 34,* 1016–1023.

Bennett, S. M., & Dickinson, W. B. (1980). Student-parent rapport and parent involvement in sex, birth control, and venereal disease education. *The Journal of Sex Research, 16,* 114–130.

Bentler, P. M., & Peeler, W. H. (1979). Models of female orgasm. *Archives of Sexual Behavior, 8,* 405–424.

Bentler, P. M., Sherman, R. W., & Prince, V. (1970). Personality characteristics of male transvestites. *Journal of Clinical Psychology, 26*, 287–291.

Benton, J. M., Mintzes, J. L., Kendrick, A. F., & Soloman, R. D. (1993). Alternative conceptions in sexually transmitted diseases: A cross-age study. *Journal of Sex Education and Therapy, 19*, 165–182.

Berdahl, J. L., Magley, V. J., & Waldo, C. R. (1996). The sexual harassment of men: Exploring the concept with theory and data. *Psychology of Women Quarterly, 20*, 527–547.

Berger, G., Hank, L., Rauzi, T., & Simkins, L. (1987). Detection of sexual orientation by heterosexuals and homosexuals. *Journal of Homosexuality, 13*, 83–100.

Berger, R. M. (1996). *Gay and gray: The older homosexual man.* Binghamton, NY: Haworth.

Berscheid, E., & Walster, E. (1974). Physical attractiveness. In L. Berkowitz (Ed.), *Advances in experimental social psychology* (pp. 157–215). New York: Academic Press.

Berscheid, E., & Walster, E. J. (1978). *Interpersonal attraction* (2nd ed.). Reading, MA: Addison Wesley.

Betzig, L. (1989). Causes of conjugal dissolution: A cross-cultural study. *Current Anthropology, 30*, 654–676.

Bieber, I., Dain, H. J., & Dince, P. R. (1962). *Homosexuality: A psychoanalytic study.* New York: Basic Books.

Billy, J. O. G., Tanfer, K., Grady, W. R., & Klepinger, D. H. (1993). The sexual behavior of men in the United States. *Family Planning Perspectives, 25*, 52–60.

Bingham, S. G., & Scherer, L. L. (1993). Factors associated with responses to sexual harassment and satisfaction with outcome. *Sex Roles, 29*, 239–269.

Blair, C. D., & Lanyon, R. (1981). Exhibitionism: Etiology and treatment. *Psychological Bulletin, 89*, 439–463.

Blanchard, R. (1989). The classification and labeling of nonhomosexual gender dysphorias. *Archives of Sexual Behavior, 18*, 315–334.

Blanchard, R. (1993). Varieties of autogynephilia and their relationship to gender dysphoria. *Archives of Sexual Behavior, 22*, 241–251.

Blasband, M. A., & Peplau, L. A. (1985). Sexual exclusivity versus openness in gay male couples. *Archives of Sexual Behavior, 14*, 395–412.

Blieszner, R., & Adams, R. G. (1992). *Adult friendship.* Newbury Park, CA: Sage.

Blumstein, P. W., & Schwartz, P. (1976). Bisexuality in men. *Urban Life, 5*, 339–359.

Blumstein, P. W., & Schwartz, P. (1983). *American couples.* New York: Morrow.

Bogaert, A. F. (1996). Volunteer bias in human sexuality research: Evidence for both sexuality and personality differences in males. *Archives of Sexual Behavior, 25*, 125–140.

Bogaert, A. F., & Blanchard, R. (1996). Physical development and sexual orientation in men: Height, weight, and age of puberty differences. *Personality and Individual Differences, 21*, 77–84.

Boles, J. (1998). My life in prostitution. In G. G. Brannigan, E. R. Allgeier, & A. R. Allgeier (Eds.), *The sex scientists* (pp. 185–200). New York: Addison Wesley Longman.

Boles, J., & Elifson, K. W. (1994). Sexual identity and HIV: The male prostitute. *The Journal of Sex Research, 31*, 39–46.

Borna, S., Chapman, J., & Menezes, D. (1993). Deceptive nature of dial-a-porn commercials and public policy alternatives. *Journal of Business Ethics, 12*, 503–509.

Bouhoutsos, J. C., Holroyd, J., Lerman, H., Forer, B., & Greenberg, M. (1983). Sexual intimacy between psychotherapists and patients. *Professional Psychology, 14*, 185–196.

Bowlby, J. (1973). *Attachment and Loss: Vol. 2. Separation, anxiety, and anger.* New York: Basic Books.

Boxer, A. M., & Cohler, B. J. (1989). The life course of gay and lesbian youth: An immodest proposal for the study of lives. *Journal of Homosexuality, 17*, 315–355.

Bradford, J. M. W. (1993). The pharmacological treatment of the adolescent sex offender. In H. E. Barbaree, W. L. Marshall, & S. M. Hudson (Eds.), *The juvenile sex offender* (pp. 278–288). New York: Guilford.

Bradford, J. M. W., & Pawlak, A. (1993). Double-blind placebo crossover study of cyproterone acetate in the treatment of the paraphilias. *Archives of Sexual Behavior, 22*, 383–402.

Brame, G. G., Brame, W. D., & Jacobs, J. (1993). *Different loving: An exploration of the world of sexual dominance and submission.* New York: Villard.

Breakwell, G. M., & Fife-Schaw, C. (1992). Sexual activities and preferences in a United Kingdom sample of 16- to 20-year-olds. *Archives of Sexual Behavior, 21*, 271–293.

Brecher, E. M., & the Editors of Consumer Reports Books. (1984). *Love, sex, and aging.* Boston: Little, Brown.

Breslow, N., Evans, L., & Langley, J. (1985). On the prevalence and roles of females in the sadomasochistic subculture: Report on an empirical study. *Archives of Sexual Behavior, 14*, 303–317.

Bretschneider, J. G., & McCoy, N. L. (1988). Sexual interest and behavior in 80- to 102-year-olds. *Archives of Sexual Behavior, 17*, 109–129.

Bringle, R. G., & Buunk, B. P. (1991). Extradyadic relationships and sexual jealousy. In K. McKinney & S. Sprecher (Eds.), *Sexuality in close relationships* (pp. 135–153). Hillsdale, NJ: Erlbaum.

Brown, G. R., & Collier, Z. (1989). Transvestites' women revisited: A nonpatient sample. *Archives of Sexual Behavior, 18*, 73–83.

Brown, J. D., & Steele, J. R. (1996). Sexuality and the mass media: An overview. *SIECUS Report, 24* (4), 3–9.

Brown, L. K., DiClemente, R. J., & Beausoleil, N. I. (1992). Comparison of human immunodeficiency virus–related knowledge, attitudes, and behaviors among sexually active and abstinent young adolescents. *Journal of Adolescent Health, 13*, 140–149.

Brown, S. S., & Eisenberg, L. (Eds.) (1995). *The best intentions: Unintended pregnancy and the well-being of children and families.* Washington, DC: Institute of Medicine and National Academy Press.

Buhrich, N. A. (1976). A heterosexual transvestite club: Psychiatric aspects. *Australian and New Zealand Journal of Psychiatry, 10*, 331–335.

Buhrich, N. A., & McConaghy, N. (1977). The discrete syndromes of transvestism and transsexualism. *Archives of Sexual Behavior, 6*, 483–496.

Bullough, B. (1994). Abortion. In V. Bullough & B. Bullough (Eds.), *Human sexuality: An encyclopedia* (pp. 3–8). New York: Garland.

Bullough, B., & Bullough, V. L. (1996). Female prostitution: Current research and changing interpretations. *Annual Review of Sex Research, 7*, 158–180.

Bullough, B., & Bullough, V. L. (1997). Are transvestites necessarily heterosexual? *Archives of Sexual Behavior, 26*, 1–12.

Bullough, V. L. (1983, November). *Presidential address: The problems of doing research in a delicate field.* Presented at the Annual Meeting of The Society for the Scientific Study of Sex, Chicago, IL.

Bullough, V. L., & Bullough, B. (1977). *Sin, sickness, and sanity.* New York: New American Library.

Bullough, V. L., & Bullough, B. (1987). *Women and prostitution: A social history.* Buffalo, NY: Prometheus.

Bullough, V. L., & Bullough, B. (1993). *Cross-dressing, sex, and gender.* Philadelphia: University of Pennsylvania Press.

Bullough, V. L., & Weinberg, J. S. (1988). Women married to transvestites: Problems and adjustments. *Journal of Psychology and Human Sexuality, 1,* 83–104.

Bumpass, L. L., Sweet, J. A., & Cherlin, A. (1991). The role of cohabitation in declining rates of marriage. *Journal of Marriage and the Family, 53,* 913–927.

Burg, B. R. (1988). Nocturnal emission and masturbatory frequency relationships: A nineteenth-century account. *The Journal of Sex Research, 24,* 216–220.

Burgess, A. W., Hartman, C. R., MacCausland, M. P., & Powers, P. (1984). Response patterns in children and adolescents exploited through sex rings and pornography. *American Journal of Psychiatry, 141,* 656–662.

Burgess, A. W., & Holmstrom, L. L. (1974). *Rape: Victims of crisis.* Bowie, MD: Brady.

Buss, D. M. (1994). *The evolution of desire: Strategies of human mating.* New York: Basic Books.

Buss, D. M. (1996). Sexual conflict: Evolutionary insights into feminism and the "battle of the sexes." In D. M. Buss & N. M. Malamuth (Eds.), *Sex, power, conflict: Evolutionary and feminist perspectives* (pp. 296–318). New York: Oxford University Press.

Buss, D. M. et al. (1989). Sex differences in human mate preferences: Evolutionary hypotheses tested in thirty-seven cultures. *Behavioral and Brain Sciences, 12,* 1–49.

Buss, D. M., & Schmitt, D. P. (1993). Sexual strategies theory: A contextual evolutionary analysis of human mating. *Psychological Review, 100,* 204–232.

Butler, C. A. (1976). New data about female sexual response. *Journal of Sex and Marital Therapy, 2,* 40–46.

Byers, E. S. (1996). How well does the traditional sexual script explain sexual coercion? Review of a program of research. *Journal of Psychology and Human Sexuality, 8,* 7–25.

Byers, E. S., & Heinlein, L. (1989). Predicting initiation and refusals of sexual activities in married and cohabiting couples. *The Journal of Sex Research, 26,* 210–231.

Byers, E. S., & Lewis, K. (1988). Dating couples' disagreements over the desired level of sexual intimacy. *The Journal of Sex Research, 24,* 15–29.

Byrne, D. (1971). *The attraction paradigm.* New York: Academic Press.

Byrne, D. (1977). Social psychology and the study of sexual behavior. *Personality and Social Psychology Bulletin, 3,* 3–30.

Byrne, D., & Fisher, W. A. (Eds.) (1983). *Adolescents, sex, and contraception.* Hillsdale, NJ: Erlbaum.

Byrne, D., Fisher, W. A., Lamberth, J., & Mitchell, H. E. (1974). Evaluations of erotica: Facts or feelings? *Journal of Personality and Social Psychology, 79,* 111–116.

Byrne, D., & Murnen, S. K. (1988). Maintaining loving relationships. In R. J. Sternberg & M. L. Barnes (Eds.), *The psychology of love* (pp. 293–310). New Haven: Yale University Press.

Byrne, D., & Schulte, L. (1990). Personality dispositions as mediators of sexual responses. *Annual Review of Sex Research 1,* 93–117.

Cadman, D., Gafini, A., & McNamee, J. (1984). Newborn circumcision: An economic perspective. *Canadian Medical Association Journal, 131,* 1353–1355.

Cado, S., & Leitenberg, H. (1990). Guilt reactions to sexual fantasies during intercourse. *Archives of Sexual Behavior, 19,* 49–63.

Caird, W. K., & Wincze, J. P. (1977). *Sex therapy: A behavioral approach.* New York: Harper & Row.

Calhoun, T. C., & Weaver, G. (1996). Rational decision-making among male street prostitutes. *Deviant Behavior: An Interdisciplinary Journal, 17,* 209–227.

Call, V., Sprecher, S., & Schwartz, P. (1995). Marital sexual intercourse frequency in a national sample. *Journal of Marriage and the Family, 57,* 639–652.

Campbell, M. K., Waller, L., Andolsek, K. M., Huff, P., & Bucci, K. (1990). Infant feeding and nutrition. In K. M. Andolsek (Ed.), *Obstretic care: Standards of prenatal, peripartum, and postpartum management* (pp. 206–221). Philadelphia: Lea & Febiger.

Cancian, F. M. (1986). The feminization of love. *Signs: Journal of Women in Culture and Society, 11,* 692–709.

Cannon, D. (1987, November). *Twenty years of sex guilt: Construct validation of the concept.* Paper presented at the Annual Meeting of The Society for the Scientific Study of Sex, Atlanta, GA.

Carlson, J., & Hatfield, E. (1992). *The psychology of emotion.* Fort Worth, TX: Holt, Rinehart & Winston.

Carmichael, M. S., Warburton, V. L., Dixen, J., & Davidson, J. M. (1994). Relationships among cardiovascular, muscular, and oxytocin responses during human sexual activity. *Archives of Sexual Behavior, 23,* 59–79.

Carnes, P. (1983). *The sexual addiction.* Minneapolis: CompCare.

Carnes, P. (1991). *Don't call it love: Recovering from sexual addiction.* New York: Bantam.

Caron, S. L., Davis, C. M., Wynn, R. L., & Roberts, L. W. (1992). "America responds to AIDS," but did college students? Differences between March 1987 and September 1988. *AIDS Education and Prevention, 4,* 18–28.

Carrier, J. M. (1980). Homosexual behavior in cross-cultural perspective. In J. Marmor (Ed.), *Homosexual behavior* (pp. 100–122). New York: Basic Books.

Carroll, J. L., Volk, K. D., & Hyde, J. S. (1985). Differences between males and females in motives for engaging in sexual intercourse. *Archives of Sexual Behavior, 14,* 131–139.

Carter, C. S. (1992). Hormonal influences on human sexual behavior. In J. B. Becker, S. M. Breedlove, & D. Crews (Eds.), *Behavioral endocrinology* (pp. 131–142). Cambridge, MA: MIT Press.

Casler, L. (1968). Perceptual deprivation in institutional settings. In G. Newton & S. Levine (Eds.), *Early experience and behavior* (pp. 573–626). New York: Springer.

Cate, R., Long, E., Angera, A., & Draper, K. K. (1993). Sexual intercourse and relationship development. *Family Relations, 42,* 158–164.

Cates, W. C., Jr., & Stone, K. M. (1992a). Family planning, sexually transmitted diseases, and contraceptive choice: A literature update—Part I. *Family Planning Perspectives, 24,* 75–84.

Cates, W. C., Jr., & Stone, K. M. (1992b). Family planning, sexually transmitted diseases, and contraceptive choice: A literature update—Part II. *Family Planning Perspectives, 24,* 122–128.

Catotti, D. N., Clarke, P., & Catoe, K. E. (1993). Herpes revisited. *Sexually Transmitted Diseases, 20,* 77–80.

Centers for Disease Control. (1993, August 6). Recommendations for the prevention and management of chlamydia trachomatis infections. *Morbidity and Mortality Weekly Report, 42,* RR–12.

Centers for Disease Control and Prevention (1995). Trends in sexual risk behavior among high school students—United States, 1990, 1991, and 1993. *Morbidity and Mortality Weekly Report, 44,* 121–123, 131–132.

Centers for Disease Control and Prevention (1996). *HIV/AIDS Surveillance Report, 8* (2), 1–39.

Cherlin, A. (1981). *Marriage, divorce, remarriage.* Cambridge, MA: Harvard University Press.

Chivers, M., & Blanchard, R. (1996). Prostitution advertisements suggest association of transvestism and masochism. *Journal of Sex and Marital Therapy, 22,* 97–102.

Chodorow, N. (1978). *The reproduction of mothering.* Berkeley and Los Angeles: University of California Press.

Christopher, F. S., Johnson, D. C., & Roosa, M. W. (1993). Family, individual, and social correlates of early Hispanic adolescent sexual expression. *The Journal of Sex Research, 30,* 54–61.

Christopher, F. S., & Roosa, M. W. (1990). An evaluation of an adolescent pregnancy prevention program: Is "just say no" enough? *Family Relations, 39,* 68–72.

Clark, R. D., & Hatfield, E. (1989). Gender differences in receptivity to sexual offers. *Journal of Psychology and Human Sexuality, 2,* 39–55.

Clement, U. (1990). Surveys of heterosexual behavior. *Annual Review of Sex Research, 1,* 45–74.

Clement, U., Schmidt, G., & Kruse, M. (1984). Changes in sex differences in sexual behavior: A replication of a study on West German students (1966–1981). *Archives of Sexual Behavior, 13,* 99–120.

Clemmer, D. (1958). *Some aspects of sexual behavior in the prison community.* Proceedings of the Eighty-eighth Annual Congress of Corrections of the American Correctional Institution, Detroit, MI.

Cochran, S. D., & Mays, V. M. (1990). Sex, lies, and HIV. *New England Journal of Medicine, 322,* 774–775.

Cohen, J. B., Hauer, L. B., Poole, L. E., & Wofsy, C. B. (1987). *Sexual and other practices and risk of HIV infection in a cohort of 450 sexually active women in San Francisco.* Paper presented at the Third International Conference on AIDS, Washington, DC.

Coleman, E. (1987). Bisexuality: Challenging our understanding of sexual orientation. *Sexuality and Medicine, 1,* 225–242.

Coleman, E. (1990). The married lesbian. *Marriage and Family Review, 13,* 119–135.

Coleman, E. (1991). Compulsive sexual behavior: New concepts and treatments. *Journal of Psychology and Human Sexuality, 4,* 37–52.

Coleman, E., Bockting, W. O., & Gooren, L. (1993). Homosexual and bisexual identity in sex-reassigned female-to-male transsexuals. *Archives of Sexual Behavior, 22,* 37–50.

Coles, C. D., & Shamp, M. J. (1984). Some sexual, personality, and demographic characteristics of women readers of erotic romances. *Archives of Sexual Behavior, 13,* 187–209.

Cooper, A. J. (1986). Progestogens in the treatment of male sex offenders: A review. *Canadian Journal of Psychiatry, 31,* 73–79.

Corey, L. (1994, March-April). The current trend in genital herpes. *Sexually Transmitted Diseases,* Supplement.

Cox, D. J. (1988). Incidence and nature of male genital exposure behavior as reported by college women. *The Journal of Sex Research, 24,* 227–234.

Cox, S., & Gallois, C. (1996). Gay and lesbian identity development: A social identity perspective. *Journal of Homosexuality, 30,* 1–30.

Cramer, D. W., Schiff, I., Schoenbaum, S. C., Gibson, M., Belisle, S., Albrecht, B., Stillman, R. J., Berger, M. J., Wilson, E., & Stabel, B. V. (1985). Tubal infertility and the intrauterine device. *New England Journal of Medicine, 312,* 941–947.

Cranston-Cuebas, M. A., & Barlow, D. H. (1990). Cognitive and affective contributions to sexual functioning. *Annual Review of Sex Research, 1,* 119–161.

Crenshaw, T. L., & Goldberg, J. P. (1996). *Sexual pharmacology: Drugs that affect sexual function.* New York: W. W. Norton.

Crepault, C., Abraham, G., Porto, R., & Couture, M. (1977). Erotic imagery in women. In R. Gemme & C. C. Wheeler (Eds.), *Progress in sexology* (pp. 267–283). New York: Plenum.

Curtis, L. (1974). Victim precipitation and violent crime. *Social Problems, 21,* 594–605.

Cutler, W. B., Garcia, C. R., & McCoy, N. (1987). Perimenopausal sexuality. *Archives of Sexual Behavior, 16,* 225–234.

Dale, J. (1986). The rape crisis center view. In A. W. Burgess & C. R. Hartman (Eds.), *Sexual exploitation of patients by health professionals* (pp. 84–96). New York: Praeger.

Daling, J. R., Weiss, N. B., Voight, L. F., McKnight, B., & Moore, D. E. (1992). The intrauterine device and primary tubal infertility. *New England Journal of Medicine, 362,* 203–204.

Darling, C. A., & Davidson, J. K., Sr. (1986). Enhancing relationships: Understanding the feminine mystique of pretending orgasm. *Journal of Sex and Marital Therapy, 12,* 182–196.

Darling, C. A., Davidson, J. K., Sr., & Cox, R. P. (1991). Female sexual response and the timing of partner orgasm. *Journal of Sex and Marital Therapy, 17,* 3–20.

Darling, C. A., Davidson, J. K., Sr., & Jennings, D. A. (1991). The female sexual response revisited: Understanding the multiorgasmic response in women. *Archives of Sexual Behavior, 20,* 527–540.

Darney, P. D., Atkinson, E., Tanner, S., MacPherson, S., Hellerstein, S., & Alvarado, A. (1990). Acceptance and perceptions of NOR-PLANT among users in San Francisco, USA. *Studies in Family Planning, 21,* 152–160.

Davenport, W. H. (1965). Sexual patterns and their regulation in a society of the Southwest Pacific. In F. A. Beach (Ed.), *Sex and behavior* (pp. 164–207). New York: Wiley.

David, H. P. (1992). Born unwanted: Long-term developmental effects of denied abortion. *Journal of Social Issues, 48* (3), 163–181.

David, H. P., Dytrych, Z., Matejcek, Z., & Schuller, V. (Eds.) (1988). *Born unwanted: Developmental effects of denied abortion.* New York: Springer.

Davidson, J. K., Sr., & Hoffman, L. E. (1986). Sexual fantasies and sexual satisfaction: An empirical analysis of erotic thought. *The Journal of Sex Research, 22,* 184–205.

Davis, C. M., & Bauserman, R. (1993). Exposure to sexually explicit materials: An attitude change perspective. *Annual Review of Sex Research, 4,* 121–209.

Davis, C. M., Yarber, W. L., Bauserman, R., Schreer, G., & Davis, S. L. (Eds.) (1998). *Sexuality-related measures: A compendium* (2nd ed.). Thousand Oaks, CA: Sage.

Davis, J. A., & Smith, T. (1984). *General social surveys, 1972–1984: Cumulative data.* New Haven: Yale University, Roper Center for Public Opinion Research.

Davis, S. F., Byers, R. H., Jr., Lindegren, M. L., Caldwell, M. B., Karon, J. M., & Gwinn, M. (1995). Prevalence and incidence of vertically acquired HIV infection in the United States. *Journal of the American Medical Association, 247,* 952–955.

Davison, G. C. (1991). Constuctionism and morality in therapy for homosexuality. In J. C. Gonsiorek & J. D. Weinrich (Eds.), *Homosexuality: Research implications for public policy* (pp. 137–148). Newbury Park, CA: Sage.

Day, R. D. (1992). The transition to first intercourse among racially and culturally diverse youth. *Journal of Marriage and the Family, 54,* 749–762.

de Carvalho, M., Robertson, S., & Klaus, M. H. (1984). Does the duration and frequency of early breast feeding affect nipple pain? *Birth, 11,* 81–84.

DeBuono, B. A., Zinner, S. H., Daamen, M., & McCormack, W. M. (1990). Sexual behavior of college women in 1975, 1986, and 1989. *New England Journal of Medicine, 322,* 821–825.

DeCecco, J. P., & Parker, D. A. (1995). The biology of homosexuality: Sexual orientation or sexual preference? *Journal of Homosexuality, 28,* 1–27.

Dekker, J. (1993). Inhibited male orgasm. In W. O'Donahue & J. H. Geer (Eds.), *Handbook of sexual dysfunctions: Assessment and treatment* (pp. 279–301). Boston: Allyn & Bacon.

DeLamater, J. D., & MacCorquodale, P. (1979). *Premarital sexuality: Attitudes, relationships, behavior.* Madison: University of Wisconsin Press.

DeLisle, S. (1997). Preserving reproductive choice: Preventing STD-related infertility in women. *SIECUS Report, 25* (3), 18–21.

DeMaris, A., & Rao, K. V. (1992). Premarital cohabitation and subsequent marital stability in the United States: A reassessment. *Journal of Marriage and the Family, 54,* 178–190.

Devor, H. (1993). Sexual orientation identities, attractions, and practices of female-to-male transsexuals. *The Journal of Sex Research, 30,* 303–315.

de Waal, F. B. M. (1995). Sex as an alternative to aggression in the bonobo. In P. R. Abramson & S. D. Pinkerton (Eds.), *Sexual nature/ sexual culture* (pp. 37–56). Chicago: University of Chicago Press.

Dhawan, S., & Marshall, W. L. (1996). Sexual abuse histories of sexual offenders. *Sexual Abuse: A Journal of Research and Treatment, 8,* 7–15.

Diamond, M. (1982). Sexual identity, monozygotic twins reared in discordant sex roles and a BBC follow-up. *Archives of Sexual Behavior, 11,* 181–185.

Diamond, M. (1993). Homosexuality and bisexuality in different populations. *Archives of Sexual Behavior, 22,* 291–310.

Diamond, M. (1996a). Prenatal predisposition and the clinical management of some pediatric conditions. *Journal of Sex and Marital Therapy, 22,* 139–147.

Diamond, M. (1996b). Self-testing among transsexuals: A check on self-identity. *Journal of Psychology and Human Sexuality, 8,* 61–82.

Diamond, M. (1997). Sexual identity and sexual orientation in children with traumatized or ambiguous genitalia. *The Journal of Sex Research, 34,* 199–211.

Diana, L. (1985). *The prostitute and her clients.* Springfield, IL: Thomas.

Dick-Read, G. (1932/1959). *Childbirth without fear* (2nd rev. ed.). New York: Harper & Row.

DiClemente, R. J. (1989). Adolescents and AIDS: An update. *Multicultural Inquiry and Research on AIDS, 3* (1), 3–4, 7.

DiClemente, R. J., Forrest, K., & Mickler, S. E. (1990). College students' knowledge and attitudes about HIV and changes in HIV-preventive behaviors. *AIDS Education and Prevention, 2,* 201–212.

Dion, K. K., & Dion, K. L. (1993). Individualistic and collectivistic perspectives on gender and the cultural context of love and intimacy. *Journal of Social Issues, 49* (3), 53–69.

Dion, K. L., & Dion, K. K. (1988). Romantic love: Individual and cultural perspectives. In R. J. Sternberg & M. L. Barnes (Eds.), *The psychology of love* (pp. 264–289). New Haven: Yale University Press.

Docter, R. F. (1988). *Transvestites and transsexuals: Towards a theory of gender behavior.* New York: Plenum.

Dodson, B. (1987). *Sex for one: The joy of self-loving.* New York: Harmony.

Doll, L. S., Peterson, L. R., White, C. R., Johnson, E. S., Ward, J. W., & the Blood Donor Study Group. (1992). Homosexually and non-homosexually identified men who have sex with men: A behavioral comparison. *The Journal of Sex Research, 29,* 1–14.

Donnerstein, E. (1984). Pornography: Its effect on violence against women. In N. M. Malamuth & E. Donnerstein (Eds.), *Pornography and sexual aggression* (pp. 53–81). Orlando, FL: Academic Press.

Donnerstein, E., & Linz, D. (1986). Mass media, sexual violence, and media violence. *American Behavioral Scientist, 29,* 601–618.

Donovan, P. (1997). Can statutory rape laws be effective in preventing adolescent pregnancy? *Family Planning Perspectives, 29,* 30–34, 40.

Dornan, W. A., & Malsbury, C. W. (1989). Neuropeptides and male sexual behavior. *Neuroscience and Biobehavioral Reviews, 13,* 1–15.

Douthitt, R. A. (1989). The division of labor within the home: Have gender roles changed? *Sex Roles, 20,* 693–704.

Dressel, P. L., & Peterson, D. M. (1982). Becoming a male stripper: Recruitment, socialization, and ideological development. *Work and Occupations, 9,* 387–406.

Dunn, M. E., & Trost, J. E. (1989). Male multiple orgasms: A descriptive study. *Archives of Sexual Behavior, 18,* 377–399.

Durkin, K. F., & Bryant, C. D. (1995). "Log on sex": Some notes on the carnal computer and erotic cyberspace as an emerging research frontier. *Deviant Behavior: An Interdisciplinary Journal, 16,* 179–200.

Dwyer, S. M. & Amberson, J. I. (1989). Behavioral patterns and personality characteristics of fifty-six sex offenders: A preliminary study. *Journal of Psychology and Human Sexuality, 2,* 105–118.

Eakins, P. S. (1989). Free-standing birth centers in California. *Journal of Reproductive Medicine, 34,* 960–970.

Earls, C. M., & David, H. (1989). A psychosocial study of male prostitution. *Archives of Sexual Behavior, 18,* 401–419.

Ecker, N., & Weinstein, S. (1983, April). *The relationship between attributes of sexual competency, physical appearance, and narcissism.* Paper presented at The Conference of the Eastern Region of the Society for the Scientific Study of Sex, Philadelphia, PA.

Edmonds, P. (1996, March 28). Teen pregnancy revives laws on statutory rape. *USA Today,* pp. 1A–2A.

Ehrhardt, A. A., & Meyer-Bahlburg, H. F. L. (1981). Effects of prenatal sex hormones on gender-related behavior. *Science, 211,* 1312–1318.

Ehrhardt, A. A., Meyer-Bahlburg, H. F. L., Feldman, J. L., & Ince, S. (1984). Sex-dimorphic behavior in childhood subsequent to prenatal exposure to exogenous progesterones and estrogens. *Archives of Sexual Behavior, 13,* 457–477.

Elicker, J. M., Englund, M., & Sroufe, L. A. (1992). Predicting peer competence and peer relationships in childhood from early parent-child relationships. In R. Parke & G. Ladd (Eds.), Family-peer relations: Modes of linkage (pp. 77–106). Hillsdale, NJ: Erlbaum.

Ellis, B. J., & Symons, D. (1990). Sex differences in sexual fantasy: An evolutionary psychological approach. *The Journal of Sex Research, 27,* 527–555.

Ellison, P. T. (1991). Reproductive ecology and human fertility. In G. W. Lasker & C. G. N. Mascie-Taylor (Eds.), *Applications of biological anthropology to human affairs* (pp. 14–54). Cambridge: Cambridge University Press.

Emory, L. E., Williams, D. H., Cole, C. M., Amparo, E. G., & Meyer, W. J. (1991). Anatomic variation of the corpus callosum in persons with gender dysphoria. *Archives of Sexual Behavior, 20,* 409–417.

Erikson, E. H. (1968a). *Childhood and society* (rev. ed.). New York: Norton.

Erikson, E. H. (1968b). *Identity, youth, and crisis.* New York: Norton.

Ernulf, K. E., & Innala, K. E. (1995). Sexual bondage: A review and unobtrusive investigation. *Archives of Sexual Behavior, 24,* 631–654.

Ewald, P. W. (1994). *Evolution of infectious disease*. New York: Oxford University Press.

Fact Sheet (1997). Sexually transmitted diseases in the United States. *SIECUS Report, 25* (3), 22–24.

Fagot, B. I. (1995). Psychosocial and cognitive determinants of early gender-role development. *Annual Review of Sex Research, 5,* 1–31.

Fairchild, H. H. (1991). Scientific racism: The cloak of objectivity. *Journal of Social Issues, 47* (3), 101–115.

Farr, G., Gabelnick, H., Sturgen, K., & Dorflinger, L. (1994). Contraceptive efficacy and acceptability of the female condom. *American Journal of Public Health, 84,* 1960–1964.

Fassinger, R. E., & Morrow, S. L. (1995). Overcome: Repositioning lesbian sexualities. In L. Diamont & R. D. McAnulty, R. D. (Eds.), *The psychology of sexual orientation, behavior, and identity* (pp. 197–219). Westport, CT: Greenwood Press.

Federal Bureau of Investigation. 1993. *Uniform crime reports for the United States, 1992.* Washington, D.C.: GPO.

Federal Bureau of Investigation. (1996). *Uniform Crime Reports for the United States, 1995.* Washington, DC: GPO.

Feeney, J. A., & Noller, P. (1990). Attachment style as a predictor of adult romantic relationships. *Journal of Personality and Social Psychology, 58,* 281–291.

Feeney, J. A., & Noller, P. (1991). Attachment style and verbal descriptions of romantic partners. *Journal of Social and Personal Relationships, 8,* 187–215.

Feild, H. S., & Bienen, L. B. (1980). *Jurors and rape.* Lexington, MA: Heath.

Fetherstone, M., & Hepworth, M. (1985). The male menopause: Lifestyle and sexuality. *Maturitas, 7,* 235–246.

Finkelhor, D. (1979). *Sexually victimized children.* New York: Free Press.

Finkelhor, D. (1980). Sex among siblings: A survey on prevalence, variety, and effects. *Archives of Sexual Behavior, 9,* 171–197.

Finkelhor, D. (1984). *Child sexual abuse: New theory and research.* New York: Free Press.

Finkelhor, D., & Browne, A. (1985). The traumatic impact of child sexual abuse. *American Journal of Orthopsychiatry, 55,* 530–541.

Finkelhor, D., & Dziuba-Leatherman, J. (1994). Victimization of children. *American Psychologist, 49,* 173–183.

Finkelhor, D., & Hotaling, G., Lewis, I. A., & Smith, C. (1990). Sexual abuse in a national survey of adult men and women: Prevalence, characteristics, and risk factors. *Child Abuse and Neglect, 14,* 19–28.

Finkelhor, D., & Russell, D. E. H. (1984). The gender gap among perpetrators of child sexual abuse. In D. E. H. Russell (Ed.), *Sexual exploitation: Rape, child sexual abuse, and workplace harassment* (pp. 215–231). Beverly Hills, CA: Sage.

Fisher, H. (1992). *The anatomy of love.* New York: Norton.

Fisher, J. D. (1988). Possible effects of reference group-based social influence on AIDS-risk prevention. *American Psychologist, 43,* 914–920.

Fisher, J. D., & Fisher, W. A. (1992). Changing AIDS-risk behavior. *Psychological Bulletin, 117,* 455–474.

Fisher, J. D., Fisher, W. A., Misovich, S. J., Kimble, D. L., & Malloy, T. E. (1996). Changing AIDS risk behavior: Effects of a conceptually based AIDS risk reduction intervention emphazing AIDS risk reduction information, motivation and behavioral skills in a college student population. *Health Psychology, 15,* 114–123.

Fisher, S. (1973). *The female orgasm.* New York: Basic Books.

Fisher, T. D. (1986). Parent-child communication about sex and young adolescents' sexual knowledge and attitudes. *Adolescence, 21,* 517–527.

Fisher, T. D. (1987). Family communication and the sexual behavior and attitudes of college students. *Journal of Youth and Adolescence, 16,* 481–495.

Fisher, T. D. (1988). The relationship between parent-child communication about sexuality and college students' sexual behavior and attitudes as a function of parental proximity. *The Journal of Sex Research, 24,* 305–311.

Fisher, T. D. (1989a). An extension of the findings of Moore, Peterson, and Furstenberg (1986) regarding family sexual communication and adolescent sexual behavior. *Journal of Marriage and the Family, 51,* 637–639.

Fisher, T. D. (1989b). Confessions of a closet sex researcher. *The Journal of Sex Research, 26,* 144–147.

Fisher, T. D. (1993). A comparison of various measures of family sexual communication: Psychometric properties, validity, and behavioral correlates. *The Journal of Sex Research, 30,* 229–238.

Fisher, W. A. (1983). Gender, gender role identification, and response to erotica. In E. R. Allgeier & N. B. McCormick (Eds.), *Changing boundaries: Gender roles and sexual behavior* (pp. 261–284). Palo Alto, CA: Mayfield.

Fisher, W. A. (1997). Do no harm: On the ethics of testosterone replacement therapy for HIV+ Persons. *The Journal of Sex Research, 34,* 35–36.

Fisher, W. A., Branscombe, N. R., & Lemery, C. R. (1983). The bigger the better? Arousal and attributional responses to erotic stimuli that depict different-size penises. *The Journal of Sex Research, 19,* 377–396.

Fisher, W. A., Byrne, D., White, L. A., & Kelley, K. (1988). Erotophobia-erotophilia as a dimension of personality. *The Journal of Sex Research, 25,* 123–151.

Fiske, S. T., & Glick, P. (1995). Ambivalence and stereotypes cause sexual harassment: A theory with implications for organizational change. *Journal of Social Issues, 51* (1), 97–115.

Fisher, W. A., & Grenier, G. (1994). Violent pornography, antiwoman thoughts, and antiwoman acts: In search of reliable effects. *The Journal of Sex Research, 31,* 23–38.

Fitzgerald, L. F., Weitzman, L. M., Gold, Y., & Ormerod, M. (1988). Academic harassment: Sex and denial in scholarly garb. *Psychology of Women Quarterly, 12,* 329–340.

Fitzgerald, L. F., Swan, S., & Fischer, K. (1995). Why didn't she just report him? The psychological and legal implications of women's responses to sexual harassment. *Journal of Social Issues, 51* (1), 117–138.

Foa, U. G., Anderson, B., Converse, J., Jr., Urbansky, W. A., Cowley, M. J., III, Muhlhausen, S. M., & Tornbloom, K. Y. (1987). Gender-related sexual attitudes: Some cross-cultural similarities and differences. *Sex Roles, 16,* 511–519.

Ford, C. S., & Beach, F. A. (1951). *Patterns of sexual behavior.* New York: Harper & Row.

Ford, N., & Mathie, E. (1993). The acceptability and experience of the female condom, Femidom®, among family planning clinic attenders. *British Journal of Family Planning, 19,* 187–192.

Forrest, J. D., & Fordyce, R. R. (1993). Women's contraceptive attitudes and use in 1992. *Family Planning Perspectives, 25,* 175–179.

Forrest, J. D., & Kaeser, L. (1993). Questions of balance: Issues emerging from the introduction of the hormonal implant. *Family Planning Perspectives, 25,* 127–132.

Forsyth, C. J., & Deshotels, T. H. (1997). The occupational milieu of the nude dancer. *Deviant Behavior: An Interdisciplinary Journal, 18,* 125–142.

Fowlkes, M. R. (1994). Single worlds and homosexual lifestyles: Patterns of sexuality and intimacy. In A. S. Rossi (Ed.), *Sexuality across the life course* (pp. 151–184). Chicago: University of Chicago Press.

Frank, A. P., Wandell, M. G., Headings, M. D., Conant, M. A., Wood, G. E., & Michel, C. (1997). Anonymous HIV testing using home collection and telemedicine counseling. A multicenter evaluation. *Archives of Internal Medicine, 157,* 309–314.

Franzoi, S. L., & Herzog, M. E. (1987). Judging physical attractiveness: What body aspects do we use? *Personality and Social Psychology Bulletin, 13,* 19–33.

Frayser, S. G. (1994). Defining normal childhood sexuality: An anthropological approach. *Annual Review of Sex Research, 4,* 173–217.

Friedan, B. (1963). *The feminine mystique.* New York: Norton.

Freud, S. (1955). *Beyond the pleasure principle, group psychology, and other works* (Vol. 18). London: Hogarth.

Freund, K., & Blanchard, R. (1986). The concept of courtship disorder. *Journal of Sex and Marital Therapy, 12,* 79–92.

Freund, K., Steiner, B. W., & Chan, S. (1982). Two types of cross-gender identity. *Archives of Sexual Behavior, 11,* 49–63.

Freund, M., Lee, N., & Leonard, T. (1991). Sexual behavior of clients with street prostitutes in Camden, New Jersey. *The Journal of Sex Research, 28,* 579–591.

Freund, M., Leonard, T. I., & Lee, N. (1989). Sexual behavior of resident street prostitutes with their clients in Camden, New Jersey. *The Journal of Sex Research, 26,* 460–478.

Fromm, E. (1956). *The art of loving.* New York: Harper & Row.

Frost, J. J., & Forrest, D. F. (1995). Understanding the impact of effective teenage pregnancy prevention programs. *Family Planning Perspectives, 27,* 188–195.

Furstenberg, F. F. (1976). *Unplanned parenthood: The social consequences of teenage childbearing.* New York: Free Press.

Furstenberg, F. F., Brooks-Gunn, J., & Morgan, S. P. (1987). *Adolescent mothers in later life.* New York: Cambridge University Press.

Fyke, F. E., Kazmier, S. J., & Harms, R. W. (1985). Venous air embolism: Life-threatening complications of orogenital sex during pregnancy. *American Journal of Medicine, 78,* 333–336.

Gagnon, J. H. (1990). The explicit and implicit use of the scripting perspective in sex research. *Annual Review of Sex Research, 1,* 1–43.

Gagnon, J. H., & Simon, W. (1973). *Sexual conduct: The social sources of human sexuality.* Chicago: Aldine.

Gaines, M. E., & Allgeier, E. R. (1993, May). *Parents' knowledge, attitudes, and responses to child sexual abuse.* Paper presented at the Annual Meeting of the Midcontinent Region meeting of The Society for the Scientific Study of Sex, Cincinnati, OH.

Gallup Poll Monthly. (1995). Legality, morality of abortion, no. 354, 30–31.

Gayle, H. D., Keeling, R. P., Garcia-Tunon, M., Kilbourne, B. W., Narkunas, J. P., Ingram, F. R., Rogers, M. F., & Curran, J. W. (1991). Prevalence of the human immunodeficiency virus among university students. *New England Journal of Medicine, 323,* 1538–1541.

Gebhard, P. H. (1977). The acquisition of basic sex information. *The Journal of Sex Research, 13,* 148–169.

Gebhard, P. H., Gagnon, J. H., Pomeroy, W. B., & Christenson, C. V. (1965). *Sex offenders.* New York: Harper & Row.

George, L. K., & Weiler, S. J. (1981). Sexuality in middle and late life. The effects of age, cohort, and gender. *Archives of General Psychiatry, 38,* 919–923.

Gerrard, M. (1987). Sex, sex guilt, and contraceptive use revisited: The 1980s. *Journal of Personality and Social Psychology, 53,* 975–980.

Gerrard, M., & Gibbons, F. X. (1982). Sexual experience, sex guilt, and sexual moral reasoning. *Journal of Personality, 50,* 345–359.

Gettelman, T. E., & Thompson, J. K. (1993). Actual differences and stereotypical perceptions in body image and eating disturbance: A comparison of male and female heterosexual and homosexual samples. *Sex Roles, 29,* 545–562.

Gilbert, N. (1992). Realities and mythologies of rape. *Society, 29,* 4–10.

Gilligan, C. (1982). *In a different voice: Psychological theory and women's development.* Cambridge, MA: Harvard University Press.

Glasock, J., & LaRose, R. (1993). Dial-a-porn recordings: The role of the female participant in male sexual fantasies. *Journal of Broadcaster and Electronic Media, 39,* 313–324.

Glass, S. P., & Wright, T. L. (1992). Justifications for extramarital relationships: The association between attitudes, behaviors, and gender. *The Journal of Sex Research, 29,* 361–387.

Glazener, C. M. A., Abdalla, M., Stroud, P., Naji, S., Templeton, A., & Russell, I. T. (1995). Postnatal maternal morbidity: Extent, causes, prevention, and treatment. *British Journal of Obstetrics and Gynecology, 102,* 282–287.

Gold, S. R., & Gold, R. G. (1991). Gender differences in first sexual fantasies. *Journal of Sex Education and Therapy, 17,* 207–216.

Gold, S. R., & Gold, R. G. (1993). Sexual aversions: A hidden disorder. In W. O'Donahue & J. H. Geer (Eds.), *Handbook of sexual dysfunctions: Assessment and treatment* (pp. 83–102). Boston: Allyn & Bacon.

Golding, J. M. (1996). Sexual assault history and women's reproductive and sexual health. *Psychology of Women Quarterly, 20,* 101–121.

Goldman, R., & Goldman, J. (1982). *Children's sexual thinking: A comparative study of children aged five to fifteen years in Australia, North America, Britain, and Sweden.* London: Routledge & Kegan Paul.

Golombok, S., & Tasker, F. (1996). Do parents influence the sexual orientation of their children? Findings from a longitudinal study of lesbian families. *Developmental Psychology, 32,* 3–11.

Gonsiorek, J. C. (1991). The empirical basis for the demise of the illness model of homosexuality. In J. C. Gonsiorek & J. D. Weinrich (Eds.), *Homosexuality: Research implications for public policy* (pp. 115–136). Newbury Park, CA: Sage.

Goodall, J. (1971). *Tiwi wives.* Seattle: University of Washington Press.

Goodheart, A. (1992). Abstinence ed.: How everything you need to know about sex you won't be allowed to ask. *Playboy, 39,* 42–44.

Goodman, R. E., Anderson, D. C., Bu'lock, D. E., Sheffield, B., Lynch, S. S., & Butt, W. R. (1985). Study of the effect of estradiol on gonadotropin levels in untreated male-to-female transsexuals. *Archives of Sexual Behavior, 14,* 141–146.

Gordon, C. M., & Carey, M. P. (1995). Penile tumescence monitoring during morning naps to assess male erectile functioning: An initial study of healthy men of varied ages. *Archives of Sexual Behavior, 24,* 291–307.

Gould, S. J. (1994). Sexuality and ethics in advertising: A research agenda and policy guideline perspective. *Journal of Advertising, 23,* 73–80.

Graber, B. (1993). Medical aspects of sexual arousal disorders. In W. O'Donahue & J. H. Geer (Eds.), *Handbook of sexual dysfunctions: Assessment and treatment* (pp. 103–156). Boston: Allyn & Bacon.

Grady, W. R., Klepinger, D. H., Billy, J. O. G., & Tanfer, K. (1993). Condom characteristics: The perceptions and preferences of men in the United States. *Family Planning Perspectives, 25,* 67–73.

Graham, K. R. (1996). The childhood victimization of sex offenders: An underestimated issue. *International Journal of Offender Therapy and Comparative Criminology, 40,* 192–203.

Green, R. (1987). *The "sissy boy syndrome" and the development of homosexuality: A fifteen-year prospective study.* New Haven: Yale University Press.

Green, R., & Fleming, D. T. (1990). Transsexual surgery follow-up: Status in the 1990s. *Annual Review of Sex Research, 1,* 163–174.

Greenwald, E., & Leitenberg, H. (1989). Long-term effects of sexual experiences with siblings and nonsiblings during childhood. *Archives of Sexual Behavior, 18,* 389–399.

Greer, G. (1971). *The female eunuch.* New York: McGraw-Hill.

Gregor, T. (1985). *Anxious pleasures: The sexual lives of an Amazonian people.* Chicago: University of Chicago Press.

Grenier, G., & Byers, E. S. (1995). Rapid ejaculation: A review of conceptual, etiological, and treatment issues. *Archives of Sexual Behavior, 24,* 447–472.

Grieco, A. (1987). Scope and nature of sexual harassment in nursing. *The Journal of Sex Research, 23,* 261–266.

Grodstein, F., Goldman, M. B., & Cramer, D. W. (1993). Relation of tubal infertility to history of sexually transmitted diseases. *American Journal of Epidemiology, 137,* 577–584.

Groth, A. N., & Burgess, A. W. (1977). Sexual dysfunction during rape. *New England Journal of Medicine, 297,* 764–766.

Grunebaum, H. (1986). Harmful psychotherapy experiences. *American Journal of Psychotherapy, 40,* 165–176.

Gutek, B. A. (1985). *Sex and the workplace.* San Francisco: Jossey-Bass.

Gutek, B. A. (1992). Understanding sexual harassment at work. *Notre Dame Journal of Law, Ethics, and Public Policy, 6,* 335–358.

Hack, M., Wright, L. L., Shankasan, S., Tyson, J. E., Horbas, J. D., Bauer, C. R., & Younes, N. (1995). Very-low-birth-weight outcomes of National Institute of Child Health and Human Development Neonatal Network, November 1989 to October 1990. *American Journal of Obstetrics and Gynecology, 172,* 457–464.

Hall, E. R., & Flannery, P. J. (1985). Prevalence and correlates of sexual assault experiences in adolescents. *Victimology: An International Journal, 9,* 398–406.

Hall, G. C. N., & Barongan, C. (1997). Prevention of sexual aggression: Sociocultural risk and protective factors. *American Psychologist, 52,* 5–14.

Hallstrom, T. (1977). Sexuality in the climacteric. *Clinical Obstetrics and Gynecology, 4,* 227–239.

Hamburg, D. A. (1992). *Today's children: Creating a future for a generation in crisis.* New York: Times Books.

Hamer, D. H., Hu, S., Magnuson, V. L., Hu, N., & Pattatucci, A. M. L. (1993). A linkage between DNA markers on the X chromosome and male sexual orientation. *Science, 261,* 321–327.

Hardy, J. B., Duggan, A. K., Masnyk, K., & Pearson, C. (1989). Fathers of children born to young urban mothers. *Family Planning Perspectives, 21,* 159–163, 187.

Harlow, H. F., & Harlow, M. K. (1962). The effect of rearing conditions on behavior. *Bulletin of the Meninger Clinic, 26,* 213–224.

Harlow, H. F., & Mears, C. (1979). *The human model: Primate perspectives.* Washington, DC: Winston.

Harry, J. (1993). Being out: A general model. *Journal of Homosexuality, 26,* 25–40.

Hartman, W. E., & Fithian, M. A. (1984). *Any man can.* New York: St. Martin's.

Harvey, S. M., & Scrimshaw, S. C. M. (1988). Coitus-dependent contraceptives: Factors associated with effective use. *The Journal of Sex Research, 25,* 364–378.

Hatcher, R. A. (1991) Female condoms

Hatcher, R. A. et al. (1994). *Contraceptive technology, 1992–1994* (16th rev. ed.). New York: Irvington.

Hatfield, E., & Rapson, R. L. (1993). *Love, sex, and intimacy: Their psychology, biology, and history.* New York: HarperCollins.

Hatfield, E., & Rapson, R. L. (1996). *Love and sex: Cross-cultural perspectives.* Needham Heights, MA: Allyn & Bacon.

Hatfield, R. W. (1994). Touch and sexuality. In V. L. Bullough & B. Bullough (Eds.), *Human sexuality: An encyclopedia* (pp. 581–587). New York: Garland.

Haub, C. (1992). New U.N. projections show uncertainty of future world. *Population Today, 20,* 6.

Hawton, K. (1992). Sex therapy research: Has it withered on the vine? *Annual Review of Sex Research, 3,* 49–72.

Haynes, J. D. (1994). Pheromones. In V. L. Bullough & B. Bullough (Eds.), *Human sexuality: An encyclopedia* (pp. 441–442). New York: Garland.

Hazan, C., & Shaver, P. R. (1990). Love and work: An attachment-theoretical perspective. *Journal of Personality and Social Psychology, 52,* 511–524.

Hechinger, F. M. (1992). *Fateful choices: Healthy youth for the twenty-first century.* New York: Hill and Wang.

Heim, N. (1981). Sexual behavior of castrated sex offenders. *Archives of Sexual Behavior, 10,* 11–19.

Heim, N., & Hursch, C. J. (1979). Castration for sex offenders: Treatment or punishment? A review and critique of recent European literature. *Archives of Sexual Behavior, 8,* 281–304.

Heiman, J. R. (1975). The physiology of erotica: Women's sexual arousal. *Psychology Today, 8,* 90–94.

Heiman, J. R. (1977). A psychophysiological exploration of sexual arousal patterns in females and males. *Psychophysiology, 14,* 266–274.

Heiman, J. R., Gladue, B. A., Roberts, C. W., & LoPiccolo, J. (1986). Historical and current factors discriminating sexually functional from sexually dysfunctional married couples. *Journal of Marital and Family Therapy, 12,* 163–174.

Heiman, J. R., & LoPiccolo, J. (1988). *Becoming orgasmic.* New York: Prentice-Hall.

Heinlein, R. (1961). *Stranger in a strange land.* New York: Putnam.

Henderson, J. S. (1983). Effects of a prenatal teaching program on postpartum regeneration of the pubococcygeal muscle. *Journal of Obstetrics, Gynecology, and Neonatal Nursing, 12,* 403–408.

Hendrick, C., & Hendrick, S. S. (1993). *Romantic love.* Newbury Park, CA: Sage.

Hendrick, S. S., & Hendrick, C. (1992). *Liking, loving, and relating.* Pacific Grove, CA: Brooks/Cole.

Henshaw, S. K. (1993). Teenage abortion, birth, and pregnancy statistics by state, 1988. *Family Planning Perspectives, 25,* 122–126.

Henshaw, S. K. (1995). Factors hindering access to abortion services. *Family Planning Perspectives, 27,* 54–59, 87.

Henshaw, S. K., & Kost, K. (1996). Abortion patients in 1994–1995: Characteristics and contraceptive use. *Family Planning Perspectives, 28,* 140–147, 158.

Henshaw, S. K., & Van Vort, J. (1992). *Abortion factbook, 1992 edition: Readings, trends, and state and local data to 1988.* New York: Alan Guttmacher Institute.

Herdt, G. H. (Ed.) (1984). *Ritualized homosexuality in Melanesia.* Berkeley and Los Angeles: University of California Press.

Herek, G. M. (1992). The social context of hate crimes: Notes on cultural heterosexism. In G. M. Herek & K. T. Berrill (Eds.), *Hate crimes: Confronting violence against lesbians and gay men* (pp. 89–104). Newbury Park, CA: Sage.

Herek, G. M., & Capitanio, J. P. (1995). Black heterosexuals' attitudes toward lesbians and gay men in the United States. *The Journal of Sex Research, 32,* 95–105.

Herek, G. M., & Glunt, E. K. (1988). An epidemic of stigma: Public reactions to AIDS. *American Psychologist, 43,* 886–891.

Herek, G. M., & Glunt, E. K. (1993). Interpersonal contact and heterosexuals' attitudes toward gay men: Results from a national survey. *The Journal of Sex Research, 30,* 239–244.

Herold, E. E., Mantle, D., & Zemitis, O. (1979). A study of sexual offenses against females. *Adolescence, 14,* 65–72.

Herold, E., Mottin, J., & Sabry, Z. (1979). The effect of vitamin E on human sexuality. *Archives of Sexual Behavior, 8,* 397–403.

Hetherington, E. M., Cox, M., & Cox, R. (1982). Effects of divorce on parents and children. In M. E. Lamb (Ed.), *Nontraditional families: Parenting and child development* (pp. 233–288). Hillsdale, NJ: Erlbaum.

Higgins, D. J., & McCabe, M. P. (1994). The relationship of child sexual abuse and family violence to adult adjustment: Toward an integrated risk-sequelae model. *The Journal of Sex Research, 31,* 255–266.

HIV comes in five family groups. (1995). *Science, 256,* 966.

Hochhauser, M., & Rothenberger, J. H., III. (1992). *AIDS education.* Dubuque, IA: Brown.

Hoenig, J. (1985). Etiology of transsexualism. In B. W. Steiner (Ed.), *Gender dysphoria: Development, research, and management* (pp. 11–32). New York: Plenum.

Hogben, M., & Byrne, D. (1998). Using social learning theory to explain individual differences in human sexuality. *The Journal of Sex Research, 35.*

Holzman, H. R., & Pines, S. (1982). Buying sex: The phenomenology of being a john. *Deviant Behavior: An Interdisciplinary Journal, 4,* 89–116.

Hooker, E. (1969). Parental relations and male homosexuality in patient and nonpatient samples. *Journal of Consulting and Clinical Psychology, 33,* 140–142.

Hostetter, H., & Andolsek, K. M. (1990). Psychosocial issues in pregnancy. In K. M. Andolsek (Ed.), *Obstetric care: Standards of prenatal, intrapartum, and postpartum management* (pp. 95–106). Philadelphia: Lea and Febiger.

Howard, M., & McCabe, J. B. (1990). Helping teenagers postpone sexual involvement. *Family Planning Perspectives, 22,* 21–26.

Hoyenga, K. B., & Hoyenga, K. T. (1993). *Gender-related differences: Origins and outcomes.* Boston: Allyn & Bacon.

Hrabowy, I., & Allgeier, E. R. (1987, May). *Relationship of level of sexual invasiveness of child abuse to psychological functioning among adult women.* Paper presented at the Midwestern Psychological Association Meeting, Chicago, IL.

Huff, P., & Bucci, K. (1990). Breast-feeding and the excretion of drugs in breast milk. In K. M. Andolsek (Ed.), *Obstetric care: Standards of prenatal, peripartum, and postpartum management* (pp. 222–236). Philadelphia: Lea & Febiger.

Hunt, M. (1974). *Sexual behavior in the 1970s.* Chicago: Playboy Press.

Hurlbert, D. F., & Whittaker, K. E. (1991). The role of masturbation in marital and sexual satisfaction: A comparative study of female masturbators and nonmasturbators. *Journal of Sex Education and Therapy, 17,* 272–282.

Hyde, J. S., DeLamater, J. D., Plant, E. A., & Byrd, J. M. (1996). Sexuality during pregnancy and the year postpartum. *The Journal of Sex Research, 33,* 143–151.

Imperato-McGinley, J., Guerrero, L., Gautier, T., & Peterson, R. (1974). Steroid 5 reductase deficiency in man: An inherited form of male pseudohermaphroditism. *Science, 186,* 1213–1215.

Imperato-McGinley, J., Peterson, R. E., Gautier, T., Looper, G., Danner, R., Arthur, A., Morris, P. L., Sweeney, W. J., & Shackleton, C. (1982). Hormonal evaluation of a large kindred with complete androgen insensitivity: Evidence for secondary 5-alpha-reductase deficiency. *Journal of Clinical Endocrinology Metabolism, 54,* 15–22.

Inciardi, J. A. (1995). Crack, crack house sex, and HIV risk. *Archives of Sexual Behavior, 24,* 249–269.

Innala, S. M. & Ernulf, K. E. (1989). Asphyxiophilia in Scandinavia. *Archives of Sexual Behavior, 18,* 181–189.

The Institute of Medicine (1996). *The hidden epidemic: Confronting sexually transmitted diseases.* National Academy Press: Washington, DC.

Jacklin, C. N., DiPietro, J. A., & Maccoby, E. E. (1984). Sex-typing behavior and sex-typing pressure in child-parent interaction. *Archives of Sexual Behavior, 13,* 413–425.

Jamison, P. L., & Gebhard, P. H. (1988). Penis size increase between flaccid and erect states: An analysis of the Kinsey data. *The Journal of Sex Research, 24,* 177–183.

Janus, S. S., & Janus, C. L. (1993). *The Janus report on sexual behavior.* New York: Wiley.

Jones, E. F., Forrest, J. D., Goldman, N., Henshaw, S., Lincoln, R., Rosoff, J. I., Westoff, C. F., & Wulf, D. (1986). *Teenage pregnancy in industrialized countries.* New Haven: Yale University Press.

Jones, J. H. (1993). *Bad blood: The Tuskegee syphilis experiment* (rev. ed.). New York: Free Press.

Jones, J. R. (1974). Plasma testosterone concentrations in female transsexuals. In D. R. Laub & P. Gandy (Eds.), *Proceedings of the second interdisciplinary symposium on the gender dysphoria syndrome.* Ann Arbor, MI: Edward Brothers.

Jorgensen, C. (1967). *Christine Jorgensen: Personal biography.* New York: Ericksson.

Joseph, J. G., Montgomery, S. B., Emmons, C. et al. (1987). Magnitude and determinants of behavioral risk reduction: Longitudinal analysis of a cohort at risk for AIDS. *Psychology and Health, 1* (1), 73–95.

Kalichman, S. C. (1991). Psychopathology and personality characteristics of criminal sexual offenders as a function of victim age. *Archives of Sexual Behavior, 20,* 187–197.

Kallmann, F. J. A. (1952). A comparative twin study on the genetic aspects of male homosexuality. *Journal of Nervous and Mental Disease, 115,* 283–298.

Kanin, E. J. (1969). Selected dyadic aspects of male sex aggression. *The Journal of Sex Research, 5,* 12–28.

Kanin, E. J. (1985). Date rapists: Differential sexual socialization and relative deprivation. *Archives of Sexual Behavior, 14,* 219–231.

Kaplan, H. S. (1974). *The new sex therapy.* New York: Brunner/Mazel.

Kaplan, H. S. (1979). *Disorders of sexual desire.* New York: Brunner/Mazel.

Karlen, A. (1971). *Sexuality and homosexuality.* New York: Norton.

Karlen, A. (1994). Aging and sexuality. In V. L. Bullough & B. Bullough (Eds.), *Human sexuality: An encyclopedia* (pp. 12–15). New York: Garland Publishing.

Karpman, B. (1954). *The sexual offender and his offenses.* New York: Julian Press.

Katz, M. H., & Gerberding, J. L. (1997). Postexposure treatment of people exposed to the human immunodeficiency virus through sexual contact or injection-drug use. *New England Journal of Medicine, 336,* 1097–1100.

Kegel, A. M. (1952). Sexual functions of the pubococcygeus muscle. *Western Journal of Surgery, Obstetrics, and Gynecology, 60,* 521–524.

Kelly, M. P., Strassberg, D. S., & Kircher, J. R. (1990). Attitudinal and experiential correlates of anorgasmia. *Archives of Sexual Behavior, 19,* 165–177.

Kenney, A. M., Guardado, S., & Brown, L. (1989). Sex education and AIDS education in the schools: What states and large school districts are doing. *Family Planning Perspectives, 21,* 56–64.

Kilpatrick, A. C. (1986). Some correlates of women's childhood sexual experiences: A retrospective study. *The Journal of Sex Research, 22,* 221–242.

Kilpatrick, A. C. (1992). *Long-range effects of childhood and adolescent sexual experiences: Myths, mores, and menaces.* Hillsdale, NJ: Erlbaum.

Kilpatrick, D. G., Best, C. L., Saunders, B. E., & Veronen, L. J. (1988). Rape in marriage and in dating relationships: How bad is it for mental health? In R. A. Prentky & V. L. Quinsey (Eds.), *Human sexual aggression: Current perspectives* (pp. 335–344). New York: New York Academy of Sciences.

Kilpatrick, D. G., Edmunds, C. N., & Seymour, N. K. (1992). *Rape in America: A report to the nation.* Arlington, VA: National Victim Center.

Kimmel, M. S., & Linders, A. (1996). Does censorship make a difference? An aggregate empirical analysis of pornography and rape. *Journal of Psychology and Human Sexuality, 8,* 1–20.

King, A. J. C., Beazley, R. P., Warren, W. K., Hankins, C A., Robertson, A. S., & Radford, J. L. (1988). *Canada youth & aids study.* Ottawa: Federal Centre for AIDS Health Protection Branch, Health and Welfare Canada.

Kinsey, A. C., Pomeroy, W., & Martin, C. (1948). *Sexual behavior in the human male.* Philadelphia: Saunders.

Kinsey, A. C., Pomeroy, W., Martin, C., & Gebhard, P. (1953). *Sexual behavior in the human female.* Philadelphia: Saunders.

Kirby, D., Barth, R. P., Leland, N., & Fetro, J. V. (1991). Reducing the risk: Impact of a new curriculum on sexual risk-taking. *Family Planning Perspectives, 23,* 253–263.

Kirkpatrick, C., & Kanin, E. (1957). Male sex aggression on a university campus. *American Sociological Review, 22,* 52–58.

Kitson, G. C., & Morgan, L. A. (1991). The multiple consequences of divorce. In A. Booth (Ed.), *Contemporary families: Looking forward, looking backward* (pp. 150–161). Minneapolis: National Council on Family Relations.

Klitsch, M. (1993). Vasectomy and prostate cancer: More questions than answers. *Family Planning Perspectives, 25,* 133–135.

Klitsch, M. (1995). Still waiting for the contraceptive revolution. *Family Planning Perspectives, 27,* 246–253.

Knoth, R., Boyd, K., & Singer, B. (1988). Empirical tests of sexual selection theory: Prediction of onset, intensity, and time course of sexual arousal. *The Journal of Sex Research, 24,* 73–89.

Kochanek, K. D., & Hudson, B. L. (1994, December 8). Advance report of final mortality statistics. *Monthly Vital Statistics Report, 43,* Supplement.

Kockott, G. & Fahrner, E. M. (1988). Male-to-female and female-to-male transsexuals: A comparison. *Archives of Sexual Behavior, 17,* 539–546.

Kolodny, R. C. (1981). Evaluating sex therapy: Process and outcome at the Masters and Johnson Institute. *The Journal of Sex Research, 17,* 301–318.

Komarow, S. (1997, February 27). Gays say military violates "Don't ask, don't tell." *USA Today,* p. 4D.

Koonin, L. M., Smith, J. C., Ramack, M., & Lawson, H. (1992). Abortion surveillance—United States. *Morbidity and Mortality Weekly Report, 41,* Special Supplement 5.

Koralewski, M. K., & Conger, J. C. (1992). The assessment of social skills among sexually coercive college males. *The Journal of Sex Research, 29,* 169–188.

Koss, M. P., & Dinero, T. E. (1988). Predictors of sexual aggression among a national sample of male college students. In R. A. Prentky & V. L. Quinsey (Eds.), *Human sexual aggression: Current perspectives* (pp. 133–147). New York: New York Academy of Sciences.

Koss, M. P., Dinero, T. E., Seibel, C. A., & Cox, S. L. (1988). Stranger and acquaintance rape: Are there differences in the victim's experience? *Psychology of Women Quarterly, 12,* 1–24.

Koutsky, L. A., Holmes, K. K., Critchlow, C. W., Stevens, C. E., Paavonen, J., Beckman, A. M., DeRouen, T. A., Galloway, D. A., Vernon, D., & Kiviat, N. B. (1992). A cohort study of the risk of cervical intraepithelial neoplasia grade two or three in relation to papilloma virus infection. *New England Journal of Medicine, 327,* 1272–1278.

Krane, R. J. (1986). Surgical implants for impotence: Indications and procedures. In R. J. Santen & K. S. Swerdloff (Eds.), *Male reproductive dysfunction* (pp. 563–576). New York: Dekker.

Kroon S & Whitley R. J. (1994, November 13–15). *Can we improve management of perinatal HSV infections?* International Herpes Management Forum, Recommendations from the Second Annual Meeting.

Kurdek, L. A. (1988). Correlates of negative attitudes toward homosexuals in heterosexual college students. *Sex Roles, 18,* 727–738.

Kurdek, L. A. (1993). Predicting marital dissolution: A five-year prospective longitudinal study of newlywed couples. *Journal of Personality and Social Psychology, 64,* 221–242.

Kurdek, L. A., & Schmitt, J. P. (1985/1986). Relationship quality of gay men in closed or open relationships. *Journal of Homosexuality, 12,* 85–99.

Kurdek, L. A., & Schmitt, J. P. (1987). Partner homogamy in married, heterosexual cohabiting, gay, and lesbian couples. *The Journal of Sex Research, 23,* 212–232.

Kyes, K. B. (1995). Sexuality and sexual orientation: Adjustments to aging. In L. Diamont & R. D. McAnulty (Eds.), *The psychology of sexual orientation, behavior, and identity* (pp. 457–470). Westport, CT: Greenwood Press.

Laan, E., & Everaerd, W. (1995). Determinants of female sexual arousal: Psychophysiology theory and data. *Annual Review of Sex Research, 5,* 32–76.

Langevin, R., Paitich, D. P., Ramsay, G., Anderson, C., Kamrad, J., Pope, S., Geller, G., Pearl, L., & Newman, S. (1979). Experimental studies of the etiology of genital exhibitionism. *Archives of Sexual Behavior, 8,* 307–331.

Langevin, R., Paitich, D. P., & Russon, A. E. (1985). Voyeurism: Does it predict sexual aggression or violence in general? In R. Langevin (Ed.), *Erotic preference, gender identity, and aggression in men* (pp. 77–98). Hillsdale, NJ: Erlbaum.

Langlois, J. H., & Casey, R. J. (1984, April). *Baby beautiful: The relationship between infant physical attractiveness and maternal behavior.* Paper presented at the Fourth Biennial International Conference on Infant Studies, New York, NY.

Langlois, J. H., & Roggman, L. A. (1990). Attractive faces are only average. *Psychological Science, 1,* 115–121.

Langlois, J. H., Roggman, L. A., Casey, R. J., Ritter, J. M., Rieser-Danner, L. A., & Jenkins, V. Y. (1987). Infant preferences for attractive faces: Rudiments of a stereotype? *Developmental Psychology,*

Laughlin, C. D., Jr., & Allgeier, E. R. (1979). *Ethnography of the So of northeastern Uganda.* New Haven: Human Relations Area Files.

Laumann, E. O., Gagnon, J. H., Michael, R. T., & Michaels, S. (1994). *The social organization of sexuality: Sexual practices in the United States.* Chicago: University of Chicago Press.

Laws, D. R., & Marshall, W. L. (1991). Masturbatory reconditioning with sexual deviates: An evaluative review. *Advances in Behavior, Research, and Therapy, 13,* 13–25.

Lawson, A. (1988). *Adultery: An analysis of love and betrayal.* New York: Basic Books.

Lazarus, A. A. (1989). Dyspareunia: A multimodel psychotherapeutic perspective. In S. R. Leiblum & R. C. Rosen (Eds.), *Principles and practices of sex therapy* (2nd ed., pp. 89–112). New York: Guilford.

Legality, morality of abortion. (1995). *Gallup Poll Monthly,* no. 354, 30–31.

Leiblum, S. R. (1993). The impact of fertility on sexual and marital satisfaction. *Annual Review of Sex Research, 4,* 99–120.

Leiblum, S. R., Pervin, L. A., & Campbell, E. H. (1989). The treatment of vaginismus: Success and failure. In S. R. Leiblum & R. C. Rosen (Eds.), *Principles and practice of sex therapy* (2nd ed., pp. 113–138). New York: Guilford.

Leiblum, S. R., & Rosen, R. C. (1989). Introduction: Sex therapy in the age of AIDS. In S. R. Leiblum & R. C. Rosen (Eds.), *Principles and practice of sex therapy* (2nd ed., pp. 1–16). New York: Guilford.

Leigh, B. C. (1989). Reasons for having and avoiding sex: Gender, sexual orientation, and relationship to sexual behavior. *The Journal of Sex Research, 26,* 199–209.

Leitenberg, H., Detzer, M. J., & Srebnik, D. (1993). Gender differences in masturbation and the relationship of masturbation experience in preadolescence and/or early adolescence in sexual behavior and sexual adjustment in young adulthood. *Archives of Sexual Behavior, 22,* 87–98.

Leitenberg, H., Greenwald, E., & Tarran, M. (1989). The relationship between sexual activity among children during preadolescence and/or early adolescence and sexual behavior and sexual adjustment in young adulthood. *Archives of Sexual Behavior, 18,* 299–313.

Letourneau, E., & O'Donohue, W. (1993). Sexual desire disorders. In W. O'Donahue & J. H. Geer (Eds.), *Handbook of sexual dysfunctions: Assessment and treatment* (pp. 53–81). Boston: Allyn & Bacon.

LeVay, S. (1991). A difference in hypothalmic structure between heterosexual and homosexual men. *Science, 253,* 1034–1037.

LeVay, S. (1993). *The sexual brain.* Cambridge, MA: MIT Press.

LeVay, S. (1996). *Queer science: The use and abuse of research into homosexuality.* Cambridge, MA: MIT Press.

Lever, J., Kanouse, D. E., Rogers, W. H., Carson, S., & Hertz, R. (1992). Behavior patterns and sexual identity of gay males. *The Journal of Sex Research, 29,* 141–167.

Levin, R. J. (1992). The mechanisms of human female sexual arousal. *Annual Review of Sex Research, 3,* 1–48.

Levin, S. M., & Stava, L. (1987). Personality characteristics of sex offenders: A review. *Archives of Sexual Behavior, 16,* 57–79.

Levine, M. P., & Troiden, R. R. (1988). The myth of sexual compulsivity. *The Journal of Sex Research, 25,* 347–363.

Levitan, M. (1988). *Textbook of human genetics.* New York: Oxford University Press.

Lewes, K. (1988). *The psychoanalytic theory of male homosexuality.* New York: Simon & Schuster.

Lewes, K. (1995). Psychoanalysis and male homosexuality. In L. Diamont & R. D. McAnulty (Eds.), *The psychology of sexual orienta-tion, behavior, and identity* (pp. 140–120). Westport, CT: Greenwood Press.

Lewis, R. J., & Janda, L. H. (1988). The relationship between adult sexual adjustment and childhood experiences regarding nudity, sleeping in parental bed, and parental attitudes toward sexuality. *Archives of Sexual Behavior, 17,* 349–362.

Lief, H. I, & Hubschman, L. (1993). Orgasm in the postoperative transsexual. *Archives of Sexual Behavior, 22,* 145–155.

Lifson, A. R. (1988) Do alternate modes for transmission of human immunodeficiency virus exist? *Journal of the American Medical Association, 259,* 1353–1356.

Lifson, A. R., Darrow, W. W., Hessol, N. A., O'Malley, P. M., Barnhart, J. L., Jaffer, H. W., & Rutherford, G. W. (1990). Kaposi's sarcoma in a cohort of homosexual and bisexual men. *American Journal of Epidemiology, 131,* 221–231.

Lightfoot-Klein, H. (1989). The sexual experience and marital adjustment of genitally circumcised and infibulated females in the Sudan. *The Journal of Sex Research, 26,* 375–392.

Linz, D. (1989). Exposure to sexually explicit materials and attitudes toward rape: A comparison of study results. *The Journal of Sex Research, 26,* 50–84.

Lish, J. D., Meyer-Bahlburg, H. F. L., Ehrhardt, A. A., Travis, B. G., & Veridian, N. P. (1992). Prenatal exposure to diethylstilbestrol (DES): Childhood play behavior and adult gender-role behavior in women. *Archives of Sexual Behavior, 21,* 423–441.

Long, G. T., & Sultan, F. E. (1987). Contributions from social psychology. In L. Diamont (Ed.), *Male and female homosexuality: Psychological approaches* (pp. 221–236). Washington, DC: Hemisphere.

Lonsway, K. A. (1996). Preventing acquaintance rape through education: What do we know? *Psychology of Women Quarterly, 20,* 229–265.

Lopez, P. A., & George, W. H. (1995). Men's enjoyment of explicit erotica: Effects of person-specific attitudes and gender-specific norms. *The Journal of Sex Research, 32,* 275–288.

LoPiccolo, J., & Friedman, J. M. (1988). Broad spectrum treatment of low sexual desire: Integration of cognitive, behavioral, and systemic therapy. In S. R. Leiblum & R. C. Rosen (Eds.), *Sexual desire disorders* (pp. 107–144). New York: Guilford.

LoPiccolo, J., Heiman, J. R., Hogan, D. R., & Roberts, C. W. (1985). Effectiveness of single therapists versus cotherapy teams in sex therapy. *Journal of Consulting and Clinical Psychology, 53,* 287–294.

LoPiccolo, J., & Lobitz, C. (1972). The role of masturbation in the treatment of orgasmic dysfunction. *Archives of Sexual Behavior, 2,* 163–171.

LoPiccolo, J., & Stock, W. E. (1986). Treatment of sexual dysfunction. *Journal of Consulting and Clinical Psychology, 54,* 158–167.

Lottes, I. L. (1993). Nontraditional gender roles and the sexual experience of heterosexual college students. *Sex Roles, 29,* 645–669.

Lowry, D. T., & Shidler, J. A. (1993). Prime time TV portrayals of sex, "safe" sex, and AIDS: A longitudinal analysis. *Journalism Quarterly, 70,* 628–637.

Luckenbill, D. F. (1985). Entering male prostitution. *Urban Life, 14,* 131–153.

Lukusa, T., Fryns, J. P., & van den Berghe, T. (1992). The role of the Y-chromosome in sex determination. *Genetic Counseling, 3,* 1–11.

Lunde, I., Larsen, K. L., Fog, E., & Garde, K. (1991). Sexual desire, orgasm, and fantasies: A study of 625 Danish women born in 1910, 1936, and 1958. *Journal of Sex Education and Therapy, 17,* 111–115.

Luria, Z., & Meade, R. G. (1984). Sexuality and the middle-aged woman. In G. Baruch & J. Brooks-Gunn (Eds.), *Women in midlife* (pp. 391–397). New York: Plenum.

MacDonald, J. M. (1973). *Indecent exposure.* Springfield, IL: Thomas.

Maguire, K., & Pastore, A. L. (1995). *Sourcebook of criminal justice statistics, 1994.* U.S. Department of Justice, Bureau of Justice Statistics, Washington, DC: GPO.

Maguire, K., Pastore, A. L., & Flanagan, T. J. (1992). *Sourcebook of criminal justice statistics—1992.* Washington, DC: GPO.

Mahoney, E. R., Shively, M. D., & Traw, M. (1986). Sexual coercion and assault: Male socialization and female risk. *Sexual Coercion and Assault, 1,* 2–8.

Major, B. (1993). Gender, entitlement, and the distribution of family labor. *Journal of Social Issues, 49* (3), 141–159.

Major, B., & Cozzarelli, C. (1992). Psychosocial predictors of adjustment to abortion. *Journal of Social Issues, 48* (3), 121–142.

Malamuth, N. M. (1981). Rape proclivity among males. *Journal of Social Issues, 37* (4), 138–157.

Malamuth, N. M. (1984). Aggression against women: Cultural and individual causes. In N. M. Malamuth & E. Donnerstein (Eds.), *Pornography and sexual aggression* (pp. 19–52). Orlando, FL: Academic Press.

Malamuth, N. M. (1996). The confluence model of sexual aggression: Feminist and evolutionary perspectives. In D. M. Buss & N. M. Malamuth (Eds.), *Sex, power, conflict: Evolutionary and feminist perspectives* (pp. 269–295). New York: Oxford University Press.

Malamuth, N. M., & Check, J. V. P. (1983). Sexual arousal to rape depictions: Individual differences. *Journal of Abnormal Psychology, 92,* 55–67.

Malamuth, N. M., & Check, J. V. P. (1984). Debriefing effectiveness following exposure to pornographic rape depictions. *The Journal of Sex Research, 20,* 1–13.

Malamuth, N. M., & Donnerstein, E. (1984). *Pornography and sexual aggression.* Orlando, FL: Academic Press.

Manderson, L. (1995). The pursuit of pleasure and the sale of sex. In P. R. Abramson & S. D. Pinkerton (Eds.), *Sexual nature/sexual culture* (pp. 305–329). Chicago: University of Chicago Press.

Mann, J. (1977). Retarded ejaculation and treatment. In R. Gemme & C. Wheeler (Eds.), *Progress in sexology* (pp. 197–204). New York: Plenum.

Marshall, D. (1971). Sexual behavior on Mangaia. In D. Marshall & R. Suggs (Eds.), *Human sexual behavior: Variations in the ethnographic spectrum.* (pp. 103–162). Englewood Cliffs, NJ: Prentice-Hall.

Marshall, W. L., Eccles, A., & Barbaree, H. E. (1991). The treatment of exhibitionists: A focus on sexual deviance versus cognitive and relationship features. *Behavior Research and Therapy, 29,* 129–135.

Marsiglio, W. (1987). Adolescent fathers in the United States: Their initial living arrangements, marital experience, and educational outcomes. *Family Planning Perspectives, 19,* 240–251.

Marsiglio, W., & Mott, F. L. (1986). The impact of sex education on sexual activity, contraceptive use, and premarital pregnancy among American teenagers. *Family Planning Perspectives, 18,* 151–162.

Martin, T. C., & Bumpass, L. L. (1989). Recent trends in marital disruption. *Demography, 26,* 37–51.

Maslow, A. H. (1962). *Toward a psychology of being.* Princeton: Van Nostrand.

Masters, W. H., & Johnson, V. E. (1966). *Human sexual response.* Boston: Little, Brown.

Masters, W. H., & Johnson, V. E. (1970). *Human sexual inadequacy.* Boston: Little, Brown.

Masters, W. H., & Johnson, V. E. (1979). *Homosexuality in perspective.* Boston: Little, Brown.

Mattson, S., & Smith, J. E. (1993). *Core curriculum for maternal-newborn nursing.* Philadelphia: Saunders.

Mauldon, J., & Luker, K. (1996). The effects of contraceptive education on method use at first intercourse. *Family Planning Perspectives, 28,* 19–24, 41.

Mays, V. M., & Cochran, S. D. (1988). Issues in the perception of AIDS risk and risk reduction activities by black and Hispanic/Latino women. *American Psychologist, 43,* 949–957.

McAnulty, R. D. (1995). The paraphilias: Classification and theory. In L. Diamont & R. D. McAnulty (Eds.), *The psychology of sexual orientation, behavior, and identity* (pp. 239–255). Westport, CT: Greenwood Press.

McCabe, M. P., & Delaney, S. M. (1992). An evaluation of therapeutic programs for the treatment of secondary inorgasmia in women. *Archives of Sexual Behavior, 21,* 69–89.

McCaghy, C. H. (1997, March). *A preliminary social history of stripping in America.* Presented at the Annual Meeting of the Popular Culture Association, San Antonio, TX.

McCahill, T. W, Meyer, L. C., & Fischman, A. M. (1979). *The aftermath of rape.* Lexington, MA: Lexington Books.

McCarthy, B. W. (1993). Relapse prevention strategies and techniques in sex therapy. *Journal of Sex and Marital Therapy, 19,* 142–146.

McCarthy, J., & McMillan, S. (1990). Patient/partner satisfaction with penile implant surgery. *Journal of Sex Education and Therapy, 16,* 25–37.

McCauley, E. A., & Ehrhardt, A. A. (1977). Role expectations and definitions: A comparison of female transsexuals and lesbians. *Journal of Homosexuality, 3,* 137–147.

McCauley, E. A., & Ehrhardt, A. A. (1980). Sexual behavior in female transsexuals and lesbians. *The Journal of Sex Research, 16,* 202–211.

McClintock, M. K. (1971). Menstrual synchrony and suppression. *Nature, 299,* 244–245.

McCormick, N. B. (1979). Come-ons and put-offs: Unmarried students' strategies for having and avoiding sexual intercourse. *Psychology of Women Quarterly, 4,* 194–211.

McCormick, N. B. (1994). *Sexual salvation.* Westport, CT: Greenwood.

McCormick, N. B., & Jones, A. J. (1989). Gender differences in nonverbal flirtation. *Journal of Sex Education and Therapy, 15,* 271–282.

McKirnan, D. J., Stokes, J. P., Doll, L., & Burzette, R. G. (1995). Bisexually active men: Social characteristics and sexual behavior. *The Journal of Sex Research, 32,* 65–76.

McKusick, V. A., & Amberger, J. A. (1993). The morbid anatomy of the human genome: Chromosomal location of the mutations causing disease. *Journal of Medical Genetics, 30,* 1–26.

McWhirter, D. P, & Mattison, A. M. (1984). *The male couple: How relationships develop.* Englewood Cliffs, NJ: Prentice-Hall.

Mead, M. (1935). *Sex and temperament in three primitive societies.* New York: Morrow.

Meischke, H. (1995). Implicit sexual portrayals in the movies: Interpretations of young women. *The Journal of Sex Research, 32,* 29–36.

Melnick, S. L., Jeffrey, W. R., Burke, G. L., Gilbertson, D. T., Perkins, L. L., Sidney, S., McCreath, H. E., Wagenknecht, L. E., & Hulley, S. B. (1993). Changes in sexual behavior by young urban heterosexual adults in response to the AIDS epidemic. *Public Health Reports, 108,* 582–588.

Meuwissen, I., & Over, R. (1992). Sexual arousal across phases of the human menstrual cycle. *Archives of Sexual Behavior, 21,* 101–119.

Meyer, J. K., & Reter, D. J. (1979). Sex reassignment. *Archives of General Psychiatry, 36,* 1010–1015.

Mickler, S. E. (1993). Perceptions of vulnerability: Impact on AIDS-preventive behavior among college adolescents. *AIDS Education and Prevention, 5,* 43–53.

Milic, J. H., & Crowne, D. P. (1986). Recalled parent-child relations and need for approval of homosexual and heterosexual men. *Archives of Sexual Behavior, 15,* 239–246.

Miller, B. C., Christopherson, C. R., & King, P. K. (1993). Sexual behavior in adolescence. In T. S. Gullotta, G. R. Adams, & R. Montemayor (Eds.), *Adolescent sexuality* (pp. 57–76). Newbury Park, CA: Sage.

Miller, B. C., & Heaton, J. B. (1991). Age at first sexual intercourse and the timing of marriage and childbirth. *Journal of Marriage and the Family, 53,* 719–732.

Miller, J., & Schwartz, M. D. (1995). Rape myths and violence against street prostitutes. *Deviant Behavior: An Interdisciplinary Journal, 16,* 1–23.

Miller, M. V. (1977). Intimate terrorism. *Psychology Today, 10,* 79–80, 82.

Miller, W. B. (1986). Why some women fail to use their contraceptive method: A psychological investigation. *Family Planning Perspectives, 18,* 27–32.

Miner, H. (1956). Body ritual among the Nacirema. *American Anthropologist, 58,* 503–507.

Minturn, L. (1995). Infanticide. In D. Levinson (Ed.), *Encyclopedia of marriage and the family* (Vol. 2, pp. 378–382). New York: Simon & Schuster Macmillan.

Misovich, S. J., Fisher, J. D., & Fisher, W. A. (1996). The perceived AIDS preventive utility of knowing one's sexual partner well: A public health dictum and individuals' risky sexual behavior. *The Canadian Journal of Human Sexuality, 5,* 83–90.

Monckton, C. (1987, January). AIDS: A British view. *American Spectator,* 29–32.

Money, J. (1976). Childhood: The last frontier of sex research. *The Sciences, 16,* 12–27.

Money, J. (1988). *Gay, straight, and in-between: The sexology of erotic orientation.* New York: Oxford University Press.

Money, J. (1991). *Genes, genitals, hormones, and gender: Selected readings in sexology.* Amsterdam, Holland: Global Academic.

Money, J., & Ehrhardt, A. A. (1972). *Man and woman, boy and girl.* Baltimore, MD: Johns Hopkins University Press.

Money, J., & Tucker, P. (1975). *Sexual signatures: On being a man or woman.* Boston: Little, Brown.

Monsour, M., Harris, B., Kurzweil, N., & Beard, C. (1994). Challenges confronting cross-sex friendships: "Much ado about nothing?" *Sex Roles, 31,* 55–77.

Montagu, A. (1969). *Sex, man, and society.* New York: Tower.

Moore, K. L. (1989). *Before we are born* (3rd ed.). Philadelphia: Saunders.

Moore, M. M. (1985). Nonverbal courtship patterns in women: Context and consequences. *Ethology and Sociobiology, 6,* 201–212.

Moore, M. M. (1995). Courtship signaling and adolescents: "Girls just wanna have fun"? *The Journal of Sex Research, 32,* 319–328.

Morokoff, P. J., & Gillilland, R. (1993). Stress, sexual functioning, and marital satisfaction. *The Journal of Sex Research, 30,* 43–53.

Morris, N. M., & Udry, J. R. (1978). Pheromonal influences on human sexual behavior: An experiential search. *Journal of Biosocial Science, 10,* 147–159.

Morse, E. V., Simon, P. M., Balson, P. M., & Osofsky, H. J. (1992). Sexual behavior patterns of customers of male street prostitutes. *Archives of Sexual Behavior, 21,* 347–357.

Mosher, D. L. (1966). The development and multitrait-multimethod matrix analysis of three measures of three aspects of guilt. *Journal of Consulting and Clinical Psychology, 30,* 25–29.

Mosher, D. L. (1988). Revised Mosher guilt inventory. In C. M. Davis,, W. L. Yarber, & S. Davis (Eds.), *Sexuality-related measures: A compendium* (pp. 152–155). Lake Mills, IA: Authors.

Mosher, D. L., & Anderson, R. D. (1986). Macho personality, sexual aggression, and reactions to guided imagery of realistic rape. *Journal of Research in Personality, 20,* 77–94.

Mosher, D. L., & Sirkin, M. (1984). Measuring a macho personality constellation. *Journal of Research in Personality, 18,* 150–163.

Mosher, W. D., & Bachrach, C. A. (1996). Understanding U.S. fertility: Continuity and change in the National Survey of Family Growth, 1988–1995. *Family Planning Perspectives, 28,* 4–12.

Moskowitz, J. T., Binson, D., & Catania, J. A. (1997). The association between Magic Johnson's HIV serostatus disclosure and condom use in at-risk respondents. *The Journal of Sex Research, 34,* 154–160.

Mott, F. L., Fondell, M. M., Hu, P. N., Kowaleski-Jones, L., & Menaghan, E. G. (1996). The determinants of first sex by age 14 in a high-risk adolescent population. *Family Planning Perspectives, 28,* 13–18.

Muehlenhard, C. L. (1988). "Nice women" don't say yes and "real men" don't say no: How miscommunication and the double standard can cause sexual problems. *Women and Therapy, 7,* 95–108.

Muehlenhard, C. L., Andrews, S. L., & Beal, G. K. (1996). Beyond "just saying no": Dealing with men's unwanted sexual advances in heterosexual dating contexts. *Journal of Psychology and Human Sexuality, 8,* 141–168.

Muehlenhard, C. L., Danoff-Burg, S., & Powch, I. G. (1996). Is rape sex or violence? Conceptual issues and implications. In D. M. Buss & N. M. Malamuth (Eds.), *Sex, power, conflict: Evolutionary and feminist perspectives* (pp. 119–137). New York: Oxford University Press.

Muehlenhard, C. L., & Hollabaugh, L. C. (1988). Do women sometimes say no when they mean yes? The prevalence and correlates of women's token resistance to sex. *Journal of Personality and Social Psychology, 54,* 872–879.

Munroe, R. L., & Munroe, R. H. (1977). Male transvestism and subsistence economy. *Journal of Social Psychology, 103,* 307–308.

Munroe, R. L., Whiting, J. W. M., & Haley, D. J. (1969). Institutionalized male transvestism and sex distinctions. *American Anthropologist, 71,* 87–91.

Murnen, S. K., & Byrne, D. (1991). Hyperfemininity: Measurement and initial validation of the construct. *The Journal of Sex Research, 28,* 479–489.

Mynatt, C. R., & Allgeier, E. R. (1990). Risk factors, self-attributions, and adjustment problems among victims of sexual coercion. *Journal of Applied Social Psychology, 20,* 130–153.

Neidigh, L., & Krop, H. (1992). Cognitive distortions among child sexual offenders. *Journal of Sex Education and Therapy, 18,* 208–215.

Neinstein, L., Goldering, J., & Carpenter, F. (1984). Nonsexual transmission of sexually transmitted diseases: An infrequent occurrence. *Pediatrics, 74,* 67–76.

Neugarten, B. L., & Gutmann, D. L. (1968). Age-sex roles and personality in middle age: A thematic apperception study. *Psychological Monographs, 72* (17, whole no. 470).

Newcomb, M. D. (1985). The role of perceived relative parent personality in the development of heterosexuals, homosexuals, and transvestites. *Archives of Sexual Behavior, 14,* 147–164.

Newcomb, M. D. (1986). Sexual behavior of cohabitors: A comparison of three independent samples. *The Journal of Sex Research, 22,* 492–513.

Newman, G., & Nichols, C. R. (1960). Sexual activities and attitudes in older persons. *Journal of the American Medical Association, 173,* 33–35.

Niku, S. D., Stock, J. A., & Kaplan, G. W. (1995). Neonatal circumcision. *Common Problems in Pediatric Urology, 21,* 57–65.

Norton, A. J., & Moorman, J. E. (1987). Current trends in marriage and divorce among American women. *Journal of Marriage and the Family, 49,* 3–14.

Novak, M. A., & Harlow, H. F. (1975). Social recovery of monkeys isolated for the first year of life. *Developmental Psychology, 11,* 453–465.

Okami, P. (1990). Sociopolitical biases in the contemporary scientific literature on adult human sexual behavior with children and adolescents. In J. Feierman (Ed.), *Pedophilia: Bio-social dimensions* (pp. 91–121). New York: Springer-Verlag.

Okami, P. (1995). Childhood exposure to nudity, parent-child co-sleeping, and "primal scenes": A review of clinical opinion and empirical evidence. *The Journal of Sex Research, 32,* 51–64.

Okami, P., & Goldberg, A. (1992). Personality correlates of pedophilia: Are they reliable indicators? *The Journal of Sex Research, 29,* 297–328.

Olds, J., & Milner, P. M. (1954). Positive reinforcement produced by electrical stimulation of the septal area and other regions of the rat brain. *Journal of Comparative and Physiological Psychology, 47,* 419–427.

Olds, S. B., London, M. L., & Ladewig, P. W. (1992). *Maternal-newborn nursing* (4th ed.). Redwood City, CA: Addison-Wesley Nursing.

Oliver, M. B., & Hyde, J. S. (1993). Gender differences in sexuality: A meta-analysis. *Psychological Bulletin, 114,* 29–51.

Olson, D. H., & DeFrain, J. (1994). *Marriage and the family: Diversity and strengths.* Mountain View, CA: Mayfield.

O'Sullivan, L. F., & Byers, E. S. (1992). Incorporating the roles of initiation and restriction in sexual dating interactions. *The Journal of Sex Research, 29,* 435–446.

O'Sullivan, L. F., & Byers, E. S. (1993). Eroding stereotypes: College women's attempts to influence reluctant male sexual partners. *The Journal of Sex Research, 30,* 270–282.

Otis, M. D., & Skinner, W. F. (1996). The prevalence of victimization and its effect on mental well-being among lesbian and gay people. *Journal of Homosexuality, 30,* 93–121.

Oyama, S. (1991). Bodies and minds: Dualism in evolutionary theory. *Journal of Social Issues, 47* (3), 27–42.

Padgett, V. R., Brislin-Slutz, J. A., & Neal, J. A. (1989). Pornography, erotica, and attitudes toward women: The effects of repeated exposure. *The Journal of Sex Research, 26,* 479–491.

Paige, K. E. (1978). The ritual of circumcision. *Human Nature, 1,* 40–48.

Parker, R. (1991). *Bodies, pleasures, and passions: Sexual culture in contemporary Brazil.* Boston: Beacon.

Pauly, I. B. (1974). Female transsexualism: Part II. *Archives of Sexual Behavior, 3,* 509–526.

Pauly, I. B. (1985). Gender identity disorders. In M. Farber (Ed.), *Human sexuality: Psychosexual effects of disease* (pp. 295–316). New York: Macmillan.

Pauly, I. B., & Edgerton, M. T. (1986). The gender identity movement: A growing surgical-psychiatric liaison. *Archives of Sexual Behavior, 15,* 315–330.

Pavelka, M. S. M. (1995). Sexual nature: What can we learn from a cross-species perspective? In P. R. Abramson & S. D. Pinkerton (Eds.), *Sexual nature/sexual culture* (pp. 17–36). Chicago: University of Chicago Press.

Peele, S., & Brodsky, A. (1974). Love can be an addiction. *Psychology Today, 8,* 22–26.

Peele, S., & Brodsky, A. (1975). *Love and addiction.* New York: Maplinger.

Pelletier, L. A., & Herold, E. S. (1988). The relationship of age, sex guilt, and sexual experience with female sexual fantasies. *The Journal of Sex Research, 24,* 250–256.

Pendergrast, M. (1995). *Victims of memory: Incest accusations and shattered lives.* Hinesburg, VT: Upper Access.

Peplau, L. A., & Gordon, S. L. (1983). The intimate relationships of lesbians and gay men. In E. R. Allgeier & N. B. McCormick (Eds.), *Changing boundaries: Gender roles and sexual behavior* (pp. 226–244). Palo Alto, CA: Mayfield.

Peplau, L. A., Hill, C. T., & Rubin, Z. (1993). Sex role attitudes in dating and marriage: A fifteen-year follow-up of the Boston couples study. *Journal of Social Issues, 49* (3), 31–52.

Peplau, L. A., Rubin, Z., & Hill, C. T. (1977). Sexual intimacy in dating relationships. *Journal of Social Issues, 33* (2), 86–109.

Perlow, D. L., & Perlow, J. S. (1983). *Herpes: Coping with the new epidemic.* Englewood Cliffs, NJ: Prentice-Hall.

Perper, T. (1985). *Sex signals: The biology of love.* Philadelphia: ISI Press.

Perry, J. D., & Whipple, B. (1982). Multiple components of female orgasm. In B. Graber (Ed.), *Circumvaginal musculature and sexual function* (pp. 101–114). New York: Karger.

Pfäfflin, F. (1992). Regrets after sex reassignment surgery. *Journal of Psychology and Human Sexuality, 5,* 69–85.

Pfeiffer, E., Verwoerdt, A., & Wang, H. (1968). Sexual behavior in aged men and women. *Archives of General Psychiatry, 19,* 756–758.

Phillips, G., & Over, R. (1992). Adult sexual orientation in relation to memories of childhood gender-conforming and gender-nonconforming behaviors. *Archives of Sexual Behavior, 21,* 543–558.

Phillips, G., & Over, R. (1995). Differences between heterosexual, bisexual, and lesbian women in recalled childhood experiences. *Archives of Sexual Behavior, 24,* 1–20.

Pithers, W. D. (1993). Treatment of rapists: Reinterpretation of early outcome data and exploratory constructs to chance therapeutic efficacy. In G. C. Hall, R. Hirschman, J. R. Graham, & M. S. Zaragosa (Eds.), *Sexual aggression: Issues in etiology, assessment, and treatment* (pp. 167–196). Bristol, PA: Taylor & Francis.

Plaut, S. M., & Foster, B. H. (1986). Roles of the health professional in cases involving sexual exploitation of patients. In A. W. Burgess & C. R. Hartman (Eds.), *Sexual exploitation of patients by health professionals* (pp. 5–25). New York: Praeger.

Pleck, J. (1983). Husband's paid work and family roles. In H. Lopata & J. Pleck (Eds.), *Research in the interweave of social roles, Vol. 3. Families and jobs* (pp. 251–333). Greenwich, CT: JAI Press.

Pocket Criminal Code. (1987). Toronto: Carswell.

Pomeroy, W. (1972). *Dr. Kinsey and the Institute for Sex Research.* New York: Nelson.

Pope, K. S., & Bouhoutsos, J. C. (1987). *Sexual intimacy between therapists and patients.* New York: Praeger.

Pope, K. S., Keith-Spiegel, P., & Tabachnick, B. G. (1986). Sexual attraction to clients: The human therapist and the (sometimes) inhuman training system. *American Psychologist, 41,* 147–158.

Possage, J. C., & Allgeier, E. R. (1992, June). *The relationship between recidivism and child sexual misuse from a learned helplessness perspective.* Paper presented at The Annual Meeting of the Midcontinent Region of The Society for the Scientific Study of Sex, Big Rapids, MI.

Potter, G. (1989). The retail pornography industry and the organization of vice. *Deviant Behavior, 10,* 233–251.

Potterat, J. J., Woodhouse, D. E., Muth, J. B., & Muth, S. Q. (1990). Estimating the prevalence and career longevity of prostitute women. *The Journal of Sex Research, 27,* 233–243.

Powell-Griner, E. (1987). Induce terminations of pregnancy: Reporting states, 1984. *Monthly Vital Statistics Report, 36,* Supplement 2.

Pratte, T. (1993). A comparative study of attitudes toward homosexuality: 1986–1991. *Journal of Homosexuality, 26,* 77–83.

Prendergast, W. E. (1994). Prisons: Sex in prison. In V. L. Bullough & B. Bullough (Eds.), *Human sexuality: An encyclopedia* (pp. 488–493). New York: Garland.

Prescott, J. W. (1975, April). Body pleasure and the origins of violence. *The Futurist,* 64–74.

Presser, H. B. (1980). *The social and demographic consequences of teenage childbearing for urban women.* Washington, D.C.: National Technical Information Service.

Preti, G., Cutler, W. B., Garcia, C. R., Huggins, G. R., & Lawley, H. J (1986). Human axillary secretions influence women's menstrual cycles: The role of donor extracts in females. *Hormones and Behavior, 20,* 474–482.

Prince, V. (1977, September). *Sexual identity versus general identity: The real confusion.* Paper presented at the Meeting of the American Psychological Association, Toronto, Canada.

Prins, K. S., Buunk, B. P., & Van Yperen, N. W. (1993). Equity, normative disapproval, and extramarital relationships. *Journal of Social and Personal Relationships, 10,* 39–53.

Pryor, J. B. (1994). Sexual cognition processes in men high in the likelihood to sexually harass. *Personality and Social Psychology Bulletin, 20,* 163–169.

Purifoy, F. E., Grodsky, A., & Giambra, L. M. (1992). The relationship of sexual daydreaming to sexual activity, sexual drive, and sexual attitudes for women across the life-span. *Archives of Sexual Behavior, 21,* 369–385.

Quinsey, V. L., & Upfold, D. (1985). Rape completion and victim injury as a function of female resistance strategy. *Canadian Journal of Behavioural Science, 17,* 40–50.

Rainwater, L., & Weinstein, K. (1960). *And the poor get children.* Chicago: Quadrangle.

Rapaport, K., & Burkhart, B. R. (1984). Personality and attitudinal correlates of sexually coercive college males. *Journal of Abnormal Personality, 93,* 216–221.

Rates of Cesarean delivery—United States, 1993. (1995). *Morbidity and Mortality Weekly Reports, 44,* 303–307.

Read, J. S., & Klebanoff, M. A. for the Vaginal Infections and Prematurity Study Group. (1993). Sexual intercourse during pregnancy and preterm delivery: Effects of vaginal microorganisms. *American Journal of Obstetrics and Gynecology, 168,* 514–519.

Reamy, K. J., & White, S. E. (1987). Sexuality in the puerperium: A review. *Archives of Sexual Behavior, 16,* 165–186.

Redfield, R. R. & Burke, D. S. (1988). HIV infection: The clinical picture. *Scientific American, 259,* 90–98.

Reed, J. (1984). *From private vice to public virtue.* New York: Basic Books.

Reinisch, J. M., Ziemba-Davis, M., & Sanders, S. (1991). Hormonal contributions to sexually dimorphic behavioral development in humans. *Psychoneuroendocrinology, 16,* 213–278.

Reiss, I. L. (1986). *Journey into sexuality: An exploratory voyage.* Englewood Cliffs, NJ: Prentice-Hall.

Reiss, I. L., Anderson, R. E., & Sponaugle, G. C. (1980). A multivariate model of the determinants of extramarital sexual permissiveness. *Journal of Marriage and the Family, 42,* 395–411.

Riessman, C. K., & Gerstel, N. (1985). Marital dissolution and health: Do males or females have greater risk? *Social Science and Medicine, 20,* 617–635.

Rind, B. (1995). An analysis of human sexuality textbook coverage of the psychological correlates of adult-nonadult sex. *The Journal of Sex Research, 32,* 219–233.

Rind, B., & Tromovitch, P. (1997). A meta-analytic review of findings from national samples on psychological correlates of child sexual abuse. *The Journal of Sex Research, 34,* 237–255.

Robbins, J. M., & DeLamater, J. D. (1985). Support from significant others and loneliness following induced abortion. *Social Psychiatry, 20,* 92–99.

Robbins, M. B., & Jensen, G. G. (1978). Multiple orgasm in males. *The Journal of Sex Research, 14,* 21–26.

Robinson, J. (1987, September 12). Senators told of family's plight with AIDS. *Boston Globe,* p. 1.

Roche, J. P. (1986). Premarital sex: Attitudes and behavior by dating stage. *Adolescence, 21,* 107–121.

Roiphe, H., & Galenson, E. (1981). *Infantile origins of sexual identity.* New York: International Universities Press.

Roiphe, K. (1993). *The morning after: Sex, fear, and feminism on campus.* Boston: Little, Brown.

Roosa, M. W., & Christopher, F. S. (1990). Evaluation of an abstinence-only adolescent pregnancy prevention program: A replication. *Family Relations, 39,* 363–367.

Rosario, M., Meyer-Bahlburg, H. F. L., Hunter, J., Exner, T. M., Gwada, M., & Keller, A. M. (1996). The psychosexual development of urban lesbian, gay, and bisexual youth. *The Journal of Sex Research, 33,* 113–126.

Roscoe, B., Cavanaugh, L. E., & Kennedy, D. R. (1988). Dating infidelity: Behaviors, reasons, and consequences. *Adolescence, 23,* 35–43.

Rosen, R. C. (1991). Alcohol and drug effects on sexual response: Human experimental and clinical studies. *Annual Review of Sex Research, 2,* 119–179.

Rosen, R. C. (1996, June). *Pharmacological treatment of male erectile disorder: Palliative or panacea?* Paper presented at the Annual Meeting of the International Academy of Sex Research, Rotterdam, The Netherlands.

Rosen, R. C., & Ashton, A. K. (1993). Prosocial drugs: Empirical status of the "new aphrodisiacs." *Archives of Sexual Behavior, 22,* 521–543.

Rosenberg, H. M. et al. (1996). Births and deaths: United States, 1995. *Monthly Vital Statistics Report, 45* (3), Supplement 2.

Rosenberg, L., Palmer, J. R., Zauber, A. G., Warshaver, M. E., Strom, B. L., Harlap, S., & Shapiro, S. (1994). The relation of vasectomy to the risk of cancer. *American Journal of Epidemiology, 140,* 431–448.

Rosenbleet, C., & Pariente, B. (1973). The prostitution of the criminal law. *American Criminal Law Review, 11,* 373–427.

Ross, M. W., & Need, J. A. (1989). Effects of adequacy of gender reassignment surgery on psychological adjustment: A follow-up of fourteen male-to-female patients. *Archives of Sexual Behavior, 18,* 145–153.

Ross, M. W. (1980). Retrospective distortion in homosexual research. *Archives of Sexual Behavior, 9,* 523–531.

Rowland, D. L., Greenleaf, W. J., Dorfman, L. J., & Davidson, J. M. (1993). Aging and sexual function in men. *Archives of Sexual Behavior, 22,* 545–557.

Russell, D. E. H. (1984). *Sexual exploitation: Rape, child sexual abuse, and workplace harassment.* Beverly Hills, CA: Sage.

Russo, N. F., Horn, J. D., & Schwartz, R. (1992). U.S. abortion in context: Selected characteristics and motivations of women seeking abortions. *Journal of Social Issues, 48* (3), 183–202.

Rust, P. C. (1993a). "Coming out" in the age of social constructionism: Sexual identity formation among lesbian and bisexual women. *Gender and Society, 7,* 50–77.

Rust, P. C. (1993b). Neutralizing the political threat of the marginal woman: Lesbians' beliefs about bisexual women. *The Journal of Sex Research, 30,* 214–228.

Sacks, S. L. (1995). Genital HSV infection and treatment. *Clinical Management of Herpes Viruses.* IOS Press.

Saluter, A. F. (1992). Marital status and living arrangements: March 1992. *Current Population Reports,* Series P20–468.

Samson, M., Libert, F., Doranz, B. J. et al. (1996). Resistance to HIV-I infection in Caucasian individuals bearing mutant alleles of the CCR-5 chemokine receptor gene. *Nature, 382,* 722–725.

Sandfort, T. G. M. (1984). Sex in pedophiliac relationships: An empirical investigation among a non-representative group of boys. *The Journal of Sex Research, 20,* 123–142.

Savitz, L., & Rosen, L. (1988). The sexuality of prostitutes: Sexual enjoyment reported by "streetwalkers." *The Journal of Sex Research, 24,* 200–208.

Schiavi, R. C. (1994). Effect of chronic disease and medication on sexual functioning. In A. S. Rossi (Ed.), *Sexuality across the life course* (pp. 313–339). Chicago: University of Chicago Press.

Schlesselman, J. J. (1990). Oral contraception and breast cancer. *American Journal of Obstetrics & Gynecology, 163,* 1379–1387.

Schoen, E. J., Anderson, G., Bohon, C., Hinman, F., Poland, R., & Wakeman, E. M. (1989). Report of the task force on circumcision. *Pediatrics, 84,* 388–391.

Scholes, D., Daling, J. R., Stergachis, A. S., Weiss, N. S., Wang, S. P., & Grayston, J. T. (1993). Vaginal douching as a risk factor for acute pelvic inflammatory disease. *Obstetrics and Gynecology, 81,* 601–606.

Schott, R. L. (1995). The childhood and family dynamics of transvestites. *Archives of Sexual Behavior, 24,* 309–327.

Schreiner-Engel, P., & Schiavi, R. C. (1986). Lifetime psychopathology in individuals with low sexual desire. *Journal of Nervous and Mental Disease, 174,* 646–651.

Schreurs, K. M. G. (1993). Sexuality in lesbian couples: The importance of gender. *Annual Review of Sex Research, 4,* 49–66.

Schreurs, K. M. G., & Buunk, B. P. (1996). Closeness, autonomy, equity, and relationship satisfaction in lesbian couples. *Psychology of Women Quarterly, 20,* 577–592.

Schumacher, S., & Lloyd, C. W. (1981). Physiological and psychological factors in impotence. *The Journal of Sex Research, 17,* 40–53.

Schwab, J. J. (1982). Psychiatric aspects of infectious diseases. *Current Psychiatric Therapies, 21,* 225–239.

Schwanberg, S. L. (1993). Attitudes toward gay and lesbian woman: Instrumentation issues. *Journal of Homosexuality, 26,* 99–136.

Schwartz, S. (1973). Effects of sex guilt and sexual arousal on the retention of birth control information. *Journal of Consulting and Clinical Psychology, 41,* 61–64.

Scott, J. E., & Cuvelier, S. J. (1993). Violence and sexual violence in pornography: Is it really increasing? *Archives of Sexual Behavior, 22,* 357–371.

Sedney, M. A. (1985/1986). Growing more complex: Conceptions of sex roles across adulthood. *International Journal of Aging and Human Development, 22,* 15–29.

Segraves, K. A., Segraves, R. T., & Schoenberg, H. W. (1987). Use of sexual history to differentiate organic from psychogenic impotence. *Archives of Sexual Behavior, 16,* 125–137.

Segraves, K. B., & Segraves, R. T. (1991). Multiple phase sexual dysfunction. *Journal of Sex Education and Therapy, 17,* 153–156.

Segraves, R. T. (1988). Drugs and desire. In S. R. Leiblum & R. C. Rosen (Eds.), *Sexual desire disorders* (pp. 313–347). New York: Guilford.

Sell, R. L., Wells, J. A., & Wypij, D. (1995). The prevalence of homosexual behavior and attraction in the United States, the United Kingdom, and France: Results of national population-based samples. *Archives of Sexual Behavior, 24,* 235–248.

Sensibaugh, C. C., & Allgeier, E. R. (1996). Factors considered by Ohio juvenile court judges in juvenile bypass judgments: A policy-capturing approach. *Politics and the Life Sciences, 15,* 35–47.

Sensibaugh, C. C., Yarab, P. E., & Allgeier, E. R. (1996, May). *Back burner relationships: Another stop on the extradyadic continuum?* Paper presented at the Annual Meeting of The Society for the Scientific Study of Sexuality, Pittsburgh, PA.

Sevely, J. L., & Bennett, J. W. (1978). Concerning female ejaculation and the female prostate. *The Journal of Sex Research, 14,* 1–20.

Severn, J., Belch, G. E., & Belch, M. A. (1990). The effects of sexual and non-sexual advertising appeals and information level on cognitive processing and communication effectiveness. *Journal of Advertising, 19,* 14–22.

Shannon, T. W. (1913). *Self-knowledge and guide to sex instruction: Vital facts of life for all ages.* Marietta, OH: Multikin.

Shaver, P. R., & Hazan, C. (1993). Adult attachment: Theory and research. In W. Jones and D. Perlman (Eds.), *Advances in personal relationships* (Vol. 4, pp. 29–70). London: Kingsley.

Shaver, P. R., & Hazan, C. (1994). Attachment. In A. L. Weber & J. H. Harvey (Eds.), *Perspectives on close relationships* (pp. 110–130). Needham Heights, MA: Allyn & Bacon.

Shaver, P. R., Hazan, C., & Bradshaw, D. (1988). Love as attachment. In R. J. Sternberg & M. L. Barnes (Eds.), *The psychology of love* (pp. 68–99). New Haven: Yale University Press.

Sherfey, J. (1972). *The nature and evolution of female sexuality.* New York: Random House.

Shilts, R. (1987). *And the band played on: Politics, people, and the AIDS epidemic.* New York: St. Martin's.

Shilts, R. (1993). *Conduct unbecoming: Lesbians and gays in the military, Vietnam to the Persian Gulf.* New York: St. Martin's.

Shusterman, L. R. (1979). Predicting the psychological consequences of abortion. *Social Science and Medicine, 13,* 683–689.

Siegelman, M. (1972a). Adjustment of homosexual and heterosexual women. *British Journal of Psychiatry, 120,* 477–481.

Siegelman, M. (1972b). Adjustment of homosexuals and heterosexuals. *Archives of Sexual Behavior, 2,* 9–25.

Siegelman, M. (1987). Empirical input. In L. Diamant (Ed.), *Male and female homosexuality: Psychological approaches* (pp. 33–79). Washington, DC: Hemisphere.

Sikkema, K. J., Winett, R. A., & Lombard, D. N. (1995). Development and evaluation of an HIV-risk reduction program for female college students. *AIDS Education and Prevention, 7,* 145–159.

Silbert, M. H., & Pines, A. (1984). Pornography and sexual abuse of women. *Sex Roles, 10,* 857–868.

Silverman, D. (1976). Sexual harassment: Working women's dilemma. *Quest, 3,* 15–24.

Silverstein, L. B. (1996). Fathering is a feminist issue. *Psychology of Women Quarterly, 20,* 3–37.

Simon, P. M., Morse, E. V., Osofsky, H. J., Balson, P. M., & Gaumer, R. (1992). Psychological characteristics of a sample of male street prostitutes. *Archives of Sexual Behavior, 21,* 33–44.

Simon, W., & Gagnon, J. H. (1987). Sexual scripts: Permanence and change. *Archives of Sexual Behavior, 15,* 97–120.

Simpson, M., & Schill, T. (1977). Patrons of massage parlors: Some facts and figures. *Archives of Sexual Behavior, 6,* 521–525.

Singer, J., & Singer, I. (1978). Types of female orgasm. In J. LoPiccolo & L. LoPiccolo (Eds.), *Handbook of sex therapy* (pp. 175–186). New York: Plenum.

Singh, D. (1994). Is thin really beautiful and good? Relationship between waist-to-hip ratio (WHR) and female attractiveness. *Personality and Individual Differences, 16,* 123–132.

Smith, M. U., & Katner, H. P. (1995). Quasi-experimental evaluation of three AIDS prevention activities for maintaining knowledge, improving attitudes, and changing risk behaviors of high school seniors. *AIDS Education and Prevention, 7,* 391–402.

Smith, T. W. (1987). The polls—a review: The use of public opinion data by the attorney general's commission on pornography. *Public Opinion Quarterly, 51,* 249–267.

Smith, T. W. (1991). Adult sexual behavior in 1989: Number of partners, frequency of intercourse, and risk of AIDS. *Family Planning Perspectives, 23,* 102–107.

Somers, A. (1982). Sexual harassment in academe: Legal issues and definitions. *Journal of Social Issues, 38* (4), 23–32.

Sonne, J., Meyer, C. B., Borys, D., & Marshall, Y. (1985). Clients' reactions to sexual intimacy in therapy. *American Journal of Orthopsychiatry, 55,* 183–189.

Spector, I. P., & Carey, M. P. (1990). Incidence and prevalence of sexual dysfunctions: A critical review of the empirical literature. *Archives of Sexual Behavior, 19,* 389–408.

Spengler, A. (1977). Manifest sadomasochism of males: Results of an empirical study. *Archives of Sexual Behavior, 6,* 441–456.

Spitz, R. A. (1947). Hospitalism: A follow-up report. In D. Fenichel, P. Greenacre, & A. Freud (Eds.), *Psychoanalytic studies of the child* (Vol. 2, pp. 113–117). New York: International Universities Press.

Sprague, J., & Quadagno, D. (1989). Gender and sexual motivation: An exploration of two assumptions. *Journal of Psychology and Human Sexuality, 2,* 57–76.

Sprecher, S., Barbee, A., & Schwartz, P. (1995). "Was it good for you, too?": Gender differences in first sexual intercourse experiences. *The Journal of Sex Research, 32,* 3–15.

Sprecher, S., & Fehr, B. (1998). The dissolution of close relationships. In J. H. Harvey (Ed.), *Perspectives on loss: A sourcebook.* Washington, D.C.: Taylor and Francis.

Sprecher, S., & McKinney, K. (1994). Sexuality in close relationships. In A. L. Weber & J. H. Harvey (Eds.), *Perspectives on close relationships* (pp. 193–216). Boston: Allyn & Bacon.

Stein, M. L. (1974). *Lovers, friends, slaves . . . : The nine male sexual types, their psycho-sexual transactions with call girls.* New York: Berkley.

Steiner, B. W. (1985). The management of patients with gender disorders. In B. W. Steiner (Ed.), *Gender dysphoria: Development, research, management* (pp. 325–350). New York: Plenum.

Stern, M., & Karraker, K. H. (1989). Sex stereotyping in infants: A review of gender labeling. *Sex Roles, 20,* 501–522.

Sternberg, R. J. (1986). A triangular theory of love. *Psychological Review, 93,* 119–135.

Sternberg, R. J. (with C. Whitney). (1991). *Love the way you want it: Using your head in matters of the heart.*

Stevens, C. E., Taylor, P. E., Pindyck, J., Choo, Q. L., Bradley, D. W., Kuo, G., & Houghton, M. (1990). Epidemiology of hepatitis C virus: A preliminary study in volunteer blood donors. *Journal of the American Medical Association, 263,* 49–53.

Stevenson, M. R. (1998). Reconciling sexual orientation. In G. G. Brannigan, E. R. Allgeier, & A. R. Allgeier (Eds.), *The sex scientists* (pp. 100–112). Boston: Addison Wesley Longman.

Stevenson, M. R., & Gajarsky, W. M. (1991). Unwanted childhood sexual experiences relate to later revictimization and male perpetration. *Journal of Psychology and Human Sexuality, 4,* 57–70.

Stock, W. E. (1982, November). *The effect of violent pornography on women.* Paper presented at the National Meeting of the Society for The Scientific Study of Sex, San Francisco, CA.

Stokes, J. P., McKirnan, D. J., & Burzette, R. G. (1993). Sexual behavior, condom use, and stability of sexual orientation in bisexual men. *The Journal of Sex Research, 30,* 203–213.

Stokes, J. P., McKirnan, D. J., Doll, L., & Burzette, R. G. (1996). Female partners of bisexual men. *Psychology of Women Quarterly, 20,* 267–284.

Stoller, R. J. (1977). Sexual deviations. In F. A. Beach (Ed.), *Human sexuality in four perspectives* (pp. 190–214). Baltimore, MD: Johns Hopkins University Press.

Storms, M. D. (1980). Theories of sexual orientation. *Journal of Personality and Social Psychology, 38,* 783–792.

Storms, M. D. (1981). A theory of erotic orientation development. *Psychological Review, 88,* 340–353.

Strassberg, D. R., & Lowe, K. (1995). Volunteer bias in sexuality research. *Archives of Sexual Behavior, 24,* 369–382.

Strassberg, D. S., & Mahoney, J. M. (1988). Correlates of the contraceptive behavior of adolescents/young adults. *The Journal of Sex Research, 25,* 531–536.

Strassberg, D. S., Mahoney, J. M., Schangaard, M., & Hale, V. E. (1990). The role of anxiety in premature ejaculation: A psychophysiological model. *Archives of Sexual Behavior, 19,* 251–257.

Stroh, M. (1996, September 1). Girls who offer sex upset Japan. *Los Angeles Times,* p. 1.

Struckman-Johnson, C. (1988). Forced sex on dates: It happens to men, too. *The Journal of Sex Research, 24,* 234–241.

Struckman-Johnson, C. (1991). Male victims of acquaintance rape. In A. Parrot and L. Bechhover (Eds.), *Acquaintance rape—the hidden crime* (pp. 192–214). New York: Wiley.

Struckman-Johnson, C. (1998). Breaking into prison: The story of a study of sexual coercion of incarcerated men and women. In G. G. Brannigan, E. R. Allgeier, & A. R. Allgeier (Eds.), *The sex scientists* (pp. 171–184). New York: Addison Wesley Longman.

Struckman-Johnson, C., & Struckman-Johnson, D. (1994). Men pressured and forced into sexual experience. *Archives of Sexual Behavior, 23,* 93–114.

Struckman-Johnson, C., Struckman-Johnson, D., Rucker, L., Bumby, K., & Donaldson, S. (1996). Sexual coercion reported by men and women in prison. *The Journal of Sex Research, 33,* 67–76.

Stuart, F. M., Hammond, D. C., & Pett, M. A. (1987). Psychological characteristics of women with inhibited sexual desire. *Journal of Sex and Marital Therapy, 12,* 108–115.

Studer, M., & Thornton, A. (1987). Adolescent religiosity and contraceptive usage. *Journal of Marriage and the Family, 49,* 117–128.

Suomi, S. J., & Harlow, H. F. (1971). Abnormal social behavior in young monkeys. In J. Hellmuth (Ed.), *Exceptional infant: Studies in abnormality* (Vol. 2, pp. 483–529). New York: Brunner/Mazel.

Suomi, S. J., Harlow, H. F., & McKinney, W. T. (1972). Monkey psychiatrists. *American Journal of Psychiatry, 128,* 41–46.

Swaab, D. F., Gooren, L. J. G., & Hofman, M. A. (1995). Brain research, gender, and sexual orientation. *Journal of Homosexuality, 28,* 283–301.

Sweat, M. D., & Lein, M. (1995). HIV/AIDS knowledge among the U.S. population. *AIDS Education and Prevention, 7,* 355–372.

Symons, D. (1979). *The evolution of human sexuality.* New York: Oxford University Press.

Tanfer, K., Cubbins, L. A., & Billy, J. O. G. (1995). Gender, race, class, and self-reported sexually transmitted disease incidence. *Family Planning Perspectives, 27,* 196–202.

Tanfer, K., Grady, W. R., Klepinger, D. H., & Billy, J. O. G. (1993). Condom use among U.S. men, 1991. *Family Planning Perspectives, 25,* 61–66.

Tangri, S. S., Burt, M. R., & Johnson, L. B. (1982). Sexual harassment at work: Three explanatory models. *Journal of Social Issues, 38* (4), 33–54.

Tanner, W. M., & Pollack, R. H. (1988). The effect of condom use and erotic instructions on attitudes toward condoms. *The Journal of Sex Research, 25,* 537–541.

Tasker, F. L., & Golombok, S. (1997). *Growing up in a lesbian family.* New York: Guilford Publications, Inc.

Telljohann, S. K., & Price, J. H. (1993). A qualitative examination of adolescent homosexuals' life experiences: Ramification for secondary school personnel. *Journal of Homosexuality, 26,* 41–56.

Temoshok, L. Sweet, D. M., & Zich, J. (1987). A three-city comparison of the public's knowledge and attitudes about AIDS. *Psychology and Health, 1,* 43–60.

Tennov, D. (1979). *Love and limerence.* New York: Stein & Day.

Thacker, T. B., & Banta, H. D. (1983). Benefits and risks of episiotomy: Interpretative review of the English literature, 1960–1980. *Obstetrical and Gynecological Survey, 38,* 322–338.

Thayer, S. (1987). History and strategies of research on social touch. *Journal of Nonverbal Behavior, 11,* 12–28.

Thompson, S. (1994). Changing lives, changing genres: Teenage girls' narratives about sex and romance, 1978–1986. In A. S. Rossi (Ed.), *Sexuality across the life course* (pp. 209–232). Chicago: University of Chicago Press.

Thompson, W. E., & Harred, J. L. (1992). Topless dancers: Managing stigma in a deviant occupation. *Deviant Behavior: An Interdisciplinary Journal, 13,* 291–311.

Thornton, A. (1988). Cohabitation and marriage in the 1980s. *Demography, 25,* 497.

Tiefer, L. (1997). Response to testosterone injection study and Fisher's concerns. *The Journal of Sex Research, 34,* 37.

Tiefer, L., & Melman, A. (1989). Comprehensive evaluation of erectile dysfunction and medical treatments. In S. R. Leiblum & R. C. Rosen (Eds.), *Principles and practices of sex therapy* (2nd ed., pp. 207–236). New York: Guilford.

Tietze, C., Forrest, J. D., & Henshaw, S. (1988). United States of America. In P. Sachdev (Ed.), *International handbook on abortion* (pp. 473–494). New York: Greenwood.

Tooby, J., & Cosmides, L. (1992). The psychological foundations of culture. In J. Barkow, L. Cosmides, & J. Tooby (Eds.), *The adapted mind: Evolutionary psychology and the generation of culture* (pp. 19–136). New York: Oxford University Press.

Torres, A., & Forrest, J. D. (1988). Why do women have abortions? *Family Planning Perspectives, 20,* 169–176.

Trends in length of stay for hospital deliveries—United States, 1970–1992. (1995). *Morbidity and Mortality Weekly Reports, 44,* 335–337.

Trivers, R. E. (1972). Parental investment and sexual selection. In B. Campbell (Ed.), *Sexual selection and the descent of man* (pp. 136–179). Chicago: Aldine.

Troll, L. E., & Smith, J. (1976). Attachment through the life span: Some questions about dyadic bonds among adults. *Human Development, 19,* 135–182.

Trussell, J., Strickler, J., & Vaughan, B. (1993). Contraceptive efficacy of the diaphragm, the sponge, and the cervical cap. *Family Planning Perspectives, 25,* 100–105, 135.

U.S. Bureau of the Census. (1996). *Statistical abstracts of the United States* (116th ed.). Washington, DC: GPO.

U.S. Department of Health and Human Services (1996). *Child maltreatment 1994: Reports from the states to the National Center on Child Abuse and Neglect.* Washington, DC: U. S. GPO.

U.S. Department of Health and Human Services (1997). *Child maltreatment 1995: Reports from the states to the National Center on Child Abuse and Neglect.* Washington, DC: U. S. GPO.

U.S. Department of Justice, Bureau of Justice Statistics. (1990). *Sourcebook of criminal justice statistics—1989.* Washington, DC: GPO.

van Kesteren, P. J., Gooren, L. J., & Megens, J. A. (1996). An epidemiological and demographic study of transsexuals in the Netherlands. *Archives of Sexual Behavior, 25,* 589–600.

Van Wesenbeeck, I., de Graaf, R., van Zessen, G., Straver, C. J., & Visser, J. H. (1995). Professional HIV risk taking, levels of victimization, and well-being in female prostitutes in the Netherlands. *Archives of Sexual Behavior, 24,* 503–515.

Van Wyk, P. H., & Geist, C. S. (1984). Psychosocial development of heterosexual, bisexual, and homosexual behavior. *Archives of Sexual Behavior, 13,* 505–544.

Vance, E. B., & Wagner, N. N. (1976). Written descriptions of orgasm: A study of sex differences. *Archives of Sexual Behavior, 5,* 87–98.

Vermeulen, A. (1986). Leydig cell physiology. In R. J. Santen & R. S. Swerdloff (Eds.), *Male reproductive dysfunction* (pp. 49–76). New York: Dekker.

Verschoor, A. M., & Poortinga, J. (1988). Psychosocial differences between Dutch male and female transsexuals. *Archives of Sexual Behavior, 17,* 173–178.

Verwoerdt, A., Pfeiffer, E., & Wang, H. S. (1969). Sexual behavior in senescence: Patterns of sexual activity and interest. *Geriatrics, 24,* 137–144.

Vogel, D. A., Lake, M. A., Evans, S., & Karraker, K. H. (1991). Children's and adults' sex-stereotyped perceptions of infants. *Sex Roles, 24,* 605–616.

Wagner, G., & Kaplan, H. S. (1993). *The new injection treatment for impotence.* New York: Brunner/Mazel.

Wagner, G., Rabkin, J., & Rabkin, R. (1997a). Effects of testosterone replacement therapy on sexual interest, function, and behavior in HIV+ men. *The Journal of Sex Research, 34,* 27–33.

Wagner, G., Rabkin, J., & Rabkin, R. (1997b). Response to commentaries. *The Journal of Sex Research, 34,* 37–38.

Wagstaff, D. A., Kelly, J. A., Perry, M. J., Sikkema, L. J., Soloman, L. J., Heckman, T. G., & Anderson, E. S. (1995). Multiple partners, risky partners, and HIV risk among low-income urban women. *Family Planning Perspectives, 27,* 241–245.

Wallace, J. I., Mann, J., & Beatrice, S. (1988, June). *HIV-I exposure among clients of prostitutes.* Paper presented at the IV International Conference on AIDS, Stockholm, Sweden.

Walster, E., Walster, G. W., & Berscheid, E. (1978). *Equity: Theory and research.* Boston: Allyn & Bacon.

Walter, H. J., & Vaughan, R. D. (1993). AIDS risk reduction among a multiethnic sample of urban high school students. *Journal of the American Medical Association, 270,* 725–730.

Walters, A. S., & Curran, M. C. (1996). "Excuse me sir? May I help you and your boyfriend?" Salespersons' differential treatment of homosexual and straight customers. *Journal of Homosexuality, 31,* 135–152.

Ward, T., Hudson, S. M., & Marshall, W. L. (1996). Attachment style in sex offenders: A preliminary study. *The Journal of Sex Research, 33,* 17–26.

Webster, D. C. (1996). Sex, lies, and stereotypes: Women and interstitial cystitis. *The Journal of Sex Research, 33,* 197–203.

Weinberg, J. S. (1994). Research in sadomasochism: A review of sociological and social psychological literature. *Annual Review of Sex Research, 5,* 257–279.

Weinberg, M. S., & Williams, C. J. (1975). *Male homosexuals: Their problems and adaptations.* New York: Penguin.

Weinberg, M. S., Williams, C. J., & Calhan, C. (1995). "If the shoe fits . . .": Exploring male homosexual foot fetishism. *The Journal of Sex Research, 32,* 17–27.

Weinberg, M. S., Williams, C. J., & Pryor, D. W. (1994). *Dual attraction: Understanding bisexuality.* New York: Oxford University Press.

Weinrich, J. D. (1994). Homosexuality. In V. L. Bullough & B. Bullough (Eds.), *Human sexuality: An encyclopedia* (pp. 277–283). New York: Garland.

Weis, D. L. (1983). Affective reactions of women to their initial experience of coitus. *The Journal of Sex Research, 19,* 209–237.

Weisse, C. S., Turbiasz, A., & Whitney, O. J. (1995). Behavioral training and AIDS risk reduction: Overcoming barriers to condom use. *AIDS Education and Prevention, 7,* 50–59.

Weizman, R., & Hart, J. (1987). Sexual behavior in healthy married elderly men. *Archives of Sexual Behavior, 16,* 39–44.

Welch, M. R., & Kartub, P. (1978). Socio-cultural correlates of incidence of impotence: A cross-cultural study. *The Journal of Sex Research, 14,* 218–230.

Wells, B. (1986). Predictors of female nocturnal orgasm. *The Journal of Sex Research, 23,* 421–437.

Whipple, B. (1994). G spot and female pleasure. In V. L. Bullough & B. Bullough (Eds.), *Human sexuality: An encyclopedia* (pp. 229–232). New York: Garland.

Whipple, B., Ogden, G., & Komisaruk, B. R. (1992). Physiological correlates of imagery-induced orgasm in women. *Archives of Sexual Behavior, 21,* 121–133.

Whitam, F. L. (1977). Childhood indicators of male homosexuality. *Archives of Sexual Behavior, 6,* 89–96.

Whitam, F. L., Diamond, M., & Martin, J. (1993). Homosexual orientation in twins: A report on sixty-one pairs and three triplet sets. *Archives of Sexual Behavior, 22,* 187–206.

Whitam, F. L., & Mathy, R. M. (1986). *Male homosexuality in four societies: Brazil, Guatemala, the Philippines, and the United States.* New York: Praeger.

White, G. L. (1981). Relative involvement, inadequacy, and jealousy: A test of a causal model. *Alternative Lifestyles, 4,* 291–309.

White, G. L., & Helbick, R. M. (1988). Understanding and treating jealousy. In R. A. Brown & J. F. Fields (Eds.), *Treatment of sexual problems in individuals and couples therapy* (pp. 245–265). Boston: PMA.

White, L. K. (1991). Determinants of divorce: A review of research in the eighties. In A. Booth (Ed.), *Contemporary families: Looking forward, looking back* (pp. 141–149). Minneapolis: National Council on Family Relations.

Whitley, B. E., Jr. (1989). Correlates of oral-genital experience among college students. *Journal of Psychology and Human Sexuality, 2,* 151–163.

Wiederman, M. W. (1993). Demographic and sexual characteristics of nonresponders to sexual experience items in a national survey. *The Journal of Sex Research, 30,* 27–35.

Wiederman, M. W. (1997). Pretending orgasm during sexual intercourse: Correlates in a sample of young adult women. *Journal of Sex and Marital Therapy, 23,* 131–139.

Wiederman, M. W., & Allgeier, E. R. (1993). Gender differences in sexual jealousy: Adaptionist or social learning explanation. *Ethology and Sociobiology, 14,* 115–140.

Wiederman, M. W., Allgeier, E. R., & Weiner, A. (1992, June). *People's perceptions of vocalizations made during sexual intercourse.* Paper presented at the Midcontinent Region meeting of The Society for the Scientific Study of Sex, Big Rapids, MI.

Wiederman, M. W., Weis, D. L., & Allgeier, E. R. (1994). The effect of question preface on response rates to a telephone survey of sexual experience. *Archives of Sexual Behavior, 23,* 203–215.

Wiles, C. R., Wiles, J. A., & Tjernlund, A. (1996). The ideology of advertising: The United States and Sweden. *Journal of Advertising Research, 36* (3), 57–66.

Will, J. A., Self, P. A., & Datan, N. (1976). Maternal behavior and perceived sex of infant. *American Journal of Orthopsychiatry, 49,* 135–139.

Winick, C., & Evans, J. T. (1996). The relationship between nonenforcement of state pornography laws and rates of sex crime arrest. *Archives of Sexual Behavior, 25,* 439–453.

Wolf, D. G. (1979). *The lesbian community.* Berkeley and Los Angeles: University of California Press.

World Health Organization Task Force on Methods for the Regulation of Male Fertility. (1996). Contraceptive efficacy of testosterone-induced asoospermia and oligozoospermia in normal men. *Fertility and Sterility, 65,* 821–829.

World Health Organization Task Force on Psychological Research on Family Planning. (1982). Hormonal contraception for men: Acceptability and effects on sexuality. *Studies in Family Planning, 13,* 328–342.

Wu, F. C. W., Farley, T. M. M., Peregoudov, A., & Waites, G. M. H. (1996). Effects of testosterone enanthate in normal men: Experience from a multicenter contraceptive efficacy study. *Fertility and Sterility, 65,* 626–636.

Yarab, P. E., & Allgeier, E. R. (1997, April). "Who" really does matter: Reactions of jealousy and perceived threat based on the characteristics of an interloper. Paper presented at the annual meeting of the Eastern Psychological Association, Washington, DC.

Yarab, P. E., Sensibaugh, C. C., & Allgeier, E. R. (1997, April). More than just sex: Gender differences in the incidence of extradyadic behaviors. Paper presented at the annual meeting of the Eastern Psychological Association, Washington, DC.

Zaviacic, M., & Whipple, B. (1993). Update on the female prostate and the phenomenon of female ejaculation. *The Journal of Sex Research, 30,* 148–151.

Zelen, S. L. (1985). Sexualization of therapeutic relationships: The dual vulnerability of patient and therapist. *Psychotherapy, 22,* 178–185.

Zellman, G. L., & Goodchilds, J. D. (1983). Becoming sexual in adolescence. In E. R. Allgeier & N. B. McCormick (Eds.), *Changing boundaries: Gender roles and sexual behavior* (pp. 49–63). Palo Alto, CA: Mayfield.

Zilbergeld, B. (1992). *Male sexuality.* Boston: Little, Brown.

Zilbergeld, B., & Evans, M. (1980). The inadequacy of Masters and Johnson. *Psychology Today, 14,* 29–43.

Zillmann, D., & Bryant, J. (1984). Effects of massive exposure to pornography. In N. M. Malamuth & E. Donnerstein (Eds.), *Pornography and sexual aggression* (pp. 115–138). Orlando, FL: Academic Press.

Zillmann, D., & Bryant, J. (1988). Pornography's impact on sexual satisfaction. *Journal of Applied Social Psychology, 18,* 438–453.

Zucker, K. J. (1996). Commentary on Diamond's "prenatal predisposition and the clinical management of some pediatric conditions." *Journal of Sex and Marital Therapy, 22,* 148–160.

Zucker, K. J., & Bradley, S. J. (1995). *Gender identity disorder and psychosexual problems in children and adolescents.* New York: Guilford.

NAME INDEX

Abbey, A., 96, 161, 350, 360, 361
Abel, G. G., 309, 393, 399, 400
Abraham, G., 87
Abramson, P. R., 310
Adams, H. E., 287
Adams, R. G., 411
Adler, N. E., 207, 214
Ageton, S. S., 351, 353, 354, 360
Agyei, Y., 280, 282
Ahlburg, D. A., 253, 258
Ainsworth, M. D. S., 405
Alfonso, V. C., 86, 87
Allen, D., 365
Allen, M., 310
Allgeier, A. R., 92, 208
Allgeier, E. R., 6, 10, 17, 21, 22,
    85, 208, 211, 249, 305, 354,
    355, 360, 366, 370, 371,
    418, 419
Allison, D. B., 86
Amberger, J. A., 33
Amberson, J. I., 398
American Cancer Society, 57, 61,
    66–67
American Psychiatric Associa-
    tion, 141
Amoroso, D. M., 307
Amparo, E. G., 385
Anderson, R. E., 257
Andolsek, K. M., 162, 165, 177,
    181
Andrews, F. M., 161
Andrews, S. L., 362
Angera, A., 243
Ansuini, C., 235
Anthony, D., 399, 400
Apfelbaum, B., 145, 154
Aral, S. O., 202, 328
Armstrong, E. G., 318
Arndt, W. B., 87, 378, 391, 392,
    394, 395
Ashcraft, D. M., 326
Ashton, A. K., 155
Asscheman, H., 383, 384
Austin, S., 366

Bachrach, C. A., 215, 216, 236
Bagley, C., 371
Bailey, J. M., 274, 280, 282, 284
Baldwin, W., 215, 217
Balson, P. M., 314

Bandura, A., 20
Banks, A., 282–283
Banta, H. D., 174
Barak, A., 363, 364, 365
Barbach, L. G., 65, 87, 105
Barbaree, H. E., 350, 351, 361,
    398, 400
Barbee, A., 243
Barlow, D. H., 138
Barongan, C., 356, 373
Barth, R. P., 236
Batra, A. K., 72
Baumeister, R. F., 388, 416–417
Bauserman, R., 11, 306, 309
Beach, F. A., 273, 399
Beal, G. K., 362
Beard, C., 411
Beatrice, J., 380
Beatrice, S., 315
Beausoleil, N. I., 325
Beck, J. G., 147
Beere, C. A., 11
Beigel, H. G., 114
Beitchman, J. H., 369
Belch, G. E., 298
Belch, M. A., 298
Bell, A. R., 234, 276, 278, 280,
    284, 285, 288, 291, 292
Belsky, J., 224
Belzer, E. G., 130
Bem, D. J., 285
Bem, S. L., 291, 341
Bennett, J. W., 130
Bentler, P. M., 129, 380
Benton, J. M., 325
Berdahl, J. L., 364
Berger, G., 277
Berger, R. M., 280
Berscheid, E., 81–82, 257, 413
Best, C. L., 357
Betzig, L., 259
Bieber, I., 284
Bienen, L. B., 355, 356, 359
Billy, J. O. G., 114, 122, 190,
    197, 275, 323, 326
Bingham, S. G., 364
Binson, D., 324
Blair, C. D., 392
Blanchard, R., 283, 381, 382,
    387, 394
Blasband, M. A., 279

Blehar, M. C., 405
Blieszner, R., 411
Blumstein, P. W., 122, 255, 257,
    274, 292
Bockting, W. O., 384
Bogaert, A. F., 10, 283
Boles, J., 312, 314, 317, 318
Borna, S., 302
Borys, D., 366
Bouhoutsos, J. C., 366
Bowlby, J., 405
Boxer, A. M., 276
Boyd, K., 85
Bradford, J. M. W., 399
Bradley, S. J., 44
Bradshaw, D., 413
Brame, G. G., 384, 387
Brame, W. D., 384, 387
Branscombe, N. R., 59
Breakwell, G. M., 107, 112
Brecher, E. M., 265–266, 267
Breslow, N., 386, 389
Bretschneider, J. G., 267
Bringle, R. G., 256, 257
Brislin-Slutz, J. A., 300
Brodsky, A., 417, 420
Brooks-Gunn, J., 216
Brown, G. R., 380
Brown, J. D., 299, 310
Brown, L., 236
Brown, L. K., 325
Brown, M., 307
Browne, A., 310
Bryant, C. D., 303
Bryant, J., 309
Bucci, K., 177
Buckley, W. F., Jr., 334
Buhrich, N. A., 380
Bullough, B., 207, 311, 317, 379,
    380, 381, 382, 383
Bullough, V. L., 4, 311, 317, 379,
    380, 381, 382, 383
Bumby, K., 281
Bumpass, L. L., 251, 253, 258
Burg, B. R., 107
Burgess, A. W., 310, 352, 357, 398
Burke, D. S., 337
Burkhart, B. R., 351
Burzette, R. G., 291, 292, 293
Buss, D. M., 17, 85, 242, 257,
    373, 390, 415, 416, 418

Butler, C. A., 129
Buunk, B. P., 256, 257, 258,
    279
Byers, E. S., 95, 145, 148, 153,
    252, 356, 361, 362
Byrd, J. M., 182
Byrne, D., 20, 85, 88, 255, 272,
    352, 413

Cadman, D., 181
Cado, S., 86
Cain, V. S., 217
Caird, W. K., 149
Calhan, C., 379
Calhoun, T. C., 314, 318
Call, V., 253, 255, 263
Campbell, E. H., 86
Campbell, M. K., 177, 179
Cancian, F. M., 409–410
Cannon, D., 89
Capitanio, J. P., 286
Carey, M. P., 136, 144, 145, 147
Carlson, J., 413, 414
Carmichael, M. S., 68
Carnes, P., 396, 397
Caron, S. L., 325
Carpenter, F., 328
Carrier, J. M., 274, 275
Carroll, J. L., 242
Carson, S., 291
Carter, C. S., 68
Casey, R. J., 233
Casler, L., 405
Catania, J. A., 324
Cate, R., 243
Cates, W. C., Jr., 197, 198, 199,
    202, 332
Catoe, K. E., 324
Catotti, D. N., 324, 341
Cavanaugh, L. E., 419
Centers for Disease Control, 332,
    335, 336, 337
Chan, S., 381
Chapman, J., 302
Check, J. V. P., 307, 310
Cherlin, A., 251, 258
Chivers, M., 387
Chodorow, N., 18–19
Christenson, C. V., 391
Christopher, F. S., 20, 237
Christopherson, C. R., 242

Clark, D., 415
Clarke, P., 324
Clement, U., 107
Clemmer, D., 281
Cochran, S. D., 326
Cohen, J. B., 315
Cohler, B. J., 276
Cole, C. M., 385
Coleman, E., 287, 292, 293, 384, 397
Coles, C. D., 300
Collier, Z., 380
Conger, J. C., 394
Cooper, A. J., 399
Corey, L., 340
Cosmides, L., 17
Couture, M., 87
Cox, D. J., 392
Cox, M., 259
Cox, R., 259
Cox, S., 277
Cox, S. L., 354
Cozzarelli, C., 215
Cramer, D. W., 202, 343
Cranston-Cuebas, M. A., 138
Crenshaw, T. L., 155
Crepault, C., 87
Crowne, D. P., 284
Cubbins, L. A., 323, 326
Culter, W. B., 261
Curran, M. C., 289
Curtis, L., 355
Cutler, W. B., 75, 261
Cuvelier, S. J., 300

Daamen, M., 249
Dale, J., 366
D'Alessio, D., 310
Daling, J. R., 202
Dane, H. J., 284
Danoff-Burg, S., 356
Darling, C. A., 114, 123, 130, 131, 146
Darney, P. D., 201
Datan, N., 223
Davenport, W. H., 274
David, H., 314, 315
David, H. P., 217
Davidson, J. K., Sr., 86, 87, 114, 130, 131
Davidson, J. M., 68, 263
Davis, C. M., 11, 306, 309, 325
Davis, J. A., 286
Davis, S. F., 335
Davis, S. L., 11
Davison, G. C., 288
Day, R. D., 241
DeBuono, B. A., 249
De Carvalho, M., 179
DeCecco, J. P., 282
DeFrain, J., 253
Dekker, J., 145

DeLamater, J. D., 106, 182, 215, 241, 242
Delany, S. M., 153
DeLisle, S., 330, 331, 332
DeMaris, A., 251, 252
Deshotels, T. H., 303
Detzer, M. J., 107
DeVita, C. J., 253, 258
Devor, H., 384
De Waal, F. B. M., 273, 422
Dhawan, S., 351
Diamond, M., 44, 49, 50, 51, 276, 282, 382
Diana, L., 314, 315
Dick-Read, G., 170
DiClemente, R. J., 325, 326
Dinero, T. E., 354, 361
Dion, K. K., 310, 417
Dion, K. L., 310, 417
DiPietro, J. A., 229
Dixen, J., 68
Dodson, B., 108
Doll, L. S., 291, 292, 293
Donaldson, S., 281
Donnerstein, E., 307, 308
Donovan, P., 360
Dorflinger, L., 198
Dorfman, L. J., 263
Dornan, W. A., 69, 75
Douthitt, R. A., 254
Draper, K. K., 243
Dressel, P. L., 303
Duggan, A. K., 217
Dunn, G. M., 86
Dunn, M. E., 131, 132
Durkin, K. F., 303
Dwyer, S. M., 398
Dytrych, Z., 217
Dziuba-Leatherman, J., 372

Eakins, P. S., 172
Earls, C. M., 314, 315
Eccles, A., 400
Ecker, N., 233
Edgerton, M. T., 382, 385
Edmunds, C. N., 357
Ehrhardt, A. A., 37, 45, 50, 382, 384
Elicker, J. M., 405
Elifson, K. W., 314
Ellis, B. J., 86
Ellison, P.T., 203
Emmers, T. M., 310
Emory, L. E., 385
Englund, M., 405
Erikson, E., 227, 229, 233, 239, 240, 247–248, 260, 263, 404
Ernulf, K. E., 387, 396
Evans, J. T., 306
Evans, L., 386, 389
Evans, M., 148
Evans, S., 223

Everaerd, W., 230
Ewald, P. W., 334

Fagot, G. I., 228
Fahrner, E. M., 386
Fairchild, H. H., 24
Farley, T. M. M., 206
Farr, G., 198
Fassinger, R. E., 278
Federal Bureau of Investigation, 350, 352
Feeney, J. A., 405, 407
Fehr, B., 258
Feild, H. S., 355, 356, 359
Feldman, J. L., 45
Fetherstone, M., 261
Fetro, J. V., 236
Fiddler-Woite, J., 235
Fife-Schaw, C., 107, 112
Finkelhor, D., 234, 310, 367–368, 371, 372, 394
Fischer, K., 364
Fischman, A. M., 359
Fisher, H., 255, 258, 259, 262, 390, 418
Fisher, J. D., 325, 326, 336
Fisher, S., 114
Fisher, T. D., 93, 236
Fisher, W. A., 59, 88, 91, 190, 299, 308, 325, 326, 336, 339, 363, 364
Fiske, S. T., 364
Fithian, M. A., 132
Fitzgerald, L. F., 364, 365
Flannery, P. J., 361
Fleming, D. T., 386
Foa, U. G., 409, 410
Foehl, J. C., 87
Fog, E., 86
Fondell, M. M., 236
Ford, C. S., 273, 399
Ford, N., 198
Fordyce, R. R., 192, 194, 196, 199, 202, 203
Forer, B., 366
Forrest, D. F., 237
Forrest, J. D., 192, 194, 196, 199, 201, 202, 203, 209, 210, 214
Forrest, K., 326
Forsyth, C. J., 303
Foster, B. H., 366
Fowlkes, M. R., 279
Frank, A. P., 337
Franzoi, S. L., 84–85
Frayser, S. G., 226, 233
Freud, S., 17–18, 24, 86, 229, 232, 233, 240, 287, 406–407, 409
Freund, K., 381, 394
Freund, M., 315, 318–319
Friedan, B., 23
Friedman, J. M., 142

Fromm, E., 408
Frost, J. J., 237
Fryns, J. P., 32
Furstenberg, F. F., 216, 217
Fyke, F. E., 168

Gabelnick, H., 198
Gafini, A., 181
Gagnon, J. H., 6, 21, 106, 240, 391
Gaines, M. E., 371
Gajarsky, W. M., 370
Galenson, E., 226
Gallois, C., 277
Garcia, C. R., 75, 261
Garcia-Tunon, M., 335
Garde, K., 86
Gardos, P., 399, 400
Gartrell, N. K., 282–283
Gauling, S., 280
Gaumer, R., 314
Gautier, T., 43
Gayle, H. D., 335
Gebhard, P. H., 58, 59, 92, 391, 393, 394, 396, 398
Gebhardt, L., 310
Geist, C. S., 234, 285, 292
George, L. K., 267
George, W. H., 299
Gerberding, J. L., 338
Gerrard, M., 89
Gettelman, T. E., 280
Giambra, L. M., 86
Gibbons, F. X., 89
Gilbert, N., 355
Gilligan, C., 19
Gillilland, R., 138, 140, 141
Gladue, B. A., 137–138, 280
Glasock, J., 302
Glass, S. P., 257
Glazener, C. M. A., 181
Glick, P., 364
Glunt, E. K., 277, 286, 334
Gold, R. G., 85, 86, 142
Gold, S. R., 85, 86, 142
Gold, Y., 365
Goldberg, A., 368, 394
Goldberg, J. P., 155
Goldchilds, J. D., 355
Goldering, J., 328
Golding, J. M., 357
Goldman, J., 29, 223, 228, 232, 235, 239, 406
Goldman, M. B., 343
Goldman, R., 29, 223, 228, 232, 235, 239, 406
Golombok, S., 287
Gonsiorek, J. C., 288, 289
Good, F. E., 87
Goodall, J., 5
Goodheart, A., 237
Goodman, R. E., 385

Gooren, L. J. G., 282, 383, 384, 386
Gordon, C. M., 144
Gordon, S. L., 279
Gould, S. J., 298
Graaf, R., 312
Graber, B., 154, 155
Grady, W. R., 114, 122, 190, 197
Graham, K. R., 351
Green, R., 284, 285, 386
Greenberg, M., 366
Greenleaf, W. J., 263
Greenwald, E., 234
Greer, G., 23
Gregor, T., 5, 29, 168
Grenier, G., 145, 148, 153, 308
Grieco, A., 364
Grodsky, A., 86
Grodstein, F., 343
Groth, A. N., 352, 398
Grunebaum, H., 366
Guardado, S., 236
Guerrero, L., 43
Gutek, B. A., 364
Gutmann, D. L., 262
Guttmacher, Allan, Institute, 216

Hack, M., 178
Hale, V. E., 145
Hall, E. R., 361
Hall, G. C. N., 356, 373
Hallstrom, T., 261
Hally, D. J., 381
Halman, L. J., 161
Hamburg, D. A., 299
Hamer, D. H., 282, 283
Hammersmith, S. K., 234
Hammond, D. C., 142
Hank, L., 277
Hardy, J. B., 217
Harlow, H. F., 404, 405
Harlow, M. K., 404
Harms, R. W., 168
Harred, J. L., 303, 304
Harris, B., 411
Harry, J., 276, 277
Hart, J., 267
Hartman, C. R., 310
Hartman, W. E., 132
Harvey, S. M., 189, 191
Hatcher, R. A., 160, 162, 189, 191, 192, 193, 194, 196, 198, 199, 200, 201, 204, 205, 206, 211, 214
Hatfield, E., 137, 255, 259, 262, 275, 409, 413, 414, 415
Hatfield, R. W., 83, 226, 407
Hauer, L. B., 315
Hawton, K., 144, 147, 148, 149
Hayashi, H., 310
Haynes, J. D., 75
Hazan, C., 224, 405, 407, 409, 413

Heaton, J. B., 241
Hechinger, F. M., 299
Heim, N., 398, 399
Heiman, J. R., 86, 91, 137–138, 149, 152
Heinlein, L., 252
Heinlein, R., 403
Helbick, R. M., 418
Henderson, J. S., 183
Hendrick, C., 409, 410
Hendrick, S. S., 409, 410
Henshaw, S. K., 207, 208, 212, 213, 214, 216
Hepworth, M., 261
Herdt, G. H., 5, 273
Herek, G. M., 277, 286, 334
Herold, E., 10–11
Herold, E. E., 393
Herold, E. S., 86, 87
Hertz, S., 291
Herzog, M. E., 84–85
Hetherington, E. M., 259
Higgins, D. J., 371
Hill, C. T., 249–250
Hills, A., 274
Hochhauser, M., 336
Hoenig, J., 385
Hoffman, L. E., 86, 87
Hofman, M. A., 282
Hogan, D. R., 149
Hogben, M., 20, 272
Hollabaugh, L. C., 97
Holmes, K. K., 328
Holmstrom, L. L., 357
Holroyd, J., 366
Holzman, H. R., 318
Hooker, E., 284
Horn, J. D., 209, 210
Hostetter, H., 181
Hotaling, G., 367
Houston, S., 363, 364
Howard, M., 237
Hoyenga, K. B., 40, 69
Hoyenga, K. T., 40, 69
Hrabowy, I., 371
Hu, N., 282
Hu, P. N., 236
Hu, S., 282
Hubschman, L., 383, 384, 386
Hudson, B. L., 178
Hudson, S. M., 350, 405
Huff, P., 177
Huggins, G. R., 75
Hunt, M., 107, 114, 117, 121, 122, 318
Hurlbert, D. F., 108, 114
Hursch, C. J., 398
Hyde, J. S., 16, 107, 182, 242

Imperato-McGinley, J., 43
Ince, S., 45
Inciardi, J. A., 312

Innala, K. E., 387
Innala, S. M., 396

Jacklin, C. N., 229
Jacobs, J., 384, 387
Jamison, P. L., 58, 59
Janda, L. H., 231
Janus, C. L., 107, 114
Janus, S. S., 107, 114
Jennings, D. A., 131
Jensen, G. G., 131, 132
Johnson, D. C., 20
Johnson, V. E., 11, 58, 108, 110–111, 112, 114, 121, 123, 124, 126, 127, 128, 129, 130, 131, 138, 148–149, 150, 152, 153, 154, 263, 264, 265, 280
Jones, A. J., 95
Jones, E., 238
Jones, J. H., 330
Jones, J. R., 385
Joseph, J. G., 326

Kaeser, L., 201
Kalichman, S. C., 394
Kallmann, K. J. A., 281–282
Kanin, E. J., 351, 352, 354, 356, 359, 362
Kanouse, D. E., 291
Kaplan, G. W., 58
Kaplan, H. S., 124, 138, 149, 151, 155
Karlen, A., 267
Karpman, B., 398
Karraker, K. H., 223
Kartub, P., 137
Katner, H. P., 325
Katz, M. H., 338
Kazmier, S. J., 168
Keeting, R. P., 335
Kegel, A., 65
Keith-Spiegel, P., 365–366
Kelley, K., 88
Kelly, M. P., 146
Kendrick, A. F., 325
Kennedy, D. R., 419
Kenney, A. M., 236
Kilpatrick, A. C., 370
Kilpatrick, D. G., 357
Kim, P., 274
Kimmel, M. S., 298, 299, 306
King, A. J. C., 241
King, P. K., 242
Kinsey, A. C., 106, 107, 110, 112, 114, 117, 121, 130, 131, 226, 230, 234, 254, 272, 275, 280, 291, 293, 298, 318, 368, 388, 395, 396, 418
Kirby, D., 236, 237
Kircher, J. R., 146

Kirkpatrick, C., 354
Kitson, G. C., 259
Klaus, M. H., 179
Klebanoff, M. A., 168, 178
Klepinger, D. H., 114, 122, 190, 197
Klitsch, M., 199, 203, 206
Knoth, R., 85
Kochanek, K. D., 178
Kockott, G., 386
Kolodny, R. C., 148
Komarow, S., 290
Komisaruk, B. R., 112
Koonin, L. M., 208
Koralewski, M. K., 394
Koss, M. P., 354, 355, 361
Kost, K., 207, 212, 213
Koutsky, L. A., 341–342
Kowaleski-Jones, L., 236
Krane, R. J., 154
Kroon, S., 341
Krop, H., 395
Kruse, M., 107
Kurdek, L. A., 259, 279, 286
Kurzweil, N., 411
Kyes, K. B., 280

Laan, E., 230
Ladewig, P. W., 170, 204
Lake, M. A., 223
Lamberth, J., 88
Langevin, R., 392, 393
Langley, J., 386, 389
Langlois, J. H., 233
Lanyon, R., 392
LaRose, R., 302
Larsen, K. L., 86
Laughlin, C. D., Jr., 22
Laumann, E. O., 6, 106, 107, 108, 114, 121, 122, 130, 131, 135, 136, 142, 144, 145, 230, 241, 247, 249, 251, 252, 253, 255, 256, 257, 263, 265, 275, 300, 302, 304, 328, 329, 330, 332, 349, 353, 354, 367, 368, 370, 371, 390
Lawley, H. J., 75
Laws, D. R., 400
Lawson, A., 257
Lawson, H., 208
Lazarus, A. A., 146
Leary, M. R., 416–417
Lee, N., 315
Leiblum, S. R., 86, 154, 160, 161
Leigh, B. C., 279
Lein, M., 325
Leitenberg, H., 86, 107, 108, 230, 234
Leland, N., 236
Lemery, C. R., 59
Lenney, E., 241

Leonard, T. I., 315
Lerman, H., 366
Letourneau, E., 142
LeVay, S., 74, 276, 282, 283
Lever, J., 291, 292, 293
Levin, R. J., 63, 72
Levin, S. M., 392
Levine, L., 87, 105
Levine, M. P., 389, 397
Levitan, M., 40
Lewes, K., 288, 289
Lewis, I. A., 367
Lewis, K., 361, 362
Lewis, R. J., 231
Lief, H. I., 383, 384, 386
Lifson, A. R., 338
Lightfoot-Klein, H., 64
Linders, A., 298, 299, 306
Linz, D., 308, 309
Lish, J. D., 45
Liu, 339
Lloyd, C. W., 140–141
Lobitz, C., 152
Lohr, B. A., 287
Lombard, D. N., 325
London, M. L., 170, 204
Long, E., 243
Long, G. T., 281
Lonsway, K. A., 352
Lopez, P. A., 299
LoPiccolo, J., 86, 137–138, 142,
    147, 149, 152, 153
Lottes, I., 242
Lowe, K., 10, 11
Lowry, D. T., 299
Luckenbill, D. F., 314
Lue, T. F., 72
Luker, K., 189, 190
Lukusa, T., 32, 36
Lunde, I., 86, 87
Luria, Z., 261

McAnulty, R. D., 396
McAuslan, P., 350
McCabe, J. B., 237
McCabe, M. P., 153, 371
McCahill, T. W., 359
McCarthy, B. W., 149
McCarthy, J., 154
McCauley, E. A., 382, 384
MacCausland, M. P., 310
McClintock, M. K., 75
Maccoby, E. E., 229
McConaghy, N., 380
McCormack, W., 249
McCormick, N. B., 23, 95, 242,
    306, 308, 312, 313, 314,
    349, 352, 354, 355, 356
MacCorquodale, P., 106, 241,
    242
McCoy, N. L., 261, 267
MacDonald, J. M., 392

McDuffie, D., 350
McKinney, K., 252, 253, 255
McKinney, W. T., 404
McKirnan, D. J., 291, 292, 293
McKnight, B., 202
McKusick, V. A., 33
McMillan, S., 154
McNamee, J., 181
McWhirter, D. P., 278, 280
Magley, V. J., 364
Magnusen, V. L., 282
Maguire, K., 315, 316, 317
Mahoney, E. R., 351
Mahoney, J. M., 145, 191
Major, B., 215, 254
Malamuth, N. M., 307, 308, 310,
    351, 356
Malsbury, C. W., 69, 75
Manderson, L., 319
Mann, J., 145, 315
Mantle, D., 393
Marshall, D., 21
Marshall, W. L., 351, 400, 405
Marshall, Y., 366
Marsiglio, W., 217, 236
Martin, C., 396
Martin, J., 282
Martin, T. C., 253, 258
Martyna, W., 241
Maslow, A. H., 403
Masnyk, K., 217
Masters, W. H., 11, 58, 108, 110–
    111, 112, 114, 121, 123,
    124, 126, 127, 128, 129,
    130, 131, 138, 148–149,
    150, 152, 153, 154, 263,
    264, 265, 280
Matejcek, Z., 217
Mathie, E., 198
Mathy, R. M., 284
Mattison, A. M., 278, 280
Mattson, S., 160, 168
Mauldon, J., 189, 190
Mays, V. M., 326
Mead, M., 229
Meade, R. G., 261
Mears, C., 404, 405
Megens, J. A., 386
Meischke, H., 299
Melman, A., 154, 155
Melnick, S. L., 326
Menaghan, E. G., 236
Menezes, D., 302
Meuwissen, I., 82
Meyer, C. B., 366
Meyer, J. K., 386
Meyer, L. C., 359
Meyer, W. J., 385
Meyer-Bahlburg, H. F. L., 45
Michael, R. T., 6
Michaels, S., 6
Mickler, S. E., 325, 326

Milic, J. H., 284
Miller, B. C., 241, 242
Miller, J. S., 284
Miller, M. V., 420
Miller, W. B., 189
Milner, P. M., 74
Miner, H., 323
Minturn, L., 37
Mintzes, J. L., 325
Misovich, S. J., 326
Mitchell, H. E., 88
Monckton, C., 334
Money, J., 37, 50, 51, 85, 234,
    397, 399
Monsour, M., 411
Montagu, A., 29
Moore, D. E., 202
Moore, K. L., 160
Moore, M. M., 11, 95
Moorman, J. E., 258
Morgan, L. A., 259
Morgan, S. P., 216
Morokoff, P. J., 138, 140, 141
Morris, N. M., 83
Morrow, S. L., 278
Morse, E. V., 314
Mosher, D. L., 88, 215, 216, 351
Mosher, W. D., 202, 236
Moskowitz, J. T., 324
Mott, F. L., 236
Mottin, J., 10–11
Muehlenhard, C. L., 97, 356, 362
Munroe, R. H., 381
Munroe, R. L., 381
Murnen, S. K., 255, 352
Muth, J. B., 318
Muth, S. Q., 318
Myers, J. G., 305
Mynatt, C. R., 354, 355, 360

Neal, J. A., 300
Neale, M. C., 282
Need, J. A., 386
Neidigh, L., 395
Neinstein, L., 328
Neugarten, B. L., 262
Newcomb, M. D., 251, 284
Newman, G., 267
Nichols, C. R., 267
Niku, S. D., 58, 180
Noller, P., 405, 407
Norton, A. J., 258
Novak, M. A., 404

O'Donohue, W., 142
Ogden, G., 112
Okami, P., 231, 367n, 368, 394
Okawa, J. B., 365
Olds, J., 74
Olds, S. B., 170, 174, 181, 204,
    205
Oliver, M. B., 16, 107

Olson, D. H., 253
Ormerod, M., 365
Osborn, C., 399
Osofsky, H. J., 314
O'Sullivan, L. F., 95
Otis, M. D., 286
Over, R., 82, 284
Oyama, S., 24

Padgett, V. R., 300, 301
Paige, K., 180
Paitich, D. P., 393
Pariente, B., 315
Parker, D. A., 282
Parker, R., 275
Pastore, A. L., 315, 316
Pattatucci, A. M. L., 282
Pauly, I. B., 382, 383, 384, 385
Pavelka, M. S. M., 273
Pawlak, A., 399
Pearson, C., 217
Peele, S., 417, 420
Peeler, W. H., 129
Pelletier, L. A., 86, 87
Pendergrast, M., 368
Peplau, L. A., 249–250, 279
Peregoudov, A., 206
Perlow, D. L., 324
Perlow, J. S., 324
Perper, T., 11
Perry, J. D., 62
Pervin, L. A., 86
Peterson, D. M., 303
Peterson, R., 43
Pett, M. A., 142
Pfäfflin, F., 386
Pfeiffer, E., 267
Philips, G., 284
Pillard, R. C., 282
Pines, A., 310
Pines, S., 318
Pithers, W. D., 400
Pithey, D. W., 307
Plant, E. A., 182
Plaut, S. M., 366
Pleck, J., 254
Pollack, R. H., 197
Pomeroy, W. B., 58, 391, 396
Poole, L. E., 315
Poortinga, J., 386
Pope, K. S., 365–366
Porto, R., 87
Possage, J. C., 370
Potter, G., 301, 302
Potterat, J. J., 318
Powch, I. G., 356
Powell-Griner, E., 216
Powers, P., 310
Pratte, T., 286
Prendergast, W. E., 351
Prescott, J. W., 407, 408

Presser, H. B., 217
Preti, G., 75
Prince, P. R., 284
Prince, V., 380, 385
Prins, K. S., 258
Pruesse, M., 307
Pryor, D. W., 291
Pryor, J. B., 364
Purifoy, F. E., 86, 87

Quadagno, D., 410
Quinsey, V. L., 361

Rabkin, J., 338
Rabkin, R., 338
Rainwater, L., 159
Ramick, M., 208
Rao, K. V., 251, 252
Rapaport, K., 351
Rapson, R. L., 255, 259, 262,
    275, 409, 414
Rauzi, T., 277
Read, J. S., 168, 178
Reamy, K. J., 163, 179, 182,
    183
Redfield, P. R., 337
Reed, J., 7
Reinisch, J. M., 45
Reiss, I. L., 21, 23, 257, 299–
    301, 418, 419
Reter, D. J., 386
Rind, B., 369, 370
Robbins, J. M., 215
Robbins, M. B., 131, 132
Roberts, C. W., 137–138, 149
Roberts, L. W., 325
Robertson, S., 179
Robinson, J., 334
Roche, J. P., 248–249, 415
Rogers, W. H., 291
Roggman, L. A., 233
Roiphe, H., 226
Roiphe, K., 354
Roosa, M. W., 20, 237
Rosario, M., 293
Roscoe, B., 419
Rosen, L., 314
Rosen, R. C., 75, 154, 155
Rosenberg, H. M., 236
Rosenberg, L., 203
Rosenbleet, C., 315
Ross, L. T., 350
Ross, M. W., 285, 386
Rothenberger, J. H., III, 336
Rouleau, J.-L., 393
Rowland, D. L., 263
Rubin, Z., 249–250
Rucker, L., 281
Russell, D. E. H., 355, 360, 368,
    395
Russo, N. F., 209, 210, 211
Russon, A. E., 393

Rust, P. C., 276, 291, 292, 293
Rywick, T., 208

Sabry, Z., 10–11
Sacks, S. L., 341
Saluter, A. F., 251, 253
Sanders, S., 45
Sandfort, T. G. M., 368–369
Saunders, B. E., 357
Savitz, L., 314
Schangaard, M., 145
Scherer, L. L., 364
Schiavi, R. C., 136, 142
Schlafly, P., 237
Schlesselman, J. J., 200
Schlueter, D., 326
Schmidt, G., 107
Schmitt, D. P., 257
Schmitt, J. P., 279
Schoenberg, H. W., 144
Scholes, D., 332
Schott, R. L., 380
Schreer, G., 11
Schreiner-Engel, P., 142
Schreurs, K. M. G., 274, 278, 279
Schuller, V., 217
Schulte, L., 88
Schumacher, S., 140–141
Schwanberg, S. L., 286
Schwartz, P., 122, 243, 253, 255,
    257, 263, 274, 292
Schwartz, R., 209, 210
Schwartz, S., 191
Scott, J. E., 300
Scrimshaw, S. C. M., 189, 191
Segraves, K. A., 141, 144
Segraves, R. T., 141, 144, 155
Seibel, C. A., 354
Self, P.A., 223
Sell, R. L., 275
Sensibaugh, C. C., 211, 249, 419
Seto, M. C., 350
Sevely, J. L., 130
Severn, J., 298
Seymour, N. K., 357
Shamp, M. J., 300
Shannon, T. W., 108
Shaver, P. R., 224, 405, 407, 409,
    413, 416
Sherfey, J., 131
Sherman, R. W., 380
Shidler, J. A., 299
Shilts, R., 286, 289, 324, 335
Shively, M. D., 351
Shusterman, L. R., 214
Siegelman, M., 284
Sikkema, K. J., 325
Silbert, M. H., 310
Silverman, D., 364
Silverstein, L. B., 254
Simkins, L., 277

Simon, P. M., 314
Simon, W., 21, 106, 240
Singer, B., 85
Singer, I., 129–130, 131
Singer, J., 129–130, 131
Singh, D., 84
Sirkin, M., 351
Skinner, W. F., 286
Smith, C., 367
Smith, J., 255
Smith, J. C., 208
Smith, J. E., 160, 168
Smith, K. H., 305
Smith, M. U., 325
Smith, T., 286
Smith, T. W., 122, 256–257, 259,
    306
Solomon, R. D., 325
Somers, A., 365
Sonne, J., 366
Spector, I. P., 136, 145, 147
Spengler, A., 386
Spitz, R. A., 405
Sponaugle, G. C., 257
Sprague, J., 410
Sprecher, S., 243, 252, 253, 255,
    258, 263
Srebnik, D., 107
Sroufe, L. A., 405
Stava, L., 392
Steele, J. R., 299, 310
Stein, M. L., 318
Steiner, B. W., 381, 383
Stern, M., 223
Sternberg, R. J., 409, 410–411,
    413, 414
Stevens, C. E., 342
Stevenson, M. R., 274, 370,
    379
Stock, J. A., 58
Stock, W. E., 147, 153, 308–309
Stokes, J. P., 291, 292, 293
Stoller, R. J., 398
Stone, K. M., 197, 198, 199,
    332
Storms, M. D., 85, 272, 285
Strassberg, D. R., 10, 11
Strassberg, D. S., 145, 146, 191
Straver, C. J., 312
Strickler, J., 189, 194
Stroh, M., 317
Struckman-Johnson, C., 281, 353
Struckman-Johnson, D., 281, 353
Stuart, F. M., 142
Sturgen, K., 198
Sultan, F. E., 281
Suomi, S. J., 404
Swaab, D. F., 282
Swan, S., 364
Sweat, M. D., 325
Sweet, J. A., 251
Symons, D., 86, 143, 418

Tabachnick, B. G., 365–366
Tanfer, K., 114, 122, 190, 197,
    323, 326, 336
Tanner, W. M., 197
Tarran, M., 234
Tasker, F. L., 287
Tennov, D., 411–412, 413
Thacker, T. B., 174
Thayer, S., 407
Thompson, J. K., 280
Thompson, S., 300
Thompson, W. E., 303, 304
Thornton, A., 251
Tiefer, L., 154, 155, 338–339
Tietze, C., 214
Tjernlund, A., 298
Tooby, J., 17
Torres, A., 209, 210
Travis, B. G., 45
Traw, M., 351, 352
Trivers, R. E., 16
Troiden, R. R., 389, 397
Troll, L. E., 255
Tromovitch, P., 369, 370
Trost, J. E., 131, 132
Trussell, J., 189, 194
Tucker, P., 50
Turbiasz, A., 325

Udry, J. R., 83
Uniform Crime Reports, 379
U.S. Bureau of the Census, 251,
    253
Upfold, D., 361

Vance, E. B., 128, 129
Van Den Berghe, T., 32
Van Kesteren, P. J., 386
Van Vort, J., 207, 208, 212, 213,
    216
Vanwesenbeeck, I., 312
Van Wyk, P. H., 234, 285, 292
Van Yperen, N. W., 258
Van Zessen, G., 312
Vaughan, B., 189, 194
Veridian, N. P., 45
Vermeulen, A., 225
Veronen, L. J., 357
Verschoor, A. M., 386
Verwoerdt, A., 267
Visser, J. H., 312
Vogel, D. A., 223
Voight, L. F., 202
Volk, K. D., 242

Wagner, G., 155, 338
Wagner, N. N., 128, 129
Wagstaff, D. A., 340
Waites, G. M. H., 206
Walburton, V. L., 68
Waldo, C. R., 364
Wall, S., 405

Wallace, J. I., 315
Waller, L., 177
Walster, E., 81–82, 257, 413
Walster, G. W., 257
Walters, A. S., 289
Ward, T., 405, 407
Ware, E. E., 307
Waters, E., 405
Watson, C., 241
Weaver, G., 314, 318
Webster, D. C., 331
Weiler, S. J., 267
Weinberg, J. S., 292, 293, 380, 387
Weinberg, M. S., 234, 278, 280, 288, 291, 292, 379
Weiner, A., 85
Weinrich, J. D., 278, 286, 288
Weinstein, K., 159

Weinstein, S., 233
Weis, D. L., 10, 243
Weiss, N. B., 202
Weisse, C. S., 325
Weitzman, L. M., 365
Weizman, R., 267
Welch, M. R., 137
Wells, B., 106
Wells, J. A., 275
Whipple, B., 62, 112, 130
Whitam, F. L., 282, 284
White, G. L., 418
White, L. A., 88
White, L. K., 258, 259
White, S. E., 163, 179, 182, 183
Whiting, J. W. M., 381
Whitley, B. E., Jr., 114
Whitley, R. J., 341
Whitney, O. J., 325

Whittaker, K. E., 108, 114
Wiederman, M. M., 17
Wiederman, M. W., 10, 85, 131, 419
Wiles, C. R., 298
Wiles, J. A., 298
Will, J. A., 223
Willerman, L., 284
Williams, C. J., 280, 291, 379
Williams, D. H., 385
Wincze, J. P., 149
Winick, C., 306
Winnett, R. A., 325
Wofsy, C. B., 315
Woite, R., 235
Wolf, L., 280
Woodhouse, D. E., 318
World Health Organization Task Force, 206

Wright, L. W., 287
Wright, T. L., 257
Wu, F. C. W., 206
Wynn, R. L., 325
Wypij, D., 275

Yachanin, S. A., 305
Yarab, P. E., 249, 419
Yarber, W. L., 11

Zaviacic, M., 130
Zelen, S. L., 366
Zellman, G. L., 355
Zemitis, O., 393
Ziemba-Davis, M., 45
Zilbergeld, B., 148
Zillmann, D., 309
Zinner, S. H., 249
Zucker, K. J., 44

SUBJECT INDEX

Aborigines, 29, 233–234
Abortion, 187, 188, 191, 206–215
  DES for, 211
  dilation and curettage for, 212–213
  dilation and evacuation for, 213–214
  emergency contraceptive pills for, 211
  of female fetuses as population control, 37
  hormones for, 211–212
  hysterotomy for, 214
  inability to obtain, 217
  intra-amniotic injection for, 214
  male role in, 214–215
  menstrual extraction for, 211, 212
  methods, 211–214
  moral and legal debate over, 207–209
  psychological responses to, 214
  reasons for, 209–211
  RU–486 for, 211–212
  saline, 214
  suction, 212–213
  vaginismus and, 147
Abstinence, in sex education, 237
Acne, 49
Acquaintance rape, 94, 190, 354–355, 357, 361–362
Acquired immunodeficiency syndrome (AIDS), 212, 249, 324, 333–340
  adolescents and, 325, 326
  anal sex and, 121, 122
  attitudes toward, 325
  bisexuality and, 292
  causes of, 335–336
  children with, 335
  dementia and, 338
  diagnosis of, 337, 339
  education on, 325, 326
  extramarital sex and, 257
  fetal development and, 160, 162
  homosexuality and, 280, 286, 290

hotlines for, A4
incidence, 327
information about, 325, 346
number of sexual partners and, 122
opportunistic infections with, 337–338
oral sex and, 115
prevalence, 333, 335
prostitution and, 312, 314
protecting against, 325–326, 339–340, 341, 343–346
risk of acquiring, 336
sex tourism and, 319
sexual intercourse after divorce and, 259
stigma associated with, 334
symptoms of, 327, 337
treatment of, 335, 338–339
young adults and, 325–326, 335
Actual failure rate, of contraceptives, 188
Addiction
  excessive sexual desire and, 139, 142–143, 396–397
  love and, 417
Adolescence
  cliques in, 234
  communicating about sexuality in, 94
  contraceptive use in, 188, 189–190, 236, 238, 239
  gender-role identification in, 239, 240–241
  gender-role socialization in, 229
  genital stage in, 224, 240
  homosexuality in, 276
  identity versus role confusion in, 224, 239–243
  marriage and, 258
  masturbation in, 241
  oral sex in, 114
  parental attitudes and sexual activity in, 93–94
  pregnancy in, 215, 216–217, 236, 238, 239
  prostitution in, 317
  puberty in, 18, 35, 47–49, 68, 225, 239, 240

rape and, 353–354, 360–361
sex education in, 235–239
sexual activity in, 236, 241, 242
sexual fantasies in, 85
sexually transmitted diseases in, 239, 325–326
sexual scripts in, 240
Adolescent Family Life Act, 237
Adoption, 215
Adrenal glands, 39, 56, 68
Adult bookstores, 301–302
Adultery, see Extramarital sex
Adulthood, see Middle age; Old age; Young adulthood
Advertisements, as erotic, 298–299
African Americans, Tuskegee study of untreated syphilis in, 330
Afterbirth, see Placenta
Aging, see Middle age; Old age
AIDS, see Acquired immunodeficiency syndrome
AIDS dementia complex, 338
AIS, see Androgen insensitivity syndrome
Alcohol
  fetal development and, 160, 161–162
  sexual arousal/desire and, 142, 143
Alveoli, 163, 177
American Academy of Pediatrics, 180
American Association for Sex Educators, Counselors, and Therapists, 155, A1
American Cancer Society, 57
American Indians, 15, 116
American Medical Association, 4
American Pediatric Society, 177
American Psychiatric Association, 141, 288, 392
Amniocentesis, 164, 165
Amniotic fluid, 171–172
Amniotic sac, 34, 46, 171–172, 173
Amygdala, 74, 75
Analingus, 114, 278

Anal intercourse, 278
Anal sex, 121–122
Anal stage, 18, 224
Androgen insensitivity syndrome (AIS), 40–42, 43
Androgens, 35, 37, 38, 39, 47, 49, 68, 69, 160, 225, 282–283
Androgyny, 241
Androstetenedione, 39
And the Band Played On (Shilts), 324
Animals
  drugs tested on, 13
  zoophilia and, 395–396
Antidepressants, for sexual dysfunction, 155
Antigay prejudice, see Homophobia
Anxiety, sexual dysfunction caused by, 72, 138
Any Man Can (Hartman and Fithian), 132
Arapesh (New Guinea), 229
Areola, 47, 163
Arousal, see Sexual arousal
Artificial insemination, 161
Asphyxiophilia, 396
Aspirin, fetal development and, 160
Association of Gay and Lesbian Psychiatrists, A1
Asymptomatic, 324
Attachment
  love and, 404–408, 409, 417
  in marriage, 255–256
Attitudes toward sexuality, see Sexual attitudes
Attractiveness, cultural diversity and, 80–81, 85
Atypical sexual activity, see Paraphilias
Australia, 285
Autoeroticism, see Masturbation
Autonomic nervous system, 71–72
Autonomy versus shame and doubt, in early childhood, 224, 227–228
Autosomes, 31
AZT, 335, 338

Back-burner relationships, 249
Bandura, Albert, 20
Bar girl, 312
Bartholin's glands, 63
Basal body temperature (BBT), 192–193
Behavioral therapy, 148
Behaviorism, 19
Bem Sex Role Inventory, 241
Bergen, Candice, 262
Bernardin, Cardinal Joseph, 368
Bestiality, *see* Zoophilia
Bias, in sampling, 9–10, 11
Biochemical measures, of arousal, 12
Birth, *see* Childbirth
Birth control pill, *see* Oral contraceptives
Birth control, 187. *See also* Contraceptives
Birthing centers, 172
Bisexuality, 51, 273, 291–293
Blended orgasm, 130
Body cells, 31
Body hair, in puberty, 35, 47, 49
Bodywork therapy, 154
Bookstores, adult, 301–302
Borderline androgen insensitivity syndrome, 43
Brain, 73, 74–75
   development of, 35, 37
   sex hormones and, 69
Braxton-Hicks contractions, 171
Brazil, 5, 29, 168, 274, 275
Breakthrough bleeding, oral contraceptives and, 200
Breast-feeding, 39, 60, 65, 68, 177, 179, 203, 335
Breasts, 60, 65–67
   cancer of, 66, 200, 212
   estrogens and, 39
   pregnancy and, 163
   in puberty, 35, 47
   self-examination of, 66–67
Brothels, 315
Bulletin-board system (BBS), erotica and, 302–303

CAH, *see* Congenital adrenal hyperplasia
Calendar method, ovulation determined by, 192
Call girls, 313, 315
Canada, 306
Cancer
   breast, 66, 200, 212
   cervical, 61, 180, 200
   endometrial, 200
   oral contraceptives and, 200
   ovarian, 200

penile, 180
prostate, 57–58
testicular, 57
Candidiasis, 342–343
Cannula, for menstrual extraction, 212
Cardiovascular disorders, sexual dysfunction caused by, 137
Case studies, sexual responses measured with, 12
Castration, for invasive paraphilias, 398–399
Casual sex, gender differences in, 16
Cell division, 31
Central nervous system (CNS), 72–75
Cerebral cortex, 75
Cerebral hemispheres, 75
Cerebrum, 75
Cervical cap, 188, 189, 196
Cervix, 60
   cancer of, 61, 180, 200
   pregnancy and, 163
Cesarean section, 178
Chancroid, 332
Chemical treatment, of invasive paraphilias, 399
Child abuse, 367n. *See also* Child sexual abuse
Childbirth, 39, 61, 68, 169–177
   babies' position during, 178
   Cesarean section and, 178
   complications during, 178
   labor during, 171–177
   late babies and, 178
   location of, 172
   personal account of, 171
   premature, 178
   prepared, 170–171, 174
Childbirth Without Fear (Dick-Read), 170
Childhood, 226–239
   acquired immunodeficiency syndrome and, 335
   anal stage in, 224
   attachment and, 404–408
   autonomy versus shame and doubt in, 224, 227–228
   awareness of gender differences in, 228
   awareness of physical attractiveness in latency in, 233
   early, 224, 227–233
   gender identity in, 227
   gender-role identification in, 227
   gender roles in, 227
   gender-role socialization in, 229–230

genital play in, 20
homosexuality in, 234, 276, 284–285
homosociality in, 234
initiative versus guilt in, 224, 229–233
language development in, 227
late, 224, 233–239
latency in, 224, 232
masturbation in, 226
natural sex education in, 228
Oedipus/Electra complexes in, 224, 229
parental responses to self-exploration in, 88–89
parental sexual intercourse witnessed in (primal scene), 231–232
pedophilia and, 394–395
phallic stage in, 224
psychosexual stages in, 18
romantic love and, 413
sex education in, 235–239
sex guilt and, 88–90
sex research and, 4
sexual dysfunction and events in, 137
sexuality in, 29
sexual knowledge in, 222, 223, 230–233
sexual rehearsal in, 233–234
toilet training in, 227–228
see also Adolescence; Child sexual abuse; Infancy
Child sexual abuse, 366–372, 373
   incest and, 366
   long-term correlates of, 368–372
   memories of, 368–369
   prevalence of, 367
   risk factors for, 367–368
   sexual assault and, 405–406
   sexual aversion and, 142
China, 37, 212
Chlamydia, 162, 327, 329–331, 336
Cholesterol, 39
Chorionic villi sampling (CVS), 165
Chromosomes, 31
   autosomes, 31
   sex, 31–33, 40
Cilia, 60
Circumcision
   female, 63, 64, 180
   male, 49–50, 58, 180–181
Classical conditioning, 19
Clinton, Bill, 289, 330, 355
Cliques, 234

Clitoral hood, 39, 63, 125
Clitoris, 6, 39, 47, 59–60, 62, 63, 92, 125, 128
   circumcision of, 63, 64, 180
   cultural diversity and, 22
   masturbation and, 110–112
   slang terms for, 93
Cocaine, fetal development and, 160
Cognitive-behavior therapies, 147–148, 399–400
Cognitive factors, learning theories and, 20
Cohabitation, 251–252
   homosexual couples and, 252, 253
   sexual intercourse and, 252–253
Cohort, 367
Coital positions, 116–121
Coitus, 86, 96
Coitus interruptus, *see* Withdrawal
Color blindness, 33
Colostrum, 164, 177
Commercial beavers, 312
Commercial sex workers, *see* Prostitution
Commission on Pornography, 307
Communication about sexuality, 92–101
   enhancing, 96–97
   gender differences in, 94
   honoring agreements and, 101
   informed consent and sexual intimacy and, 97–99, 100
   management of sexual feelings and behavior and, 99
   sexual dysfunction caused by difficulties in, 139–140
   sexual intimacy and, 94–97
   socialization for, 92–94
Companionate love, 414
Compulsive sexual behavior, 396–397
Computer, erotica and, 302–303
Comstock, Anthony, 305
Comstock Act, 305
Conception, cross-cultural views on, 4, 5
Concordance rates, homosexuality and, 282
Conditioned response (CR), 19
Conditioned stimulus (CS), 19
Conditioning, 19–20
Condoms, 188, 189, 191, 196–198
   adolescents' use of, 236, 238, 239

female, 198, 340, 341
prostitution and, 314, 315
sexually transmitted diseases and, 197, 326, 340, 341, 345
young adults' use of, 249
Congenital adrenal hyperplasia (CAD), 43–44
Congestive prostatitis, 331
Connery, Sean, 262
Consummate love, 411, 412, 414
Contraceptive foams, 189, 190–199
Contraceptives, 117, 186–206
actual failure rate of, 188
adolescents' use of, 188, 189–190, 236, 238, 239
after childbirth, 183
attitudes toward sex and, 190–191
cervical caps, 188, 189, 196
contraceptive foams, 189, 198–199
contraceptive sponge, 189
contraceptive suppositories, 189, 198–199
Depo-Provera, 189, 201
development and use of modern, 187–191
diaphragms, 188, 189, 191, 194–196, 340
douching, 188, 202–203
erotophilia and, 88
female condoms, 198, 340, 341
female sterilization, 188, 189, 191, 204–205
future methods of, 205–206
informed consent for, 98
intrauterine devices, 188, 189, 190, 201–202, 211
male sterilization, 188, 189, 191, 203–204
male vaccines, 206
Norplant, 189, 200–201
oral, 7–8, 13, 160, 188, 189, 191, 199–200, 211
prostitution and, 314, 315
religious affiliation and, 190
rhythm method, 189, 192–194
selecting, 188–189
self-help organizations for, A3
sex guilt and, 89
sexual intimacy dealing with, 98
sexually transmitted diseases and, 326, 340, 341, 345
sexual relations inhibited by, 140
spermicidal agents, 188, 194–196, 341, 345

spontaneous sex versus use of, 190
testosterone derivatives, 206
theoretical failure rate of, 188
tubal ligation, 51, 188, 189, 191, 204–205
vaginal ring, 206
vaginal suppositories, 189
vasectomy, 188, 189, 191, 203–204
withdrawal, 58, 188, 189, 202
in young adulthood, 249
see also Abortion; Condoms
Contraceptive sponge, 189
Contraceptive suppositories, 189, 198–199
Contractions, during childbirth, 171–174, 175
Control, love and, 416–418
Control variables, 9
Convicted rapists, 350, 351, 352
Copper T, 202
Coprophilia, 397
Copulation, 14. *See also* Sexual intercourse
Copulins, 83
Corona, 58
Corpora cavernosa
of clitoris, 63
of penis, 58, 73
Corpus luteum, 39, 71
Corpus spongiosum, 58, 73
Correlational method, 10–11
Courtship, women initiating, 94–95
Couvade, 164
Cowper's glands, 58
Crack, prostitution and, 312
Cremaster muscle, 55
Cross-cultural research, *see* Cultural diversity
Cross-dressing, *see* Transvestism
Cruising, lesbians and, 279–280
Cultural diversity, 5, 21–24, 25
aborigines and, 29, 233–234
abortion of female fetuses as population control and, 37
American Indians and, 15, 116
anal sex and, 122
attachment and, 407–408
attractiveness and, 80–81, 85
bodily odors and, 84
Brazil and, 5, 29, 168, 274, 275
childhood sexual knowledge and, 232
circumcision and, 180
coital positions and, 116
conception and pregnancy and, 4, 5

divorce and, 258–259
erectile dysfunction and, 143
erotica and, 310
extramarital sex and, 258
female circumcision and, 63, 64
gender-role socialization and, 229
genital differences and, 228
homosexuality and, 22, 273–275, 285
Indonesia and, 274
Japan and, 310, 317
love and, 22, 407–408, 410, 416
masturbation and, 22, 107
mate selection and, 416
Melanesia and, 274
Netherlands and, 258
New Guinea and, 5, 229, 273
oral sex and, 114
prostitution and, 317, 319
sex during pregnancy and, 168–169
sex education and, 237, 238
sexual arousal and, 80–81
sexual dysfunction and, 137
sexual intercourse and, 5, 21, 22, 29
sexual play and, 233–234
South Pacific and, 5, 21, 116
Sudan and, 64
Sweden and, 232, 285, 410
Thailand and, 319
Trinidad and, 226
Uganda and, 21, 22, 80, 168
women's enjoyment of sexual intercourse and, 21, 22
Cunnilingus, 96, 114–115, 168, 195–196
Curettage, 212
Curette, 212, 213
Cushing's disease, 212
Cyberspace, erotica and, 302–303
Cystitis, 327, 331
Cytomegalovirus (CMV), 338

Dancing, erotic, 303–304
Dancing Grannies, 264–265
Darwin, Charles, 14–15
Date-rape drugs, 354–355. *See also* Acquaintance rape
Dating
criteria for, 416
infidelity and, 419
Defense of Marriage Act (DOMA), 289
Deoxyribonucleic acid (DNA), 31

Dependence, love and, 416–418
Dependent variables, 8–9, 10, 12
Depo-Provera, 189, 200
Depression
hypoactive sexual desire and, 142
postpartum, 181
sexual dysfunction and, 141
DES, fetal development and, 160
DHT, *see* Dihydrotestosterone
Diabetes, fetal development and, 160
Diagnostic and Statistical Manual, 141
Dial-a-porn industry, 302
Diaphragm, 188, 189, 191, 194–196, 340
Dick-Read, Grantley, 170
Diethylstilbestrol, *see* DES
Dihydrotestosterone (DHT), 38
Dihydrotestosterone-deficiency syndrome, 43
Dilation, in first-stage labor, 172
Dilation and curettage (D&C), 212–213
Dilation and evacuation (D&E), 213–214
Dildos, 278, 304
DINS (double income, no sex) dilemma, 253
Directed masturbation therapy, 400
Direct observation, sexual responses measured with, 11
Discrimination, homosexuality and, 289–290
Diversity, *see* Cultural diversity
Divorce, 250–251, 258–259
DNA, *see* Deoxyribonucleic acid
Dominant genes, 32–33
Doppler, 165
Double standard
of aging, 261–262
jealousy and, 420
sexual, 241–243
Douching, 188
as contraceptive method, 202–203
Down syndrome, in fetus, 165
Dreaming, erections during, 226
Drugs
fetal development and, 160, 161
sexual dysfunction caused by, 137
Dyspareunia, 136, 146–147

Eagle Forum, 237
Early childhood, 224, 227–228
Ectopic pregnancy, 161, 165, 202

Effacement, in first-stage labor, 172
Egg(s), *see* Ovum(a)
Ego, 18
Ego integrity versus despair, in old age, 248
Ejaculation, 72, 73–74, 125–126
  female, 130
  premature, 144–145, 149, 152–153
Ejaculatory ducts, 36, 56–57
Ejaculatory incompetence, *see* Inhibited male orgasm
Electra complex, 224, 229, 232
Embryo, 34
Emergency contraceptive pills (ECPs), 211
Emission phase, of male orgasm, 72, 73, 125
Emotional intimacy, sexual intimacy and, 249–250
Empty love, 413–414
Endocrine disorders, sexual dysfunction caused by, 137
Endocrine glands, 67–68. *See also* Ovaries; Sex hormones; Testes
Endometriosis, 212
Endometrium, 60, 71
  cancer of, 200
Endorphins, 74–75
Enemas, during labor, 173
Engagement, in first-stage labor, 172
Epididymis, 36, 38, 56, 57, 225
Episiotomy, 147, 173–174, 182, 183
Equal Employment Opportunity Commission (EEOC), sexual harassment and, 363–364
Equity, in marriage, 257
Erectile dysfunction, 143–144, 149, 154–155, A4
Erections, 39, 58–59, 73, 74, 125, 144, 226
Erikson, Erik, 222, 224, 227, 229, 233, 239, 240, 247–248, 260, 263
Erogenous zones, 83
Eros, 17, 413
Erotica, 297–311
  adult bookstores and, 301–302
  advertisements, 298–299
  children and, 310–311
  cultural diversity and, 310
  cyberspace and, 302–303
  erotic dancing, 303–304
  hard-core, 298
  legal aspects of, 305–306, 307, 310–311

magazines and newspapers, 298
  movies and videos, 299–301
  nonviolent, 306
  prolonged exposure to, 309–310
  rape and, 307–309, 355
  romance novels, 300
  sexual aids as, 304–305
  soft-core, 298
  *store offering, APP 5
  telephone sex, 302
  television programs and, 299
  violent, 307–309
Erotic dancing, 303–304
Eroticism, in infancy, 225–227
Erotophilia, 88
Erotophobia, 88
Escort services, prostitution and, 313
Estradiol, 37, 39
Estrogens, 35, 37, 39, 47, 56, 60, 68, 69, 71, 160, 181, 199, 200, 225, 261, 262, 264
Ethical issues
  in sex research, 4, 7–8
  study of untreated syphilis and, 330
Ethnic differences, *see* Cultural diversity
Eve's Garden, A3
Evolutionary theory of sexuality, 14–16, 24, 25. *See also* Gender differences
Excessive sexual desire, 139, 142–143, 396–397
Excitement phase, of sexual response, 125, 127, 128
Exhibitionism, 391–393, 400
Exocrine glands, 67
Exotic Becomes Erotic model, of sexual orientation, 285
Experimental method, 10
Expulsion phase, of ejaculation, 72, 73
Extramarital sex, 256–258, 266
  jealousy and, 418, 419

Face-to-face coital position, 116, 117–120
Fallopian tubes, 35, 47, 59, 60
  fertilization in, 30, 33
  in infants, 225
  tubal ligation and, 188, 189, 191, 204–205
Family
  division of labor and formation of, 253–254
  dream versus reality of, 252, 253
  homosexuality and, 252, 284

sexual dysfunction and, 137
  sexual intercourse and, 253–254
  see also Marriage; Single parenthood
Fantasies, 14, 73, 75, 79, 85–87, 112
Fatuous love, 414
Federal Bureau of Investigation, 302
Federal Commission on Crimes of Violence, 355
Fellatio, 96, 114–115, 278
  homosexuality and, 274, 275
Female-above coital position, 116, 117, 118–119
Female condom, 198, 340
Female Eunuch, The (Greer), 23
Female sexual mutilation, 63, 64
Feminine Mystique, The (Friedan), 23
Feminists, 23
  erotica and, 305–306
  lesbians as, 279
  X-rated movies and, 300–301
Femme Productions, 300
Fertilization, 29–31
Fetal alcohol syndrome (FAS), 161–162
Fetishism, 378–379
Fetus, 45–46. *See also* Prenatal development
Fight or flight response, 72
First Amendment, 311
Fitness, 15
Flirtation, in bars, 11
Foams, *see* Contraceptive foams
Focus groups, sexual responses measured with, 12–13
Follicles, 60, 69, 71
Follicle-stimulating hormone (FSH), 35, 39, 49, 68, 69, 70, 206
Follicular phase, 69, 70, 71
Food and Drug Administration (FDA), 155, 196, 199, 200, 206, 211, 212, 337
Forebrain, 74
Foreplay, 115–116
Foreskin, of penis, 58, 63. *See also* Clitoral hood
Fornication, 311
France, RU–486 in, 212
Frenulum, 58
Freud, Sigmund, 6, 17–18, 24, 86, 222, 224, 229, 232, 233, 240, 287, 293, 406–407, 409
Friedan, Betty, 23
Friendship, love and, 409, 411
Frigidity, 142. *See also* Sexual arousal disorders

Frotteurism, 393–394
FSH, *see* Follicle-stimulating hormone

Gametes, *see* Germ cells
Gardnerella vaginalis, 327, 332
Gay Liberation Front, 290
Gay liberation movement, 290–291. *See also* Homosexuality
Gebhard, Paul H., 4–6
Gender, 16
Gender differences, 16–17, 230
  in adjustment to separation and divorce, 259
  in attitudes about love, 410
  in attitudes toward casual sex, 16
  awareness of in childhood, 228
  in communication of feelings, 94
  cultural diversity and, 21, 22
  in gender-role socialization, 229–230
  in homosexuality, 279–280
  in masturbation, 10, 90, 107, 109–112
  in mate selection criteria, 416
  parental-investment theory and, 16–17
  in power, 23
  in puberty, 47–49
  in sadomasochism, 387–388, 389
  in sex guilt, 90
  in sexual arousal, 12, 90–91
  in sexual attitudes and behaviors, 88, 228
  in sexual behavior in young adulthood, 248–249
  in sexual coercion, 373
  in sexual fantasies, 85–86
  in sexual intercourse, 242–243
  in sexual intimacy, 96–97, 415–416
  in sexual response, 127
  in values and morality, 229
Gender identity
  in childhood, 227
  sexual differentiation and, 49–52
Gender-role identification
  in adolescence, 239, 240–241
  in childhood, 227
  homosexuality and, 272, 276–278
  rape and, 356
Gender-role nonconformity, homosexuality and, 284–285
Gender roles
  in childhood, 227

erotica and, 301
  in middle age, 262–263
Gender-role socialization, 229–230
Gender stereotypes, 230
  in infancy, 223, 225
  in sexual interactions, 242
  in young adulthood, 248
Gender-typed identification, 241
Generalizability, self-report bias and, 10
Generativity versus stagnation, in middle age, 248, 260–261
Genes, 15, 31
  dominance and recessiveness and, 32–33
Genetic diseases, in fetus, 165
Genetics, homosexuality and, 281–283
Genetic sex, 31–33
Genital herpes, *see* Herpes simplex type II
Genitals
  ambiguous, 50–52
  females with progestin-induced masculinized external, 45
  in puberty, 35, 47, 49
  see also Sexual system
Genital stage, 18, 224, 240
Genital tubercle, 38, 39
Genital warts, 327, 341–342
Gentlemen's Clubs, 303
German measles, *see* Rubella
Germ cells, 31
Gestation, 33. *See also* Prenatal development
Gigolo, 314
Glans
  of clitoris, 63
  of penis, 58
Glory holes, 301–302
GnRH, *see* Gonadotropin-releasing hormone
Gonadal sex, 35–36. *See also* Sexual system
Gonadotropin-releasing hormone (GnRH), 35, 39, 68, 69
Gonadotropins, 39, 68
  follicle-stimulating hormone, 35, 39, 49, 68, 69, 70, 206
  luteinizing hormone, 35, 39, 49, 68, 69, 70
Gonorrhea, 324, 327, 328, 330, 336
Gräfenberg spot, 60, 62, 130
Great Britain, 212
Greece, 274
Greer, Germaine, 23
Group therapy, 153
Growth hormone, 68

Growth spurt, 47
Guilt, *see* Sex guilt

Habituation, sexual desire disorders and, 142
Hard-core erotica, 298. *See also* Erotica
Hearing, sexual arousal and, 85
Helms, Jesse, 6–7
Hemophilia, 33, 165
Hepatitis B, 327, 342
Heredity, *see* Genes; *under* Genetic
Hermaphroditism, 50–51
Heroin, fetal development and, 160
Herpes Resource Center, 341, A4
Herpes simplex type II, 160, 162, 327, 340–341, A4
Heterosexuality, 273
Hindbrain, 74
HIV, *see* Human immunodeficiency virus
Homophobia, 234, 271, 286–287
Homosexuality, 271–295
  acquired immunodeficiency syndrome and, 280, 286, 290, 340
  adjustment and, 286–289
  aging and, 280–281
  biological correlates of, 281–283
  in childhood, 234, 276, 284–285
  cohabitation and, 252, 253
  coming-out process and, 276–277
  cross-species perspective of, 273
  cultural diversity and, 22, 273–275, 285
  discrimination and, 289–290
  family experiences and, 252, 284
  fear of, 251
  gay liberation movement and, 290–291
  gender-role identity and, 272, 276–278
  glory holes and, 301–302
  homophobia and, 234, 271, 286–287
  legal issues and, 289–290
  lesbians, 272, 274, 278, 279–280, 282–283, 284, 286, 287
  marriage and, 289
  as mental illness, 288
  military and, 289–290
  mutual masturbation and, 113
  oral sex and, 115

parenthood and, 252
prevalence of, 275–276
  in prisons, 281
  prostitution and, 314
  safer-sex practices and, 326
  self-help organizations on, A4
  sexual expression and, 278–281
  sexually transmitted diseases and, 280, 286, 290, 340
  therapy and, 155–156, 288–289
Homosociality, 234
Honeymoon cystitis, *see* Cystitis
Hormonal sex, development of, 36–37, 39
Hormone-replacement therapy, 261, 264
Hormones, 67–68. *See also* Sex hormones
Hotel prostitutes, 312–313
Hot flashes, 261
HPV, *see* Genital warts
Hudson, Rock, 324
Human chorionic gonadotropin (HCG), 160–161, 206
Human immunodeficiency virus (HIV), 162, 312, 319, 334, 335–336, 337. *See also* Acquired immunodeficiency syndrome
Human Life Amendment, 208
Human papilloma virus, genital warts and, 341–342
Human Sexual Response (Masters and Johnson), 6
Hymen, 63–64
Hyperactive desire, *see* Excessive sexual desire
Hyperfemininity, 352
Hypermasculinity, 351
Hypoactive sexual desire disorder, 136, 141–142, 149
Hypothalamus, 39, 49, 68, 74–75
Hypothesis, 8
Hysterectomy, 61
Hysterotomy, 214

Id, 17, 18
Identity versus role confusion, in adolescence, 224, 239–243
Immunosuppression, acquired immunodeficiency syndrome and, 334
Implants, for erectile dysfunction, 155
Impotence Information Center, A4
Impotency, 142, 155, A4. *See also* Sexual arousal disorders

Impotents Anonymous, A4
Incest, 137, 366. *See also* Child sexual abuse
Inclusive fitness, 15
Independent variables, 8–9, 10
India, 37
Indonesia, 274
Industry versus inferiority, in late childhood, 224, 233–239
Infancy, 223–227
  attachment and, 404–408
  biosexual development in, 225
  breast-feeding and, 39, 60, 65, 68, 177, 179, 203
  circumcision in, 49–50, 58, 180–181
  erections and lubrication in, 226
  eroticism during, 225–227
  gender stereotyping and, 223, 225
  intersexed infants and, 51–52
  masturbation in, 226
  oral stage in, 224
  romantic love and, 413
  sensual development in, 226–227
  trust versus mistrust in, 223–227
Infanticide, 188
Infatuation, love and, 411–412
Infectious prostatitis, 331
Infertility, 161
Infidelity, dating and, 419
Informed consent
  in sex research, 7
  sexual intimacy and, 97–99, 100
Inhibin, 39
Inhibited female orgasm, 136, 145–146, 151, 152
Inhibited male orgasm, 136, 145
Initiative versus guilt, in early childhood, 224, 229–233
Inner lips (labia minora), 62, 63
Instincts, 17
Integrity versus despair, in old age, 263
Intercourse, *see* Sexual intercourse
Interfemoral intercourse, 278
Intersex Society of North America (ISNA), 50, 51, 52, A4
Intersexuality, 40, 49–52
  self-help organizations for, A4
Interstitial cells, 39, 49, 56, 225
Interstitial cell stimulating hormone, 39

Interstitial cystitis, 331
Interviews, sexual responses measured with, 11
Intimacy, love and, 410. *See also* Sexual intimacy
Intimacy versus isolation, in young adulthood, 248
Intra-amniotic injection, for abortion, 214
Intrauterine devices (IUDs), 188, 189, 190, 201–202, 211
In vitro fertilization/embryo transfer, 161
IUDs, *see* Intrauterine devices

Japan, 310, 317
Jealousy, love and, 418–420
Joan of Arc, 379
Johns, prostitution and, 316, 318
Johnson, Virginia, 6, 148–149
Johnson, Lyndon, 307
Johnson, Magic, 324
Jorgensen, Christine, 382
Jorgensen, George, 382
Journals, research on sexuality in, A2–A3

Kaplan, Helen Singer, 149
Kaposi's sarcoma (KS), 337, 338
Kegel, Arnold, 65
Kegel exercises, 65, 183
KinkNet, 303
Kinsey, Alfred C., 4–6
Kissing, 113–114
Klinefelter's syndrome, 41
Klismaphilia, 397

Labia, 47
Labia majora, *see* Outer lips
Labia minora, *see* Inner lips
Labioscrotal swelling, 38
Labor, childbirth and, 171–177
Lamaze, Bernard, 170
Language development, in childhood, 227
Laparoscope, for tubal ligation, 204–205
Larynx, 49
Lascivious material, 305
Latency, 18, 224, 232, 233
Learning theory, of sexuality, 19–20, 24, 25
Legal issues
    erotica and, 305–306, 307, 310–311
    homosexuality and, 289–290
    prostitution and, 315–317
    rape and, 359–360
Lesbians, 272, 274, 278, 279–280, 282–283, 284, 286, 287. *See also* Homosexuality

Leukorrhea, 332
Lewd material, 305
Leydig cells, *see* Interstitial cells
LH, *see* Luteinizing hormone
LHRH, *see* Luteinizing hormone releasing factor
Liberace, 324
Liberal feminism, 23
Libido, 17, 18
Librium, for sexual dysfunction, 155
Limbic system, 75
Limerence, 411–412
Lochia, 182
Longitudinal research, 249
Long-term relationships, 254
    vitality in, 421–423
    see also Marriage
Love, 402–424
    attachment and, 404–408, 409, 417
    commitment and, 410
    companionate, 409, 414
    constructions of, 409–410
    consummate, 414
    cultural diversity and, 22, 407–408, 410, 416
    dependency and control and, 416–418
    deprivation and, 405–408
    early experience with, 403–408
    empty, 413–414
    fatuous, 414
    forms of, 410–414
    friendship and, 409, 411
    infatuation and, 411–412
    infidelity and, 419
    intimacy and, 410
    jealousy and, 418–420
    loving sexual interactions and, 403, 420–423
    lust versus, 414–416
    mature, 420–423
    of others, 409–414
    passionate, 409, 410
    pregnancy and, 163
    punishment versus, 20
    romantic, 412–413, 417
    self-, 408
    two-stage process of, 81–82
    unrequited, 413
Lubricant
    as sexual aid, 304
    of vagina, 39, 61, 72, 136, 143, 144, 183, 226, 261, 264, 265
Lust
    love versus, 414–416
    two-stage process of, 81–82
Luteal phase, 69, 70, 71
Luteinizing hormone (LH), 39, 49, 68, 69, 70

Luteinizing hormone releasing factor (LHRH), 206
Lymphadenopathy, 337

McCormick, Naomi, 23
MacKensie, Bruce, 155
MacKensie, Eileen, 155
Magazines, as erotic, 298
Male-above coital position, 116, 117–118
Male menopause, 261
Mangaian people (Polynesia), 21
Marijuana
    fetal development and, 160
    sexual arousal/desire and, 142, 143
Marriage, 247, 252–259
    in adolescence, 258
    age at first, 250
    attraction versus attachment in, 255–256
    cohabitation and, 251
    dream versus reality of, 252, 253
    homosexuality and, 289
    separation and divorce and, 250–251, 258–259
    sexual intercourse in, 252–256
    sexual pleasure and longevity of, 254–255
    see also Extramarital sex
Martin, Clyde E., 4–6
Masochism, sexual, 386–388, 389
Massage, for simultaneous orgasm, 123
Massage parlors, 313, 318
Masters, William, 6, 148–149
Masturbation, 6, 86, 88, 90, 107–113, 230
    in adolescence, 241
    in childhood, 226
    cultural diversity and, 22
    erotic material and, 304
    excessive sexual desire and, 143
    female methods of, 110–112
    gender differences in, 10, 90, 107, 109–112
    homosexuals and, 278
    in infancy, 226
    mutual, 112–113
    in old age, 266, 267
    prevalence of, 107
    training in, 151–152
    Twain on, 110
Mature love, 420–423
May, Rollo, 409
Medroxyprogesterone acetate, *see* Depo-Provera
Meese, Edwin, III, 307

Meese Commission, 307
Mehinaku (Brazil), 5, 29, 168
Meiosis, 31
Melanesia, 274
Menarche, 35, 47–48, 69
Menopause, 261, 262
Menstrual extraction, 212
Menstruation, 69–71, 75
    menarche, 35, 47–48, 69
    menopause and, 261, 262
    pregnancy and, 163
Mercury-in-rubber strain gauge, 12
Metal-band gauge, 12
Methadone, fetal development and, 160
Mexico, 274, 275
Micropenis, 58
Microsurgery, for erectile dysfunction, 155
Midbrain, 74
Middle age, 259–263
    affection and loyalty in, 255
    changes and assessments in, 260–261
    double standard of aging in, 261–262
    ego integrity versus despair in, 248
    gender roles in, 262–263
    generativity versus stagnation in, 248, 260–261
    homosexuality in, 280–281
    intimacy versus isolation in, 248
    menopause in, 261, 262
    sexual intercourse in, 263
Midwives, 172
Mifepristone, *see* RU–486
Military, homosexuality and, 289–290
Minorities, acquired immunodeficiency syndrome and, 335
Minor tranquilizers, for sexual dysfunction, 155
MIS, *see* Müllerian-inhibiting substance
Miscarriage, 164, 165
Mitosis, 31
Modeling, 20
Mons pubis, 62
Morality
    development of, 229
    theories of sexuality and, 24–25
Morning-after pill, *see* DES
Morning sickness, 163, 164
Mosher Guilt Inventory, 80, 88
Motile, sperm as, 30
Movies, erotic, 299–301
Müllerian-duct system, 35, 36

Müllerian-inhibiting substance (MIS), 37
Multiculturalism, *see* Cultural diversity
Multiple orgasms, 131–132
Mundugamor (New Guinea), 229
Muscle tension, in sexual response, 124
Mutual masturbation, 112–113
Myographs, 12
Myometrium, 60

National Gay Task Force, A4
National Health and Social Life Survey, 6–7
National Institute for Child Health and Human Development, 6
National Opinion Research Center, 300
National Right to Life Committee, 209
Natural selection, 14–15
Necrophilia, 396
Negative reinforcement, 20
Nervous system, 71–75
    autonomic, 71–72
    central, 71, 72–75
    parasympathetic, 71, 72
    peripheral, 71
    spinal cord, 72, 73–74
    sympathetic, 71–72
    see also Brain
Netherlands, 258
Neurological disorders, sexual dysfunction caused by, 137
New Guinea, 5, 229, 273
Newman, Paul, 262
Newspapers, as erotic, 298
NGU, *see* Nongonococcal urethritis
Nicotine, fetal development and, 160
Nipples, 60
Nocturnal emissions, 49
Nocturnal orgasm, 106–107
Nocturnal penile tumescence test, 144
Nondemand pleasuring, 150, 151
Nongonococcal urethritis (NGU), 327, 330, 331
Norplant, 189, 200–201
Novelty, temporary effects produced by, 13
NSP–270, 304–305
Nurse-midwives, 172
Nymphomania, 143

Object-relations theory, 18
Obscene telephone calls, 393

Obscenity, 305–306. *See also* Erotica
Observation, *see* Direct observation
Obsessive-compulsive reaction, excessive sexual desire and, 143
Oedipus complex, 224, 229, 232
Office of Adolescent Pregnancy Programs, 237
Oil glands, in puberty, 35, 49
Old age, 263–267
    ego integrity versus despair in, 248
    female sexual system in, 265
    generativity versus stagnation in, 248
    homosexuality in, 280
    integrity versus despair in, 263
    intimacy versus isolation in, 248
    male sexual system in, 264, 265
    physiological changes in, 263–264
    sexual activity in, 263–267
    social stereotypes and self-image in, 264–265
Operant conditioning, 19–20
Operational definition, 8
Opportunistic infections, with acquired immunodeficiency syndrome, 337–338
Oral contraceptives, 7–8, 13, 160, 188, 189, 199–200, 211
Oral-genital sex, 114–115
Oral sex, 113–115
    cunnilingus, 96, 114–115, 168, 195–196
    fellatio, 96, 114–115, 274, 275, 278
    kissing, 113–114
    oral-genital sex, 114–115
    during pregnancy, 168
    prostitution and, 315
    in young adulthood, 248
Oral stage, 18, 224
Orgasm, 39, 63, 65, 68, 72, 74, 85, 87, 124, 125–126, 128, 129–132
    blended, 130
    breast-feeding and, 178
    in childhood, 230
    cultural diversity and, 22
    female, 116, 124, 125, 126, 129–131
    female masturbation and, 112
    male, 116, 124, 125–126, 131–132
    male masturbation and, 110
    multiple, 131–132

nocturnal, 106–107
    pretend, 130–131
    quality of time following, 123
    simultaneous, 123
    uterine, 130
    vulval, 129–130
Orgasm disorders, 136, 144–146
    inhibited female orgasm, 136, 145–146, 151, 152
    inhibited male orgasm, 136, 145
    premature ejaculation, 144–145, 149, 152–153
    retrograde ejaculation, 145
Orgasmic phase, of sexual response, 39, 68, 74. *See also* Orgasm
Osteoporosis, 264
Outer lips (labia majora), 62–63
Ovaries, 39, 60
    cancer of, 200
    development of, 35, 36, 47
    in infants, 225
Overlapping distributions, 230
Ovulation, 29, 39, 60, 68, 69, 70
    calendar method determining, 192
    rhythm method determining, 192–194
Ovum(a), 29, 60
    as germ cells, 31
    sperm fertilizing, 29–31
Oxytocin, 39, 68, 177, 178

Pain centers, in brain, 74, 75
Pandering, 315
PAP test, 61
Paraphilias, 376–401
    asphyxiophilia, 396
    chemical treatment of, 399
    cognitive-behavior therapies for, 399–400
    compulsive sexual behavior, 396–397
    excessive sexual desire and, 143
    exhibitionism, 391–393, 400
    fetishism, 378–379
    frotteurism, 393–394
    invasive, 388–400
    necrophilia, 396
    noninvasive consensual, 378–388
    obscene telephone calls, 393
    pedophilia, 394–395
    psychotherapy for, 398
    sadomasochism, 386–388, 389
    surgical castration for, 398–400
    transsexuality, 273, 381–386
    transvestism, 273, 379–381
    treatment of, 398–400

uncommon, 396, 397
    voyeurism, 389–391
    zoophilia, 395–396
Parasympathetic nervous system, 71, 72
Parental-investment theory, 16–17
Parents
    child sexuality and, 227
    gender-role socialization and, 229–230
    homosexual behavior in childhood and, 234
    infant sensuality and, 226–227, 228
    sex education from, 92, 93–94, 235–236
    sex guilt in children and, 88–90
    sexual intercourse between, 231–232, 253
    toilet training and, 227–228
Parents and Friends of Lesbians and Gays (PFLAG), A4
Partialism, 397
Passionate love, 409, 410
Passive immunity, from breast milk, 177
Past experiences, sexual dysfunctions and, 137–138
Paul, St., 409
Pavlov, Ivan, 19
Pediculosis pubis, 343
Pedophilia, 394–395
Pelvic inflammatory disease (PID), 202, 327, 332
Pelvic nerve, 73
Penile plethysmograph, 12
Penis, 38, 49, 55, 58–59, 63, 92
    cancer of, 180
    circumcision of, 49–50, 58, 180–181
    erections and, 39, 58–59, 73, 74, 125, 144, 226
    slang terms for, 93
    see also Ejaculation; Masturbation
Penthouse, 298
Perimenopausal stage, 261
Perimetrium, 60
Peripheral nervous system, 71
Personality development, Freud and, 17–19
Perversion, 377. *See also* Paraphilias
Phallic stage, 18, 224
Phallus, 38. *See also* Penis
Pharonic circumcision, 64
Pheromones, 75, 83
Philia, 409, 411
Phimosis, 180
Physical attractiveness, awareness of in childhood, 233

Picasso, Pablo, 395
PID, *see* Pelvic inflammatory disease
Pill, *see* Oral contraceptives
Pimp, 312, 313, 317, 318
Pituitary gland, 39, 49, 68–69, 74
Placebos, 13
Placenta, 34, 39, 160, 174
Planned Parenthood Federation of America, 299, A3
Plateau phase, of sexual response, 125, 127
Platonic love, 409, 411
Play, sexual learning through, 230–231
Playboy, 298
Pleasure centers, in brain, 74–75
Pneumocystis carinii pneumonia (PCP), 337–338
Politics
  sex research and, 4–7
  theories of sexuality and, 24–25
Pomeroy, Wardell B., 4–6
Population control, abortion of female fetuses as, 37
Pornography, 297
  rape and, 307–309, 355
  see also Erotica
Positive reinforcement, operant conditioning and, 20
Postpartum, 159
Postpartum depression, 181
Power, gender differences in, 23
Pregnancy, 39, 60, 71, 159–169
  acquired immunodeficiency syndrome and, 335
  in adolescence, 215, 216–217, 236, 238, 239
  adoption and, 215
  babies' position during, 178
  children's ideas on, 235
  coital positions in, 119
  complications during, 178
  cross-cultural views on, 4, 5
  early symptoms of, 159–161
  ectopic, 161, 165, 202
  herpes simplex type II and, 341
  infertility and, 161
  miscarriage and, 164
  postpartum adjustment and, 181
  progestins during, 45
  sexual intercourse and, 140, 168–169, 181–183
  single parenthood and, 215
  stages of, 162–168
  tests and, 159–161
  unintended, 215–217
  unwanted, 217, *see also* Abortion; Contraceptives

see also Childbirth; Fertilization; Prenatal development
Premarital sex
  in adolescence, 236, 241, 242
  sexual double standard and, 241–243
  in young adulthood, 248–249
Premature birth, 178
Premature ejaculation, 144–145, 149, 152–153
Premenstrual phase, 69, 70, 71
Prenatal development, 33–46, 224
  tests for, 164, 165
  threats to, 160, 161–162, 168–169
  see also Sexual differentiation
Prepared childbirth, 170–171, 174
Prepuce, *see* Foreskin
Preschool years, 224, 229–233
Priapism, 144
Primal scene, 231–232
Primary orgasmic dysfunction, 151
Prisons, homosexuality in, 281
Proceptivity, 94
Procuring, 315
Professional organizations, about sexuality, A1–A2
Profit, sex for, *see* Erotica; Prostitution
Progestasert, 202
Progesterone, 37, 39, 60, 71, 181, 261
Progestins, 35, 37, 39, 45, 47, 70, 71, 160, 181, 199, 200, 261
Prolactin, 39, 68, 177, 225
Prostaglandins, 212
Prostate gland, 39, 57
  cancer of, 57–58
Prostatitis, 327, 331
Prosthesis, for erectile dysfunction, 155
Prostitution, 311–319
  adolescence and, 317
  bar girls and, 312
  brothel and, 315
  call girls and, 313, 315
  clientele and, 317–318
  contraceptive use and, 314, 315
  crack use and, 312
  cultural diversity and, 317, 319
  decriminalization of, 317
  description of trade of, 314–315
  economics of, 315
  escort services and, 313
  factors associated with entry into, 317–318
  homosexuals and, 314

hotel prostitutes and, 312–313
  johns and, 316, 318
  legal issues of, 315–317
  males prostitutes (gigolos) and, 314, 318
  massage parlors and, 313, 318
  as oldest profession, 311
  oral sex and, 315
  pandering and, 315
  pimps and, 312, 313
  procuring and, 315
  Rome and, 311
  sex tourism and, 319
  storefront variety of, 313
  streetwalkers and, 312, 315
  Victorian England and, 311
Prurient, 305
Pseudohermaphrodite, 51
Psychoanalysis, for sex therapy, 147
Psychoanalytic theory, of sexuality, 17–19, 24, 25
Psychosexual stages, 18–19
Psychotherapy, for invasive paraphilias, 398
Puberty, 18, 35, 47–49, 68, 225, 239, 240
Pubic hair, in puberty, 35, 47, 49
Public Health Service, 330, A4
Pubococcygeus muscle (PC muscle), 65
  Kegel exercises for, 65, 183
Pudendal nerve, 73
Punishment, operant conditioning and, 20

Questionnaires, sexual responses measured with, 11
Quickening, 165, 166

Radiation, fetal development and, 160
Radical feminism, 23
Rape, 349–362
  acquaintance, 94, 190, 354–355, 357, 361–362
  adolescents and, 353–354, 360–361
  aftermath of, 357–359
  criminal justice system and, 359–360
  exaggerated gender-role identity and, 356
  fantasies on, 87
  female victims of, 353–355
  gender differences in, 373
  by husbands, 355, 357
  male victims of, 353, 354
  procedure for victim of, 357–359
  rapist and, 350–352

reducing risk of, 361–362
  risk factors associated with, 360–361
  sexual aversion and, 142
  sexual dysfunction and, 137
  statutory, 359–360
  stereotypes on, 350
  uncontrollable lust or aggression and, 356
  vaginismus and, 147
  victim precipitation and, 350, 355
  victims of, 352–355
  violent erotica and, 307–309, 355
  young adults and, 354–355
Rape-crisis centers, 357–358, 359, 360
Rape-trauma syndrome, 357
Rape Victim's Privacy Act, 360
Rapid eye movement (REM) sleep, erections during, 144
RAS, *see* Reticular activating system
Rear-entry coital position, 116, 120–121
Recessive genes, 33
Rectal myograph, 12
Reducing the Risk (RTR) program, 237
Refractory period, 126, 131
Reinforcement, operant conditioning and, 20
Reliability, of research measures, 11
Religion, theories and, 24
Replication, of results of sex research studies, 13
Repression, 17
Reproductionism, 17
Reproductive bias, 5
Reproductive organs, *see* Sexual system
Reproductive success, 15
Research on sexuality, *see* Sex research
Resolution phase, of sexual response, 126
Response variables, *see* Dependent variables
Retarded ejaculation, *see* Inhibited male orgasm
Reticular activating system (RAS), 75
Retrograde ejaculation, 145
Retrovirus, 335
Revictimization, 369–370
Rhythm method, of contraception, 189, 192–194
Risk-benefit principle, in sex research, 7–8
Roe v. *Wade*, 207, 208

Rohypnol, 354–355
Roman Catholic Church, conception and, 5
Romance novels, as erotic, 300
Romantic love, 412–413, 417
Rooming, 177
Roth v. *United States,* 305
Royale, Candida, 300
RU–486, 211–212
Rubella, 34, 160

Sadomasochism, 87, 386–388, 389
Safer-sex practices, 325–326, 339–340, 343–346
Saline abortion, 214
Sambia (New Guinea), 5, 49, 273
Sampling, 9–10
Satyriasis, 143
Scales, sexual responses measured with, 11
Scissors coital position, 121
Scripts, for sexual behavior, 14, 21, 23, 106, 240
Scrotum, 39, 55
Sebum, 49
Secondary orgasmic dysfunction, 151, 153
Secondary sexual characteristics, 35, 47–49
Self-administered measures, sexual responses measured with, 11
Self-help organizations, A3
  for erectile dysfunction, 155
Selfishness, self-love versus, 408
Self-love, 408
Self-report bias, 9, 10
Self-stimulation, *see* Masturbation
Semen, 49, 55, 57
Seminal vesicles, 36, 38, 57
Seminiferous tubules, 49, 56
Sensate focus, in sex therapy, 150
Senses
  development of in infancy, 226–227
  sexual arousal and, 83–85
Sensuous Seniors, 264
Sex chromosomes, 31–33, 40
Sex education, 228, 234, 235–239
  parents and, 92, 93–94, 235–236
Sex for One: The Joys of Self-Loving (Dodson), 108
Sex guilt, 86, 88–90
Sex Guilt Scale, *see* Mosher Guilt Inventory
Sex hormones, 37, 55, 56, 60, 68–69, 74

for abortion, 211–212
androgens (testosterone and androstetenedione), 12, 35, 37, 38, 39, 47, 49, 56, 60, 68, 69, 160, 255, 262, 282–283
endocrine glands and, 67–68
estrogens, 35, 37, 39, 47, 56, 60, 68, 69, 71, 160, 181, 199, 200, 225, 261, 262, 264
fetal development and, 160
follicle-stimulating hormone, 35, 39, 49, 68, 69, 70, 206
gonadotropin-releasing hormone, 35, 39, 68, 69
homosexuality and, 282–283
inhibin, 39
luteinizing hormone, 35, 39, 49, 68, 69, 70
as male contraceptive, 206
menopause and, 261, 262
oxytocin, 39, 68, 177, 178
progestins (progesterone), 35, 37, 39, 45, 47, 60, 70, 71, 160, 181, 199, 200, 261
prolactin, 39, 68, 177, 225
for sexual dysfunction, 155
testosterone, *see* androgens (testosterone and androstetenedione), *above*
vasoactive intestinal polypeptide, 39
Sex Information and Education Council of the United States (SIECUS), A2, A3
Sex linkage, 32
Sex-reassignment surgery, 381, 382–383, 384–386
Sex research, 3–14
  case studies in, 12
  with children, 4
  direct observation in, 11
  ethical issues in, 4, 7–8
  evaluating results of, 13–14
  focus groups in, 12–13
  interviews in, 11
  *journals publishing, APP 3–5
  measurement in, 11–13
  methods of, 10–11
  physiological response measures in, 12
  political and social barriers to, 4–7
  process of, 8–13
  questionnaires in, 11
  sampling in, 9–10
  scales in, 11
  surveys in, 11
  terms in, 8
  variables in, 8–9

Sex therapists
  certified, A4
  qualifications and ethics of, 155–156
  sexual harassment by, 365–366
Sex therapy, 147–156, 227
  behavioral approaches for, 149–150
  for erectile dysfunction, 144, 149, 154–155
  evaluation of, 148–149
  group therapy and, 153
  for homosexuals, 155–156, 288–289
  hormones in, 155
  for hypoactive sexual desire, 149
  implants for, 154
  Kaplan's approach to, 149
  Masters and Johnson's approach to, 148–149
  masturbation training in, 151
  medications for, 155
  nondemand pleasuring in, 150, 151
  for orgasmically inhibited women, 151, 152
  for premature ejaculation, 149, 152–153
  sensate focus in, 150
  sexual arousal enhanced with, 151
  sexual surrogates in, 154
  squeeze technique in, 152–153
  surgery and, 154–155
  systematic desensitization in, 153
  for vaginismus, 147, 149
Sex tourism, 319
Sex-typed identification, 241
Sexual abuse, *see* Child sexual abuse
Sexual addiction, *see* Excessive sexual desire
Sexual aids, 304–305
Sexual arousal, 39, 55, 58, 61, 63, 79–91
  attitudes towards sexuality and, 87–90
  breasts and, 65, 67
  circumcision and, 180
  cultural diversity and, 80–81
  erotic material and, 304–305
  fantasies and, 14, 75, 79, 85–87, 112
  gender differences and similarities in, 12, 90–91
  learning, 80–82
  measuring changes from, 12
  pelvic muscles and, 65
  penis length and, 59
  purposes of, 82

senses and, 83–85
sex therapy and, 151
sources of, 83–90
toward someone outside primary relationship, 101
two-stage model of, 81–82
violent erotica and, 307–309
Sexual arousal disorders, 143–144
  erectile dysfunction, 143–144, 149, 154–155
  priapism, 144
Sexual assault, 349, 359
  childhood experiences and, 405–406
  sexual sadism and, 386, 388
  see also Rape
Sexual attitudes, 87–90
  contraceptive use and, 190–191
  gender differences in, 88, 228
Sexual aversion disorder, 142
Sexual Behavior in the Human Female (Kinsey group), 5
Sexual Behavior in the Human Male (Kinsey group), 5
Sexual coercion, 348–375. *See also* Child sexual abuse; Rape; Sexual assault; Sexual harassment
Sexual compulsion, *see* Excessive sexual desire
Sexual desire, 75
Sexual desire disorders, 136, 139, 141–143
  excessive sexual desire, 139, 142–143, 396–397
  hypoactive sexual desire, 136, 141–142, 149
  sexual aversion disorder, 142
Sexual desire phase, of sexual response, 124
Sexual deviance, *see* Paraphilias
Sexual differentiation
  atypical, 40–45
  development of, 35–36
  intersexuality and, 49–52
  typical, 34–39
Sexual double standard, 241–243
Sexual dysfunction, 134–157
  anxiety or fear causing, 72, 138
  biological causes of, 136, 137
  causes of, 135–141
  communicating about sexuality and, 94, 139–140
  drugs causing, 137
  dyspareunia, 136, 146–147
  erectile dysfunction, 143–144, 149, 154–155, A4
  inhibited female orgasm, 136, 145–146, 151, 152

Sexual dysfunction *(continued)*
  inhibited male orgasm, 136, 145
  masturbation for, 108
  misinformation causing, 138–139
  past experiences causing, 137–138
  premature ejaculation, 144–145, 149, 152–153
  priapism, 144
  psychosocial causes of, 136–141
  self-help organizations for, A4
  in sexual arousal, 143–144
  sexual pain, 136, 146–147
  stress causing, 140–141
  vaginal lubrication, 136, 143, 144
  vaginismus, 146, 147, 149
  see also Sex therapy; Sexual desire disorders
Sexual exclusivity, 98–99
Sexual exploitation, children involved in erotica as, 310–311
Sexual expression, homosexuality and, 278–281
Sexual harassment, 349, 363–366
Sexual information, organizations offering, A4
Sexual intercourse, 63
  child witnessing parents having, 231–232
  cohabitation and, 252–253
  coital positions during, 116–121
  as copulation, 14
  cultural diversity and, 5, 21, 22, 29
  divorce and, 259
  emotional intimacy and, 249–250
  fantasies during, 86, 87
  first, 242–243
  foreplay and, 115–116
  frequency of, 122
  gender differences in, 242–243
  in marriage, 252–256
  in middle age, 263
  mutual masturbation as alternative to, 113
  in old age, 265–267
  painful (dyspareunia), 136, 146–147
  parenthood and, 231–232, 253
  pregnancy and, 140, 168–169, 181–183
  script for, 106
  sounds during, 85
  "token no" and, 97

  in young adulthood, 248–249
  see also Extramarital sex; Premarital sex; Sexual intimacy; Sexual response
Sexual intimacy
  gender differences in, 96–97, 415–416
  informed consent and, 97–99, 100
  interpersonal communication and, 94
  purposes of, 123
  see also Sexual intercourse
Sexual learning, in childhood, 230–233. *See also* Sex education
Sexually transmitted diseases (STDs), 140, 322–347
  in adolescence, 239
  attitudes toward, 323–325
  bacterial infections, 326, 327, 328–332
  bisexuality and, 292
  candidiasis, 342–343
  chancroid, 332
  chlamydia, 327, 329–331, 336
  contraceptive foams and suppositories and, 199
  cystitis, 327, 331
  fetal development and, 160, 162, 168–169
  gardnerella vaginalis, 327, 332
  genital warts, 327, 341–342
  gonorrhea, 324, 327, 328, 330, 336
  hepatitis B, 327, 342
  herpes simplex type II, 160, 162, 327, 340–341, A4
  homosexuality and, 280, 286, 290, 340
  nongonococcal urethritis, 327, 330, 331
  parasitic infections, 342–343
  pediculosis pubis, 343
  pelvic inflammatory disease, 327, 332
  prostatitis, 327, 331
  prostitution and, 314, 315, 317
  protecting against, 98, 197, 325–326, 339–340, 341, 343–346
  self-help organizations for, A4
  sex tourism and, 319
  shigellosis, 327, 332
  syphilis, 160, 327, 328–329, 330, 336
  trichomoniasis, 343
  viral infections, 327, 340–342, *see also* Acquired immunodeficiency syndrome (AIDS)

  see also Acquired immunodeficiency syndrome (AIDS)
Sexual masochism, 386–388, 389
Sexual Opinion Survey (SOS), 87, 88
Sexual orientation, 271–272
  bisexuality, 51, 273, 291–293
  transsexuality, 273, 381–383
  transvestism, 273, 379–381
  see also Homosexuality
Sexual pain disorders, 136, 146–147
  dyspareunia, 146, 147
  vaginismus, 140, 146, 147
Sexual partners, number of, 122
Sexual rehearsal, in childhood, 233–234
Sexual response, 55, 72, 124–129
  excitement phase, 125, 127, 128
  gender differences in, 127
  menopause and, 261
  in old age, 263–264, 265
  orgasmic phase of, 39, 68, 74, *see also* Orgasm
  patterns of, 127
  plateau phase, 125, 127
  resolution phase, 126
  sexual desire in, 124
  variations in, 128–129
  see also Nervous system
Sexual sadism, 386, 388
Sexual Salvation (McCormick), 23
Sexual satisfaction, 121–122
Sexual scripts, 14, 21, 23, 106, 240
Sexual surrogate, in sex therapy, 154
Sexual system
  female, 59
  male, 55–59
  prenatal development of, 35–39, *see also* Sexual differentiation
  pubescent development of, 18, 35, 47–49, 68, 225, 239, 240
Sexual violence, violent erotica and, 307–309, 355. *See also* Sexual assault
Shared Intimacies (Barbach and Levine), 87, 105
Shepard, Cybill, 262
Shigellosis, 327, 332
Sickle-cell anemia, in fetus, 165
Side-by-side coital position, 119–120
Side effects, studying, 13
Sight, sexual arousal and, 84–85
Sildenafil, for sexual dysfunction, 155
Simultaneous orgasm, 123

Single lifestyles, 250–251
Single parenthood, 215, 252
  adolescent pregnancy and, 215, 216–217, 236, 238, 239
Smell, sexual arousal and, 83–84
Smoking, oral contraceptives and, 200
So (Uganda), 21, 22, 80
Socialization, 21
  communicating about sexuality and, 92–94
  gender-role, 229–230
Social learning theory, 20, 229
Society, sex research and, 4–7
Sociological theories, of sexuality, 21–24, 25. *See also* Cultural diversity
Sodomy, 289
Soft-core erotica, 298. *See also* Erotica
South Pacific, 5, 21, 116
Spectating, sexual dysfunction caused by, 138
Sperm, 39, 49, 55, 56, 57, 58, 68
  egg fertilized by, 29–31
  as germ cells, 31
  puberty and, 47
Spermatic cord, 55
Spermicidal agents, 188, 194–196, 341, 345
Spina bifida, in fetus, 165
Spinal cord, 72, 73–74
Spontaneous abortion, *see* Miscarriage
Sports Illustrated, 298
Squeeze technique, 152–153
Statutory rape, 359–360
STD National Hotline, A4
STDs, *see* Sexually transmitted diseases
Sterilization
  female, 188, 189, 191, 204–205
  male, 188, 189, 191, 203–204
Stimulus variables, *see* Independent variables
Stonewall Inn, 290
Strange Situation, 405
Streetwalkers, 312, 315
Stress, sexual dysfunction caused by, 140–141
Stripteasing (erotic dancing), 303–304
Subincision, 180
Suction abortion, 212–213
Sudan, 64
Superego, 18
Supreme Court, U.S.
  on abortion, 207, 208, 214
  on child erotica, 311
  on contraceptives, 188
  on obscenity, 305

Surrogate motherhood, 161
Surveys
    on sexual arousal, 90–91
    sexual responses measured
        with, 11
Sweat glands, in puberty, 35, 47
Sweden, 232, 285, 410
Sympathetic nervous system, 71–72
Sympto-thermal contraception, 189, 192–194
Syphilis, 160, 327, 328–329, 330, 336
Systematic desensitization, 153

Tay-Sachs disease, in fetus, 165
Tchambuli (New Guinea), 229
Telephone calls, obscene, 393
Telephone clubs, in Japan, 317
Television programs, as erotic, 299
Telljohann & Price, 276
Tenting effect, 125
Testes, 39, 49, 55–56, 68
    cancer of, 56
    development of, 35, 36–37, 38, 49
    in infants, 225
    self-examination of, 57
Testicular feminization, *see*
    Androgen insensitivity
    syndrome
Testosterone, 12, 35, 37, 38, 39, 47, 49, 56, 60, 68, 69, 160, 225, 262, 282–283
Tetracycline, fetal development
    and, 160
Thailand, 319
Thalamus, 74, 75
Thanatos, 17
Theoretical failure rate, of con-
    traceptives, 188
Theories of sexuality, 14–25
    evolutionary, 14–16, 24, 25,
        see also Gender differences
    feminist, 23
    learning, 19–20, 24, 25
    morality and, 24–25
    politics and, 24–25
    psychoanalytic, 17–19, 24, 25
    sociological, 21–24, 25, *see
        also* Cultural diversity

Therapists, *see* Sex therapists
ThrobNet, 303
Tissot, Simon André, 107–108
Tiwi (Melville Island), 5
Toilet training, 227–228
Touch, sexual arousal and, 83
Toxic shock syndrome, 196
Transition, in first-stage labor,
    173
Transsexuality, 273, 381–386
Transvestism, 273, 379–381
Triangular family system, homo-
    sexuality and, 284
Tribadism, 278, 279
Trichomoniasis, 343
Trinidad, 221
Triple-X syndrome, 41
Trust, in sexual relationship, 140
Trust versus mistrust in infancy,
    223–227
Tubal ligation, 51, 189, 191,
    204–205
Turkey, 274
Turner's syndrome, 40, 41
Turner, Tina, 262
Tuskegee study, of untreated
    syphilis, 330
Twain, Mark, 110
Two-stage model, of sexual
    arousal, 81–82

Uganda, 21, 22, 80, 168
Ultrasonography, of fetal devel-
    opment, 165
Umbilical cord, 34, 46
Unconditioned response (UCR),
    19
Unconditioned stimulus (UCS),
    19
Unidentified rapists, 350, 351,
    352
U.S. Commission on Obscenity
    and Pornography, 307, 309
Unrequited love, 413
Urethra, 36, 39, 56, 57
Urethral tube, 38
Urinary bladder, 36, 39
Urogenital folds, 38, 39
Urophilia, 397
Uterine orgasm, 130
Uterus, 33, 34, 35, 39, 47, 59,
    60–61, 225

Vacuum aspiration, *see* Suction
    abortion
Vacuum pump, for erectile diffi-
    culties, 155
Vagina, 36, 39, 47, 57, 59, 61,
    62, 72
    after childbirth, 183
    lubrication of, 39, 72, 125,
        136, 143, 144, 183, 226,
        261, 264, 265
    tenting effect and, 125
Vaginal lips, 39
Vaginal myograph, 12
Vaginal ring, 206
Vaginismus, 146, 147, 149
Vaginitis, *see* Gardnerella
    vaginalis
Validity, of research measures, 11
Valium, for sexual dysfunction,
    155
Values, development of, 229
Variables, 8–9, 10
Vas deferens, 36, 38, 39, 55, 56
Vasectomy, 188, 189, 191, 203–
    204
Vasoactive intestinal polypeptide,
    39
Vasocongestion, 124, 125
Vasovasectomy, 204
Venereal diseases (VDs), 324.
    See also Sexually transmit-
    ted diseases
Vibrators, 111–112, 304
Victim precipitation, rape and,
    350, 355
Victim recidivism, 369–370
Videos, erotic, 299–301
Vitamin A, fetal development
    and, 160
Vitamin E, sexual performance
    and, 10–11
Voice change, in puberty, 35, 49
Volunteer bias, 9–10, 11
Voyeurism, 389–391
Vulva, 47, 59, 60, 62–64, 72
Vulval orgasm, 129–130

Waist-to-hip ratio (WHR), repro-
    ductive fitness and, 84
Watson, John, 19
Wet dream, *see* Nocturnal
    orgasm

White, James Platt, 4
Withdrawal, 58, 188, 189, 202
Wolffian-duct system, 35, 36, 37,
    38
Womb, 59. *See also* Uterus
Women-above coital position,
    123
Woodward, Joanne, 262
World Health Organization, 191,
    206
World Wide Web, erotica and,
    302–303

X chromosome, 31–33, 40
X-rated movies, 299–301
XYY syndrome, 41

Y chromosome, 31–33, 35, 36,
    40
Young adulthood, 247–254
    acquired immunodeficiency
        syndrome in, 335
    back-burner relationships in,
        249
    cohabitation in, 251–252
    contraceptive use in, 249
    dating in, 248–249
    ego integrity versus despair in,
        248
    generativity versus stagnation
        in, 248
    intimacy versus isolation in,
        248
    lifestyle choices and shifting
        norms in, 250–252
    passion and sexual intimacy in,
        255
    rape in, 354–355
    sexual activity in, 248–249
    sexual harassment in, 365
    sexually transmitted diseases
        in, 325–326
    sexual versus emotional inti-
        macy in, 249–250
    single lifestyles in, 250–251
    see also Marriage

Zidovudine, *see* AZT
Zoophilia, 395–396
Zuni (New Mexico), 15
Zygote, 33

CREDITS

Chapter Opening Photographs

p. 2, The Granger Collection; p. 28, Barbara Campbell/Gamma Liaison; p. 54, Barry Yui/Gamma Liaison; p. 78, Barry Yui/Gamma Liaison; p. 104, Sohm/Sohm/Stock Boston; p. 134, Lien Nibauer/Gamma Liaison; p. 158, T. Henstra/Gamma Liaison; p. 186, Deborah Gilbert/The Image Bank; p. 220, Jerry Koontz/The Picture Cube; p. 246, M. Siluk/The Image Works; p. 270, Lien Nibauer/Gamma Liaison; p. 296, Barbara Alper/Stock Boston; p. 322, Robert Ginn/Picture Cube; p. 348, Allen Mcinnis/Gamma Liaison; p. 376, Dr. M. Diamond/InterAction Stock; p. 402, Frank Siteman/Stock Boston.

Other Photographs

p. 4, Reproduced by permission of The Kinsey Institute for Research in Sex, Gender and Reproduction, Inc.; p. 6, Ira Wyman/SYGMA; p. 9 (3 photos), Andrew Brillant/Carol Palmer; p. 12, top (2 photos), © 1994 Dr. M. Diamond/InterAction Stock; p. 12, bottom, Courtesy Perry Meter Systems/Biotechnologies; p. 15, top, Steward Halperin/Animals, Animals; p. 15, bottom, Jose Carrillo/Photo Edit; p. 16, John Eastcott, Yva Momatiuk/ The Image Works; p. 30, Jason Burns/Ace/Phototake; p. 32, BiophotoAssociates/Photo Researchers; p. 34, Phototake; p. 42 (2 photos), *Sex Errors of the Body* by John Money, 2nd Edition, Baltimore, Brookes Publishing, 1994; p. 44 (2 photos), *Sex Errors of the Body* by John Money, 2nd Edition, Baltimore, Brookes Publishing, 1994; p. 46, Custom Medical Stock Photo; p. 80: Brad Pitt—Gregory Pace/SYGMA, Tyra Banks—Guccione/G. Heri/SYGMA, Maasai Woman—Bachmann/Photo Edit, Indian Man—Michele Burgess/Stock Boston, k. d. lang—Gregory Pace/SYGMA; p. 84, Les Stones/SYGMA; p. 89, Robert V. Eckert, Jr./The Picture Cube; p. 95, David Ulmer/Stock Boston; p. 108, National Library of Medicine Bethesda, MD; p. 112, Keister/Gamma Liaison; p. 140, Vic Bider/Photo Edit; p. 164, Joyce Tenneson 1993/FPG; p. 166, left, Joyce Tenneson 1993/FPG; p. 166, right, Michael Newman/Photo Edit; p. 168, Joyce Tenneson 1993/FPG; p. 176, top, Jim Daniels/Picture Cube; center, Phototake; bottom, Sharon Fox/Picture Cube; p. 179 (2 photos), Thomas Rywick; p. 182, Mark Richards/Photo Edit; p. 193, Thomas Rywick; p. 195, Custom Medical Stock Photo; p. 196, Custom Medical Stock Photo; p. 198, Markow/SYGMA; p. 201, © 1997 Dr. M. Diamond/InterAction Stock; p. 209, A. Ramsey/Stock Boston; p. 213, Thomas Rywick; p. 215, J. L. Atlan/SYGMA; p. 221, David Young Wolff/Photo Edit; p. 225, Cindy Charles/Photo Edit; p. 228, © Dr. M. Diamond/InterAction Stock; p. 231, Myrleen Ferguson/Photo Edit; p. 235, Jeff Persons/Stock Boston; p. 236, Michael Newman/Photo Edit; p. 242, Lien Nibauer/Gamma Liaison; p. 255, Kathleen Ferguson/Photo Edit; p. 256, Rhoda Sidney/Stock Boston; p. 260, R. Hutchings/Photo Edit; p. 262, left, Kirkland/SYGMA; p. 262, right, Mark Richards/Photo Edit; p. 263 (3 photos), *Gender and Life Cycle* from Gechlechtskunde by Magnum Hirschfield. Photo from the New York Public Library. p. 266, Paul Conklin/Photo Edit; p. 267, David Austen/Stock Boston; p. 277, Mark Howes; p. 278, Ramey/Stock Boston; p. 279, *Le sommeil* by Gustave Goubet, Musée du Petit Palais, Paris—Photo by Bulloz/Art Resource; p. 287, Chris Maynard/Gamma Liaison; p. 290, Mark Howes; p. 298, J. Sohm/The Image Works; p. 301, Elizabeth Rice Allgeier; p. 302, Bonnie Kamin/Photo Edit; p. 304, Nik Kleinberg/Stock Boston; p. 313, The Everett Collection; p. 316, Mark Ellen Mark Library; p. 324, James D. Wilson/Gamma Liaison; p. 328, Courtesy, Massachusetts Department of Public Health/Division of Communicable and Venereal Diseases; p. 329, Atlanta Center for Disease Control; p. 338, Phototake; p. 340, Phototake; p. 341, Medichrome/The Stock Shop; p. 345, Esbin Anderson/ The Image Works; p. 357, Michael Newman/Photo Edit; p. 362, Cindy Charles/Photo Edit; p. 370, Bob Daemmrich/Stock Boston; p. 379, left, Evan Agostini/Gamma Liaison; p. 379, right, John Nordelli/Picture Cube; p. 383, Dr. Donald Laub; p. 384, Dr. Donald Laub; p. 388, Ted Soqui/SYGMA; p. 390, Roswell Angier/Stock Boston; p. 392, Bonnie Kamin/Photo Edit; p. 395, *Sculptor with Centaur and Women* by Pablo

Picasso, Sotheby Parke Bernet/Art Resource, NY; p. 404, Harry F. Harlow, University of Wisconsin Primate Laboratory; p. 406, top right, Frank Siteman/Picture Cube; p. 406, top left, MacDonald/Picture Cube; p. 406, bottom right, Steven Frisch/Stock Boston; p. 406, bottom left, M. Ferguson/Photo Edit; p. 407, Barbara Jaffe; p. 414, Marilyn Ferguson/Photo Edit; p. 417, Michael Newman/Photo Edit; p. 422, Frans de Waal.

Text and Figures

p. 18, Table 1.1: Albert R. Allgeier and Elizabeth R. Allgeier, *Sexual Interactions*, Fourth edition, p. 76. Copyright © 1995 by D. C. Heath and Company. Used by permission of Houghton Mifflin Company. p. 29: Exerpt from Ronald Goldman and Juliette Goldman, *Children's Sexual Thinking* (New York: Routledge & Kegan Paul, 1982), p. 194. Reprinted by permisssion of Routledge Ltd. p. 35, Table 2.1: Albert R. Allgeier and Elizabeth R. Allgeier, *Sexual Interactions*, Fourth edition, p. 102. Copyright © 1995 by D. C. Heath and Company. Used by permission of Houghton Mifflin Company. p. 41, Table 2.2: Albert R. Allgeier and Elizabeth R. Allgeier, *Sexual Interactions*, Fourth edition, p. 110. Copyright © 1995 by D. C. Heath and Company. Used by permission of Houghton Mifflin Company. p. 70, Figure 3.8: Albert R. Allgeier and Elizabeth R. Allgeier, *Sexual Interactions*, Fourth edition, p. 141. Copyright © 1995 by D. C. Heath and Company. Used by permission of Houghton Mifflin Company. p. 87: Excerpted with permission from L. G. Barbach and L. Levine, *Shared Intimacies: Women's Sexual Experiences.* Copyright © 1980 by Doubleday, a division of Bantam Doubleday Dell Publishing Group, Inc. p. 93, Table 4.1: Albert R. Allgeier and Elizabeth R. Allgeier, *Sexual Interactions*, Fourth edition, p. 174. Copyright © 1995 by D. C. Heath and Company. Used by permission of Houghton Mifflin Company. p. 105: Excerpted with permission from L. G. Barbach and L. Levine, *Shared Intimacies: Women's Sexual Experiences.* Copyright © 1980 by Doubleday, a division of Bantam Doubleday Dell Publishing Group, Inc. p. 128, Highlight Box: Excerpted from E. B. Vance and N. N. Wagner, "Written Description of Orgasm: A Study of Sex Differences," *Archives of Sexual Behavior*, 5, pp. 87–98. Copyright © 19 . Used by permission of Plenum Publishing Corporation. p. 146, Table 6.2: Albert R. Allgeier and Elizabeth R. Allgeier, *Sexual Interactions*, Fourth edition, p. 246. Copyright © 1995 by D. C. Heath and Company. Used by permission of Houghton Mifflin Company. p. 160, Table 7.1: Albert R. Allgeier and Elizabeth R. Allgeier, *Sexual Interactions*, Fourth edition, p.

266. Copyright © 1995 by D. C. Heath and Company. Used by permission of Houghton Mifflin Company. p. 189, Table 8.1: Albert R. Allgeier and Elizabeth R. Allgeier, *Sexual Interactions*, Fourth edition, p. 266. Copyright © 1995 by D. C. Heath and Company. Used by permission of Houghton Mifflin Company. p. 191, Table 8.2: Reprinted with permission of Irvington Publishers, Inc. Copyright © 1994. p. 210, Table 8.3: From Russo, et al., "U.S. Abortion in Context" *Journal of Social Issues, 48,* No. 3, pp. 183–202. Reprinted by permission of Blackwell Publishers. p. 216, Table 8.4: Albert R. Allgeier and Elizabeth R. Allgeier, *Sexual Interactions*, Fourth edition, p. 363. Copyright © 1995 by D. C. Heath and Company. Used by permission of Houghton Mifflin Company. p. 223, Research Controversy Box: Ronald Goldman and Juliette Goldman, *Children's Sexual Thinking* (New York: Routledge & Kegan Paul, 1982), pp. 62–63, 73–74. Reprinted by permission of Routledge Ltd. p. 224, Table 9.1: Albert R. Allgeier and Elizabeth R. Allgeier, *Sexual Interactions*, Fourth edition, p. 374. Copyright © 1995 by D. C. Heath and Company. Used by permission of Houghton Mifflin Company. p. 238, Across Cultures Box: Albert R. Allgeier and Elizabeth R. Allgeier, *Sexual Interactions*, Fourth edition, p. 309. Copyright © 1995 by D. C. Heath and Company. Used by permission of Houghton Mifflin Company. p. 236, Table 9.2: Reproduced with permission of the Alan Guttmacher Institute from F. L. Mott, M. M. Fondell, P. N. Hu, L. Kowaleski-Jones, and E. G. Menaghan, "The Determinants of First Sex by Age 14 in a High-Risk Adolescent Population," *Family Planning Perspectives*, Vol. 28, No. 1, January/February 1996. p. 241, Table 9.3: Albert R. Allgeier and Elizabeth R. Allgeier, *Sexual Interactions*, Fourth edition, p. 403. Copyright © 1995 by D. C. Heath and Company. Used by permission of Houghton Mifflin Company. p. 248, Table 10.1: Albert R. Allgeier and Elizabeth R. Allgeier, *Sexual Interactions*, Fourth edition, p. 416. Copyright © 1995 by D. C. Heath and Company. Used by permission of Houghton Mifflin Company. p. 264, Health Box: Albert R. Allgeier and Elizabeth R. Allgeier, *Sexual Interactions*, Fourth edition, p. 441. Copyright © 1995 by D. C. Heath and Company. Used by permission of Houghton Mifflin Company. p. 265, Health Box: Albert R. Allgeier and Elizabeth R. Allgeier, *Sexual Interactions*, Fourth edition, p. 442. Copyright © 1995 by D. C. Heath and Company. Used by permission of Houghton Mifflin Company. p. 266, Table 10.3: Albert R. Allgeier and Elizabeth R. Allgeier, *Sexual Interactions*, Fourth edition, p. 444. Copyright © 1995 by D. C. Heath and Company. Used by permission of Houghton Mifflin